From Mission to Church

Eugene P. Heideman

The Historical Series of the Reformed Church in America
No. 38

From Mission to Church

The Reformed Church in America Mission to India

Eugene P. Heideman

Wm. B. Eerdmans Publishing Co.
Grand Rapids, Michigan

The Historical Series of the Reformed Church in America

This series has been inaugurated by the General Synod of the Reformed Church in America, acting through its Commission on History, for the purpose of encouraging historical research and providing a medium wherein this knowledge may be shared with the academic community and with the members of the denomination in order that a knowledge of the past may contribute to right action in the present.

Global mission has played a prominent role in the history of the Reformed Church in America. Many of the volumes in this series, including this one, illuminate the history of RCA mission. These volumes are published in cooperation with the Mission Services Committee, General Synod Council, Reformed Church in America.

General Editor

The Reverend Donald J. Bruggink, Ph.D.
Western Theological Seminary

Commission on History

The Rev. Melody Meeter, M.Div., Grand Rapids, Michigan
Christopher Moore, New York, New York
The Rev. Jennifer Reece, M.Div., Princeton, New Jersey
Jesus Serrano, BA, Norwalk, California
The Rev. Robert Terwilliger, M.Div., Kalamazoo, Michigan
Dr. Jeffrey Tyler, Ph.D., Hope College, Holland, Michigan

Contents

Illustrations

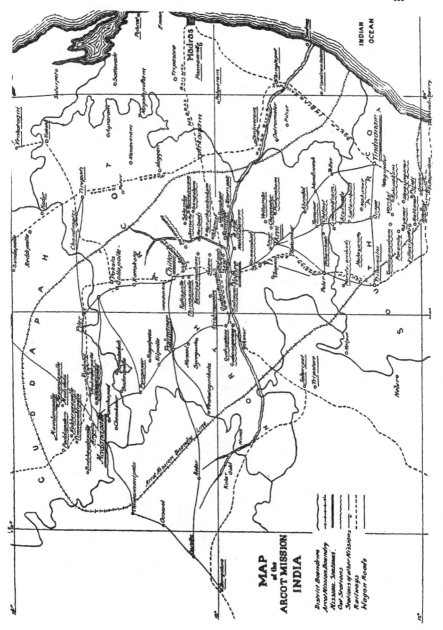

MAP
of the
ARCOT MISSION
INDIA

INDIAN OCEAN

Author's Preface

This book chronicles a history of the Reformed Church in America's mission in India between the years 1819-1987. It begins with the period in which the mission societies and the missionaries held the initiative in their hands. It quickly moves to the decades when the Arcot Mission began to work in partnership with the church as organized in the Classis of Arcot. Cooperation between the mission and the classis meant that, in certain respects, missionaries and Indian Christians served together as equals in God's mission in India, although the missionaries always were the "elder brothers," to use a phrase familiar in the traditions of India.

After India became an independent country and the Church of South India was inaugurated in 1947, the initiative was understood henceforth to lie in the newly united self-governing, self-propagating, and self-supporting Church of South India, with the overseas missions and the missionaries playing a supporting role. The century-long movement from mission to church was understood to be a success story, but it was not without its conflict and pain as Indians and foreign missionaries learned to be cross-culturally sensitive and gracious as they walked together in mission.

The period from 1819 to the present has been one of great turmoil and social and economic change. Not the least of these changes has been the changing role of women in human society and in the church. This book also chronicles the crucial role that women played in the Reformed Church in America's mission in India from the very beginning, in spite of the fact that for the first eighty years they were no more than "assistant missionaries" without the right to vote or at times even to speak in the deliberations of the mission. The caliber of their work proved to be so high that they came to enjoy full status as partners in the mission. Their achievements not only rivaled, but in some respects outstripped, those of the men.

Throughout the whole period from 1819-1987, male missionaries wrote almost all of the reports and correspondence. Only now and then do we discover in the official files any letters or reports written by women. Even fewer reports were written by Indian Christians. As a result, our account of the mission in India necessarily is entitled, *"A* History" rather than *"The* History." We must hope that, now that there are others who are carrying out detailed research into the lives of Reformed Church missionaries, they will enable us to gain additional insight into the contribution of women.

This is also *"A* History" because it needs to be supplemented by histories written from an Indian perspective. We are fortunate that a number of Indian scholars are now engaged in the process of writing monographs relating to the entrance of Christianity among the Tamil and Telugu people in south India. A number of those studies have served as valuable resources for this book, and they are cited in the footnotes.

It is important to express my appreciation to those who have provided assistance in the research and production of this book. A number of persons connected with India have shared insights and materials with me. They include Dora Boomstra, John Buteyn, Marcine and Keith De Jong, David De Vries, Joyce Dunham, Gladys Kooy, Janet Pofahl, Blaise Levai, Ruth Ten Brink, Stanley and Darlene Vander Aarde, Harold and Yvette Vande Berg, and Frank and Ann Zwemer.

Russell Gasero, Reformed Church in America archivist, has gone beyond the call of duty in providing me with access to materials in the Reformed Church archives and in utilizing his wide knowledge of Reformed Church official minutes and reports and missionary correspondence to guide me to lesser known resources. The staff of the Gardner Sage Library of New Brunswick Theological Seminary has always been more than willing to assist me in the use of the library's resources, as well as being generous in allowing me to borrow resources from the library for an extended period of time. Dr. Norman Kansfield, president of the seminary, provided me with a room to stay overnight while conducting research in the archives and library.

The staff at the Joint Archives of Holland, Michigan, was similarly helpful whenever I spent time conducting research there.

It is impossible to be too grateful to the editor of the Reformed Church Historical Series, Donald J. Bruggink, who is responsible for my taking up the task of writing this history. I had hoped for many years that someone would write a history, both because it would be crucial for the institutional memory of the church in India as well as for the Reformed Church in America, and because it would provide an important case study in issues faced in the modern missionary movement. Without his request that I engage in the project, I would never have begun it. His editorial skill and knowledge have provided direction for me in the writing of each chapter. Laurie Baron, who has carefully read the entire manuscript for matters of style and felicity of language, has offered many suggestions that make for clarity and precision.

My wife, Mary, read through each chapter as it was being written. Her ability to make suggestions concerning organization, grammar, clarity of thought, and her sensitivity to the needs of readers immeasurably improved the manuscript. Her patience and good humor, together with her refusal to accept my seventy-five word sentences and objections to her gentle criticisms, merit appreciation by the editors as well as by myself.

In conclusion, I am above all thankful to God, from whom Mary and I felt the call to serve as Reformed Church missionaries under the direction of the Diocese of Madras in the Church of South India. We treasure the years between 1960 and 1970 and the friendship of the many persons with whom we served as colleagues in India. They greatly enriched our lives, broadened our faith, deepened our theology, and taught us much about how to live together with sensitivity across cultures and national boundaries.

Foreword

by Charles Van Engen

From Mission to Church is a fascinating history and a case study in missiological reflection on complex mission action. Only someone with long-term, international, cross-cultural missionary experience could have written this book, and to do so Dr. Eugene P. Heideman is eminently qualified. He received his theological education in Holland, Michigan, and Utrecht, the Netherlands; served a Dutch immigrant congregation in Edmonton, Canada; and was sent to India as a missionary. After serving for a decade, he joined the religion faculty of Central College, Pella, Iowa; then served as academic dean at Western Theological Seminary, Holland, Michigan; authored a concise history of Reformed Church missions; and served as the denomination's secretary for world mission.

Heideman's history of the Reformed Church mission in India is written with candor and detail. It is carefully researched, human, and readable. It describes complex mission practices with clarity, and balances a concern for the big picture with sensitive stories of concrete situations which the missionaries faced in India during the past 180 years.

There are more than twenty major issues with which missiologists wrestle illustrated in this history of the Reformed Church's work in India. Four will be cited as examples.

First, winding its way throughout the entire story is the matter of the "three-self formula" as a viable and acceptable goal of mission. In this view, developed by Rufus Anderson, a mature church was to be self-propagating, self-supporting, and self-governing. Heideman shows that the missionaries in India understood the three-self formula to be advocating proclamational evangelism for conversion, the growth of the church, and leadership formation over against establishing Christian institutions in education, medicine, agriculture, and industry. I would consider this interpretation of the three-self to be somewhat unique to India. In other places in the world, the three-self formula was not assumed to be so strongly supportive of evangelism as apparently the missionaries in India understood it. However, due to the heavy institutionalization of the mission endeavor in India, faithfulness to the three-self vision was an issue that was never resolved. Heideman explores why it was that missionaries who were committed in their heart of hearts to proclamational evangelism ended up founding, running, supporting, and then being constrained by a host of ponderous institutions. Could it be that the people to whom the missionaries were sent and whom the missionaries loved needed medical, agricultural, educational, and vocational training in order to experience a transformation of all aspects of their lives that would offer them a way to contribute to the transformation of Indian society? In terms of the three-self, it is interesting to think of the story of Reformed Church mission in India in three periods: 1820s to 1880s—a time of self-propagation, early evangelization, and church formation; 1880s to 1920s—when missionaries and Indian nationals alike search (often unsuccessfully) for ways for the churches and institutions to become self-supporting; and 1920s to1960s—the churches and institutions in India walk the rough road toward becoming completely self-governing.

A second very important issue permeating almost every page of this book is the relation of gospel, European and Indian cultures, and inter-religious dialogue (with both Hindus and Muslims). Here is a very complex matter in the Indian context. It requires the historian to deal with the missionaries' and Indian pastors' approach to the caste system so embedded in Indian Hinduism, as well as their search for appropriate ways to respond to ancient Hindu religious and cultural wisdom. To this day, the debate on this issue has not been resolved in India or elsewhere. Pastors, missionaries, mission executives, and evangelists will find in this book a fascinating case study of contextualization—and they will find more questions than answers.

Third, there is the matter of the relationship of the missionaries to the Classis of Arcot in India, to other Indian church leaders, to international missionary churches and agencies, and to the Reformed Church in America's General Synod. With the exception of Canada, the Classis of Arcot was the only classis belonging to the General Synod that was established outside the U.S. The structural relationships among all these bodies seemed often to be simultaneously stormy and loving, creative and deadening, supportive and divisive. Drawing from his own wisdom and experience, Heideman offers the reader profound insights and compelling observations based on concrete cases in this history. As a case study in mission-church partnerships alone, the book is worth reading.

Finally, Heideman helps the reader understand more deeply the role that Christian missionaries and churches played in building modern India. However one reads the matter of the three-self in relation to the institutions founded by Reformed missionaries, one thing is clear: Christian institutions in health, education, agriculture, and industry contributed positively and fundamentally to the preservation, cultivation, and affirmation of Indian culture. They contributed directly to building a nation that eventually declared its independence from England and took its place as one of the great nations of the world. Reformed Church in America missionaries made an indispensable contribution to the development of leaders and social structures in modern India.

Heideman's story is written in a style similar to Stephen Neill's in *A History of Christian Missions*, one of the classic works in the field. Like Neill, Heideman paints his canvas in such a way that the mission endeavor in India can be seen as a picture-within-a-picture, a sketch of the mission set within India's history, set within the picture of the Reformed Church in America, and framed by global Christianity.

This style allows Heideman to highlight aspects of the story that are both global and local. For example, he describes the trusting friendships built among hundreds of international missionaries from several communions during their summer vacations in the mountains at Kodaikanal. He then rightly points out that these friendships were possibly the most significant factor contributing to the strong support on the part of expatriate missionaries for the formation of the Church of South India in 1947. Playing tennis at Kodaikanal was good for church union in India.

One of the refreshing aspects of this book is the way Heideman interweaves those many connections—linking what was happening in India with events taking place in the churches of North America. For example, the "Baby Roll," a tradition in many churches for many years, originally began as a way to support denominational world mission efforts. The World Day of Prayer was begun by women in several denominations as a prayer movement for world missions. The Reformed Church's participation in global ecumenism stems from its involvement in cooperative mission-sending from the U.S. through the American Board of Commissioners in the mid-1800s. From that grew ecumenical mission cooperation in India and elsewhere, involvement in the Student Volunteer Movement, and eventually membership in global ecumenical structures like the World Council of Churches. All of this was a direct product of Reformed Church missions. Other issues, like the relationship of evangelism and social transformation, the witness of Christians to persons of other faiths, and the relationship of Christian institutions to church structures, were arenas in which the church was also directly influenced by its missionaries. Time and again throughout this book, Heideman helps us see the influence that mission in India had on the formation of the Reformed Church in America. He also shows us that prevailing trends and popular perspectives in the U.S. had an impact on the denomination's mission support and practice in India.

At the end of the book Heideman suggests that it may now be time for the churches in India to re-evangelize North America. I would go a step further. It is time for the Reformed Church in America to join churches and Christian institutions in India for world evangelization, including Europe and North America. The Church of South India needs to become a mission-sending church in its own right. The Reformed Church would be greatly enriched by a partnership with the Church of South India in such an endeavor.

Eugene Heideman is to be congratulated for this outstanding contribution to the history of Christian mission. I commend it to anyone who wants to understand the Reformed Church in America and its global missionary endeavor.

Charles E. Van Engen
Arthur F. Glasser Professor
of Biblical Theology of Mission
Fuller Theological Seminary

A complete list of all those who served as missionaries of the Reformed Church in America in India, arranged in chronological order of their entry into the field, can be found in the *Historical Directory of the Reformed Church in America, 1628-2000*, Wm. B. Eerdmans Publishing Company, on pages 708 to 711.

Introduction
A United Church
in a Free Country

Independence Day, August 15, 1947

On the evening of August 14, 1947, the British government officers packed up and left their offices. The Union Jack came down from the flagpole. When the sun arose, the new tricolor flag was raised over India.

Throughout the whole of the Chittoor and the North and South Arcot Districts, members of the South India United Church and missionaries from the Reformed Church in America joined in the celebrations on that first Independence Day in India. Orators everywhere proclaimed the symbolism of the flag, which had been designed by Gandhi, Nehru, and other national leaders. The green stripe was for the 85 percent of India's people who worked among green fields and villages. The white stripe was for the principles of peace and *ahimsa* (nonviolence). The orange stripe was India's saffron shade symbolizing renunciation and self-sacrifice. The lion design in the center, taken from ancient king Asoka's pillar, connected the new India with its glorious past. "For the first time

1

Indians experienced the thrill of saluting their own flag and of singing their own song."[1]

The Inauguration of The Church of South India, September 27, 1947

Six weeks after the new flag was raised in India, four thousand people gathered in the compound[2] of the St. George's Cathedral in the city of Madras to celebrate the inauguration of the Church of South India. Methodist, Anglican, Presbyterian, Reformed, and Congregational churches would on that day merge themselves into one united Church of South India. The setting was grand for the historic event. It had rained on the night of September 26. The roads had been washed clean; the grass was a luscious green. The cathedral doors were open for the seven hundred who could be seated inside. Its tall steeple welcomed those who were coming from a distance. Its eighteen ionic columns and broad porches provided a sense of grandeur and awe at what was about to occur.

Missionaries and Indian Christians sang together great hymns of praise as the long-awaited day arrived. Unlike the English officials, no missionary had packed a bag and left an office on this day of unity. Words in "The Governing Principles of the Church" expressed both a sense of continuity with the past and a hope for the future on that day.

> The Church of South India thankfully acknowledges that the Churches which have been united to form it owed their existence mainly to the faith, zeal and prayers of many who either came themselves from other lands to India in order to preach the Gospel and build up the Church of Christ; or gave liberally of their time and money for the furtherance of that work. It believes that the Holy Spirit has guided

---

[1] Charlotte C. Wyckoff, *A Hundred Years with Christ in Arcot: A Brief History of the Arcot Mission in India of the Reformed Church in America* (printed for American Arcot Mission Centenary Celebration, 1953), 121.

[2] A "compound" in India is an area ranging in size from a small city lot to ten acres or more; it is often surrounded by a wall or fence. One or more buildings are located in the compound.

St. George's Cathedral

those Churches into this union in order that this same work of evangelization may be the more effectively fulfilled, in accordance with the prayer which Christ prayed that by the unity of His disciples the world might know that He had been sent to be its Saviour.[3]

This was truly a day for which Reformed Church missionaries in India had been hoping for many decades. As early as 1879, Jacob Chamberlain had read a paper for the South India Missionary Conference in Bangalore, India, in which he set forth his hope for unity. He longed for an organized "Church of Christ in India" which would not be American, English, German, or Danish, but "of India and suited to India." It would be a church not Scots Presbyterian, English Anglican, German Lutheran, or Dutch

---

[3] *The Constitution of the Church of South India,* II, 3. The first long section of *The Constitution of the Church of South India* is entitled, "The Governing Principles of the Church." It states the basic principles according to which the churches entering the union intended to guide the Church of South India for at least the first three decades of its existence. The Governing Principles remain unchanged to the present day.

Reformed. It would be free of foreign control to develop as God would lead it.[4]

In the inaugurating service of union, the Reverend Dr. C. R. Wierenga, president of the former South India United Church, a Reformed Church missionary and president of the Arcot Theological Seminary, led the prayer of confession of sin. Later, he questioned the newly appointed bishops on their assent to the Basis of Union and their acceptance of the Church of South India.[5] In the evening meeting, Dr. F. M. Potter of the Board of Foreign Missions of the Reformed Church in America, who was also present as a representative of the Indian Mission Conference of North America, congratulated the Church of South India for its unity in a time when brotherhood and cooperation were so badly needed in the world.[6]

The year 1947 was thus a high point in the history of the Reformed Church's mission in India. The terrible world war had come to an end. People in America were showing renewed interest in sending and supporting missionaries in Japan, China, India, the Middle East, and throughout the world. In India, the churches related to the Arcot Mission, which had been founded in 1853, were enjoying greater strength than ever. Forty-five missionaries were working in partnership with twenty-one ordained Indian ministers, while 302 male and 215 females were employed as teachers, catechists, Bible women, and in other related ministries. There were eighteen pastorates with 283 congregations, 32,020 members in the Christian community. In the previous year, 831 adults and 1,117 children had been baptized.

There existed one college, six boys' and seven girls' high schools and elementary boarding schools, 137 village elementary schools, a men's and a women's normal teacher training school, and one theological seminary. Besides the great Christian Medical College and Hospital in Vellore under the leadership of Dr. Ida Scudder,

---

[4] Jacob Chamberlain, *Native Churches and Foreign Missionary Societies,* 7-8.
[5] Rajaiah D. Paul, *The First Decade: An Account of the Church of South India* (Madras: The Christian Literature Society, 1964), 24.
[6] Ibid., 32.

there were three other hospitals and two rural dispensaries that provided more than 100,000 treatments during the year. Rural economic development and Christian stewardship were being encouraged through the widely recognized efforts of the Katpadi Industrial Institute and the Katpadi Agricultural Institute for men and boys, and the Women's Industrial Institute for women and girls. As the Christians and missionaries in the old Arcot Mission area entered the Church of South India, they had much for which to be thankful to God.

Underneath the celebrations of national independence and church union, however, there was also great anxiety among Indian Christians and missionaries alike. A leading Indian pastor, the Reverend Arthur John, who was chairman of the Indian Church Board in the Arcot area in 1948, reported on the mixed feelings of Christians, especially those living in villages. On the one hand, they were joining people of other languages and faiths in the great task of nation-building in India. On the other hand, they were anxious about how they would be treated in the new India. Most of them were members of "untouchable" castes, and they were concerned that their rights would not be protected in courts of law, that schools would no longer be open to them, and that the missionaries who had often been their protectors would leave.[7] In spite of the reassurances given to them by the new leaders of India, they were not sure what to expect.

The missionaries also struggled with uncertainty. In the new India there were charges that Christianity was a foreign religion. New Christian leaders were arising in the church who were well qualified to take positions as superintendents of hospitals and schools and leadership roles in the church. There was a restlessness in the air as Indian Christians and missionaries both sensed that a changing of the guard was at hand in many places. C. R. Wierenga had already expressed both welcome and concern two years earlier in a letter to Dr. Potter, when he commented, "Clearly the Indians are in charge

---

[7] Arthur John, *American Arcot Mission Report* (hereafter "AAR"), 1947-1948, 1-2.

now."[8] In spite of the many official and unofficial affirmations of the need for missionaries by Indian Christians, the missionaries themselves were unsure of their continuing role. Mina Jongewaard, director of the thriving Women's Industrial Institute in Palmaner, could not conceal her concern and pessimism about the future. She wrote to Potter about her fear that several mission institutions would have to close and then commented, "I do not feel that we are really wanted here, even by our own Indian Christians."[9]

Among the supporters of the mission back in America, another set of concerns surfaced. A hot controversy was raging in the Reformed Church in America about theological and social liberalism within the Federal Council of Churches. Many pastors, especially in the Midwest, were urging that the denomination should withdraw from the council. As the controversy went on, ecumenism and church union was tainted with charges of modernism, softness on communism, and lack of concern for evangelism. The Church of South India, as a symbol of the success of the ecumenical movement, was viewed with great suspicion among some.

In early 1947, one of the most articulate spokesmen in the Midwest, the Reverend Henry Bast, resigned from the Board of Foreign Missions, stating that he objected to Reformed Church attitudes towards traditional doctrines and membership in the Federal Council of Churches. He and several other pastors charged that in establishing so many educational, medical, and economic development institutions, the Arcot Mission had lost its first love, that of the priority of evangelism. This last charge was particularly troubling because in the promotion of mission, evangelism and stories about conversions had consistently played a central role in encouraging financial contributions. Thus, the question had to do not only with the priority of evangelism as such, but also with whether the Board of Foreign Missions and the missionaries had reported with integrity to the churches.

8 C. R. Wierenga to F. M. Potter, Jan. 2, 1945.
9 Mina Jongewaard to F. M. Potter, June 30, 1948.

Even those who were not critical, including Indian church leaders and missionaries themselves, were concerned about the constantly increasing cost of maintaining mission institutions in an era when government regulations and advances in technology were forcing the Arcot Mission and church to upgrade facilities, retrain staff, increase salaries, and change curriculum. Mission was entering a new era and the way forward was not at all clear.

At the moment when the advent of national independence and a newly united church provided occasion for celebration, a great tangle of issues made for an underlying anxiety. Many questions were being raised in the minds of the missionaries, the Indian Christian leaders, and the Reformed Church in America. Had the priority of evangelism been lost? Was the church in India a foreign, western body in an Asian land? Was there still a need for missionaries? Should missionaries go home? Was the emphasis on church union a sign of a loss of direction in mission? Would the theological contributions of the Reformed Church be lost in the new church? Were schools, hospitals, and industrial and agricultural training institutes becoming too expensive? How much authority should those who contribute funds for mission have in setting priorities for mission? What must be the relationship between missionaries and the Indian leadership of the church in India? What was the nature of the relationship between the Board of Foreign Missions and the missionaries? Were they all so burdened by the past that it would be almost impossible to move forward into the future? Some missionaries and members of supporting churches were also asking why they had to worry about all these questions when all they wanted to do was simply share the gospel and offer charity to the poor people of India.

The questions being raised in 1947 have not gone away. They arise wherever cross-cultural missions take place anywhere in the world. Most of the issues were there almost from the very moment when the Arcot Mission and the Arcot Classis of the Reformed Church in America were organized almost 150 years ago. In our study of the history of the Reformed Church mission in India, we will be constantly wrestling with the tangled skein of these and other issues as they constantly presented themselves. We will take note of how these issues came to take the particular shape that led to the events of 1947. We will then follow through to the year 1987, when Dr. Stanley and Darlene Vander Aarde and Dora Boomstra retired as the last Reformed Church missionaries assigned to work under the direction of the Church of South India.[10]

The story is one of missionary zeal and sacrifice, of the deaths of missionaries and their children, and of salvation especially for the poor and oppressed. It contains romance and excitement as well as dry detail and tedium. It is a story of the simple gospel entering into the complexities of Indian life and the mission enterprise. It is filled with men and women of high ideals and human frailty, of good intentions and unwitting racism and resolute paternalism. Long-forgotten people of humble birth and caste enter the story, along with well-known American missionaries and highly educated Indian church leaders. It is a story without an end because the task is yet unfinished, the mission not fully understood.

The story begins in India, with the coming of ships from the West carrying sailors, merchants, soldiers, colonial agents, and missionaries. Among those missionaries we discover John and Harriet Scudder, accompanied by their daughter, Maria, and their faithful "colored servant," Amy, who insisted on going to the mission field with them.

---

[10] Keith and Marcine De Jong continued to serve as Reformed Church missionaries in India after 1987, under assignment to the Kodaikanal International School rather than the Church of South India. Rani Vande Berg and Bruce and Tamara De Jong also were assigned to serve in Kodaikanal after 1987.

1

The Founding Family

On June 8, 1819, John and Harriet Scudder, Maria, and Amy boarded the brig *Indus* under command of Captain Wills, bound to Calcutta, India. That date can be said to mark the beginning of the Reformed Church in America's mission to India. With the Scudders were three other missionary couples, Messrs. Winslow, Spaulding, and Woodward with their wives, also under new appointment by the American Board of Commissioners for Foreign Missions (ABCFM). They were ultimately bound for Ceylon, which had become a British crown colony in 1802. Given the perils of tropical diseases and sea voyages in those days, they did not expect ever to see their homeland or families again. On May 19, after he had already said farewell to his saintly mother, John Scudder wrote, "I have parted with my dear mother for the last time. It would have gratified you to have seen how cheerfully she gave me up."[1]

In 1819, the Reformed Protestant Dutch Church, as it was then named, did not yet have a mission board of its own. It was still a very small American denomination located almost entirely in the states

---

[1] Dorothy Jealous Scudder, *A Thousand Years in Thy Sight: The Story of the Scudder Missionaries of India* (New York: Vantage Press, 1984), 7.

John Sr. and Harriet Scudder

of New York and New Jersey. Its history reached back to its first congregation in New Amsterdam in 1628. In 1810, it had joined with Presbyterian and Congregational churches in establishing the ABCFM. In 1815 ABCFM had sent four ministers and their wives to start work in Ceylon, after the British East India Company had (in 1812) refused to give permission to begin mission work in Calcutta.

The predecessors of the East India Company had been chartered by Queen Elizabeth in 1600 to open trade with India and other Asian countries. In 1757 the company's army under the leadership of Robert Clive had won a great victory at Plassey and thereby laid the foundation for its ultimate supremacy over the territory that today constitutes India and Pakistan. The company was established for the sake of trade and profit. It consequently proved to be antagonistic to the presence of missionaries, fearing that their evangelizing activities would raise animosity among the local Hindu and Muslim populations and disrupt trade and profit. One of its directors, a Mr. Bensley, objected to the presence of pioneer missionary William Carey in Calcutta. He declared,

The sending of missionaries into our Eastern possessions is the maddest, most extravagant, most costly, most indefensible project which has ever been suggested by a moonstruck fanatic. Such a scheme is pernicious, imprudent, useless, harmful, dangerous, profitless, fantastic. It strikes against all reason and sound policy; it brings the peace and safety of our possessions into peril.[2]

By 1813, when the East India Company had to apply for the renewal of its charter, pressure from Evangelicals[3] in England forced the company to open the doors to English missionaries. It was not until 1833, however, that missionaries of other nations were granted permission to carry out their activities in India. For this reason, John and Harriet Scudder began their service in Ceylon, remaining there from 1819-1836.

The Missionary Motivation of John and Harriet Scudder

John Scudder was born September 3, 1793. His parents were Joseph and Maria Scudder. His maternal grandfather, Colonel Johnston, had fallen in the Revolutionary War at the battle of Long Island while bravely storming a strong position of the enemy. Maria Scudder dedicated her son to God in his infancy as Hannah had once dedicated her son Samuel in the days of the Old Testament.

---

[2]   Quoted in John De Boer, *The Story of the Arcot Mission* (New York: The Board of Foreign Missions of the Reformed Church in America, 1938), 7.

[3]   The "Evangelicals" in England must be distinguished from the more narrow use of the term applied to Evangelicals in the United States today, although there is continuity between the two. William Wilberforce and Charles Grant were two of the most important English Evangelicals who encouraged the change in policy. The evangelical attitude in England owed much to the Puritans and to the work of John Wesley. Evangelicals sought to lead persons to conversion to Christ and encourage a life of holiness. They emphasized the importance of certainty of salvation. "The three most important features of the Evangelical mind were its intense individualism and exaltation of individual conscience, its belief that human character could be totally transformed by a direct assault on the mind, and finally that this required an educative process" [Sushil Madhava Pathak, *American Missionaries and Hinduism,* (Delhi: Munshiram Manoharlal, 1967), 11]. John Scudder is to be numbered among the Evangelicals.

She stated that she never knew when he was converted, "for he seemed always to be possessed with the Christian temper."[4]

His sisters later remembered that he had from his boyhood manifested a very devotional spirit and would at times gather sticks for the fires of the destitute. In his time as a student at Princeton College he was attentive to opportunities to win his fellow students over to the cause of Christ.

His heart's desire was toward the sacred ministry, but his father, a lawyer of repute and "a gentleman of the old school," was opposed. Somewhat out of a sense of duty toward his father, he went on to study medicine at New York Medical College under a leading doctor of that time, Dr. David Hosack. At the completion of his studies, he opened a practice in New York City that soon became very successful.

When he opened his practice, he lived in the home of Mrs. Gideon Waterbury, a widow with four daughters and two sons. He was concerned that this family, though of religious background, did not give enough evidence of personal piety. He was particularly interested in the oldest daughter still living at home, Harriet Waterbury, who was the first, with his encouragement, "to show signs of contrition." As personal attachment grew, their prayers led to her "conversion." She was joyous and practical; John needed that leaven in his life.[5]

As a means to lead her into faith, John encouraged her to read a book, the old Puritan tome by Thomas Boston of Scotland, entitled *Boston's Fourfold State.* Any theologian would acknowledge that this book is strong meat rather than milk for infants in the faith. It is open to question as to whether any young man in love today would dare hazard asking his chosen one to read that volume and thereby put her love and faith to the test. In this case, however, it served well. Throughout the course of their married life, John and Harriet

4 J. B. Waterbury, *Memoir of the Rev. John Scudder, M.D.* (New York: Harper & Brothers, Publishers, 1870), 12. I am indebted to this memoir for much of the material which follows regarding the early life and theology of John Scudder (pp. 13-25).

5 Scudder, *A Thousand Years,* 6.

exhibited a remarkable unity of love and purpose in family life, faith, and mission.

In New York, John Scudder attended the Reformed Dutch Church on Franklin Street where the Reverend Christian Bork was pastor. Mr. Bork, by this time an old man, had come to America as a Hessian soldier serving with the British army in the Revolutionary War. His conversion took place under the preaching of the Reverend Dr. John Livingston, the leading minister in the denomination. Bork held firmly to the high doctrine of predestination. In his concern for strictly recognizing that all spiritual renewal and conversion is a work of the Spirit of God rather than of human agency, Bork preached entirely to believers. He said that if he could edify them, he would leave sinners in the hands of God.

Scudder was not able to convince Bork that it was the duty of a preacher to call sinners to repentance. But Bork did agree that, while he was not willing to do it himself, he did not object if Scudder wished to do so. With that concession, John Scudder was free to give exhortations to sinners in weekly meetings conducted in the church and soon was rewarded with signs of spiritual awakening, especially among the young people. Among the materials he used were some of the most pungent of the revivalist Jonathan Edwards's sermons, the most famous being that of "Sinners in the Hands of an Angry God." Within a year or two, from one to two hundred converts were added to the church.[6]

One day as Dr. Scudder was visiting a patient, he saw on a table the pamphlet, *Conversion of the World, or The Claims of the 600,000,000 and the Ability and Duty of the Churches Respecting Them*. As he read it, he became convicted that he was called to be a missionary in response to the command to go into all the world to preach the gospel and heal the sick. After some time of thought and prayer, Harriet agreed to go along, so they applied and were accepted as missionaries by the American Board of Commissioners or Foreign Missions, in association with the Reformed Church in America.

[6] Waterbury, *Memoirs*, 22-25.

Unfortunately, John's father, Joseph Scudder, could not reconcile himself to the decision. He threatened to disinherit John if he persisted in going. When they went, Joseph Scudder followed through on his threat.

Jaffna Mission, 1819-1836

After a long sea voyage, the Scudders arrived in Calcutta in October, 1819, where they had to wait for passage to Ceylon. The four missionary families on board made use of their time to worship and study. They urged the ship's crew to repent and come to faith in Christ, even though many crew members had feared at the beginning of the voyage that the "holy brotherhood" would give them a sharp elbow if they used one of their many colorful oaths. One commented, "we shall forever be tormented with these men."[7] The ship became a literal Bethel (a "house of God") as the days passed and the crew one by one became converted to the gospel. Unfortunately, after they arrived in Calcutta most of the sailors reverted to their old ways.

John Scudder used some of the time in Calcutta to meet with the famous pioneer missionary, William Carey. But then sorrow filled the new missionaries when little Maria was stricken with dysentery October 22 and died after three days. The Scudders sailed to Ceylon and reached there in December, 1819. They were assigned to work in the Tamil-language Jaffna area, which consisted of a peninsula and islands on the northern part of Ceylon. In contrast to much of Ceylon which was Buddhist in religion, Jaffna was largely Hindu.[8] In February, Harriet gave birth to a second child. After one week it died on February 25, 1820. But John and Harriet remained steadfast. John wrote, "Perhaps our dear parents may be ready to

[7] Ibid., 37.

[8] The church which came into being in Jaffna through the work of the ABCFM and other missionaries became the Jaffna Diocese of the Church of South India in 1947. In recent years there has been much political conflict in that area, with the result that there has been much suffering. Members of the diocese have been called upon to carry on a great deal of humanitarian work, often at great risk to themselves.

say that we are sorry, and repent of our coming to this heathen land; that if we had remained at home we should have been less afflicted. You may rest assured that we do not repent of our coming....No; blessed be God, I hope to be the unworthy instrument of bringing souls to the dear Redeemer."[9]

In July, 1920, the Scudders opened a new mission station in Panditeripo, Jaffna. The ABCFM had not been able to send the necessary funds for the station, so Dr. Scudder drew upon his own reserve funds and opened a hospital and school there. Panditeripo had been an important place for Roman Catholic Portuguese missionaries two centuries earlier, when the Portuguese traders had been the major European power there. A number of Roman Catholics continued to live in the area. A large stone church was in ruins. Another thirty churches had been built in the surrounding area, but now all had been deserted. The government had given permission for the Scudders to live in an old bungalow with a thatch roof. Mats covered the floors and ropes were placed around the house to protect them from snakes, which did not like to cross the roughness of the ropes.

John Scudder was the first American to be sent overseas as a medical missionary. He was convinced that medicine was a means to an end: the body was healed so that the soul might be saved.[10] In those first decades of the nineteenth century, medical practice was still primitive by modern standards. The vaccine against smallpox had only recently been developed. There were as yet no vaccines against epidemic diseases such as typhoid, yellow fever, cholera, or bubonic plague. There was no effective treatment of malaria (jungle fever), polio, tuberculosis, leprosy, tetanus, or rabies. Anesthetics were still unknown; operations had to be done without them. The need for pure water supplies was not yet recognized.

Nevertheless, Scudder's knowledge of and skill in the practice of medicine was quickly recognized and accepted in the area. He wrote

[9] Ibid., 35.
[10] Scudder, *A Thousand Years*, 17.

that in his medical practice, "I prescribe for the sick at an early hour every morning and have prayers and conversation with them before I administer to their wants. I find it an excellent time to compare their present situation with what it will be in eternity, if they reject the only sacrifice for sin."[11]

His surgical skill was in particular demand. Repair of broken bones, treatment of cataracts, removal of tumors numerous and huge, and treatment of wounds of all sorts called for his attention. In times of epidemics, especially cholera, John and Harriet Scudder worked among the sick, bathing the sufferers, burying their dead, and doing whatever they could to relieve distress. In her journal, Harriet described their ministry in the time of an epidemic:

> Rode with the doctor this afternoon to visit some poor people who were this morning taken with the cholera. Oh, the misery and distress we witnessed! The mother met us, having but a few minutes before followed her child to the grave—her husband apparently dying, her father in the same situation, her only child sick, lying by the side of an old man—no human being near them, no comforts, scarcely a cloth to wrap around them! We spent four hours there in administering medicine, applying hot sand, and rubbing them….Their neighbors lived very near, but none dared to come to their assistance.[12]

Despite the need for his medical ministry, John Scudder's central concern remained preaching the gospel. He had studied theology on the ship to India, preparing to be examined for ordination. On August 8, 1820, he was licensed to preach the gospel and on Sunday, September 3, he preached at the school bungalow and hospital in the morning and in two villages in the afternoon. He was ordained in 1821 in a Wesleyan chapel with Congregational, Baptist, and Methodists ministers performing the ordination.[13]

11 Waterbury, *Memoirs*, 62.
12 Ibid., 108
13 Scudder, *A Thousand Years*, 23.

He soon began the practice of making tours of one or two weeks through the surrounding district, preaching the gospel and dispensing medical assistance as he went. This practice was to become one of the hallmarks of Reformed Church missionaries throughout the whole of the nineteenth century. It would come to represent the very heart of missionary activity. He would take two or three of his students with him, using boats with sails to go from island to island. The sails, however, could take them along only with a fair wind, so they often had to remain with people on an island for several days. When the wind died, they had only an umbrella to break the scorching rays of the sun.

At times he took trips by "palanquin," which resembled a small stagecoach without wheels, about 6 feet long by 2 ½ feet wide, with a top and side door to shield the passenger from the hot sun or rain. The coach was fitted with poles which four bearers took up to carry the passenger, who had to sit squarely in the center and dared not move more than slightly when muscles began to cramp. Using this mode of travel, he was able to conserve his strength for preaching and medical practice when he arrived in a village. Even so, he drove himself so hard that he was often ill with fatigue and terrible headaches. One Sunday he preached against doing any work on Sunday. A Hindu then asked him whether he was not inconsistent in requiring the bearers to carry him to the place of worship on the Sabbath. Scudder confessed that his critic was right. From that time on he always walked, sometimes for hours, rather than ask others to work on Sunday.[14] Unfortunately, the additional demands on his health from walking in the hot sun apparently became a major factor in the breakdown of his health by 1824.

Harriet Scudder, the Ideal Missionary Wife

Harriet Scudder proved to be the ideal missionary wife, totally dedicated to her family, to her husband's work, and to sacrificial missionary service of her own. Even when their third child died

[14] Ibid., 24.

shortly after birth, she went on without complaining. In subsequent years, the ten additional children born to them lived and grew up under her care. All of them except one, Samuel, who drowned while in theological seminary, would give service as missionaries in India. Most of the credit for their desire to follow their parents' example in missionary life must go to Harriet. John's affirmation of the necessity of maternal influence clearly reflects the opinion of both of them:

> We have seen that the means now employed are now inadequate for the world's conversion; and such, we have reason to fear, will continue to be the state of things until the church is blessed with a different race of mothers...who, while dandling them upon their knees, and rehearsing to them the history of the suffering and death of Christ....The hope of the church in our own land and the world rests, in a great degree, under God, on the infant sons and daughters of pious mothers.[15]

In his address to Christian mothers, he admonished them:

> There is a oneness between you, which resembles that between the branch and the vine, and the same kind of sap will be in the offshoot as is found in the trunk. The ideas which your child receives from you, with regard to the relative importance to be attached to different things, will generally retain their influence even to its death, shaping and modifying its course at every step of its existence.[16]

In light of Dr. Scudder's intense involvement in his medical work and his preaching ministry, the task of maintaining the home, nurturing their children, and managing the school which they had begun was left almost entirely to Harriet Scudder. Using their own

---

[15] John Scudder, *An Appeal to Christian Mothers in Behalf of the Heathen* (New York: American Tract Society, 1844), 8-9.
[16] Ibid., 13.

funds, John had in July, 1920, already opened a hospital and school
in Panditeripo. By December, 1921, in her seventh month of her
fourth pregnancy, John wrote that Harriet was providing for the
children in the school, "taking care of almost whole of (our)
domestic concerns, which are neither few nor small. She has ten
females under her care. These she teaches to sew in the afternoon.
In the morning she begins to hear the boys recite in English, which
is no small labor. She hears three different classes. She sometimes
visits the people."[17]

She was often left alone with all of these duties. In her journal she
would on one occasion write that he had been absent on a preaching
tour for about eighteen days, during which time she experienced
considerable anxiety about him. She had been left alone at home
with the care of about forty persons, many of whom were children
actually living in their home.[18] The majority of these were either
orphans or from extremely impoverished families. She would not
have been able to manage all of that without the assistance of Amy,
who in Ceylon became her friend, as well as an able assistant and
faithful servant.[19]

One of the American stereotypes of female foreign missionaries
has often been that of women who were out of fashion, dressed in
antiquated and drab clothing. One gains some understanding of
how this view came about. In her journal, Harriet wrote that their
clothing consisted chiefly of white cloth, made on the coast and
brought to their place for sale. "It is similar to our long-cloth at
home. There are colored ginghams made in Jaffna, but they do not
stand washing. Every piece of European gingham or calico which
I brought from home I value highly." She went on to describe her
husband's clothing and then showed by her appreciation of a new
hat that she had not lost her sense of fashion. "The doctor's daily
suits are white vests, when he will wear any, white jacket and nankin
pantaloons, which are preferable to white. I have received a very

[17] Waterbury, *Memoirs,* 79.
[18] Ibid., 100.
[19] Ibid., 81.

beautiful English straw bonnet as a present, a few days since, from our good friend, Mrs. Mooyaart."[20]

Mission in Madras, 1836-1854

In 1833, the East India Company changed its policy and opened India to missionaries of all lands. This enabled the American Board of Commissioners for Foreign Missions to fulfill its dream of beginning missionary activity in India itself. In 1836, John and Harriet Scudder moved to Madras, a city of perhaps 700,000 people, located about four hundred miles from the southern tip of India on the coast of the Bay of Bengal.

Madras, which in 1836 had a population twice that of New York City, had been acquired by the East India Company in 1639. It contained a small colony of British officials and businessmen who lived on the outskirts in spacious homes. The old part of the city was called Black Town, thickly settled with narrow streets. By the time the Scudders arrived, there were already two important Anglican churches in the city. The first was St. Mary's Church, consecrated in 1680 inside Fort St. George, with a bomb-proof roof which would serve as a safe place should the French or any other fleet attack with cannon. The second was the magnificent St. George's Cathedral, four miles from the fort, built for the use of British merchants living in that area. Patterned after St. Giles in London, it had been consecrated January 8, 1816. It became a cathedral in 1835 when Archdeacon Daniel Corrie of Calcutta was consecrated first Bishop of Madras.[21]

Prior to the arrival of the missionaries of the ABCFM in 1836, there had already been a long history of Christian presence in the Tamil-speaking area. Tradition had it that the Apostle St. Thomas had been martyred and buried at St. Thomas Mount, just south of Madras. It is certain that there were Syrian Christians on the west coast of India in what is now Kerala by the fourth century A.D. The

[20] Ibid., 102.
[21] Paul, *The First Decade,* 21.

first great movement to Christianity within the Tamil language area took place when a Christian mass movement broke out among the Paravas, a poor Tamil fishing community on the southernmost shore. In 1532, 20,000 were baptized by Roman Catholic Portuguese missionaries. When the Portuguese left, no teacher remained to tell them the meaning of Christian baptism. Nevertheless, the community remained open to Christian instruction. Francis Xavier of the Jesuits left Goa to go to work among them from 1542-44 until he went to China. Work was continued among that community by successors in the Jesuit mission. Particularly noteworthy was the work of Constantine Joseph Beschi (1680-1747). He developed a grammar of Tamil prose, which was much used by the first Protestant missionaries.[22]

Descendants of these and other early Roman Catholic converts moved to various areas throughout the Tamil area, including Madras and the Arcot area. Because they were left without pastoral support, they usually had little understanding of the Christian faith. As a consequence of the Portuguese having been there, there were also a considerable number of "Christian" descendants of Portuguese-Indian marriages or other sexual liaisons. One estimate is that there were approximately 15,000 Indo-Europeans in Madras at the time the Scudders arrived, many of whom would have still have been Roman Catholic.

The first Protestant missionary to India, the Lutheran Bartholomaeus Ziegenbarg, arrived in the Danish trading station at Tranquebar, a port on the east coast about two hundred miles south of Madras, July 9, 1706. Following his arrival, other German and Danish missionaries, often with financial support of the high Anglican Society for Propagating Christian Knowledge (SPCK), joined him and translated the Bible into Tamil. They also translated some of the great Lutheran hymns and Luther's catechism. However, the Danish authorities who were in charge at Tranquebar did not

---

[22] N. C. Sargent, *The Dispersion of the Tamil Church* (Delhi: ISPCK, 1962), 6.

wish to allow the missionaries to extend their ministry beyond the Christian community in the settlement, lest trade relations be upset.

When the Reverend William Stevenson was appointed as chaplain to Fort St. George in Madras in 1712, he found that the Danish missionaries had already begun work on the east coast. He ascertained that these Danish missionaries would be more suitable for the pastoral care of the English garrisons with their Indian and Portuguese wives than were the English military chaplains with their short terms of service in India. His influence resulted in a very cordial relationship between the East India Company chaplains and the Danish and German Lutheran missionaries supported by the SPCK.[23] On September 1, 1726, the Lutheran Benjamin Schultze landed in Madras and began a Tamil school. Before the end of 1728 he had a congregation of seventeen communicants and twenty-seven catechumens. He took up residence in Black Town and had a congregation of nearly one thousand by 1750.[24]

Thus, at the time when the Scudders arrived in Madras in 1836, the history of Roman Catholicism in South India was already three hundred years long, and that of Protestantism more than a century. One result was that there was immediately available to them a Tamil translation of the Bible, a well-developed outline of Tamil Grammar, and a good Tamil lexicon, as well as a serviceable Christian theological vocabulary, however misleading it could be at times. This meant that ABCFM missionaries could immediately begin writing, printing, and distributing religious tracts in the Tamil language. In fact, the morning after his arrival in Madras, Scudder had filled his hands and pockets with leaflets to distribute as he visited established schools. Before a month had passed, he had persuaded several Indian teachers to put their schools under his direction. He hoped to turn several of these into boarding schools.[25]

---

23 Eugene Ten Brink, *History of Vellore Fort and St. John's Church* [privately printed, on file at the Archives of the Reformed Church in America, New Brunswick, N.J. (hereafter Archives of the RCA) 1961], 37-38.

24 Sargent, *Dispersion of Tamil Church,* 10.

25 Scudder, *A Thousand Years*, 42.

In Madras he met the Church of Scotland missionary, Dr. John Anderson, who later was to found Madras Christian College. John Scudder also became an ardent advocate of the development of a Christian college. Therefore he made a trip through the jungle to the west coast to visit British officials and get their approval and donations. On his return trip, he came down with "jungle fever," probably malaria. Word was sent to Harriet that his life was in danger and he was not able to travel. Her faith and character is illustrated by her immediate decision to go see him, even though she was in the eighth month of pregnancy.

A friend loaned her a tent. Bearers were engaged to carry her and her youngest son, John, on a palanquin. Since she did not want to lose time, relays of coolies were hired to carry her by day and night. While they were in deep jungle one night, the roaring of wild animals was heard nearby. The bearers became frightened and fled, leaving Harriet and John exposed to the beasts. Taking her son by the hand, she spent the night in prayer while she heard the tread of wild elephants not too far away, as well as the growl of tigers and other beasts. When morning came they were still safe. Her bearers returned, and they went on their way until they came to her husband, who by that time was out of danger of death, but with his health badly impaired. They then returned to Madras, where Harriet gave birth to her thirteenth and last child, whom the couple named Louisa.[26]

Following their arrival in Madras, John Scudder continued to be as tireless in his evangelistic touring through a wide area as he had been in Ceylon. On these tours, he went from town to town, changing his itinerary as he heard of opportunities to go where he might find a welcome. Often his wife and the other missionaries in Madras did not know where he was.[27] In response to an anxious letter from her, he wrote,

[26] Ibid., 44-45.
[27] Harriet Scudder was not always fully accepting of her husband's frenetic touring. On one occasion she wrote, "If this is your duty and the labor which the Lord would have you perform, I do trust it may be made more plain to me. I would not oppose if I could see your duty plain" (Scudder, *A Thousand Years*, 50).

....you seem to think that I keep you in the dark as to the places where I go, and on this account you have not been able to tell your inquirers where I had gone or am going. I am not aware that you have been more in the dark, my dearest, than myself. I do know that, when I left home, I had any more idea of visiting Negapatam than I have of going to the *moon* tonight. The thought first probably entered my mind at Sethemparum...I am going just where the pillar of cloud by day and the pillar of fire by night lead me.[28]

In other letters, he described how he and his Indian evangelist helpers worked often from sunrise to sunset, preaching, discussing with Hindus, doing medical procedures and dispensing medicines, and distributing scriptures and tracts.

Now as to myself and helpers. I have had hard work for a week. Raaman has, until yesterday, been laid *aside*—could do nothing. I have had to preach, and preach, and preach, and this, too, with a bad cold, so that my lungs are almost worn out....We preach all the time, we may say, as well as give out portions of the Scriptures and tracts....We shall have crowds of people before night. I do not know, my dearest, when I shall see you. It will, I think, take up my full six weeks before I can in any way reach home. [29]

Touring missionaries often distributed large numbers of scriptures and tracts. John tells how on June 26, when the sun is very hot, they were busy from three to six distributing literature to a throng of people. The next day, he was in a small room screening people who wanted scriptures or tracts. The screening was a literacy test, so that only literate persons would qualify to receive materials. By the 28th they were busy in Conjeevaram near a large Hindu temple, where their stock of literature was almost exhausted.

28 Waterbury, *Memoirs,* 160.
29 Ibid., 161.

On one of his tours John saw Vellore in the North Arcot District for the first time. He climbed the mountain adjacent to the town and described the view.

> The view of the plain from this mountain is most charming. I had a most commanding sight of the whole city. It is very large; not, however, to be compared to Black Town as to size. I also had an excellent view of the villages in the vicinity of Vellore. The tops of the trees, which appeared at a distance; the paddy fields, in perfect green or yellow; the white bed of the river, which is nearly dry; the shades cast over a part of the plain by the passing cloud, while the full sunshine was on the other side; the fort, with its surrounding water and so forth, presented a scene which beggars all description.[30]

His visit to Vellore was found to be promising. He was busy distributing the Scriptures from 7:00 a.m. to 6:00 p.m. Since everyone had to be examined for the ability read, his helpers gave out a ticket in response to each person making a request, according to which piece of literature the person wanted. The ticket system enabled them to keep order in making a fair distribution to literate persons. "This, when presented to me, was redeemed by a Gospel. Of course two thousand tickets and more passed through my hands, and a thousand Gospels, with the same number of tracts."[31]

Vellore was eventually to become the center of the Reformed Church in America's mission area in India. John Scudder had immediately seen its possibilities. He wrote, "Vellore is an excellent place for missionary labor. It needs a dozen laborers, as there cannot be less than eighty or ninety thousand inhabitants in it and its vicinity."[32]

Dr. Scudder's health had been rather precarious ever since 1824. At that time his fellow missionaries had insisted that he and his

[30] Ibid., 139-140.
[31] Ibid., 141.
[32] Ibid., 142.

family go from the heat of Ceylon to the cool climate of the seven-thousand-foot Nilgiris mountains in India for rest and restoration. In 1841, when he was had been almost five years in the Madras area, his health broke again. His severe headaches became chronic. His digestive system was ruined by an unbalanced diet on his frequent tours. Though only 48 years old, he suffered from inflammation of the tendons of his left arm and had lost the use of the first joints of his fingers before his whole arm had become paralyzed. He had six or seven small tumors removed from his arm, had circulatory troubles, and suffered from a constriction in the region of his heart as well. He constantly wanted to sleep, but he refused to do so as long as he was in India.

Finally, he was persuaded that the only hope for a restoration of health was a return to America. By March 1842, five of the Scudder children had already been sent to America to receive their education. In that month, John and Harriet, with their other five children, sailed back to America, to the land and the family that they had never expected to see again. "One evidence of God's providence marked their homecoming. Joseph Scudder, who had sworn to have nothing more to do with his son if he went to India, who had refused to write to him and had ignored the claims of his grandchildren, now met the exile on his return, opened his arms and, embracing him, restored him to the home he had surrendered."[33]

Presenting in America the Call to Foreign Mission, 1842-1846

John and Harriet Scudder and the five children with them rented a large house in Elizabeth, New Jersey, fairly near Harriet's mother in Westfield. John began to recover his health. His arm no longer troubled him, but he still had a severe cough and what appears to have been amoebic dysentery, for which at that time there was no simple remedy. Nevertheless, in spite of his need for a longer period of rest, he found inactivity abhorrent. He lived with a sense of urgency about making known to Americans the pressing need for

[33] Ibid., 51.

missionaries in India in the face of the actual conditions prevailing there. A number of major lengthy speaking tours were carried out. Once again, Harriet Scudder had to remain at home to cope with the realities of taking care of a large family while her husband was away.

John began a tour in the winter in the southern part of the United States; then he spoke in almost every major city on the eastern seaboard; then on to Ohio, Kentucky, and Illinois, returning by way of the Erie Canal to New England. During their more than twenty years in India, the Scudder missionary name had spread throughout the country, so he was given a hero's welcome wherever he went. He especially loved to speak to children. It is claimed that he preached to over a hundred thousand children during their four years in America.

Two small books were written and published by the American Tract Society in 1844. These give us some insight into Scudder's motivation for mission and his response to what he saw in America. In *The Redeemer's Last Command,* his starting point is Matthew 28:19, "Go ye into all the world and preach the Gospel to every creature." Prior to the beginning of the modern missionary movement and the writings of William Carey who went to India in 1792, most Protestant churches had understood this command as one which Jesus had given to the Apostles rather than to believers generally. In the centuries following the Protestant Reformation, the rulers and churches of Europe had for the sake of religious peace agreed to the rule that "the religion of the prince is to be the religion of the people." On this principle, they understood it to be the duty of the civil authorities to establish churches in each place in their realm and to support the ministers. It was the duty of a "true church" to carry on the pure preaching of the gospel and administration of the sacraments. The Reformed tradition usually included a third duty or "mark" which was to maintain ecclesiastical discipline in relation to the sacraments of baptism and the Lord's supper.

Within this framework of thought, persons such as Carey or Scudder who went to a foreign land unsupported by the civil authorities could readily be seen as disturbers of the peace and as political subversives. The church and its preachers had the duty to remind the civil authorities of their duty to support the Christian religion and establish the church in their realm. Because of the close relation of church and state, the church was not supposed to undertake the task of foreign missions.[34] The stance of the East India Company worked in harmony with this understanding. It supported chaplains who had the duty to preach, celebrate the sacraments, and provide pastoral care for the Christians alone in each place where it established itself. The rule provided a reason for the East India Company to refuse to allow foreign missionaries to work where it had formed alliances with local rulers. The English Evangelical opponents of the company's policy refused to admit, however, that the rule, "the religion of the prince is to be the religion of the people" should be applied by the company to India.

John Scudder taught that Matthew 28:19-20 is a command to every follower of Christ. He wrote that it makes every believer a preacher and a missionary, "or at least obliges him to see it, so far as his ability extends, that the labors of diffusing evangelization are actually performed by a substitute....all the energies of the Son of God were enlisted to this end, and all who are his must follow his example."[35]

A second motivation named by him is the Christian's knowledge that those who die apart from Christ are eternally lost: "Do not the souls of fifty thousand of the perishing heathen pass from time to time into eternity every day, unprepared to meet God? Shall hell continue to receive such accessions without a single effort on your

---

34 John Piet, in *The Road Ahead* (Grand Rapids, Mich.: Eerdmans, 1970), has provided a full scale attack on this understanding of the "true church's" role and shown that it is a misunderstanding of the New Testament doctrine of the church and mission; see esp. 21-47. John and Wilma Piet served as Reformed Church missionaries in India, 1940-1960.

35 John Scudder, *The Redeemer's Last Command* (New York: The American Tract Society, 1844), 6.

part to induce yours sons to do all in their power to prevent it?"[36]
That John Scudder felt a sense of personal guilt when he did not
take every opportunity to present the gospel of Christ to the lost
souls of this world was clearly one of his motivations for mission
and for the frenetic touring which proved so hazardous to his
health.

In his *Appeal to Christian Mothers on Behalf of the Heathen,* one can
discern a third motivation for mission which he especially lays
before mothers in America. In this tract is an appeal to Christian
mothers that from the time of birth, especially during the first four
years of childhood when the direction of a person's character is set,
they should place before their children the plight of the heathen in
order that their sons would consider the call of Christ to become
missionaries and that their daughters would be ready to marry men
called to be missionaries. He seeks to motivate mothers to have
deep sympathy for their sisters, the suffering Hindu women and
girls of India. He provides almost lurid examples of the way in
which the women are beaten by their husbands, abused by their
mothers-in-law, girl babies killed, and widows mistreated, in order
to encourage them to train up their children to be missionaries.[37]

> Christian mothers, do you care for the temporal comfort of
> the heathen? Have you any compassion for their perishing
> souls? Have you any gratitude to the Son of God, who has
> so abundantly blessed you? Have you any desire to honor
> him, any delight in his glory, any burnings of heart to carry
> out the great purpose of his death? Then I beseech you, by
> each and all of these considerations, to train your sons for
> Christ; to educate them from infancy for him; for ministers
> or missionaries, as he shall call them to his service."[38]

Although John Scudder seems never to have traded on his own
life of sacrifice of his health and a prosperous American medical

[36] Ibid., 26.
[37] Scudder, *An Appeal to Christian Mothers,* 28-50.
[38] Ibid., 48.

practice, not to mention the death of their first three children, he was appalled at what appeared to him to be the American Christian's self-indulgence and search for affluence and luxury. He observed that Paul's comment that "the love of money is the root of all evil" applies not only to the wicked, but must be extended to the great majority of the household of faith.

> My brethren, how it is with you? Are you living unto yourselves, or unto Him who died for you and rose again? All of you are engaged in seeking the treasures of the world. What are you seeking them for? Is it that you may hoard them up for your own gratification and for the use of your heirs? If this is your object, the day is coming when nothing but unmingled regret will be the consequence....your heirs would have been much more benefited, had you thought less of them and more of the cause of your Savior."[39]

Returning to Missionary Life in India, 1847-1854

By 1846, John Scudder's health had improved sufficiently to allow the family to return to India, which they reached in early March, 1847, after an extremely stormy sea voyage. Their return had been preceded by that of his eldest son, Henry Martyn Scudder, and his wife, Fanny Lewis. When John and Harriet Scudder and their daughters Harriet and Louisa disembarked in Madras, they were informed by Henry and Fanny that their little son, the first Scudder grandchild, had died. In April, John and Harriet were asked to go to the city of Madura,[40] somewhat inland about three hundred miles south of Madras, to serve for a time with the newly established Madura Mission of the American Board. There was a cholera epidemic in that area and no physician in the vicinity. The Scudders' presence there was the beginning of the long and fruitful relationship

[39] Scudder, *Redeemer's Last Command,* 64.
[40] In transliterating Indian names, I have generally used the most recent accepted spellings. However, I have made an exception in the case of Madura (now generally "Madurai"), because of frequent references in the missionary reports to the "Madura Mission."

between what was to become the Arcot Mission of the Reformed Church in America and the Madura Mission, which was related to the ABCFM and the Congregational churches in America.

In Madura, John Scudder once again was fully occupied with his medical work while at the same time using every opportunity to go into the surrounding areas to preach and distribute literature. He became involved in a caste controversy that developed between the Madura Mission and the Jaffna Mission. This involvement had long-term consequences for the development of the Arcot Mission regarding the practice of caste.

At this point it is important to digress for a moment to note how the caste system functioned in the areas in South India where Reformed Church missionaries served. Theoretically, in classical Hinduism, there are four main castes. The Brahmins at the head of the structure of caste were the priests of the early Aryans who came to India from the north. As the Brahmins were supposed to have sprung from the head of their god, the second caste, the Kshytrias, sprang from his shoulders and became the warriors and civil rulers. The Vaisyas sprang from the thighs and were the agriculturists and landowners, who also were the merchant class. These three castes are the "twice-born" castes from a ceremony of rebirth through which every male member passes. They are invested with a sacred cord to be worn over the left shoulder. The Sudras came from the feet and formed the basis of the structure as the artisans and tradesmen.

Beneath these four castes there were a great mass of people who, in the time of the Scudders, were commonly known as "untouchables" or "Pariahs" whose very shadow could pollute the upper castes. As outcastes, it was questionable as to whether they were Hindus. They lived outside the caste village in their own village, known as the "cheri," separated by a short distance from the main village. It was from this last group that eventually perhaps 90 percent of the Christians in the Arcot area would come.

According to the Hindu concepts of *karma* (you reap what you sow) and *samsara* (the wheel of births, "re-incarnation"), one's present position in the social structure in this life is determined by one's actions in previous lives. Thus one must accept the caste into which one has been born with its related duties and not presume to seek a higher status in life. Included in this understanding is the idea that one should not presume to have the right to change one's religion by converting to another. Within the Hindu structures also, the Sudras should not seek to carry out the religious duties which have been apportioned to the Brahmin caste.

What has been outlined above sets forth the theoretical structure of the caste system. In practice, however, the system is far more complex than the theory admits. There are about three thousand castes scattered throughout India, many of which are not easily classified into one of the four castes. Over time, a caste can also rise or descend on the social scale as conditions change. An American reader can be helped to understand the role of caste by noting that caste in India in daily life functions very much like race and ethnicity function in American society, except that with its long history in India it is much more rigid. In the United States in the nineteenth century, marriages, religious practices, and social relationships tended to take place within one's own ethnic communities. The elite in Boston were often spoken of as the "Brahmans" of society. The legal and social position of the black slaves in the United States in 1850 was not all too different, although probably somewhat worse, than the "untouchables" in India.

The outcastes were not allowed to enter Hindu temples, to use the same wells, to ride public transportation, or to enter restaurants and hotels with caste people. No caste people would eat with them. They were not permitted to wear certain kinds of clothing. In some villages women were not to wear clothing above the waist. They usually did not own land but were at the mercy of the local landowners for times and conditions of employment. In many cases they were virtually the slaves of the caste people. Interestingly enough, there were also caste distinctions among the outcastes, so that they too would discriminate against others lower on the caste scale than themselves.

When Indians who were of Hindu origin became Christians, there was a strong tendency among many of them to continue to practice customs of caste following their baptism. For example, those of originally higher caste would refuse to eat with those lower or discriminate against them in other ways. When Scudder was in Madura, the Madura Mission made the rule that all caste distinctions should be done away with in the use of the sacraments in the church. The majority of Christians there accepted the rule, but seventy-two people refused to show their acceptance of the rule, which required them to eat food with all the others. One catechist named Cooley not only refused to eat but publicly stated that he would never give up his caste. After some months he was dismissed from the church and from his job as catechist in Madura. Cooley, however, then went to Jaffna where he was accepted as a member of the church and employed as a catechist, even though two of the members of the Jaffna mission had been present when he was dismissed in Madura.

Scudder, as a corresponding member of the Madura Mission in late 1848, took it upon himself to reprimand the members of the Jaffna Mission. Jaffna in mild terms replied that as he was not a full member in Madura he had no business interfering, since the Madura Mission itself had not taken any action against them. Eventually he appealed to the executive committee of the ABCFM, but its secretary wrote back "censuring Dr. Scudder for 'arraigning and prosecuting the Jaffna Mission' and for being 'too demanding' on what he termed a 'national custom.'"[41]

Throughout the last half of the nineteenth century, missionaries from the various missions came together to hold conferences. The issue of caste occupied the Madras Missionary Conference of 1850,

[41] Scudder, *A Thousand Years,* 60. In the above, I am indebted to her full description of this event, pp. 56-61.

attended by six Wesleyan, three Church of Scotland, two Church of England, two London Mission, one Baptist, and four American missionaries. The missionaries resolved that

1. Candidates for baptism should be well instructed in regard to its evils and before receiving the Sacrament should be required to renounce Caste usages forever, both in principle and practice.
2. The renunciation of Caste ought also to be demanded of all Christians before their coming for the first time to Communion.
3. ....Among the special means now alluded to, one, which all the members of the Church including their Pastor and teachers, shall partake of a simple and suitable repast....[42]

The position taken by Scudder and the Madras Missionary Conference in 1850 became one of the most important policies of the Arcot Mission when it was organized three years later. It was maintained with utter firmness throughout the history of the mission.

John Scudder, Sr.'s, health continued to be a serious problem after his return to India. He tired easily. His eyesight began to fail, but in his journal he wrote that he would prefer to lose his eyesight than his voice, which continued to be strong. "Though I should become blind, if spared, I trust that I shall be able to preach."[43]

In those years, death was never far away. Their second son, William Waterbury, and his wife, Katherine Hastings, had returned to India with them. William and Kate were assigned by the ABCFM to missionary work in Ceylon, where a daughter, Kitty, was born in 1848. In 1849 they went to Madura to visit William's parents. On their way back to Ceylon, Kate died of cholera. Two months later a daughter born to Henry and his wife died two days after birth.[44]

42 Ibid., 342
43 Waterbury, *Memoirs*, 241.
44 Scudder, *A Thousand Years*, 68.

The heaviest blow of all fell, however, on November 29, 1949, when Harriet Scudder died after three days of severe illness. The family took comfort in her last testimony of faith. Just before she died, she opened her eyes and exclaimed, "Glorious heaven! Glorious salvation!" and "sweetly fell asleep in Jesus."[45]

John Scudder never really recovered from the death of his wife. He continued to work hard in his practice of medicine and preached whenever opportunity offered and strength allowed. By 1854 his health had declined to the point that he was no longer able to bear a journey to the healthier climate of a hill station. He agreed to take a sea journey on a ship going to South Africa, accompanied by his third son, Joseph, who had come as a missionary to India two years earlier. His health improved on the sea voyage to Capetown. There he immediately began to preach to the English-speaking people, especially to the children. On the night of January 12, 1855, he complained of pain in his side, but the following morning was quite comfortable. He preached that morning and came back to his room to rest. When Joseph went in to awaken him for the evening service, he found that his father had apparently died in his sleep, aged 62 years. [46]

The Founding of the Arcot Mission, 1853

During the years that John and Harriet Scudder were serving in India under the umbrella of the American Board of Commissioners for Foreign Missions, there was a growing sentiment in the Reformed Church in America that it should adopt a mission area of its own. For that reason, by 1851 it was agreed that a mission should be established in the Arcot area, with a center in the town of Arcot, about eighty miles inland, west of Madras. From 1853, when it was organized, until 1857, when the Reformed Church formed its own Board of Foreign Missions, the mission remained under the administration of the ABCFM.

[45] Letter to Dr. John Anderson, Nov. 22, 1949, quoted in Waterbury, *Memoirs*, 245.
[46] Scudder, *A Thousand Years*, 72.

As we have already noted, the eldest son of the Scudders, Henry Martyn, had arrived in India in 1844. He and his wife, Fanny, lived in Madras for six years, during which time in addition to his missionary activity he studied medicine at the recently founded Madras Medical College. He would later receive his M.D. degree from New York University and thus follow his father in becoming both an ordained minister and a physician and surgeon. In June, 1850, he and the Reverend John Dulles of the Madras Mission were deputed to take an extended preaching and prospecting tour inland from Madras, to preach to those who had not previously heard the gospel, to explore the countryside, and to report on the best place for establishing an outstation of the Madras Mission. They reported that a favorable place for such a station would be the town of Arcot, or the adjacent one of Wallajanagar, then a place of about twenty-five thousand inhabitants.

In the following year, Henry M. Scudder and his wife moved to Wallajanagar, since no house was available at the time in Arcot. At his town of residence, he established a medical dispensary with the purpose of winning a more favorable entrance for the gospel, as well as to relieve the miseries of the people. He occupied the new field alone for two years, following the example of his father by giving himself to both medical and evangelistic work in the North Arcot District.[47]

The second Scudder son, William Waterbury Scudder, had returned to America in 1851 with his daughter, Kitty. In 1852 he married again, this time to Elizabeth Knight, and returned to join his brother in the Arcot District in early 1853. Unfortunately Elizabeth died of malaria in 1854, after spending less than two years in India. While in America he and the third brother, Joseph, had met with members of the Reformed Church to draw up plans for the new mission of Arcot.[48]

---

[47] Jacob Chamberlain, *Sketch of the Arcot Mission* (New York: Board of Foreign Missions, Reformed Church in America, 1915), 23-24.
[48] Scudder, *A Thousand Years,* 92.

On May 31, 1853, Henry Martyn Scudder and William Waterbury Scudder met together in Arcot, India, and drew up the charter of the American Arcot Mission. Within a few months, they were joined by the third brother in the family, Joseph Scudder. The three of them are considered the founding members of the Arcot Mission. At that time, missionary wives were considered to be "associated missionaries" but not missionaries in their own right. Therefore, their wives were not listed as members.

Their father, John Scudder, was very much disappointed that he was not allowed by the American Board of Commissioners for Foreign Missions to join his sons as a member of the Arcot Mission. By this time he and his sons spoke of him as an "old man." He had been very much weakened by his years of toil and sickness in Jaffna and in India, and saddened by the death of his wife four years earlier. He was lonely. He had written to Dr. Rufus Anderson, secretary of the ABCFM, requesting permission to be with his sons in Arcot where he could, as he wrote, "be with his chickens" in his last years.

This request brought a sharp negative rejoinder from Anderson, who decreed:

> The young men are no longer "chickens." They are full grown, of full age, of full individual responsibility. It is essential to the satisfactory working of the plan that they should not work as sons under paternal superintendence, but as men, as ministers, as missionaries, each with the fullest play of his own individual judgment that is compatible with the existence of the missionary community and with the responsibilities committed to the joint associated community of minds. We have never contemplated a family mission in the sense of carrying on the work on the patriarchal plan.[49]

Anderson expanded at some length on the thinking of the ABCFM in permitting the three Scudder brothers to go to Arcot

[49] Anderson to John Scudder, May 21, 1853.

together to form a mission separate from Madras and Madurai. He stated that the ABCFM was on the whole reluctant to assign several members of the same family to the same mission for obvious reasons. However, they had agreed to allow the three brothers of the same family as an experiment to begin a new (rather than to join an existing) mission, and even, if matters worked out well, to add other brothers to that mission. "If the three brothers should not be able to work happily together, *as missionaries*, which we do not expect, then the experiment will of course stop short and probably not soon be repeated."[50]

These remarks coming from Anderson brought forth a sharp response from the brothers, who resented the "dictatorial" tone of Anderson's letter. They also objected to the inference that their father was domineering and perhaps equally to the implication that they were not able to stand up to their father and express their own minds. They further claimed that Anderson had specifically said to William the one reason William was being transferred from Jaffna to Madras was so that he could be near his father, who was suffering much from his weakened condition.[51] This appeal did not sway Anderson, however, in refusing permission for John Scudder to become a member of the Arcot Mission.

Anderson then went on to state that the ABCFM had no objection to establishing in Arcot a "Dutch Mission" similar to the Amoy Mission in China. He agreed with the Scudders that the founding of the Arcot Mission did not entail ecclesiastical control over either the mission or the church to be established through the efforts of the mission. It was one of the principles of Anderson, who was Congregationalist in his understanding of church polity, that the church in each land should be free to make its own decisions.[52] He stated a basic principle of the ABCFM in this regard:

50 Ibid.
51 Henry M. and William W. Scudder to Rufus Anderson, August 4, 1853.
52 Rufus Anderson was the corresponding secretary and eventually senior secretary of the American Board of Commissioners for Foreign Missions from 1832 to 1866 and the

You know it would give the Dutch Reformed Ecclesiastical bodies no control of the mission whatever. You are aware, too, that it is one of our principles of belief that churches formed among foreign nations should not be subjected to the ecclesiastical rule of any bodies, whether voluntary or ecclesiastical in the United States. Missionaries may, of course, retain their own personal connection with ecclesiastical bodies in the United States and may change, or form new connections of that sort, according to their pleasure as individuals, but the *churches* formed in India, Sandwich Islands, Western Asia, China, etc. should be independent as such of all foreign control.[53]

The Scudders were in full accord with these principles stated by Anderson. The principles remained fundamental to the self-understanding of the Arcot Mission throughout its entire existence. At one point, however, there was a difference. Reformed Church ministers are presbyterian rather than congregational in their understanding of church polity. When Anderson went on to state that he had no objection to the formation of the Classis of Arcot as well as the Arcot Mission, he wrote from his congregational perspective. By contrast, as members of the Classis of Arcot in the Reformed Church in America, the local congregations in India were bound to act according to the constitution of that denomination in matters of liturgy, theology, ordination of ministers, and discipline. A classis or congregation cannot be fully independent of foreign control when one is working across national boundaries.

The founding principles of the Arcot Mission are found in the first annual report of the American Arcot Mission: "The work of

most influential American mission leader during that period. For a brief biographical sketch of his life and work, see R. Pierce Beaver, "Rufus Anderson, 1796-1880: To Evangelize, Not Civilize," in Gerald H. Anderson, et.al., *Mission Legacies: Biographical Studies of Leaders of the Modern Missionary Movement* (Maryknoll, N.Y.: Orbis Books, 1994), 548-53.

[53] Anderson to John Scudder, May 21, 1953.

this Mission is threefold." This statement was to be so fundamental
to its existence that the full text must be quoted:

1. *The preaching of the Gospel.*—This is our great leading idea.
   The Word of the Lord must be proclaimed to the
   masses. We cannot encumber ourselves with institutions
   which will hinder this work. Christ's commission, "Go
   preach to every creature," is the true law of Missionary
   labor.

2. *The preparation and extensive diffusion of Vernacular Tracts
   and Books.*—As we mingle much with the people, we
   trust God will enable us to compose tracts and treatises
   specially adapted to the Hindu mind and character. We
   have commenced a series in the Tamil and Telugu
   languages. We are deeply impressed with the importance
   of vernacular distribution. We can send the tract far on
   beyond us into masses where our voice has not yet
   reached.

3. *The education of those who join us.*—We have no schools for
   heathen children. If three or more families in any place
   renounce heathenism and put themselves under our
   instruction, we erect a small building for them, in which
   a school is opened for their children, and where parents
   and children attend on the Sabbath and learn the way of
   the gospel. Such bodies are called "village
   congregations." The worship of the true God is thus
   introduced among them. If any of them become truly
   converted we admit them as communicants. To teach
   these nominal Christians the truths of God's words,
   and to give their children a plain practical education are
   objects of great interest to us. The work has begun: we
   trust that it may increase to the glory of Him who is our
   God and our Redeemer. [54]

[54] *American Arcot Mission Report* (hereafter "AAR"), 1854, 6-7.

One must note in this statement of the threefold work of the Arcot Mission that priority is given to the evangelistic preaching of the gospel along with the distribution of scriptures and Christian literature to Hindus. Reports of how this work was carried out by the missionaries and their Indian helpers will be examined in chapter 2.

The second point to note is that the Scudders state as a policy that they will not encumber themselves with the establishment of institutions such as schools and hospitals that will hinder their work of preaching the gospel. Anyone who was acquainted with the results of the work of the Arcot Mission in 1947 at the time of the inauguration of the Church of South India would have been amazed to read this provision. At the time of the inauguration, the Arcot area may well have been the most heavily institutionalized mission area in the whole of the Church of South India. It will be necessary in subsequent chapters to trace the course by which the Arcot Mission moved from its original policy to what actually came to pass in the twentieth century. The shift of emphasis also was responsible for considerable tension following World War II.

The first report of the Arcot Mission, issued in 1854 at the end of its first year, gives evidence of how sincere the first missionaries were in giving priority to evangelism, preaching, and scripture distribution over establishing institutions. Much of the fame of the Scudder family in India was and still is due to their medical mission service. John Scudder, Sr., was the first American to be appointed as a medical missionary. His son, Henry Martyn, was also a medical doctor. He was the first to move to the Arcot District. He began by opening a medical clinic at Walajanagar, located about twenty miles from Vellore. In the first report, the missionaries state that they have closed the dispensary that had been opened the previous year. One reason given is that the health of Henry was such that he would not have been able to carry on other, more important duties.

The report also states that there is a more important reason for their rejoicing in the dispensary being closed. The government had opened new dispensaries in Vellore and Arcot (five miles from Wallaganagar) in addition to its former dispensary at Chittoor (twenty miles away in a triangular distance from both Vellore and Wallaganagar). "The necessity for ours therefore is gone. Provision is made for the sick, and the energies hitherto expended by us in that direction are more suitably employed in other departments of mission work."[55] The missionaries go on to state that because the government had thus freed them from the necessity of doing medical work, they would have closed the dispensary even if Henry Scudder had remained in good health. Now they know themselves to be free to remain true to their fundamental principle.

> We can but rejoice that God in His Providence has taken away our Dispensary, and thrown us more entirely upon the preaching of His Word—divested even of this auxiliary— so that the fundamental principle of our mission may shine out in its simple oneness.[56]

Consonant with their priority for evangelism was the missionaries' report that, following the closing of the medical dispensary, there was a balance of Rs. 87-7-0 in the account. This they placed in the tract and book fund, which, they supposed, "no one will be displeased by our doing so." Moreover,

> The very complete set of surgical instruments ordered in 1853, arrived in 1854, and is now in possession of the mission. If any of the set should be sold, the funds will be credited to our Tract and Book fund. The same is to be said in regard to the stock of medicines on hand. We, at present, think, however, that both medicines and instruments should be retained to meet the exigencies of the mission.[57]

---

55 Ibid., 8.
56 Ibid., 9.
57 Ibid.

It is perhaps ironic that one hundred years later the largest Protestant mission hospital and medical college in the world was growing rapidly in Vellore, under the leadership of Dr. Ida Scudder.

The third point of the threefold work of the mission makes clear that its concern, alongside evangelistic preaching and distribution of literature, was that believers should be gathered into churches and village congregations. People are not only called to hear the Word of God and be converted; they also need to be instructed in the knowledge and discipline of the faith and in the worship of God. Thus the first annual report devotes the greatest amount of space to reporting about the settlement of the missionaries in three stations, Vellore, Chittoor, and Arni. It includes much information about the congregations already organized according to the rules of the Reformed Church in America. These congregations were in Vellore and Chittoor. A third, in Arni, they hoped to organized upon the return of Joseph Scudder from South Africa following the death of their father.

The report includes a plea for funds for church buildings in each of the three towns, at a cost of Rs. 4000 each (about $1,300).[58]

> Our design is to build them in the midst of the heathen population, and not far away in a secluded spot. The most public place we can secure in the heart of the town, is the suitable site for their erection. Then many heathen will come to hear the Word as it is regularly preached....A neat commodious substantial building will be a perpetual declaration to the heathen that Christians have taken possession of the land in the name of the Lord Jesus.[59]

In appealing for funds for the immediate erection of church buildings, the Scudders showed their recognition of the importance

---

[58] The foreign exchange rates between the English pound, the American dollar, and the Indian rupee varied considerably over the course of the years. We will indicate the approximate exchange rate from time to time for comparative purposes, but our figures should be understood as approximations, not as exact rates.
[59] Ibid., 7-8.

of a place of worship in Tamil culture. One of the proverbs in that language asks, "If it has no temple, is it a village?" The church buildings would serve to communicate that the gospel of Jesus Christ had come to stay.

Formation of the Classis of Arcot, 1854

On the same day in 1853 that the Scudders established the American Arcot Mission, John Scudder and his two sons asked the Particular Synod of New York to approve their being organized into the Classis of Arcot. This request was in accord with the action of the Board of Foreign Missions report to the Reformed Church General Synod in 1852, recommending that such a classis be formed in both mission fields of the denomination, in Amoy, China, as well as in Arcot. The service of organization took place in 1854, with the three Reformed Church ministers and three Indian Christians from Madras representing the eldership. As so constituted, the Classis of Arcot of the Reformed Protestant Dutch Church (the name of the denomination until 1867, when the Reformed Church in America adopted its present name) came into existence with an anomalous national or cultural identity.[60] The classical reports of the Classis of Arcot appear annually thereafter in the Reformed Church's *Minutes of General Synod*, 1854-1902, when its churches were transferred to the South Indian United Church.[61]

When they sent their first classis report to the General Synod in September, 1855, the Scudders reflected on what had brought them to the desire to form the Classis of Arcot in India. "Far away in the

[60] The General Synod of the Reformed Church in 1857 requested its missionaries in Amoy to take the same step in forming a classis there. However, the Amoy missionaries had developed a close mission partnership with English Presbyterian missionaries and refused to do so. The controversy that ensued continued until 1863, by which time the General Synod accepted the judgment of the missionaries. As a result, the Classis of Arcot was the only classis organized by the denomination on a mission field. A full account of the controversy in China can be found in Gerald F. De Jong, *The Reformed Church in China, 1842-1951* (Grand Rapids: Eerdmans, 1992), 62-77; cf. Arie R. Brouwer, *Reformed Church Roots* (New York: Reformed Church Press, 1977), 129-133.
[61] The Reformed Church's actions on this train of events are reported in the *Minutes of the General Synod, RCA,* 1852 (279-280), 1853 (392), 1854 (474), and 1902 (99-100).

Henry M. Scudder, William W. Scudder, Joseph Scudder

desert lands of heathenism, we long to hear the expressions of our affection, and to enter within the sphere of your sympathy. The strong desire of our hearts that you should encompass us with you love, must be our apology."[62]

They wrote about how they had come to be related to the Reformed Church. Henry M. and William W. had been sent to the United States for their education when they were still fairly small boys. They lived separately with different relatives. In their letter to the General Synod, they pointed out that in God's providence, Henry had belonged to the New School Presbyterian Church and had studied in Union Theological Seminary in New York, at that time a Presbyterian seminary favored by adherents of the New School. William, however, had grown up in Old School circles and had received his theological training at Princeton Theological Seminary. Both were ordained in the Presbyterian Church prior to beginning their missionary service. In the course of his career, however, Henry had come to love the Dutch church of his adoption as the "deliberate choice of his riper years." Similarly, William, as a

[62] Arcot Classis, *Letter to the General Synod of the Reformed Protestant Dutch Church in the United States of America,* September, 1855.

missionary in Jaffna, and finding himself "unable to sympathize with the Congregational form of church government, yearned for union with the mother church." The younger brother, Joseph, meanwhile found himself within the Reformed Church and became a graduate of its New Brunswick Theological Seminary.[63] It is possible that few classes have been formed with such joy and anticipation as the Scudders felt in the establishment of the Classis of Arcot. They wrote,

> Pour some of your tides of affection towards us. Sustain us by your prayer. Give us counsel and sympathy. We need it. We need something more than formal official connection with a Missionary Board. There is such a thing as ecclesiastical sympathy. We need to stand in intimate relationship to our own church, to have her arms of strength put around us and to feel the beating of her heart and her warms lips of holy love. We must have a classis. The Dutch church is our Zion, beautiful for situation, the joy of our hearts. We must be permitted to look towards her distant summits, and say, Behold the house of our habitation [64]

While not allowed to become a member of the Arcot Mission, John Scudder, as an ordained minister in the Reformed Church, could not only be a member of the classis, he was appointed to preach the inaugural sermon and to organize the classis. By 1854 he was very weak, and only three days after the day of organization he would be taken by his son, Joseph, to South Africa in his final journey. The description of the organization of the classis and John Scudder's role in it is so poignant that we quote it at length:

> Our father, the Rev. Dr. John Scudder was appointed to preach the sermon and organize the classis. He was stretched

63 Ibid. We will later consider more carefully possible implications of the New School and Old School Presbyterian training for the theological direction maintained by the Arcot Mission.

64 Ibid.

upon a bed of sickness. He had no hope of living. The materials for forming the classis were brought together. Monday was the appointed day. On the Sabbath, fearing that he could not live until the next day, he insisted on anticipating the great and delightful duty assigned to him, but was persuaded to wait until the day and the hour predetermined, when he rose in pain and weariness, and preached the sermon, seated in a chair.[65]

John Scudder's sermon on that day was the last act of his missionary life in India. The Scudder brothers went on to write about the formation of the Classis of Arcot and his last days in India before he boarded the ship bound for the Cape of Good Hope:

He conceived it to be a work every way befitting the close of his career. He had planted the standards of his own beloved church in India. He committed them to his sons. He charged them to be faithful. In three days he was carried on board of a ship, and at the Cape of Good Hope he died in the bosom of the church which he so much revered. Before he left the shores of India, he asked one of his sons to write as follows:

My last request to the Dutch Church is that they may live and labor and pray for the salvation of a lost world, and that they may train up their children for this great object.[66]

In moving toward forming both a mission and a classis on the same day, the Scudders were dealing with an issue which would be the focus of controversy as well as polite dialogue for more than a century. The central issue was how to honor the proper role and authority of the church and classis while the mission had overwhelming resources in relation to the church. The Arcot Mission was formed to complete certain tasks, as described in its

[65] Ibid.
[66] Ibid.

statement on it "threefold work." It was to be a task which
supposedly could some day be completed, as was the case in
America and Europe, where the churches existed without an
organized mission working in partnership with them.

According to the Reformed Church *Constitution*, the classis, like a
presbytery in the Presbyterian tradition, is the body that exercises
superintendence over the churches within its bounds and over the
ministers who are members of it. In 1854, a classis consisted of all
the ministers enrolled and an elder delegated from each consistory
within its bounds. It had the power to approve or disapprove calls
of ministers on the part of the consistory (the church board
composed of elders and usually deacons also), to ordain and to
discipline ministers, to form new congregations, and to serve as a
judicial body in cases of disciplinary matters. It also was responsible
to see that the ministers and elders in the churches maintained
regular public worship, properly administered the sacraments, and
carried on a ministry of pastoral care and Christian education
among the members. In a classis, all ordained ministers, whether
they be missionary or Indian, have equal rank and authority; all
ministers and elders present have one vote, meeting together in one
body.

Given the nature of the responsibilities of the classis in relation
to its organized churches and village congregations, it was regarded
as essential that there always be a classis (or a successor body with
similar functions, such as a presbytery or diocese), so long as there
were individual congregations. In the mission situation in the
nineteenth and much of the twentieth century, the difference in
financial resources and resources of personnel was usually immense.
The financial resources for carrying out the missionary task, for
paying salaries of ordained ministers and village catechists, teachers,
and other "helpers" all came from the Arcot Mission, in which male
missionaries, but no Indians, were members. A high percentage of
the cost of supplies, of travel expenses for evangelistic touring,
resources for medical and educational materials and church building,

even the cost of the meetings of the Classis of Arcot, had to be met by the Arcot Mission.

As ordained ministers in the Reformed Church in America, the Scudders had a high regard for the authority of a classis to make its own decisions independent from outside interference. They also believed that all ministers and elders who held membership in the classis were equal in rank and authority, with equal rights of voting and speaking. Thus there could be no distinction between missionary and Indian in the classis. From the very beginning, therefore, the Scudders believed that they had formed a church which met the test of self-governance. Nevertheless, however such self-governing was officially the case, it was impossible to ignore the fact that for a number of years most of the elders were employed by the Arcot Mission as teachers or catechists and the salaries of the ministers were likewise paid by the mission. Furthermore, the missionaries had long experience with Reformed Church order, theology, and worship while the Indians were new to the Reformed Church. Under those circumstances, the Indians were naturally hesitant to challenge the missionaries in meetings of the classis, however much the missionaries encouraged them to feel free to do so. As a result, throughout the decades in which the Classis of Arcot existed, the power of the Arcot Mission was immeasurably greater than that of the classis.

The problem of the relation of an organized missionary society to an organized church was not new to missionaries of the Reformed Church. In fact, Rufus Anderson, foreign secretary of the American Board of Commissioners for Foreign Missions (1832-1866), to whom Reformed Church missionaries were accountable until 1857, had developed what has come to be known as the "three-self" theory to guide the missions. His formulation provided a clear statement of the aim, means, and recognition of the time of completion of missionary activity, when the missionary would have worked himself out of a job and could either go home or enter into a new mission field in a region beyond. In the colonial situation of the nineteenth century, he maintained that the proper test of success in missions is not the progress of civilization but the evidence of a religious life. Missionaries should not build institutions but should focus on bringing individuals to faith and planting "self-governing, self-supporting, self-propagating churches." When such churches came into existence in foreign lands, the missionaries would be free to leave to serve elsewhere in "regions beyond." He stated his position succinctly:

> Such is the simple structure of our foreign missions, as the combined result of experience, and of the apostolic example: in all which the grand object is to plant and multiply self-reliant, efficient churches, composed wholly of native converts, each church complete, with its pastors of the same race with the people. And when the unevangelized nations are so filled with such churches, that all...have it within their power to learn what they must do to be saved, then may we expect the promised advent of the Spirit, and the conversion of the world...[67]

The members of the Arcot Mission were fully in accord with the thesis of Rufus Anderson. In forming both a mission and a classis, they from the outset had provided structure and direction for their subsequent efforts. The Arcot Mission would provide the initial impetus for the conversion of individuals, the planting of churches, and the training of an educated and evangelistic ministry and the development of a sense of stewardship of time, talents, and money. All of such activity was carried out, looking forward to the day when the church in India would be self-governing, self-supporting, and self-propagating, at which time the Arcot Mission would turn over all its responsibility to the church. The Classis of Arcot immediately met the first test, that of being self-governing, although it was in

---

[67] Rufus Anderson, quoted in Norman E. Thomas, *Classic Texts in Mission and World Christianity* (Maryknoll, N.Y.: Orbis Press, 1995), 69.

1853 still in need of Indian ordained ministers. It would be many decades before it became self-supporting and self-propagating.

In the theory proposed by Rufus Anderson, institutions such as schools and hospitals did not fit well into mission work unless they had a clearly defined evangelistic purpose. Institutions had a strong tendency to distract missionaries from their primary task of evangelism and planting churches. Moreover, they required financial assistance in such amounts that the church which should become self-supporting would never be able to afford them.

Establishment of the Board of Foreign Missions of the Reformed Church in America, 1857[68]

During the first years of the American Arcot Mission and the Classis of Arcot in India, a movement toward the incorporation of the Reformed Church's Board of Foreign Mission was also going forward. A Board of Foreign Missions had already been formed in 1832, but it operated through the American Board of Foreign Missions. In that year it was assisting missionaries in Borneo as well as John and Harriet Scudder in Jaffna. Anticipated additional support for a Borneo Mission from the Dutch East India Company did not materialize, and conditions were devastating there for missionary health. Consequently, missionaries remaining on the field after 1842 were transferred to Amoy, China. However, the level of contributions from Reformed churches remained low, being $3,905 in 1833 and increasing only slowly thereafter. By 1850 there had developed a strong sense that financial support for foreign missions would be considerably greater if the denomination had its own incorporated Board of Foreign Missions.

The General Synod approved the Constitution of the Board of Foreign Missions in its meeting of October, 1857, thereby

---

[68] For a brief history of the Reformed Church in America's relationships with foreign missionary societies prior to the establishment of the Board of Foreign Missions, see Marvin D. Hoff, *The Reformed Church in America: Structures for Mission* (Grand Rapids: Eerdmans, 1985), 23-37.

committing to that board the management and control of foreign missions of the denomination, subject to the "revision and instruction of the General Synod." The preamble to the constitution is a clear statement of the purposes of the board and in basic philosophy is consistent with the purposes of the Arcot Mission. Within a very few years, some tensions would arise between the board and the mission regarding the authority of the board, but it would be a long time before there were important theological differences. The preamble reads:

> *Whereas* the Lord Jesus Christ, as the Divine Head of the Church, has enjoined on all His people the duty of giving the Gospel to every creature; and, *Whereas* the condition of all men without the Gospel is one of exposure to eternal death, as well as of present suffering and sorrow—Therefore, under the conviction of duty, and with earnest desire for the best interest of our fellow-men here and hereafter—the General Synod of the Reformed Dutch Church, acknowledging with gratitude what God has been pleased to accomplish by the Church, deems it important in entering on a distinct and separate management and support of Foreign Missions, to remodel its Board of Foreign Missions, with a view to greater efficiency and a more faithful conformity to the Divine requirement....[69]

One can note here that the reason given for forming a Board of Foreign Missions is "greater efficiency and a more faithful conformity to the Divine requirement." Thus the Board of Foreign Missions exists for the sake of the church and its witness, but it exists for the sake of efficiency rather than because it is a necessary component of the church's life. In this respect, its role is similar to that of the Arcot Mission. That body also is recognized to exist for the sake of planting a self-governing, self-supporting, self-propagating church,

---

[69] *Minutes of the General Synod*, 1857, 263.

while the Arcot Mission's role as one of the church's official
assemblies is closer to that of the General Synod. As the decades
rolled on, a number of issues related to these interrelationships of
the classis, the mission, the board and the General Synod became
at certain times important points of tension.

2

The Founding Principles
Confirmed, 1853-1860

By 1853, the basic principles and direction for Reformed Church mission activity in India were in place. The threefold work of the Arcot Mission—the preaching of the gospel, the preparation and extensive diffusion of vernacular tracts and books, and the education of those who joined—provided a set of priorities. Rejection of caste and caste discrimination within the church was a firm policy. The three-self theory of a self-governing, self-supporting, and self-propagating church provided a concrete set of criteria by which the progress of the missionary endeavor could be measured. It looked toward a day when the mission's goal would have been reached and the missionaries could carry on in new regions. The formation of the Classis of Arcot provided a firm structure for the continuing ministry and witness of an indigenous church that was a full participant in an international, intercontinental church.

The first decade of the American Arcot Mission and the churches that formed the Arcot Classis begins to reveal the shape of the work that was built on these sturdy foundations. Before considering that work, however, it is important first to consider the geographical location of the Arcot Mission, the historical colonial setting of its activity, and the history of missions in that area prior to the arrival of Reformed Church missionaries.

The Geographical Location of the Arcot Mission

Vellore was located at the geographical center of the Arcot Mission, which occupied the districts of South Arcot, North Arcot, and Chittoor in the Madras Presidency, with a small amount of territory beyond the boundaries of those districts. Vellore lies about ninety miles west of Madras. The territory extended beyond the towns of Tindivanam, eighty miles south of Vellore, and Madanapalle, eighty miles north, for a total distance of 160 miles. Its width varied from twenty to sixty miles, for a total area of 8,277 miles, which is somewhat similar to the size and shape of the state of New Jersey. Vellore is located about four hundred miles north of the southern tip of India. The population was estimated at about 1.5 million in 1853.

Tamil is the major language spoken in the larger part of the area, from Tindivanam in the south to a line about ten or fifteen miles north of Vellore. Telugu is the language spoken north of that line, including the towns of Chittoor, Palmaner, Punganur, and Madanapalle. The congregations that came into existence in the areas of Chittoor and Palmaner, however, were for the most part Tamil speaking. Tamil and Telegu are both part of the south Indian group of languages known as Dravidian. They are related to each other as German is to Dutch or French is to Italian. They are quite different from the north Indian languages that are related in origin to Sanskrit and are part of the Indo-German language grouping.

Throughout its history, the Arcot Mission had to take into account the fact that it served people who spoke two different languages. After India became independent in 1947, state lines followed the linguistic boundaries, with the result that the Tamil area became part of Madras State, later named Tamilnadu (i.e. Tamil country), while the Telugu area became part of Andhra State. This political division became particularly important in the field of education, where quite different policies regarding funding and curriculum had to be taken into account by the church.

The Colonial Context

Two of the charges that have often been leveled against missionaries are that they have been agents of colonialism and western imperialism, and that they have been destroyers of native cultures. The missionaries of the American Board of Commissioners for Foreign Missions (ABCFM) who went to the Sandwich Islands (Hawaii) have been criticized rightly or wrongly by numerous scholars and in popular writings on these counts. Since the Scudders went to India under the ABCFM, it is important that we explore the extent to that they were guilty of one or both charges.[1] We will bear these charges in mind as we move through the next several chapters.

The Reformed Church missionaries who began to enter India in 1836 served during the colonial era, when India was under the control of England. The purposes and extent of that rule changed over time, however, and those changes affected the roles and responses of Christian missionaries in India. We have already noted that during the period 1600-1813 the East India Company was hostile to missionaries, fearing that their presence would create religious tensions and thereby undermine the profitability of the company. Throughout much of that era, the company had "a policy of non-interference with local custom."[2] Its transition from almost exclusive concern for profit shifted to a need to rule over territory when conflict arose with other European traders, especially the French. A series of alliances were made by the East India Company with various Indian rulers, with the result that a number of battles

---

[1] Arie Brouwer, who was executive secretary for the General Program Council of the Reformed Church in America in 1977 and thus carried supervisory responsibility over its world mission program when his book, *Reformed Church Roots,* was published, entitled the chapter dealing with John and Harriet Scudder, "Imperial Mission" (94-99).

[2] Hal W. French and Arvind Sharma, *Religious Ferment in Modern India* (New York: St. Martins Press, 1981), 8-9.

were fought. The ultimate result was that the French had to retreat from broad involvement in India and, one by one, the Indian authorities were forced to become subordinate to the East India Company.[3]

As the company officers followed ever more aggressive policies in establishing their power in India following their victory at Plessey in 1757, their aggressive movements forced the English conscience to develop a rationale for its expanded rule in India. Differences of opinion developed between the "utilitarians," the "evangelicals," and the "orientalists," although all agreed that England must rule in India for the foreseeable future.

Utilitarians

Governor-general Richard Wellesley represented a utilitarian point of view when he told the Board of Directors of the East India Company on July 9, 1800,

> We feel that it would not only be unpolitic, but highly immoral to suppose that Providence has admitted of the establishment of British power over the finest provinces of India, with any other view than that of its being conducive to the happiness of the people, as well as to our national advantage.[4]

The view of Wellesley was more fully articulated by persons such as Jeremy Bentham, James Mill, and his son, John Stuart Mill, whose utilitarian philosophy is often summed up in the popular slogan, "the greatest good for the greatest number." The utilitarians taught that one must labor for a reciprocal good in which all participating

[3] It is interesting to note that these alliances and conflicts between the English and the French were taking place in India in the same years that the French and Indian War, using American Indians as allies, was being fought in America. The Treaty of Paris signed in 1763 by England and France brought a degree of resolution to matters in India as well as in America. It is also worthy of note that the real beginning of the colonization of India took place in same decades as the beginning of the independence movement took place in America.

[4] French and Sharma, *Religious Ferment*, 10-11.

parties prosper (the "win-win" result, in today's parlance). The
utilitarians believed that one must look for the underlying unity of
humanity that can be found in every nation. Nations such as India,
that were "backward," were not inherently inferior but were
"backward" because they were not yet modern. The Indians were
still living under "oriental despotism," under personal rule in a
master-servant relationship rather than under the rule of law.[5]
Therefore the utilitarians understood it to be their duty to provide
a system of laws for the development of a modern India. "In
devising legal codes for India, the Utilitarians did not seek merely
to adapt British legal precedents to local circumstances. They saw
themselves as independent of legal models from any country,
seeking rather to implement insights from the universal science of
jurisprudence."[6]

All of the British were horrified by some of the customs that they
met in India. Among these were the practice of *sati* (the immolation
of Hindu widows on the funeral pyres of their dead husbands), *thugi*
(ritual murder by strangling and highway robbery in the service of
the Mother Goddess Kali), child marriages, and the practice of
forbidding very young widows to remarry.[7] The utilitarian Lord
William Bentinck, who served as governor-general from 1828 to
1835, promulgated the Act of Abolition in 1829 abolishing *sati* and
thereby established a precedent for government intervention into
the most sacred areas of Indian ritual practice.[8]

Evangelicals

The evangelicals were equally horrified by the abuses that they
saw, but they ascribed the decadence to the sinfulness of the human

---

[5] Thomas R. Metcalf, *Ideologies of the Raj* (Cambridge: Cambridge University Press, 1994),
  6-7.
[6] French and Sharma, *Religious Ferment*, 12; cf. Metcalf, *Ideologies of the Raj*, 39.
[7] The practice of celebrating a marriage between a very young girl to an older (even old
  man) was not uncommon. When the man died, the woman became a widow without
  opportunity to remarry, even though she could be as young as eight years or less. Many
  believed that the man may have died because of some fault in the wife. Widows were
  often treated very badly.
[8] Stanley Wolpert, *A New History of India*, 4th ed. (New York: Oxford University Press,
  1993), 212.

race and to the depravity and idolatry they saw in much of Hinduism. William Wilberforce, who in England was one of the leaders in the movement for social reforms and the abolition of slavery, in 1813 declared that it was crucial that the East India Company relax its prohibitions on missionary work. He stated, "Our Christian religion is sublime, pure and beneficent. The Indian religious system is mean, licentious, and cruel....It is one grand abomination."[9]

When the East India Company Charter came up for renewal in 1833, the situation had reached the point where Parliament asserted its authority to make policy for India but essentially gave the company the role of administering India according to those policies. By 1833, utilitarians and reform-minded evangelicals could work together to pass progressive legislation. The Liberal Charter of that year established a number of reforms. It abolished slavery (actually passed for India in 1843), limited the age at which children could be employed in mines and mills, and established the right of every person in India to have equal access to employment by the company. The committee of Parliament in 1833 also stated the opinion that the interests of the "Native Subjects" must be respected.

> On a large view of the state of Indian Legislation, and of the improvements of which it is susceptible, it is recognized as an indisputable principle, that the interests of the Native Subjects are to be consulted in preference to those of Europeans, whenever the two come in competition; and that therefore the Laws ought to be adapted rather to the feelings and habits of the Natives than to those of the Europeans.[10]

Though these noble sentiments were often quoted by Indian nationalists as evidence of the hypocrisy of the British, as they certainly were, they did set a standard on which Indians could call their English overlords to account.

9 French and Sharma, *Religious Ferment*, 14.
10 Wolpert, *History of India*, 213.

Orientalists

The orientalists also were dismayed at what they saw, but they believed that India and Hinduism itself had the resources to develop a system of laws suitable to India. Foremost among the orientalists was Sir William Jones, who died in 1794. Jones was a translator and profoundly appreciative of the cultural heritage of India. It was, in fact, through his own and his successors' translation of Hindu texts into English that Indians themselves found these materials more accessible and thereby gained a greater respect for their own spiritual heritage. Surprisingly enough, the missionary William Carey can in some ways be considered to be among these orientalists. Through his studies of the vernacular languages, he came to have a great feeling for the life and dignity of the common people. His *Dialogues,* produced as a Bengali reader for his Fort William students, was a document of intense social significance. "It would not be far-fetched to call Carey, as a result of this work alone, India's first cultural anthropologist."[11]

The orientalists made two important contributions that were of great significance for Reformed Church missionaries in India. First, they believed that there was something that could be identified as a separate religion called "Hinduism." This differed from the understanding of the word in the texts of the Muslim rulers who ruled India prior to the coming of the East India Company.

> Yet the term "Hindu" though of Perso-Arabic origin, was not used in Muslim texts to mark out a religion, but rather referred generally to the inhabitants of the Indian subcontinent, the lands across the Indus river. Even when

[11] French and Sharma, *Religious Ferment,* 16. Jawaharlal Nehru has said of the work of Carey and Christian missionaries, "The desire of the Christian missionaries to translate the Bible into every possible language thus resulted in the development of many Indian languages. Christian mission work in India has not always been admirable or praiseworthy, but in this respect, as well as in the collection of folklore, it has undoubtedly been of great service to India" [Nehru, *The Discovery of India* (Garden City, N.Y.: Doubleday, 1959), 229].

the term "Hindu" was used to set off those adhering to a non-Islamic faith, the perception each group had of each other, as Romila Thapar has written, "was not in terms of a monolithic religion, but more in terms of distinct and disparate castes and sects along a social continuum."[12]

In the Tamil language, the word *Indu* refers to the people, while the word somewhat equivalent to the English word "religion" is *matham*. In this sense, whatever is the religion of the people who live in that land can be properly called "Hindu" religion. Thus "Hinduism," designating a religious community distinct from other religious communities, took on a fixed definition only with the coming of British rule. Such a definition enabled the British to "devise comprehensive systems of law that would at once respect the customs of their new subjects and yet reduce them to a manageable order."[13]

The second significant contribution was the orientalists' conviction that it is the ancient Sanskrit texts that reveal the doctrinal core of the Hindu faith. For that reason they turned for advice on the interpretation of those texts to those whom they saw as the "priests" of the religion, the Brahmin pundits. Those texts were understood to embody not only moral teachings, but also precise legal prescriptions. This use of Brahmin pundits together with the Brahminical orientation of the texts themselves encouraged the British and missionary view that the Brahmins are the predominant group within Hindu Indian society.[14]

Anti-Brahminism in the Madras Presidency

In the latter half of the nineteenth century and the first half of the twentieth century, resentment against the predominant Brahmin community intensified, especially in Tamilnadu. Caste systems in

[12] Metcalf, *Ideologies of the Raj*, 132.
[13] Ibid., 133.
[14] Ibid., 11.

south India tended to be more extreme and rigid than in the north, with a greater separation between Brahmins and non-Brahmins. The untouchable members of society suffered from elaborate forms of discrimination enforced by both Brahmins and non-Brahmins.[15] A non-Brahmin movement that crystallized politically into the Justice Party surfaced. It included as major participants members of the Nadar caste and other intermediate castes, such as the Vellalas, Mudaliars, and Chettiars, as well as Telugu Reddis. The predominance of the Brahmin community becomes apparent in a review of the 1912 statistics. These show that in Madras Presidency, the Brahmins made up only 3.2 percent of the population, yet they held 55 percent of deputy collectors and 72.6 percent of district munsiff posts (both positions being crucial in cases of local concern). Many of them were also the major landowners.[16] After 1947, the anti-Brahmin bias in Tamilnad led to a cultural movement that sought to purify the Tamil language[17] by eliminating all Sanskrit-based words and substituting for them words with pure Tamil roots, much as an English-speaking purist would substitute Anglo-Saxon root words for words derived from Latin. In the 1960s, the Tamil Progress Party, with its anti-Brahmin platform, would replace the Congress Party as the ruling party in the state.

As we will see in following chapters, Reformed Church missionaries responded somewhat ambiguously to the predominance of the Brahmins. On the one hand, they had a grudging admiration for the Brahmins, as they recognized in many of them cultural and philosophical or theological wisdom and the ability to move in polite social society. They were particularly eager to see in the latest Brahmin convert evidence of the movement of India to Christianity.

---

15 Kenneth W. Jones, *Socio-religious Reform Movements in British India* (Cambridge: Cambridge University Press, 1989), 154.

16 Sumit Sarkar, *Modern India: 1885-1947* (New York: St. Martin's Press, 1983), 159.

17 The Tamil language is claimed to be the oldest language continually in use and spoken anywhere. It is highly developed grammatically and has a large classical vocabulary. Speakers of Tamil like to point out that the word "Tamil" means "sweet," hence it is the sweetest of all languages, although many missionaries attempting to master its intricacies felt differently.

On the other hand, their complaints about injustices and superstitions in the religion often were addressed in terms of opposition to the evil system of "Brahminism," rather than Hinduism in general.

Economic Impact of Colonialism

Reformed Church missionaries consistently informed their supporters in the United States about the abject poverty of the people among whom they worked. They often implied that this poverty could be overcome only as people turned to Jesus Christ. They seldom spent much energy analyzing reasons for the lack of economic development. What they failed to note was that right up to the eighteenth century, when the Industrial Revolution began in England, the Indian economy and standard of living was probably not that much different from Europe's. In fact, trade with India was so desirable to European nations precisely because India had an efficient and well organized banking and commercial system, with excellent shipbuilding and cloth manufacturing industries, as well as desirable agricultural products and spices. Jawaharlel Nehru claimed in 1945 that at the beginning of the Industrial Revolution, "India was, in fact, as advanced industrially, commercially, and financially as any country prior to the Industrial Revolution."[18]

The Charter Act of 1833 opened India to unrestricted enterprise as well as to the coming of American missionaries. While it abolished the company's monopoly over all trade except opium and salt, it also enabled the cheaper machine-made cottons from England to gain an advantage over and bring about the collapse of the home-spun cotton industry in India, and thereby threw millions of Indian men and women out of work.[19] Nehru, along with many other Indian nationalists after1885, maintained that the net effect of the British domination of India was to make India a colonial and agricultural appendage of the British structure. This not only severely damaged the self-sufficient economy, it also prevented

[18] Nehru, *Discovery of India,* 192.
[19] Wolpert, *History of India,* 213-14.

Indians from making the adjustments necessary to advance
economically and socially in the age of the Industrial Revolution.[20]
The result was the economic impoverishment of India, in the view
of Indian nationalists.

East India Company Involvement in Hindu Temple Administration

One of the complaints that evangelicals in England made against
the East India Company prior to the Charter Act of 1833 was that
the company's involvement in temple administration in India was
actually a bias in favor of Hinduism to the disadvantage of
Christianity. The company had not really desired to become involved
in such administrative detail but in the previous fifty years had been
drawn into it. Over the centuries, temples in India had accumulated
wealth and lands, often under the control or supervision of the local
raja or other ruler. The raja often took responsibility to see that
salaries for the temple employees such as cooks and dancing girls
as well as those performing priestly functions were paid, to collect
interest on mortgages held by the temple, and to collect rents from
lands. His duty was also to ensure that villagers within the realm
would respond to the need for help in the time of the great festivals.
Since the great Jagannath car festivals sometimes required several
thousand men to guide and pull the heavy cars by means of long

---

[20] Nehru, *Discovery of India*, 217-22. Nehru compared ironically the economic development
of India with that of the United States after Britain's victory at the Battle of Plessey in
1757 and the American independence declared in 1776: "The independence of the
United States of America is more or less contemporaneous with the loss of freedom
by India. Surveying the past century and a half, an Indian looks somewhat wistfully and
longingly at the vast progress made by the United States during this period and
compares it with what has been done and what has not been done in his own country.
It is no doubt true that the Americans have many virtues and we have many failings,
that America offered a virgin field and almost a clean slate to write upon while we were
cluttered up with ancient memories and traditions. And yet perhaps it is not
inconceivable that if Britain had not undertaken this great burden in India, and, as she
tells us, endeavored for so long to teach us the difficult art of self-government of which
we had been so ignorant, India might not have only been freer and more prosperous
but also far more advanced in science and art and all that makes life worth living" (197).

ropes, this call to labor for the temple could be one that the villagers tried to avoid. [21]

Under the Raj, when temple administration became inefficient and/or corrupt, the raja's control over temple administration was transferred to district officials appointed by the British officials. In North Arcot District, in 1833, the British collector[22] reported on his duties for temple administration. "Our interference has extended over every detail of management; we regulate their funds, superintend the repairs of their temples, keep in order their cars and images, purchase and keep in store the various commodities required for their use, investigate and adjust all disputes, and at times, even those of a religious nature."[23] The collector reported that he was "highly esteemed" for the manner in which he cared for temple administration and enabled it to flourish under his management.

Thus, by 1833, local company officials tended to be heavily involved in carrying out the duties that were formerly the responsibility of the local ruler. Evangelicals in England complained that this was an excessive and inexcusable support for and encouragement of idolatry. The company bowed to the pressure and sought ways to discontinue insofar as possible its involvement in the management of temples and to place that management with the revenues in the hands of native Indians. Unfortunately, this meant that there was a lack of accountability over the committee members appointed to administer the temples, with the result that many conflicts arose and complaints about mismanagement and corruption multiplied. To deal with the situation, the Religious Endowment Act XX of 1863 was eventually adopted, and further revisions in auditing accounts and government oversight took place after that to ensure good and equitable administration of temple finance and services. While many problems remained, the act of

---

[21] Cf. Geoffrey A. Oddie, *Hindu and Christian in South-east India* (London: Curzon Press, 1991), 43-56. One estimate was that it took 10,000 men with ropes 1,600 feet long to move the great temple car at Tiruvalur in Negaparam taluk (47).

[22] The "collector" was the chief British government officer in a district.

[23] Donald Eugene Smith, *India as a Secular State* (Princeton: Princeton Univ. Press, 1963), 74.

1863 set a pattern for continued legal governmental concern for temple funds and management that remained in force after independence. Following independence, the government of India has often been criticized for giving Christian churches a freedom from government control in the management of their property and funds that had not been granted to the other religions. This issue will come before us again in our last chapter.

British Support for English Language Education

Three men, Thomas Macauley, law member of the council in Calcutta in 1835, governor-general William Bentinck, and Alexander Duff, a missionary of the Church of Scotland in Calcutta, bear major responsibility for the introduction of English education in India. Until the arrival of Duff in Calcutta in 1830, the official view seemed to be that "whatever of European literature and science might be conveyed to the native mind should be conveyed chiefly through native media, that is to say, the learned languages of India—for the Muslims, Arabic and Persian; and for the Hindus, Sanskrit."[24]

Duff had received very little instruction about India before his arrival there, but he did have several basic ideas. He knew that caste and idolatry were rife in India. He said later that he had planned with the blessing of God to devote his time to preparing a mine that would one day explode the whole structure of Hinduism. He also resolved that in his educational efforts he would insist that every class that was able read some portion of the Bible daily. He prayed that by this reading of the Scriptures the truth might be brought home and some at least would turn from their idols to serve the living God.[25]

He further believed that education must not be confined to Bible or religious reading. He planned to teach every variety of useful knowledge, from the most elementary to the higher branches,

[24] A. A. Millar, *Alexander Duff of India* (Edinburgh: Canongate Press, 1992), 35.
[25] Ibid., 34.

including history, literature, logic, and moral philosophy. He would use the "Baconian," or scientific, method in natural history, mathematics, natural philosophy, and other sciences. The foundation of all of this would be the religion of his Christian faith, upon which the superstructure of all useful knowledge was to be reared, for the highest welfare of the race in time and eternity.[26]

While most of his missionary colleagues disagreed with his plan, Duff went to visit the aged William Carey and gained his approval. When he founded his school in 1830 in Calcutta, it was an immediate success in drawing outstanding young men to study and in producing outstanding results both in terms of educational advancement and moral and religious wrestling with issues of Christian faith and morality. A number of students were converted to the Christian faith, the most famous a Hindu named Ram Mohan Roy, whose story is told in a later chapter.[27]

By 1833, Duff was convinced that his educational approach was the dynamite that would explode the very foundations of Hinduism. Western education should be understood as preparation for the gospel. He declared,

> Only use English as the medium, and you will break the backbone of caste, you will open up the way for teaching anatomy and all other branches fearlessly, for the enlightened native mind will take its own course in spite of all the threats of the Brahmanical traditionalists.[28]

He also laid before the British Governor-general additional reasons for using the English language. He reasoned:

> In reference to the acquisition of European science, the study of languages mentioned would be a sheer waste of

[26] Ibid.
[27] An excellent account of Duff's work can be found in the Millar biography, 33-59 (see also note 23 above). A good summary of the life and contribution of Duff can be found in Michael A. Laird, "Alexander Duff, 1806-1878: Western Education as Preparation for the Gospel," in Anderson, et.al, Mission Legacies, 271-76.
[28] Ibid., 58.

labour and time; since, viewed as a media for receiving and treasuring the stores of modern science, there is no possible connection between them....The sole reason why the English is not even more a general and anxious object of acquisition among the natives, is the degree of uncertainty under which they (the natives) still labour as to the ultimate intentions of Government, and whether it will ever lead them into paths of usefulness, profit or honour....[29]

In proposing that English become the medium of instruction, Duff did not wish to exclude knowledge of the literature of the vernacular languages. He had also developed considerable respect for Bengali learning, but he did not believe such learning would be adequate for the modern age that was arriving in India.

Knowing the experience and enthusiasm of Alexander Duff, and at the same time encouraged by the efforts of Macauley, Bentinck decreed on 7 March, 1835,

1st. His Lordship in Council is of opinion that the great object of the British Government ought to be the promotion of European literature and science among the natives of India, and that all the funds appropriated for the purposes of education would be best employed on English education alone.

2nd. But it is not the intention of his Lordship in Council to abolish any college or school of native learning, while the native population shall appear to be inclined to avail themselves of the advantages which it affords; and his Lordship in Council directs that all the existing professors and students of all the institutions under the superintendents of the committee shall continue to receive their stipends....

4th. His Lordship in Council directs that all the funds which these reforms will leave at the disposal of the committee be henceforth employed in imparting to the

29 Ibid., 59.

native population a knowledge of English literature and science through the medium of the English language....[30]

The experience of Duff and the advocacy of Macauley and Duff for English as the medium of instruction may well have made for more change in the country of India than anything else that occurred there in the last two centuries. It provided the Indian people with an instrument for communication with each other across linguistic lines and opened their educational institutions to the whole scope of modernization and technical knowledge required for scientific advancement. It also provided a legal and political vocabulary that India needed as it moved into its status as an independent nation.

The intent of the British in developing their educational system was not to nurture an independent Indian nation, however, but to be the means of preserving their own ability to manage and profit from their reign over India. By undertaking the education of its subjects in western sciences, languages, and literature, Britain was able to insert Indians into the colonial administrative apparatus and make them useful servants of the empire. The British educational policy was essentially a secular project to transform Indian into "deracinated replicas of Englishmen, even while they remained affiliated with their own religious culture....The strategic objective of turning Hindus into non-Hindu Hindus, or Muslims into non-Muslim Muslims, has been memorialized in Macauley's infamous pronouncement on the goal of an English education for Indians: "Indian in blood and colour, but English in taste, in opinions, in morals, and in intellect."[31]

After 1947, language remained a major political, social, and educational issue, as controversy broke out over whether Hindi should become the language of India and what roles the leading vernacular languages should play in relation to English.

[30] Ibid., 55-56.

[31] Gauri Viswanathan, *Outside the Fold: Conversion, Modernity, and Belief* (Princeton: Princeton Univ. Press, 1998), 5.

Against this background of British support for English education, the American Arcot Mission arrived with a contrasting vision. With its determination to establish a self-governing, self-supporting, self-propagating church, the mission decided from the beginning to work in the vernacular languages of Tamil and Telugu, rather than to establish schools with English as the medium of instruction.

The Mission Context

By the time the first annual report of the Arcot Mission was issued in 1855, the missionaries were already able to record that a church was organized in Vellore. It had thirteen communicants and a total of about seventy people in the congregation. There was also a church at Chittoor that had a congregation with thirteen communicants and a congregation numbering more than one hundred, of whom seventy were nominal Christians. The Arni church was waiting to be organized until Joseph Scudder returned from South Africa. There was a catechist in each location and a total of five teachers in the three vernacular schools.[32]

The reason the Arcot missionaries were able to report the existence of organized churches with communicant members and related schools at the end of the first year is that they were not the first people on the scene. Prior to their coming, there was a fairly long history of missions in Tamilnadu. As a result, a small number of Christians were already present in the area when the Scudders arrived. Very little evidence exists regarding the backgrounds of those Christians, but information is available concerning the wider mission movements to which they would have been related.

In chapter one, the presence of Roman Catholics in Jaffna as a result of the work of Portuguese missionaries in the sixteenth century was noted, as well as the fact that a number of those persons had converted to Protestantism with the coming of the nineteenth-century missionaries. The same movement of Portuguese origin had taken place in south India. Then, in the seventeenth century,

[32] "AAR," 1854, 4-5.

the Jesuits had begun proselytizing among the pearl fishers of the Tuticorin Coast. In 1680, members of the Nadar caste had come in touch with that work of the Jesuits, with the result that the Jesuits were able to organize a congregation largely composed of Nadars at a village named Vadakkankulam and, five years later, to erect a church. The Nadars were a low caste associated with making toddy, the liquor produced from the fermented sap of the Palmyra tree. Since the production and sale of toddy was seen as polluting, the Nadars held a position in the social structure as untouchables. They were not allowed to enter Hindu temples, to use public wells, or to approach members of the higher caste within a specific distance. They were limited in the type of dress they could wear and had to live outside the village proper. They were a small subdivision of the larger Nadar community, called Nadans, who lived as landlords over the others of their caste.[33]

The Jesuits then established a permanent mission in that area and by 1713 counted over four thousand in that parish. After the Jesuits were suppressed by the pope in 1771, their work was carried on by catechists, but the Roman Catholic influence diminished. Nevertheless, the Roman Catholic population for a long time remained at least nine times as great as the Protestant.[34] When the Reformed Church missionaries toured the North Arcot District with their evangelistic preaching, they met many who were nominally Roman Catholics.

Anglican missionaries appeared in Tanjore and Trichinopoly. Some Indian converts, especially a man named David Sundaranandam, succeeded in converting more than five thousand Nadars.[35] After his death, others took his place. By 1850, there were

---

[33] Kenneth W. Jones, *Socio-religious Reform,* 156-57.

[34] Oddie, *Hindu and Christian,* 17.

[35] An excellent account of the ministry of David Sundarandam and the large movement of the Nadars to become Christians is to be found in D. Arthur Jeyakumar, "Christianity Among the Nadars of Tirunelvelly" in E. Hrangkhuma, ed., *Christianity in India: Search for Liberation and Identity* (Delhi: CMS/ISPCK, 1998), 124-37. Actually, the name of the caste prior to the twentieth century was "Shanar:" "...the Shanars were officially known as Nadars from the year 1921. This [change] was because of Christianity. Education, made accessible to all, was much utilized by the Nadars, and

nearly forty thousand Christian converts in the Tinnevelly district under the guidance of two Anglican societies, the Church Missionary Society (CMS) and the Society for the Promotion of Christian Knowledge (SPCK). There were another twenty thousand in neighboring southern Tranvancore. Many of the descendants of these Christians would eventually become members of the Church of South India.[36] A number of them also entered employment as government workers or as personal or domestic servants of British officials and consequently moved to various parts of Tamilnadu, including the North Arcot area. There were also British military garrisons in each of the places where the Arcot Mission planted churches; included among the Indian Sepoys were often a number of Christians.

The first known visit to Vellore by a Christian chaplain took place in 1766. The chaplain of Fort St. George in Madras, the Reverend John Thomas, made a pastoral visit in that year to the 350 British troops who had been stationed there following their defeat of the Nawab of Arcot in 1761. More regular pastoral visitations began in 1771 by the Reverend C. W. Gericke, a German missionary of the SPCK stationed in Cuddalore to the south. He baptized a number of the Indian wives of English soldiers and organized a congregation consisting of members of the garrison, their English wives, and a few Christians who had come to Vellore from Trichinopology, 140 miles to the south. Some of the local Roman Catholics later joined this group.[37]

education brought in social upliftment. Social upliftment brought social freedom. Christian Nadars migrated to Sri Lanka and Malaysia from about the middle of the Nineteenth century. Their remittances enabled them as well as their relatives to rise up in the social ladder" (135).

36 Jones, *Socio-religious Reform,* 157-58.

37 Ten Brink, *History of Vellore Fort,* 38-39. During the eighteenth century, the SPCK had been unable to find enough English clergymen willing to go overseas, so it turned to the Royal Danish Missionary Society for men to assist in providing pastoral care for its garrisons. The company chaplain in the Madras Presidency area found that these Danish missionaries were more suitable for the pastoral care of English garrisons with their Indian and Portuguese wives than were the military chaplains, with their short terms of service and constant coming and going (ibid., 37-38).

Following the visit of Gericke, a pastoral visit was made in 1773 by the Reverend J. P. Fabricius, who had been trained at the great university and theological faculty at Halle under the leading pietist mission scholars of that time. He proved to be a great Tamil scholar, remembered for his Tamil translation of the New Testament and the English and Tamil dictionary that is still used today, a book of hymns and metrical psalms and many other works in Tamil. Thus, by 1773, the Vellore Christians already had available to them a basic Christian literature and hymnody in the Tamil language. In his second visit, Fabricius celebrated the holy Communion, baptized five of the soldiers' children, married five couples, preached in Tamil to the local congregation, and administered holy Communion in German to some German mercenary soldiers who were in the garrison.[38]

Between 1773 and the arrival of the Scudders in 1853, there continued to be a Tamil congregation in Vellore. Several different buildings were used over the course of the decades. In 1825, the management of the mission in Vellore was transferred from the SPCK to another Anglican society, the Society for the Propagation of the Gospel (SPG), that was under the leadership of the Reverend P. Wessing, who was the second resident European missionary in Vellore. Three years later, the military commandant wanted to move the Tamil worship services to a room in the Vellore General Hospital, but the congregation so strongly resisted meeting there that Wessing decided to hold the services in his own bungalow. That bungalow would after 1900 be used by Ida Scudder as the bungalow for the Schell Memorial Hospital. In 1830, two hundred pounds were given for a Tamil church building that the English as well as the Tamil congregation used after 1835.[39]

By 1843, the building had become too small to accommodate the English Protestants who then numbered 230. The building could hold no more than seventy. The English congregation also objected

38 Ibid., 38-40.
39 Ibid., 43-44.

to the building because it was close to the cantonment slaughter house and lacked adequate ventilation. As a result, the Madras government in 1844 sanctioned the building of a new church within the Vellore Fort. This was built in 1846, with a seating capacity of 280. It proved to be an excellent building that required little maintenance. After independence in 1947 and the inauguration of the Church of South India, the St. John's Church, as it was called, became a pastorate in the Church of South India. [40] Throughout the time of the British rule in North Arcot, there was considerable fear that the Indian sepoy troops would mutiny. There was a serious mutiny in Vellore in 1806 and a small participation in the much wider mutiny of 1857. One result of this unrest was that Indians were not allowed to be in the fort except while on duty or with special permission. Thus the Tamil congregation could not use the church inside the fort for Christian worship, so it continued to worship in the 1835 building.

When the Scudders arrived in 1853, the SPG missionary was no longer in Vellore, having been transferred to Chittoor in 1845. The Tamil congregation was under the care of an Indian catechist. The SPG was at the time suffering financial difficulties, so in 1855 the Madras Diocesan Committee of the Anglican Church sold to the American Arcot Mission the SPG buildings at Vellore and Chittoor for Rs. 2,500. In 1858, Joseph Scudder reported on the transfer at the 1858 Missionary Conference at Ooctacamund:

> Early in 1855 a church of about 13 communicants was organized at Vellore,....About the close of the year 1855 the Gospel Propagation Society, having been unable for a number of years to place a European Missionary over their stations at Chittoor and Vellore, withdrew from those places, and committed its congregations to our care. The transference was made with great cordiality. The members

---

[40] Ibid., 45-46. Three Reformed Church missionaries have served as pastors of the St. John's Church between 1954-1966: Blaise Levai, Eugene Ten Brink, and Eugene Heideman.

of the Vellore church withdrew in a body, and for a time
stood aloof. They are, however, gradually returning."[41]

There was ambiguity in what had actually been intended in the
sale of the property. When the SPG Tamil Christians were left
without a pastor, as Joseph Scudder reported, some of them joined
the Arcot Mission church, while others continued to adhere to the
Church of England.[42] The Scudders understood that the intent had
been that the SPG would be withdrawing fully from Vellore and
that the members of the congregation would all become members
of the church established by the Arcot Mission. The SPG felt an
obligation to those who continued to want to belong to the
Anglican communion.[43] A dispute arose over these different
interpretations. While we will take note of the controversy in
following chapters, which continued sporadically for several decades,
we quote here how the Arcot Mission understood the matter:

> We are therefore happy to congratulate the Board on the
> fact that the field has been cordially and entirely conceded
> to us, and that we are now the only Missionary Society
> occupying this district. A vast tract of densely populated
> land extends on every side of us and no other missionary
> body is likely to establish missions in it. In transferring the
> field to us, the Gospel Propagation Society requested us to
> purchase their Mission buildings at Vellore and Chittoor.
> The buildings at Vellore consist of a small chapel and a
> school house…The only building at Chittoor that the
> Society wished us to purchase is a very good and
> commodious dwelling house….The transfer of the
> congregations at Vellore and Chittoor by the Gospel

[41] Ibid., 49.
[42] Ibid., 48.
[43] Since the Society for the Propagation of the Gospel was "high church" Anglican, using
candles, surplices, incense, and crosses in their liturgy, while the Reformed Church
missionaries strongly suspected all such practices as "popery," it is not surprising that
some members of the congregation in Vellore resisted the transfer.

Propagation Society obliges us to ask for an additional appropriation to meet the attendant expenses."[44]

As a result of the earlier missionary endeavors, the stationing of British garrisons for the previous seventy-five years in the area, and the transfer from the Society for the Propagation of the Gospel, the Scudders found it possible to organize congregations in Vellore, Chittoor, and Arni within the first two years of their establishing residence in each of those towns. The history of the Chittoor congregation was somewhat different from that of Vellore, however. In Chittoor, mission work had been carried on by Anthony Norris Groves, a Plymouth Brother who had gathered a little congregation, mostly of native cultivators.[45] Groves had died and this small nucleus of a congregation had been handed over to the new mission even before the SPG had withdrawn in its favor.[46]

"In the very midst of the heathen, the worship of Jehovah is regularly maintained" ("First Annual Arcot Mission Report," p. 4)

Since nineteenth century missionaries consistently used the word "heathen" to refer to people outside the Christian fold, it is important to note more precisely how they understood that term. They did not intend by that word to cut themselves off from the people among whom they labored. On the contrary, they felt themselves and their call to mission to be in some measure a result of their linkage with the heathen. Henry Martyn Scudder's article, "The Heathen," written apparently sometime in the 1870s, was a thirteen-point statement concerning missionary preaching among the heathen. Concerning an American missionary's relation to the heathen, points ten and twelve are important statements:

10. We are not Jews, but Gentiles. Our lineage is heathen. The missionary enterprise rescued us from paganism.

44 W. W. Scudder to Anderson, December 11, 1855.
45 "Cultivators" were people who were engaged in planting and harvesting a variety of crops, such as bananas, coffee, tea, coconuts, mangoes, and papaya.
46 Chamberlain, *Sketch,* 24.

Gratitude for our own emancipation and love for our brethren, the heathen of all countries, should move us with a mighty impulse to engage in missionary work.

12. We ourselves are the offspring of the missionary enterprise. To turn against it is like a man's turning against his own mother.[47]

Regarding the heathen, Scudder stated that they "are conscious of sin" and yearn for deliverance. They feel the need of some satisfaction to be made for their sins. They need a divine deliverer. Because the Lord has commanded that the missionary go into all the world to preach the gospel, success is certain. Many heathen will respond when they hear the message. Since one goes in obedience to the command, the person or the church that does not go forth in the missionary spirit is dead.[48]

Congregations, Catechists, Teachers, and Evangelists

When they settled down in the Arcot Mission area, the Scudders knew that it was crucial that the heathen who heard the gospel preached should also be introduced to the regular worship of the true God. They believed that those who expressed an interest in the Christian faith needed instruction in the faith prior to baptism. It was their policy that "if three or more families in any place renounce heathenism and put themselves under our instruction, we erect a small building for them, in which a school is opened for their children, and where parents and children attend on the Sabbath and learn the way of the gospel. Such bodies are called 'village congregations.'"[49]

The policy of these first Arcot missionaries to recognize village congregations wherever there were three families ready to renounce

---

[47] *Mission Field,* March, 1908, 397-98. An editorial note at the top of the article states that it was submitted to the *Christian Intelligencer* "over twenty-five years ago."
[48] Ibid.
[49] "AAR," 1854, 6-7.

heathenism and put themselves under Christian instruction already marked the beginnings of what became a hierarchy of Christian workers. By early 1855, three Indian catechists and five Christian schoolmasters were employed to assist the missionaries in meeting the pastoral and instructional needs of the town and village people. As the system developed, the roles of the catechist, who exercised pastoral and leadership in the congregation, and the teacher, who instructed the Christian children in the schools, would often be combined. That person, the teacher/catechist, would teach school during the week and lead worship on Sunday and at other times. This was a system that other foreign mission societies, including the ABCFM, had adopted prior to 1850. Within a few years, as the number of villages under instruction increased, the volume of work for the missionary who had supervisory responsibilities often became overwhelming. The cost of maintaining the ever-expanding network of employed Indian workers also became a severe impediment to continuing numerical growth. Twenty years later, in 1875, there were forty-five schools, two ordained Indian ministers, twenty-one catechists, twenty-four "readers," fourteen male teachers, eight female teachers, eleven colporteurs, and three Bible readers employed in fifty-one town and village congregations, under the supervision of seven missionaries living in mission stations at some distance from the scattered villages.

In the twentieth century, great effort would be put forth in seeking ways to carry out the ministry of the church with a less expensive system, such as training lay volunteers to provide leadership for village congregations. The early missionaries would often be criticized for having a devised a system that rested on teachers and catechists who, even while receiving very low salaries, were nevertheless a heavy financial burden on the mission and the church. In spite of their concern about the cost of the system, the early missionaries were not able to devise any adequate alternative. As our study of the history of Reformed Church mission in India continues, we will find ourselves repeatedly encountering issues and dilemmas inherent in the system that continues to operate to the present day.

Because the male missionaries were usually extremely busy with their evangelistic touring and other duties, the day-to-day maintenance of public worship, instruction, and pastoral care came to rest on the Indian pastors, catechists, and teachers. Their faithful labors were really the key to the continuing growth of the church and development of its spiritual life. The story of missions cannot be told in terms of the missionaries alone. Unfortunately, as is so often the case, those who did the most faithful work were not the ones who wrote the reports, letters, and other materials that mission historians can use.

The Reverend Andrew Sawyer, the first ordained Indian minister, reported in 1862 that at his congregation at Arcot, two services of worship were held on the Sabbath. Prayer meetings were held in the houses of Christians on Tuesday and Friday evenings. A woman's prayer meeting was conducted on Wednesday, at which time the females of the congregation were catechised and instructed. Communion was administered once in three months.[50]

Andrew Sawyer's pastoral approach and Christian piety can be appreciated through reading his words in the 1862 Report:

> That the people committed to my charge might guard themselves from sin, and walk by the divine rule, I established meetings in every house, where by the setting forth of the truth and by prayer, all hearts were opened, and refreshed. The old men and the young have been been of one heart and purpose, and have grown in faith and love. The Christian women have also been affectionate toward each other, and have, as they were able, made known to other women, the love and power of their Lord. By the help of the Lord I have preached the Gospel in all the heathen villages around Arcot.[51]

[50] "AAR," 1862, 9-10.
[51] Arcot Mission Report for 1861, 9.

In that same year, Sawyer included an account of the valuable service rendered by Andaravedi, an Indian soldier the 41st Regiment located in Arcot, by whose ministry the church at Arcot had been much edified:

> In the year 1850, a little book fell into his hands, by means of which he was brought to believe upon the Lord Jesus, and publicly to confess His holy name. He suffered much persecution, but found strength to bear it. From the time he believed he has endeavoured to serve his Master faithfully. Knowing six languages he has been able to proclaim the Gospel to many people, and has been used by the Holy Spirit as the instrument of leading many precious souls to Jesus.[52]

Reformed Church missionaries knew from the very outset that the church in India could not be dependent on the presence of missionaries permanently. That is why their aim was a self-governing, self-supporting, self-propagating church. One move toward that goal was to develop a system of education that would train men to be catechists who would be married to women with at least a basic education. A second move was to discern among the catechists individuals who could benefit from additional training. After meeting the basic requirements for ordination under the rules of the Classis of Arcot, these catechists could then be ordained as ministers.

The First Indian Ordained Minister

Andrew Sawyer was catechist at Chittoor when the Arcot Mission was organized in 1854. As mentioned above, he was the first such catechist to be ordained and to function in the classis as a minister equal in rank with the ordained missionary members. He was ordained in 1858. Ezekiel (E. C.) Scudder stated concerning Sawyer's ordination examination by the Classis of Arcot in November 1857,

52 Ibid., 9-10.

a more satisfactory and well sustained examination I never had the pleasure of listening to. Questions were answered on all the cardinal points of our faith, with a degree of confidence and promptitude that showed a thorough acquaintance with each subject. He proved himself to be a Dutchman upon the doctrines of the Inspiration of the Scriptures, the Trinity, Creation, the Fall, Depravity, Providence, Decrees, Rewards and Punishments, and what more do we want to establish his orthodoxy?[53]

Andrew Sawyer was held in high regard by missionaries and Indians alike for his knowledge, humble piety, and faithful ministry. He remained an active pastor until his death in 1886. Following his death, the Classis of Arcot adopted a minute, the second paragraph of which reads:

Andrew Sawyer was the first native pastor ordained by the Classis of Arcot. He was a member of it from its organization more than thirty years ago. His reports to it, year by year, show that he has received and baptized hundreds of converts and their children. He has broken the bread of life to tens of thousands in all parts of our district. More than this he walked before men wholly and consistently in the footsteps of Christ, and the example he has left to his fellow workers and the whole Church is a lasting treasure. He preached the whole counsel of God and lived as he preached.[54]

As the missionaries became acquainted with the children in the village schools and as they came to know other young men who were interested in being instructed in the Christian faith, they were constantly on the lookout for persons who showed aptitude and an inclination to become evangelists, catechists, and teachers. Those who showed such abilities were enrolled in what they termed at first a "praeparandi class."

[53] E.C. Scudder to Rev. Porter, March 11, 1858.
[54] "Board of Foreign Missions Report" (hereafter "BFMR") 1887, 29.

The second annual Arcot Mission report, for the year 1855, contains the information that the praeparandi class was meeting in Vellore. Instead of English, the Christians "lads" were learning Tamil, Telugu, and a little Sanskrit. They were also regularly trained in systematic theology by the missionary in Vellore, Henry M. Scudder. The Heidelberg Catechism, with its scripture proof texts, formed the basis of instruction. "They also study Geography, Arithmetic, and Grammar," the missionaries reported. "Great attention is paid to music. They are taught to sing both European and Native tunes. Once in the year they go with the Missionaries on a preaching tour among the heathen."[55]

In the following year, the name of the praeparandi class was changed to Arcot Seminary, and it included eleven students. The course of study remained the same as the previous year. Two of the "youths" are reported to be nearly ready to act as schoolmasters. They had also gained the services of one Mr. Holzwarth, "assistant missionary."[56] By 1859 the Arcot Seminary had been moved to Palmaner, forty-five miles from Vellore, and E. C. Scudder was now in charge. Henry M. Scudder had suffered a breakdown in health and had moved to the hill station of Coonoor in order to spend some time in a cooler and healthier climate. In order to have more efficient use of Arcot Mission resources, the boys in boarding school at Arni had also been moved to the seminary in Palmaner. All the students in the school received room and board, and often clothing as well, from the mission.

The same report includes the basic policy of the seminary, which was that no boy was admitted for fewer than six years, "in which time we hope they will be thoroughly trained and fitted for the work for which they are designed. It is to this school that we must look for our future Native Assistants....Each Mission needs men of its own training, and one great want with us this day is native helpers."[57] Those boys in the day schools who showed some

55 "AAR," 1855, 9.
56 "AAR," 1856, 5-6.
57 "AAR," 1859, 12.

interest and promise of becoming catechists or ministers were selected to be in the Arcot Seminary boarding and to attend for a period up to six years. If after three or four years they did not give evidence of piety deep enough for a catechist, they could still be employed as schoolmasters under the immediate supervision of a missionary. "Those whom it pleased the Lord to draw unto Himself pursue their studies with a view of becoming catechists or ministers. We live not in a land of colleges and seminaries. We are therefore forced to have one institution of this kind in our mission."[58]

Joseph Scudder wrote on behalf of the mission requesting that the board would provide funds to hire a European as an "assistant missionary" for the staff of the seminary, in order that the missionaries would be set free to do the highest priority work of direct evangelism. Mr. Holzwarth, who had served so well, had died a several months ago.[59] Joseph Scudder, in discussions with a German missionary, the Reverend Dr. Gundert, had learned that there were Germans thoroughly trained and dedicated for missionary service who were not ordained but were good linguists, married, and not likely to leave missionary service for higher paying government employment. In light of the availability of such persons, he wrote:

> Would it be right for one of our missionaries to devote the largest portion of his time to this institution and give up in a great measure his pastoral and itinerant duties? We think not. A missionary we believe is one sent to the heathen, not to revolve in a compound and devote his time and energies to a limited number of nominal Christian lads for the purpose of cultivating their minds. His is a nobler work. It is to enter in among the masses day after day and proclaim the unsearchable riches of Christ to every creature he can reach.[60]

[58] Joseph Scudder to Isaac Ferris, October 9, 1858. Isaac Ferris was a leading minister in the Reformed Church in America and served on the Board of Foreign Missions. He was chancellor and professor at New York University, 1853-1870. His son, John Mason Ferris, served as secretary for the Board of Foreign Missions, 1865-1883.
[59] E. C. Scudder to Isaac Ferris, February 19, 1858.
[60] Joseph Scudder to Isaac Ferris, October 9, 1858.

The Female Seminary

In the missionaries' view, the importance of catechists and teachers lay not only in their ability to conduct worship and teach, but also in the example they could set through the Christian marriages and homes they would established. To that end, the missionaries knew that they would have to make it possible for those men to have literate Christian wives. Already in 1855, Sarah (Mrs. Ezekiel) Scudder had taken three orphan girls as boarders in her home and instructed them daily, along with three other girls. She reported, "These will probably form the germ of a Girl's Boarding School. We should be glad to increase the number, but have not the means for their support. Those already taken are supported by private charity."[61]

By 1860, her hopes had been realized. The report for that year was sent from the "Female Boarding School." By the following year, the name of the school had been changed to the "Female Seminary." In that year there was a full-time matron for the girls, a Eurasian named Mrs. Lackey, who remained with the school for a number of years. The reason for the existence of the school is clearly stated,

> The object of this school is to train up a class of girls who will be fitted to become the wives of our native helpers. While we strive to give them a good plain education, we do not neglect those things which the wife of a native should know. They learn to cook, to sew, and to do all kinds of house work. We do not wish to raise them above, but to fit them for the position they will be called to fill.[62]

The girls were given three hours of instruction in religious and secular subjects daily, as well as being taught to sew and carry out other domestic responsibilities.[63]

[61]"AAR," 1855, 12.
[62] "AAR," 1860, 11.
[63] Ibid., 1861, 15.

By naming their school a "female seminary," the Arcot missionaries showed that they were familiar with developments in the field of female education in America. After 1830, "female seminaries" began to replace "female academies." Unlike "academy," the word "seminary" carried with it the connotation of professional preparation. Rather than emphasizing "ornamental" branches of knowledge, the female seminary tried to prepare young women for life through religious, domestic, and teacher training. The realization had begun to dawn that women were better equipped than men to train young minds, and they were willing to work for less pay. The seminaries encouraged the systematic, graded acquisition of knowledge and believed that the female mind was capable of maintaining the mental discipline provided by subjects such as mathematics.[64] The training given in the Female Seminary, therefore, not only met the needs of the "native helpers"[65] for Christian homes, but it also was consistent with the American woman missionary's understanding of her own role in missionary service.

The Female Seminary represented a real advance in the role of women. For the first time, young girls were given the opportunity to gain a basic education, as well as a role alongside their husbands in the life of the village church. It also fulfilled its purpose of providing wives for catechists, teachers, and other "native workers." After 1861, the seminary annually reported on the number of girls who married such persons: one in 1861, one in 1862, three in 1863. Jared Scudder provided a vivid account of the marriage ceremony

[64] Dana L Robert, *American Women in Mission: A Social History of Their Thought and Practice,* (Macon, Ga.: Mercer Univ. Press, 1996), 92-93.
[65] Missionaries used the term, "native helper," to indicate all those who were employed in mission service by the mission. The word "native" was not intended to refer to aboriginal people, as it is often heard by Americans today. In that colonial era, it was used to refer to the people of India, much as the word "national" began to be used after independence. The missionaries of that era heard it not as a pejorative word, but as indicating respect for their role and position. The phrase, "native helper," does, however, clearly indicate that the mission being carried on belonged to the missionaries, who were being helped by those employed. However the missionaries may have felt about using the phrase, it is clear from our perspective that it belongs to the colonial era, a time of paternalism in the church and mission.

Jared W. Scudder

for six men from the Arcot Seminary and four other men and ten
women from the Female Seminary:

> Last Friday I married ten couples in the Vellore church. The
> bridegrooms were six from the Arcot Seminary and the
> brides from the Female Seminary. A gallant sight it was to
> see the twenty—all dressed in their graceful and brilliant
> Oriental costume standing in a circle around the pulpit with
> a packed audience as a background! I wish friends in
> America could have been present and witnessed the gay
> scene. It took me nearly an hour and a half to tie and register

Camp of missionary on tour

the ten knots. That's a pastoral feat that few ministers at home are ever called to perform.[66]

Evangelistic Touring

In the minds of the Arcot missionaries of the nineteenth century, public evangelistic preaching and distributing scriptures and Christian tracts was the very pinnacle of their calling. Nothing compares with the enthusiasm in their reports of their evangelistic tours that could last six weeks or more. It was in such evangelistic preaching tours that the real romance of mission could be found. They sent long reports of such tours to the Board of Foreign Missions' corresponding secretary in New York. John Scudder's health had broken under the strain of walking and standing in the hot sun, speaking hour after hour, crossing streams swollen with recent rains, encountering wild animals, and meeting friends and foes in the towns and villages. Those who followed him were no less willing to enter into the adventures of evangelistic touring.

Jacob Chamberlain, one of the most intrepid touring missionary evangelists, reported that in 1868 he had been away from home on tours and in evangelistic work in outstations altogether 122 days

---

[66] J. W. Scudder to Henry Cobb, March 19, 1889. Henry Cobb was corresponding secretary of the Board of Foreign Missions, 1883-1910.

during the year. The native helpers under his charge had spent 395 days in itinerating. Altogether they had preached 1,375 times to 1,142 different audiences, in 1,061 different towns and villages, to 20,012 people. In more than one-half of those, they were sowing the seed for the first time. In their tours to outlying areas, they had covered territory between three and four hundred miles. In his opinion,

> It is safe to say that more than 80 per cent of the converts from Hinduism received in the Arcot Mission have been brought in by this 'public proclamation' of the Gospel in the vernaculars. These have, indeed, come mostly from the lower classes, but a large percentage of our high caste converts have also thus been brought to Christ."[67]

In 1861, William W. Scudder described the mode of street preaching that they carried out as he, accompanied by the catechists and two or three seminary lads, went from village to village. As they entered a village, they would select a place where they thought the people would assemble, such as at an intersection or near the temple or bazaar area. The seminary boys would then sing Christian songs to Indian tunes. A number of people would gather around. Then one of the catechists would read aloud an appropriate portion of scripture and briefly address the people. Next, Scudder himself would speak at greater length, striving to show the lost state of the human race, the futility of all human devices to save themselves, and the sin and folly of polytheism and idolatry. He then would give a brief exposition of God's plan of redemption. At times the people would listen without saying a word; at other times they would interrupt and urge objections.[68]

One afternoon, ten or twelve young men on whom he had urged the claims of the gospel came to Scudder to present their objections to the Bible. The conversation went something like this:

[67] Jacob Chamberlain, *Sketch,* 30.
[68] W. W. Scudder to Philip Peltz, May, 1961. Philip Peltz served as corresponding secretary for the Board of Foreign Missions, 1860-1865.

Preaching in an Indian village

Young man:"You declare that God is unchangeable and at the same time teach that he became man. This implies change of form."

Answer: "God has no form. He is a spirit. The fact that he assumed the human nature does not imply that his divine nature underwent change. We may pour water into a vessel and it still remains water and retains all its qualities. So God becoming manifest in the flesh retains all his attributes."

Young man: "Why should God assume the human nature? Is he not Almighty and capable of saving us by a simple command? Can he not do all things?"

Answer: Though God is all powerful, there are things which he cannot do. He cannot lie, nor steal, nor be guilty of impurity. Neither can he do anything which would be prejudicial to a single attribute of his character."[69]

Two days later they were in another village, standing in front of a Hindu temple, preaching to about 150 people, who listened attentively. One man spoke up to say that if Scudder should show

[69] Ibid.

them any benefit that would come to those who have embraced Christianity, then all would turn to that religion. He indicated by his comment that he was referring "simply to temporal good. Very few of the people have ideas that rise above this. I endeavored to should him how much superior spiritual are to temporal benefits."[70]

The missionaries never knew what to expect next in these dialogue sessions, where the issues raised by supposedly simple villagers could be profound. William Scudder reported concerning one such dialogue that he was confronted by a haughty self-appointed spokesman, who asked the people what this babbler was saying. Then he showed himself to be a pure materialist as he made the sage announcement, "Whatever would digest in the stomach is truth and whatever would not is false." We are not told what response Scudder gave.[71]

On that same tour they ran into another problem. While they were camped and in their tents in a village near Punganur, several policemen came and summoned them to appear before the local magistrate. The charge was that one of their evangelist tour members, a *pariah*,[72] had drawn water from their village "tank" (reservoir) and thus ritually polluted it. Ezekiel Scudder told them that the man had acted in the matter without the missionary's knowledge and that he would see to it that they would not repeat

---

70 Ibid.

71 W. W. Scudder to P. Peltz, July 30, 1863.

72 *Pariah* was one of the lowest of castes among the untouchables. It could also be a word used to apply to the untouchables in general. Terms applied to the lowest level of Indian society varied over the course of the decades. As Indians and westerners sought to use less pejorative language, other terms came into use. *Avi-Dravida* was proposed to signify that the outcastes were the original inhabitants of India and had been pressed down by their conquerors, as the America Indians were treated by the arriving Europeans. M. K. Gandhi proposed the word *harijans* ("God's people") in order to bring them into the Hindu social structures in recognition their full humanity. *Harijan* was widely accepted during the era leading up to and following independence. More recently, many members of what legally are known as the "scheduled castes" have objected to *harijan* as in turn paternalistic, applied to them by members of the higher castes. They would now want to be called *Dalits*, which had been a pejorative word. Americans can be helped to understand the course of these shift of language by comparing it to their own situation, where "Black" is the equivalent of *Dalit*, "Negro" with that of *harijan*, and so on with their predecessor word choices.

their use of the well. This satisfied the matter so far as the case against the evangelistic tour group was concerned. However, the people of the village would not use the tank again until they had drawn out all the water and called a Brahmin to remove the defilement by use of his incantations. Scudder stated that in point of fact his group had a legal right by order of the government to use such reservoirs, but that he believed the course of wisdom was to respect the wishes of the people who lived there.[73]

The Arcot missionaries were more indefatigably committed to evangelistic touring than those of any of the surrounding missions. Others doubted whether such preaching and debates had many positive results. Certainly most of the public debates seem to have ended in draws, although the missionaries often believed they had won the debate. Whatever the effect of the street preaching itself, the missionaries did in many places find that there were people who expressed interest in their preaching and literature and invited them to return. In fact, one of their great frustrations was that there were so many places where they had been invited to return, but for lack of time had never done so.

The First Converts

Orientalists, western scholars, and colonialists were enthusiastically discovering the spiritual resources of Asian religions and cultures in the eighteenth and early nineteenth century. They were translating ancient scriptures and writing from Sanskrit into English, German, and other languages. European philosophical idealists were exploring the similarities of their idealism with the religious monism of Indian religious thought. In the United States, at the time members of the second generation of Scudders were completing their education, thinkers such as Thoreau and Emerson were developing a transcendentalist philosophy that was much influenced by Indian spirituality as they understood it.[74] During the 1850s, England was

[73] W. W. Scudder to P. Peltz, July 30, 1863.
[74] Pathak, *American Missionaries*, 84-89.

expanding its hold on India, at the same time recognizing how fragile that hold could be. In the interests of empire consolidation, it sought to discourage missionary efforts to bring Indians into the Christian faith.

In contrast to the spirit of the times, the Scudders remained unabashedly fervent in calling people to conversion to Christ. Ingrained in their evangelical faith there was a profound sense that we are all from birth, "inclined to hate God and our neighbor," as their beloved Heidelberg Catechism taught them. Since we are all in that sense "heathen," we are all in need of conversion. John and Harriet Scudder therefore were concerned for the conversion of their own children. On her deathbed, Harriet Scudder expressed her own readiness to die and soon meet again the loved ones who had preceded her in death. Her only concern was for her three as yet unconverted children. She said, "'My only burden in dying is the thought that three of my children are yet in an impenitent state,' and she besought her daughter Louisa, in the most affectionate and impressive manner, to yield her heart to the Saviour: adding, 'This is my dying request. I have done all I can for you.'"[75]

Missionaries in the Arcot Mission in 1853 knew that both in independent America and in colonial India, all are from birth depraved in sin against God and their neighbors. It is crucial, therefore, that each one be converted to Jesus Christ, whose atonement for sin is our only hope of salvation. This universal human condition, rather than any political, religious, or cultural context, is what renders personal conversion essential. Just as there is rejoicing in heaven over one sinner who repents, so one must give

[75] Letter of John Scudder, Sr., to John Anderson, dated Nov. 22, 1849, quoted in Waterbury, *Memoirs,* 243-44. Harriet Scudder's concern for the salvation of her children was shared by many evangelical women of her era. The mother in the home carried major responsibility for providing a "nursery for heaven" and leading her children to true penitence and faith; see Firth Haring Fabend, "Pious and Powerful: The Evangelical Mother in Reformed Dutch Households, New York and New Jersey, 1926-1876," in Renee House and John Coakley, eds., *Patterns and Portraits: Women in the History of the Reformed Church in America,* Historical Series of the Reformed Church in America, no. 31 (Grand Rapids: Eerdmans, 1999), 70-80.

thanks to God for everyone who turns to God in Jesus Christ for salvation. Thus it was with considerable joy that the Arcot Mission was able to tell the story of the converts in its report for the year 1854.

Francis, converted from Roman Catholicism

The first was a man named Francis, the school master at Arni, who had formerly been a Roman Catholic. He first heard the evangelical gospel when it was preached in the streets and had come to doubt the truth of his religion. He came at first secretly to the missionary, then boldly began to attend public worship, and "finally threw off Roman Catholicism and embraced the religion of the Bible." He was greatly persecuted by the Roman Catholics. His wife was induced to desert him and join her friends in Madras. But his faith had not wavered. "At the last communion, he publicly took upon him the vow of God's children and was admitted as a member of the church."[76]

In this account of Francis's conversion, the conviction of the Arcot missionaries that Roman Catholicism is superstitious popery and false religion is manifest. In making this assumption, the missionaries reflected both their American roots and their India experience. With regard to India, the Roman Catholicism that they encountered had first been introduced by Counter-Reformation Portuguese and firm Jesuits who had vigorously taught all that the Protestant reformers had opposed. The missionaries knew from Question and Answer 80 of the Reformed Church's Heidelberg Catechism that the papal mass "is fundamentally a complete denial of the once and for all sacrifice of Jesus Christ and as such an idolatry to be condemned."[77]

[76] "AAR," 1855, 13-14.
[77] The Heidelberg Catechism was adopted in Heidelberg, Germany, in 1563 in an era of severe tension between Protestant and Roman Catholic churches. At that time, much superstitious practice had entered into Roman Catholic practices. The church had tried to deal with a number of the issues at the Council of Trent (1545-1563) but had not satisfied Protestant objections. Only in the twentieth century, following the decrees of the Vatican II Council (1962-1964) and the election of President Kennedy, did most

With regard to their American experience, both Henry Martyn and William Waterbury Scudder were completing their theological education in New York and Princeton respectively between 1840 and 1844, when anti-Roman Catholicism was at its height in America. Roman Catholics, including the new immigrants so feared by the Protestant "nativists,"[78] were opposing the use of the King James Version of the Bible in the new public common schools. The rising tensions in those years led to severe riots and the closing for a time of the schools in Philadelphia. The *Christian Intelligencer*, published weekly in New York by Reformed churchmen, included from 1830 and thereafter numerous virulent articles against Roman Catholic "popery." For example, at the conclusion of a series on "Prelacy,"[79] one reads the following:

> …another development of covert, deadly hostility of Popish Jesuitism against the Protestant religion, as well as against the use of the Bible, the liberties of the people of our country and the form of our Republican government, where liberty and despotic Popery cannot dwell together peaceably,…and to subvert our liberty, so to deprive us of our Bibles and of the enjoyment of our civil liberties!!…with its tyranny, its masses and bloody inquisition in our dear beloved land.[80]

of the old rancor between Protestants and Roman Catholics disappear in the United States. The severe condemnation of the Roman Catholic Mass had not been included in the first edition of the Heidelberg Catechism but was added in the second edition. The Reformed Church in America has dropped the severe condemnation since Vatican II.

78 The "nativists" in the United States in the 1840s carried out agitation against immigrants. They were especially antagonistic against the Roman Catholics who were coming in great numbers to the cities on the eastern seaboard.

79 "Prelacy" was a hostile term that was used by Protestants in opposition to a hierarchical order of ministry with bishops, particularly as it was manifested in the Roman Catholic Church, but also as it had developed in the Church of England in the centuries following the Protestant Reformation. Many Americans believed that the presence of "prelates" would lead inevitably to the demise of democracy and the restoration of monarchy.

80 *Christian Intelligencer*, June 1, 1844, 181.

Two weeks previous, the *Christian Intelligencer* had included several paragraphs from the memoir of Harriet L. Winslow, whose family had been colleagues of John and Harriet Scudder in Jaffna and Madras. The article entitled, "Hindooism and Popery," attempted to show that there were clear similarities between Hinduism and Roman Catholicism. It summarized the point in a list, showing that each used images (idols), lights and candles, incense, festivals (including processions carrying the images in the streets), vain repetitions in prayers and chants, superstitious practices relating to purgatory and ceremonies for the dead, and "mummery" such as fast and feast days, ringing bells, and idolizing priests. The editors added a note to Harriet Winslow's list, stating that one of the best ways to show the evils of popery in America would be to bring a Hindu priest to America and let the Americans see the similarities for themselves.[81]

In their negative attitude toward Roman Catholicism, as in their positive attitude toward women's education for the uplift of family life, the Scudders are revealed as uncritical of many of their own cultural assumptions. Many Americans since then have been exceedingly critical of nineteenth-century missionary endeavors on that account. These critics tend to ignore the fact that such activity on the part of the missionaries serves to bring to light the basic flaws in the American culture of that day and since that time. A question that will concern us from time to time in what follows is the extent to which the Arcot missionaries themselves began to recognize their own American western presuppositions that could be destructive in India. One can only wonder whether the American population in general, and American Christians in particular, have been as open to hearing the criticisms as have missionaries.

Shengalrayan, converted from Hinduism

The case of Shengalrayan is reported in two Arcot Mission annual reports—for the years 1854 and 1855. He was "a lad of good caste"

[81] Ibid., May 18, 1844, n.p.

in the town of Wallajanagar who came to the dispensary for treatment. After about a month of treatment he was discharged. As he heard about the Great Physician, he became convinced that his own Hindu religion was false and that the atonement of Jesus is the only hope of the soul. When he made known his intention to convert to Christianity, his father and mother pleaded with him against it and tried every means to stop him. Then he broke caste of his own accord, and he himself requested that the tuft of hair on his head, being a mark of Hinduism, be removed. A few days later, he and the missionary were summoned to appear before the magistrate to determine whether the missionary had exercised undue influence over him. The boy gave such clear testimony of his understanding of what he had done and his conviction to live and die as a Christian "that even the head of his caste and other influential Hindus signed a paper declaring that they considered him abundantly capable of forming an enlightened determination in regard to the subject of religion."[82]

The boy, now without the support of family connections, was placed as a member of the praeparandi class and was baptized. "He has forsaken home, father, mother, friends and caste, for Christ's sake.[83] In this account, the consequences of conversion for the new believer become clear. One not only was disinherited from one's immediate family but also lost one's social position in Indian society. Conversion represented a change of community. In a society in which marriages were arranged for young men and women by their parents, prospects for marriage became dim indeed. Insofar as occupation was still related to caste, possibilities for suitable employment became slim. As in the case of Shengalrayan, the convert was often reduced to becoming dependent on the missionary for receiving a new place in a new community.

[82] "AAR," 1854, 11.
[83] "AAR," 1855, 17.

A believer who has not become a convert

A third case concerning a believer is reported in the Arcot Mission Report for 1855. This unnamed person was first met by Henry M. Scudder at Vellore when he was on a preaching tour in Vellore. When some Hindus had opposed Scudder, this young man had defended him. That evening he told the missionary that he had possessed a Tamil Bible for many years, knew it well, meditated on it daily, and no longer worshiped idols. Yet he was not ready to come out openly and be baptized because of the opposition of his caste, his wife, and the shame of the cross. Henry Scudder stated his belief that the problem in this case was that the Christian with whom the man spoke when he received his Bible had left him to infer that he "would get to heaven with his present course."[84]

The issues raise by the case of this man would continue to call for much thought in the mission and church as the decades went by. The issues become particularly acute in the context of a Hinduism that taught that all religions ultimately lead to the same goal and therefore was ready to encapsulate the Christian religion within its own, overarching tent.

Extending the Boundaries of the Arcot Mission

Coonoor

When the Arcot Mission was established in 1853, its boundaries were the districts of Chittoor and of South and North Arcot, but they did not as yet extend as far into the Telugu language area as the town of Madanapalle. By 1860, the Arcot Mission had taken on responsibility for that Telugu area, as well as for work among Tamil-speaking people in the hill station of Coonoor, almost two hundred miles from Vellore. In considering how these two fields of responsibility came to rest with the Arcot Mission, we will note once again how fully the activities of the Reformed Church

[84] Ibid., 16.

missionaries were carried out in coordination with those of other missionary societies.

In 1856, both Joseph Scudder and his wife, Anna, were suffering from ill health so serious that it was decided that they should go to Coonoor in the Nilgiris Hills. The Nilgiris Hills form part of the Western Ghats, a mountain range that rises to a height of more than eight thousand feet and therefore provided a malaria-free area and an escape from the heat of the plains. The developing railway system of India provided a good connection between Vellore and Coonoor. The Basel Evangelical Lutheran Mission had taken that area as its mission field, but their work was exclusively among the mountain tribes who did not use the Tamil language.

At the hill station itself, to which English government and military officials, merchants, and tea and coffee planters would come to reside or take vacations and rest from the heat of the plains, the Reverend P.P. Shaffter of the Church Mission Society had opened a church in 1855. The congregation consisted of Tamil-speaking people, but Shaffter conducted services for the English-speaking people as well. After Joseph Scudder's arrival in Coonoor, the Church Missionary Society decided it could not afford to keep a missionary there, and Scudder was asked to take responsibility for the ministry in the local English congregation and for the Tamil work.[85]

The Arcot Mission formally adopted Coonoor as one of its stations in 1857. This station was at the time unique among the stations of the mission in that it had resources of personnel and economic strength. The English residents contributed liberally and erected a fine church edifice. A retired English officer, Major-General Kennett, built an excellent house for the missionaries as a gift to the mission. It was named "Wyoming" by the missionaries and was used by the missionaries well into the twentieth century.[86] The Tamil people also were of a "good class, artificers, merchants,

---

[85] Joseph Scudder to Rufus Anderson, March 14, 1957.
[86] Chamberlain, *Sketch*, 25.

and the better sort of laborers. They are living away from most of their caste relations. There are no Brahmins here to frighten them into submission, no mighty temples to allure them to remain in the fastnesses of heathenism."[87]

In December, 1859, Joseph and Anna Scudder both suffered complete breakdowns in health and were compelled to leave India, never to return. At that time W. H. Stanes, an English tea planter in Coonoor, who had married the Scudder sister, Harriet, in 1855, offered his services to look after the interests of the mission in Coonoor. The second sister, Louisa, was also in Coonoor at the time and at the urgent request of the church there was permanently assigned by the mission to be in charge of the school and "Christian females." Henry Martyn Scudder, upon his return to India in 1859, had once again suffered a breakdown in health, so he was assigned to take charge of the Coonoor station, where he was also given responsibility to devote himself to the preparation of vernacular books and tracts.[88]

Coonoor remained a station of the Arcot Mission until 1912, when the Basel Mission indicated that it was willing and able to take up the Tamil work. The Arcot Mission at that time transferred its church, school, and property to that mission that by reason of location was able to give it fuller attention and adequate care.

Madanapalle

After Jacob and Charlotte Chamberlain arrived in India and were assigned to work in the Telugu language area, the attention of the Arcot Mission was drawn to the area around Madanapalle. That area had formerly been occupied as an out-station of the London Missionary Society from 1847 to 1856. After several years of communications, the London society directors adopted a cordial resolution formally relinquishing the field to the Arcot Mission. The Chamberlains were then assigned to Madanapalle and spent

[87] Joseph Scudder to Rufus Anderson, March 14, 1957.
[88] "AAR," 1860, 14.

the rest of their more than four decades in India in close relationship with the work there. Within a few months they had gathered a worshiping congregation of between twenty-five and forty people and were in the process of opening a school.

One problem the Chamberlains encountered was that there was no house suitable for them there, so for several years they had to live in very unhealthy surroundings. Their house had a roof that leaked when it rained and became too hot when the sun shone.[89]

Throughout the Arcot Mission area, Reformed Church missionaries entered a field where Christians had preceded them in bearing witness to Jesus Christ. The groups of Christians who had been gathered into small congregations had first come into the faith through the activity of missionaries of various denominations. High Anglican Society for the Propagation of the Gospel Christians worshiped in Vellore; low Anglican Church Missionary Society Christians belonged to the congregation in Coonoor. A person who was Plymouth Brethren began the Chittoor congregation. Madanapalle had first been congregational under the London Missionary Society. By 1857 the ABCFM was largely congregational in its stance. In each place Indian believers had become Reformed as a result of mission diplomacy rather than personal conviction about the relative merits of specifically Lutheran, Reformed, Anglican, or Wesleyan theologies.

Financing the Mission

The Arcot missionaries always needed more money to carry on their mission. They constantly pleaded with the corresponding secretary of the Board of Foreign Missions in New York to send more money to India, so that they could pay the salaries of more catechists, teachers, evangelists, and Bible women. They needed money to build buildings, buy buildings, whitewash buildings, or pay rent. Evangelistic tours required money to purchase tents and conveyances and to feed horses. More boys and girls had to be

[89] "AAR," 1863, 24-25.

boarded and educated in the Arcot Seminary and the Female Seminary.

In 1857 the Board of Foreign Mission's appropriation for the Arcot Mission totaled $13,101. The Arcot Mission's budget for that year provides considerable information about salary scales and other expenses. All missionaries received the same salary, $900 per year for married couples, plus $70 per child. Native assistants' salaries varied slightly, with Andrew Sawyer, catechist in Chittoor, paid the highest salary of $12.50 a month, or $114 per year. Thus the salary for a missionary couple was approximately nine times that of the average salary of a native assistant. As time went on and the discrepancy increased between standards of living in Europe and the United States, on the one hand, and India, on the other, the salary differential between the missionaries and the native workers tended to increase rather than decrease. As a result, major tension arose around this issue in the twentieth century.

The cost of maintaining schools and other institutions was always a matter of concern. In 1857 it cost $463 to maintain five schools, $325 for boarding fifteen boys in the prepaerandi class, and $275 for twelve girls in the female boarding school. In that year $2,000 was used for building a missionary house in Vellore, $1,000 for the Chittoor church building, $250 for enlarging the church in Vellore, $500 for renting houses, and $100 for whitewashing and repair on existing buildings. Another $330 was appropriated for touring and traveling. [90]

The Arcot Mission did not regard itself as primarily a charitable organization. The missionaries believed that they were doing a valuable service in proclaiming the gospel in India and that the mission service was worthy of the support of the people in India. One of their priorities, as we have already noted, was that the church should grow toward self-support. In light of the poverty of almost all of the Indian members of the congregations, they turned

[90] Statement of Appropriations for the Arcot Mission, 1857, undated, in E.C. Scudder's handwriting.

first of all to the English and European government and military officers, merchants, and agricultural planters, who often were personally quite favorable to the activities of the missionaries. The amounts received from such persons could be significant, particularly in responding to special appeals to meet local needs. In 1857, when two rupees were equal to one dollar, the English and Europeans contributed Rs. 3,075, of which Rs.1,345 was designated for the new church building in Coonoor.[91]

Four years later, the missionaries were appealing to the board for an increase in their salaries, in spite of an increase that had already been given in 1858. The 1857 Sepoy Mutiny in India had brought about a rapid escalation of prices, especially for materials and food used by foreigners in India. At the same time, the outbreak of the Civil War in America had caused the dollar to loose value in relation to the English pound and the Rupee. As a result, every one hundred dollars the board sent from America in salaries was reduced to sixty-seven dollars by the time it had passed through currency exchange and reached the missionaries in India.

Ezekiel Scudder sent a letter in August 1861 that vividly described his situation. In it, he contemplated whether he would be forced to sell his books and furniture in order to survive financially. We quote only from the first page of his four-page tale of woe:

> I have been in India five years and a half and my condition is daily growing worse and more alarming though I have done everything in my power to curtail my expenses and been reduced to a limit beyond which I supposed I could ever be called to go. I stand today Rs. 850 in debt and instead of gaining on my debt, my debt is gaining on me. The stock of clothes I brought out with me is about exhausted and it is impossible to replenish my wardrobe in the present state of our finances. I do not wish to complain, but I must say that both my wife and myself are sometimes

[91]"AAR," 1857, 14-16.

ashamed to meet decent people, and there is no hope of making a better appearance.[92]

Missionary Attitudes towards the British Raj in the 1850s

As was noted above, in the modern era missionaries have often been accused of being agents of western colonialism. In response to this charge, it is possible to contend that the American Arcot missionaries in India were not colonialists as such, but that much of the time they were willing collaborators with British "Raj," as the colonial rule came to be known. As American missionaries, however, they would not have been naturally inclined to favor the English colonization of India.

The Scudders went to India in a time of considerable tension between England and the United States. John and Harriet Scudder's ancestors had been on the side of the American colonies' revolt against England at precisely the time England was establishing the Raj in India. The missionaries of the ABCFM had been refused permission to enter Calcutta in 1813 when the War of 1812 was still going on against England.[93] The Scudders had to remain in Jaffna until 1836, when the English finally allowed them to go to Madras. In the years leading up to the Civil War and during the war, the interests of England favored the South rather than the North. American missionaries of that era had few reasons to favor the extension of the British Empire. John Scudder, Jr., commented on the English attitude toward the North following reception of the news about the northern defeat in the Battle of Bull Run in the Civil War:

The first accounts we received made it out to be a most disastrous and shameful flight. One of the most disgraceful routs that ever occurred in any war. But this is owing to the

[92] E. C. Scudder to P. Peltz, August 20, 1861.
[93] *First Ten Annual Reports of the American Board of Commissioners for Foreign Missions*, (Boston: Crocker and Brewster, 1834), 1813 Report, 63.

source from which we received our information, viz. the English account. The English seem to delight in picturing every reverse of the Northern troops in the very worst light. Nor are they at all scrupulous in making statements whether true or not, if the statement will make the picture appear worse and more disgraceful to the Americans.—Their account has to be taken *cum grano salis*.[94]

On the other hand, the missionaries' position in India was secured by the legal permission granted to them by the British authorities. Moreover, one of the conditions of their remaining was that they promise not to work to undercut or participate in activities against the Raj. Such a promise would not have concerned the Scudders. In their firm conviction that it was their calling always to give first priority to calling people to repentance and faith in Christ, they had no interest in playing a political or economic role with regard to British rule in India. They developed a love for India and her people. In spite of his forceful criticisms of Hinduism, John Scudder could write to the American board on March 11, 1848:

I love India...I love her people. I repudiate as a calumny many things that have been said of this country...The Hindoos are an interesting people. They are kind and polite...they generally carry themselves toward the missionaries with much civility. The better classes of them have a great deal of dignity.[95]

As isolated English-speaking Americans in India, the missionaries naturally found that friendship with other English-speaking people who followed American or British social customs and claimed Christian faith was important to them for companionship and mutual assistance. When they went to a hill station such as Coonoor for health reasons or vacations, they moved in social circles with the

[94] John Scudder, Jr., to P. Peltz, October 9, 1861.
[95] Quoted in Pathak, *American Missionaries*, 71.

British and Europeans there. They found many of the British and Europeans to be personally favorable to their missionary activities and, as we have seen above, often disposed to make financial contributions to the needs of the mission.

Their sense of the importance of the British Raj as a stabilizing and positive element in India became much greater after 1857. In that year, the great Sepoy Mutiny, which centered in North India in a wide area around Delhi for several years, traumatized the white people living in India.[96] In the months prior to May 1857, there had been many signs of restlessness and agitation among the sepoys[97] in the Bengali regiments. Rumors were circulating among the sepoys, as well as among the general populace, that the British were intending to make all the sepoys share a common diet without regard to caste or religion. It was rumored also that the East India Company's plan was to destroy the religion of the country. It was being said that the cartridge for the new Enfield rifle had been lubricated with a mixture of pig and cow fat and that the army was grinding a mixture of pig and cow bones into the sepoy's flour and adding cow's blood to the salt.[98]

While these rumors provided the immediate occasion for the outbreak of the mutiny, they were given credence by the promulgation in 1850 of the Caste Disabilities Removal Act. Hindus were suspicious of this act, which declared that any law or usage that

> inflicts on any person forfeiture of rights or property, or may be held in any way to impair or effect any right of inheritance, by reason of his or her renouncing or having been excluded from the communion of any religion, or

[96] The mutiny and reactions to it have recently been vividly described in Lawrence James, *Raj: The Making and Unmaking of British India* (New York: St. Martin's Press, 1997), 233-300.

[97] A sepoy was an Indian soldier serving in the British army in India or other places in the interests of the empire. During the Raj, the officers in the army were British, but the overwhelming percentage of the soldiers were Indian.

[98] Ibid., 234-36.

being deprived of nadar, shall cease to be enforced by law."[99]

This law meant that legal rights of inheritance were not lost by a person who renounced her faith or who converted to another faith. While this legislation was viewed by many as a freedom of religion act, orthodox Hindus protested that it interfered most grievously with their religious usages, for the right to inherit property was accompanied by religious obligations that only a Hindu could fulfill. Since the main result of the act was to protect those who had converted to Christianity from loss of inheritance or other rights or property, it was viewed by many as a step on the road to the establishment of Christianity.[100]

On May 10, a Sunday, after several weeks of great tension and severe disciplinary measures by British commanders, cavalrymen broke into the gaol and rescued their sepoy comrades. This encouraged a mob, including many sepoys, to rush through the town of Lucknow and the British cantonment, burning bungalows and murdering every European man, woman, and child they encountered. The arson and murder directed against members of a race that had hitherto represented authority and demanded obedience destroyed the mystique of British supremacy.[101] It served to unify the rebels, while at the same time forcing the members of the white race to huddle more closely together in the face of the danger threatening them from people whose loyalty they could no longer trust.

The actual course of the mutiny need not concern us further. The situation in the northern part of India remained chaotic and turned into a full scale war for eighteen months before the mutiny was eventually put down and order restored. The legacy of the War of 1857-58 was of fundamental importance to British India. On August 1, 1858, the British Parliament passed the Government of

[99] Smith, *India as a Secular State*, 70.
[100] Ibid., 71.
[101] James, *Raj*, 239.

India Act, transferring all rights that the British East India Company had hitherto enjoyed on Indian soil directly to the British crown. In order to put to rest the suspicions that it was the purpose of the British government to establish Christianity as the religion for India, Queen Victoria issued her momentous proclamation of religious neutrality in the state's relations with its Indian subjects:

> Firmly relying ourselves on the truth of Christianity, and acknowledging with gratitude the solace of religion, we disclaim alike the right and desire to impose our convictions on any of our subjects. We declare it to be our royal will and pleasure that none be in any wise favored, none molested or disquieted, by reason of their religious faith or observances, but that all shall alike enjoy the equal and impartial protection of the law; and we do strictly charge and enjoin all those who may be in authority under us that they abstain from all interference with the religious belief or worship of any of our subjects on pain of our highest displeasure.[102]

After 1858, Arcot missionaries agreed with other missionaries in India on two points. The first was that the rule of the British was a blessing. India was going through many positive changes due to the introduction of western education, the legal system, and the railways, and British rule maintained order in a divided land. The second point was that the British government had failed in its Christian duty.[103] In the new situation after 1858, as previously under the rule of the company, the professed neutrality actually discriminated against the Christian faith and encouraged Hindus who were organizing opposition against the Christians. Three letters sent by Arcot missionaries to Isaac Ferris following the mutiny show clear evidence of these two points.

---

[102] Smith, *India as a Secular State,* 71-72.
[103] Immanuel David, *Reformed Church in America Missionaries in South India, 1839-1938* (Bangalore, India: Asian Trading Corporation, 1986), 48.

The great anxiety felt by missionaries and Christians in the year of the mutiny pulsates through Ezekiel Scudder's report concerning events in the London Mission area in Travancore in the far south. That area was not under direct control of the British; it was under the rule of the Rajah of Travancore, who was in alliance with the British. When the mutiny broke out in the north, Scudder reports, eleven chapels of the London Mission were burned, teachers were beaten, imprisoned, and deprived of their property. Clothes were torn off Christian men and women. Many of their schools were broken up and worship interrupted.[104]

In this case, the underlying cause, Scudder believed, was that the inhabitants were of two different classes, "the one proud, ignorant and overbearing, yet wealthy and possessed of influence from their connection with the government; the other degraded and oppressed." The second group, among whom were the Christians, were not allowed to wear sandals, carry an umbrella, or have men or women wear any clothing above the waist. The fact that these persons in becoming Christians were gaining a measure of dignity caused the attacks upon them. "The Christianizing and civilizing influences of the gospel upon these poor people…had taught them to become in a measure independent and self-respectful. The missionaries had secured for the Christian women the privilege of wearing a jacket." When complaints were sent to the Rajah about the attacks on the churches and the Christians, the Rajah in the post-mutiny situation did nothing. The report of what had happened in Travancore fueled the anxieties of the people in the Arcot area.

In a letter dated November 26, 1858, Scudder again wrote to Ferris. This time he described an incident in Vellore, where a Muslim sepoy, on guard at the fort while drunk, suddenly discharged his musket twice and rushed inside. There he shot the European jailer, whose wife was a "native woman and a beloved member of our church in Vellore." This incident, while an isolated act of one

[104] For this and subsequent paragraph, we follow a letter (undated but found together with correspondence of 1858) of E. C. Scudder to Isaac Ferris.

individual, only served to raise anxieties and rumors in the area. It also "exhibits the deep antipathy and hatred of the native toward the European and the desire he has to free himself from the dominion of the latter. I believe however that the Lord has given this land into the hands of a Christian government for his own purposes and glory, and that though they have often proved unworthy of the charge committed to them."[105]

Scudder then went on to say that the Queen's proclamation of religious neutrality was having negative consequences in the area. Unfortunately, he wrote, the translation of the text of that proclamation into Tamil was misleading and open to wrong interpretations. "Some of the interpretations are quite alarming. My brother Jared writes that the natives around Arnee (his station) say that any one who promulgates Christianity shall receive 500 lashes. Others have got the impressions that the government is about to adopt the Christian religion."

W. W. Scudder also wrote an undated report about the situation. He told of how some of the soldiers in the 24th Regiment in his area had been pressing forward eagerly, inquiring into the subject of Christianity. They drew back when they heard that the British government was directly discouraging such interests and refusing to allow any further baptisms in the corps. Moreover, the officers were not permitted to converse with even the native Christians about Christianity. As an example of the boasted "neutrality" of the British government, he wrote, "A Christian gentleman in government employment sees fit to attend in a private capacity the baptism of a sepoy. He is reprimanded for it by the Governor-General and an order issued on the subject that convinces the native soldiers that Government are opposed to others becoming Christians and officers are warned not to hold religious conversation with their men....*And this is called neutrality!*"[106]

---

[105] For this and following paragraph, we follow the letter of E. C. Scudder to Isaac Ferris, Nov. 26, 1858.

[106] W. W. Scudder, *Hindrances of the British Government* (on file with 1858 correspondence in Archives of the RCA, undated).

By 1860, Reformed Church missionaries had a clear sense of direction in their expectation that the church was being planted and could move toward being self-governing, self-supporting, and self-governing. The church was beginning to gain its own Indian leadership, with one Indian ordained minister and with elders delegated from the Classis of Arcot congregations holding equal rank, as well as speaking and voting privileges, with the missionary ordained ministers. With the Raj still firmly in control, the missionaries could look forward to continuing their evangelistic and pastoral service in India, however disappointed they were in the stance of the Raj with respect to religion.

In the next decades the gains made in the first decade were consolidated. More missionaries arrived, and whole villages began to ask to be instructed in the Christian faith. The movement toward Christ had begun in the Arcot area, as the Classis of Arcot of the Reformed Protestant Dutch Church began to reach out more fully into the field to which it knew itself called.

3

Village Movements in
Response to the Gospel

In 1861, one of the native helpers working with Reformed
Church missionary Joseph Mayou in the area of Arni came into
conversation with a Roman Catholic man from the village of
Sattambady, located twenty-two miles from Arni. The helper spoke
with the man about the way of salvation through Christ as it is
taught in the Bible. Thereupon the man invited him to visit his
village and teach the people the truths of the Bible. A number of
months later, twenty-nine adults and thirty children were baptized
in Sattambady, and that group became the first village congregation
established in India through the mission of the Reformed Church
in America.

An account of a whole group of people deciding together to be
instructed in the faith, to be baptized, and to live as a village
congregation is not unusual in the annals of the church in India. On
the contrary, in a major research study led by J. Waskom Pickett in
1933, it was concluded that "one half of the Roman Catholics in
India are descendents of mass-movement converts, and that not
less than 80 percent of the 1,800,000 Protestants are the product of

mass-movements."[1] Although the term "mass movement" became popular, it is more accurate to speak of "group movements."[2] Such movements toward Christianity occurred more often in a small group of several families within a village, or perhaps an entire a small village, than they did among a "masses" of thousands, although there were also a number of such larger movements as well. A number of the Christians in the Telugu language area of the Arcot Mission did come into the faith as the result of one such large movement in the Madigas and Mala castes.[3]

The Arcot missionaries, like other American and English missionaries, were thankful for the movements of groups of people into the faith, but they also had problems with such movements. They were concerned that members of the groups were simply following a leader or going along with the crowd without knowing what was involved. They feared that perhaps these were "rice Christians," offering to become Christians only in order to get some free food or other economic assistance. They sought means to test the people's sincerity in their expressed faith.[4]

Group movements not only brought to the fore issues about motivation and adequate understanding on the part of the converts,

---

[1] J. Waskom Pickett, *Christian Mass Movements in India* (Cincinnati: Abingdon, 1933), 5. The Board of Foreign Missions provided a grant toward funding this research. The missionaries at first were hesitant about such a grant because there was a shortage of funds in the years of the great depression, and they believed that priority ought to be given to the work of the mission, which was experiencing retrenchment on every front due to the economic situation. After Pickett visited the area and produced the results of his work, the missionaries found it to be helpful (letter of Wierenga to Potter, Sept. 10, 1936). Pickett's work has become a classic on the subject of mass movement converts.

[2] Ibid., 21.

[3] Ibid., 128-30.

[4] In Pickett's study, converts were asked about their motives for becoming Christians. The study lists forty motives, ranging from "because I was tired of the devil," to "because God worked in me and I had to do it," "for Jesus' sake," "to marry a good girl," and "because our missionary helped us against the Brahmans and the Rajputs." In addition to the forty motives listed, Pickett also quotes one person who said, "So that I could be a man. None of us was a man. We were dogs. Only Jesus could make men out of us" (155-68). These responses in turn raise intriguing questions about how each could be evaluated for sincerity in faith.

but they also raised theological questions for the missionaries themselves. Reformed Church missionaries in the mid-nineteenth century had all been reared on the American eastern seaboard in areas that had been heavily influenced by the two Great Awakenings of the eighteenth and early nineteenth centuries, as well as by currents of eighteenth-century Reformed pietism.[5] In those traditions, conversion was an extremely intense and personal event. It involved profound sorrow for sin, a response to the call of Christ in a time of spiritual wrestling, and a great sense of gratitude and joy at the removal of guilt and the knowledge of salvation and eternal life.

In that era, Europe and the United States were still considered to be Christian nations, however far they might have fallen short of that ideal. Most children in the respectable society in which the missionaries had been nurtured were baptized as infants. But many strayed away from the faith, became "backsliders," even "black sheep." Others continued the practice of religion but remained "nominal Christians" who attended church more out of custom than conviction. In such a society, people needed to be brought to a spiritual awakening, to revival of the faith into which they had been baptized. Conversion brought about restoration to community, to parents and family. Wandering boys came home; black sheep returned to the fold. Harriet Scudder on her deathbed still feared the eternal separation that would result if her three as yet unconverted children would not come to faith. With their conversion after her death, the unity of the family was made whole.

Conversion to the Protestant faith in India included a set of social dynamics foreign to such missionaries. In India, conversion for a Hindu meant estrangement from family, from one's caste relations, from the religious exercises of the surrounding community. Rather than representing the wandering boy coming home or the black sheep returning to the fold, the conversion of a Hindu boy was interpreted by his family as a previously obedient son now deciding to forsake his home. He was perceived to have renounced the true morality of the family's caste and to have laid aside the religious marriage and funeral rites that were so important to the continuity of the family and the salvation of its members. In the experience of the missionaries, conversion represented the victory of faith; in the families of the individual convert in India, it meant the tragedy of a broken home.

The experience of such a young man still fit within the missionary's own American experience of conversion. It was not at all unusual for a new convert to be ridiculed and urged by his former friends to once again join them in their riotous and wicked ways. There were many families who did not appreciate the new spiritual zeal of the converted one. There also had been many martyrs in England in the Reformation and post-Reformation centuries. *Foxx's Book of Martyrs* was a favorite piece of literature for those who knew that persecution often came to the one who was converted. Thus, the following story of a backsliding convert to and from Roman Catholicism in Coonoor was well within the framework of their experience:

> After three years yielding to the enticements of the Romanists, he joined them. Though I spoke to him at the time, he did not give heed to my advice, but said,
>
> "Go, go, yours is Luther's religion. Romanism is the true religion. Miracles were formerly wrought in it and still may be witnessed. I came to your religion through ignorance." A few days after this, his own mother and stepfather quarreled with him and charged him with theft through malice, and established the same before the magistrate by false witnesses, and he was sentenced to three years' rigorous imprisonment....Yet this unjust punishment was not only useful to turn his mind, but the means of opening

his eyes to see the errors of Romanism, and stirred him up to seek the true light. After he was released, he came to me and confessed, with tears that he had sinned against God and truth.[6]

As individuals who had come to know conversion as an intense personal experience, however, nineteenth-century missionaries remained uneasy about group conversion movements. They could not help but take satisfaction when whole families or villages expressed their desire to be instructed in the faith and be baptized, but they were very much concerned about motivation, sincerity, and whether there was real sorrow for sin and a personal knowledge of Christ for salvation.

Their deep suspicion of the Roman Catholic Church only made it more difficult for them. The Roman Catholic Church had long experience with the problems that the missionaries now faced. In western Europe during the early medieval period, Europe had been Christianized along tribal lines, often as the result of monastic or military activities. When a king or a tribal leader would decide out of pure or impure motives that he and his people should become Christian, the whole group or area would be obliged to follow his lead. The response of the Roman Catholic missionaries had been to baptize the great masses of people who were ready to submit to the yoke of Christ and then to seek to instruct them following their baptism. The church had dealt with the issue of whether people really understood what they were doing by developing a doctrine of "implicit faith." Those who made use of the sacraments as means of grace and implicitly believed what the church believed, even if they did not know or really understand just what the church believed, were thus incorporated into the community of salvation.

Protestants were very much aware of the deficiencies of the Roman Catholic system. They saw that in the Roman Catholic churches in Latin America and much of Europe the veneration of

6 Report from Zechariah John, pastor at Coonoor, included in Board of Foreign Missions Report, 1871, 36-37.

the saints often showed considerable continuity with the worship of their former pagan deities. They recognized that the use of the sacraments was in many cases simply magic and superstition. They believed that the doctrine of implicit faith is often a cover for lack of any real faith at all. It enabled the clergy ("the teaching church") to maintain control over the laity ("the listening church"). Upon meeting the Roman Catholic descendants of the Portuguese missionaries in India (who had often been left like sheep without a shepherd), all of these suspicions were confirmed. The Roman Catholic practice of quickly incorporating large numbers of people into the church through baptism appeared to encourage a very defective, even apostate, Christianity.

Group conversion movements thus confronted the American missionaries with problems similar to those posed to Rome in the early medieval period, but on a radically smaller scale. In the 1860s the number of group movements in the Arcot area remained relatively few, with the result that it was possible to find resources more or less adequate to assist the villagers to grow into the faith.[7] After 1877, when the number of villages asking for instruction in the faith multiplied, the mission's financial resources were inadequate to the opportunities before it, to the chagrin of the missionaries. However, that came later. First, the Arcot Mission had to deal with these issues in the Tamil-language group at Sattambady and the new Telugu area around Madanapalle.

The Group Conversion Movement at Sattambady

Although missionaries were often accused of being aggressive and eager to baptize people, the case of Sattambady is much more typical of their mode of operation. People whose motivations they

[7] The number of people involved in the mass conversion movements in Telugu language areas at some distance from Madanapalle was much larger. In the area of the American Baptist Mission, the number of conversions increased from 23 in 1861 to 153,440 in 1900. The increase for all reporting missions was from 1,899 in 1861 to 201,213 in 1900 (Pathak, *American Missionaries*, 103). Some of those converts entered congregations in the Arcot Mission area.

questioned at first often approached them.[8] Once convinced that people asking to be instructed in the faith were sincere, a missionary would make arrangements for a period of instruction by placing a catechist or teacher in the village and opening a school for the prospective Christians' children. Upon being satisfied that the people did have a basic understanding of the faith, they were baptized and enrolled as a village congregation. Those who had a more mature understanding of the faith would be admitted into the communicant membership of the church.

We have noted above that a worker employed by the Arcot Mission was the first to be approached by a man from the village of Sattambady. When the Indian evangelist went to the village for a first visit, he took some Christian literature with him. On his return to Arni, the evangelist took the same man with him as a representative of his village to introduce him to the missionary there, Joseph Mayou. At first, Mayou was suspicious of the story and sent the catechist at Arni with another native helper to the village to ascertain its truth. The catechist returned and reported that the villagers there were "poor people, who had been entirely forsaken— that they desired us to come among them and teach them and their children."

Joseph Mayou was still uncertain, so he went to the village himself to investigate the situation, along with the Indian pastor Andrew Sawyer. He summarized his conclusions in the Arcot Mission Report, 1861:

> I...explained to them freely the outlines of the Christian faith as recorded in the Bible, and the difference between

---

[8] Hindus also remained suspicious of low caste people showing interest in the Christian faith. M. K. Gandhi was to write in 1937, "Presentation, with a view to conversion, of a faith other than one's own, can only necessarily be through an appeal to the intellect or the stomach or both. I do maintain that the vast mass of Harijans, and for that matter, Indian humanity, cannot understand the presentation of Christianity, and that generally speaking their conversion wherever it has taken place has not been a spiritual act in any sense of the term. They are conversions for convenience" [M. K. Gandhi, *Christian Missions: Their Place in India* (Ahmedabad, India: Navajivan Publishing House, 1941), 61.]

the teachings of the Scriptures and the Romish system of
religion, and then asked them if they assented to what their
representatives had signed for them. Each family then gave
a formal assent. They were warned that they might meet
with opposition and even suffering on account of what they
had done. They said they knew this, but that they would try
to bear it if I would help them. I received them under my
charge on the fourth day of December. I have visited them
twice since. The principle landowner for whom they labor
is hostile to the movement, and threatens to turn them out
of employ if they do not work on the Sabbath, and to sue
them for advances of any extra monies they and their
fathers may have obtained from his family. If he really
should do this the poor people will be reduced to destitution.[9]

Joseph Mayou was fully conscious of the importance of the steps
that he now undertook in receiving this group of people under his
care. Sattambady would prove to be a very positive example of how
important pastoral care and firm support of newly converted
groups is to their sustained faithfulness and spiritual growth. The
need for careful attention to the spiritual maturation of village
congregations would soon demand much of the time of the
missionaries and their Indian helpers. Within a few years, these
congregational needs came into tension with the central missionary
concern for evangelistic touring in previously unreached villages
and people. By 1870 there were already nearly forty villages needing
such sustained care. The financial burden on the Arcot Mission also
increased rapidly, because as more and more villages applied for
instruction in the faith, vernacular schools had to be established in
accordance with the mission's principle that such a school should
be opened wherever there were three Christian families.

Mayou listed his requirements for receiving people under his care.
He stated that a schoolhouse, which may be used as a place of

9 "AAR," 1861, 12.

worship, must be built. A catechist and a teacher must be placed there, and a house built for each of them. Even though the salaries would be low (about fifty dollars per year for each one) and village houses and school buildings would be basically mud huts with thatched roofs, the cost still was beyond what the Board of Foreign Missions had appropriated. He knew that no additional funds would come from America, where the Civil War had broken out. His hope was that financial resources could be found in India for the project. In Mayou's appeal for funds, his favorable attitude toward the British Raj can also be seen.

> We cannot turn to America at this time for aid, and we look no where but to the true friends of Missions among the English in India. Religion and Education are the two great pillars of the state, and every Missionary, be he an Englishman or an American, is endeavoring to confer these on the masses of India. He is then a friend to the Government, and deserves the sympathy, encouragement, and aid if necessary, of every well wisher of the Government. Let it be remembered that every Native Christian in the land is a stanch royalist.[10]

In the 1862 report, we read that Mr. Yesadian has been placed in the village as the catechist and Mr. Joshua as the teacher. Joseph and Margaret Mayou have moved from Arni to the town of Gingee, so as to be within "driving distance" of Sattambady. The number of people who came under care in December 1861, was fifty-nine, in ten families. The prospect that the landowner would no longer employ them had indeed come to pass and the people had suffered much. However, they were managing to survive, thanks to the liberality of several English gentlemen and the native church in Coonoor. Twenty-five children had been enrolled in school and were making good progress. A spot of ground had been given for

---

10 Ibid, 13.

a chapel and schoolhouse, for which contributions had been received.[11]

By 1863, the Mayous were back in Arni because Gingee proved to be so unhealthy a place that they could not remain there. But the work in their central station of Arni was somewhat weakened by the need to attend to the needs of the out-stations, such as those at Aliandal and Vellambi. Aliandal consisted of five families with twenty-three people. A catechist and a teacher had been placed there. Vellambi had eight families with forty-one people and had a "reader" and a teacher. A number of Hindu families in the town of Chetpet, eight miles from Sattambady, had also pledged themselves to renounce heathenism.[12]

In Sattambady, the congregation had now grown to seventy-eight. Twenty-nine people had been baptized as adults, as well as thirty of their children. They had also been organized into a Christian church. They now enjoyed the privileges of the Christian church and were subject to its discipline, including that of abstaining from work on the Sabbath day. Some additional Hindu families had signified their desire to renounce heathenism. Twelve boys and eleven girls were in school. What is perhaps especially remarkable is that already three girls had been placed in the Female Seminary at Chittoor and were thus on their way to becoming wives of catechists or teachers.[13]

Mayou stated that he had not yet accepted the Hindu families because they had not yet "statedly" observed the Sabbath: "This is their first test. In their ignorance and poverty it is very hard for them to give up the profits of one day in seven for a good that appears to them very indefinite. We believe however they will soon join us."[14] In another village, Parachoor, five families had for some time

---

[11] "AAR," 1862, 23.

[12] For this and the next two paragraphs, see "AAR," 1863, 11-16.

[13] The history of Sattambadi's first fifty years after the first converts were baptized is remarkable. By 1910, 110 Christian workers had come out from the village to serve in the Arcot Mission ("BFMR," 1912, 62).

[14] "BFMR,"1861, 14.

pondered the question of embracing Christianity. The teacher Francis was laboring among them. However,

> ...the people are very poor, entirely dependent on their capricious masters; they are liable at any time to be left without the means of support if they observe the sabbath....They are men who have been accustomed to weigh little temporal matters, not spiritual realities. They may believe Christianity to be true, but they want to know how it will affect them temporally.[15]

In the following year, 1864, further progress was reported, in spite of a crop failure that their Hindu neighbors said was due to their having become Christians. Apparently nine families had slid back into Hinduism, but one of those had returned. The other Christians were remaining firm in their new faith. When the Hindu priest came for his usual visit to the village, the people told him that his services were no longer needed, that his religion was a lie, and that they were all anxious to become Christians. They had a secure site for a church that they hoped to erect quite soon.[16]

The statistics reported for Sattambady indicate that there were twenty-seven communicants, twenty-three baptized children, fourteen catechumens, fourteen children of catechumens, and one under suspension. For the other new village of Aliandal there were twelve communicants, two baptized adult noncommunicants, sixteen baptized children, eleven catechumens, and three children of catechumens. In Aliandal we see clearly reported the widespread practice of baptizing adults without admitting them to the Lord's Table. This practice ran counter to the Reformed Church liturgy and church order, which required of adults a public response to questions. Positive answers to the questions indicated that such individuals should not only be baptized, they should also be invited to partake of the Lord's Supper with all of the other communicants.

[15] "BFMR," 1864, 23.
[16] Ibid., 20.

However, in the village situation, missionaries believed that it was important to not keep people waiting for baptism who had indicated willingness to be instructed in the faith and who had by their lives shown for a time a measure of faith. Thus one sees here a two-stage catechumen process, the first leading to the point of baptism along with the group, and the second to the point when the person can provide an account of her or his personal, individual spiritual growth and understanding of the faith. The second stage opened the way to admission to the Lord's Table. In making this distinction, the missionaries were attempting to integrate their American individualism with Indian corporate community understanding.

As noted in several of the missionary reports, trouble arose in Sattambady and several other villages when the new Christians refused to work on the Sabbath for the landowners to whom they were obligated. Here again the influence of American religious experience on missionary policies in India can be felt. The complete cessation from unnecessary work on Sunday was one of the defining characteristics of American Protestantism, at least in its Calvinistic, Methodist, and Baptist traditions. The General Synod of the Reformed Church in America, beginning in 1792, had adopted a whole series of resolutions affirming the importance of the Lord's Day as a day of rest from labor. The General Synod of 1843 approved a report opposing the running of railroads, stagecoaches, and canal boats on Sunday. It stated,

> We believe that the sanctification of one day in seven is indispensable to the very existence of religion, and that the neglect of such observance leads not only to irreligion, but to crime—that nature and revelation both teach that man has of *right* but six days in which to do his own work, and that he cannot take more without exposing himself to the peculiar pleasure of God—that man's highest, social, civil and religious interests demand the observance of the Lord's Day....[17]

[17] *Minutes of the General Synod, RCA,* 1843, 192.

Most Reformed Church missionaries in India had received their early Christian education in areas in the United States where strict Sabbath observance was a way of life. They were utterly convinced that for the good of believer, the church, and humanity, they could not retreat from firm discipline on the rhythm of six days of labor and one of rest. Opposition from Hindu landowners did not sway them.

In their efforts to enable the villagers to observe the Sabbath, the missionaries were quite ready to enlist the power of the government. The weekly bazaar at Chetpet was held on Sunday, which meant that the Christians of Sattambady were unable to go there to supply themselves with their necessary weekly supplies without violating the fourth commandment. "This proved a sore hardship, and they looked to the Lord for a change. Efforts were made by the Missionary to have the bazaar meet on Monday instead of Sunday, and by the grace of God this was effected on the 11th day of November, 1866."[18] More than a decade later, the Reverend Enne Heeren, a Reformed Church missionary in Palmaner, rejoiced because the Sunday weekly market day there was changed to Monday. That Sunday market had been of particular disturbance to the Christian community because it was held next to the church. The Christians had appealed to the collector of the district to have it changed to another day, so the Sabbath was now better observed there and the Christians could worship in peace.[19]

However, at Sattambady in 1865, severe harassment of the converts continued. Their former employer had cut them off from many hereditary rights and privileges, and his action brought them to the edge of starvation. They were denied the right to use water from the village wells, to catch fish in the village pond, to cultivate their land, or to appeal to the village for charity. While the Arcot Mission was meeting one day in Arni, a messenger brought news that the high-caste landowners of the village continued to persecute

18 "AAR," 1866, 34.
19 "BFMR," 1877, 23.

the Christians, and he pleaded for help. With that the missionaries adjourned their business session, mounted their horses, and galloped away down twenty-two miles of road to the village. The sight of seven white men in long beards riding into their village on big horses such as government officials used was enough to impress the elders of the village. They promised to leave the Christians alone for the time being.[20] Within a short time, however, the harassment began once more.

The report from Sattambady in 1866 notes a dramatic change. The report lists the village as a pastorate in its own right, with the Reverend Andrew Sawyer present. However, he was living in a new village called Gnanothiam, which came into being though the efforts of Joseph Mayou. He secured from the collector a grant of sixty acres of jungle land halfway, about four miles, between Sattambady and Chetpet. The location placed them on the main road alongside Gingee. Travelers on that road were pleased to have the village located there, because it previously had been an area frequented by tigers, thieves, and bandits. It became a place where such travelers could be told the message of Jesus Christ.[21]

Eight families from Sattambady were resettled in Gnanothiam, because they continued to be oppressed by the landowner Narayanan Reddi. Although they met opposition from the Hindus when they left Sattambady, they remained faithful as they re-located in their new area. In their first days and nights there, Sawyer and others remained with them because they feared thieves and wild animals. The missionaries helped them with food, materials for houses, and also agricultural implements until they could clear the land, dig wells, and secure their first harvest. Several of the Christian families decided to remain in Sattambady, and they had been joined by four families "from heathenism," wrote the missionaries. "Thus is God blessing and increasing His Church in all places." Two more new

---

[20] Wyckoff, *A Hundred Years*, 11.
[21] For this and the following paragraph, "AAR," 1866, 32-34.

villages were then reported, Thalambandi and Pariantangal. By this time the group conversion movements were reinforcing one another in the area.

The pattern established in the planting of the church in Sattambady was followed repeatedly in its basic form as the number of occupied Christian villages increased rapidly over the next century. In summary, six points can be listed.

1. Missionaries were often hesitant to accept villagers asking to come under instruction, either because they were suspicious about the real motives for the request or, as the number of villages making the request increased, because there were no resources available to supply a teacher or catechist for the village.

2. Missionaries were hesitant to baptize persons prematurely. In contrast to the practice of Roman Catholic missionaries of previous centuries, they instituted a three-step process into full church membership. It began with acceptance of the villages to be brought under instruction and continued with baptism after a more or less extended period of two or more years and a careful examination of individuals as to whether they should be admitted to celebrations of the Lord's Supper.

3. Attention was given to the development of a disciplined Christian life. Such a life included forsaking the worship of idols, breaking of caste by eating together, and obeying the Ten Commandments, including cessation of work on the Sabbath day.

4. Schools were established for the children of those who had come under instruction.

5. In cases where the villagers experienced particularly difficult impoverishment due to persecution and/or refusal on the part of landowners to employ them, new

land would be sought where they could resettle as a new Christian village.

6. The Arcot Mission found it increasingly difficult to find the financial resources to follow this pattern.

Criticism has often been directed against missionaries particularly for point 5. Such criticism often tends to imply that resettling new believers on mission compounds was the rule rather than the exception. In reading through the Arcot Mission reports and missionary correspondence, one gains the clear impression that converts were brought into the compounds or missionary homes in cases when there was severe animosity toward them. Such was the case particularly with young unmarried boys, who were then placed into one of the boarding schools. The number of places where villagers were resettled were relatively few, although such villagers often did provide more young people to be educated and assume leadership in the Christian community as time went on.

This first point of criticism often is related to a second one, which is that the mission compound mentality has produced denationalized Christians. This is a far more complex issue than the previous one. From our contemporary vantage point, the Arcot missionaries in the nineteenth century were clearly unable to recognize their cultural blinders. They had a strong tendency to universalize their own experience as simply being the reasonable situation of a universal humanity. They also believed that the villagers in India were sinners like themselves and had natural abilities equal to their own, but that the Indians had been kept in ignorance, poverty, and superstition by the heathen system in which they found themselves.

The Arcot missionaries did not go to India to civilize the people; they went to evangelize them. But when the people came asking to be instructed in the faith, the missionaries assumed that the Ten Commandments were to be included in those instructions. The missionaries' interpretations of the Ten Commandments were shaped by American church and public life. The comment of David

Bosch concerning nineteenth-century American missionaries in general also applied to those who went to Arcot: "The problem was that the advocates of mission were blind to their own ethnocentrism....They were, therefore, predisposed not to appreciate the cultures of the people to whom they went."[22] It is perhaps enough that we admire those early Arcot missionaries for the large measure of respect and assistance they gave to those villagers at the bottom of their society who had not remembered previously receiving any real respect and assistance from anyone. It would remain for future generations to wrestle with issues of how best to live the faith as Indians in the country of India.

Preaching the Gospel in Villages Surrounding Madanapalle

The first decade of Arcot Mission activity in the Telugu language area of Madanapalle stands in contrast with that of Sattambady in that it ended with disappointment and had to wait for the following decade to show more positive results. Arcot missionary activity in the Madanapalle area essentially began in 1863, when the Reverend Jacob Chamberlain was asked to take up residence there after spending several years in Palmaner. It was an era of great budget stringency in the Board of Foreign Missions and the Arcot Mission, due to the Civil War in the United States. Chamberlain had to struggle with the need to build a missionary house, a school, and houses for a catechist, a reader, and a Christian schoolteacher when he and his wife Charlotte arrived. They had to live in a small, dark, inadequate house that was very damp in times of rain and extremely hot when the sun shone. Under the strain, his health broke to the extent that he had to go to the hill station to recover in a more favorable climate. Although the Chamberlains would be India missionaries until his death in 1908 and hers ten years later, Jacob had to struggle constantly with his poor health, periodically spending time in the hills or even in the United States.

[22] David J. Bosch, *Transforming Mission: Paradigm Shifts in Theology of Mission* (Maryknoll, N.Y.: Orbis Press, 1991), 294.

In 1865, Chamberlain reported that he was thankful that his health had permitted him to remain in his Madanapalle mission station throughout the year. Four Indian workers were also with him: Souri, catechist and elder; John Souri, reader; Ryal, Christian schoolteacher; and Alexander, Bible colporteur. The congregation had been organized with eight communicants, two baptized adult noncommunicants, eight baptized children, forty-one catechumens, and nine children of catechumens. All of the communicant members were received by letter of transfer from other churches. Six families from heathenism had joined them at the close of the year. Evidently they had waited to declare themselves until it appeared that the mission had come to stay. Chamberlain reported, "Some of these have long heard the truth, and their coming was not the result of a sudden impulse, but of a growing conviction and deep seated purpose; and we trust that in some the change is more than outward, and that a short term of probation will prove them worthy to receive the sealing ordinance of baptism."[23]

No missionary was more enthusiastic in his missionary touring than was Jacob Chamberlain, but in 1866 the doctor had ordered him not to engage in such strenuous activity. As a result, he decided to keep regular hours of medical practice. "I could thus, while administering physical relief, tell them of the Great Physician who takes away the maladies of the soul. I have kept this up through the year, with ten to thirty patients a day. These have heard the great truths of the Gospel, and taken Tracts and Scriptures to many villages that would not otherwise have been reached." [24]

In contrast to the Sattambady area, where the missionary Joseph Mayou and the Indian pastor Andrew Sawyer remained throughout the whole period, the Madanapalle area suffered from an inconsistent missionary presence and no Indian ordained pastor on the scene, although P. Souri was an experienced catechist. In 1867, we find Chamberlain once again located at Palmaner, thirty miles from

---

[23]"AAR," 1865, 24.
[24] Ibid., 24-25.

Madanapalle. He did make four visits to Madanapalle during the course of the year. However, it had been a year in which he and his family experienced considerable illness, including typhoid suffered by his three oldest children. The number of communicant members had increased by two, but the number of catechumens had decreased to eleven, because they managed to get into a quarrel with each other just before they were to have been baptized.[25]

A village about a mile and a half from Madanapalle had sent word to Chamberlain in Palmaner that "they would join us if I would come and receive them. I came at once, but their courage failed them. They still declare themselves thoroughly convinced of the truth of Christianity, and ready to cast away their idols and become Christians were it not for the people around them."[26]

While things were not going well around Madanapalle, an important development was taking place in the Palmaner out-station named "Arunodaya" (Dayspring) by vote of the inhabitants. This was a new village located on a tract of wasteland four miles southeast of Palmaner. It was laid out for a group of new Christians who had been turned out of their homes and village. A church of mud and thatch capable of seating sixty had been built. Several of the catechumens had turned out to be scoundrels and were turned out, but a number of others had joined, so the village was off to a good start. In December, Chamberlain baptized eight adults and seven children in addition to the previous three communicants and six baptized adult noncommunicants. The highlight of the day before the baptism was a "love-feast." The congregations of Palmaner and Arunodaya attended, including included people of various castes. In his report we learn of the unity that came to the congregations as they ate together across caste lines.

> We thought it important that they should signify their entire renunciation of all caste feeling and distinctions by eating together as brothers before being admitted by baptism into

25"AAR," 1867, 34-39.
26 Ibid., 37.

the Church of God. Forty-three persons, originally of eight different castes and from fourteen different towns, thus sat together and partook in brotherly love of the feast spread for the occasion in the school house. The Lord's Supper was also administered on the Sabbath for the first time in the new village, and twelve communicants took part.[27]

In reading Chamberlain's report about the new village of Arunodaya, one gets some feeling for the dilemma felt by the missionaries when they saw new converts turned out of their villages and in need of some type of income. Chamberlain wrote,

> It has been one of our greatest difficulties to find a means of honest and independent livelihood for those whom, on forsaking their heathen idols and becoming Christians, have been turned out of their homes and driven from their former employment. Of course, to support such persons in idleness, even were it in our power, would be to put a premium on hypocrisy. While, on the other hand, if we could not put the means of obtaining an honest livelihood in the way of those who forsake everything for Christ, it would be an almost insuperable barrier to others following their example.[28]

In this case, as we have seen, the solution adopted was to help them to settle on their new land. Unfortunately, in this first year the rains failed them, so there was no harvest, and they had to receive charitable assistance for several months. "They have worked hard and proved themselves worthy."[29]

Chamberlain said in 1868 that it was still too early to reap a harvest; it was still the season for sowing the seed. "It is yet with us the seed-time, and we go forth scattering the Gospel seed, fully believing that the harvest of souls will in due time appear."[30] Since

[27] Ibid., 41-42.
[28] Ibid., 40.
[29] Ibid., 42.
[30] "AAR," 1868, 35.

he was sick for five months of the year, he was able to go on only five tours, which together with his time spent at outstations meant that he was away from home 122 days in the year. He and his companions had on those five tours preached the gospel in 822 villages. In most villages they received a pleasant welcome and people listened willingly. As they turned to leave one village at dusk one evening, however, some in the crowd threw a shower of small stones. With that, Chamberlain turned back into the village and told the people that he had been telling these same things all over the Telugu area, but to their village belonged the honor of being the first to have stoned them. With that, the village elders apologized for what had happened and said they would not let it happen again.[31]

Chamberlain in 1861 adopted the plan on tour of selling the Scriptures and tracts for a small price instead of distributing them gratuitously, as he had previously done. His object was not to recover the cost of the books but to secure their being properly used. After nine years of trial of this method of distribution, he still believed it was a more effective way to distribute literature. He also discovered that as the time went on people came to know that they would not be given the books free of charge. In 1870 the mission sold 28 Bibles, 19 New Testaments, 999 Scripture portions, 2,137 tracts large or small, and 396 school books.[32] The policy of selling rather than giving Scriptures continued to grow in favor after this time.

During 1872 Chamberlain's health was such that he had to spend much of his time in the hill station, but he still provided valuable service by working with the Bible Society on a new Telugu translation of the Bible. In spite of his absence, a new movement, which began in July, enrolled twenty new villages during the course of the year in the vicinity of Madanapalle.[33] The joy of this good

31 Ibid., 37.
32"AAR," 1870, 44-45.
33"AAR," 1872, 6.

news was short-lived, for in the following year's report, when Chamberlain was not at the station, investigation revealed that only seven of the villages remained, with the rest having gone back to their old religion. When the Indian evangelists were questioned about what had happened they admitted that they had used improper influences in what they had said to the villagers. When the villagers discovered the duplicity, almost all of them had returned to their old ways and no longer wanted the native mission helpers in their village.[34]

The Chamberlains had to spend several years in the United States for health reasons, and they returned to Madanapalle in December, 1878. During the interim, the Reverend Enne and Aleida Heern, who arrived in India in 1872, lived in Madanapalle for a brief period, but he too became seriously ill and had to return to America. He died soon after his return. Thus, due to the constant shift of residence and illness of the missionaries, people were left like sheep without a shepherd. Chamberlain found, after his long absence, "the village buildings all in ruins, and the congregations, those who had escaped the famine, scattered, and but one native assistant on the ground." But Chamberlain, ever the optimist, went on to say, "I was encouraged, however, by finding as much of a desire as I did, among the deserted villages, after better things, and set resolutely to work."[35] Within four years his faith and optimism would be justified.

In the first decade of Reformed Church missionary in the Madanapalle area, it became apparent that faithful attention to evangelistic preaching tours was not by itself adequate. Where people responded positively to what they had heard, they needed the support of faithful pastoral care. The Arcot Mission at that time had no other person it could release for the Telugu area when Chamberlain became ill, so a decade was lost there. It was the first rumbling of the question, later to come up for debate, of whether

[34]"AAR," 1873, 30-32.
[35]"BFMR," 1880, 21.

the Reformed Church would be able to grant sufficient funds and whether the Arcot Mission would have adequate resources to carry out missionary activity in two different language areas.

Church Growth, Evangelistic Touring, and Statistics after Fifteen Years

The Reformed Church missionaries believed that the experience of the mission during its first fifteen years confirmed its "principle that preaching the gospel to the masses is the divinely appointed agency for evangelizing heathen and has expected its missionaries to regard this as their primary and most important work." "God has here put upon it the seal of success."[36]

In accord with their first principle of preaching the gospel to the masses, the simple proclamation of the gospel throughout the towns and villages had brought in more than two thousand adherents to Christianity and established fifteen churches. But more impressive in the minds of the missionaries was the fact that to hundreds of thousands of the inhabitants of the area, Christianity was no longer a new and strange thing. Missionaries no longer were met with blank stares or treated as curiosities. Intelligent questions were asked. Confidence in pagan myths and hoary superstitions were manifestly shaken. "The leaven has entered the masses of the people, and we are content to watch and aid its working, confident that it will go on, until in God's own time the whole lump shall be leavened."[37]

In tracking the progress of their labors, the missionaries took great care to maintain detailed statistical records of their membership; number of churches and out-stations; students in the schools; number of Indian workers by categories; number of sermons preached in services of worship and number of persons present; number of Scriptures and pieces of Christian literature produced, distributed, and sold; as well as complete statistical records of

[36] "AAR," 1869, 4.
[37] Ibid., 5.

preaching tours. They were interested in numerical growth and rejoiced when by God's grace the numbers grew.

At the end of their seventeenth year, 1870, the missionaries reflected once again on what had happened since 1853. Like the report at the end of fifteen years, the affirmation is made that when one goes out preaching in season and out of season, God's promise holds true: "My word shall not return to be void, but it shall accomplish that which I please....We have met with scoffing and abuse in many instances, but as the result of our preaching there have come to us from the high and the low, the learned and the ignorant, those who have heard our message and believed it, and left all to follow Christ."[38] The 1870 statistical stable tells the story of numerical growth.

STATISTICS	1854	1869	1870
Stations	3	8	8
Out Stations	1	35	35
Missionaries*	3	8	7
Native Ministers	...	3	3
Catechists	3	24	26
Assistant Catechists	...	8	4
Readers	...	18	25
Teachers	5	29	33
Colporteurs	...	19	22
Churches	2	15	17
Communicants	26	564	659
Baptized Adults, not Communicants	...	214	227
Baptized Children	...	671	708
Catechumens	...	396	354
Children of Catechumens	...	298	302

[38]"BFMR," 1871, 23.

Total of			
Congregations	170	2,163	2,274
Arcot Seminary	13	52	44
Female Seminary	...	53	55
Preparandi School	...	36	43
Day Schools	4	36	36
Scholars in Day			
Schools	...	573	633[39]

(* "Missionaries" include only the males. Not included in the statistical report is the number of "Assistant Missionaries" who were the wives of the missionaries.)

The missionaries who remembered the early days in Arcot could take heart in reading the statistical reports. People were coming to Christ. The number of workers in the fields white unto harvest was increasing, and there were a good number of people being prepared for future service. Nevertheless, one can detect as an undercurrent in this report, as in the report of two years previous, a slight tone of defensive uneasiness. In both one feels the need to defend the policy of giving such exclusive priority to preaching the gospel in the surrounding districts. One suspects that the missionaries were somewhat disappointed that the numbers were not growing more rapidly, in light of their firm conviction that Hinduism was weak in comparison to the power of the gospel. One can wonder why they felt the need to defend themselves repeatedly in comparison to missions that were opening English-language schools with large enrollments. Here is one example: "Our Mission is seventeen years old. And although what is sometimes called a 'Preaching Mission,' in distinction from those which have large English Schools to aid them in getting a hold on the people, we do not think that a glance at our comparative statistics will tend to show that the vernacular preaching system is a failure."[40]

[39] Ibid.
[40] Ibid., 22-23.

Perhaps the missionaries had some justification for their disappointment, in view of the heavy schedules they and their Indian colleagues were maintaining. During the year 1870, in spite of the fact that many of them were in poor health, the report shows that they preached a total of 10,706 times in services of Christian worship, many of which also included a number of Hindu inquirers, and also preached 3,169 times in nearly 2,000 villages to the amazing total of 337,385 people while on their twenty-six evangelistic tours. Even if one questions how it was possible to count with accuracy the number of villagers who listened to the open-air preaching on the tours (for villagers had a strong tendency to come and go during the sermons), this still represents an amazing amount of mission labor. During the year, they also sold 4,056 Scriptures and items of literature and gave for free distribution 11,500, of which half of the latter were given to those in the congregations.[41]

The missionaries were sadly overburdened in their missionary labors. In 1870, seven ordained male missionaries held responsibilities across an area roughly equal to the size of the state of New Jersey in an era when roads to villages were poor or nonexistent and travel was by foot, horseback, or ox cart, often in the hot tropical sun with the temperature near a hundred degrees. They were responsible for the supervision of the Indian workers, for erection and maintenance of buildings, keeping records and accounts, teaching in the seminaries, writing tracts, carrying on medical practice if they were physicians, keeping good relationships with government officials, communicating with other missions, and providing for the needs of their families, among other things.

The situation got worse before it got better. The Board of Foreign Missions had a deficit in 1872. Then in 1873 there was a financial panic in the United States, which meant continued reductions in the appropriation for India for several years. Several more missionaries had to return to the United States for reasons of health, with the result that for a number of months in 1878 there were only two male

41 "AAR," 1870, 5.

missionaries in India in a year that there was a terrible famine in the country. The fact that the membership of the church grew rapidly during the years 1876-1879 is a sign of how much the growth of the church was due to the work of the catechists and teachers who were located in the towns and villages. During the last five years of the decade, the Christian community membership grew to more than six thousand. By 1879, there were almost three times as many Christians as a decade earlier.

Group Conversion Movements in a Time of Famine

Famines were endemic in India in the nineteenth century. Reformed Church missionaries repeatedly found it necessary to respond to the terrible suffering around them when famine came into the land. A more local famine in 1865 was perhaps the first after the mission was founded. There was a severe famine at the end of the nineteenth century and several other times of severe food shortages, with the latest of the famines affecting the North Arcot area when the rains failed after World War II between 1947-1952. The worst of all of the famines, however, may have been that of 1877-1879. It is important to sense the suffering that occurred in this famine, the ways in which some of the suffering was relieved, the cruelty that was inflicted on some of the victims, and the resultant growth of the church.

In every famine, the pitiable condition of the people makes the first impression. Missionaries sought to communicate their plight to the people in America every time there was a famine. The descriptions are terribly repetitive from famine to famine. L. B. Chamberlain's account sent during the 1899 famine could describe any of the famines. The people become impoverished as they sold their possessions and even most of their meager clothing for food. Chamberlain told of a woman seated in darkness in her house who would not bring her pot out to receive a little rice because she did not have enough clothing to appear in public. He saw tree leaves in a pot with a few roots that would be eaten after being cooked for

four hours. Children lying in a house had bands tied tightly around
their loins to keep them from feeling the pangs of hunger.[42]

In such times, the people left their villages to look for work in less
affected regions, with the result that villages would be emptied and
congregations simply vanish. P. Souri, the catechist at Madanapalle,
reported in 1878 that "there has been a great falling off in numbers
in the various villages, and the people in two have entirely
disappeared. They have suffered greatly from the famine, and many
having wandered away in search of food have not returned and
probably never will, as no doubt many have perished."[43]

Those who have not lived in a famine-stricken area often are not
aware that there is still some supply of food, but the prices have
risen to the point where poor people no longer have money to buy
any food. Those who are in positions of power can use food
shortage conditions to make money by selling food at very high
prices and gain further power by discriminating socially and
economically against groups that are out of favor. In 1878, John
Scudder II told of his experience in a village outside Arni.

> The distress has been very great in this county. During my
> visit to this place in the latter part of July, I learned that 25
> children and a number of adults had died from starvation
> among the Pariahs. The condition of the people was most
> deplorable. I have not seen anything more heartrending
> during the famine. All were mere walking skeletons. The
> native official of the village had received orders to give
> relief in money to the needy, but I learned that, with a few
> exceptions, he had refused aid to the poor Pariahs, and had
> given relief to the higher castes, who were not in such great

[42] L. B. Chamberlain, "Famine Funds," *Mission Field*, January, 1899, 284. Lewis Birge
Chamberlain (1864-1942) was the second son of Jacob Chamberlain to serve in India.
He served in India 1891-1915 and with the American Bible Society 1915-1935. His
brother, William Isaac Chamberlain (1862-1937), served in India 1887-1905. After a
short time teaching at Rutgers College, he served in the Reformed Church Board of
Foreign Missions, 1910-1935.
[43] "BFMR," 1878, 19.

distress. This I found to be the case in other places. The Pariah has been allowed to die like a dog, and his life is not worth saving.[44]

In early 1878 two things happened that brought a measure of improvement. The first was that missionaries gained access from two sources to funds that could be used to purchase and distribute food. When Christians in England and America heard about the suffering, they contributed to famine-relief funds that missionary societies sent on to the missionaries in India. The second was that missionaries brought complaints to government officials when local leaders refused to help the lowest caste people. When John Scudder complained to the local officials, they refused to change. He then appealed to the Revenue Board, but received no help there either.

> Lastly, I brought it to the notice of the Governor, asking that something might be done to keep the people from starving. His Grace the Duke immediately by telegraph ordered the district officials to inquire into the matter. This was done, relief works were opened, and food supplied to the children, the sick and infirm, for a few weeks. When these were stopped, I was enabled by the money I received from America and the Mansion Home Fund to open nurseries for the children, give money to the people, and aid them in cultivating their land. Encouraged by this aid, the people immediately went to work in their fields, and now have fine crops growing, which I trust will give them a good harvest in due time.[45]

Missionaries weren't the only ones complaining to the government. Many Indians also complained that when the government first began to give assistance of about three million dollars, it did so through Indian officials and Brahmin leaders. It was soon found

[44] Ibid., 16.
[45] Ibid., 18-19.

that they were putting the money into their own pockets, and only a small portion was actually being distributed. Upon learning of the corruption, the government committed responsibility for distribution to the missionaries.[46] Missionaries then carried out assistance with those funds without regard to caste or creed.[47]

One of the problems involved in evaluating human disasters and humanitarian relief efforts is that things often are not what they seem on the surface. Symptoms can easily be confused with causes, and leading philanthropists are often not free from complicity in the disaster. In the case of the 1877-1878 famine, it is possible that the missionaries were seduced into confusing symptoms with causes. Already in early 1878, they were expressing great admiration for the noble response of the people of England to the appeal for funds. Through their response multitudes had been spared. John Scudder wrote, "These people owe a debt of gratitude that they can never pay to all who have contributed toward their aid, and especially to the people of England who have surpassed by their noble and munificent gifts all other nations in generosity."[48]

Dorothy J. Scudder, in her book on the history of the Scudder family in India, gives credit to Viceroy Lord Lytton, "a man of great intelligence and force," who came down to South India to study the situation personally and to enforce a freer distribution of rice than was being carried out. He formed the first Famine Commission in India, which became the foundation of famine administration in the land. Without his assistance the situation would have grown much worse.[49] One can only wonder whether Viceroy Lord Lytton really deserves as much credit as he is here given. Stanley Wolpert contended that Lytton had promoted a policy of inequitable competition in cotton manufacturers that favored the Lancashire mills over the India's home production, with the result that the Indian cottage industry in cotton was all but destroyed. In 1879,

---

46 Ibid., 13.
47 Ibid., 25.
48 "AAR," 1877, 3.
49 Scudder, *A Thousand Years,* 138.

when the famine was still raging in much of India, "he actually overruled his entire council to accommodate Lancashire's lobby by removing all import duties on British-made cotton, despite India's desperate need for more revenue in a year of widespread famine and tragic loss of life in Maharasthra."[50]

It would go too far to blame Lytton's policies directly for the famine in North Arcot, but his actions regarding the suffering in Maharasthra in 1879 show his priority for the English economy over the needs of India. Similarly, while the English people made generous contributions toward famine relief, the government in its tax policy did not show such compassion.[51] On the contrary, even when the people were destitute and starving, the government insisted that the people in Gnanodiam and Arulnadu continue to pay taxes on their lands. Even when they had to sell their only bullocks to do so, the officials refused to make any concessions. John Scudder paid their taxes that year from his private funds.[52]

The missionaries recognized almost from the beginning of their involvement with victims of famine that it was important to provide assistance in such a way as to preserve their independence and dignity. When possible they implemented "food for work" projects. John Scudder employed people in deepening their wells, cultivating their fields so as to have them ready when the rains came, and in any other occupation that could be found. Nurseries were opened for the sick and the children.[53]

The problem of how to distribute food and other necessities whenever famine came continued to bother the consciences of missionary and Indian leaders alike. L. B. Chamberlain stated it concisely in 1899, when he said that it was necessary to provide aid.

[50] Wolpert, *History of India,* 248.

[51] Taxes on agricultural harvests were high by any standard. In the Madras presidency in 1840, of the proceeds of the harvest, 40 percent went to the cost of production, 14 percent for sustenance of the family, and 46 percent for the government. Taxation rates had not been lowered in following years. When the rains failed, collection of taxes forced the farmers into ruinous debts (James, *Raj,* 192-193).

[52] "BFMR," 1877, 20-21.

[53] "BFMR,"1878, 16.

"When their chronic poverty is increased by a semi-famine we are bound to help, and then come the questions how far is aid necessary, how to render it so as not to do harm, when to stop, how to give so that the people will not always look for such aid, etc."[54]

In struggling with these questions, some missionaries wondered whether they had perhaps become too reticent about giving help or, on the other hand, whether such aid actually undercut the move toward a church that was self-reliant and self-supporting. Chamberlain struggled with these questions in the article quoted in the previous paragraph. Ten years later, J. H. Wyckoff raised the question once more in light of his two decades of experience with periodic famine relief. He wrote, "From the beginning of this year appeals for aid have been growing in number and importunity. Private succor has been rendered to the most needy individual cases; but the doling out of general aid plays such havoc with the spirit of self-respect and self-support, both in individuals and churches that we have refrained from aid perhaps for too long."[55]

The problem has never gone away. The leaders of the church in India to this day struggle with the issue of how to provide assistance to those in dire need without promoting longer-term dependence and without depriving them of their self-respect and self-reliance. Reformed Church missionary John Piet, during the last great famine in the area in 1952, described his approach to the issues with several half-humorous comments. He wrote, "Relief as you may well realize is one of the most difficult things to handle. As someone has said, 'I give to fifty people, but that means that number 51 and all that follow after are no longer my friends.' In order to have a few friends left we of the Western Circle have done things differently." He then goes on to tell of the projects completed, such as building a meditation hall on top of a hill, building a wall around a compound, and working on building a parsonage at Gudiyattam. Having run out of immediate projects, he said, "I'm putting

54 Chamberlain, *Mission Field,* January, 1899, 282.
55 Wyckoff to Cobb, June 9, 1908.

villagers to work cracking stones. I don't know what we use them for just yet—perhaps another parsonage in the new field or perhaps a village church. In any case we'll have stones." Cracking stones required a special skill, and the stones provided road base and building blocks in India. Piet went on, "Further, the Christians will be trained for road work and later can get jobs earning up to Rs. 2-8-0 per day coolie."[56]

The work of the missionaries, Indian pastors, catechists, and teachers in administering the famine relief program brought about a major shift in the attitudes of people in the Arcot Mission area.

> The contrast between the self-denying action of the servants of Christ and the heartless indifference, dishonesty and selfishness of their own religious leaders, made a profound impression upon the people. Nearly one hundred villages, comprising about ten thousand persons, besought the Mission to give them instruction in the truths of the Christianity which had made so attractive an exhibition of its character.[57]

The Arcot Mission was faced with new concerns even while it rejoiced in the movement in the villages. First of all, the new workload was enormous. There were at the end of 1878 only four male Reformed Church missionaries in India. The number of catechists and teachers employed had been scarcely enough for the villages already occupied; now many more were asking for instruction. John Wyckoff found that he would have to be supervising thirty-two villages besides the congregation at Tindivanam. He had more villages on the waiting list, which he dared not promise more assistance in instruction than he had resources. He also wanted to wait until the famine was over in order to be more satisfied with their motivation.

---

[56] John Piet to B. Luben, October 15, 1952. "Coolie" is the word for wages paid to ordinary laborers, also called "coolies." Barnerd M. Luben served as a secretary for the Board of Foreign Missions 1941-1961.
[57] "BFMR," 1878, 13.

John H. Wyckoff

Moreover, the missionaries were becoming so involved in supervising the catechists and teachers and in caring for the new Christians that they had little time left for their primary evangelistic task of preaching the gospel in surrounding villages. In 1881 Wyckoff reported that there has been so much work that he had not been able to make a single tour that year. He had, however, kept the catechists and readers "pretty faithfully" at such work. They had preached during the year to 64,480 people.[58] The same delegation of preaching tours was happening in other places. Jacob Chamberlain reported in 1883 that, while he was not able to make any tours owing to illness and pressure of work, his assistants had made

[58]"BFMR," 1881, 31.

several extended tours, speaking 722 times in 258 villages to audiences of 15,924.[59]

As he became overwhelmed with the enormity of the task before him, John Scudder spoke of his mood as being that of "discouragement from success." He had already received nine new villages under instruction, including 137 families, 612 people, whom he did not include in his statistical report. "Other villages have applied to us for instruction, but thus far I have not been able to do anything for them, as I have not the men or means to extend our work. This is a sad and discouraging state of things—*a discouragement from success*. We have not sufficient men for the places already received, and where the means are to come from I cannot say."[60]

The concern Scudder and Wyckoff felt about the lack of catechists to instruct the people as well as about the villagers' motivation proved to be justified. In 1881 Wyckoff reported on the one hand that the number of Christians was growing. During the past year he had baptized 117 people, of whom 53 were adults. On the other hand, the number of catechumens or people under instruction had decreased by 226. This decrease consisted for the most part of people who had come during the famine and who had not received competent instruction. "A good proportion of them could, I think, have been retained, had there been competent teachers to instruct them. The accession of so many people has obliged us to employ teachers of very little education and no experience, and the villages have suffered in consequence. In two villages the congregations have been almost wholly ruined by the bad conduct of those sent to instruct them."[61]

The villagers who had previously come to faith now lived with a new confidence that they had made the right decision. The village of Yehamur, which would produce many leaders for the church,

[59]"BFMR," 1883, 34.
[60]"BFMR," 1881, 25.
[61]"BFMR," 1881, 29.

had become a village in which every person had become a Christian. They had torn down their old sacred stones and made them into steps for their church building. Vellambi received fifty-four new catechumens and, although nineteen persons had died from starvation, the people had pulled down their temples and idols. The same had happened in the near-by village of Kumalantangal. Henry M. Scudder wrote that he had received a total of eighteen new villages in the Arcot pastorate area, including 375 households with 1,239 people, including some of high caste who had broken caste by eating and drinking with him.[62]

Another issue confronting the mission was whether the people in this great movement could be trusted to understand what they were doing. Perhaps they were coming to instruction in the faith only in order to get temporal blessings. J. H. Wyckoff believed a cautious response was required. The villages that already had congregations had doubled in size, and he had accepted nine more for instruction. "Many other villages have applied, but I have put them off until after the famine....These villages require teachers and they cannot be expected to support them immediately. We must appeal to our friends in America for help."[63]

Comparison of the statistical reports of 1879 with that of a decade earlier, 1869, indicates that the missionaries' fears that they were would not be able to meet the needs of the villagers for instruction were on target. They claimed in 1878 that there were ten thousand making such requests, but the statistical summaries over the next several years indicate that a only small percentage of those persons were ultimately received into the membership of the church. In 1879, the membership of the Christian community was almost three times that of 1869—6,083 as against 2,164. However, the number of missionaries had decreased by two, from seven to five. Ordained Indian ministers increased from two to four. The number of churches had increased from fifteen to twenty-one, village out-

62"BFMR," 1878, 14.
63 Ibid., 22.

stations from thirty-one to eighty-eight, but the number of catechists, assistant catechists, readers, and teachers combined remained exactly the same at eighty-eight. These statistics show that the resources necessary to integrate those who requested instruction into the life of the church were extremely inadequate.

When consistent instruction and pastoral care was made available in a village, many of the people remained steadfast in their new faith. The southern area of the Arcot Mission between Arni and Tindivanam remained under the care of Wyckoff and his experienced Indian colleagues. Growth continued to be seen in the villages of that area, in contrast to several of the other areas, where missionary presence and consistent pastoral care was less available. A problem that bothered Wyckoff was how to know when to baptize people in the new villages. In a letter dated March 30, 1881, he gave thoughtful consideration to the issues involved.

He wrote that he had had the pleasure of baptizing thirty-three people, of whom twenty were adults, at the new village of Panjalam. They had been under instruction since 1877 and had made such progress in the knowledge of Christianity that he no longer could consistently delay responding positively to their requests to be baptized. Nevertheless, in this case as in so many others, it was difficult to decide to accept them for baptism. "The moral sense of the people is so darkened, owing to their long period of degradation and ignorance, that it is extremely difficult for them to grasp the plainest truths and even after several years of instruction they seem to have made but very little advance in Christian knowledge." He went on to say that in dealing with these matters, it was important not to receive them into the church too soon, before their motivation has been tested and they have learned the fundamental truths of the gospel. On the other hand, there is also error in waiting too long and requiring too much of the uneducated villager who cannot be expected to answers with the same clarity as do others who have been less disadvantaged.[64]

[64] Wyckoff to J. M. Ferris, March 30, 1881. John M. Ferris served as corresponding secretary of the Board of Foreign Missions, 1865-1883.

What is the Good News of Christ for the Pariahs?

We have several times already heard the concerns of the missionaries that in their poverty and distress people in the villages were asking for instruction and baptism in order to gain some financial, material, or other temporal advantage. The term of opprobrium for such persons was "rice Christians." Arcot missionaries resisted early baptisms. Wyckoff had delayed for four years, from 1877 to 1881, before administering baptism to thirty-three people and even then was not clear whether he may have baptized too soon. They still did not have the clarity of understanding of the basic doctrines of the Christian faith that he would have liked to see.

At this point it may be important to ponder the question, "What is the Gospel—the Good News of Jesus Christ—to the pariah, the outcaste of society, the virtual agricultural slave of the high-caste people?" We cannot forget the sorrowful words of John Scudder II above, who wrote that in the village he visited, "The Pariah has been allowed to die like a dog, and his life is not worth saving." However great were the sins and the degradation of those pariahs, one must still say that Jesus in the New Testament treated such people as those who were more sinned against than sinning.[65] A vivid description of how much they were sinned against was set forth in a report to the Reformed Church General Synod in the time of an on-going famine in 1893. The report says:

> They are outcastes from society in the full meaning of that term without any rights or privileges which are to be respected by that community. Despised, abused, abhorred by all, they do not receive the consideration allowed to the cattle and dogs of the land. Their touch, yea, their shadow also is considered pollution. ...Many of these are found to

---

[65] This theme of the gospel for the sinned against has been beautifully elaborated by Raymond Fung, "Mission in Christ's Way," *International Review of Mission,* January, 1989, 4-29, esp. 18-19.

have sold themselves with their families for few rupees into a servitude practically perpetual inasmuch as they can never even hope to command the paltry sum which would redeem their liberty.[66]

For those who have never received any respect, who have always been told that they are ignorant, good-for-nothing polluters of the environment, the message that they are miserable sinners in need of salvation is as such neither news nor good news. Such a message of sinners needing salvation is good news for those who have enjoyed a measure of respect in society and who do not live under the oppression of others. The missionaries had come from respected families living in respectable communities. Those communities, in their self-satisfaction and self-righteousness, needed to hear the message of Christ for sinners, so that they could be called to recognize the depths of sin remaining within them, awakened out of their spiritual torpor, and called to love their neighbors while living among them with justice and peace.

The missionaries recognized that the villagers received the respect shown along with the food given and the advocacy for them as good news. The missionaries also knew that the villagers were convinced by such actions that the gospel of Jesus Christ was truth for the world in a time when their idols were powerless to help them. What was lacking in the instruction given to them was an integration of the theology of forgiveness of sin with a theology of love and respect for the sinned-against.

What was beginning to be understood by the men of the Arcot Mission in the 1870s was that their point of origin in defining the role of the mission had been too narrow and exclusive. In affirming that they would preach the gospel of Jesus Christ on its own merits without using any economic incentives to bring people to faith, they had followed the example of Jesus. They were responding to his teaching that human beings cannot live by bread alone, and that one

---

[66] Quoted in David, *Reformed Church Missionaries*, 103.

cannot treat one's relation to God in terms of gaining rewards for offerings and sacrifices given. But in giving almost exclusive priority over all other types of service to such preaching, they tended to negate—even in their medical practice—the important .truth that God's love and respect for those in need is often mediated through food, healing ministries, and the search for justice in the face of oppression.

After 1870, the men of the Arcot Mission began to reconsider their original formulation of the threefold work of the mission. The coming of two young single women to serve as assistant missionaries brought some of the issues to light. Their coming brought to the fore the situation of the women of India. It is to their story, and to the assistant missionaries who came to live and serve in their land, that we will turn next.

4

The Role of Women in the
Threefold Work of Mission

The men of the Arcot Mission had a problem. It was difficult for them to preach the gospel to the high-caste Hindu women who were secluded in the *zenana,* women's quarters in high-caste homes. Other missionary societies in India faced the same problem. The British Society for Promoting Female Education in the East was founded in 1834 to send female missionaries to Asia, particularly India.[1] At that time, American missionary societies were still dubious about sending out unmarried female missionaries. Most had policies that required any unmarried woman serving as a missionary to live in a home with a married couple, however difficult that might be for all concerned. A woman who felt called to go overseas in mission was encouraged to marry a missionary and serve as an assistant missionary alongside her husband.[2] Prior to 1870 only two unmarried women served as assistant missionaries in India, but these were exceptions. Harriet and Louise Scudder were the daughters of John and Harriet Scudder and lived the with families of their brothers during their years of service until they were married.

[1] Robert, *American Women in Mission,* 126.
[2] Ibid., 14.

The welcome the missionaries gave to Martha Mandeville and Josephine Chapin when they arrived to work in the schools and begin special efforts in visiting the wives and daughters of the higher classes of Hindus in the zenanas thus represented a shift in attitude on the part of the Scudders and the other missionaries.[3] These two young women were soon breaking new ground for the Arcot Mission. Contrary to the original policy of the mission that stated that educational efforts would be confined to vernacular schools for the children of Christians and others being instructed in the faith, the women opened a Hindu Caste Girls' School in Vellore for girls of families who were not Christian. This venture was seen as a revolutionary one at the time and understood to be a doubtful experiment. In spite of the universal prejudice among Hindus against the education of girls, it met with such immediate and unusual success that two additional schools were opened, although two out of the three went out of existence in a relatively short time. On the basis of the Vellore experience, within the next thirteen years five additional Hindu girls' schools were opened in the Arcot Area.[4]

The Role of Reformed Church Women Missionaries, 1819-1869

In order to understand the importance of the arrival of Josephine Chapin and Martha Mandeville, it is helpful to take note of the role of women in mission between the period of John and Harriet Scudder's arrival in India in 1819 and 1869. At this point we can be

---

[3] "AAR," 1870, 8. This statement of welcome represents the official position of the Arcot Mission. However, Ethel (Mrs. L. R.) Scudder, writing in 1928, had a different understanding of how the men felt about the coming of single women. She wrote, "In that year (1869), Miss Chapin and Miss Mandeville arrived, the forerunners of the very large number of unmarried ladies who have since been responsible for such a large part of the work of the Women's Board. *Received rather coldly at first,* they have won their way, till they now outnumber the men" [author's italics] ("Work for Women," in *The Arcot Assembly and The Arcot Mission of the Reformed Church in America Jubilee Commemoration, 1853-1928* (Madras, India: Methodist Publishing House, 1931), 193.

[4] Mary Anable (Mrs. W. I.) Chamberlain, *Fifty Years in Foreign Fields* (New York: Woman's Board of Foreign Missions, RCA, 1925), 27.

assisted a great deal by the careful research into that role by Dana L. Robert in her outstanding book, *American Women in Mission,* published in 1996. Robert makes five points that are significant in understanding the growth of woman's work in the Arcot Mission.

The first is that when the American Board of Commissioners for Foreign Missions (ABCFM) sent its first group of missionaries to India in 1812, "missionary women were expected both to assist their husbands in the primary missional responsibility of spreading the Gospel and to evangelize the women, teaching them of Christ, enlightening their minds, raising their characters, and challenging their social customs."[5] The charge given to women by the Reverend Jonathan Allen included subverting indigenous customs injurious to women, such as the burning of widows on their husbands' funeral pyres in the practice of *sati.* In urging them to effect such social transformation, Allen charged women with a *civilizing* role as well as an *evangelizing* role.[6] By contrast, John Scudder understood his male role to be almost exclusively that of an evangelizer. The women who went out at that time had in most cases first felt a call to become a missionary wife and then chose to marry the man who was going as a missionary. Harriet Scudder was an exception among the first ABCFM missionary wives, in that she was already married prior to considering the call to becoming a missionary.[7]

The second point is that on the basis of the experience of ABCFM missionaries in the Sandwich (Hawaiian) Islands, Rufus Anderson gave high priority to the existence of the missionary wife as a role model in a Christian home. He wrote,

> The heathen should have an opportunity of seeing Christian families. The domestic constitution among them is dreadfully disordered, and yet it is as true there as everywhere else, that the character of society is formed in the family. To rectify it requires example as well as precept.

[5] Robert, *American Women in Mission,* 3.
[6] Ibid.
[7] Ibid., 21.

(The heathen wife) must have female teachers, living
illustrations....And the Christian wife, mother, husband,
father, family must be found in all our missions to pagan
and Mohammedan countries.[8]

The model Christian family in the mind of Anderson and the
missionaries was naturally that of the New England evangelical
nuclear family, where the children in the home were neatly dressed,
well-disciplined, and kept clean under the care of a loving mother.
Harriet Scudder in Jaffna was able to provide such a model family
environment when shortly after their arrival there she took young
girls into her home where they could day by day and even hour by
hour experience a true Christian home. Sarah Scudder provided the
same Christian home experience in 1855 for the three orphan girls
who came to live with them.

Third, in their mission to raise the status of Indian women, they
had an important role as educators. While her husband preached
and distributed tracts, the missionary wife had four goals in
educating women. First, starting schools for girls would be the best
way to gain access to the female half of the population for the
purpose of evangelization. Second, teaching females would
demonstrate to the men of that society that women were capable
individuals who did not have to be kept secluded. Third, there
would be a pool of women suitable to be wives to the Indian
catechists, teachers, and other helpers. Finally, the education of
women would subvert the very foundations of heathen society and
bring about broad social changes accompanying conversion to
Christianity.[9]

The fourth point to be noted from Dana Robert's research is the
impact on missionary policy that came through the work of Mary
Lyon, who opened Mount Holyoke Female Seminary in South
Hadley, Massachusetts, in 1837. This institution was highly regarded

---

[8] Rufus Anderson, "An Introductory Essay on the Marriage of Missionaries," quoted in
    ibid., 67.
[9] Ibid., 83.

by Rufus Anderson. John Scudder gave several lectures there in 1844 and was profoundly impressed by what he saw there. He asked the students to consider coming to serve as missionaries in India.[10] Mary Lyon believed that in a female seminary girls should receive a good education fitting them to become teachers. The seminary should give them training in domestic skills and sewing, teach them self-discipline, and stress the importance of sacrificial Christian service in the world. This school became a center from which many young women went out to be missionaries.[11] It also provided a model for the female seminary in India.

Fifth, as time went on the burden on the missionary wife in her multiple roles as assistant missionary proved to be overwhelming. By the time Chapin and Mandeville arrived in India, ABCFM missionaries in Turkey, Ceylon, and India were asking for help for their wives. At that time various missions began to send out single women as trained educators to work as colleagues of missionary wives. The missionary wives acted as matrons in the female seminaries and boarding schools in which the single women teachers did the actual teaching.[12]

When Sarah (Mrs. Ezekiel) Scudder opened her home to three orphan girls and then took the additional steps that led to the establishment of the Female Seminary in Chittoor, she was clearly operating according to the models that had prevailed at Mount Holyoke Female Seminary and the American Board of Commissioners for Foreign Missions. She remained in charge of the school that was first known as the Female Boarding School, which became the Female Seminary in 1861. In that year, Jared W. Scudder was placed in charge of the Chittoor mission station. His

[10] Scudder, *A Thousand Years,* 53-54.
[11] Robert, *American Women in Mission,* 96. Charlotte Chamberlain, the wife of Jacob Chamberlain, was a graduate of Mount Holyoke, as was Alice Van Doren, who served as a Reformed Church missionary in India, 1903-1952. A brief sketch of Charlotte Chamberlain's life as the wife of a missionary is found in Una H. Ratmeyer, *Hands, Hearts, and Voices: Women Who Followed God's Call* (New York: Reformed Church Press, 1995), 140-43.
[12] Scudder, *A Thousand Years,* 107.

wife, Julia Goodwin Scudder, who was from Atlanta, Georgia, and was the sister of the governor of the state of Georgia, had great concern for the women of India. Under the supervision of her husband, she took over the management of the Female Seminary and had the good fortune to have Mrs. Lackey, a Eurasian woman, as the experienced and faithful matron of the girls in the boarding school.

While the school was operating well, the seminary had grossly inadequate accommodations for the girls. After several years of expressing complaints, Jared Scudder's report for 1865 took on a tone of exasperation. "Nearly thirty girls are yet crowded into two small low godowns (storage sheds) contracted and without ventilation. Health, cleanliness and morals are all at stake. For two years, I have made loud appeals for relief. But there has been no adequate response."[13]

This time his appeal was heard by Susan Gridley of Utica, New York, who provided the funds necessary for the construction of a "a large and commodious edifice, consisting of a court surrounded by verandhas, giving access to ten comfortable dormitories, a large school room, apartments for the matron, who is a faithful East Indian widow, and a kitchen, store-room and bath-room, the last furnished with three large tubs." Shortly thereafter Mrs. R. J. Brown of New York City provided funds for completing a playground and exercise area with a wall around it to provide for the privacy of the girls.[14] This concern for exercise and play is another indication of the influence of the Mount Holyoke model, according to which women and girls for the sake of their health needed to engage in such activities just as men and boys did. Two things were still lacking in the facilities. "We have a beautiful school-room, large, light and airy; but there is no furniture in it, and what is worse, no money to get it. We also need simple apparatus to illustrate the

---

13"AAR," 1865, 18.
14 Julia Scudder, "The Chittoor Female Seminary," in Margaret E. Sangsster, *A Manual of the Missions of the Reformed (Dutch) Church in America* (New York: Board of Publications of the Reformed Church in America, 1877), 101-102 (hereafter, *Manual*).

teachings of our text-books. We merely hint at these facts to our friend. 400 or 500 Rupees would do the thing nicely."[15]

The Female Seminary, at which the girls would reside for as long as five years, kept the girls on a rigorous schedule. Some of the girls would rise at 5:30 a.m. and set themselves to clean the building while others would draw water from two deep wells for cooking and bathing. Every girl would take a bath and be dressed for school by 8:00 a.m. After assembly and prayers, they studied a curriculum of subjects including history, dictation, geography, grammar, arithmetic, Bible verses, and catechism in the Tamil language. Between noon and 3:00 p.m. they studied Telugu and English. After a short recess, they would gather on the verandah of the missionary house to sew or do fancy work until 4:30, following which they were free to go to the playground or otherwise amuse themselves until dark, which is usually around 6:30 p.m. in that tropical zone. They also enjoyed Indian music.[16] The outline of their daily routine and curriculum displays how progressive the seminary was in its early years, when both in the United States and in India many still had grave doubts about the capacity of women to master subjects such as mathematics, which required concentrated thought.

In contrast to the often strong missionary words condemning Hinduism, we find a surprising comment by Jared W. Scudder about the purpose of the school. He expresses the school's intent to keep the girls well suited to the conditions in which they will live after they complete their course of study and are married. He states:

> The design of this Institution is not so much to make brilliant scholars or to produce striking results, as to fit its members to fill practically and efficiently the station in life which the most of them will probably occupy. In general, our aim is to give them a good vernacular education, to break up pernicious habits, to extirpate foolish prejudices, to train them for household and other future duties, and

[15] "AAR," 1867, 26.
[16] Scudder, "Chittoor Female Seminary," 103.

above all, to lead them to consecrate themselves wholly to Jesus. *Withal, we try not to anglicize; but, on the contrary, to keep them simple-minded Hindoo girls, retaining all Hindoo customs which are innocent, beneficial, or otherwise suited to the spheres they are expected to fill* [author's italics].[17]

As a parenthesis, we should note here that the use of the word "Hindoo" (Hindu) refers to the customs of the people of India rather than to a religion at odds with the gospel.

In 1867, besides the Female Seminary in Chittoor there were also two vernacular schools, one for boys (with twenty-five students) and one for girls (with fifteen). Sarah Scudder was also in charge of the proper operation of those schools, and she watched over them very carefully. She went to the schools to examine the children once a week in order to check on their progress.[18] Missionary wives in the other stations busied themselves equally with the progress of the children in the schools.

Missionary wives also could relate to some of the vernacular schools in surrounding villages as well as to schools in the mission station. Sarah Scudder provided a description of such a school for the *Manual*, published in 1877. Four low mud walls with a thatched roof and a mud floor formed the schoolhouse itself, which in many cases also served as the church. Small openings in the walls admitted light and air. The furniture consisted of a plain table and chair for the teacher, with a small box for books and slates for the use of the children. The children sat crossed-legged on the floor. The parents were so poor that the children wore very meager clothing, sometimes almost nothing at all. Study was carried on out loud, which made for a very noisy classroom. The curriculum included simple rules of grammar, arithmetic, and elementary geography. A simple catechism was taught orally to the younger scholars. Scripture texts and Bible history were given a large amount of time. Sarah Scudder was pleased to inform her readers that from such simple and inadequate

17"AAR," 1867, 25-26.
18 Ibid., 26.

schools came many who were able to go on for further education in one of the seminaries. However, one of the great problems was how to encourage the parents to continue to send the children to school. "A child who is old enough to frighten away the crows from a field of grain, or to lead a cow or a goat out to graze, has a pecuniary value to the family; and so, to often, he is taken from the school, just as he is beginning to learn, and is sent to earn his living in the fields."[19] Some teachers took to evening sessions to encourage continued attendance; at times adults also attended in the evenings.

The Woman's Board of Foreign Missions of the Reformed Church in America[20]

At this point we must interrupt our review of the work of women in the threefold work of the Arcot Mission in order to take note of what was happening in the United States. The mid-nineteenth century was an era in which there were not only growing opportunities for women to acquire higher education, there was also a developing sense of the rights of women. The first stirrings of the movement for women's suffrage with the right to vote began to be felt. Women were taking leadership in many crusades for social reform, such as the anti-slavery movement and temperance leagues, the Sunday schools, and the fields of nursing and education. The first Woman's Rights Convention was held in the home of Elizabeth Cady Stanton of Seneca Falls, New York, in 1848.

Women were also among the leading advocates for foreign missions. Within the Reformed Church in America, Sarah Doremus had opened her home to the Reverend David Abeel, who was to become the first Reformed Church missionary in China. She was

[19] Sarah Scudder, "Village Work in the Arcot Mission," in *Manual*, 113.
[20] A brief account of the role played by the Woman's Board of Foreign Missions is to be found in Russell L. Gasero, "The Rise of the Woman's Board of Foreign Missions," in House and Coakley, *Patterns and Portraits*, 95-102. The Woman's Board regularly reported on the activities of its missionaries in its magazine, the *Mission Gleaner*; Renee House, "Women Raising Women: The Urgent Work of the *Mission Gleaner*, 1883-1917," ibid., 103-118.

Sarah Doremus

involved in a multitude of philanthropic endeavors. She sought ways to care for the sick, to assist in city missions, to create homes for the aged, to develop schools for Italian-Americans, to minister to people in prisons, and to encourage a variety of reform movements, in addition to taking care of her household with her nine children.[21] In 1834, Sarah Doremus and other women in New York formed the first Protestant woman's foreign missionary society ever founded for definite, independent missionary work in foreign lands, called the "Society for Promoting Female Education in China and the Far East." This society was destined to set free the unsuspected energies of multitudes of women on behalf of the less fortunate women of the Far East. Over the next twelve years, forty American

21 Chamberlain, *Fifty Years,* 5-7.

women of different denominations were sent out by this one missionary society.[22]

Sarah Doremus had wanted to found a woman's board of foreign missions as early as 1836, but she refrained from doing so because of the resistance to the idea by Rufus Anderson. When Anderson's opposition reached the ears of women who were meeting to organize, strong passions were aroused. In a letter written to the Woman's Board of Foreign Missions of the Reformed Church, Doremus recalled one of those meetings.

> A meeting was called in the parlors of Dr. Matthews in the South Dutch Church, then Garden, now Exchange Street. The meeting for the final arrangement was at the house of Mrs. Bethune, Dr. Bethune's mother. Dr. Abeel opened the meeting and then remarked that he had a message for them. The Secretary, Dr. Rufus Anderson, wished the ladies to defer. "What!" said Mrs. Bethune, "is the American Board afraid the ladies will get ahead of them?" Some were for going on; others, out of respect for Dr. Anderson, were willing to wait; and Dr. Abeel, with tears rolling down his face, exclaimed: "What is to become of the souls of those who are ignorant of the offers of mercy and of the Bible?"[23]

In 1861, however, Doremus ignored the objections of Anderson and went ahead to found the Woman's Union Missionary Society, an independent, interdenominational mission board run by women to send out women missionaries. By that time, public opinion was no longer satisfied with the views of women as weak physically and not suited for public life mentally or socially. Their advancing education and leadership in the wide range of voluntary societies gave them confidence to move ahead to further their views with regard to foreign missions as well. The two major reasons for the decision to form their own board in 1861, however, was that they

22 Ibid., 4.
23 Ibid., 7.

had become impatient with the reluctance of Protestant mission boards to send out unmarried women and also impatient with the limitations of Anderson's three-self theory for the particular missionary contribution of women.[24] We have already seen that the Reformed Church did not send any unmarried women to India until 1869, except for the two Scudder sisters who were there with their brothers. We must now consider the other matter, the limitations of Anderson's three-self theory with respect to the missionary contribution of women.

In the evolution of his own thought, by 1850 Anderson had fully developed the theory that the primary aim of foreign missions must be the planting of self-governing, self-supporting, self-propagating churches. The founders of the Arcot Mission were in complete agreement with this aim. They also agreed with a corollary of this theory, which was that the primary work of a missionary is that of preaching the gospel to those outside the church. In accordance with the three-self theory, all other mission activity, whether it be medical or educational or something else, must be directly related to evangelism and the planting of churches.

It was for this reason that the Scudders could accept with rejoicing the fact that in the first year of the Arcot Mission's existence, God's providence had taken away their dispensary and they could sell their medical instruments in order to strengthen their tract and book fund. It is also the reason that in the Arcot area they ruled out establishing English-language schools and intended to open schools in the Tamil and Telugu languages only. At the lowest level in the villages, it was important that people become literate in order to read the Bible and Christian literature. At the seminary level, vernacular education was required for the studies that would enable the churches to have trained ministers, catechists, teachers, and related mission helpers. Evangelizing rather than "civilizing" India was the purpose for the presence of the Arcot Mission in India.

24 Robert, *American Women in Mission,*115.

The position of the Scudders was reinforced when in 1854-1855 Anderson and Augustus Thompson made a deputation visit to India, Ceylon, Syria, and Turkey. The goal of the deputation was to help the missions evaluate the activities and programs developed over the past forty years in light of the top priority of church planting. The most controversial problems had to do with the educational institutions that had grown up. One of the concerns of the members of the deputation was that from their perspective the number of converts in India and Ceylon was depressingly low and that a comparatively small number had been converted in those institutions.

The deputation concluded that it was time to streamline the education and make it directly subservient to evangelism. No non-Christians should be allowed henceforth to teach in mission schools. The number of schools above the elementary level would be reduced and given the sole purpose of training indigenous preachers and teachers. The teaching of English would come to an end in order to keep those trained for mission service grounded in their own culture rather than in a foreign culture.[25]

The implication of the theory for the role of women became clear in the deputation's decision about the Oodooville Female Boarding School in Ceylon, the only mission institution supervised by missionary women at that time. The Oodooville school had been founded by Harriet Winslow in 1824. After her death in 1833, the school had come under the direction of Mr. and Mrs. Levi Spaulding. It will be remembered that the Winslows and the Spauldings had gone to Calcutta on the same ship as John and Harriet Scudder. The Oodooville Female Boarding School would have been well known to the Scudders and could have been one of the reasons that the Female Boarding Home was opened in Chittoor so soon after the Arcot Mission was founded.

The Oodooville Female Boarding School was becoming recognized as providing superior education for young girls, with the

25 Ibid., 118-20.

result that its student body grew to seventy-five. Young men other than ministers and catechists were eager to receive brides from the graduates of the school. Although it still had a long way to go, the school was on its way to becoming an institution of quality higher Christian education, similar to the course being taken in America by schools such as Wellesley, Mount Holyoke, and Vassar. For two months, the deputation stayed in Ceylon holding meetings with the Ceylon Mission. The women were permitted to be present but not to speak, vote, or write mission policy. "First the missionary brethren eliminated English from the curriculum at Oodooville. The biggest blow came, however, when the brethren decided that instead of having as its goal the raising of 'a suitable native missionary agency,' the sole goal of Oodooville would be to educate wives for native pastors and evangelists."[26] Although the decision raised a storm of protest in some circles in America as well as among some of the missionaries in Ceylon, most notably the Spauldings, it did for a time remain in force.

For the Scudders in India in 1855, the decision served to reaffirm their principle of the threefold work of the mission. It confirmed their decision to open only vernacular schools and to have a female seminary for the sole purpose of educating girls to be wives for Indian ministers, catechists, teachers, and other native workers. The net result of the decisions regarding education was that the missionary women working in the field of education were clearly made subordinate to the men, whose primary work was that of evangelism and the planting of churches. As a result of the policy, mission boards in America were reluctant to send unmarried women as missionaries unless they were assigned to work alongside a missionary wife in a single-purpose female seminary. Without a married woman alongside her, an unmarried woman in such a situation would find it difficult to know how to prepare young Indian girls for marriage.

[26] Ibid., 121.

Given the priority for single-minded attention to the goal of developing a self-governing, self-supporting, self-propagating church, Anderson had good reason for being reluctant to give approval to the formation of a women's board of foreign missions. Nineteenth-century appeals to women to give support for foreign missions had usually emphasized the degraded and pitiable status of heathen women. They called on American Christian women to send missionaries to save such women from their hopeless situation in this life as much as in the life to come. John Scudder, Sr., in his sixty-four page *Appeal to Christian Mothers*, used thirteen pages for the chapter entitled, "Degradation of Heathen Women," followed by a ten-page chapter, "Condition of Christian Females Contrasted with that of the Heathen."

Typical also is the description of the status of Hindu women to be found in *A Manual of the Missions of the Reformed (Dutch) Church in America*, published by the Woman's Board of Foreign Missions in 1877. It includes statements such as:

> How weary and tedious must have been the hours spent by listless unoccupied women, within the walls of the zenanas! Their sole employment, the preparation of food for their husbands, and the light tasks of housekeeping; their minds inactive, or filled with childish jealousies, it was small wonder that some of them clung to idolatry as their only refuge.[27]

> So soon as she reaches the verge of womanhood, a husband is found for her, and she is married. Frequently the betrothal ceremony has taken place long before, so that a girl of six or eight may have been given away by her parents to a man of sixty or seventy. Should the prospective husband die before his child-bride grows old enough to become his wife, she is condemned for life to the position of a widow.[28]

[27] *Manual*, 115.
[28] Ibid., 116.

Women are looked upon as a necessary article of household
furniture, to be tolerated accordingly; but the men treat
them often worse than they treat their own cows and
oxen....Then she cooks his food, but must wait patiently till
he has finished his repast, before she can eat a morsel. Then
she feasts on what he may have left.[29]

Influenced by such descriptions of the degraded status of women
in India, Christian women in America were motivated to assist in
ameliorating their sufferings. Their vision for women's place in
India was the same as it was for their own place in America.[30] They
believed that a woman, whether in India or America, should be
educated, respected in the home, free to participate in making her
contribution to the welfare of the whole society, and have access to
good health care. She should be free to remarry after the death of
her husband and essentially to be a person in her own right. In other
words, women's advocacy for foreign missions can rightly be
understood to be an extension of the nineteenth-century movement
for women's rights in America. Anderson correctly saw that if a
woman's board for foreign missions sent unmarried missionaries
women to India, the goal for mission would have to be enlarged to
include the "civilizing" ministry of educating women out of their
subservient, even degrading, situation.

Between 1861 and 1875, Reformed Church women followed the
lead of Sarah Doremus in supporting the interdenominational
Woman's Union Missionary Society. That society, founded during
the Civil War, inevitably took on some of the characteristics of the
woman's movements of those years as women were revising their
ideas of their role in society.

[29] Ibid., 117-18.
[30] Barbara Fassler, "The Role of Women in the India Mission, 1819-1880," in James Van
Hoeven, ed., *Piety and Patriotism: Bicentennial Studies of the Reformed Church in America,
1776-1976*, Historical Series of the Reformed Church in America, no. 4 (Grand Rapids:
Eerdmans, 1976), 157. The reader is referred to Fassler's excellent treatment (149-62)
of the subject indicated in the title of her chapter, which contains many details not
repeated in our review.

The ministry of women to soldiers in the war had proved that they possessed great executive ability and an amount of energy which, once set free, could not and ought not to be suppressed. The vision of national need which they had so clearly seen in the struggle of the war, developed at its close into a wider comprehension of world demands and they were ready at the end of that decade to begin the most strategic and far-reaching enterprise in which they had ever yet engaged—the work of carrying their vision to the women and children of other lands.[31]

Meanwhile women in other denominations were organizing their own women's boards while the interests of Reformed Church women were becoming dissociated from the work of the Reformed Church's Board of Foreign Missions. Reformed Church women felt a need to become more directly supportive of activity of Reformed Church missionaries in the schools for female education in India, China, and Japan. "At eleven o'clock and forty minutes" on the morning of January 21, 1875, the Woman's Board of Foreign Missions of the Reformed Church in America was born in the lecture room of the Marble Collegiate Church in New York City.[32]

The Woman's Board stated clearly in its *Constitution* that it regarded itself as an auxiliary organization to the Board of Foreign Missions. Its missionaries would be subject to the approval of the Board of Foreign Missions in their appointment and assignment. It would promote increased study of and financial support for Reformed Church missions. Article 2 read:

Its object shall be to aid the Board of Foreign Missions of the Reformed Church in America, by promoting its work among the women and children of heathen lands; and for

---

[31]Chamberlain, *Fifty Years*, 8.

[32] Ibid., 11. Mary Chamberlain's narrative of the process leading to the birth of the woman's board (10-11) is a lively account of the perseverance of the women in bringing it to fruition.

this purpose it shall receive and disburse all money which shall be contributed to this Society, subject to the approval of the Board, in the appointment of missionaries supported by this Association, and in fixing their locations and salaries. To the furtherance of this end, it shall also endeavor to organize similar associations in all Reformed Churches, and these associations shall bear the name of the Auxiliary Societies to the Women's Board of Foreign Missions of the Reformed Church in America, and shall report their work to this Board at such times as the By-laws may direct.[33]

In spite of the unambiguous language in its *Constitution,* apparently some still feared that "the ladies were stepping out of their proper sphere," so the "ladies" accepted the admonition of Dr. Inglis, the minister of the Church on the Heights, Brooklyn, who expressed his opinion that they could give their "spare moments" to this work. "Home duties need not conflict." Furthermore, at that first meeting Dr. Ormiston, pastor of the Marble Collegiate Church, presided, and all of the prayers were spoken and reports were given by men. This practice of men doing the speaking and presiding continued for a number of years. Dr. Isaac Ferris, corresponding secretary of the Board of Foreign Missions, was usually present. When he was present, he presided and gave the opening prayer. At the very first meeting a number of contributions were reported, including twenty-eight dollars for the support of two girls in the Female Seminary in Chittoor. [34]

The Woman's Board developed a system of encouraging the woman's auxiliaries in Reformed churches to accept responsibility for a specific aspect of the mission work, such as providing an agreed-upon amount annually for a specific missionary. The number of women missionaries supported increased rapidly. In 1893, a year of financial panic in the United States when the Foreign Missions Board was once again experiencing a severe budget problem, the

33 "Woman's Board of Foreign Missions Report," 1875, 17.
34 Chamberlain, *Fifty Years in Foreign Missions,* 15-16.

women listed forty female missionaries whom they were assisting wholly or partially with contributions. Supporting pupils in the girls' boarding schools proved to be especially popular. Depending on the school, the support level per girl in 1893 ranged from $20 to $60 per year. The high-caste Hindu Girls' Schools in India had the highest cost, at $150 each. It was also possible to support a Bible woman and Zenana teacher in India at $30 or a hospital bed in China at $35.[35] As we will see, maintaining this system of designated contributions became a matter of some frustration for missionaries and board secretaries alike.

The men's suspicion that "the ladies were stepping out of their proper sphere" was not totally groundless. Within two decades, the men in both the Arcot Mission and the Board of Foreign Missions discovered that they had to take the wishes and power of the Woman's Board into account in making decisions about budgets and girls' schools. More important, however, is the fact that the slogan, "woman's work for woman," was current in the women's circles of which the leaders of the Woman's Board of Foreign Missions participated.[36] In an address that was printed in the annual report of 1886, Mrs. C. E. Crispel affirmed that while the work of foreign missions as a whole requires the entire strength of Christendom, special parts call for special workers. The phrase, "woman's work for woman," highlights woman's "peculiar fitness for woman." "Her keen perception, her lively sensibilities, her persistence and tact in effort, her patience in endurance and hope, are some of the qualities that peculiarly fit her for this work." Another thought is "that millions of women will never hear of the blessed Redeemer unless their sisters tell them."[37]

[35] "Woman's Board of Foreign Missions Report," 1893:124-25.

[36] The slogan, "Woman's Work for Woman," developed especially in American Methodist women's missionary societies to emphasize that "the theoretical opposition between evangelization and civilization in American mission theory was in fact irrelevant" (Robert, *American Women in Mission,* 133).

[37] Mrs. C. E. Crispell, "God's Method of Evangelizing the World," in "Woman's Board of Foreign Missions Report," 1887, 76-77. "Woman's work for woman" was still used as a unifying theme for woman's work in the seventy-fifth year Jubilee anniversary commemoration book published in 1928; cf. Scudder, "Work for Women," 191.

A further motive for woman's work for woman was found in the fact that women, in heathendom as elsewhere, however degraded, exerted a molding influence upon the home, and, as a necessary consequence, upon the community and upon the state. In elevating women, Crispell said, "we cleanse the streams of life at their fountain head."[38] In these comments, Crispell showed herself to be firmly within the stream of nineteenth-century women's motivation for foreign mission. Reformed Church mission leaders, both in the United States and in their overseas settings, seem to have always been conversation partners with mission leaders of other churches in matters of mission theology and practice. Crispell's lecture articulated well what Reformed Church women were thinking, and it echoed the thoughts of women in other mission societies. Her use of the phrase, "woman's work for woman," "was based on a maternalistic, albeit idealistic belief that non-Christian religions trapped and degraded women, yet all women in the world were sisters and should support each other."[39] Her thought reflected that of Jennie Fowler Willing's article in the first volume of the woman's mission journal, *Heathen Woman's Friend,* published in 1869.

> If all men are brothers, all women are sisters. Yet, the wretched widow, looking her last upon this beautiful world through the smoke of her suttee pyre, driven by public opinion to the suicide's plunge into the darkness of the future, and the one throwing her babe to the crocodiles— tearing from her heart its only joy, the joy of maternity— these women are our sisters....When we look at the domestic, civil, and religious systems of Pagandom, we sicken at their rottenness. We feel greatly moved to give them the blessings of Christian civilization.[40]

---

38 Crispell, "God's Method," 78.

39 Robert, *American Women in Mission,* 133.

40 Quoted in ibid., 133. The story about the mother sacrificing her baby to the crocodile seems to have been one of the favorite tales used to impress audiences with the depravity of Hinduism. John Scudder, Sr., apparently used it regularly. He also recommended that mothers tell it to their children in order to inspire them for

Dana Robert has shown that "one searches in vain for positive references to Rufus Anderson's three-self principles in the formative years of the late-nineteenth-century woman's mission movement."[41] Women rejected the opposition between preaching and teaching to people of other religions. In their work with girls who were subject to their parents and women in zenanas subject to their husbands, the women sought to bring them to salvation, but with those women planting churches could not be an immediate goal. Evangelization had to be intertwined with "civilizing," that is, elevating Hindu women into social equality with western women and into positions of respect in their own society. Woman's work for woman looked to the liberation of women from their degradation. The core of that work had to be education in schools and in the homes of women. Those things that men had made subordinate and secondary became primary in the woman's movement.[42]

The Hindu Girls' Schools and Zenana Visitation

Present day readers can easily miss the significance of the fact that in the 1877 volume, *A Manual of the Missions of the Reformed (Dutch) Church in America*, published by the Women's Board of Foreign Missions, three of the articles about women's work were written by women under their own names. The appearance of these articles is remarkable because, at that time, all of the material in the annual reports of the Arcot Mission was submitted by men. In 1877, in the Woman's Board own meetings, the roles of presiding, leading the prayers, and submitting reports also were filled only by men.

It may well be that the article in the *Manual* entitled, "The Caste Girls' Schools at Vellore," was written by Josephine Chapin at the request of the editors. They may have decided to include articles

missionary service and support of missions (*The Redeemer's Last Command*, 23). I am not aware of the origin of the story. I do not know whether it was understood to be a story to illustrate the despair felt by Indian women in their plight or whether the tellers of the story somehow related it to Hindu worship of a deity.
41 Ibid., 131
42 Ibid., 130.

written by women themselves, and Chapin was conveniently in the United States after her resignation and return in 1874 for reasons of health. The Board of Foreign Missions remained hesitant about appointing unmarried women to serve in India, although two young Scudder women did arrive on the field. Julia C. Scudder, daughter of Jared W. and Julia G. Scudder, arrived in 1879, and M.K. (Kitty) Scudder, daughter of William W. and Katherine, arrived with her father on his return to India in 1884. Apart from these members of the Scudder family and the two young women, Martha Mandeville and Josephine Chapin, appointed in 1869, no other unmarried woman was appointed to the Arcot Mission until Ida Scudder returned with her father in 1890, Lizzie Van Bergen came in 1893, and Louisa Hart arrived in 1895.

While the mission did request a replacement for Josephine Chapin when she left, until 1890, the Arcot Mission often let it be known that they much preferred married couples. Their opposition to unmarried men was stronger than their hesitation about unmarried women, and it was based on the experience of the men of the mission whose wives had died in India. Ezekiel Carman Scudder, Jr., whose wife, Minnie, had died in 1883, wrote a strong letter to the corresponding secretary, John Cobb, in 1887 to relate how difficult it was for an unmarried male missionary to live in India. In the letter, Ezekiel stated that he was returning to the United States to find a wife. He strongly advised, on the basis of his and others' experiences, that no unmarried man should be sent as a missionary to India.[43] We can be quite certain that the all other men would have agreed with him at that time. The Reformed Church sent no unmarried male missionary to India until the second decade of the twentieth century.

Whatever may have been the attitudes of various members of the Arcot Mission to having unmarried women assistant missionaries

---

[43] Ezekiel Carman Scudder, Jr., to John Cobb, February 23, 1887. He did find a wife, Mabel Jones, and returned with her to India in 1889. After her death in 1918, he established a scholarship fund, the "Minnie and Mabel Scholarship" in honor of his two wives. The fund continued to provide scholarships through the twentieth century.

among them, once present, Chapin and Mandeville were welcomed and put to work learning the language. It was anticipated that when they had gained a basic grasp of the language, they would engage "as they are able in the work of the schools and seminary there, hoping soon to begin their special efforts in behalf of the wives and daughters of the higher classes of the Hindus. May the Lord open the way before them, and enable them to gather many a hidden flower and precious gem to adorn the crown on our Redeemer's brow."[44] The Arcot Mission expected that the two young women would provide assistance to the missionaries' wives in the vernacular schools and the seminary in Vellore, while also finding ways to enter into the zenanas to talk about the Bible with Hindu wives in seclusion. The opening of a school for high-caste Hindu girls does not seem to have been in the plan before they arrived, although they would not have been able to do so without the permission of the mission.

The opening of the Hindu girls' schools in Vellore played a crucial role in bringing the mission to a gradual re-evaluation of its founding principles. For the first time, institutions were founded by the Arcot Mission that did not have as their primary purpose vernacular education for Christian children or seminary training for service in the mission's evangelistic and pastoral activities. Their founding ran counter to what the mission said in its 1855 report, as well as to the three-self principles of Anderson that were so fundamental to its whole orientation. We should for the moment recall what was said in 1855:

> The chief object of our Mission being the preaching of the Gospel, we cannot establish schools for heathen children. We have not the time, nor the means to enter upon this work, which more properly belongs to those who have the charge of the secular interests of the Hindus.[45]

[44]"AAR," 1870, 8.
[45]"AAR," 1855, 6.

Not only were the Hindu Girls' Schools expressly established for the education of "heathen children," but, in contrast with the 1855 Anderson-Thompson deputation's decision and the Arcot Mission stance since then that Hindus should not be permitted to teach in mission schools, the Hindu Girls' Schools by their very nature could not avoid having some caste Hindu men on their teaching staff. There would have been no Christians apart from the missionaries themselves who would have been acceptable to Hindu caste prejudices. One result of the Arcot Mission's acceptance of the existence of these schools under its mantle was that the door had now been opened a crack to the establishment of other institutions, in spite of the long-standing policy of the mission. As the mission's history unfolded, that small crack became as wide as a barn door.

Josephine Chapin wrote that the Caste Girls' School in Vellore was opened in 1871.[46] This was an amazingly short time after the women's arrival in India. Since the Arcot Mission reports for the next two years give only cursory mention of the schools, one can wonder whether the men who wrote the reports were paying much attention to the school's growth. The first detailed report, only one paragraph long, about the school appears in the 1874 report, by which time Josephine Chapin's health had already forced her to return to America. The relatively low priority accorded to the Hindu Girls' Schools is made clear by the fact that in the same year that Chapin had to leave, Martha Mandeville was transferred to Chittoor to teach and be in charge at the Female Seminary. The report affirms that her "experience and success in teaching will, we are confident, preserve its good name and prosperity."[47] With regard to the Hindu Girls' Schools, "Mrs. E. C. Scudder has consented to do what she can for these schools, but her already numerous duties will render it impossible for her to give them the care and attention they need. We hope the 'Women's [sic] Board of

[46] Josephine Chapin, "The Caste Girls' Schools at Vellore," in *Manual*, 106.
[47] "AAR," 1874, 6.

Hindu Girls School, Punganur

Foreign Missions' will see our necessity and kindly send us out a lady for this work without delay."[48]

In spite of the fact that Sarah Scudder did not have the time necessary to superintend the schools, the annual reports for the next four years state that they are rendering good service. By 1878, however, we are told that the schools have

"deteriorated in some degree, owing to the lack of proper attention." It was anticipated, however, that the schools would improve in the near future when Julia Scudder arrived from America. The value of the schools was recognized. "These schools are carrying enlightenment, and a knowledge of Christianity into many Hindu homes, that could be reached by no other means within our power."[49] These words make it clear that by 1878 the Hindu Girls' Schools had come to be appreciated as vital components of the work of the Arcot Mission. Education under the supervision

[48] Ibid., 9.
[49] Ibid., 26.

of women, including "civilizing" goals, had become important alongside preaching as a means to the evangelization of India. However, there was still an undercurrent of resistance to these schools that would lead to a major confrontation about two decades later.

Having considered how the Hindu Girls' Schools came to be established and how their presence represented a shift in the mission's historic stance concerning its aims, it remains to take note of the purpose of the schools as stated by one of their founders and to look for a moment at the curriculum of the schools. The evangelization of the girls and the Hindu community was affirmed as the aim of the schools, with all of their activities related to that goal. Chapin clearly spelled out the purpose:

> The aim of these schools is to carry the word of God to the daughters and families of the better classes of Hindus, whose caste, a social and religious distinction, makes them almost inaccessible to missionary effort. While we instruct them in secular studies and in needle work, the one object for which the schools were founded, is made paramount to every other. All the children who are old enough to read, are studying the Bible daily and learning the way of salvation through Christ....A large number of the pupils are now reading the Bible in their homes to their fathers and mothers, brothers and sisters.[50]

The schools had to include a basic curriculum set by the government. Beginning students used the First Reader, studied arithmetic (addition and the multiplication table as far as five times five), and also learned sewing (hemming and stitching). From there students advanced through the second and third readers, and added subjects such as grammar and geography. At all levels there was study of the Bible.

---

[50] Chapin, "The Caste Girls' Schools," 106-107.

Financial assistance from the government was awarded annually by an inspector of the school as a "grant-in-aid" according to a schedule fixed according to the number of students in school and the progress that the students were making. The cost to the Arcot Mission was approximately fifty dollars for each twenty-five or thirty girls enrolled, or a total of about $300-$350 in 1874. [51]

While foreign missionaries have often been accused of destroying the cultures of the people among whom they ministered, the founders of the Arcot Mission specifically sought to avoid getting caught up in "civilizing" activities, such as the establishing of schools or other institutions for those who were not Christians. It is difficult today to grasp the nature of changes in social and cultural as well as religious attitudes that were required in order for members of the Hindu communities to send their daughters to a school established by missionaries.

In the *Manual* published by the Women's Board for Foreign Missions in 1877, a writer comments on the fact that twenty years previously, the only Hindu women who were literate were the temple dancing girls, who were often involved in prostitution.

> It must be remembered that so early as twenty years ago, to ask a Hindu lady whether she could read and write was to offer her the vilest possible insult. Women, fortunate enough to have acquired any education, were careful to hide the fact from all but their immediate relatives. The only class among females who received instruction were the dancing girls of the temples, whose position was parallel with that of the ancient festal virgins."[52]

The next chapter will consider more fully the nature and extent of Hindu reform movements in the nineteenth century. We must now note that the direction of changes in the social position of Hindu women in India was the same as that in America, although

[51] Ibid., 108.
[52] *Manual*, 115.

the Hindu women on the whole had a far less favorable position at the beginning of that century than did American women. Few aspects of Hindu life in the early nineteenth century were subject to as much criticism as was the position of women. Censure of temple prostitution and the system of child marriage were especially strong and persistent. In the marriage system, a girl of six years or younger would be made the bride of a man as old as sixty years, and often such girls became widows even before reaching puberty. As the justice of these criticisms was accepted by a number of reform-minded Hindus, the role of women began to change. As Hindus came to see what was happening among women in the Christian community, they also became more open to the possibility of their own daughters becoming educated.

Reformed Church missionary Alice Van Doren in 1922 credited the work of missions with having played a role in bringing about reforms and opening the door to education of the women of India.

> The achievements of Christianity in India are not to be confined to the four millions who constitute the community that have followed the new Way. Perhaps even greater has been the reaction it has excited in the ranks of Hinduism among those who would repudiate the name of Christian. Chief among the abuses of Hinduism to be attacked has been the traditional attitude toward woman. Child marriage and compulsory widowhood are condemned by every social reformer up and down the length of India. The battle is fought not only for women, but by them also. Agitation for the sufferance has been carried on in India's chief cities.[53]

Several of the male members of the Arcot Mission came to see the value of educating the Hindu girls of India. J. H. Wyckoff was one

---

[53] Alice B. Van Doren, *Lighted to Lighten: The Hope of India* (West Medford, Mass.: The Central Committee on the United Study of Foreign Missions, 1922), 26-27. It should be noted that the United States' constitutional amendment guaranteeing women the right to vote was adopted August 26, 1920, less than two years before Van Doren's book was published.

of the first to speak appreciatively of this broader educational activity of the mission. In 1878, the Hindu Girls' School in Tindivanam was the only girls' school among a population of 500,000 people. Following the annual government inspection of the school in November, a public meeting was held for the distribution of prizes for outstanding achievement by the various girls. A "native gentleman" gave a lecture entitled, "Female Education," that was enthusiastically received, in spite of the fact that much prejudice against the education of females still existed in the community. Wyckoff had come to believe that such education was crucial to the missionary's calling. "We cannot hope for India's conversion to Christ unless the women are brought under the influence of Christianity. Notwithstanding the degradation of woman in India, she is a power in the family and practically rules the household."[54]

The girls' school on Circar Mandy Street was in the wealthiest and most aristocratic section of Vellore. On its annual prize distribution days, the school was usually "crowded with native gentlemen and a few native ladies." The girls were examined publicly in several subjects, including the Bible. They sang songs and exhibited their needlework and embroidery. It was also a social occasion.

> The pupils looked charming in their rich dresses and costly jewels, and the whole occasion was one of great interest and pleasure, not only to the missionaries, but to the large and influential audience of natives, who had gathered to witness a scene which is still rare in this land of women's degradation. The influence of such schools as these in shattering time-hardened prejudices, and in introducing light and knowledge into Hindu homes, cannot be overestimated.[55]

The Hindu girls' schools, like the other schools that had Hindu pupils, always walked a fine line between approbation and rejection.

[54]"BFMR," 1878, 21.
[55]"BFMR," 1883, 47.

Hindu parents were pleased to send their children to such schools to get an education that was not available in the community. They were quite ready to agree that the children would receive instruction in the Bible and Christian music. But the line was always drawn at the point of conversion—and sometimes well before that line was reached. It was not unusual for opponents of the girls' schools to open their own school in clear competition with the mission school. This happened in Vellore in 1887. In that year a committee of Hindu gentlemen started a school very near to the mission school with the avowed purpose of breaking up the "missionary's school." Julia Goodwin Scudder, who was in charge of the school, sent a polite letter to the gentlemen requesting them "to open it in some place sufficiently removed from us to prevent a clashing of interests." This request was refused and a vigorous campaign was waged "to capture our pupils and injure our school." While a few students joined the new school, no real damage occurred, and the mission school enrollment increased.[56]

Perhaps the most dramatic confrontation regarding the purposes of Hindu boys' schools and girls' schools took place in Chetpet in 1896. When Ezekiel Carman Scudder, Jr. (known as Carman), who was always forthright and strict in his management, took over supervision of the schools in Chetpet in 1896, he decided that as soon as vacancies occurred, he would appoint Christians to fill positions previously held by Hindus. When the first two Christians were placed, everything remained calm. But then, just before the second two were placed, he received word at his residence in Arni that his presence was urgently required in Chetpet, sixteen miles distant. He left at 6:00 the next morning and reached Chetpet at 9:00 a.m. He discovered that the girls' school building was empty, except for four weeping lady teachers.

Carman Scudder said that he wanted to talk with the leading men of the town about the situation, and soon most of the influential

[56]"BFMR," 1887, 48.

men of the town and the fathers of the sixty-five girls were there. It is well to have his description of the scene in his own words:

> I asked them what was the matter and they replied that I was invading their rights by sending non-Christian teachers, that possibly I was trying to convert the girls and perhaps even themselves. I then asked them what they supposed I was in India for except to bring all I could to Christ and told them thus that, altho' I should use no force or underhanded means to accomplish the end, they need have no doubt as to what the end was; it was to induce them all to become Christians.
>
> They were rather astonished at the plain declaration and said if I did not transfer the new Christian teachers and promise not to send any others they would not send their girls any more. I assured them that their dictation as to persons and methods in our mission schools would not be accepted and if they persisted in their course I should simply close both schools and open them in the neighboring town of Polur, where I had long been waiting to have some work of this sort and where the people were ready to accept any terms if I would give them a Boys' and a Girls' school.[57]

Following that exchange, Scudder gave them fifteen minutes to make a decision. He had to go back home soon, because the river was rising and there was no time to waste before it became too deep to cross. When the fifteen minutes elapsed with no decision, he announced that the schools were closed and ordered the Indians accompanying him to load the furniture and equipment on the carts. When the carts were loaded, he locked the school door and returned the key to the owner of the building. No sooner had he begun to leave than the men all came to him, saying that they wanted the schools and would accede to any wishes he might have.

---

[57] E. Carman Scudder to Henry Cobb, November 24, 1896. Excerpts from the letter appeared as an article in *Mission Field,* August, 1897:387-88.

The only final humble request they made was that I would appoint from the people of the town a Committee of Inspection to see that all things went on properly. To this I was only too glad to assent, and the five gentlemen appointed are taking a deep personal interest in both the schools, reporting to me occasionally and seeing to it that the boys and girls attend our Sunday School on Sundays. [58]

At the time he wrote the letter, two months after the crisis, the girls' school had seventy girls enrolled, with three Christian and three non-Christian teachers. He included in the letter also the comment that by the time he got to the river, it had become a roaring torrent where in the morning it had only been a bed of dry sand.

Zenana Work and Bible Women

Arcot missionaries believed the "wives of missionaries" should work among the women of India by visiting them in their homes. One of its fundamental rules was that

The companions whom God has graciously given us are expected, as far as health, family duties and other circumstances may allow, to labor among heathen women by visiting them at their houses and using other appropriate means to bring them for a knowledge of the truth. [59]

In 1863, Mary Anna (Mrs. Silas) Scudder invited women from a neighboring village to come every day to her house for Bible study, and she promised a piece of cloth to all who could read a verse from the Bible by the end of the year. Four attended, two won the prize, and all became Christians. [60] Margaret Mayou in Arni became the first to employ educated Christian women to visit Hindu women in

---

[58] Ibid.
[59] "Rules of the Arcot Mission," quoted in Chamberlain, *Fifty Years*, 56.
[60] Ibid.

their homes and read the Bible to them.[61] By 1888, eighteen Bible women were employed by the mission to visit in homes and other places to read and discuss the Bible with women.

The zenana movement among women received much of its impetus from the recognition that it was important to keep in touch with girls who no longer could attend the Hindu girls' schools. After a high-caste girl had attended the school for a few years, she would in most cases be withdrawn, often around the age of twelve and in some cases even earlier. From that point in her life, she would live in the seclusion of the zenana portion of the home. Sensing that as the girls grew into womanhood they would welcome the opportunity to continue their studies at home, the mission began home classes taught by zenana teachers in the homes of the young women. In these classes, the secular subjects taught in the schools were pursued to a higher grade, including reading, writing, arithmetic, sewing, geography, hygiene, and domestic economy. The Bible was also studied with each visit to the home.[62]

Zenana work could also develop among women who had not been enrolled in a Hindu girls' school. In Wallajah, the girls' school was opened and regular zenana work began in the same year, 1886. The people there were at first reluctant to send their daughters. Thirteen were enrolled in the first year, but thirty-seven came in the second year. Most of them were very young girls. As soon as the girls' school was opened, the teachers of the Government Girls' School began to gather in all the girls they could and nearly doubled their number. Thus the opening of the mission school served to influence the Hindus of the town to a more positive attitude toward education for girls.[63]

Opposition to zenana work at Wallajah soon declined, with the result that after two years, the zenana woman had twenty-eight homes to visit. Her work was to read and explain the Bible and to

[61]"AAR," 1866, 20.
[62] Chamberlain, *Fifty Years,* 90.
[63] "BFMR," 1888, 46.

teach the women to read, sew, and do fancy work. The women listened respectfully and were glad to have the zenana woman in their homes. Elizabeth Conklin, the missionary at Arcot, frequently visited the houses in company with the zenana woman.[64] The teamwork between the zenana woman and the missionary proved to be an effective arrangement, in that the missionary woman gave added prestige to the zenana woman, while the zenana worker's comprehension of the language and culture made for effective communication.

Julia Scudder and Mrs. Isaac Henry, a volunteer, visited the zenanas in Vellore for a number of years, along with paid assistants. They often visited young women of thirteen and fourteen years of age who had previously attended the schools. These women were able to continue their studies to some extent through such visits. They discovered that it was important for them to introduce Christian Tamil language magazines and small books to them as well as the Bible, so that they would read such material rather than "literature of their own that is not fit for anyone to read."[65]

Although their functions overlapped to a considerable degree, there was a slight difference between the work of the Bible woman and the zenana teacher. The Bible woman tended to work over a large area, in the village, along the roadside, beside village ponds and wells where women would go for water, in hospitals as well as in house-to-house visitation. The zenana teacher followed a more regular schedule in visiting former pupils and homes where the women carried on more systematic ways of learning.

It was difficult to evaluate the effectiveness of the Bible women and zenana teachers. The Arcot missionaries had grown accustomed to measuring their progress through the reporting of statistics: number of places preached and how often, number of persons added to the membership of the church, number of village congregations, financial contributions, and so on. Those who

[64] Ibid.
[65] "BFMR," 1889, 68-69.

visited the zenanas could report how many houses they had visited, but the effectiveness of their work could never be measured by statistical means. A Hindu woman who was required to be obedient to her husband could tell the zenana teacher that she now believed in Jesus, but she was not free to be baptized or to participate in the worshiping life of the church.

Julia Scudder did report in 1890 about one zenana pupil in Bangalore, 140 miles from Vellore, who had been converted to Christianity. Upon her conversion she did the only thing she was free to do, which was to leave her home and join herself to the missionaries and refuse to leave them. When news of the conversion reached Vellore, the homes of the zenana pupils were closed to the teachers. "Some of our old pupils also expressed a wish to discontinue their duties, so there was nothing for us to do but to work on with the few scholars who remained, patiently waiting and praying until the doors should be open to us again....And we believe God's own word is doing its silent work, even though we do not see much outward advancement."[66]

The outreach into Hindu villages and homes continued to be faithfully carried out for many decades, especially by unmarried missionaries and Indian women. The accounts of their work are similar from decade to decade, as they were forced to do their most valuable service behind the scenes.

> They were often called upon to settle family disputes; they were encouraged to discipline refractory children, to advise perplexed mothers, to placate indignant husbands, to rescue forbidden books from the earthen pot in which they had been concealed....A Hindu writer has said of this work, 'If we do not find many Christians among the Hindus, we find a very large number Christianized in spite of themselves.'[67]

---

[66]"BFMR," 1890, 72.
[67]Chamberlain, *Fifty Years*, 57.

Mary A. Chamberlain served in the Arcot Mission from 1891 until 1906, when the severe health problems of her daughter made it necessary for the family to return to the United States. She worked with a number of the Bible women and zenana teachers. In writing the history of the first five decades of the work of the Woman's Board for Foreign Missions, she remembered the great contribution of several of those women.

She tells about three such women in Madanapalle—Rebecca, Esther, and Susanna. Those three along with three others regularly visited a total of 250 homes. She tells of Charlotte, the Bible woman in Palmaner, who in one year reached over six thousand hearers. Through the work of one Bible woman, "there seemed to be many secret disciples in Chittoor, people who confessed in their hearts that Jesus was the true Son of God but who had not the courage to give up home, husband, children, kindred, reputation and everything that they held dear in life for this new religion."[68]

Annie Hancock, who served as a missionary in Vellore from 1899 until her death in 1924, and her Indian colleagues developed a wide network of relationships among the women of Vellore. She had as a colleague a Mrs. Subramaniam, a converted Brahmin of a sweet Christian character who worked especially among Muslim women. At first she had entrance to only one house, but gradually the number increased to forty. Once again conversion was the boundary that a woman was not allowed to cross. When two young Muslim women were anxious to profess their faith in Christ, their relatives threatened to kill them and Mrs. Subramaniam had to discontinue her visits.[69] By 1912 there were ten Bible women at work visiting nearly five hundred houses in Vellore.

Four Bible women, Rachel, Caroline, Rebecca, and Manomani, were carrying on similar work in the Arcot and Ranipet region. They told the story of the beginning of their work there when one of them went along the streets in an area that had never before been visited.

68 Ibid., 163.
69 For this and the following paragraph, ibid., 164-65.

Her hands were full of books and lace, and men and women looked at her in surprise. She told them that she was a Christian woman who had come to teach. All who wished to do so could join her and learn to read and make lace and sew. After examining her lace and books, they expressed the opinion that it would be better to learn such things than to spend the whole day in idleness and gossip. With this beginning, the number of Bible women needed in that area increased to six.

Through the work of the Bible women and the zenana teachers, a whole segment of the population came into the knowledge of the gospel who could not otherwise have done so through the evangelistic activity of the men alone. On the whole, its impact was more "civilizing" than evangelizing, if one thinks in terms of the growth of the church. The women who were visited in their homes in many cases were among those who, while remaining Hindu, became leaders in development and reform within their own communities. Many of them would continue to speak appreciatively of the teachings that they had learned from the Bible and their teachers.

The Creative Leadership of the Unmarried Women Missionaries

We have seen that in 1870 considerable reluctance still existed about the appointment of unmarried missionaries, female or male. There was a firm conviction that it was not good for a man to be alone without a wife in India. It was understood that a woman could make her greatest contribution through her role as a missionary wife. Prior to 1890, only two unmarried women, apart from members of the Scudder family, had been appointed to serve in India. Appreciation for the contribution of unmarried women began to grow after 1890. Assistant women missionaries were accorded the right to participate in official mission discussion in 1896 and "to vote on all questions related to the work in which they are engaged."[70]

---

[70] *Manual of the Board of Foreign Missions of the Reformed Church in America,* 1895, III, 2, p. 14.

Louisa Hart   *Ida S. Scudder*

After the arrival of Lizzie Von Bergen, Louisa Hart, and Ida S. Scudder between 1890 and 1895, any residual reluctance to welcome unmarried women disappeared. Lizzie Von Bergen proved to be a faithful visitor with the women in the village and town areas. Ida Scudder, then still very young and related to her parents, uncles, and aunts among the members of the Scudder family, was much appreciated for the way in which she provided assistance for her parents in their responsibilities. Louisa Hart, a physician, brought medical skills that proved to be practically indispensable in the time of an epidemic of bubonic plague in 1899. The government requested at that time that she go on plague duty, a very risky task at the time when the vaccine was still new and one could not be sure that it was yet fully tested.[71] Such duties consisted of inspecting women in their houses and inoculating all who would accept the vaccine.

It is not necessary to repeat the story of homes made desolate by this disease. Often one seemed to be walking

[71] Five years later, in 1904, Mary Gnanamani, an Indian doctor in mission service in Madanapalle, died of the plague while treating patients.

through a death stricken city, seeking whoever would accept of a means of escape. Sometimes one brave enough to be treated would appear. More often one fled at the very sight of the doctor. Those who had the courage to be inoculated were treated out in the open street so that all might see. Then perhaps the doctor would be invited into the house to see and treat the women. Again some influential and more enlightened men would invite the doctor to come and inoculate them. Thus it happened that in one week Dr. Hart had inoculated one thousand people.[72]

Dr. Hart was also the first to approach the Woman's Board about the great need for a hospital for women and children to be placed at Vellore, the largest and central town in the Arcot Mission area. She had experienced great difficulty at Ranipet in getting any of the zenana women in or even near the hospital, owing to their dread of being thrown into any contact with men. She estimated that such a hospital would cost about $8,000 to construct, with another $1,500 needed annually for running expenses.[73] The speed with which both the Arcot Mission and the Woman's Board approved the request demonstrates how quickly Dr. Hart and the other women had won the confidence of those around them.

A number of very creative young unmarried women were appointed by 1910, among them Alice Van Doren, Annie Hancock, Margaret Rottschaefer, and two sisters, Josephine and Sarella Te Winkel, who labored in the areas of education, medicine, zenana work, and women's social service centers. Their appointments anticipate the great expansion of the Arcot Mission's range of service over the next several decades, as well as the expanding involvement of women missionaries. Within a couple of decades, the number of women in the mission would be considerably more than the number of men. In the fiftieth anniversary year of the Woman's Board of Foreign Missions, 1925, there were twenty-one

[72] Chamberlain, *Fifty Years*, 93.
[73] Ibid.

unmarried women and fifteen married women, compared to two unmarried and fifteen married men.[74] In 1947, the year of the inauguration of the Church of South India, there were thirty-one unmarried and eleven married women, and two unmarried and eleven married men.

A Shift in the Arcot Mission's Understanding of its Threefold Work

When Reformed Church missionaries in India in 1903 looked back over the half century that had passed since the founding of the Arcot Mission, they discerned three periods in the history of the mission. The first, from 1853-1860, they designated "The Initial or Rudimental Period"; the second was "The Village Movement or Rapid Development Period, 1861-1878." The third period, beginning in 1878, was "The Development of Institutional Work, or the Period of Concentration." They used the year 1878 as the beginning point of the third period because that was the year in which the mission took action permitting Hindu children to enter the Christian school for boys at Tindivanam. This action of the mission was not in accordance with the third principle of the mission—to educate only the children of Christian parents or those under instruction in the faith. In recognition of that fact, the mission altered its third principle in 1884. With that amendment to its rules, the door was opened wide to the establishment of other mission institutions as well.

> This has produced momentous changes in the Mission. The number of non-Christian students has constantly grown, until [in 1903, auth.] there are 3,305 more Hindu than Christian students in our educational institutions. This one cause, perhaps more than any other, has so shaped the conditions of our work in the Mission that we have applied

[74]"BFMR," 1925, 23. The Board of Foreign Missions in 1925 was still listing the missionary wives as "assistant missionaries." As early as 1888, however, the Arcot Mission was listing all missionaries as "personnel of the mission," and thus avoided the distinction in rank. None of the women had the right to vote, however, until 1896.

the name to this period. A partial result, as noted below, has been the relaxing of evangelistic efforts in the districts by the Missionary forces."[75]

The 1903 mission report recognizes that pressures for a change in policy to admit institutions as a legitimate aspect of the work of the mission had been building prior to 1878. By then there were already the two seminaries and fifty-six day schools and three Hindu girls' schools in existence, as well as the small hospital in Ranipet. Of these, it was the Hindu girls' schools that clearly violated the working principle. The other schools served the Christian community, whereas the hospital was still in its beginning stages. The lower priority for woman's work surfaced in 1878 with the Anglo-vernacular boys' school in Tindivanam under the supervision of J.H. Wyckoff. It was the presence of the boys' school rather than the larger Hindu girls' schools that finally brought the mission to recognize the need to change its policy. Wyckoff commented on the importance of such a school:

> Boys of all classes, Christians, Brahmins, Sudras, Pariahs and Mohammedans, read together with no distinction of caste, and the effect this has wrought in removing caste differences is very marked. Much interest has been taken in the Scripture lesson....Nearly all the boys pay fees, which have amounted to Rs. 207, not a small sum considering the famine times. I am firmly convinced of the usefulness of such a school at a Missionary station. Nothing serves so well as a stepping-stone to work among the higher classes as a school which admits all castes.[76]

By 1881, Wyckoff was supervising two Anglo-vernacular boys' schools, having added the supervision of the school in Chetpet to that in Tindivanam. By this time he had been convinced of the important role of the schools in the mission's approach to Hindus.

[75]"AAR," 1903, 3.
[76]"BFMR," 1878, 20.

He also saw that when Hindu and Christian boys studied together in the same school, confidence grew among the Christians that they could compete with high-caste Hindus. Moreover, the schools could be managed with very little expense to the mission. He commented, "Of the Christian boys connected with the School, all except one passed. This is an encouraging fact and shows that the sons of our Christians are able to compete with Hindus of the highest castes. The total cost of the institution has been Rs. 1,424-11-3. Of this sum, Rs. 656-5-0 has been met from school fees; Rs. 560-12-0 from Result grant, and the balance of Rs. 207-10-0 has been paid by the Mission."[77]

J. H. Wyckoff was not the only one who accepted responsibility for managing an Anglo-Vernacular boys' school whose students were Hindus. Jared Scudder in Vellore was approached in 1880 by the Brahmin superintendent of such a school in Vellore with a plea for the mission to take charge of it. The Brahmin had for a time been employed as a teacher in a mission school and recognized its value. He had started his school in Vellore a little more than a year before and had gained an enrollment of two hundred students. But it was too much responsibility for him. He was willing that the mission would follow its normal practice of teaching the Bible to all students. The school was largely self-supporting with student fees and government grants, so the mission accepted responsibility for it with a request that the board add five hundred dollars for the school to its annual appropriation. Scudder commented that

> We cannot but think that there are individuals in our church, who, if made aware of the circumstances, and especially of the exceptionally favorable opportunity afforded us by Providence of bringing a large number of Hindu youth under Biblical instruction, would gladly give the money necessary to supplement the means already at our disposal for carrying on the school.[78]

77 "BFMR," 1882, 27.
78 J.W. Scudder to J.M. Ferris, September 15, 1880.

Managing the schools not only required some funds from the board, but it also took time away from the missionary's evangelistic work. In spite of the fact that Wyckoff had high regard for the value of evangelistic touring and, to judge from his journal, very much enjoyed the adventure of such activity, in 1882 he found he had little time for touring. It had been carried on largely by five of the native assistants. "The time of the Missionary and Helpers is so taken up with the congregations and school, that at present it is not possible to do as much of this work as could be wished."[79] In this comment, it becomes clear that Scudder's fear that the opening of schools and other institutions would diminish the time available for direct evangelistic work was justified. The tension between the original principle and its revision in 1884 to allow for institutional development would not go away.

The revision in 1884 had the great advantage of making it possible for many more women to find opportunities to render missionary service. The women as well as the men needed an organizational or institutional framework in which to carry on their work. It had not been adequately recognized that the establishment of the Arcot Mission and the Classis of Arcot had provided such a framework only for the ordained male missionaries. No man who was not ordained was appointed to serve in the mission until A.C. Cole was assigned to Voorhees College in 1905. The Female Seminary and the village schools had, almost from the beginning, provided an outlet for the service of the missionaries' wives and a very limited number of unmarried women, all of whom except Chapin and Mandeville were daughters or granddaughters of John and Harriet Scudder. When schools, hospitals, and other institutions were established, the need for unmarried women grew rapidly and gave them their significant place in the Reformed Church's mission in India.

Having seen that the period after 1878 was the era of the development of institutional work, we must review that activity in

79 Ibid., 25.

more detail. Prior to doing so, however, we will devote a chapter to the theology of the Arcot missionaries and their attitude toward the religion of the Hindus, as well as some developments in the nature of the relationship between the Arcot Mission, the Classis of Arcot, the Board of Foreign Missions, and the General Synod of the Reformed Church in America.

5

Defining the Mission

The Arcot Mission made a policy change in 1884 that enabled the
founding of institutions and that opened the door to teaching
Hindu boys and girls in the English language as well as in the
vernacular languages. During its first half-century, several
controversies also arose that called upon the Arcot Mission and the
Board of Foreign Missions to define more clearly their relationships
to and responsibilities toward each other. In that same period, the
missionaries developed a better knowledge of the Hindu culture
and religion as well as a broader definition of their missionary task.
In this chapter we will explore these developments in the self-
understanding of the Reformed Church in America's calling to
service in India.

The Religious Climate in Which the First Arcot Missionaries were Educated

At the end of 1860, there were four Scudder brothers and their
wives in India: Henry Martyn in Coonoor, William Waterbury and
Silas Downer in Vellore, and Ezekiel Carman in Chittoor. Two
other brothers and their wives had sailed to America in 1860
because serious illness required that they leave India. Joseph

Rev. & Mrs. Jared Scudder, Rev. & Mrs. Jacob Chamberlain,
Mrs. Sophia Scudder

Scudder's health was such that he was never able to return to India. Jared Waterbury's wife, Julia Goodwin, recovered her health, but the couple remained in America long enough for Jared to earn a degree in medicine.

The seventh and youngest brother, John Scudder II, and his wife, Sophia Weld, arrived in India in March 1861. Like several of his older brothers, John was both a medical doctor and an ordained minister. Two other Reformed Church missionary families were in India to welcome John and Sophia Scudder. They were the Reverend Joseph and Margaret Mayou, who arrived in 1858, and the Reverend Jacob and Charlotte Chamberlain, who arrived in 1859.

An outsider looking at these eight ordained Reformed Church missionaries would at first sight have been impressed with how much they all seemed alike in thought and goal. Except for the two oldest sons—Henry, who graduated from Union Theological Seminary in New York in 1843, and William Waterbury, who graduated from Princeton in 1845—all of them had received their college and theological education in the 1850s. Jared and Ezekiel Scudder graduated from Western Reserve University in 1850. Jacob Chamberlain graduated from Western Reserve in 1855. Silas and John Scudder graduated from the Reformed Church college, Rutgers, in 1856 and 1857, respectively. Joseph Mayou also graduated from Rutgers, in 1855. Apart from the two old brothers, all were alumni of the Reformed theological school, New Brunswick Theological Seminary: Jared,'55, Ezekiel, '55, Joseph Mayou, '58, Jacob Chamberlain, '59, and Silas, '59-60.[1] Since all of the schools they attended had small student bodies in those years, there would have been ample opportunity for all except the two older brothers to have come to know each other well and to agree about the missionary calling prior to their service in India.

However, in their letter to the General Synod in 1855, the three founding brothers of the Classis of Arcot called attention to the differences among the theological seminaries that they had attended. Union Theological Seminary, which Henry attended, was a New School Presbyterian seminary while Princeton, at which William studied, was Old School Presbyterian. Dutch by birth, the brothers had been reared by relatives in the United States, having been sent there for their education when Henry was ten and William was nine. Despite this American upbringing, they were both pleased that "the Dutch Church, like a great magnet, exerting its silent, quiet but powerful influence upon us in our different courses, drew us to a common center."[2] The third brother, Joseph, had been related to the Reformed Church in America through his college and seminary years by his study in Rutgers College and New Brunswick Theological

[1] Russell L. Gasero, *Historical Directory of the Reformed Church in America, 1628-1992* (Grand Rapids: Eerdmans, 1992), 37, 150, 209.
[2] Letter to the General Synod of the Reformed Protestant Dutch Church in the United States from the Arcot Classis, September, 1855.

Seminary and had been ordained in that denomination by the Classis of New York.

Although both Henry and William Scudder had been attracted to the Reformed Church as by a "great magnet," we could go wrong by ignoring too easily the situation in the Presbyterian Church between 1830 and 1860. The Presbyterian Church had suffered a major division at its General Assembly in 1837. The Old School party had gathered a sufficient number of votes to abrogate retroactively the 1801 Plan of Union agreement with the Congregational churches. This action eliminated from the denomination the Synod of Western Reserve in Ohio and the New York synods of Utica, Geneva, and Genesee, all of which had been formed under the plan and were New School churches. This action struck nearly one-fifth the membership of the denomination from its roles and reduced the voting strength of the New School party by one-half. The remaining New School delegates then withdrew from the assembly. Thereafter for three decades there were two Presbyterian assemblies, each claiming to be "The General Assembly of the Presbyterian Church in the United States of America."[3] The theological seminaries attended by Henry and William Scudder in the decade following the division were thus in opposite camps.

The theological controversies that led to the division also had a long and complex history. Issues concerning free will and predestination, the doctrine of the atonement, and revivalism as practiced by persons such as Charles Finney,[4] all were involved. For our purposes, it is sufficient to note that

---

3 For the complete story of this controversy, see George M. Marsden, *The Evangelical Mind and the New School Presbyterian Experience* (New Haven: Yale University Press, 1970), esp. 59-86.

4 Charles Finney had said that while conversion is properly said to be the work of God, "It is also the appropriate work of the sinner himself." The actual turning to God, he explained with an emphasis that suggested that a person saved himself through choice, is the work of the individual. It is what God requires of the individual, and what God requires of him must be something that God cannot do for him." Finney was impatient with the debates at the General Assembly. He said, "Their contentions and janglings are so ridiculous...that no doubt there is a jubilee in hell every year about the time of the meeting of the General Assembly" [Winthrop S. Hudson, *American Protestantism*

The real issue was the proper content of the appeal that the evangelist or pastor could make to the members of his congregation. Could he tell the sinner who was deeply concerned about the state of his soul, 'Choose Christ this day'? Or must he risk discouraging the sinner by telling him that it is God alone who chooses those whom he will save and that without the gracious regenerating work of the Holy Spirit the sinner can do nothing toward his salvation? Here, the seeming abstract theological question took on an intensely practical significance.[5]

The New School held to the first alternative, while the Old School held to a strict interpretation of the denomination's Westminster Confession and the second alternative.

The *Christian Intelligencer,* the Reformed Church weekly newspaper published in New York, followed the controversy closely and kept its readers well informed by printing long articles for their information. The material included in the *Christian Intelligencer,* as the controversy went on in the 1850s, would certainly have been available to the remaining Scudder brothers, as well as to Chamberlain and Mayou during their years in New Brunswick Theological Seminary.[6] In the Scudder family history, we have already seen that in debate with his pastor, the Reverend Christian Bork in New York City, John Scudder, Sr., had essentially taken what was to become the New School position, while Bork had been Old School. Their very pragmatic way of working together in Franklin Street Reformed Church also was favored by many others in the Reformed Church, which did not divide over the issue. Textbooks written by such Old School professors as Charles Hodge of Princeton came to be used in the Arcot Theological Seminary, while in their preaching the

(Chicago: Univ. of Chicago Press, 1972), 101-102]. Finney's language was such, however, as to give New School as well as Old School advocates some pause.
[5] Marsden, *Evangelical Mind,* 81-82.
[6] That the division in the Presbyterian Church touched the lives of Jared Scudder and Jacob Chamberlain is indicated by the fact that both of them pursued their college education at Western Reserve University, which is related to the Western Reserve Synod in Ohio, one of the synods abrogated by the General Assembly in 1837.

Scudders followed the practice of their father and the New School teachings.

The Old School Presbyterians were also suspicious of the American Board of Commissioners for Foreign Missions as one of the evangelical voluntary societies that sought to bring about cooperation among Christians across denominational boundaries. Such societies organized for specific purposes and avoided taking a stance on specific doctrinal points on which there was division. New School Presbyterians, who were interested in church growth on the American frontier as well as in other evangelical efforts at evangelism, personal piety, and social reform, were ready to maintain a more tolerant doctrinal stance. The Old School became increasingly convinced that "the operations of the independent agencies within the bounds of Presbyterianism were a major source of divergent opinion and doctrinal laxity."[7]

The New School champions of voluntary mission societies believed that such societies were the best way to move forward in domestic and foreign evangelization. Absalom Peters of the New School argued, "We are constrained to believe that the voluntary, associated action of evangelical Christians, as far as it is practicable, is much better suited to the object of the world's conversion, than any form of church organization for this purpose, ever has been or can be."[8] In this statement of the role of the voluntary Christian mission society, one can see theoretical formulation for the action of the Scudders in establishing two distinct bodies. On the one hand, they formed the Arcot Mission with responsibility to reach out to the "heathen" and to train people to give Christian leadership. On the other hand, they organized the Classis of Arcot to provide means for maintaining stated times for worship, preaching, administering the sacraments, church discipline, and the work of sanctification.

Charles Hodge of the Old School party conceded that for certain activities, such as the promotion of Scripture and literature

7 Ibid., 72.
8 Ibid.

distribution, voluntary societies had a legitimate place. However, he objected to the independent roles of the American Home Missionary Society, which had established Union Churches on the American frontiers, and foreign missionary societies that sought to plant churches. Planting churches was to be the work of the churches or denominations themselves. The Presbyterian denomination must have its own mission board rather than work through voluntary mission societies; therefore, at the General Assembly of 1837 the Presbyterian Church established its own foreign mission board.[9] In contrast, the Reformed Church in America, which had formed its own foreign missions board in 1832, continued to work through the American Board of Commissioners for Foreign Missions until 1857, rather than set up a separate administrative structure for overseas relationships.

The Reformed Church missionaries in India in 1860 had all been nurtured in the postmillenial theology that was then dominant in the Reformed Church as well as among New School Presbyterians. They accepted the optimistic vision of preachers such as the leading Reformed Church minister, John H. Livingston, who taught that the Holy Spirit was working powerfully to bring the world to salvation in preparation for the millenial reign of Christ at the close of the age. John H. Livingston believed that the two centuries from 1800-2000 AD were to be the age of mission.

> We are compelled...to look forward for the accomplishment; and are now reduced to the short remaining space of two hundred years. Within this compass there can be no mistake. At some point of time, from, and including the present day, and before the close of two hundred years, the angel must begin to fly in the midst of Churches and preach the everlasting Gospel to all nations, and tongues, and kindred, and people in the earth.[10]

9 Ibid., 74.
10 John H. Livingston, "The Everlasting Gospel," in John W. Beardslee III, ed., *Vision from the Hill*, Historical Series of the Reformed Church in America, no.12 (Grand Rapids: Eerdmans, 1984), 10.

This millenial vision led leaders of the Reformed Church to speak optimistically about the assured success of the mission in America and in India. The confidence of the Reverend Peter Stryker, who in 1800 urged the Reformed Church to open up new mission fields in the western frontiers of the emerging nation of America, was also present in the Arcot missionaries.

> The Lord in the course of his Providence is opening a large field in the Western Territory for the Extension of his Church and the Spread of the Gospel....The Period is not far distant when the Fullness of the Gentiles shall come to the Knowledge of divine Truths as they are revealed to us...to insure to Thousands and Millions all temporal, Spiritual, and heavenly blessings.[11]

Confidence that the Spirit of God was active across the face of the earth in bringing the nations to faith in preparation for the coming of Christ was the driving force that encouraged Reformed Church missionaries to go on in their mission in the face of opposition, disease, and death. The innumerable optimistic statements which they made about the decay of Hinduism and the increase of Christianity in India were not based on political, sociological, cultural analysis, or in confidence in the superiority of their own culture and wisdom. It was the nature of their faith in the coming of the Lord that sustained them.

From the perspective of the twentieth century, the lack of any serious reference to slavery in America by members of the Arcot Mission is a glaring omission. Their annual reports contain no comments about slavery in America, while their only references to the Civil War have to do with diminished contributions in America and the great need in India for increased funding.[12] Such lack of comment is understandable in light of their intense concentration on evangelism to the neglect of other concerns. It is possible, however, that a deeper reason for their silence was that Reformed

---

[11] James W. Van Hoeven, "The American Frontier," in Van Hoeven, *Piety and Patriotism*, 34. For postmillenialism among New School Presbyterians, see Marsden, *Evangelical Mind*, 185-90.
[12] "AAR," 1861, 8; 1862, 8; 1863, 7.

Church missionaries in India in 1860 were in accord with the stance of the Reformed Church in America and the Presbyterian General Assembly. Prior to the outbreak of the Civil War, both of these bodies held that hope for overcoming the slavery issue was to be found in support for the African Colonization Society, rather than through abolition.

Until the outbreak of the Civil War, the Presbyterian General Assembly's strongest and most comprehensive statement had been passed in 1818. It had declared that slavery is a sin of the first order, being "a gross violation of the most precious and sacred rights of nature," "utterly inconsistent with the law of God." The assembly urged that it was "manifestly the duty of all Christians…as speedily as possible to efface this blot on our holy religion, and to obtain the complete abolition of slavery throughout Christendom, and if possible throughout the world."[13]

Although the General Assembly's stand against slavery had been made clear, no steps were taken to bring about an immediate end to slavery, as the Abolitionists were demanding. It was felt by many in the North as well as in the South that a more gradual course should be followed in granting freedom as the slaves were prepared for it. The General Assembly in 1818 endorsed the colonization movement of assisting freed slaves to resettle in Liberia, stating, "In the distinctive and indelible marks of their colour, and the prejudices of the people, an insuperable obstacle has been placed to the execution of any plan for elevating their character, and placing them on a footing with their brethren of the same common family."[14]

After 1830 the Abolitionist movement became stronger, while the futility of the campaign to assist American blacks to go back to Liberia in Africa was becoming apparent to those who were willing to see it. Within the Reformed Church in America, which had no churches in the American South, there was little desire to see it. The General Synod continued to be interested in the African Colonization

13 Marsden, *Evangelical Mind,* 90.
14 Ibid., 92.

Movement almost to the outbreak of the Civil War, while the *Christian Intelligencer* was ever ready to inform its readers of the positive progress of the movement.[15] When the Civil War broke out, the Arcot missionaries were on the side of the Union, since in their context in India they found themselves in favor of law and order and opposed to "insurrection,"[16] whether in India or among the southern states in America. They took essentially the same position with the outcastes in India who could rise in society through education and justice in the law and order of the British Raj, rather than through violent agitation.

To Whom is an Ordained Missionary Accountable? The Case of John Scudder, Jr.

The Reverend Dr. John Scudder and his wife, Sophia Weld, arrived as missionaries in India in March, 1861. At the age of twenty-six, John was in a sense coming back home to the place where he had spent his first years of life. His return to India brought back to him many pleasant memories. He also realized that his wife would have to make many adjustments to her new land, and he remembered the impoverished circumstances in which the Scudder family had lived much of the time. When he saw the dire straits in which his brothers were living in India, many emotions swept over him. Like his father, he was known to be impetuous and ready to speak his mind. He knew that the missionaries had written a letter asking for a raise in salary. He believed that the missionaries needed a raise in salary and believed that the board should act on their request.

Not long after his arrival, he sent to Philip Peltz, corresponding domestic secretary of the Board of Foreign Missions, an angry, personal letter in which he stated his position. He began by stating that he remembered that before leaving the United States, Peltz had told him that it was important to have communication with

---

[15] *Minutes of the General Synod, RCA*, 1850, 107.
[16] "AAR," 1861, 8.

missionaries and that one should be free to speak and write "heart to heart." Scudder then went on to write:

> Every day's experience has tended to strengthen me in the opinion that we cannot live on our salaries....I have at times almost wished myself at home on this account....It seems to me that one of two things must be true: either the Board did not believe the statements given in the letter written by all members of the Arcot Mission; or the Board does not feel willing or will not support its missionaries. If the former be the case, is not the Committee duty bound to recall all the members of the Arcot Mission who signed that letter? And if that be the case, the sooner the Arcot Mission is recalled, the better it will be for all of them individually....To be compelled to get down on their knees almost, and beg the committee for the sum of two hundred rupees to enable them to live, they feel to be humiliating in the extreme.[17]

The impertinence of the newest, youngest missionary did not please Peltz. According to the rules of the Board of Foreign Missions, all correspondence with the mission and the missionaries was to be made available to the executive committee of the board. The letter was shared, and the executive committee took firm and immediate action to help the new missionary understand the importance of respect for authority. It voted a motion of censure, "Resolved that the Committee have heard this letter with pain and mortification and cannot but regard its trifling as unworthy of the position of a Christian teacher who know the necessity of rules of government."[18]

John Scudder was deeply hurt by the response. The Arcot Mission at that time had a rule that all correspondence with the board should be shared with all members of the mission. John had not shared his letter with the mission because he had intended it to be a personal, private letter in which he shared his opinions and feelings "heart to heart," as he understood Peltz had suggested. He felt betrayed by

[17] John Scudder, Jr., to P. Peltz, September 11, 1861.
[18] Board of Foreign Missions Executive Committee action, January 8, 1862.

Peltz, who had submitted it to the executive committee. He was not sure whether he should stay in India. Since his letter had now become an official piece of correspondence, he shared it and the reply with the other missionaries.

Now the other missionaries had their dander up. They did not intend to allow one of their brethren to be trampled in that way. In their minds, the response of the executive committee raised several matters of principle. First, they objected that a private letter of a new missionary had immediately been shared with the executive committee. Second, they affirmed that the executive committee had gone beyond its authority. In pronouncing "censure" and stating that John Scudder had written in a way "unworthy of a Christian teacher who knows the necessity of rules of government," it had assumed to itself ecclesiastical authority that in Reformed polity belongs to a classis rather than to a board. By the words "Christian teacher," the committee had clearly meant to censure John Scudder as an ordained minister, something only a classis had the right to do.[19]

In forming both a mission and a classis, the Arcot missionaries had put into place their understanding of the quite separate roles each had to play. The action of the executive committee in censuring John Scudder, Jr., had in the minds of the Arcot Mission confused the roles and allowed the committee to usurp the role of the classis. They were in total accord with what Rufus Anderson had written when he gave approval to the distinct role the Reformed Church was to play in mission in the Arcot area. With regard to the respective roles, Anderson had written:

> As to having the mission regarded as a reformed Dutch
> Mission, in the same sense with the Amoy Mission, there is
> no objection to such a thing. You know it would give the
> Dutch Reformed Ecclesiastical bodies no control of the
> mission whatever. You are aware, too, that it is one of our
> principles of belief that churches formed among foreign

[19]Arcot Mission members to the Executive Committee of the Board of Foreign Missions,
    June 20, 1863.

nations should not be subjected to the ecclesiastical rule of any bodies, whether voluntary or ecclesiastical in the United States....[20]

Jared Scudder was in the United States at the time, so he and the executive committee discussed the matter. He asked that the committee erase from its record the vote of censure and stated that John would retract his letter, as John had indicated he was ready to do. The committee, however, was less agreeable. It insisted that John make the first move, but the Arcot Mission refused to let John do so. The missionaries were not going to let a committee of laymen on the board pass judgment on one of their number.

Two years passed, with exchanges of correspondence but no retreat on the part of the executive committee. In 1863, all of the Arcot missionaries resigned in protest against the executive committee's pre-empting for itself an action that they insisted was the prerogative of a classis. They also stated that they intended to appeal to the General Synod for a ruling on the correct interpretation of the church's constitution on the issue.

This action by the members of the Arcot Mission brought to the fore a set of issues about the roles and interrelationships among the Board of Foreign Missions, the Classis of Arcot, the Arcot Mission, and the General Synod of the Reformed Church in America. These issues did not go away as time went on. On the contrary, they became more complex. Specific issues arose from time to time. Who has authority to assign a missionary to a specific task? Who has authority to recall a missionary from the field or to refuse to allow or permit the missionary to return? What is the relative power and authority of each body with regard to financial matters? In the twentieth century, following the merger of the Classis of Arcot in the South India United Church in 1906, what is the relation to be between mission and church and between church and church?

In the case of John Scudder, most of these issues remained for the time being unresolved. The Board of Foreign Missions refused to

20 Rufus Anderson to John Scudder, May 21, 1853.

accept the resignations of the members of the Arcot Mission. It affirmed its right to have taken the actions it had, because it believed that General Synod in making the board its agent had delegated that right. It denied that resignation was the way to deal with a problem such as this.[21] It also appealed to the missionaries to recognize that the worst possible course was to take this matter to the General Synod. That course would only bring the mission in India into question and could mean that all their work here had been in vain. The board affirmed that it had only the good of the work in India and the Arcot Mission in mind:

> Resolved that this Board, believing that they are moved solely by a proper respect for their own established rules, by a tender regard for the Arcot Mission, for our Church and for the great interests of the Kingdom of Christ which are involved in this most trying difficulty, do most earnestly entreat the Mission and every member of it, to review their proceedings in the light of the explanations embodied in this paper which are the only true and authorized interpretation of the action of the Board.[22]

By this time, the participants in the case seem to have been exhausted by it. No further actions were taken. The mission did not appeal to the General Synod. John and Sophia Scudder remained in India until their deaths. Three of their children and several of their grandchildren also became missionaries in India. The missionaries continued in their work. The issues about roles and relationships would reappear in one way or another for a hundred years.

---

21 Both the Board of Foreign Missions and the members of the Arcot Mission were undoubtedly aware that all of the missionaries in China had firmly resisted the order of the General Synod to form a Reformed Church Classis in Amoy and that in 1863 they had stated that if the synod insisted on it, they should all be recalled since they themselves would not form the classis. If the missionaries had insisted on following through on their appeal, the whole foreign mission program of the Reformed Church in America would have been at stake in 1863, while the nation was going through the crisis of the Civil War.

22 Board of Foreign Missions Executive Committee action, January 8, 1862.

The Heidelberg Catechism and The Bazaar Book

Throughout the twentieth century, missionaries and Asian and African churches have often been criticized for their lack of attention to developing contextual or indigenous theologies intimately related to the culture within which the people live. Included in such criticism has been a negative attitude toward the use of catechism books developed in the age of the Reformation. Reformed Church missionaries in India opened the door to such reproach by using the Heidelberg Catechism as their basic textbook next to the Bible itself. In its first annual report, the mission clearly stated how it intended to carry out its it basic instruction in the Christian faith.

> The education of our Praeparandi class, from which we trust God will give us teachers, catechists, and preachers, is to be carried on and completed in the vernaculars. They all learn two languages. When the missionary is not absent on preaching tours he daily instructs them in the Scriptures and Systematic Theology. Taking the vernacular Bible, and the standards of our Church, as exhibited in that admirable compendium of Theology, the Heidelberg Catechism, we intend to train them to think and reason and express themselves in their own tongues.[23]

The Heidelberg Catechism was the basic document used not only in the schools, but also in the life of the congregations, since Reformed Church order required that the points of doctrine included in the catechism be considered in preaching at least once in a cycle of four years. Andrew Sawyer reported in 1873 that in Gnanodiam, "Besides the Sabbath services, daily prayers, morning and evening, with instruction in the catechism, have been maintained." In the same report, Samuel Sawyer, catechist, states that in Sattambadi, "Divine service with preaching is held every Sabbath. On these occasions the people assemble with eagerness

[23] "AAR," 1854, 5.

and joy. Those that cannot read, recite from the Sweet Savors of Divine Truth, those who can from the Heidelbergh Catechism."[24]

In view of the fact that the Heidelberg Catechism remained in such wide use through the decades, we must pause to consider what it teaches and the extent to which it related to the culture of the Indian world. The first thing to note is the basic method and structure of the catechism. Its teachings are presented in a series of 129 questions and answers, beginning with the question, "What is your only comfort in life and in death?" The answer, one of the longest and most complex in the catechism, is:

> That I belong—body and soul, in life and in death—not to myself but to my Savior, Jesus Christ, who at the cost of his own precious blood has fully paid for all my sins and has completely freed me from the dominion of the devil; that he protects me so well that without the will of my Father in heaven not a hair can fall from my head; indeed, that everything must fit his purpose for my salvation. Therefore, by his Holy Spirit, he also assures me of eternal life, and makes me wholeheartedly willing and ready from now on to live for him.[25]

The remainder of the catechism covers those areas of Christian faith and life that have through the ages been considered to be most important. The three longest sections cover the Apostles' Creed, the Ten Commandments, and the Lord's Prayer. There is also a section on the nature of faith, the two sacraments, and church discipline. Thus, in using the comparatively brief Heidelberg Catechism as its basic instructional book, the mission enabled the believers in India to enter the ecumenical tradition of the whole church as mediated through the Protestant Reformation.

The catechism was taught in the believer's own language, whether that be Tamil or Telugu, with the intent also that believers should be "taught to think and reason and express themselves in their own

[24]"BFMR," 1873, 22-23.
[25]"Heidelberg Catechism," in Gerrit T. Vander Lugt, ed., *The Liturgy of the Reformed Church in America* (New York: The Board of Education, RCA, 1968), 461: Q and A 1.

tongues." Thus the hope was expressed that concepts originally expressed in Latin and German and known to Arcot missionaries through the English language would now also serve to edify the Indian church. Since missionaries had been translating the Scriptures and Christian literature for more than a century previous to the establishment of the Arcot Mission, the Reformed Church missionaries did not have to develop their own lexicons for translation purposes, but they used the Christian theological vocabulary already available to them. That vocabulary and idiom was deficient in many ways and was to become known as "Christian" Tamil or Telugu.

As we soon shall see in our review of *The Bazaar Book,* the Arcot missionaries were aware of the need to relate the Christian message more intimately to the theological language of the Hindu people. Nevertheless, they regarded the clear questions and answers in the Heidelberg Catechism as a good beginning point to help the new believers to a better understanding of the basic teachings of the faith as formulated in the Apostles' Creed, the Ten Commandments, and the Lord's Prayer.

The opening section of the catechism (Q and A 2-22) was fundamental to the way in which the missionaries presented the claims of the Christian faith. Q and A 2 sets forth the outline of their presentation:

> Question: How many things must you know that you may live and die in the blessedness of this comfort?
>
> Answer: Three. First, the greatness of my sin and wretchedness. Second, how I am freed from all my sins and their wretched consequences. Third, what gratitude I owe to God for such redemption.
>
> Questions and answers 3-9 then go on to state that while the law of God requires us to love God above all and our neighbor as ourselves, we are by our fallen nature inclined to hate God and our neighbor. Answer 10 states that God must punish those who transgress the

law and sin against God. Questions and answers 11-18
then teach that in our sinfulness we owed a debt to God
that is so great that only God can pay it, yet it must be
paid by the human sinner. Thus only a true mediator
who is both fully divine and fully human could wipe out
the debt. "Who is this mediator who is at the same time
true God and a true and perfectly righteous man? Our
Lord Jesus Christ, who is freely given to us for complete
redemption and righteousness" (Q and A 18).

In questions and answers 3-18, the Heidelberg Catechism teaches
a doctrine of atonement for sin which was first formulated in this
basic form by St. Anselm in the twelfth century AD in terms of
honor and reworked by the Protestant Reformers in terms of law.
Through the centuries the church has taught the meaning of Jesus'
atoning death and resurrection through the use of a variety of
metaphors, such as redemption from slavery, victory over Satan
and death, or being the true sacrificial offering. It has recognized
that no one metaphor is adequate to the full scope of the atoning
work of Jesus Christ. The Heidelberg Catechism, like many of the
leaders of the Reformation, gave full priority to the "Anselmic"
formulation of the doctrine of the Atonement. As we shall learn
later in this chapter, the first generation of missionaries in the
Classis of Arcot insisted that all of its members must hold firmly to
the Anselmic doctrine of the Atonement.

According to the Anselmic doctrine as reformulated in the
Heidelberg Catechism, the founders of the Arcot Mission taught
that all human beings as descendants of Adam are inclined by their
very fallen nature to hate God and their neighbors. They have
broken the law of God and are subject to the penalty of eternal
death. The only hope for any human being is that Jesus Christ as the
only Son of God died on the cross as a substitute for us, making a
"vicarious atonement" for sin. Therefore, it is essential that
individuals come to faith in Jesus Christ and thereby be united with

Christ in order that the righteousness of Christ may be counted or "imputed" to their credit for their salvation.

In the theological schools where the founders of the Arcot Mission had studied, the Anselmic doctrine was often contrasted with the teachings of the medieval scholar Abelard. He was understood to have taught a "moral influence" doctrine of the Atonement, which meant that Jesus died to show the love of God to human beings who in seeing his example would love God and their neighbors in return. The Scudders believed that the moral influence theory underestimated the depth of human sin and also failed to emphasize the uniqueness of Christ in that there could also be other great examples of the love of God for human beings.

While using the Heidelberg Catechism as a basic textbook for the instruction of the members of the church, the Arcot missionaries in their evangelistic preaching and literature distribution among Hindus searched for language which would communicate the meaning of the gospel and bring them to faith in Jesus Christ. When Henry Martyn Scudder's health became such that it was necessary for him to reside in the hill station of Coonoor out of the heat of the plains, he was commissioned to write tracts that would communicate in the language of the Hindus. To that end, he sought to become familiar with some of the Hindu scriptures and especially with the rich tradition of the Tamil poets of previous centuries. He had already in 1855 produced a series of tracts in the Tamil language. That series of thirteen was bound together in one volume under the title, *The Bazaar Book,* and it provided material for use in preaching as well as for distributing when they visited bazaars. It was translated into English by his Henry Martyn's brother Jared and published by the Religious Tract and Book Society in Madras in 1869.

Several of the thirteen tracts bear titles with Hindu terms, such as *The Guru, The Sastra,* and *Mantras.* Scudder regularly quotes with approval from Hindu scriptures and the Tamil poets and follows by showing that the truth contained therein is illuminated more fully and often corrected in some way by the gospel message. Following the method of Paul in Acts 17, he urges his hearers or readers to recognize that their own poets point them in the direction of Jesus Christ. We can take note of a few examples of his procedure.

The first tract in the English edition of *The Bazaar Book* is entitled "The Guru."[26] This tract begins with the affirmation, "'All men everywhere agree in acknowledging and affirming their need of our guru.'[27] We need a Guru because our stay in this world is not permanent, because we are destitute of knowledge, because we are destitute of merit, and destitute of pure joy. The saintly poets recognize this. The *Tiru Kural,* a book of sayings resembling the biblical book of Proverbs, says, 'The glory of this world may all be summed up in saying, that he who was born yesterday died today.'" On this, Scudder comments, "This is only too true. Our body is destined to death and decay. Not so, however, the soul, which resides within it. That is deathless, eternal. When the body dies, the soul will be forced to leave its tenement, and passing away, seek some other place beyond the bounds of this world."[28]

After further interaction with the poets on the theme of the Guru, Scudder moves to show that the Guru in the full sense of the word is Jesus Christ. We quote at some length to show how the theme is developed. Scudder begins by quoting the Hindu saint Agastya:

> "Approach, Oh my soul! And worship the self-existent and eternal God, the Illuminator of the universe, who having in the twinkling of an eye created this vast world, and placed thereon perfect men, afterwards himself appeared upon it as its incarnate Guru, lived in it as an ascetic without family relatives or pomp, practiced religious austerities, established the school of his loving disciples, and finally returned to the eternal abodes of heaven."

26 H.M. Scudder, trans J.W. Scudder, *The Bazaar Book* (Madras: The Religious Tract and Book Society, 1869). The pagination in the book is separate for each tract. Most of the tracts are approximately sixteen pages long.

27 "The Guru," *Bazaar Book,* 1. It is important to remember that *The Bazaar Book* was first written in the Tamil language, which is Hindu in terminology. In the English translation there is a considerable shift in the direction of Christian overtones, which would not have been there for the Hindus who read it in Tamil.

28 Ibid.

Is there indeed such a Guru as this one of whom Agastya sings? Yes there is one, and only one. Jesus Christ is that Guru. Sinful Soul! Meditating on Him, pray these words, "Oh Thou Eternal Guru! Take possession of me, in such wise, that my soul, my body, and my all may be entirely and for ever thine.[29]

The second tract, *The Sastra,* deals with the relation of the basic scriptures of Hinduism, the four *Vedas,* to the Bible. The four Vedas include a huge amount of material in a very ancient and terse form. The very sounds of the Vedas were sacred and had to be recited precisely. Thus the Vedas are essentially untranslatable from the Sanskrit. The Vedas are holy and not to be read or heard by everyone. Scudder quotes the *Manava Dharma Sastra,* "The three-fold Veda is not a thing (intended) for the ears of women, of Sudras, or of the twice-born who also have their caste,"[30] to show the contrast with the Christian scriptures that are given for everyone. In contrast, the "true Sastra is none other than the Christian Veda. This Christian Veda is within such a compass, that all can easily read it through. Its nature is such, that it can be readily translated and published in every language of every country in the world. It is written in prose so simple, that all persons can read it without difficulty."[31]

Two of the tracts are directed against idol worship. The Tamil poet Pattanattu Pillai is quoted concerning true worship.

"No longer will I adore chiseled stones, nor plastered images fashioned to resemble the Deity, nor copper idols polished with acids. I have clearly demonstrated, that true worship consists in fixing firmly in one's mind the two feet (of the divine Being) which glitter like fine gold. (Therefore) I desire nothing more."[32]

Scudder's comment reads, "Idolatry is not worship. Heart worship alone is true worship."[33] He was aware of another poet who had

[29] Ibid., 9.
[30] "The Sastra," *Bazaar Book,* 17.
[31] Ibid.,10.
[32] "Idolatry Sinful," *Bazaar Book,* 13.
[33] Ibid.

said regarding idolatry, "Vainly imagining such worship to be a sacred law of antiquity, they, by practicing it, lose heaven and fall into a burning hell."[34] He made a passionate appeal to turn from idols and to embrace Jesus Christ.

> Oh People! Cast away your worthless idols. Accept the Lord Jesus Christ, the all powerful and all-loving Saviour of the world, as your God, your soul's friend, and your sin-destroyer. Embrace His holy religion. If you do so, you will by His grace attain to the transcendent joys of heaven. If not, you must inevitably fall into the flames of hell.[35]

The foregoing passages are sufficient to indicate that the Reformed Church missionaries found within the Hindu and Tamil poets many passages and concepts which indicated the nature of true religion. The discovery of many such concepts would not have surprised them. They found passages in the Bible that indicated that God "has not left himself without a witness in doing good" (Acts 14:17, NRSV). The Belgic Confession, one of the standard confessional statements of the Reformed Church, also taught them that God can be known by a general revelation to all people as well as by special revelation.

> We know him by two means. First, by his action of creating, sustaining, and directing the whole world, seeing it is before our eyes as a beautiful book, in which all creatures, great and small, are as so many letters that give us to *see the invisible things of God, namely, his eternal power and deity,* as the Apostle Paul says, Romans 1:20. All these things are sufficient to convince men and leave them without excuse. Secondly, to his glory and our salvation, he makes himself more clearly and fully known, (so far as we need to know him in this life), by his holy and divine Word.[36]

[34] "Idolatry Ruinous," *Bazaar Book,* 9
[35] "Idolatry Sinful," *Bazaar Book,* 12.
[36] "The Belgic Confession" in Vander Lugt, *Liturgy,* Art. 2, 433.

On the basis of their theological tradition, the Arcot missionaries were free to appreciate whatever truth and beauty was present in Hindu thought and life as well as to be critical of its deficiencies. Because they believed that God had never left any people without some revealed knowledge of the truth about the will of God, they could speak with positive valuation of whatever truth they found in the Hindu tradition.

In their zeal for evangelism, however, their natural tendency was to focus on the worst aspects of what they heard, especially in the early decades of the Arcot Mission. John Scudder, Sr., in particular, was inclined to report the worst in Hinduism. He accused Hindus of lacking basic honesty in the British courts of law and of being especially quarrelsome. He attacked practices of child marriages, oppression of widows, refusal to allow child widows and any widow the right to remarry, female infanticide, *sati,* and temple prostitution among other degrading customs.[37] In the first half of the nineteenth century, the British colonial rulers and the missionaries had an equal interest in portraying Hinduism in the worst possible light and therefore highlighted such abuses, especially to their publics abroad.

Hindu Reform Movements in the Nineteenth Century

The colonial rulers and the missionaries were not the only ones who saw the abuses going on in India. After 1820, a number of Hindu reform movements were established. The first and best known of these is the Brahmo Samaj, begun by Ram Mohan Roy (c. 1774-1833), who had become associated with the work of the Scottish missionary, Alexander Duff. The movement toward reform actually began, however, prior to his relationship with missionaries. Even as a child he had become dissatisfied with Hinduism as he saw it being practiced. It seemed to him resistant to change, decadent in its idolatrous and superstitious practices. Once or twice he was banished from his father's house because of his outspoken criticisms.

---

[37] Scudder, *An Appeal to Christian Mothers,* 20-40.

In 1816-1817, he published *Defense of Hindoo Theism,* in which he suggested that the worship of Krishna encouraged nudity, debauchery, and murder. The worship of Kali, he said, was characterized by intoxication, criminal intercourse, and licentious songs. He argued that Hindu idolatry destroyed the texture of society more than any other pagan worship.[38]

He began to have contact with the Serampore missionaries William Ward and Joshua Marshman in 1816 and was impressed with the teachings of Jesus, although he never severed his roots in Hinduism or the Brahmin caste. In 1820, he crowned his critical study of the New Testament with the publication of *Precepts of Jesus, the Guide to Peace and Happiness.* He stated that he believed these teachings more than any other to be capable of elevating human behavior and motivation. The Serampore missionaries did not appreciate his efforts; instead they attacked him for his separation of Jesus as teacher from his identity as Son of God and Savior in the gospels.[39]

Roy became active in the movement to prohibit *sati* and with Evangelicals opposed many other practices in popular Hinduism that he regarded as superstitious and degraded. He maintained that such things as idol worship and the low status of women in Indian society were not part of original and true Hinduism. On the contrary, they were aberrant corruptions that had entered into the society partly through previous foreign conquests. Original Hinduism, he believed, was a pure, tolerant monotheism, which, if Indians would follow it, would permit India to appropriate the useful learning of the West for its own advantage.[40] Ram Mohan Roy's attempt to reform Hinduism can be seen as the first in a tradition that continued for the next century through persons such as Rabindranath Tagore, Vivekananda, M. K. Gandhi, and Aurobindo. They declared that the corrupt elements were not

[38] French and Sharma, *Religious Ferment,* 22.
[39] Ibid., 22-23.
[40] Embree, *Utopias in Conflict: Religion and Nationalism in Modern India* (Berkley: Univ. of Calif. Press, 1990), 144.

integral to the Hindu religion. They also asserted that all religions have a common core of truth, so there is no need for conversion to another religion. Roy thus was one of the first of those who lay the groundwork for the Indian secularism in the national constitution, which does not deny the claims of religion but asserts that there is truth in all religions.[41]

In 1830 Ram Mohan Roy supported Alexander Duff's desire to open an English-language school in Calcutta and paid the rent for the hall in which the classes were held. He encouraged his Brahmin friends to attend the courses in the curriculum of English education. He opposed the British Orientalists who favored Sanskrit-based education, saying that the Sanskrit "system of education would be the best calculated to keep this country in darkness, if such had been the policy of the British legislature."[42] Shortly thereafter, he went to England to speak in support of the reform legislation that was passed in Parliament in 1833.

The circle in which Roy moved organized the Hindu reform movement, the Brahmo Samaj,[43] which stimulated many of the

---

[41] Ibid., 44.

[42] French and Sharma, *Religious Ferment*, 25.

[43] The first people to attempt an indigenous interpretation of Christ in India were neither missionaries nor Indian Christians but leaders of the Brahmo Samaj. "It is important to note that the origins of Indian-Christian theology can be located in the context of the intense popularity and the extensive influence of the Brahmo movement. Thus, the agenda for Indian-Christian theology was set by caste Hindu (mainly Brahmin) intellectuals" [Sathianathan Clarke, *Dalits and Christianity: Subaltern Religion and Liberation Theology in India*, (Delhi: Oxford Univ. Press, 1998), 37]. In the early twentieth century a number of Christian thinkers, including A.S. Appasamy Pillai, P. Chenchiah, V. Chakkarai, and A. J. Appasamy sought "to harmonize Hindu and Christian theologies as the authentic expression of a truly indigenous Church community....not into a new syncretistic religion but into a Christianity which is simultaneously faithful to the *scruti* and yet culturally 'at home' in India" (ibid., 38-39). Although *The Bazaar Book* represented a point of view quite different from the Indian Christian thinkers of the early twentieth century, it provided encouragement to their position that for the Christian faith to become indigenous in India it was necessary to give primarily emphasis to intellectual dialogue with Brahminism. S. Clarke has pointed out that in doing so, the Christian thinkers were, in fact, in alliance with the upper castes of India and not taking seriously the local indigenous Dravidian "Pariah" culture. "Theology, thus, was done from the perspective and for the welfare of the caste Christians by drawing from their religious and cultural brahminic traditions....the reflective and

educated Hindus to rethink their social and religious doctrines. Although the Samaj was attractive to many, its outright rejection of idolatry went too far for many Hindus. In 1864, the Veda Samaj was founded in Madras. It accepted the theistic ideals of the Brahmo Samaj but was careful to remain within the borders of Hinduism. It stated that marriage and funeral rituals were matters of routine, destitute of all religious significance. Its recruits promised gradually to abandon all caste distinctions, to tolerate the views of strangers, to abstain from polygamy and child marriage, and to campaign for widow remarriage. The Veda Samaj agreed to use the vernacular languages and to encourage the study and use of Sanskrit "by means not calculated to promote superstition."[44] The Veda Samaj did not have a long organizational life in Madras, but it did serve to reinforce efforts at reform within Hinduism.

The efforts at reform introduced by Arumuga Navalar of Jaffna (1822-1879) were located much closer to the Arcot area. Navalar became well acquainted with some of the work of the American and English missionaries in Jaffna. His writings in excellent Tamil were published in Madras and Jaffna at a time when John Scudder and his two older sons were serving in those areas in the 1840s and 1850s. We will examine briefly his career and arguments against Christianity in order that we may have a greater sense of the nature of the opposition which Arcot missionaries would meet in the towns where they preached.

Arumuga Pillai, his original name, belonged to a high-status caste known as Vellalas, a class that along with Brahmins had produced most of the Tamil literary elite for centuries. He grew up within the Shaiva[45] culture of southern India. In the seventh century A.D., the

critical construals of the vast majority of its constituents were not brought into the discursive arena. In so doing, it invalidates and repudiates the culture and religion of the Dalits ["outcastes"] (ibid., 40).

[44] Kenneth Jones, *The New Cambridge History of India: Socio-religious Reform Movements in British India* (Cambridge: Cambridge Univ. Press, 1989) III, 1, 164.

[45] The "Shaivites" chose to worship God in the form of Siva (or Shiva), one of the three major gods alongside Brahma and Vishnu. The Shaivites were especially concerned to follow the path of religious devotion, in contrast to those who gave primary emphasis

Shaivites had been favored with many deeply religious and gifted Tamil poets, a number of whom were quoted with approval by Henry Martyn Scudder in *The Bazaar Book*. At the time of his birth, Protestants from England and America had established stations in nine villages on the Jaffna peninsula. John Scudder was living in one of those villages. From their base in those villages, they waged vigorous campaigns to convert Hindus and Muslims to Christianity.[46]

At the age of twelve, Arumuga entered a Christian mission school to study English. He did so well that he was asked to stay on at Jaffna Wesleyan Mission School to teach English and Tamil. The missionary principal, Peter Percival, asked him to serve as his own Tamil assistant, to assist him in writing and editing treatises and hymns and, more importantly, in translating the prayer book and the Bible. Arumuga worked with Percival from 1841 to 1848, during the eight years in his early manhood when he was wrestling with the question, What does it mean to be Hindu?[47] During his years with Percival, he also came to a good knowledge of the Christian scriptures and Protestant liturgy.

Severe tensions arose between Shaivites and Christian missionaries after 1828, when the American Missionary Seminary at Batticotta decided to teach the Shaiva scripture, *Skanda Purana*, in their school. The decision to teach this work angered the Tamil Shaivites, who doubted that Christians would use it in a sympathetic way. Within the seminary, the Tamil instructor, a Hindu, refused to teach it on the grounds that the book was one of the most sacred in the country and that it should be taught only in sacred places where the accompanying ceremonies would be performed along with the teaching. The seminary proceeded to have it taught, however, by a

to the way of religious wisdom or way of religious action. Because their poetry was filled with profound sentiments expressing love of God, it was not difficult for Henry Martyn Scudder, who knew the experiential piety of Puritan and evangelical Christianity, to find parallel sentiments to be quoted in *The Bazaar Book*.

[46] D. Dennis Hudson, "The Hindu Renaissance Among the Tamils," in Kenneth Jones, ed., *Religious Controversy in British India: Dialogues in South Asian Languages* (State Univ. of New York Press, 1992), 29.

[47] Ibid.

senior student. A portion of it was translated from poetry to prose, thus stripping it from its ritual context and laying it bare for what Hindus regarded as "profane" study. The seminary was pleased with the results, although the study was soon discontinued. It reported, "Enough, however, was read to convince all who would reflect, that the book is filled with the most extravagant fictions, many of which are of an immoral tendency, (just as the Bible says,) 'for the people will walk every one in the name of his god.'"[48]

In the midst of the controversy, two long, anti-Christian poems appeared in Tamil in Jaffna, entitled *Kummi Song on Wisdom* and *Abolition of the Jesus Doctrine.* The events in Jaffna encouraged Hindus in Madras to circulate polemical literature as well. In about 1841, a Vellala Hindu in Madras published a condemnation of the Bible entitled, *The Misunderstanding of Veda.* In that same year, two Tamil Christians at the American Mission Seminary launched a Tamil periodical, the *Morning Star,* with which the editors intended "to fill the educational gap between ordinary Tamils and Europeans, 'imitating the Europeans in the improvements they have made by such means.'"[49]

The editors also took efforts to translate the Bible and distribute it among Tamils. They were confident that those who read the Bible would see the truths, choose them, and reject evil. They persistently challenged Catholics, Muslims, and Shaivites to open their sacred books to public scrutiny and judgment. When they did not do so, the only conclusion that could be drawn was that their scriptures were too weak to withstand such scrutiny.[50]

In September, 1842, more than two hundred Hindu men gathered at the Shiva temple in Jaffna to make plans to open a school to teach Shaivism. At this point, Arumuga entered the scene with letters to the editors of the *Morning Star* to report this event. He explained what the founders meant when they said, "Christian doctrine is

[48] Ibid., 30.
[49] Ibid., 31.
[50] Ibid., 32.

doctrine fabricated by the missionaries." He said that though he was a Shaivite, he read the Bible regularly, but in doing so began to have some questions about it. He signed himself anonymously as "The lover of good doctrine who is a son of a Shaiva."[51]

His first question had to do with the striking parallels he noticed between the liturgies of the temple in Jerusalem and the temples of Shiva in Sri Lanka and India. He asked what the differences were between the rites and ceremonies of the Shaivites and those of the Bible. Therefore he wanted to ask this question.

> The Israelites who were chosen by God as his own children believed that the Lord who dwelt in the ark made of wood and who lived between the cherubims had bestowed grace upon them. The Shaivas believe that God dwells in the image. They (the Israelites) made a sanctuary for the worship of God. The Shaivas build temples. The Israelites worship Cherubim and the bronze serpent. The Shaivas worship the images made of gold, and silver. The Israelites had shew bread and wine in their sanctuaries. The Shaivas keep fruit as prasade. The Israelites had incense. The Shaivas have it too. The Israelites burnt heifer and took its ashes for their use. The Shaivas use ashes from the dung of a heifer. [52]

He asked whether the Shaivites were not in their worship closer to the Israelites in the Old Testament than was the Christian worship introduced in Jaffna by the missionaries. Since God in the Bible had said that the rites and ceremonies of temple worship were to continue forever and Christ and the early Christians had gone to worship in the temple, how could the missionaries abandon such worship? One could not say that the Shaivites were ridiculous in their temple worship without also ridiculing the Old Testament and Jesus. Therefore Protestants were inconsistent in their understanding

---

51 Ibid., 33.
52 Ibid., 33-34.

of the Bible. "Protestants need not give up their path and follow Shiva's, he maintained, but they did need to see that on the basis of their own scriptures they had every reason to respect the Shaiva path and to leave it alone."[53]

Arumuga Navalar wrote many commentaries and other works in exposition of Shaivism and is regarded by many as the "father" of Tamil prose. His most effective weapon against Christianity was something of a training manual for use in opposition to the missionaries, entitled, *The Abolition of the Abuse of Shaivism,* printed in 1854. It was widely used in Sri Lanka and Madras. It was reprinted at least twice in the nineteenth century and eight times by1956. In the booklet, he shows that the missionaries had not bothered to study Shaivism in its own terms, and that their publications had attacked only their false understanding of it. He maintained that the Shaivite hymns proclaim that it is a great sin for Shaivites to sit back and accept such abuse.[54]

The Hindu Tract Societies

Hindu reform movements encouraged Hindus to develop defenses and new self-respect in the face of attacks by foreigners and missionaries. In the last half of the nineteenth century, organized forms of opposition to missionary preaching came into being, often using methods familiar to missionaries, such as street preaching and literature distribution. Jared W. Scudder published an article in 1888 in which he discussed the significant and widespread movement known as the "Revival of Hinduism." He commented that, for a time, the natives of India had regarded the efforts of missionaries with "mixed apathy and contemptuous amusement," because they assumed that nothing would ever come of such foreign preaching and teaching. With the growth of the church and the pervasive influence of Christianity, however, they were becoming alarmed.

[53] Ibid., 35.
[54] Ibid., 45.

They grew zealous in "buckling themselves to the task of averting threatened calamity."[55]

Scudder reported that a Hindu Preaching and Tract Society had been organized in Madras. Its intention was to send missionaries everywhere to preach the gospel of the Vedas. Committees were to be formed to warn people against listening to the foreign preachers. Tracts and books in defense of Hinduism were to be scattered throughout the land. The society had plans to establish branches in all the large towns of the Madras Presidency and to employ paid agents to go into the villages. Their tracts were no less spirited than were the Christian tracts. Scudder gives a translation of a paragraph from one of them, including the following lines:

> How many thousands of thousands have these padres turned to Christianity and keep on turning? How many hundreds of dear children have they swallowed up? How many more have they cast their nets? How much evil is yet to come upon us? If we sleep, as heretofore, in short time they will turn all to Christianity without exception, and our temples will be changes into churches....It is because of our carelessness that these strangers insult our gods in the open streets during our festivals....We must therefore, oppose the missionaries with all our might. We must not fear them because they have white faces, or because they belong to the ruling class.[56]

The Hindu Preaching and Tract Society was well organized and effective in breaking up meetings and opposing the work of Christian Indians and missionaries alike. Carman Scudder provided lively details concerning the society's activities. We will follow his description of two such accounts. Several missionaries and Indian associates "sallied forth to preach in a nearby village." They took with them the new curiosity, the "magic lantern," and set up their

---

[55] Jared W. Scudder, "The Revival of Hinduism," *Mission Field,* October, 1888, 24.
[56] Ibid., 25.

equipment in the bazaar area with the intention of showing their Christian pictures at 8:30 p.m. Soon a crowd of fifteen hundred people gathered for the occasion. He reports what happened next in some detail.

> Things went smoothly enough for a while, and the Gospel was poured in on them like hot shot! Sebastian, the Catechist of Tindivanam, spoke most eloquently. In the midst of an impassioned application of the truths connected with the picture of the "Brazen Serpent," a stone fell almost at his feet, then another, and then a scene occurred perhaps not very unlike that described in Acts 19:23ff.[57] The word, "Govinda," being substituted for the expression used in verse 28. "Govinda" is the name of one of the heathen deities. This uproar was occasioned by certain members of the Hindu Tract Society, who made "no small stir." Tindivanam is one of the most heathenish places in our Mission, and had only recently been visited by the Tract Society men, who had abused Christianity until some of the heathen residents themselves protested. Of course, our preaching was stopped, and though we went on again, some more stones, one of which fell with great force upon a man's head near the screen, convinced us that we had better leave that night. On the succeeding Tuesday and Wednesday nights, however, we showed the lantern again in another place, and were unmolested, a goodly number sitting quietly and listening....[58]

A more complex account of the Hindu Tract Society was provided by E. Carman Scudder three years later. His account

---

[57] Acts 19:23-32 describes the riot that occurred in Ephesus when Paul and his companions preached there. Verses 28-29a read, "And when they heard these sayings, they were full of wrath and cried out, saying, Great is Diana of the Ephesians. And the whole city was filled with confusion..." (KJV).

[58] E. Carman Scudder to Henry Cobb, April 29, 1890. Henry Nitchie Cobb served as secretary of the Board of Foreign Missions, 1883-1910.

provides insight into the anxieties of parents who placed their children in Hindu girls' schools, as well as into the nature of the Hindu Tract Society opposition.[59] The account begins with a magic lantern exhibition in the Hindu Girls' School in Arni. The building was crowded with parents and friends of the school children. A number of pictures of Bible stories were shown. One of these was the miracle of the feeding of the five thousand people by Jesus using just five biscuits and two fish. The story of the feeding was told beautifully by a Hindu girl who was a student in the school. When she was asked how such a great miracle was possible, the girl immediately said, "Why, Jesus is God and of course He could do it." This caused a considerable disturbance, led by a young man, and resulted in the closing of the magic lantern exhibition that evening.

Within a short time, a rival school for Hindu girls was opened across the street and a public proclamation was made that if any of the girls were allowed to attend the mission school, the parents would be ostracized. The result was that almost all the girls left the mission school. The source of the opposition was the Hindu Tract Society, supported locally by several Brahmin lawyers and government officials. A Brahmin preacher was also hired specifically to preach against the work of the mission and to try to stop Christian street preaching.

The establishment of the Hindu Tract Society in 1887 proved to be effective throughout the 1890s in interfering with or drawing attention away from Christian meetings, often by organizing rival meetings and processions. The civil authorities established a number of rules to maintain order. One such rule was that rival Hindu and Christian preaching teams had to remain at least forty yards apart.[60] During the time of the great Hindu festival in Punganur in 1891, the Christians went forth to preach the gospel and managed to gain large crowds especially because they also had a bicycle and "baby organ" with them as added attractions. The Hindu Tract Society

[59] E. Carman Scudder to Henry Cobb, May 20, 1893.
[60] "BFMR," 1891, 51.

organized their own preaching band to counteract the Christian efforts.

> For three days the claims of Christianity and Hinduism were proclaimed through every land and street of the town. The Hindu party usually followed ours, and endeavoured to remove the "evil impression" made. The bicycle always collected a good crowd, and the "baby organ" quieted it, while the magic lantern at night drew large numbers of people together in the courtyard of the palace, the Rajah's band playing in the intervals. An amusing incident may here be mentioned. Our Hindu friends thought something must be done in the way of a counter attraction of our bicycle and "baby organ." Thereupon they procured an accordion, the player perched upon a wall, and when we commenced our "one finger exercises," over which our music teacher exercised so much patience in former days, the accordion bellowed forth with great enthusiasm.[61]

The Hindu Tract Society was particularly active in publishing tracts. For example, in 1889 it published eleven tracts, usually in editions of ten thousand. After the turn of the century, their attention turned to other issues.[62]

The Controversy with Joseph Mayou

While organized opposition to evangelistic preaching and Christian literature distribution was growing among the Hindus, an internal dispute broke out between Joseph Mayou and the other missionaries. Joseph Mayou had been assigned to India in 1858. After completing some time studying the Tamil language, he and his wife, Margaret, were assigned to live in Arni. His accounts in the Arcot Mission Annual reports are clear and incisive. On reading his accounts, one comes to appreciate his dedication, enthusiasm for evangelism, and

[61] Ibid.
[62] Jones, *Socio-religious Reform Movements,* 163.

faithfulness in caring for those who are in the process of becoming Christian. When the villages of Sattambadi and Gnanodiam became Christian, he and Margaret moved to that area in order to be closer to them. They were susceptible to the diseases in that area, however, and after eighteen months they moved back to Arni for reasons of health.

As an evangelist and pastor, Mayou was a true success story. The mission station at Arni served a very large field, stretching to the southernmost border of the mission area, beyond Tindivanam. In 1869, it had the largest number of occupied and unoccupied villages,[63] with twenty-one congregations located in seven different townships. The strain of overwork was beginning to tell. His reports for 1869 and 1870 show signs of increasing impatience and tension. In the account of his work for 1870, he told of having had responsibility for building eight churches and schoolhouses. He had opened work in six new villages and made six evangelistic tours. In the course of the tours, he and his assistants had made 21 encampments, visited 601 villages, preached to 24,799 people, and distributed 1,974 books. It had also been a year of drought, which meant an increased need to assist people in days of hunger.[64]

Moreover, there had been over two hundred converts from Romanism and heathenism. One man, A. Anthony, a convert from Romanism, was beaten by his father, even though Anthony was over forty years old. His wife and children were taken from him, and he was driven from his house. Mayou had placed a catechist in the new village of Nungatoor. Other villages desired instruction as well, but there were no funds or people to send to them. The need was urgent. He repeated several times his plea of the previous year for help, for the workload had increased. "I trust that the Mission and the Board will soon see their way to place a missionary at Tindivanam

---

[63] An "occupied village" was one in which a teacher and school or a catechist had been placed; an "unoccupied village" was one in which there may have been Christians but there was no teacher or catechist.
[64] "BFMR," 1869, 26; 1870, 20.

to work the whole field."[65] This report with its plea is particularly poignant because it appeared after Mayou had left the field.

When one reads Mayou's 1870 report in light of what he wrote in 1869, one feels the stress behind his words. In 1869, he had reported that ninety new converts had come in the previous year, and that forty of them had returned to their previous religion. In the village of Vellambi there had been a number of lapses, and the blame fell on the reader in charge, who was under Mayou's supervision. Mayou also felt the need to defend himself because he had refused to take his turn in the hill station of Coonoor for three or four months as the other missionaries had agreed to do. Then come words of complaint about what he believed to be the neglect of the southern area of the Arcot mission.

> The absence of the Missionary from his field for three or four months often leads to great disaster. Constant supervision is necessary for the direction of the helpers as well as the Churches. Some of the helpers become very remiss in their duties during the absence of the Missionary. The ablest among them had to be dismissed last year from service altogether, and others had to be removed to other places for dereliction of duty or bad conduct. The fact is we need more Missionaries to work the field....Policy as well as necessity *demands* that one Missionary be placed there [in Tindivanam] at once.[66]

The other missionaries did not heed Mayou's plea, for they and their wives were all under very heavy loads. They too had been pleading with the Board of Foreign Missions for more missionaries and more funds for the work. They had also become impatient with Mayou because he had seemed less than cooperative in agreeing

65 Ibid., 1869:26-27.
66 Ibid., 1868:20.

move to another station when they had wanted him to do so. They were tired of hearing him raise questions about mission policy.[67]

The stressful situation in which all the missionaries labored exacerbated tensions that would issue in the Mayou's return to America. But the heart of the breach lay in real differences between Mayou and the others concerning mission policy and theology, as well as mission and classis authority. The controversy was recorded in an exchange of letters. Mayou stated his position in his letter of resignation to the secretary of the board dated April 13, 1869; his accompanying letter to the secretary of the mission on the same date; and his letter to the secretary of the Arcot Mission dated May 13, 1869. The other missionaries responded with a letter to the Board of Foreign Missions, September 16, 1869, and with the action of the Classis of Arcot, November 26, 1869.

The correspondence clearly indicates that Joseph Mayou had for a number of years spoken in less than fully respectful language to his colleagues. His words and demeanor irritated the others, who came to regard him as a young upstart among men of long experience. They resented a sentence in one of his letters, in which he implied that the Scudders always took a united front against him on matters of assignment and policy. He had written, "It is a genuine proof that if I differ from one, I differ from all; that if I touch one, I touch all."[68] In making this comment, Mayou touched a sensitive point. He implied that the Arcot Mission was a family mission, which was exactly the fear that Rufus Anderson had expressed in refusing to permit John Scudder, Sr., to become a member of it.

Beyond the personal dynamics, however, deep issues resided— issues that touched the very heart of the threefold work of the Arcot Mission. The first to emerge looked like a very small issue, but it served to raise larger questions. The Arcot Mission and the Classis

---

[67] W. W. Scudder, J. W. Scudder, J. Chamberlain, S.D. Scudder and John Scudder, Jr., (hereafter W.W. Scudder, *et. al.*) to the Board of Foreign Missions, September 16, 1869.
[68] Ibid.

of Arcot held the doctrine of rest from labor on the Sabbath in very
high regard. Mayou agreed with his colleagues on this point and had
disciplined a number of villagers for Sabbath breaking. But many of
his villages were far from his home, so late on Sunday evenings he
had traveled home instead of remaining overnight in the villages.
Such travel would have required those with him to do some work
carrying equipment or tending carts and animals. The other
missionaries insisted that this was a violation of the Sabbath and
passed a rule to the effect that no one should engage in travel before
Sunday midnight.[69] When Mayou objected, two powerful members
of the mission remarked to him that "if one cannot agree to rules,
one should withdraw." They claimed that every missionary should
make "conscientious submission" to the rules of the mission.[70]

The call for "conscientious submission" touched a crucial point
in the relationships among the missionaries as well as in the church.
Missionaries constantly had to make decisions and rules about each
other's work assignments, official correspondence, fund raising,
family circumstances, personal health, and personal privileges. The
question of the extent to which a missionary was bound to submit
to rules made by the majority of the mission members was not
resolved in this first major controversy within the mission. The
issue would arise constantly throughout the history of the
involvement of the Reformed Church in India.

The second issue raised by Mayou concerned the fundamental
policy of the mission only to open vernacular schools, and those
only for the children of Christians. Mayou disagreed with this
policy, and early in his years in India he had broken with it by
establishing a small school for children of his Hindu workers at the
mission station. Moreover, he challenged the policy that no English-
language education should be given. W. W. Scudder, in advocating
for the position that if one could not follow a rule, one should
withdraw from the mission, had stated that "if the mission should

introduce English into the Schools," he would withdraw from the mission. His statement left the implication that, if someone was in opposition to the present policy, he should leave.[71]

Mayou raised a third issue by calling into question the rule of the mission that new converts had to break caste by eating with all others regardless of caste, and that they must cut off the "kudumi," or top knot, and the sacred cord that symbolized membership in a higher caste. He objected to this policy on pragmatic grounds, saying that new Christians could not be expected to become mature all at once. Many people in his area would have been ready to accept Christ and become members of the church, but the consequences of breaking caste and thereby cutting their social and family relationships were too heavy. He pointed out that churches in America do not apply this rule to white people who do not accept "Negroes" into their congregations. So long as this rule—along with the rule forbidding English-language education—was applied, there would be very few higher-caste Hindus among the converts. That in turn would mean that the church would draw members only from the lowest income group and would never be able to support itself. He also objected on theological grounds, saying that the church did not have the right to place additional rules on converts beyond the basic affirmation of repentance for sin and faith in Jesus Christ.

A fourth issue arose out of Mayou's concern about the mission's policy of placing a paid teacher in every village in which there were three Christian families. On the basis of his experience, this practice erected an expensive system that the board would not be able to sustain and that would never result in a self-supporting church. The

---

[71] Mayou to J. M. Ferris, April 13, 1869. In 1961, Donald A. McGavran would advocate that in starting new churches and accepting converts, one should make a distinction between the work of "discipling" and "perfecting" and thereby refrain from requiring new converts to accept immediately all the Christian morality of the church but rather assist them to grow into the faith. He stated that one must recognize that there is a "homogeneous" principle operating when people enter into the church [*The Bridges of God: A Study in the Strategy of Missions* (London: World Dominion Press, 1961), 94-102].

other missionaries may well have agreed with him, but like Mayou they did not see any alternative. As with many other questions raised in the mission, this one did not go away. Indian Christians and several missionaries raised this issue again the twentieth century.[72]

Finally, Mayou called into question the right of the classis to install an ordained minister to be the pastor of a church without having received a call from the congregation. The practice arose in a situation in which ordained missionaries were stationed in towns according to the needs of the work of the mission. Having been stationed there, the classis would then dissolve the relationship between the church and the previous missionary in that place and then proceed to install the newly stationed missionary to be pastor of the church as well. Mayou correctly pointed out that this was contrary to Reformed Church order. He implied that the Classis of Arcot had acted improperly in interfering with his pastoral relationships in Arni by appointing another missionary there. The other members of the mission recognized that Reformed Church procedures were not being followed carefully, but they insisted that the mission situation had not been adequately taken into account at the time the church order was written.[73]

It is not surprising that the Arcot missionaries suggested to Mayou that the time had come for him to consider withdrawing from the mission. His challenge to their rules and their authority went too deep. In some ways he was ahead of his time, for within two years, after the arrival of Josephine Chapin and Martha Mandeville, the mission would somewhat reluctantly accept the presence of Hindu girls' schools. In challenging the right of the mission and the classis to make rules requiring "conscientious submission" by all the missionaries, he threatened the high priority for mutual accountability so essential to mission work in the nineteenth century. In raising questions about the financial burdens of placing employed men in the villages and about the placement

[72] Mayou to F. M. Ferris, April 13, 1869.
[73] W. W. Scudder, *et. al.*, to Board of Foreign Missions, Sept. 16, 1869.

of ordained ministers, he attacked policies for which neither he nor the other missionaries had alternative answers.

But most basic of all was his questioning of mission's requirement that new Christians must immediately break caste. Although the missionaries had many criticisms of abuses in Hindu religion and society, their fundamental objection to Hindu religion was really twofold: idolatry and caste. They were not ready to compromise in any way on the matter of caste. On this point and Sabbath breaking, the missionaries had to stand together, or their ability to maintain discipline in the life of the congregations would come to an end. Therefore, although the other missionaries refused to make a formal statement to the effect, Mayou knew that he either had to state his acceptance of the principle of conscientious submission or leave. He chose to resign.

Nevertheless, the members of the Classis of Arcot were not yet willing to let Mayou leave India. They had one more item of business with him, which was the charge of heresy. Earlier in this chapter, we saw how crucial in the mission was the role of the Heidelberg Catechism and the Anselmic doctrine of the Atonement. We also took note of the conflicts in the United States between the Old School and New School Presbyterians. Before he would be allowed to leave India, Mayou had to answer charges that he held a heretical view of the atoning work of Jesus Christ.

Suspicion that he was heretical had arisen one day when John Scudder was in the home of Mayou and saw on the table the book, *Christian Nurture*, by Horace Bushnell. This book emphasized the need to nurture children in the Christian faith, rather than seeing them as sinners in need of conversion as the evangelists and revivalists did. The idea was growing in influence in the field of Christian education in America. It also reflected the theological views of European liberalism and romanticism and as such was not appreciated by Old School or even New School Presbyterians. Many evangelical scholars in America regarded it to be based on an Abelardian "moral influence" doctrine of the atonement rather than an Anselmic "vicarious sacrificial" understanding. Scudder asked Mayou what he thought about that book. Mayou replied that although he did not agree with all of Bushnell's position, there were many good ideas in it. That was enough to raise the suspicion of heresy. Charges were brought to the classis, which proceeded to conduct a full trial, with a transcript over eighty pages in length.[74]

Mayou was declared guilty of heresy by unanimous roll call decision on five counts at the end of the trial. The members of the classis believed that they were meticulous in following proper trial procedures and that they had been more than fair to Mayou. The key statement of Mayou that proved the charge was, "The Old Testament sacrifices procured the forgiveness of sins without any knowledge of Christ by the worshiper."[75] The classis concluded that this statement meant that the atonement of Christ was not necessary for the Jewish worshipers of the Old Testament and thus called into question the universal need for Christ's atonement. In his defense, Mayou claimed that by this statement he meant that God, looking toward the atoning work of Christ, did not require such knowledge of Christ by the worshiper.

Mayou did not satisfy the classis with his defense, in light of the fact that he had spoken favorably of Bushnell's book. Mayou asked the Scudders, on the witness stand, whether they had actually read Bushnell, but the question was ruled out of order. Nevertheless, the impression was clearly left that they had not. Finally Mayou was declared guilty unanimously on all five counts against him. It was declared that he was guilty of heresy in praising Bushnell, by using incorrect theological nomenclature concerning the Atonement, in his view of the Old Testament sacrifices, in his expression of the idea of how Christ made satisfaction to God, and in whether the evidence against him had been proven true.[76]

---

[74] The full transcript is available in the Archives of the Reformed Church in America, New Brunswick, N.J.

[75] W. W. Scudder *et. al.* to Board of Foreign Missions, Sept. 16, 1869.

[76] Minutes of the Classis of Arcot, November 26, 1869:82-84.

Mayou was dissatisfied with the verdict. He maintained that, although there had been nineteen Indian ministerial and elder delegates and only four missionaries voting, the missionaries exercised almost total control of the proceedings. All of the Indian delegates from the various churches were employees of the mission and had missionaries as supervisors. He appealed the decision to the Particular Synod of New York and left India for the United States. In that appeal, he wrote that he had not received an impartial trial. His letter gives us some insight into the power of the missionaries over the Indian members of the classis, even though all were equal in rank and in their right to speak and vote:

> The five gentlemen [that is, the missionaries] of it had already decided the case themselves, as they had previously slandered me in their letter to the Board of Foreign Missions dated July 31, 1869, and therefore felt bound to make good their statements. They called upon their dependents, the native members of classis to sustain them in their decision. Rev. Z. John is the only one who is partially supported by a congregation; all the rest are Mission Agents. Any one acquainted with the Hindoo character knows that they will decide on the side of the strong, on the side that their salary comes from.[77]

On April 14, 1870, Joseph Mayou sent a message through the Board of Foreign Missions to the Particular Synod of New York in which he retracted his appeal, so the decision of the Classis of Arcot remained the final Reformed Church action in the case.[78] The Presbyterian Church accepted him as an ordained minister. Thereafter, he served for a number of years with distinction in a congregation on the mission frontier in Kansas.

---

[77] Joseph Mayou to The Reverend, the Particular Synod of New York of the Reformed Church in America, December 1, 1869.

[78] J. M. Ferris to Rev. P. D. Van Cleef, Stated Clerk of the Particular Synod of New York, April 22, 1870.

As they worked their way through the issues raised by Joseph Mayou, the members of the Arcot Mission and the Classis of Arcot found it necessary to examine once again their founding principles. In doing so, they reaffirmed their original positions concerning vernacular schools, teaching English, caste, the authority of the mission as distinct from the authority of the classis, the role of the classis as the body responsible for maintaining the theological integrity of the church, and the right of both the classis and the mission to make rules to which their members had to exercise conscientious submission. Nevertheless, the issues remained. Within two years there would be schools for Hindu children and within a decade Anglo-Vernacular schools using English. In the next several decades, even the missionaries most dedicated to the system of catechists and teachers in every village would be facing dilemmas about how to accept new villages for instruction. By the turn of the century, even the rule about caste would be somewhat softened.

Amending the Kudumi Rule

In the final decades of the nineteenth century, a number of members of the mission and the Christian church in the Arcot area began to have reservations about the rule that when new converts broke caste, the *kudumi* or top knot of hair on their heads, had to be cut off. Finally, in August, 1898, the mission agreed to hold a full-scale, formal debate on the subject. By this time, Carman Scudder was openly disregarding the rule, while J. H. Wyckoff was holding to it but advocating that it be changed.[79] Each side in the debate was allocated seventy-five minutes to present its case on a Thursday afternoon. Jared Scudder presented a paper in opposition to change and Wyckoff a paper on behalf of those who desired change. The discussion resumed the next day, and, "A very spirited, but courteous discussion consumed the afternoon."[80]

[79] It is probably coincidental but nevertheless interesting that Wyckoff in Tindivanam and Carman Scudder in Arni were located in the area that was the responsibility of Mayou in 1869.
[80] Jacob Chamberlain to Henry Cobb, August 22, 1898.

The item was also on the agenda of the Classis of Arcot, scheduled to meet the next day, Saturday. J. C. Pakianathan had been appointed to read his paper to the classis. He did so,

> presenting a very strong paper against yielding an iota to the kudumi. The paper on the other side was weak. A four-hour discussion followed. Every native minister took strong ground against its being allowed among the Native Mission agents, but some urged its relaxation in the case of the new adherents. No action was taken in Classis, as it was felt that it belonged to the Consistories. But the air was cleared by the discussion."[81]

The mission meeting was resumed on Monday. Finally the mission resolved to soften the rule against the kudumi by leaving the decision concerning baptism or reception into the church to the consistories, but it resolved that the mission would not employ anyone who wears the kudumi to be a Christian agent.

> RESOLVED that the Arcot Mission, while adhering to its historic position that it cannot employ as Christian Agents, nor entertain in its Boarding Schools pupils who wear the kudumi, leaves the matter of requiring the excision of the kudumi in every case before baptism or reception into the church, in the hands of the consistories, where it belongs.
>
> RESOLVED that the removal of one portion of the hair of the head, above the forehead, or the growing of any

---

[81] Ibid. It is of interest to note that a similar controversy was taking place in the same decades concerning whether a person who was a member of the Masonic Order could be admitted into membership in the Reformed Church in America. The General Synod in 1880 expressed strong disapproval of membership in oath-bound secret societies but voted to leave the matter to the consistories, without setting up new rules for admission to membership. For our purposes, the relative paragraph in the action is number 4: "Resolved, that this Synod also advises Consistories and Classes of the Church to be very kind and forbearing and strictly constitutional in their dealings with individuals on this subject, and that they be and are hereby affectionately cautioned against setting up any new or unauthorized tests of communion in the Christian Church" (*Minutes of the General Synod, RCA*, 1880, 335).

portion of the hair long enough to tie a knot, be considered a kudumi.[82]

All of the members of the mission present, with the surprising exception of Carman Scudder, voted for this resolution, which concerned how strict the church and mission should be about abolishing all signs of caste among them.[83] This shift in attitude would, in the twentieth century, be followed by broader moves to seek ways to relate to Indian cultural traditions, especially those not so intimately connected with the practice of caste.

Noah and the Vedas

The mission's action concerning the kudumi is indicative of its growing sophistication in understanding the nuances of Hindu religion. On furlough in 1896, Jacob Chamberlain delivered an address before the International Missionary Union in Clifton Springs, New York. In it, he holds firmly to the uniqueness of Jesus Christ as the crucial point of difference between Christianity and other religions. "This is the key: this son of God bearing our sin; this great high priest touched with the feeling of our infirmities; this God-man stretching his hand of love far down to us, to help us up. It is this that causes Christianity to stand out, among the world's religions, alone, without a peer or second."[84]

Chamberlain believed that the great religions of the world agree in many things, such as that the Godhead is one; that God is holy, good, and pure; and that humanity is in a state of sin and in need of purity and holiness. The difference is that "not one of the religions

---

82 J. Chamberlain to Henry Cobb, August 20, 1898.

83 A few years prior to the mission meeting in 1898, the father of Bishop A. J. Appasamy, while of high caste, became a Christian convert. Much interest was shown in his conversion, because he became a strong Christian leader and an effective evangelist among high-caste Hindus. He continued to wear the kudumi, to be a vegetarian, and to practice yoga in his meditation [cf. A. J. Appasamy, *The Gospel and India's Heritage* (London: Society for Promoting Christian Knowledge) 1942, 1-3].

84 Jacob Chamberlain, "Religions of the Orient: Their Beauties and Their Fatal Defects," (on file at the Joint Archives of Holland, Hope College, Holland, Michigan), 1.

of the world save Christianity, the religion of Jesus, furnishes any help *outside of ourselves* for the accomplishment of this stupendous task."[85]

He found much that is beautiful in the Vedas and other Hindu scriptures. The reason for this, he believed, was that in the time of Noah all human beings had the "divine oracles," which have continued to re-echo down the ages since that time. The Rig Veda can be dated "from near the time of Moses, in the upper table-land of central Asia, before all Noachian tradition had been lost, before man had wandered so far away from God" and therefore it contains, in the main, true ideas of God, of man, of sin, and of sacrifice.[86]

Chamberlain then goes into more detail about the truth he has found. In the *Rig Veda*, God is the creator, upholder, and controller of all. "May He not destroy us, He the Creator of the earth; He the righteous, who created the heaven; He also created the bright and mighty waters; Who is the God to whom we shall offer our sacrifice."[87] In the Vedic hymns, God is portrayed as the bountiful benefactor, omniscient, omnipresent, and eternal.[88]

Chamberlain was certain that God had not left himself without a witness. Human beings in every continent continued to be called back from their sinful ways. God's perfections and human beings' alienation were taught not only in the Vedas but also by the Tamil poet, Sivavakyar, who wrote, "Oh God! I once knew naught of what thou art, and wandered far astray. But when thy light pierced through my dark, I woke to know my God. Oh Lord! I long for thee alone; I long for none but Thee to dwell within my soul."[89]

Chamberlain said that the problem is not so much in what is included as in what is left out. There remains a chasm beyond which human beings cannot go. There is no way human beings can find

85 Ibid., 2.
86 Ibid., 4.
87 Ibid., 5.
88 Ibid., 4-5.
89 Ibid., 10.

the power within themselves to go farther. The only way to bridge the chasm is to accept the bridge which God has given, Jesus Christ, who is our high priest, our elder brother, the Lamb of God who takes away the sin of the world.[90]

In this address of Chamberlain, the shift from the polemics of the early decades to a more sympathetic understanding of Hinduism is apparent. By the end of the nineteenth century, the missionaries and the Indian Christians believed that Hinduism itself was moving in the direction of the Christian faith. It was becoming possible for the Christians to be more sensitive to the values in the ancient cultures and religious writings of India. At the same time, the evangelistic impulse that defined the self-understanding of the early missionaries had not been lost. Chamberlain put the message in words of invitation, in a whisper more than a shout,

> Come unto me, all ye that labor and are heavy laden, and *I* will give you rest," whispers Jesus; "For God so loved the world that He gave His only begotten Son, that whosover believeth in Him should not perish but have everlasting life."[91]

At the end of the century, the message was the same as it was in the beginning, but the tone was a little mellower.

[90] Ibid., 11.
[91] Ibid., 11.

6

The Growth of Institutions
and Dilemma of Self-Support

The Arcot Mission did not regard itself as a charitable institution. It believed that it was making known in India a message that was valuable to India. In biblical language, it was proclaiming the gospel of salvation in Jesus Christ, the pearl of great price. The congregations that came into being as people responded to the gospel could therefore be challenged as well as expected to bear any costs that were entailed by their needs for instruction in the faith and for pastoral leadership. The Reformed Church knew that for a number of years financial assistance would be required by new congregations comprised of village people living in extreme poverty, but it encouraged even the poorest to give something.

The parable of the widow's mite provided biblical material for many a sermon in India. Within a decade after the founding of the mission, the annual reports begin to provide information about sacrificial giving in congregations. Jared Scudder, in Chittoor, reported that a marked increase in the practice of stewardship had taken placed between 1863 and 1864.

> The members of the congregation are all poor. No one of
> them has an income of more than Rupees 14 a month; and

many barely contrive, in an almost miraculous way, to keep body and soul together on a pittance of a Rupee or a Rupee and a half a month. Yet from these depths of poverty, they have during the year contributed Rs. 57-3-1 to various benevolent objects. This sum does not include anything given by me or my family. The sums given in 1863 amounted to only Rupees 18-9-5….One member of the church gives his tenth regularly and systematically to the Lord. His example may be safely recommended to thousands of his brethren, who carry a whiter skin and a tighter purse.[1]

The basic policy for self-support was that the day must come when the Indian church would take care of its own expenditures, including the salaries of pastors and leaders of village congregations, as well as buildings and other supplies required for the life of the church. The costs for maintaining missionaries in India would remain the responsibility of the Reformed Church in America. While at first the mission would be responsible for the expenditures of the church as well, that responsibility was to be transferred to the church as soon as possible.

In one of the first moves toward developing a sense of financial stewardship in the church, some of the Indian leaders organized a benevolent society named the *Sahodara Sangam* (Band of Brothers) in 1867. The immediate object of the society was to minister to the necessities of those poor converts who required aid. They were often left in the most destitute of circumstances, renounced by their friends, dismissed by their employers, and with their property confiscated by others. The Sahodara Sangam assisted by providing small loans to enable the new converts to start over. The Indians

---

[1] "AAR," 1864, 26-27. In 1864, the exchange rate was fluctuating due to the American Civil War, but on average two rupees were about equal to one dollar. Thus the highest income of any member of the congregation was about seven dollars a month, or twenty-three cents a day. In 1861 John Scudder sent his angry letter about the low salaries of missionaries, who were then receiving a little less than $100 a month, or about $3.35 a day, and going into debt. The missionaries of that era were a thrifty group, so the board did not dispute his concern, though the tone of his letter was not appreciated.

themselves managed the fund. They contributed to it and sought contributions from others, including the missionaries. The Sahodara Sangam raised Rs. 1,550 in the first year.[2] No funds were ever appropriated to this society by the Arcot Mission. [3] The funds at the disposal of the society remained small, so the number of people whom it could help was necessarily limited. The society was important, however, because it increased the self-respect of the Indian villages who participated by giving them an opportunity to reach out with a helping hand to their brothers and sisters in need.

The missionaries remained ambivalent about how hard they should press the members of the churches to achieve self-support, given the impoverished condition of most of the believers. Developing a sense of stewardship was hard work and held little of the romance of mission. Carman Scudder, one of the missionaries most concerned for moving toward self-support, decided to write an article in 1894 to the supporters of mission in the Reformed Church, although he knew that his story would be less inspiring than those about tigers, opposition, or conversions.

> Many…are apt to look for the "romantic" and many others for the "profit and loss" sides, and to tell the truth, I haven't much to relate about either of those sides. The "romantic" was done with, at least in my field, before my time. I have never had any hair-breadth escapes or startling adventures, and my eloquence has never been sufficient to "melt an audience to tears" or cause them to renounce their heathenism on the spot! As to the "profit and loss" side, there is that certainly, but I hate to think of it. I don't believe our church cares much about it—so many souls for so many dollars…To be sure, they want results, not for their money, but for the Kingdom. So do we![4]

[2]"AAR," 1868, 6.
[3]"AAR," 1869, 8.
[4] E. Carman Scudder to Henry Cobb, October 2, 1894.

Scudder was stationed at Arni in 1894, the same station where, twenty-five years earlier, Joseph Mayou had written that the Arcot Mission policy of placing a catechist or teacher in every village with at least three families was too costly to be maintained. Scudder encountered the same problem with the expanding number of villages. He emphasized the importance of encouraging self-support and self-reliance from the very beginning of a congregation's life. He stated:

> The idea grows on me more and more each year, that the Home Church has been carrying the Mission Church too much. A thirty-five-year-old baby ought to begin to walk soon; more, I think than it does. In fact I have been so strenuous on this that my own field has not grown as much as I wish it might....Possibly I am in the wrong, but as a matter of fact I have not received several villages—that is, I have not enrolled them as "Christian" villages—because I think it right that they should begin to help themselves and the Mission from the very start, and I have been waiting for them to come to it! As a result I have one good sized village where there are two Helpers, whose houses have been supplied almost entirely—all but a total of Rs. 8 by the people themselves, and another large village the people of which have promised to build a school house and provide a house for a teacher.[5]

On the other hand, the emphasis on requiring self-support measures as one requirement for enrolling villages as "Christian" also raised the concern that sincere people were being inhibited from gaining the instruction they needed to grow into the faith. J.H. Wyckoff was a strong advocate for self-support measures; nevertheless, thirty-three years after his first arrival in India, he could still express doubt about the shift to institutional work and the pressure for self-support. In 1907 he wrote,

5 Ibid.

It is now several years since we have had any general movement toward Christianity in the villages, and it behooves us to enquire for the cause....The Missionaries are largely absorbed in the care of institutional work, and but little aggressive effort is being made in the villages, where we must chiefly look for growth. I am not sure but that we are making a fetish of self-support, to the neglect of personal evangelistic endeavour.[6]

Throughout the last three decades of the nineteenth century, various attempts were made to encourage people to contribute to the financial needs of the church. As attitudes toward some of the Hindu customs became less harsh, one of the more successful self-support efforts was the move to hold harvest festivals.[7] Throughout the earlier nineteenth century, missionary attitudes toward the Hindu festivals were negative. Such festivals attracted very large crowds, both of serious pilgrims and of people out for excitement and a good time. The missionaries were often appalled at what they saw going on. In great temple-car processions they saw idol worship, drunkenness, wild dancing, and sexual licentiousness. The noisy, carnival atmosphere of many festivals seemed far from true piety. The missionaries were also disheartened by the costs of holding such festivals and of the long pilgrimages people took to the festival sites to fulfill their vows.

In the last decade of the century, however, J.H. Wyckoff and some others agreed that Christian villages also needed festivals to encourage them in the midst of the tedium of their lives. Many of the Christians lived as minority populations in their villages and needed to feel themselves part of a larger Christian community. Wyckoff believed that the time had come to accept the Hindu tradition of festivals into the life of the Christian church.

[6] J.H. Wyckoff to Henry Cobb, October 23, 1907.
[7] For another report about the important role of harvest festivals, see David, *Reformed Church Missionaries*, 118-20.

The festival is as dear to the Hindu as a national holiday to a European. Yet, so much of religious significance pertains to them that Christians have to forego Hindu festivals. To supply this want and make it the means of uniting the Christians while stimulating their spiritual life, a Christian festival, combining athletics, prayer meetings, tamashes and street preaching was held in Tindivanam with promising results.[8]

The congregations in the Tindvanam-Gingee-Arni area gathered for the harvest festival in a small grove on the banks of the Gingee River, with 350 people present. Everyone remained overnight for the two-day meeting. It had been planned that all would bring their own food, but two well-to-do Christians followed an Indian custom that at festivals the wealthy should make food available for the poor, so they supplied good plain food for those most poor. Some of the people came twenty miles for the festival, the women carrying their babies and the men their two-day supply of food.[9]

During the days, lectures were given on hygiene, Christian thrift, and stewardship; on opposition to borrowing money and spending lavish amounts on marriages and funerals; and on spiritual growth. A collection basket was placed on a table, and young and old pressed forward to give their offerings, "the poor widow likewise casting in her mite." Then sports and recreation events were held, a display of fireworks began, and finally a magic lantern exhibition closed the first evening of the festival. The next morning, about 150 men climbed to the abandoned fort at the top of the hill "where earnest prayers were offered that the whole region might be speedily given to Christ. It was interesting and significant to hear the old fort that had so often resounded with the noise of cannon, ring with the music of gospel hymns."[10]

---

[8]"BFMR," 1894, 20. *Tamash* is a difficult word to translate. It refers to joyful celebrations complete with music, drums, processions, and good food, with a sense of excitement in the air. Village people especially enjoyed a tamash that broke the routine of their lives.
[9] J. H. Wyckoff to Henry Cobb, April 15, 1895.
[10] Ibid.

In the following decade, harvest festivals became a focal point of the life of the Christian community. These can perhaps best be described as a combination spiritual growth convention, market, and large family reunion lasting three or four days. The largest of these was held on the banks of the Ponnai River. This festival was attended annually after the harvest. Several thousand people usually came on the first day, with a smaller attendance thereafter because many people had to return to their daily work. The first day was the one in which, village by village, they brought their offerings. We gain a feeling for the event from a description written by Margaret Beattie. She wrote that after the morning devotional meeting, the presentation of the offerings in kind were brought and auctioned off under the shade of tamarind trees on the high sandy bank of the river.[11]

> And such a collection of goods to be disposed of—goats, sheep, chickens, a few calves, a young buffalo, cocoanuts, sugar cane, grains, vegetables, eggs, a few parrots, brooms, peanuts, etc., etc. Each village was taken in turn; the auctioneer was a teacher or native pastor and the buyers were principally the missionaries and the catechists and helpers. We bought bundles of sugar cane and bags of peanuts for our boarding school girls, bundles of brooms and lots of pumpkins.[12]

After the auction, an evening meeting was held, and then those who had to return home left the site. During the following two days, attention was given to congregational singing, lectures on various subjects, an evening procession with singing and torches to light the way, and a banner awarded to the village that had brought the largest offering. The final day ended with fireworks in a ceremony

[11] The Ponnai River looks like a dry bed of sand much of the year. It usually flows only in the rainy monsoon season, so the people from both sides of the river could easily arrive at the campsite. Shallow wells in the riverbed enabled people to draw clean water for their needs from the flow a number of feet beneath the riverbed.
[12] Margaret Beattie, *Mission Gleaner,* July/August 1903, 11.

attended by many Hindus as well, and a time of preaching for their benefit. "The coming together of these Christians once a year is a great thing for them. It is a change, they hear and see much that is new, and realize that after all the Christians are not such a feeble folk."[13]

In spite of the emphasis on self-support and the pride the village Christians realized in being able to bring the first fruits of their harvest to the festival, one cannot fail also to note how fully dependent the church was on the Arcot Mission for its financial support. The customers at the auction were the employees of the mission and the missionaries themselves. The missionaries were in a position to bid for the items in the auction because they needed to supply food and other materials to the children in the boarding school. At the end of the nineteenth century, the vast majority of the Christians were living at a meager subsistence level, working in the fields and their garden plots in the villages. Only those who were employed by the mission enjoyed receiving regular and almost equally meager salaries. In its 1906 annual report, which celebrates the seventy-fifth year of the founding of the Board of Foreign Missions, the Arcot Mission confessed its failure to achieve its goal of self-support.

> The term "poor Christian" has undoubtedly much delayed the development of self-support. It has taught the Christian to expect everything for nothing....For the first twenty years no return of contributions from the churches appeared in the annual reports....This has undoubtedly been the weak spot of the mission administration; but a study of the problems of Missions has led us to correct our mistake....Our Harvest Festivals have gone a long way to help solve the problem. Insistence on the people doing their share in the erection and repair of village buildings, is beginning to bear fruit.[14]

13 Ibid., 13.
14 "AAR," 1906, 2-3.

Self-support remained a vision for the future; harvest festivals confirmed the hope that the vision would one day become reality.

The Emergence of Medical Institutions

Medical missionaries have often enjoyed pride of place in stories of missionary heroes. Stories abound of how they performed almost miraculous acts of healing on deathly ill patients and how complex operations were done by lamplight with only the simplest instruments available. We read of their devoted service in times of plague at risk of their own lives. Such narratives can be found also in the letters and reports of the medical personnel in the Arcot Mission, and we will take note of several such events.

Nevertheless, the Arcot Mission did not understand itself to be a "medical mission," in spite of the fact that John Scudder, Sr., and six out of the first nine men to serve in the Arcot Mission were medical doctors. In its first half century, the mission never wavered from its original purpose of forming and developing a self-supporting, self-governing, and self-propagating Indian church. It stated its position once again in the 1906 Annual Report:

> The ultimate aim of all intelligent, well thought out missionary effort in all its departments of work is the formation and development of a self-supporting, self-governing, and self-propagating native Church. Any other object, such as merely acting as witnesses among all nations, or the conversion of individual souls to Christ, is inadequate and incomplete. To establish an indigenous Church, which shall grow from its own root, which shall be a living testimony to Christ, and worthily represent to the world the Christian ideal, is the object for which our mission stands.[15]

The missionary doctors in the Arcot Mission continued to believe that they were first called as missionaries to preach the gospel to those who did not yet believe in Jesus Christ. While they knew they

15 Ibid., 1-2.

had an obligation to use their medical knowledge for the welfare of the people among whom they served, they consistently followed what they understood to be the practice of Jesus, who refused to allow his healing ministry to assume priority over everything else. Jacob Chamberlain's reflections on this matter are typical of the other physicians as well.

> In the early part of the year, when the doctors had forbidden my going out touring and preaching in the villages, I determined to make use of my medical and surgical knowledge in bringing the villagers to us. From my first coming to Mudnapilly I had had frequent and earnest applications for medical and surgical treatment. These I had discouraged except in extreme cases. I now, after prayerful consideration, determined to devote certain hours each day to dispensing medicines to the sick. I could thus, while administering physical relief, tell them of the Great Physician who takes away the maladies of the soul....These have heard the great truths of the Gospel, and taken Tracts and Scriptures to many villages which would not otherwise have been reached.[16]

Chamberlain recognized that his own resources were inadequate to meet the great need in the Madanapalle area, so by persistent efforts he persuaded the government to establish a hospital in Madanapalle. Later, he was able to secure the establishment of another hospital at Palmaner, both of which he continued to oversee for years on behalf of the government.[17]

The first small shift in raising the priority for medical mission occurred when the mission recognized the great need for a hospital in Ranipet. Ranipet was three miles from Wallajapet, where Henry Martyn Scudder, in 1851, had opened his dispensary as the first Reformed Church missionary to locate in the Arcot District. In

16 Ibid., 24-25.
17 De Boer, *Story of the Arcot Mission,* 19.

1860, the mission approached Dr. Silas Scudder, asking him to come to India and start this great work. Silas had visited clinics in Europe to broaden his medical knowledge and then had settled down, like his father, John Scudder, Sr., to a lucrative practice in New York City. However, he could not resist the appeal of his brothers and sailed for India in 1860. Unfortunately, owing to the Civil War, the Board of Foreign Missions did not have funds for the hospital after his arrival there.[18]

Silas Scudder was naturally profoundly disappointed to learn that financial support was not available, after he had given up his practice in New York to become a medical missionary in India. One cannot help but sympathize with his plight as one reads his sense of abandonment:

> I have no money, no place in which to receive patients, no apothecary, and no medicines. Not one Christian friend has, during the past year, sent me pecuniary aid. I do not write, however, as one despairing. The Lord will not permit me to abandon this most important work. My heart is in it; my most earnest desire is to carry it on. I spent many, long, hard working years, and visited foreign lands for the sake of medical knowledge. The knowledge obtained, shall through no lack, on *my* part, go to nought. As a physician, I can preach the Gospel to thousands, whom I could not reach, merely as a *Minister* of the Gospel. I mean to have a dispensary, and I call upon the Lord's people to aid me in carrying out my intention.[19]

The Board of Foreign Missions in 1863 was still extremely short of funds and therefore not in a position to respond positively to Silas Scudder's plea. But there was another reason as well for the hesitation. In that year, the board was not yet ready to give a higher

[18] Dorothy J. Scudder, "The History of the Ranipet Hospital," in *A History of the Ranipet Hospital and A Survey of the Work at the Scudder Memorial Hospital* (printed in Ranipet, North Arcot, India, 1935), 7.
[19] "AAR," 1863, 33.

priority to medical mission service. It feared that establishing
hospitals and dispensaries would lead to ever larger outlays of funds
for such work, in contrast to the original idea that medical training
for ordained ministers would "give the medical Missionary such
simple means of administering to the physical ills of those around
him as might be necessary to procure an entrance for the truths of
the Gospel."[20] Since the Ranipet hospital that was to be established
under Silas Scudder's leadership was the first institution founded
that moved beyond the "threefold work" of the mission, we will
here follow the developments in the life of the hospital over the
next four decades.

Silas was persistent. The following year, 1864, he set forth his firm
opinion that the Lord was on his side in this matter. In light of the
fact that two of his brothers and Jacob Chamberlain were quite
satisfied to keep their medical work at the level of "such simple
means of administering to the physical ills of those around him" and
continued to plead with the government to open hospitals, it is not
surprising that Silas felt somewhat let down by his fellow missionaries.
And perhaps they were surprised that he was not ready to settle into
their mode of service. He wrote,

> The Lord will yet open the way. It is an object I cannot lay
> aside, feeling, as I do, its paramount importance. I am sure
> that the dignity, the whole status of the mission, would be
> greatly raised in the eyes of the native population of this
> country if a large dispensary and hospital were connected
> with it. Many of their fears, many of their foolish prejudices,
> can be overcome through this department of missionary
> labour. Friends cannot understand or appreciate this object;
> otherwise I should have more money than I need to carry
> on this work.[21]

---

[20]"BFMR," 1863, 11.
[21] "AAR," 1864, 33.

When the Civil War ended, the Board of Foreign Missions was finally able to appropriate $1500 (Rupees 3,100) for the hospital's work. Silas Scudder opened it in March 1866, in a rented building. Objections to its opening came from the civil dispensary there, under the charge of an apothecary who did not want competition. Rumors were spread that Scudder's object in coming was to force Christianity upon the people and that to accomplish that end he would stop at nothing. Allegations were made that he would injure their caste standing, interfere with their customs, mix unclean water with the medicines dispensed, employ the lowest class servants to wait upon patients and put up prescriptions, and that the local government authorities would be angry with those who went to the hospital.[22]

For a time the opposition was successful in persuading the poor and illiterate to refrain from attending the hospital. The higher and educated class of Indians recognized the superior medical services available and came for treatment, but the numbers remained small. At that point the mission encouraged by some Christian medical personnel in the government petitioned the Inspector General of Hospitals to close its dispensary in Ranipet and requested that "the whole district be delivered over to us." In making this request, they asked for no assistance of any kind from the government, but said that if any such help were to be offered, the mission would gratefully accept it. The inspector general hesitated, but asked the advice of the local government subcollector who advised in its favor.[23] On July 20, 1866, the government ordered that the petition be granted. Furthermore, one-half of the amount of expenditure formerly allowed to the dispensary would now be available to the hospital.

The government also made available in August a building that the mission used for the hospital free of rent until the new Scudder Memorial Hospital building was completed in 1928. It was a large building that had formerly been the government cavalry barracks

Scudder Memorial Hospital, 1928

and riding school and therefore was hard to adapt to the purposes of a hospital. On the whole, it served its new purpose fairly well until with the advances in medical care the requirements of a modern hospital made it thoroughly outmoded.[24] Soon the false rumors were overcome and the patient load rapidly increased.

Two years later, in 1868, the number of outpatients served for the year reached 21,170 and the number of in-patients was 12,000. Of the in-patients, 10,920 were supplied with food while 1,080 supplied their own food. Moreover, the patients welcomed receiving the Christian message. People came freely and filled the benches for the morning reading of the scriptures before treatment began. "They come to us freely, missionaries though we are; they hear our words, if not with belief, with seeming eagerness, and receive portions of Scripture and other books with avidity, very often of themselves asking for them."[25]

---

[24] S.R. Scudder, "The Building of Scudder Memorial Hospital, 1935," Golden Jubilee Souvenir (privately printed, 1973), 12.
[25] "AAR," 1868, 63.

The building was large enough to house sixty to eighty in-patients, but they could admit only as many as they had funds to care for, since no fees were charged to the patients. The government had cut back its subsidy from Rs. 193 per month to Rs. 172, so the number of patients had to be cut back to an average of 5-6 in-patients a day. "Sometimes we have had more than 40 patients at a time, all of whom were housed, fed, allowed the use of hospital clothing, blankets, bedding, and otherwise cared for."[26] Some additional financial help had come from the assistant district collector who gave Rs. 20 per month and a Hindu, V. Luchmia Naidoo, who gave a total of Rs. 185 during the year. He was a former student in the school in Madras led by Dr. John Anderson, the friend of John Scudder, Sr., and contributed in appreciation of what he had received from his education there.[27]

Silas Scudder also reported on surgical operations that he found particularly interesting because they were cases he was not likely to see in America where people had doctors closer at hand. One many had been admitted with an enormous hydrocele, or collection of serous fluid in the scrotum, on both sides. After the hospital built up his strength with a nourishing diet and tonics, he was operated first on the left side, where Scudder drew off 160 ounces or ten pounds of fluid. The next week they operated on the other smaller side and drew off only five pounds of fluid. After that a spontaneous cure took place and the man was perfectly well.[28]

When the hospital was opened Silas Scudder recruited five young men to be medical students under his tutelage. One problem was their lack of knowledge of the English language, that was necessary for them in order to read and write prescriptions as well as to read the textbooks. By the time the end of their second year had been reached, six works on anatomy, medicine, hygiene, surgery, and midwifery had been translated by other persons into Tamil. There were a few disappointments. One student had been dismissed. The

26 Ibid., 64.
27 Ibid., 65.
28 Ibid., 69.

other students had some conflict among themselves, but Silas Scudder was still hopeful for a good outcome for their studies.[29] Owing to their lack of knowledge of English and equipment, their progress remained slow. In 1870 they were still plodding through their studies, but the arrival of the books, anatomical and physiological plates, and skeletons purchased from a supplier in America the previous year was still awaited.[30]

The Board of Foreign Missions' fear that they would not be able adequately to support a hospital in India was substantiated in 1870 when it suffered a shortfall in anticipated income and had to inform the Arcot Mission that the annual appropriation had to be cut back by $5,000. Since the mission could not cut back easily or quickly in its pastoral and village work, there was nothing to do but close the hospital, in which event Silas Scudder would also return to the States. The government by this time had developed high regard for the work of the hospital and decided to assist in keeping the hospital open. It increased the monthly allowance, gave permission to draw medical supplies from the government depot and gave a grant to make repairs and increase the light in the operation room. The grant also made it possible to increase the accommodations for high caste patients and for the needs of the police. It also dug a well and provided some cots for patients.[31]

For the next fifteen years the hospital went through difficult circumstances as the resources of the Board of Foreign Missions and the Arcot Mission were strained to the limit. Another one of the cyclical financial crises in the United States meant that the Board of Foreign Mission would continue to be in debt. Poor health on the part of the missionaries added to the crisis in India. Silas Scudder had to leave India permanently in 1872 because of poor health. Dr. John Scudder, Jr. carried on the work of the hospital along with his evangelistic work with the help of one or two students trained by Silas. Nevertheless, for lack of personnel and finances, the hospital

29 Ibid., 66-67.
30"BFMR," 1870, 35.
31"BFMR," 1870, 34.

went into a measure of decline. For several years the government through the local county board met all the expenses of the hospital apart from the missionary's salary.[32]

The Board of Foreign Missions sent Dr. Henry Martyn Scudder, Jr., grandson of John and son of the oldest Scudder brother, Henry Martyn, Sr., to serve at Ranipet as the first missionary appointed exclusively for medical work. In his first year he doubled the number of in-patients and in his second year added a maternity department, that proved to be very successful in spite of the fears of many that Hindu and Muslim men would not permit their wives to go to the hospital in maternity cases.[33] He worked with great energy and soon was at the height of his popularity in the surrounding area. The dispensary that his father had opened more than two decades ago in Wallajapet was restarted and quickly gained great numbers of patients. In addition he began a traveling dispensary that he took out to the villages, accompanying the station missionary on some of his tours.[34]

Unfortunately, between the years of 1876 and 1880 the number of Reformed Church missionaries in India was very low, with only four ordained missionaries and one or two young women who were present along with Henry Martyn Scudder, Jr. During the famine years of 1875-77, Henry worked alongside his uncle John in the villages around Ranipet. John Scudder was heavily involved in doing whatever he could to relieve the sufferings of the people and Henry also busied himself with providing medical relief to the people in the villages as well as in the town. But after a couple of years it was discovered that during that period Henry had been speculating in rice with his private funds. He bought the rice at a comparatively low price and then hoarded it while waiting for a major rise in its price. Such practice was totally contrary to his calling as a missionary. It is difficult to understand how one

[32]"AAR," 1874, 10.
[33]"AAR," 1875, 8.
[34] Scudder, *The History of the Ranipet Hospital,* 9.

seemingly so dedicated to relieving human suffering could hold onto rice for a higher price while he saw people he served starving. His actions were also contrary to Board of Foreign Mission policy that strictly forbade members of the mission from making money on a private venture.[35]

The Arcot Mission demanded that the board remove him. Henry resigned and left for America. He had done nothing strictly illegal, but his conduct was not acceptable in the calling of a missionary. He was the only one of the Scudder family who can be considered to be a failure and had to be removed for misconduct.

With Henry's departure, the mission had no one to put in charge of the hospital and medical work in the area, so it handed over the work temporarily to the government's Local Fund Board. In 1883 Dr. Lambertus Hekhuis arrived in India as a replacement for Henry Martyn, but the Local Fund Board refused to give up the hospital. Two years later the Madras government prevailed upon the Local Fund Board to hand it back to the mission, while the Wallaja dispensary was given back in 1886.

Hekhuis was also an ordained minister who took a great deal of interest in the development of the broad scope of mission work. In that sense, he still belonged to the generations of medically trained persons who regarded medical work as one of their tasks, rather than their primary responsibility. The annual report that he gave for the Arcot Station in 1888 includes ten paragraphs, of which the medical paragraph is one of the shorter ones. The hospital work was still supported with the help of government funds.

Nevertheless, Lambertus Hekhuis was to be one who furthered the establishing of mission institutions whose scope was beyond the original threefold work of the mission. In 1886 he proposed to the mission that an "industrial school" be opened and that a class in rug-making be offered.[36] Such a school would require a teacher

---

[35] Dorothy J. Scudder, *A Thousand Years,* p. 152.
[36] John Conklin had suggested the need for a mechanic/carpentry/trade school two years earlier, but he was then still ahead of the mission (Conklin to Isaac Ferris, Feb. 22, 1884).

to instruct the boys and a plant and material to work with. To his
surprise, his proposal passed unanimously.

> The plan is to get a class of 8 to 10 boys, provide them with
> board, clothing, teacher and materials to work with to make
> rugs for which I hope to find a market in America....The
> reason for starting an industrial school is obvious. Our
> Christians are very poor, and often have no work to keep
> them busy for the whole year, so that a new industry will be
> a blessing to them in helping them on in the way of self-
> support. I proposed rug-making because I expect to find a
> ready market for these in America.[37]

The industrial school was opened in Arcot at the close of 1886
with a rug class. A carpentry class was added in October, 1887. The
rug class had six boys, three of whom went to day school half the
time. The carpenter class had eleven, some of whom went to day
school part of the time. The opening of the school required an
outlay of start up expenditures for materials. It was expected,
however, that in a short time the school would pay most of its own
expenses. Hekhuis also saw the opening of the school as an
opportunity for friends in America to participate in mission by
sending out tools, including machinery for circular and scroll saws
and a good wood lathe.[38]

This industrial school proved to be one of three such institutions
established by the Arcot missionaries. All of them began with the
idea of teaching young boys or girls a skill that would enable them
to enhance their livelihood while at the same time strengthening the
Christian church in its movement toward self-support. The hope
that the institutes would pay their own expenses would not be
realized. As we shall see, it often proved to be a point of considerable
irritation as the missionaries in charge found it necessary to defend
themselves for continuing to need subsidies from the mission to

[37] L. Hekhuis to Henry Cobb, September 4, 1886.
[38] "BFMR," 1888, 47.

Lewis R. Scudder

meet expenses. The three institutions were to play a very important role in the Arcot Mission area for a number of years.

Unfortunately for the Ranipet hospital and the industrial school, however, Hekhuis was bitten by his beautiful retriever dog in July, 1888, but it was only a scratch and little thought was given to it even though the dog died shortly thereafter. In September he came down with rabies and after a few days he died. Since a mission meeting had been planned for that time, most of the missionaries were present. His request for a final communion service was remembered in his eulogy. He said, "I want you to promise to give me communion tomorrow. You need not worry, I will take the cup last."[39]

In the year that Hekhuis died, Dr. Lewis R. Scudder, son of William Waterbury Scudder arrived in India, still loyal to the tradition of being both a medical doctor and ordained minister. With his appointment, the hospital finally came to enjoy stability and has continued its very significant service to the present day. He came to feel that the dual management of the hospital by the mission and the Local Fund Board was an arrangement unsatisfactory

[39] J. W. Conklin, "Dr. Lambertus Hekhuis," *Mission Field,* January, 1889, 26.

to both. From the mission perspective, the affiliation tended to secularize its religious work as well as hamper his management of the institution. In 1899 he succeeded in gaining agreement that the Local Fund Board would withdraw from the management and allow the hospital to become truly a mission institution. Assistance from the government would continue at about Rs. 2,000 per year plus the use of the government buildings.[40]

One condition in the transfer was that the Reformed Church in America would take over the balance of the costs of running the hospital that had previously been funded by the Local Fund Board. This required an annual appropriation of $2,000. At that time the board was still struggling with a serious debt and, throughout the 1890s there had already been a number of serious reductions in the Board of Foreign Missions appropriations to the mission. At the end of 1898 the mission had been struggling with how to cut back in its expenditures by 14.5 percent because of the reduction in appropriation for 1899. The fear of the early missionaries that the establishment of institutions would interfere with the evangelistic work of the mission had proved to be justified. Although all of the missionaries by this time had come to see the value of the hospital, a number of them were reluctant to allow any of the annual appropriation of funds to the mission be used for the work of the hospital. They continued to believe that the work of the hospital should be funded by sources within India.

The letter of L. R. Scudder to Henry Cobb, secretary of the Board of Foreign Missions, proposing that funds from the Reformed Church be used annually for the hospital was circulated to all members of the mission for comment. J. H. Wyckoff said that he agreed with most of Scudder's letter and the action of the mission in accepting the change in management pattern, but that he disagreed that the $2,000 annually should be granted to the hospital

---

[40] Scudder, *History of the Ranipet Hospital,* 9. See also L. R. Scudder to Henry Cobb, Feb. 22, 1899, for an 11-page letter detailing the negotiations the transfer to full mission control of the hospital.

for its work. He believed that the $2,000 could better be used for evangelism and village work. He further stated that Lew Scudder's work as a district missionary with the churches and in evangelism was even more valuable than his medical work. Carman and Jared Scudder agreed with Wyckoff. Henry J. and John Scudder sided with Lew. James Beattie asked whether it would be possible for the board to raise the money outside the regular budget. Jacob Chamberlain agreed with Beattie and suggested that a special group of interested persons become a "syndicate" of supporters, as was the case in support of the Arabian Mission that had been adopted by the Reformed Church in 1893.[41] The hesitation and even opposition shown by a number of the missionaries is a clear signal that the arrival of institutions requiring subsidy was still not a totally welcome development by all.

Henry Cobb acted decisively in the matter. He sent a cablegram stating that the board would consider the hospital a mission institution and take that point into account in making its annual appropriations. The movement toward establishing medical institutions as full and legitimate partners in the work of the mission now gained momentum. In that same year, Louisa Hart and Ida Scudder were putting forth their vision of a woman's hospital in Vellore, and the Woman's Board of Foreign Missions was showing great interest in the project. In September, J. H. Wyckoff transmitted to Henry Cobb the mission's action calling for the establishment of a woman's hospital in Vellore, with a capital budget of $8,000 and an annual appropriation of $1,500.[42] Three months later the mission learned that a gift had been received for a woman's hospital in Vellore to be named the Mary Tabor Schell Hospital, with annual appropriations to be granted by the Woman's Board.[43]

Two weeks later the mission treasurer, Henry Scudder, son of John Scudder, Jr., wrote a letter to Cobb expressing his utter dismay

[41] J. H. Wyckoff to Cobb, March 15, 1899, accompanied by the remarks by the others.
[42] J. H. Wyckoff to Henry Cobb, Sept. 21, 1899.
[43] J. H. Wyckoff to Henry Cobb, November 13, 1899.

Henry R. Cobb

that the budget appropriation for 1900 would once more be cut. It required a 43 percent cut in work funds. It "means not disaster but death; it is almost useless to remain here."[44] In agreeing to appropriation for the hospitals, the missionaries who were usually cautious about accepting new projects had obviously not thought through the impact on the budget as a whole. One can only wonder whether the winsome personalities of L. R. Scudder, Ida Scudder, and Louisa Hart had won them over too easily.

Jacob Chamberlain also wrote a letter stating that he had not realized the impact on the other work because of the large annual expenditure for hospitals. In light of the new budget cuts, he no longer believed that they could afford the hospitals or Voorhees College that has also recently become a responsibility of the

[44] Henry Scudder to Henry Cobb, November 29, 1899.

mission.[45] L. R. Scudder also was shocked by the implications for the budget of the additional financial requirements for the hospital. He wrote to Cobb asking that the board would please accept his offer to reduce or eliminate his own salary because it would be wrong to reduce the salaries of the native helpers without reducing the missionary force as well.[46]

The Increasing Number of Educational Institutions

Events in India always tended to move in parallel with those in Great Britain and the United States. The period 1850-1910 in the United States was one in which churches were establishing high schools or academies and colleges particularly in the Midwest. Within the Reformed Church in America, Hope College in Holland, Michigan, was established in 1866. The Pleasant Prairie Academy was opened in German Valley, Illinois, in 1894. Wisconsin Memorial Academy began instruction in Cedar Grove, Wisconsin, in 1900. The last two were closed prior to World War II. Northwestern Classical Academy was founded in 1882 and following World War II was upgraded to be a four-year college. Central College in Pella, Iowa, was founded by Baptists, and became a Reformed Church college in 1916. Thus an atmosphere was created in the Reformed Church that looked with some favor upon the growth of educational institutions in its foreign missions work.

Educational institutions grew in parallel with hospitals and clinics or dispensaries in the Arcot Mission. By 1910, the mission was offering a full range of educational fare, from elementary education to high school and junior college level for Christians, Hindus, and Muslims, plus theological seminary training and normal school training for men and women teachers. Boarding homes played an important role in its educational program. Offering such a range of educational opportunities required a change of mission policy as well as additional funds to support the programs.

[45] Jacob Chamberlain to Henry Cobb, December 13, 1899.
[46] L. R. Scudder to Henry Cobb, December 14, 1899.

We have already traced the change in policy regarding Hindu girls' schools and seen that by 1880 the mission had also accepted Anglo-Vernacular boys' schools at Vellore and Tindivanam. It had been possible to accept these schools because much of the cost of running the schools could be met by educational grants received from the government, while the initial grants needed from the mission were relatively modest. There was another factor at work as well. However much the mission would continue to give priority to evangelism, it was not possible for the long term to ignore the responsibility to participate in renewing the culture and building up the national welfare. Only through such participation could the church ultimately escape the charge that it was the bearer of a foreign religion.

J. H. Wyckoff, who at Tindivanam was the first to incorporate an Anglo-Vernacular school into the work of the Arcot Mission, had by 1878 come to the conclusion that there was much to be said for the position of Alexander Duff of the Church of Scotland, who opened English medium schools for high-caste Indians. As one who remained an enthusiastic evangelist, Wyckoff wrestled for a long time with the issues of the relation between his evangelistic purposes and his educational efforts. At a time when a number of the Arcot missionaries were still critical of the Church of Scotland Mission's priority of maintaining schools particularly for higher caste Hindu boys, Wyckoff began to advocate for closer cooperation with that mission. Eventually the Arcot Mission entered into partnership with the Church of Scotland Mission in support of the Madras Christian College, which became one of the leading educational institutions in India at the turn of the century. As he approached the end of the nineteenth century, Wyckoff was convinced that the original stances of the Arcot Mission and the Church of Scotland Mission were to be understood as complementary rather than mutually exclusive. After a visit to Madras Christian College where he had given a lecture, he contrasted the educational needs of that urban area with his work in rural areas.

There could be no greater contrast than between the work these [Church of Scotland] men are doing, and that in which I am engaged. Theirs is exclusively in English among the high and the noble; mine entirely in the vernacular amidst the outcaste and depressed. Both are equally essential and one rejoices that a broader view of foreign missionary effort than formerly prevailed, now admits the necessity of both branches of labor. As I stood before these young men and realized what possibilities lay before them, I was led to appreciate more fully the value of the educational work our Scotch brethren are doing, and to rejoice that through our college at Vellore we are now putting forth similar efforts.[47]

One of the things that often bothered missionaries, not to mention their supporters back in America, was the fact that on the whole comparatively few conversions took place through the work of the educational institutions. Wyckoff had come to appreciate the fact that the schools had to be evaluated in their Christian role as educational institutions, rather than on the basis of evangelistic results. After a meeting with the principal of Madras Christian College, Dr. William Miller, he commented,

"Dr. Miller's idea is becoming more and more to be accepted; that these institutions are a *help* to other forms of work rather than converting agencies. To make them aggressively evangelistic as in the days of Anderson would be to soon empty them and drive the young men into the Hindu and Government Colleges."[48]

[47] J. H. Wyckoff to Henry Cobb, October 20, 1898.
[48] J. H. Wyckoff to Henry Cobb, October 28, 1896. William I. Chamberlain correctly said of Miller, "No individual, not excepting Government officials, has had greater power in the moulding and directing of education in India in recent times.... A worthy successor of Dr. Duff, of Calcutta, and Dr. Wilson, of Bombay, Dr. Miller has long been Principal of the Madras Christian College, the most popular and successful, if not also the best equipped collegiate institution in all India"[William, I. Chamberlain, *Education in India* (New York: MacMillan, 1899), 90]. Chamberlain wrote these words in the same era that his missionary colleague Wyckoff was making his comments.

As we now consider the growth of educational work in the Arcot Mission in the last two decades of the nineteenth century, we will see how the view of Wyckoff won the day. The issue of the relationship between the educational mission, on the one hand, and the evangelistic mission, on the other, did not go away. Throughout the twentieth century, the tension remained, the issues at times becoming sharp and divisive.

It is important to understand the context in which the missionaries worked after 1880. Christian mission societies operating in India were encouraged to open schools by the comparatively generous grant-in-aid policy of the government, according to which schools received annual grants based on attendance and achievement. The Indian Education Commission of 1882 spelled out once again the three reasons for encouraging education.

> We have, moreover, always looked upon the encouragement of education as peculiarly important, because calculated not only to produce a higher degree of intellectual fitness, but to raise the moral character of those who partake of its advantages, and so to supply you with servants to whose probity you may, with increased confidence, commit offices of trust in India, where the well-being of the people is so intimately connected with the truthfulness and ability of officers of every grade in all departments of the State.[49]

Three reasons for British government support of India's educational system thus were shown to be raising the intellectual standards of Indians, developing their moral character, and training people to be good and loyal employees in the administration of the Raj. The Arcot Mission at times would find it difficult to meet the costs and personnel requirements when the government raised the standards of education. It was confident that it could develop moral character, although often disappointed when confronted by apathy or moral laxness on the part of certain teachers. Since the missionaries

[49] Quoted in Chamberlain, *Education in India*, 43-44.

believed that the Raj was on the whole helpful for the time being in India, they were not troubled very much by the third reason. In taking this attitude they found themselves in agreement with many educated Indians in the nineteenth century.

When the mission accepted Anglo-Vernacular schools, they also found themselves in agreement with the government policy that education should be placed within the reach of the great mass of people. As they began to establish and operate the whole range of mission schools, the missionaries recognized that, while the government allowed them considerable latitude, there were certain restrictions on their conduct of the schools. The basic rule for receiving a grant-in-aid had to be accepted.

> The system of grants-in-aid is to be based on the principle of perfect religious neutrality. Aid is to be given (so far as available funds may render it possible) to all schools imparting a good secular education, provided they are under adequate local management, and subject to Government inspection, and provided that fees, however small, are charged in them.[50]

The government was quite open to offering religious instruction in the schools. It did not hold to a rigid distinction between church and state as is the case today in the United States. Christian teachers and administrators tended to avoid direct efforts to bring students to conversion, instead allowing the teachings of the Bible and Christian teachings to work slowly in the minds of the students. The restrictions of the government were not the problem at this point so much as was public opposition to conversion and to the violation of parental rights that conversion could entail. When "Mrs. G." wrote to Kitty Scudder in 1888 asking how government restrictions affected what missionaries taught in the schools, Scudder answered in terms of the rigidity of the curriculum rather than in restrictions on religious teaching. She wrote,

[50] "The Summary of the Despatch of 1854," quoted in Chamberlain, *Education in India,* 45.

As far as the prescribed studies are concerned it is an incentive to both teachers and scholars. But it also cramps us in certain directions as we have to conform to certain rules. For instance, in the case of our girls, I should give them more fancy work, and different kinds of sewing than I can now do, as they must spend a good deal of time in learning to cut and make rapidly the miniature models required for the government.[51]

The generous policy of the government in providing grants to schools enabled the Arcot Mission to conduct a large number of schools at relatively low cost. In its fiftieth anniversary year report, 1903, its statistical chart shows that the mission was operating 161 day schools with 79 Christian male teachers, 77 Christian female teachers, and 113 Hindu teachers, of whom only three were female. The schools had a total enrollment of 6,623 students, of whom 1,315 were Christians and 5,305 of other religions, almost all Hindu. In that year there were 389 boys and 173 girls in the mission boarding schools. Most of the children in the boarding schools were Christians.[52]

In 1903, the schools had received as income Rs. 18,022 in fees from students and Rs. 27,697 as grants.[53] The total contribution of the Reformed Church for those schools in that year was about Rs. 24,000, of which about Rs. 10,000 was for the maintenance of the nine boarding schools.[54] When one compares these income figures with the total contribution to the self-support of the churches by Indian Christians in the amount of Rs. 7,065 for that year, the financial significance of the government and fee income becomes especially clear.[55] Moreover, most of the Christian teachers would also have been serving as leaders in worship and pastoral care in the

---

51 M. K. Scudder, "My Dear Mrs. G," *Mission Gleaner,* Nov./Dec., 1888, 3.
52 "AAR," 1903, statistics chart at end of report.
53 Ibid.
54 "BFMR," 1903, 109.
55 "AAR," 1903, statistics chart at end of report.

villages where they taught. Rather than the church supporting the schools, the schools enabled the mission and the church to sustain the life of Christian worship in most of the villages. In summary, the presence of the village schools receiving government grants enabled the mission to maintain Christian worship and pastoral care in the villages. At the same time, given the financial stress and deficits under which the board was functioning, this annual subsidy for education was a drain on the mission's ability to support other essential activities, especially evangelism. Supervision of the schools also occupied much of the time of the missionaries and thus diverted them from other work.

The Village Day Schools

The day schools and boarding schools functioned at a crucial point in the work of the Arcot Mission. When they fulfilled their purposes, the church gained a generation versed in a basic understanding of the Bible, trained in the principles of personal hygiene and social skills, and skilled in basic reading, writing, and arithmetic. When members of the mission looked back over fifty years, they affirmed the central role of village schools.

> These little schools, however crude, are not to be despised. The vast majority of our pastors, catechists, evangelists, and teachers laid the foundation of their education in them. The missionary as he visits the villages keeps his eye on the brightest boys and girls, and when they have made some advance in their education, selects the best for a higher course of instruction in the boarding schools.[56]

The village school usually was held in a simple, one-room building formed by four low mud walls with a thatched roof and a mud floor. Small windows in the walls and openings under the eaves admitted light and air. The furniture consisted of a plain table and chair or

[56] "AAR," 1906, 9.

bench for the teacher and a small box to hold books and slates for the children. The children sat cross-legged on the floor and often learned their letters by writing with their forefingers in the sand. The children often studied by reciting together out loud, which could bring forth a seemingly intolerable din. But one would be surprised at how well students could repeat their lessons when called on to recite individually. Much time was given to religious instruction. A simple catechism was taught to the younger scholars, and the older ones learned Scripture texts and stories.[57]

Conditions in the villages schools remained very much the same over the years. In the annual reports, the same words are used repeatedly about progress in some villages, teacher apathy in others, and greater interest or lack of support among parents in still others. Illiterate parents in villages that had existed for time immemorial without literacy were not always easily convinced that book learning should take priority over watching the cattle and working in the fields. Several examples of the types of reports given year after year serve to give a sense of the strengths and weaknesses of the schools.

The year 1877 was the third of a great famine that had led many people to leave their villages to seek work and food. It was difficult to maintain the educational level in the schools because there were fewer students, and those had frequent absences and suffered from lower energy levels due to the lack of a good diet. The teachers were discouraged. Nevertheless, the day school in Palmaner had been well attended during the first and last part of the year. Station missionary E. J. Heeren commented, "It gives us pleasure to add that the teacher has…, judging from numbers and progress made, gone to work in earnest."[58] His report on the school in Madanapalle was mixed. "The school has had a daily average attendance of 15, and would have had a larger number had not the health of the Teacher been so unsteady, he having frequently suffered from

---

[57] Ibid.
[58] "BFMR," 1877, 23.

fever. Notwithstanding this drawback, the scholars have made encouraging progress."[59]

In view of the severe drought and famine conditions, it is surprising that the teachers were able to accomplish anything at all in the schools. In his report on the congregations and schools in the Vellore area, John Scudder included a paragraph about the famine. He advocated strongly with the local government officials, who were Hindus, that food had to be made available to the pariah Christians who were being discriminated against, but his efforts had little success.

> Many of the Christians in this part of the field have also suffered more or less, for want of food. Their crops have failed, still they are compelled to pay their taxes. Help has been given them, or some of them must have died of starvation. We do not intend to let any of them die for want of food. We must continue to aid them for months to come. I have made one application to the Government for aid, but in vain. Still I do not despair of receiving it, as I intend to apply again, and, if need be, a third time, as I feel that the Government is as much bound to support the starving Christians as the starving heathen.[60]

In that context, Scudder reported that with one or two exceptions the schools in his area were in satisfactory condition. However, due to the famine, they had deteriorated somewhat in the last several months. "Many who, in usual times, have been able to support their children and send them to school, have been compelled to withdraw them, for a time at least, in order to make them earn their own living."[61] A similar report came from Gnanodiam, where the

---

59 Ibid., 22. Without knowing more specifically the symptoms of the teacher's illness, one suspects that he was suffering recurring bouts of malaria for which at that time there was little treatment available. If it was malaria, one can only admire the fact that the teacher was able to accomplish anything at all.

60 Ibid, 28.

61 Ibid., 27.

number of pupils had declined, "owing to the necessity of the children's earning their own living in this time of necessity."[62]

The Boarding Schools

Reflecting on the first half century of the Arcot Mission, the missionaries affirmed that no branch of the mission work was more vitally connected with the development of the Indian church than the boarding schools. Boys and girls came to the homes from villages where they were surrounded by very little that is "uplifting and much that is harmful." Christian teachers in charge of the boarding homes made every effort to keep them from harmful influences and to train young lives in the ways of right and truth. The matrons in the homes insisted on habits of cleanliness and labored to develop the good and suppress the evil. "It is no doubt true that no equal effort in our entire mission work yields such direct results as our work in the Boarding Schools."[63]

In 1906, the mission was running four boarding schools for 235 boys and three boarding schools for 195 girls. In the course of the years, nearly all of the men and women who were employed as Christian workers had been educated through these boarding schools. Their sons and daughters had also been placed in the boarding schools, with the result that there were hundreds of Christian homes providing Christian influence throughout the area. Out of this experience, it continued to be felt that boarding schools were vitally necessary in that they provided for a healthy Christian environment for children in their years of maturation. "The necessity of segregating Christian children into such schools, where they will be weaned from heathen associations, come into contact with some of the refinements of civilization, and develop a healthy Christian character, is considered of first importance."[64]

[62] Ibid. 20.
[63] "AAR," 1904, 17.
[64] "AAR," 1906, 9.

Life in boarding homes changed but little over the years. Prior to the second half of the twentieth century, village schools at best enabled the children to progress through the fifth grade, and few children reached even that level due to the need for their labor by the family. Furniture in the boarding home was virtually nonexistent for the children, but they could depend on a consistent, nourishing diet in secure and generally pleasant surroundings. Entrance into a boarding home by a girl opened up a new life to her, but it also could be somewhat traumatic. Alice Van Doren gives us a sense of what was involved for the girl and her family.

> "Many…come from poor unlettered village homes. It is often pathetic to see the father as he brings his little girl for the first time. The two have trudged many miles from their village away back in the country. She has never been away from home and the school building with its wide rooms and verandah, and its multitudes of strange faces is more wonderful than anything she has ever seen. She is the first child from that village who has been away to school, and the father himself unable to read and write, can scarcely contain himself for pride when the time comes to say good-bye and go back the long way home. There are tears in his eyes, as with trembling voice he turns to the missionary and says, "What will her mother do without her? She will weep for loneliness when night comes."[65]

North American visitors in India were often surprised to see how little furniture there was in a boys' or girls' boarding home. No beds were needed. In a girls' boarding home, each girl brought her own mat to sleep on and had her own trunk for storing her possessions. The mat was rolled up neatly during the day, thus making the room available for other purposes. She had only the bare minimum of clothing, so she had no need for a closet beyond her trunk. There were no tables or chairs for the girls either. They sat on the floor to

[65] Ibid., 10.

eat, using their fingers rather than silverware. They also learned to cook and keep their home clean. Each day besides going to school they studied at home, did some work—such as sweeping, grinding raggi, or carrying water. On Saturday they did a little extra cleaning and bathed.[66]

While emphasizing the positive benefits of the boarding schools, the missionaries were not unaware of some of the dangers as well. The major problem was that the boys and girls who were fed, clothed, and educated by the mission lost contact with the struggle to make ends meet, as their families in the villages had to do. Even in times of famine, the mission always found funds to purchase sufficient food, so that the children did not sense the suffering in the villages. Moreover, as the boys and girls progressed in their education, they began to hope for clerical, teaching, or pastoral work rather than manual labor.[67] Much as the boarding homes sought to overcome these dangers by expecting the children to assist in food preparation, cleaning, and various forms of manual labor as well as by their teaching emphases, the students after completing their studies looked toward living and working in the towns rather than returning to their villages.

Vellore High School purchased from the Church of Scotland Mission

The action of the Arcot Mission in 1878 permitting Hindu children to enter the Christian school for boys at Tindivanam proved to be the decisive move away from the original policy of the mission to provide education only for Christian children. The rule was modified officially in 1884, with the result that in 1903 there were 3,305 more Hindu students than Christian ones in its educational institutions. This change of policy more than any other shaped the conditions of the work of the mission. At the fifty-year mark, the writer of the annual report bemoaned the change of emphasis.

[66] Nellie Van Vranken, "A Budding Boarding School," *Mission Field,* October 1920, 152.
[67] "AAR," 1906, 11.

What are the consequences? The neglect of evangelistic
efforts in the backward districts, where the richest harvests
have been gathered in the past. The result—the village
work has not grown as rapidly as formerly. Apart from the
efforts of our earnest native brethren, this work has received
comparatively little attention from the Misisonary force. In
1903 only two Missionaries were able to tour for a short
time among the unevangelized.[68]

The momentum for increasing the educational mission could not
be stopped. As more children completed their work in the primary
schools, the mission had to face the fact that if high schools were
not opened, the successful students would in all likelihood not be
able to go on with their education. The church in the Arcot mission
area could become an educational backwater in Indian society.
Wyckoff, in the 1890s, continued to send from to time his twenty-
page reports about his latest evangelistic tour, but he also became
an ardent advocate for Christian higher education. In October,
1893, he informed Henry Cobb that the Arcot Mission was
negotiating with the Church of Scotland Mission (CSM) to
amalgamate the CSM Vellore High School and the Arcot Academy
in Ranipet. This move had been generally affirmed by the mission,
but two Arcot missionaries were hesitant. They were concerned
that Christian boys would suffer in a college where the majority of
students were Hindu.[69]

The background of their fear was located in the difference
between the two schools. Previous to 1884, the Arcot Seminary had
provided both a vernacular education in secular subjects and
theological education for those who were to become catechists or
ordained ministers. When the Arcot Seminary sought to raise an
endowment fund in the Reformed Church in the amount of
$50,000 in order that it might become a theological seminary on a
par with the two Reformed Church seminaries in the U.S., the

[68] "AAR," 1903, 4.
[69] J. H. Wyckoff to Henry Cobb, October 6, 1893.

Arcot Theological Seminary

General Synod suggested separating the two departments in the school. Similar separations had occurred between New Brunswick Theological Seminary and Rutgers College in New Jersey and between Western Theological Seminary and Hope College in Michigan. In 1887 Arcot Academy, as it became known, was moved to Ranipet and functioned as a high school within the original mission policy to provide such education for Christians.[70]

The Vellore High School, on the other hand, had been established in Vellore in the 1860s by the Church of Scotland Mission at a time when it was still carrying on evangelistic and pastoral work as well as educational mission there. In 1882 it entered into an agreement with the Arcot Mission that it would bring to an end its evangelistic and pastoral work and turn that over to the Arcot Mission while continuing to operate the school. The Vellore High School thus worked on the basis of the principles of Alexander Duff. Its enrollment was almost entirely made up of higher caste Hindus. Most of its teachers were Hindus, as was its principal. Thus there were grounds for the fears of the missionaries who hesitated to combine the two schools.

[70] "BFMR," 1887, 34.

In presenting the mission's proposal to the Board of Foreign Missions that funds in the amount of $1,600 be allocated to enable the two missions in India to share equally in the ownership of the buildings and management of the school, Wyckoff offered the information that in 1882 the Church of Scotland Mission had requested the Arcot Mission to share management of the school. At that time, the mission was not yet ready to establish schools for non-Christians. Wyckoff went on to say that in the decade since then there had been considerable advance in the Indian church along educational lines, "so much as to attract universal attention."

> Our own mission has caught the spirit of the times, and the separating of the Theological class from the Academy, and the development of the latter into a High School under a Principal from home has marked an era in the educational history of our mission. But we cannot stop here. The matriculation standard, although considered high a few years ago, can no longer be regarded as such now when nearly every town of any size has one or more institutions of the high school grade. Nothing less than a college at least of second grade [junior college in America] can meet the requirements for a growing Christian community and place our mission on a level with other American societies in South India.[71]

Wyckoff went on to point out that the Church of Scotland High School at Vellore had students coming from an economic level of society who could afford to pay fees, so the school had been self-supporting for the past several years. Vellore was also the district center and therefore the proper place for a high school and junior college, whereas Ranipet was somewhat off the center. "Moreover," he wrote, "because the boys in the school at Ranipet are almost all poor and can pay little in the way of fees, the school there will remain a heavy expense for the Board."[72]

[71] J. H. Wyckoff to Henry Cobb, October 31, 1893.
[72] Ibid.

Wyckoff then went on to deal with the objection that the Christian students would be a minority in their own school. In response to this, he first insisted that the establishment of a college with a majority of Hindu students was not as much a departure from Arcot Mission tradition as it may have seemed. Furthermore, it would be wrong to continue to segregate Christian students from others at higher levels.

> Our primary object in establishing the college is the education of our Christian boys; but if we can at the same time reach Hindus and Mohammedans as well as secure their help toward expenses, why should we not do it? The old plan of segregating Christian children in schools by themselves, although adapted to the first stage of mission work, has long since been abandoned by nearly all missions.[73]

Events moved quickly after Wyckoff wrote his letter. Six months later, in March, 1894, he wrote that the Church of Scotland Mission wanted to withdraw completely from Vellore and allow the Arcot Mission to have full management of the school.[74]

The Vellore High School almost doubled in enrollment in the first year after the Arcot Mission took it over, reaching nine hundred students. William I. Chamberlain was named principal, and a new missionary, the Reverend Henry Huizenga, was sent by the Board of Foreign Missions to become principal after he had gained a knowledge of the language and some experience in India. In that year, intense opposition arose in the Hindu community, however, because they recognized that the Arcot Mission would seek to make the high school more Christian and because they did not want the Christians to strengthen their influence by establishing a second grade (junior) college in Vellore.[75] J. H. Wyckoff, on the other hand, looked for changes to be made in view of the fact that in the school

---

[73] Ibid.
[74] J. H. Wyckoff to Henry Cobb, March 22, 1894.
[75] Jacob Chamberlain to Henry Cobb, November 19, 1896.

Voorhees High School

with its "heathen headmaster and largely heathen staff, the positive Christian influence is not very marked yet."[76]

Henry Cobb, secretary of the Board of Foreign Missions in New York, was also concerned about the fact that the Arcot Mission continued to employ Hindus as teachers in its schools. Jacob Chamberlain, as secretary of the mission in 1897, tried to answer Cobb's concern. Chamberlain and the mission were also troubled by the situation but did not know how to get out of the dilemma. The same problem had arisen in the fledgling high school in Punganur under William Chamberlain's supervision. He had advertised and written in all directions when the Hindu headmaster there had died. He was determined to appoint a Christian, but, after a number of months without success, he was forced to put in a non-Christian or leave the post vacant Other schools had the same problem because the supply of qualified Christian teachers did not

76 J. H. Wyckoff to Henry Cobb, October 28, 1896.

at all equal the demand. "If we cannot utilize non-Christians to teach science and Mathematics and Logic and grammar we would probably have to close our schools. With might and main we are working for the happy consummation, but it will take time."[77]

In spite of the optimism that the school would be self-supporting through fees and government grants, it proved to require some financial assistance from the Board of Foreign Missions. The first cost was for the purchase of the property, but in view of the very favorable price desired by the Church of Scotland Mission, that expenditure turned out to be one of the best bargains the mission ever received. The property remains in a very central location in Vellore, with the original building still in use. In its first year, the school collected enough fees and grants to end the year with a substantial balance on hand. Unfortunately, the situation did not continue. In 1898 some of the teachers' salaries had to be raised, but the government refused to sanction additional grants for those raises or for salaries for newly appointed teachers. The net result was that the school had a deficit of about 14 percent, or Rs. 1,896, about $600 at the exchange rate of that time.[78] The deficit was all the more troubling in light of the increased institutionalization of the mission, of which the industrial school was another instance.

The Industrial School as a Necessary Portion for our Mission Effort

In their search for ways to assist the poverty-stricken Christians in the villages, missionaries began to look to the establishment of industrial institutes and schools where boys and girls could be taught crafts and vocational skills. The first such institute grew out of the rug-weaving course that was opened by Lambertus Hekhuis in 1886. For several years, the industrial school was related to the Arcot Academy. Those enrolled in its program often were a little older than those in the academy and were enrolled "chiefly for technical education, as they are too old or have not sufficient

[77] Jacob Chamberlain to Henry Cobb, August 21, 1897.
[78] "AAR," 1898, 49.

natural resources to make them a startling success in a distinctively literary career!"[79] Study and work were combined in the curriculum, with three and one-half hours a day allotted to each of the two components. The boys were permitted to select for themselves study in one or more of five different crafts and trades offered. The accommodations for the school in those early days were very meager, and funds for construction of a building were greatly limited. However, the boys of their own accord participated in work such as carrying bricks and dirt in order to assist in completing the building.[80]

Henry Cobb in New York had some concerns about the opening of the industrial school. He feared that this new work would become an additional drain on the mission's finances and that this could become another move toward educating those who were not Christians. He was assured by John Conklin, the missionary in charge of the school, that (a) all of the boys were Christians, and (b) the school obtained grants from the government subject to inspection and to the government's curriculum. The government was encouraging the opening of such schools.[81]

For the first three or four years, the existence of the industrial school was dependent to a considerable extent on the enthusiasm of the missionary in charge of the project, but by 1890 the mission as a whole had come to appreciate its merit. The industrial component of the curriculum helped break through the old problem that boys who went to school wanted to become clerical workers or find employment with the mission, rather than engage in physical labor. Therefore, the mission adopted the principle that "industrial training is necessary to the complete education of our native helpers, and every boy in our Boarding schools, unless specially excepted, is now obliged to pass through the industrial department before entering the High School."[82]

[79]"BFMR," 1893, 66.
[80] Ibid., 66-67.
[81] J. W. Conklin to Henry Cobb, September 15, 1890.
[82] J. H. Wyckoff to Henry Cobb, September 1, 1894.

The mission took the next logical step in 1894 when it resolved that industrial education is necessary for three purposes: "(a) for the full training of our native agency; (b) the development of self-supporting native churches, and (c) to exhibit to the Hindus a complete gospel." It was further resolved "that the Board be requested to recognize the Industrial Department at Arni as a necessary portion of our mission plant, and allow us to include it in the estimates for appropriations along with the other departments of our educational work."[83]

In making its request to recognize the school, the mission estimated that the annual cost to the Board of Foreign Missions would be low. The average cost to the mission budget for the first four years of operation was approximately $800, including start up costs. In 1893 the net cost to the mission was only $160. The expenses to date had been met by private donations from individuals, but the mission wanted to have $175 appropriated for 1895, since the school had by then passed the experimental stage.[84] In this case, as in many others when the missionaries provided estimates of the future cost of the operation of an institution, the original projections would prove to have been too optimistic and the need for financial assistance greater than had been first anticipated. The history of the Arcot Mission makes clear that missionaries share with humans in general a strong aptitude for underestimating the costs of a program they desired to carry out.

The annual reports for the years 1895-1898 on the industrial school continued in the optimistic line that was apparent in the original projections. The manager of the school was Carman Scudder, who carried many other responsibilities along with the school. By 1897 the school's building was completed, and seven trades were in the curriculum, although no students had enrolled in the rug-weaving course. It had been a prosperous year in which the government had given a grant of Rs. 3,120. The literary branch of

83 Ibid.
84 Ibid.

the school was being discontinued. "It has been decided that hereafter only those who intend to take up a trade for their living will be admitted, and the school be made a purely technical one."[85]

In the following year the report remained optimistic, but there were signs of problems. Carman Scudder reported that the industrial school "has been doing very well and the prospects for it are brighter than ever before." Nevertheless, a committee of the mission had visited the school, and, according to instruction from the mission, made a complete change in its organization. The manager did not approve of the changes in theory and approved even less after a few months of implementation. But the report said that he was accepting the decisions: "It is for him to go on with his work, on the new lines, according to orders, until the happy day arrives when he can pass the job on to new hands and brains."[86]

A new missionary, W. H. Farrar, arrived in India in the final months of 1897. In light of his abilities, the mission assigned him to serve with Scudder in Arni. After gaining some experience in India and some proficiency in the Tamil language, he was made "Manager, Technical Department" in the industrial school. While still engaged fully in his language study, he also "for a diversion" went over to the industrial school for about three hours each day. He wrote an unofficial letter to Cobb in which he expressed his opinion that many improvements were required.

> I can tell you in confidence that to my mind the school is no longer a school, but a poor kind of factory in which the mission is doing (perhaps unwittingly) a sort of manufacturing business with no stock and very little capital, the maistries [foremen] and a few employees doing the work and the main body of students acting as coolies at the expense of their education, the school meanwhile being known as a "school" in the eyes of the gov't for the sake of grants.[87]

85 "BFMR," 1897, 31.
86 Ibid., 1898, 39.
87 W.H. Farrar to Henry Cobb, June 22, 1898.

Farrar soon presented a new plan for the industrial school to the mission.[88] The mission recognized that Farrar had an understanding of what was involved in running an industrial school and accepted his recommendations with his higher expectations for the school. His recommendation included an emphasis on carpentry, printing, and tailoring, with the hope to develop more fully the weaving, blacksmith, and masonry courses.[89] Carman Scudder was pleased to have Farrar take charge of the work.

The original optimistic projection of a self-supporting industrial school came back to haunt its managers for a good number of years. Farrar came under criticism in his first year for having run a serious deficit. He admitted that one part of the problem was that he lacked experience in dealing with accounts for an institution that was half school and half factory. In spite of his criticism two years previously that the mission was running a factory but not a school, he now found himself forced to do what Carman Scudder had done. "But I have experience now, and am beginning this year very differently. I shall have to sacrifice the school to the factory, which I hate to do, but the Mission says it must pay, and I shall do my utmost diligence to have no deficit at the end of this year if such a thing be possible in the world."[90]

Farrar had to suffer the purgatory of a knowledgeable young man who must listen to those who are older and wiser but do not really understand the business they are talking about. He sought the advice of others experienced in the field of industrial institutes and learned from a well-versed school inspector that there were very few industrial schools that did not run deficits. The inspector told

[88] Farrar suffered a serious illness in August, 1898, and had to remain in the hills for more than six months. "It is the hope of the Mission that before the end of the year he will have become so well and strong that he can be put in entire charge of the Industrial School and leave Mr. Scudder free to throw himself exclusively into his chosen evangelistic work, when we shall look for large results in the Arni field, on which the burden of the Industrial School has prevented Mr. Scudder expending as much labor as he has wished" (Jacob Chamberlain to Henry Cobb, August 20, 1898).
[89] "BFMR," 1900, 47.
[90] W. H. Farrar to Henry Cobb, January 29, 1901.

him that the popular prejudice was that articles made in such schools were inferior; therefore, people would only buy the articles at a lower price when made at a school. Meanwhile, the other missionaries were encouraging Farrar to raise his prices for articles made, even though Farrar knew that his prices were already above comparable articles in the Madras bazaar. He also had made a bad judgment when he made a deal with a man in Madras to sell some aluminum articles in Arni on commission. Sales of the aluminum articles were slow because the Indians were familiar only with zinc, tin, and lead. The net result was that he ended the year Rs. 142 or $48 behind.[91]

The other missionaries were not sympathetic. In a time when the board had cut its appropriations, the mission had made a rule that anyone who ran a deficit would have to make up the loss out of his own personal funds. The mission refused to sanction the overexpenditure. Farrar commiserated,

> The hardest thing for me to bear is a just punishment. I suppose it is always so....Although, as I said, the punishment was just and deserved, it was hard to bear and has discouraged me very much in my efforts to build up Industrial work or Industrial Education. The new boys that have been sent here this year are for the most part little tiny boys 10 years old that can produce nothing of value until they are taught and cannot be taught because the school must pay. I have no money to carry on the aluminum industry and so I must see it die, just when it was getting to be in good working order.[92]

Henry Cobb also thought he had a solution to the problem; he suggested that the industrial school go into agriculture and farm the land that it owned, rather than continue to rent it out to a local landowner. Farrar thanked him for the suggestion but pointed out that

[91] Ibid.
[92] Ibid.

the local landowner could deal with those who controlled the water supply that was provided by the hour to those who grew rice. The industrial school did not have enough land to contract on an economic basis for water, so it gained more income from the rent than it would from growing crops. Farrar believed he could "surprise these natives by what I could turn out per acre," but it would require more capital than was available at that time.[93]

The struggle over financing the industrial school continued. In 1903, the mission agreed that it should request the board to permit Arcot missionaries on furlough to ask for support for a $5,000 endowment fund for the institute and thereby relieve the board and mission of providing annual appropriations to it. This desire to raise endowment funds for institutions was becoming a favorite idea since an endowment in the amount of $50,000 had been raised for Arcot Theological Seminary. It was also easier at times to get the mission to agree to ask for an endowment than to ask for an increase in appropriation.[94]

The board agreed to allow the missionaries to try. Unfortunately for Farrar, he learned in November, 1903, that Wyckoff on furlough in the United States had declared that he would not have time to seek money for the industrial institute. L. B. Chamberlain also informed Farrar that he would not be able to raise money for the institute because he had responsibility to raise funds in America for the Madanapalle Church Fund. Farrar felt that he could not hold on much longer.[95] But all was not lost. In 1904, the Board of Foreign Missions itself decided to make a special effort to raise a $10,000 endowment for the industrial institute, plus $250 for the school's previous year's deficit.[96]

Not all of the missionaries were pleased with the growing need to meet the costs of running institutions of various types. Even J. H. Wyckoff, who had inspired some of the institutionalization of the

[93] W. H. Farrar to Henry Cobb, June 18, 1902.
[94] W. H. Farrar to Henry Cobb, January 27, 1903.
[95] W. H. Farrar to Henry Cobb, November 3, 1903.
[96] Wm. I. Chamberlain to Henry Cobb, January 27, 1904.

work of the Arcot Mission, was losing patience. In 1906, when Farrar ran another deficit and was feeling run down, Wyckoff urged that a furlough be granted to Farrar; he was tired of hearing about a deficit every year from Farrar.[97]

In fact, Wyckoff was becoming increasingly troubled about the amount of energy required to run the institutions as well as the financial costs. He feared that the Arcot Mission was building what could turn out to be a house of cards on foreign money. At the end of the first decade of the twentieth century, he pondered the situation:

> I am troubled at the way we are all becoming absorbed in institutional work. We are having indigenous growth but are building up only at the centers of foreign money. If the foreign missionary and foreign money should suddenly be cut off, we would have a heap of empty buildings....The glory of the work has been in the uplifting of the outcaste. We are in danger of going to the opposite extreme.[98]

At this point we must pause to ask why it was that the Reformed Church missionaries in India were ready to move ahead into the institutionalization of the work of the Arcot Mission. In their hearts they still resisted such developments, because they were holding firmly to the priority of evangelism as the work of the mission and resolutely to the goal that the church must become self-governing, self-supporting, and self-propagating. One can surmise that by establishing various institutions they were half-consciously recognizing that a self-supporting, self-governing, self-propagating church would persevere in India only when it was surrounded by a environment that was conducive to Christian intellectual, mental, physical, and cultural growth. Given the fact that most of the Christians came from the pariah caste, they were not accepted in or permitted to enter into the full life of the Madras Presidency. Either

[97] J. H. Wyckoff to Henry Cobb, February 20, 1906.
[98] J. H. Wyckoff to Henry Cobb, April 1, 1909.

because of outright discrimination against them or because of their own lack of knowledge, skills, and social development, they could not hope to be accepted as students in schools of higher education, to be allowed to gain entrance into the ranks of skilled craftsmen, or to be employed in government service. Therefore, whether or not missionaries wanted to establish educational, medical, and vocational institutions, when the opportunity came to do so they could not resist. In the twentieth century, as the institutions gained strength, visibility, and respect in the larger Indian community, they would become the meeting points in which the Christians' lives would day by day intersect with their neighbors of other faiths.

The Future of the Telugu Field Challenged

Jacob Chamberlain always had great hopes for the Telugu area, while the Scudders were primarily focused on the Tamil field. By 1881, Chamberlain had come to believe that the Arcot Seminary located in the Tamil-language area could not adequately educate young men to be teachers and catechists in the Telugu area. He brought his concerns to the mission. The other missionaries agreed that "if the Telugu department of our Mission is to be successfully worked, and be in accordance with the cultus and spirit of our Church, we must no longer delay taking steps to educate helpers for the Telugu field in the Telugu country."[99] At that time only two of all the helpers in the Telugu field were graduates of Arcot Seminary. All the rest of them had been trained outside the Arcot Mission area by one of the English missionary societies. Boys sent from the Telugu area to the Arcot Seminary tended to stay in the Tamil area.

Chamberlain went on to say that he had always looked forward to the day when the Telugu work would grow and when there would be both a boys' and a girls' boarding school in Madanapalle. In fact, when some land had become available for mission premises, he had purchased ten acres. He was pleased that the most recent mission

[99] J. Chamberlain to J. M. Ferris, February 25, 1881.

meeting resolved to ask the Board of Foreign Missions and the Woman's Board for $250 each for a boys' and a girls' school. He was pleased also to report that there were fifteen promising boys ready to enter such a school and be educated to become teachers or catechists. With his usual flair for the dramatic, Chamberlain pointed out that his letter was being written while they were in their tent on an evangelistic tour. His wife was away from the tent working among the women at the moment he was writing.[100]

Jacob and Charlotte Chamberlain had first moved to the Telugu area in 1861, two years after their arrival in India. Much of the time they were alone in the area. Jacob's health was precarious, and he often had to go to the hills to recover. It also was necessary for them to spend several years in America for the sake of his health. Upon his return to India, the mission's medical committee had decided that he should work in a hill station where he could continue his writing and translation work. Alternatively, they could reside again at Madanapalle, which was at three thousand feet of altitude and somewhat cooler than the Tamil area. The Tamil area was located at one thousand feet, and the temperature rose to ninety-five or one hundred degrees or more daily for most of the year. They chose to reside again in Madanapalle. But Jacob's sufferings continued. "I have never, except in one instance spent ten days on the plains without a bilious attack and fever and continued pains and distress in may head."[101]

The Chamberlains' move to Madanapalle occurred in 1863, when the Board of Foreign Missions' funds were limited because of the Civil War. They had been granted sufficient money to build a house for themselves, but, to the chagrin of some of the other missionaries, Jacob Chamberlain used the money to build a number of other small houses for Indian workers. One of these buildings became his and Charlotte's home. It had a floor made of rough bricks, over which a grass mat was placed and a low, tiled roof. "After living, as

100 Ibid.
101 J. Chamberlain to J M. Ferris, Feb. 25, 1882.

we had, in a tent through the hot season and through one month of the monsoon, while building, it seemed to us like a palace." The disadvantages of the low roof became apparent, however, when the hot season came. The heat in the house was such as to affect his health, but they continued to live in the house until he asked for money to build a new larger one in 1880.[102]

By the time he sent his requests for money for a house and for a boys' and girls' school in 1881, Jacob and Charlotte Chamberlain were among the most-loved missionaries in the Reformed Church. In lectures and sermons during his furloughs in the United States, Jacob related tales about escapes from tigers and cobras, as well as his debates with Hindus on his on evangelistic tours. He became well known for his work in Bible translation. He was also gaining respect in other missions for his insight into mission strategy. People in the Reformed Church trusted his words. When he spoke, they responded. This did not, however, endear him to his fellow missionaries when he was able to garner contributions for his work without always consulting the Arcot Mission.

The only request the mission had approved for the schools in Madanapalle was $250 each for the girls' and the boys' schools. However, in one of Chamberlain's letters to the president of the Woman's Board of Foreign Missions he just happened to mention his dream of erecting a building for a girls' school. Almost by return mail, the Woman's Board sent a check to Chamberlain in the amount of $1,000 for the building. The incident made the mission nervous about Chamberlain's big plans to develop the Telugu field separately. Jared Scudder, as secretary of the Arcot Mission, wrote to J. M. Ferris asking whether the Board of Foreign Missions was aware of the probable future costs of opening the schools and expanding the Telugu field. He was also not sure that the mission was empowered to erect the building, since it had never requested money for it.

---

[102] Jacob Chamberlain to J. H. Ferris, November 2, 1880.

Independently of the fact that the Mission do not consider themselves empowered to erect such a building without the sanction of the Board, the Mission feels that the question of the erection of this building carries with it the larger question of the expansion of the work in the Telugu field; and that, in order to (have) an intelligent decision of the whole matter the Board should be made acquainted with all that the proposed enlargement involves....But, is the Board prepared to meet the increased outlay which the establishment and carrying on of these institutions will demand. This is a matter, not for us, but for the Board to decide....[103]

The Board of Foreign Missions was going through another of its periods of financial difficulties. The growth of mission work in Japan, China, and India was moving on a pace that far exceeded the will or power of the members of the Reformed Church to increase their contributions. In 1881, the board took an innovative approach to the problem. It ruled that the mission apply its "premium" gains on foreign exchange as part of the board's annual appropriation remittances, stating that the board "requests the Mission to confine its expenditures for the last six months of 1881 to the amount appropriated."[104] Dealing with exchange of currencies was a much more complex matter in the nineteenth century than it is today. Board of Foreign Missions remittances in dollars would often be exchanged in London for pounds that, in turn, would be converted to rupees for use in India. Since the rates were subject to change during the time that it took for the money to move across the seas and continents, the board often set the amount in dollars it would send, calculated at an exchange rate presumed to be at least equal to the mission budget stated in rupees.

As the board sought to be fair to the mission in matters of foreign exchange, it often calculated its estimate of the rate in a manner

103 J. W. Scudder to J. M. Ferris, July 7, 1881.
104 J. W. Scudder to J. M. Ferris, July 22, 1881.

slightly favorable to the mission, lest the mission be embarrassed for funds in the event of an adverse change of rate. What the mission gained in the time of a favorable rate was called the "premium." In 1879 Ferris had written that, while the board could not increase its appropriation for the year, the mission would be allowed to use any premium gain for work beyond its original budget. This had been a windfall for the mission. For a couple of years, when exchange rates were very favorable for the mission, it could move forward a bit. The 1881 ruling took this financial cushion away from the mission and in fact forced an immediate reduction of Rs. 6,000 in expenditures for the final six months of the year.[105]

This action of the board brought to a head the fear of the missionaries in the Tamil area that Chamberlain was moving ahead too rapidly in the Telugu area, which was about one-sixth the size of the Tamil area. To fund his dreams would force them to cut back in the Tamil area. Jared Scudder alerted his brother John in the United States about the danger. He feared that money put into buildings in Madanapalle would be wasted, because the mission would probably not be able to continue the work there should Chamberlain have to leave due to his continuing ill health. Jared had been under pressure from other missionaries already in 1878 to ask the board for permission to withdraw at once from Madanapalle, and the subject was being brought up more often.

> I still think he ought to be allowed to continue there while he lasts. But, nonetheless, my confident opinion is that our Mission will leave the place when he does. It is, as it were, a foreign country to us. Owing to differences of language, we and our Helpers cannot work there; and he and his helpers cannot work here. It is far away from the center of the Mission; and is accessible only by a very long, expensive and disagreeable journey. Chamberlain excepted, we have

105 Ibid.

not, and probably never will have a missionary, who would
care to go and work there rather than here.[106]

Jared Scudder went on to suggest that Madanapalle was really
within the bounds of the London Missionary Society, although the
Arcot Mission had accepted responsibility for it when Chamberlain
moved into the Telugu area twenty years earlier. But by 1881 the
London Missionary Society (LMS) was "very anxious to get it back.
One of their missionaries told me so only the other day." But Jared
knew that there was not the slightest possibility that the LMS would
pay the Arcot Mission for any extensive houses and the like in what
would be for them a subordinate station.[107] John Scudder shared
the letter with Ferris in New York.

A half-year later, Jared Scudder expressed his concerns directly to
Ferris. He suggested that the only way he saw through the need to
cut back Rs. 6,000 in the expenditures of the mission was either to
give up the Tindivanam territory in the southern end of the mission
or Madanapalle in the north. But Tindivanam was the most rapidly
growing area in the Tamil field. Therefore he suggested that the
Madanapalle and Telugu works be returned to the LMS and the
Arcot Mission become a one-language mission.[108] Jared Scudder
shared his single-page letter by circulation to all the other members
of the mission, as required by mission rules for personal opinions
expressed to the board.

Chamberlain responded with his own long letter four days later.
He did not want to advocate for the abandonment of any of the
work of the mission, and especially not the Telugu field. The LMS,
in his opinion could not handle the mission work in Madanapalle,
which was located more than seventy-five miles from any of their
mission stations. Moreover, closing down the Telugu work would
save only Rs. 2,500 in native helpers' salaries. Most important of all,
he believed, was the fact that when the mission had unanimously

106 J. W. Scudder to John Scudder, July 30, 1881.
107 Ibid.
108 J. W. Scudder to J.M. Ferris, February 20, 1882.

asked him to take the Telugu work in 1861, he had consented to accept that as his "life-work." His commitment to that work was non-negotiable.

> That consecration I still hold. I have vowed to my Master to work for Him among the Telugus until my God comes to be their God or until *He* takes me hence. I feel it laid upon me to fulfil that vow, and purpose so to do. I expect to live, and God willing, to die among any Telugus. I would fain do it under our Board and in the Arcot Mission. If that cannot be,—If the Board feel compelled to abandon the Telugu field I shall very respectfully, through the Mission, ask the Board to allow me to resign my connections with them and to make such arrangements with some other society that shall be able and willing to keep up the work here as shall allow me to spend my remaining years working for this people.[109]

The Board of Foreign Missions had no inclination to remove its most popular Indian missionary from the field to which he knew himself to be called. The other missionaries were ready to continue the work in the Telugu area so long as Chamberlain was there. In spite of his continuing ill health, he remained in India related to Madanapalle until his death in 1908. Charlotte Chamberlain lived until 1915. Moreover, although not as prolific as the Scudders had been in bringing into the world children who were ready to serve as missionaries in India, Jacob and Charlotte were not without resources on that score. Their two sons soon joined them as missionaries in India: William I. and his wife, Mary Anable, in 1887 and Lewis B. and his wife, Julia Anable, in 1888. With their arrival, the future of the Telugu field was assured.

[109] J. Chamberlain to J. M. Ferris, February 24, 1882.

298 *From Mission to Church*

The Decision to Close the Hindu Girls' Schools

During the last decade of the nineteenth century, the expansion of the work of the Arcot Mission was on a collision course with the increasingly difficult financial position of the Board of Foreign Missions. The board had never fully recovered financially from the difficult years of the Civil War. Its position became worse after an American economic crisis in 1873. It ended 1891 with a debt of over $30,000. Its income for that year was $110,396.[110]

A financial panic again hit the American economy in 1893, with the result that there was a deficit in that year of about $7,000. The two years after that were equally bad, so the debt ballooned to $46,097.[111] The Board of Foreign Missions had to consider whether to abandon one of its mission fields. The General Synod of 1895 instead urged the members of the Reformed Church to make additional contributions in order to wipe out the long-standing debt. The members responded generously, and at the end of 1896 only $4,699 remained to be paid.[112]

The optimism of 1896 soon vanished, however. By 1898 the debt had climbed to $27,036. The result of all this debt and annual deficits was that, by the turn of the century, the board was profoundly disturbed by the disparity between the requests of the missions for funds and its ability to respond adequately. The board reported to the General Synod:

> In view of these facts, and of the severe retrenchments the Board has been obliged to order for the last seven years— severest of all last year—it should not excite wonder that, in some important respects, our work is actually going backward. Careful oversight of the helpers and visitation of the churches has, in some fields, been impossible. Valuable helpers have been lost through the inability of the Missions

110 "BFMR," 1893, 17.
111 "BFMR," 1895, xxv.
112 Ibid., xxiv.

to employ them. Aggressive evangelistic work has been retarded and in some instances prevented. Last and worst of all, the North Japan Mission is convinced that, if help does not come, the large and promising field in Shin-shiu, so long occupied by it, must be given up, and the Arcot Mission, for the third time urges that, if the "cuts" are to continue, the Telugu portion of its field, so long occupied by Dr. Chamberlain and later by his sons, be relinquished and handed over to another Missionary Society.[113]

The dreary litany of deficits in the accounts of the board resulted in equally despairing pleas from the Reformed Church missionaries in India. We will now consider the impact of the reductions in appropriations between the years 1896 and 1901.

The first reduction in expenses ordered by the Board of Foreign Missions was given at the end of 1893, the year of the financial panic in America. It was a cutback of 6.5 percent. The Arcot Mission was disappointed but accepted the situation. Jacob Chamberlain said that the mission would do what it could to cut expenses, such as printing only a very brief annual report of its activities in 1893.[114]

Two years later the board once again informed the mission that its appropriations for the current year, 1896, would be reduced by 11.5 percent, which equaled $4,000, or Rs. 13,800. J. H. Wyckoff, secretary of the mission, wrote back to say that the reduction has "filled us with consternation and dismay" as various alternatives were considered. "When we consider that a school or a native helper costs on the average only about Rs. 350, or $100 a year, the serious results of retrenchment are manifest. Put in simple language, it means that forty schools must be closed and their teachers dismissed."[115]

The mission could not decide to close forty schools and dismiss forty teachers in light of the role those teachers and schools played

---

[113] "BFMR," 1896, xv-xvi.
[114] J. Chamberlain to Henry Cobb, January 31, 1894.
[115] Reported in the editorial, "What Retrenchment Means," *Mission Field,* April, 1896, 350.

in the life of the village congregations. The mission met three times to find alternatives. It decided that the best alternative was to close all the Hindu girls' schools, plus such schools for boys that were not at that time self-supporting. The editor of the *Mission Field* commented on this action,

> We have not now space to tell all that this action of the Mission implies. To close some of these schools will be to practically abandon work among the higher classes in the towns, and surrender footholds that we have been years in securing. The Hindu girls' schools are stepping stones to Zenana work, and without them it is hard to see how our ladies can get access to the high-caste women.[116]

The Vigorous Dissent of the Woman's Board of Foreign Missions and their Fundraising Efforts

The men of the Arcot Mission responsible for the decision to the close the Hindu girls' schools were about to come to a better understanding of the power of the Woman's Board of Foreign Missions and to the limits of their own authority. Clara Burrell represented both the actions and the emotions of the Woman's Board, as well as women all across the denomination. In a letter to Wyckoff, she first reported that the Woman's Board could not consent to the closing of the Hindu girls' schools. Their board was planning to issue $2,500 worth of bonds at $5 each, to be made available at the May meeting of the board. This amount would guarantee support for the schools and keep them open.[117]

This good news was only the opening shot, however. Burrell continued, "Now I want to take some of your valuable time for a question or two. In the consideration of this cut we secretaries [of the Woman's Board] especially are met with this question, Why should the work of the Woman's Board be cut? If they meet their

[116] Ibid., 350-51.
[117] Clara Burrell to J. H. Wyckoff, March 10, 1896.

pledges is it right to subject their work to the general rule? We went to the Synod's Board to receive the reply that, first, our work was larger than our pledges and, secondly, that the cuts were made at the discretion of the missionaries."[118] The Woman's Board refused to accept this explanation. It did not believe that it was providing less than full funding for woman's work in the Arcot Mission, and it refused to let the male personnel of the Board of Foreign Missions simply pass the blame for the decision on to the missionaries. But the Woman's Board was obviously also disappointed in the action of the male missionaries in the mission.

Although some of the missionary women in India had been present when the Arcot Mission made its decision to close all sixteen Hindu girls' schools, they were very disappointed. Mary Chamberlain, Gertrude Wyckoff, Mabel Scudder, and Margaret Beattie all wrote articles to be published in the *Mission Gleaner*. Gertrude (Mrs. J. H.) Wyckoff began her letter in a manner that leaves the impression that there may have been some intense discussions about the decision in the Wyckoff household. "I must put in my urgent plea against the closing of our Hindu Girls' School in Tindivanam, leaving the other ladies to speak for their own Schools, and leaving the gentlemen to talk about the matter in the abstract."[119] Mary Chamberlain wrote, "It strikes at the very heart of my work. It closes the avenues of approach to the home, that is the heart of the people. It will amaze the Hindus, it will frighten and discourage the Christians, it will reach everywhere against us....It will be a plain case of putting the hand to the plow and looking back. Our position will be one of painful humiliation, and I tell you frankly, that I do not know how to face it."[120]

By the time the Arcot women's letters were published in the *Mission Gleaner*, the Woman's Board had already won the day. However, the letters provided incentive to the women in the denomination to purchase the $5 bonds issued by the Woman's

[118] Ibid.
[119] Gertrude Wyckoff letter, *Mission Gleaner*, May/June, 1896, 9.
[120] Mary Chamberlain, ibid., 8.

Board to keep the schools open. The Hindu girls' school controversy thus became one more illustration of the ability of the women to raise funds at a time when the men of the Board of Foreign Missions were consistently falling short. The Woman's Board was able to report increases in contributions even in the year of the financial panic.

The Woman's Board was able to maintain a consistent record because it sought to work closely with the woman's missionary societies, which claimed a total membership of more than twelve thousand in more than five hundred congregations. Those societies all had a common aim, as stated in their constitutions: "Its object shall be to aid the Board in sending out and maintaining Female Missionaries, Bible-readers, and Teachers, who shall work among heathen women and children."[121] The Woman's Board also encouraged the women to maintain the "Baby Roll." Mothers were encouraged to enroll their babies in the baby roll. Those who did so received a membership card in the child's name and pledged twenty-five cents a year for five years. The membership card had on it a picture of Jesus with a group of little children around him. The purpose of the Baby Roll was clearly stated: "It is our earnest desire that all the baptized children of our Church should become members of this precious circle, that from it a missionary influence may surround the cradle of babyhood and, through a mother's prayers, be early taught to send to the Christless ones God's precious truth."[122]

The Woman's Board also encouraged the formation in congregations of associations of young ladies called "Mission Bands." Any young lady was eligible to become a member by paying twenty-five cents annually. Each Mission Band obligated itself to be responsible to send a mission contribution of at least twenty dollars a year to the Woman's Board.[123] Children could also be included in

121 *Constitution for Auxiliaries of the Reformed Church in America,* Art. 2, 1876, 24-26.
122 "Woman's Board of Foreign Missions Report," 1898, 10.
123 "Directions for Forming Mission Bands," ibid. 26.

the mission effort. They were to be organized into a "Mission Circle" that was to contribute at least five dollars annually. As an alternative to the five dollars, members of the Mission Circle could make the following pledge and send whatever was raised: "We desire to help in sending the Gospel to heathen children, that they may hear of Christ, who died to save them. We promise to give one cent a week to the Missionary box, and to come together once a month, to hear about missions, and to work for the cause."[124]

In order to sustain its wide network of auxiliaries, the Woman's Board came to recognize how crucial it was to sustain interest by encouraging the missionary societies in the congregations to take special responsibility for a particular school or person on the mission field. It also encouraged the persons or institutions who were recipients of such support to write letters to the missionary society that provided support. Such letters were always the highlight of the monthly meeting of the auxiliaries when they arrived.

In 1893, as in other years, there was a list of "special objects" as well as women missionaries worthy of support. There were approximately forty women missionaries on the list. The Woman's Board had particular responsibility for the financial support of the unmarried women, of whom there were fourteen. "Special Objects" had a variety of mission endeavors. Support of a pupil in a girls' boarding school in China or Japan called for a $20 annual contribution. The Girls' Boarding School in Madanapalle needed $30 per pupil, as did the Female Seminary in Vellore. Support of an entire Hindu Girls' School required a gift of $150, while a zenana teacher needed $30.[125]

The Missionaries' Resistance to the "Special Objects" Contribution Method

In voting to close the Hindu girls' schools, the Arcot Mission had indicated that it regarded the central concern of the Woman's Board, to reach the "heathen women" of India, as being its lowest

124 "Missions Circles of Children," ibid., 26-27.
125 "Woman's Board of Foreign Missions Report," 1893, 124-25.

priority. Not only that, but the mission had resisted for a number of years the Woman's Board's encouragement of its auxiliaries to designate support for specific unmarried women missionaries, or for a "special object." In doing so, the mission was attacking a basic and very successful strategy used by the women to maintain a high level of contributions at a time when the Board of Foreign Missions itself was losing ground financially. In her letter to Wyckoff, Clara Burrell could not resist letting him know that the Woman's Board had also lost some of its financial momentum in 1893 because it had not asked for "specials."

> There has been one serious mistake made this year and we are just beginning to realize it. This is that in obedience to the directions of Synod's Board we have asked for no "specials" and have lost money everywhere. We should have specialized our general work and it does not help any for the five of us who thought so to say, I told you so.[126]

Behind her comment that the Board of Foreign Missions had asked the Woman's Board to cease its "specials" appeal was her knowledge that the board had made that request in response to the missionaries' resistance to "specials."

The issue Burrell raised, whether contributions should be designated for particular persons or programs, was already one of long standing at the time she wrote her letter, and it remains one to the present day. Therefore, it is well to review the history of "special objects" in the Reformed Church work in India up to the time when she wrote her letter.

One of the ironies of the situation is that the missionaries themselves repeatedly advocated the use of "specials" as a means of increasing contributions when they wanted to open some new work for which there was no room within the annual appropriation. Thus, in spite of their objections to the amount of work involved in keeping track of "specials," they were also responsible for

---

[126] Clara Burrell to J. H. Wyckoff, March 10, 1896.

encouraging such fundraising. They had suggested, for example, that large endowments be raised for the Arcot Theological Seminary and the Industrial Institute at Arni by requesting designated contributions outside the annual budget of the board. Also, in 1894 the Arcot Mission had sent a request to the Woman's Board for an additional $1,800 for a bungalow to serve as the residence of unmarried women missionaries in Ranipet.[127] In making this request, the mission would have known that such additional funds would in all likelihood be raised as a "special object." Burrell had taken obvious pleasure in communicating the Woman's Board's positive response to this special request in the very opening paragraph of her letter to Wyckoff.[128]

As an aside, we may note that after the mission received the $1,800 for the bungalow, it discovered that the building it had hoped to use for the girls' school being transferred to Ranipet would not be available. Therefore, it requested and received permission to use the $1,800 for a new school building rather than a bungalow and stated that it would later put in a new request for funds for the bungalow.[129]

The Board of Foreign Missions throughout its history had encouraged designated contributions as a means of stimulating interest in missions. During the Civil War, it stated, "Our Foreign Missionary Work has the advantage of being capable of subdivision, so that each school or band of Christian workers may have a specific object. Thus we find one Sabbath School supporting a native helper, another a school, a third a scholar in one of our seminaries."[130] Designated contributions for particular persons and designated programs proved to be a favored way of participating in the work of missions by congregations and missionary societies.

The board and missionaries alike had underestimated the amount of time and effort required to maintain such a system of designated

[127] L. R. Scudder to Henry Cobb, September 12, 1894.
[128] Clara Burrell to J. H. Wyckoff, March 10, 1896.
[129] L. R. Scudder to Henry Cobb, January 27, 1896.
[130] "BFMR," 1864, 5.

contributions. Already in 1871 the board was aware of its problems and listed five in its report to the General Synod: (a) donors desire to make specific designations at the cost of general contributions; (b) it narrows the interest of contributors to one locality; (c) it brings about confusion, such as when a letter becomes directed to the wrong person or school; (d) its takes valuable time of the missionaries; and (e) the system cannot be expanded adequately. Missionaries have to correspond with as many as two or three hundred congregations and Sunday schools.[131]

The board then presented a new policy, which was to establish a "Mission School Fund" into which all the previously designated gifts would go. Those schools, teachers, and pupils in India who had previously been individually supported by a specific Sunday school in America, for example, would henceforth be supported through this fund into which the Sunday school's designated gift would be placed. Instead of an individual letter being sent to a donor Sunday school in appreciation, each donor would now receive six letters a year with information about missions and what was happening in the mission schools.[132] This was a good solution in the minds of the board and the missionaries, but congregations, missionary societies, and Sunday schools continued to seek out ways to make designated contributions for specific persons or projects. After it was formed in 1875, the Woman's Board in particular continued to encourage support of special objects by its auxiliaries.

The dilemma of designated contributions has never been resolved. Financial support of missions involves the contributor in a very personal and emotional concern to be related to the place where the mission is actually taking place and to the people among whom it is happening. It erodes when it becomes merely a part of a bureaucratic process or a simple financial transaction. On the other side, it becomes a major headache for those who must track the flow

131 "BFMR," 1871, 6-7.
132 Ibid.

of designated gifts and encourage missionaries to write the letters of appreciation expected by the donors.

The Arcot missionaries constantly complained about the difficulties of maintaining the system. When a specific "native worker" was supported, the missionaries had to keep track of which missionary society supported her. In that century before anyone had heard of a computer, it meant keeping manual records of the changes in lists of supporters, as well as informing all of the supporters whenever a change of employment took place in India. In 1894, Jacob Chamberlain in exasperation informed the Board of Foreign Missions that maintenance of the system really required the full-time service of one missionary. "If the churches are going to require us to run such lists of specials, I am not sure but that they will have to send out a special missionary whose sole work shall be to manage this voluminous and unsatisfactory business and require those who insist on such correspondence to pay his or her salary."[133]

Chamberlain went on to ask questions about several items in the latest list of special contributions that need "elucidation." In order to show the complexity of the accounting problem, we quote just two paragraphs from a much longer list of details about the accounting for the specials:

> The 7th item in the list reads "Y.P.S.C.E. 1st Ch. Schenectday, for Theol. Student, $15.00." This is given us as *within* the appropriations. So of course I am not at liberty to credit it to the Theological Seminary and without that we can hardly apply it to a Theol. Student, for there is nothing in the appropriations of the Board or the Mission for Theol. Students whose expenses are all being borne by the Theol. Sem. Fund. If *within* the appropriations it seems to me that it will have to be applied to a student in the Arcot Seminary. But will that suit the donors? Please direct us what to do.

[133] J. Chamberlain to Henry Cobb, March 31, 1894.

In your list of "Payments for Members of the Mission" is this: "Mission Treasurer: p. 2 Miss Bertha von Bergen....$15.00." The value of this ($15.00) viz., Rs. 47-3-5, was paid in to the Mission Treasury Nov. 22nd 1893 and was credited to the Board in the accounts for 1893, it being the last item by one in the credits to the Board on page 1 of the Annual Bill, so that no credit of that amount can appear in the Missions Bill for 1894 although you have reported its payment in 1894....I fear however there may have been a clerical error in copying that item into the bill, for I find that in the duplicate which I have the sum is entered as $5.00 instead of $15.00 but the amount in Rupees is correct, viz. Rs. 47-3-5.[134]

It is not difficult to understand why the missionaries expressed some impatience with the system of designated special objects. But the missionaries could not have it both ways. If they wanted to have their program supported, they had to accept the system. Clara Burrell wanted to make sure that Wyckoff and the Arcot Mission understood that.

The Board of Foreign Missions and the Arcot Mission had no alternative but to surrender to the wishes of the Woman's Board. The mission was instructed to discriminate between the Board of Foreign Missions' appropriation and that of the Woman's Board of Foreign Missions. Wyckoff wrote back to Burrell that the mission was accepting its instruction and would honor the specific designations from women's contributions.[135]

Balancing Missionary Costs with Mission Work Costs

The $2,500 additional funds received from the Woman's Board in 1896 enabled the mission to avoid a destructive retrenchment of its outreach (although Clara Burrell did point out that the calamity

[134] Ibid.
[135] J. H. Wyckoff to Clara Burrell, April 14, 1896.

had been avoided only because the women who had contributed paid twice for the Hindu girls' schools in that year).[136] Nevertheless, deep financial problems remained. In 1898 the appropriation remained approximately level, but the cost of two unmarried women missionaries, Annie Hancock and Ida Scudder (for her second term following her leave of absence for medical study), had to be incorporated into the mission budget at a level of $4,000 for 1898.[137] The situation became worse in 1899, when the appropriation called for an additional reduction of 14.5 percent.

The 1899 cut was particularly disastrous because the mission was not allowed to cut down on woman's work. That meant an 18 percent cut in allocations to boarding schools, reduction in evangelistic itinerating, delay of repairs, no new villages to be taken under instruction, and seventeen native assistants to be dismissed. This situation alarmed the mission. It suggested that the board should consider recalling one or more of its missionaries instead of cutting the funds for mission program.[138]

Individual missionaries went further. One suggestion that was in the air was that the mission should abandon the whole Telugu field rather than try to make cuts across the board and allow everything to languish. Henry J. Scudder, son of John Scudder, Jr., opposed abandoning the Telugu field. He wrote to Henry Cobb,

> Rather than abandon the Telugu portion of the Vineyard God has given our Church through the Arcot Mission to cultivate and care for, I feel it would be far better for my wife and me to withdraw from the service of the Mission and the Board, so that our salary could be given for the maintenance of the Telugu work....The number of teachers that could be employed on our salary to preach the Gospel under the directions of the missionaries in charge would be much greater for the interests of Christ's Kingdom, than for

136 Clara Burrell to J. H. Wyckoff, March 10, 1896.
137 J. H. Wyckoff to Henry Cobb, July 26, 1897.
138 J. Chamberlain to Henry Cobb, December 3, 1898.

me to remain on, worried and depressed and handicapped
because of want of funds to carry on the work.[139]

Henry Scudder was not alone in his concern about the relation of
missionary costs to other expenditures. L. R. Scudder in Ranipet
offered to work without salary. He said it was wrong to reduce the
number of native helpers without at the same time reducing the
missionary force.[140] In spite of the fact that the mission had for four
decades pressed the board for the appointment of more missionaries,
in light of the financial situation, it asked that the proportion of
work funds be at least equal to the cost of supporting missionaries.
It desired that, when the board considered appointing additional
missionaries, an equal amount be appropriated for the program of
the mission.[141] In contrast to that hope, application of the budget
cuts meant that the general work of the mission began receiving
considerably less than its share. In 1898, the proportion was 53
percent for general work, 48 percent for missionary costs. In 1900
it would be 56 percent for missionaries, 44 percent for general work
in dollar terms. Because in the meanwhile the foreign exchange
rates had shifted from twenty-nine cents for a rupee in 1898 to
thirty-three cents for a rupee in 1900, there was an additional loss
of Rs. 5,120, or 30 percent of work funds.[142]

Fortunately for the work of the Arcot Mission, there was from
time to time a positive response to their appeals for mercy. The
situation at the end of 1898 was relieved somewhat by a contribution
from Ralph Voorhees of $10,000 for the general work of the board.
The missionaries expressed their appreciation for a measure of
relief from the budgets cuts.[143] At the end of 1899 the mission
acknowledged the restoration of Rs. 7,500 to the 1900
appropriation.[144] At the beginning of 1900, the mission learned that

139 Henry J. Scudder to Henry Cobb, December 6, 1899.
140 L. R. Scudder to Henry Cobb, December 14, 1899.
141 J. H. Wyckoff to Henry Cobb, August 15, 1900.
142 Ibid.
143 J. Chamberlain to Henry Cobb, February 1, 1899.
144 L. R. Scudder to Henry Cobb, December 14, 1899.

the Woman's Board had agreed to support one-third of the cost of married missionaries.[145] The negative effects of the reductions in appropriations in the decade thus were to some extend avoided, and the essential activities of the mission continued.

After the turn of the century, the worst of the financial troubles came to an end. With the help of several large individual donations and other special efforts, the balance of the board's long-standing debt was eliminated by the end of 1902. The board expressed its appreciation to those who had so generously helped end its long struggle to reach financial equilibrium again. Yet it wanted the members of the Reformed Church to know that it was the overseas missions that had borne much of the burden.

> It is true, in a sense, that the Missions have after all paid it in suffering and tears. The relief now gained should be an inspiration to the church to relieve its Missions from the burdens which they have borne, to free their hearts from the care which has weighed them down and their hands from the bonds with have confined them, to send them all the help they need by way of re-enforcements and to supply them with the means necessary for the development of the native agency which is so seriously needed, and so seriously lacking, to publish more widely the glad tidings of the Word of God.[146]

Although the board was as yet in no position to provide much in the way of increased financial assistance, the small gain represented to the missionaries and the churches in India a sign of better days ahead. A new tone began to be heard in the letters of the missionaries to the Board of Foreign Missions. A new spirit of self-confidence was growing in the churches. Rather than relying on the mission for support, Indian Christians began to develop new patterns of taking initiative. The missionaries likewise gained a new respect for what

---

145 J. H. Wyckoff to Henry Cobb, January 27, 1900.
146 "BFMR," 1902, xxiii.

could happen when they placed responsibility for maintaining mission property in Indian Christian hands. There is a new wind blowing through the fiftieth anniversary report of the Arcot Mission.

The crucial change was that, in 1903, "the Mission departed, for the first time, from the time-honored principle of administering foreign moneys only by foreign hands, and made a definite grant-in-aid to several churches, that in turn took upon themselves the care and responsibility of a definite work."[147] This step, so long in coming, marked the beginning of changes that would ultimately result in the presence of a church that was self-governing, self-supporting, and self-propagating. There was still a long road ahead, but we can pause to rejoice in the first small steps toward changes in missionary attitudes and the response of Indian Christians.

The churches and catechists' houses in Madanapalle were in need of repair in 1903, so the mission voted Rs. 100 grant-in-aid to the Madanapalle church to make the repairs. When the Board of Deacons in Madanapalle learned of the grant, they resolved to make all repairs to the building without accepting the grant by using harvest festival money for that purpose. Unfortunately, late in the year there were exceptionally heavy rains with the result that more repairs were needed, so the Board of Deacons then accepted the grant-in-aid lest the buildings suffer further damage.[148]

The Yehamur Church made encouraging progress in self-support and self-government in 1903. It took responsibility to pay the salary of the pastor as well as his travel allowance. With regard to its buildings, the mission voted to give them a grant-in-aid in the amount of Rs. 200. The Yehamur pastorate then carried the responsibility for the erection and upkeep of all mission buildings and for the taxes on all mission property used by the church. In accepting this responsibility, the Yehamur pastorate made rules to watch over the property with more care than the mission could have done.

147 "AAR," 1903, 8.
148 Ibid.

They first drew up a number of rules with regard to the care of village buildings prohibiting, under penalty of fines, all things that would be likely to injure the buildings, such as allowing pumpkin vines to run over the roofs and tying cows to the verandah posts. They warned all that carelessness in allowing white ants to injure the rafters would be severely dealt with.[149]

Similar grants-in-aid were made to the churches in Ranipet and Vellore, with similar results. In Vellore, the church bore the entire expense of building a house in a village for a catechist. Ranipet carried out more work on the buildings than was anticipated and spent from its own funds Rs. 217-11-0 more than the grant-in-aid from the mission.[150]

In the first decade of the twentieth century, the mission of the Reformed Church in America entered a new phase in India. A union of churches related to various missions brought into being the South India United Church, a forerunner of the Church of South India. New forms of cooperation among the various missions took place as union institutions were established. Authority and power began to shift from the missionaries to the Indian Christians. Some of the early romance of mission was gone, but there was a new excitement in the air.

[149] Ibid., 10.
[150] Ibid.

7

From the Classis of Arcot to
the South India United Church

The Arcot Mission, in its report of 1891, expressed amazement at the changes that had occurred during its four decades of mission in India. There were now railway and electric lines connecting all of the towns in which there were mission stations. Macadamized roads had been built. Bridges were being placed over rivers. Hospitals and dispensaries were available in more and more places. Sanitary laws were being written and at times even enforced. There was also intellectual progress, as evidenced by the growing number of schools and newspapers, and increasing knowledge of the English language. Railways made it possible for people to broaden their outlook as they traveled. Members of different castes were learning to sit next to each other as they rode. Furthermore, missionaries had played no small role in advocating for the moral and social changes that had accompanied these developments.[1]

During that same period new political winds had begun to blow as Indians grew into a new consciousness of national identity. They resented the racist attitudes of their colonial rulers and the high-handed ways in which new laws and regulations were introduced.

[1] "AAR," 1892, i, iv, 3.

They also saw how much waste was caused by the constant military campaigns being carried out on the frontiers of India. Seventy-three men met together in 1885 at the first annual meeting of the Indian National Congress, the group that would become the leading body in the independence movement. They came as representatives of every province of British India.

The delegates met for three days. All proclaimed their loyalty to the English crown, but everyone who spoke expressed some political grievance toward the government of India. The president of the Congress said that what they all desired was "that the basis of the Government should be widened and that the people should have their proper and legitimate share in it."[2]

Thereafter, the Indian National Congress met annually to pass resolutions to send on to the government. Initially, under the Congress's moderate early leadership, these resolutions were framed in a spirit of loyal cooperation. As time went on, the Congress became increasingly revolutionary and independent, especially after 1905. By 1920 it had become totally uncooperative with the government.[3]

The Arcot missionaries watched the growth of Indian nationalism with a sense of appreciation coupled with anxiety. To the extent that the movement was the result of educational progress, of the traditions of English law, and of moral uplift it was to be welcomed. But they were anxious about the growing impatience of the movement that after 1905 sometimes led to rioting, terrorism, and even the throwing of bombs. The Indian Christians in the Arcot area did not participate in the political developments of the late nineteenth century. Nevertheless, missionaries and Indians alike recognized that events in the social and political realms would have an impact on the church and the mission. As far as the church was concerned, the new consciousness and self-respect was to be

2 Wolpert, *A New History of India*, 258-59.
3 Ibid., 259.

welcomed as an aid in the movement of the church toward becoming self-governing, self-supporting, and self-propagating.

Jacob Chamberlain's Call to Unity in Mission

Jacob Chamberlain sensed the need for the Christian missionary societies operating in India to serve in harmony with each other and to work toward greater unity. Six years before the Indian National Congress met in Bombay, Chamberlain was thinking of the relationships that ought to exist among the missions and churches of a revitalized India. In a lecture given at the meeting of the South India Missionary Conference on June 16, 1879, he became the first to propose that there should be one church of Christ in India.

> I may not live to see the day, but my sons now in college preparing to come to India as missionaries may, when there shall be organized a *"Church of Christ in India,"* not American, not English, not German, not Danish but *of India and suited to India,* in which we shall see not Scotch Presbyterianism, nor English Anglicanism, nor German Lutheranism, but the best features chosen out of all denominations and incorporated into one visible Church of Him of Nazareth. To this end it seems to me we should all of us work. This may not be feasible *now* but I do believe that greater organic unity than we now possess is feasible and should be earnestly sought for in the near future.[4]

Chamberlain went on to tell about how, on his return to India in 1878, he had spent two months in Japan and China studying the question of unity. He had met there with representatives of the "Church of Jesus Christ in Japan" and with the churches living together as one body in the Amoy area of China.[5] He pointed out that in 1879 at least twenty-eight different church organizations or

4 Jacob Chamberlain, "Native Churches and Foreign Missionary Societies" [lecture on file at the Joint Archives of Holland, Michigan (hereafter Joint Archives), 1879], 5.
5 Ibid., 6.

missions were operating in India. He believed that they should agree on several principles. One was "to make much of the essentials in which we all here agree, and less of the non-essentials in which we chance to differ."[6] A second was, "There should then in Ecclesiastical matters, be the greatest maximum of liberty to the Native Churches, with the smallest minimum of authority over them exercised from home lands."[7]

In his vision for mission cooperation and unity, Chamberlain called for a beginning to be made by reducing the number of independent and isolated church organizations. He suggested that there be one for Presbyterians, one Methodist, one Baptist, one Episcopalian and Lutheran, and one Congregational and that they should all meet from time to time in one assembly.[8] Chamberlain's vision struck a responsive chord as time went on. Within thirty years, the Classis of Arcot would lose its identity as it entered into the larger unity of the South India United Church.

The Presbyterian Alliance in India

The issue of increased cooperation and union with other Reformed and Presbyterian churches and missions was not new to the missionaries of the Reformed Church when Chamberlain made his appeal in 1879. E.C. Scudder had forwarded to the General Synod in 1867 a letter from "certain Presbyterian brethren in India" that proposed that a convention be held in 1868 to consider the expediency of uniting Presbyterians generally in one General Assembly in India."[9] The General Synod of the Reformed Church agreed with the proposal, saying that "this Synod sees no reason why missionaries of our Church in India should not hold themselves open to any suggestions that may be made on the subject of

6 Ibid., 5.
7 Ibid., 7.
8 Ibid.
9 Edward Tanjore Corwin, *A Digest of Constitutional and Synodical Legislation of the Reformed Church in America* (New York: Board of Publications of the Reformed Church in America, 1906), 55.

Presbyterial relations between the several mission churches in India, but that the whole matter is entrusted to the discretion of our missionaries...."[10]

The Presbyterian Alliance was formed in India in 1875, with representatives present from the various Presbyterian and Reformed mission organizations and churches. The alliance was in its origin a very loose coalition of Presbyterian and Reformed bodies in the subcontinent of India. The Arcot Mission joined the alliance and regularly sent one or more of its members to attend the meetings. Jacob Chamberlain was the leading advocate for the alliance, and the other Arcot missionaries supported participation with varying amounts of enthusiasm.

The General Synod of 1886, undoubtedly with the encouragement of Chamberlain (who was present), spoke even more decisively in favor of an organic union of Presbyterian church bodies in India to replace the loose coalition structure of the alliance. It advised the Classis of Arcot to move ahead in pursuit of such cooperation.

> *Resolved,* 1. That the Classis of Arcot be permitted and advised to initiate such measures as shall tend to bring together the churches of the Presbyterian polity in India;
>
> And 2. That the Classis of Arcot will endorse the union of the Classis of Arcot with such a union Church of Christ in India composed of those holding the Reformed faith and Presbyterian polity.[11]

A Plan of Union had been formulated the previous year. The plan required that the parent bodies in Scotland and the United States give approval to move ahead, since in the case of the Reformed Church, for example, the Classis of Arcot could act to unite with another church or alliance only with the synod's assent. Therefore, the General Synod further resolved to commission Chamberlain to stop in Scotland on his return journey to India to present to the

10 *Minutes of the General Synod, RCA,* 1867, 276-77.
11 *Minutes of the General Synod, RCA,* 1886, 122.

Presbyterian General Assemblies the fraternal greetings of the Reformed Church in America. He was also instructed "to draw their attention to the unanimous action taken by this body in favor of Organic Union on Missions Fields of those holding the Reformed Faith with Presbyterian Polity, in the hope that similar permissive action may be taken by their respective bodies authorizing their missions in India to take part in such a union."[12]

In advising the Arcot Mission and the Classis of Arcot to take part in the organic union of Presbyterian bodies, the General Synod had moved ahead of most of its missionaries in India, who had been expressing reservations about the idea of organic union. J.H. Wyckoff, who had represented the Reformed Church at several of the meetings of the Presbyterian Alliance and who was in favor of cooperation, had expressed his hesitation in a letter to the Presbyterian delegate William Miller, with a copy to Henry Cobb. Miller had addressed the Classis of Arcot with reference to a plan that the alliance should found a Presbyterian Theological Seminary for India in the city of Allahabad in the north central part of India.

Wyckoff replied in his capacity of clerk of the Classis of Arcot by communicating the action of the classis: "Resolved, that while the Arcot Classis approve generally the scheme of the Alliance, they do not at present see their way clear to recommend it to their home Society for pecuniary support."[13] The classis was hesitant because the Arcot Mission was a vernacular mission, while the proposed seminary, which would serve missions throughout India, would have to conduct its courses in the English language. People in the Arcot area did not yet have adequate command of English to enable them to benefit from theological study in that language.[14]

The Presbyterian Alliance presented to the Classis of Arcot a second and more far-reaching question. It proposed with regard to ordained office bearers that the parent judicatories "be asked to

[12] Ibid., 123.
[13] J. H. Wyckoff to William Miller, November 29, 1883.
[14] Ibid.

recognize the judicial authority of this council, so far as to authorize it to decide finally cases of appeal in matters of discipline referred to the council by the parties concerned, in accordance with the rules of their respective churches, in regard only to native churches' office bearers and members...."

The Classis of Arcot considered this proposal at length in several of its sessions. If it was adopted, appeals by Indian ordained ministers (but not ordained missionaries) against decisions of the Classis of Arcot, such as that made by Joseph Mayou to the Particular Synod of New York, would go to the Presbyterian Alliance. The change would have been a major step in the process of turning the Presbyterian Alliance into an independent denomination in India. The classis did not take any action on this proposal because it learned that the Presbyterian Alliance had also sent the proposal directly to the General Synod. The classis felt that it had to await the action of the General Synod.[15]

While the classis did not believe it should take action, Jared Scudder, who was secretary of the mission, did feel free to send his opinion to Henry Cobb. He said that he heartily hoped the day would come when there would be an Indian Presbyterian Church embracing all who hold to that form of government. Nevertheless, he thought the plan as presented was not really practicable. He did not believe that the classis could sustain a dual relationship with the Reformed Church and the Presbyterian Alliance in which the ordained missionaries would be amenable for discipline to the Reformed Church while the Indians would be to the alliance in some things and to the Reformed Church in others. This arrangement, he believed, would lead to the disintegration of the classis as it sought to follow two sets of rules applying to two different categories of members. He further believed that the only way to become a component part of the alliance was to sever relations with the overseas judicatories, so that appeals by Reformed

15 Ibid.

Church in America ordained missionaries would also go the Presbyterian Alliance. Jared Scudder was not yet ready to do that.[16]

Scudder expanded his thought in another direction when he linked the role of the self-government of the alliance to the matter of self-support. "I think the churches here must become self-supporting before such an independent footing can be assumed. As long as churches in India are sustained, in whole or in part, by contributions from abroad, they must, it seems to me, remain under the ecclesiastical control of the judicatories of the foreign churches making those contributions."[17] In Scudder's mind, accountability on the part of churches accepting contributions from their members still required that the churches have adequate control to ensure that the funds were actually spent for the purposes for which they were contributed. In the twentieth century, there would be strong movements to cut that linkage in order to enable the Indian churches to be fully self-governing and free from foreign control. But the question did not go away. Even when the autonomy of the Indian church was fully recognized after 1947, Bishop Hollis, the first bishop in Madras in the Church of South India, would write a whole book on the subject, entitled *Paternalism and the Church*.[18]

The proposal to move forward into a more organic union met resistance in other Presbyterian missions and overseas churches as well as among the Arcot missionaries, so interest in the alliance waned for a number of years. Meetings of the Presbyterian Alliance continued to be held regularly until 1889, but after that it did not meet for more than a decade.

Negotiating and Protecting the Arcot Mission Boundaries

In spite of the interest that the Arcot missionaries expressed in greater cooperation among the missions, they also took pride in

16 J. W. Scudder to Henry Cobb, April 2, 1884.
17 Ibid.
18 Michael Hollis, *Paternalism and the Church: A Study of South Indian Church History* (London: Oxford Univ. Press, 1962).

having secured their own mission field and vigorously defended its geographical boundaries. In the very beginning, when the possibility had arisen for the Reformed Church in America to develop its own mission field in India, Rufus Anderson had strongly advised the Scudders "as to the desirableness of our Mission cultivating fields where they would be the sole and undisputed occupants; and on one occasion, you made the remark to the Rev. H. M. Scudder, that it would be well worth while to pay the Gospel Propagation Society something in case they would abandon this District to us."[19]

The Arcot Mission took this advice from Rufus Anderson very seriously. In spite of the fact that several of its missionaries became leaders in ecumenical cooperation in India, they also proved to be zealous in remaining "the sole and undisputed occupants" of the field to which they believed they had been called. As we have previously noted, the field that they occupied was vast, especially in an era when transportation and communications were still slow and difficult. At the beginning, there were only three ordained men to cover an area the size of the state of New Jersey. Fifteen years later, there was a short time when only two ordained men were present. In 1882, questions were being raised about whether to abandon the Madanapalle and Telugu field.

Rather than abandon any part of their field to others, the missionaries worked exceedingly hard, often at the cost of their own health, while complaining to the Board of Foreign Missions that it was failing to heed the need for more missionaries. The complaints could become quite bitter. John and Elizabeth Conklin had arrived in India in 1881 and almost immediately became quite ill. They often had to leave their work to go to the hills or elsewhere to rest and recover. Two of their children died shortly after birth. Nevertheless they persevered and accomplished much. At the end of ten years, however, the mission decided that they must leave India for sake of their health. It wrote to the board in New York January 30, 1890, that the Conklins must leave the following week,

---

[19] Rufus Anderson to William W. Scudder , December 11, 1855.

"crushed under their load." The letter accused the board of allowing John Conklin "to immolate himself to save Christ's work." The mission went on to add that Carman Scudder had returned to India a short time ago, but he also was already "crushed under the load."[20]

In spite of their tremendous burden, the missionaries firmly and repeatedly protected their field from the encroachments of other missionary bodies. On other occasions, they entered into negotiations with other missions looking to transfer one or another town to another mission. The question of the field and its boundaries was a matter of active concern between 1880 and 1900. A review of the specific actions will reveal the mission's thinking on the subject.

The Society for the Propagation of the Gospel returns to Vellore, 1882

The first case arose when the Society for the Propagation of the Gospel (SPG) purchased a house across the road from the Vellore mission church in 1882. It settled a person in the house, conducted a school in it, and held divine worship there. The mission regarded this action on the part of the SPG to be in violation of the agreement made in 1855. At that time, the Arcot Mission had purchased the SPG chapel and other buildings in Vellore and Chittoor and had accepted the promise of the bishop in Madras to deliver the congregation over to the mission.[21] The SPG at that time had withdrawn from mission work in the area. It did, however, continue to provide pastoral services in the English language church within the Vellore fort and to the Indian Christians in Vellore who refused to join the Reformed Church following the transfer of the congregation. The mission had no objection to the continuation of those pastoral services.[22]

There were people in the SPG who were not pleased with the withdrawal from Arcot District in favor of the Arcot Mission. The

---

[20] Arcot Mission to Board of Foreign Missions, January 30, 1890.
[21] See chap. 2, 74-76.
[22] J. W. Scudder to J. M. Ferris, March 27, 1883.

SPG represented the high Anglican theology that believed that ordination by the hands of a bishop in the unbroken tradition of the church catholic was of the essence of the faith. Therefore, in their opinion the Reformed Church ministers, who had not been ordained by a bishop, did not have a valid ministry of the sacraments. Those who held such a view found a loophole in the 1855 agreement in which the SPG promised to withdraw from the field. The loophole was that there was no promise that the SPG would not at some future date return to work in Vellore.[23] Since the mission expected to make little progress with the SPG missionaries in India, it asked the Board of Foreign Missions to enter into direct correspondence with the SPG leaders in England and request them to order their mission in India to honor not only the letter but the spirit of the 1855 agreement.

The first exchange of letters between the SPG and the board produced little result. Henry Cobb stated that he had little hope of any good coming from further correspondence. After reviewing copies of the correspondence sent to him by Henry Cobb, Jared Scudder vented his disgust with the arrogance of the SPG's reply.

> Its members live in a self-constructed sphere of arrogance in which they look down with undisguised contempt on all who are not of their way of thinking. Availing themselves of the prestige which their connection with Government gives them here, they manage to make it uncomfortable for those who will not pronounce their Shibboleth. The only point in our favor is that they *took our money* at the transfer. This ought certainly to make *gentlemen* hesitate to do what they have done. But in their *religion,* these men are not gentlemen. So I imagine they will rather sacrifice honor than withdraw.[24]

23 Ibid.
24 J. W. Scudder to Henry Cobb, December 4, 1883.

When one remembers that in 1947 the SPG and the Arcot Mission would embrace each other in celebration of their being united in the Church of South India, one must give thanks again at the reconciling power of the Spirit of God, who repeatedly overcomes human arrogance and suspicion. But the Vellore controversy did not have to wait until 1947 for resolution. Tempers soon cooled, and Christian reasonableness returned. On June 12, 1885, Jared Scudder wrote to the board that the SPG controversy had more or less been resolved. They had reached agreement reached about how to achieve cooperation without competition.[25] The SPG continued to provide pastoral services in Vellore for those who wanted to remain within the Anglican church, but it did not compete with the Arcot Mission in evangelistic outreach.

The Church of Scotland Mission Stays in Vellore, 1882.

One comes to a better understanding of the Arcot Mission's desire to be the sole occupants of a territory by examining the mission's 1865 experience of taking under its care the village of Kundipatoor, located about nine miles northeast of Vellore. Kundipatoor had first been visited by native helpers of the Arcot mission six years earlier, who had distributed a number of tracts. At that time the missionary in Vellore was temporarily absent, but the village came to the notice of native helpers of the Church of Scotland Mission. They took spiritual charge of those villagers who were expressing their desire to become Christians. After the Arcot missionary returned to Vellore, he was repeatedly urged by other "heathen" of the same village to receive them under instruction.

Since there was already a catechist and teacher of the Church of Scotland in the village and they had already built a place of worship, the missionary did not agree to their request. Instead, he suggested that the new group join with the others who were receiving instruction from the catechist and teacher who were already there.

---

[25] J. W. Scudder to Henry Cobb, June 12, 1885.

Nevertheless, the new group persistently asked the missionary to take them under instruction. After about a year, the church that had been built burned and was not rebuilt. Finally the people of the village said that if the Arcot Mission would not respond, they intended to remain in heathenism. The result was that the mission stationed a catechist and teacher there to serve those persons. They were joined by two families of the Church of Scotland, for a total of fifty-four persons.[26]

The Arcot Mission and the Church of Scotland Mission had enjoyed good relationships with each other ever since John Scudder, Sr., and John Anderson had become friends in Madras many years before. Still, the Church of Scotland was not ready to recognize the exclusive role of the Arcot Mission in the work of evangelism and planting churches in the Vellore area, and it ignored for many years the protests of the Arcot Mission to its presence there. The Arcot Mission then proposed that the Church of Scotland Mission devote itself to educational work and leave all the evangelistic work to the Arcot Mission, but the Church of Scotland Mission would not agree.

Finally, in 1882, the two missions agreed that educational work would be the responsibility of the Church of Scotland Mission and evangelism the responsibility of the Arcot Mission. Jared Scudder admitted to J.M. Ferris after the agreement had been reached that the Arcot Mission had found a way to apply a little pressure. He reminded Ferris that he had taken over the management of the Anglo-Vernacular school when offered it by its Brahmin founder in 1880.[27] "It was, *partly,* to bring pressure upon them that we took over the Anglo-Vernacular School in Vellore, when it was offered to us in 1880."[28]

The Church of Scotland Mission felt the pressure of the competition that the Anglo-Vernacular School had the potential to

26 "AAR," 1865, 40-41.
27 See chap. 4, 192.
28 J. W. Scudder to J. M. Ferris, August 19, 1882.

place upon the enrollment of the high school it was operating in Vellore. The secretary of its mission wrote to the Arcot Mission to say that it was transferring its Indian minister located in Vellore to Arkonam, fifty miles to east, and leaving the few families in connection with his congregation to the care of the American Arcot Mission. In response, the Arcot Mission stated that it was giving up its Anglo-Vernacular school in Vellore in favor of the Church of Scotland Mission. Thus an amicable understanding was reached, and each mission was now free to do that work that it did best without further tension between them.[29]

The Salvation Army Invasion

The Arcot Mission also felt called upon to defend its territory against the invasions of the Salvation Army, which at that time had not been a party to comity agreements establishing boundaries among the various mission societies. Already in 1885, Lambertus Hekhuis wrote a long complaint to the board in New York about the "Salvationists" invasion of the Arni area. He grumbled that "they have strange ways."[30]

He described their attempt to adapt to the customs of the people:

> They dress like natives, in a long coat, a turban and a loose pair of trousers, or, as I saw the Captain going along the street today, with simply a cloth tied around his waist and hanging loosely down to his knees, or a little lower, leaving the lower parts of his legs bare, his feet being encased in a pair of native shoes, which look more like slippers with the toes narrow and turned up. This is a very becoming dress for a native, but for a European it looks anything but decent and respectable....[31]

> The way they count converts is novel indeed....When they enter a village they use all the means at their command

29 Ibid.
30 L. Hekhuis to Henry Cobb, August 29, 1885.
31 Ibid.

to draw a crowd, then after preaching a little and explaining the object of their coming, they ask them to kneel down with them to pray, which if they do they are immediately enrolled as converts and said to be saved.[32]

A more serious invasion occurred ten years later. The Salvation Army, without any consultation, entered the villages within the area of the triangle formed by the towns of Vellore, Arcot, and Chittoor. It placed one or two of its agents in a number of the villages in which there were congregations established by workers of the Arcot Mission. The Arcot Mission catechists and teachers were instructed to walk in peace with the uninvited guests and to watch and report developments.

A little more than a year later, the founder of the Salvation Army, General Booth, came to India to gain more knowledge of how the work of the Salvation Army was progressing. A "Village Demonstration" was scheduled to be held in the Arcot area for his benefit. The demonstration included a great reception for the distinguished visitor, processions with torches and banners, and the sale of Salvation Army jerseys. The banner at the head of the procession bore the words, "Serkadu and Victory." Several of the Arcot missionaries had come to watch the proceedings. They were bemused by the reference to Serkadu, where a congregation had already been formed in 1867. The Christians there made up one of the strongest village congregations. They had their own pastor and had built their own church at a cost of Rs. 550. Most of the people who participated in the demonstration were not very clear about who the Salvation Army was, but they came to enjoy the reception and excitement. The missionaries heard General Booth address the crowd of about five hundred people.

It was at once amusing and most pitiful to hear this really great Leader of the Salvation Army Hosts, in addressing them through an interpreter, tell these people that he had

32 Ibid.

heard of the wonderful work of the Salvation Army in the Arcot District, and the large recruiting [sic] of soldiers, news of which had come to him over the seas, and he was greatly rejoiced now to see these Salvation Army soldiers! After this Demonstration the people settled down again into their usual manner of life, with no desire for further association with the Salvation Army.[33]

The interference of the Salvation Army agents continued after the demonstration, so the Arcot Mission sent three of its most senior pastors to Madras to speak with the colonel of the Madras Division. The missionaries told him about the way in which the Salvation Army was proving to be a divisive force among the Christians in the area. The colonel and his chief of staff went to the area to investigate. The colonel agreed that most of the "soldiers" there were already members of congregations related to the Arcot Mission. He disclaimed any intention to interfere with the work of the Arcot Mission and withdrew the Salvation Army officers from the area. For a time there was peace.

A short time later, however, the Salvation Army returned and established new headquarters in Katpadi, complete with a training school, and announced that vigorous work would be carried on from that center. It was further announced that the commissioner in charge of the London Foreign Office of the Salvation Army would soon be visiting the new center. The mission lamented, "Thus is our last state worse than our first, and thus are the complaints of other Missions against the Salvation Army confirmed by our own experience."[34]

The course of events described in the Serkadu village area is not at all unusual in the history of Protestant mission efforts over the past two centuries. Evangelists working in a locality often feel heavy pressure to show results and report converts. In order to achieve

[33] "BFMR," 1897, 43.
[34] Ibid., 43-44.

quick results, they begin work in places where there are already a fairly large number of Christians. By offering various incentives and some entertainment they gather for themselves a congregation, while implying to their overseas supporters that these are new converts from heathenism. Fortunately, the Salvation Army changed its tactics in India and within a comparatively short time became a respected member among the missionary societies there. In the nineteenth century, when there was great hostility between Protestants and Roman Catholics, the Arcot missionaries never considered the objections they were making to the efforts of the Salvation Army in relation to their own successful efforts in gaining their first congregations at the expense of the Roman Catholic Church.

Cooperation and Controversy at Coonoor

In 1857, the Arcot Mission had agreed with the Basel Evangelical Lutheran Mission to take responsibility for the English language congregation and the Tamil work at Coonoor, three hundred miles from Vellore.[35] Coonoor was important to the Arcot Mission because it provided a place in the mountains where missionaries could stay to recover their health. As time went on, the mission adopted a policy that there should be a missionary in Coonoor at least three or four months every year. If there was no missionary who had to reside there for a time for health reasons, then, the mission decided, one of its missionaries should spend the months there. The mission also provided a catechist and teacher for the Tamil work.

Coonoor had a resident English-speaking congregation consisting of planters and officials who were able to contribute to the support of the church. In times of distress on the plains, such as famine or destruction due to fires or floods, the members were often ready to provide financial assistance to the victims of the disasters. They also

[35] See chap. 2, 98-99.

made contributions to purchase materials for church buildings and schools. At the same time, there often were conflicts within the church, so the missionaries who went there found themselves struggling with how to resolve the issues. While they appreciated the faithfulness of the Arcot Mission in providing care for the congregation, a majority of the English people in Coonoor were members of the Anglican Church, and, if they had had a choice, may well have preferred to be ministered to by an Anglican priest.

There were signs of problems in 1885, when Jared W. Scudder spent three months in Coonoor and did not find things in an encouraging condition. He removed the catechist and other helpers and sent a new catechist, C. David, who worked energetically and brought about some improvement. At the end of the year, however, the Church Missionary Society, in connection with "The Church Committee of All Saints Church, Coonoor," occupied the Coonoor station and attempted to replace the work of the Arcot Mission. Although the Church Missionary Society was Anglican "low church" and held that the episcopally ordained ministry is important to the church rather than absolutely essential, it still looked askance at non-episcopally ordained ministers, especially when they were ministering to those who had been Anglicans. The Arcot Mission printed a "remonstrance" against the action of the Church Missionary Society. The church committee of All Saints Church then published a letter in the newspaper, the *Madras Mail*, defending its action, but, in the opinion of Jared Scudder, suppressing the facts in the case. The Arcot Mission published its own side of the story, and there were other public attacks and defenses set forth by both sides. The heat with which the controversy was waged can be felt by reading Scudder's words:

> Their action in Coonoor was undoubtedly an outrage against all that is right and courteous; but with them both right and courtesy seem always to be at a discount in matters relating to *the Church*. We would feel very much humiliated if we did things which they do most freely. You in America

can have but faint idea of the arrogant scorn with which
English Churchmen treat those who are outside their pale.
All such, in their estimation, have no rights which they are
bound to respect. It is too bad that we have to waste so
much time and effort in resisting the encroachments of
those who rightly ought by every Christian principle, to
work with, and not against us. But so it is.[36]

The facts of the case and the arguments pro and con need no
longer concern us. The attempt by followers of the Church
Missionary Society to gain control was not successful. In fact, the
Reformed Church congregation gained twenty-nine members for
the year. Services were well attended and the schools were also in
good condition.[37]

The Coonoor hill station was used less by Reformed Church
missionaries after the beginning of the twentieth century. Then the
Kodaikanal hill station became a more convenient and prominent
place for Arcot missionaries to rest and recuperate. The Arcot
Mission entered into negotiations with the German Basel Mission
to take over responsibility for the Coonoor station, since the
German mission already had a station six miles from Coonoor. The
transfer took place November 26, 1911.

William Farrar of the Arcot Mission preached on the text,
"Beloved, I do not consider that I have made it my own; but this one
thing I do: forgetting what lies behind and straining forward to what
lies ahead, I press on toward the goal for the prize of the heavenly
call of God in Christ Jesus" (Phil. 3:13-14). Carman Scudder
described the transfer of the Congregational Register and church
key:

> After graceful farewell addresses to Pastor Jacob Solomon
> (who leaves them at the end of the year) and to the
> American Arcot Mission, it fell to my lot to speak to the

---

[36] J. W. Scudder to J. M. Ferris, March 23, 1886.
[37] "BFMR," 1886, 54-55.

From the Classis of Arcot to the South India United Church   333

people from Exodus 14:15, and to hand the Congregational Register and Church Key to Rev. Mr. Risch, of Kaity, who took them with the remark that he hoped the Basel Mission would so fulfill the trust committed to them that all those on the roll in the register and many more would be found on the right side in the great hereafter.[38]

At this point we cannot help but note that eventually the churches founded by the Arcot Mission, the Church Missionary Society, and the Basel Mission would all become one in the Church of South India.

Trading Responsibilities with the Hermansburg Evangelical Mission

In their desire to cooperate with other societies without competing in mission, the Arcot Mission at times entered into negotiations concerning boundaries with neighboring missions. One such set of negotiations came to a successful conclusion with the Hermansburg Evangelical Mission, a Lutheran mission with its base in northern Germany. That mission's territory bounded the Arcot Mission boundary to the northeast of Chittoor and Madanapalle in the Telugu area. On several occasions, missionaries and Indian evangelists had unwittingly crossed the boundaries that had been fixed between the two. They had occupied villages in the other's territory. A Hermansburg missionary had established an outstation in the town of Piler inside the Arcot mission area. When the Arcot missionary raised a question about it, the Hermansburg mission withdrew in favor of Arcot. On another occasion, the Arcot Mission had asked that the boundary be adjusted so that the towns of Pakala and Damalcheru become its responsibility, but Hermansburg declined, as it had a right to do. Meanwhile, Arcot missionaries L.R. Scudder and James Beattie had been conducting evangelistic tours and placing teachers in villages close to Puttur,

---

[38] "BFMR," 1912, 49. Ex. 14:15 reads, "Then the Lord said to Moses, 'Why do you cry out to me? Tell the Israelites to go forward.'"

James Beattie

northeast of Chittoor. Hermansburg had intended to make Puttur one of its main mission stations.[39]

When the railway connection was made among Madanapalle, Chittoor, and Tirupati, it became apparent that some boundary adjustments would make it simpler for both missions to fulfill their responsibilities. Several conferences between representatives of the two missions were held, with the result that a new boundary was established between them.

> The boundaries were settled by villages for the whole length of contact. They gave over to us Pakala and all the region that we had asked for, and we gave over to them a part of the Koorvetnagar Zamindari in which we had begun work, including the village of Sauteguntur taken up by Brother Beattie six months ago, they paying the cost of the

[39] J. Chamberlain to Henry Cobb, March 3, 1898.

buildings....Mr. Beattie was authorized to occupy Pakala as an outstation at once. A number of native Christians connected with the railway [sic]. Some of them members of the Chittoor church are already there as the nucleus of a congregation.

We have thus secured what we have long desired, the whole territory on the S. I. Railway from Villupurman to the N.W. boundary of the Madanapalle field, and the arrangement has been made with perfect cordiality on both sides. We are very glad.[40]

It is ironic that these negotiations, friendly from beginning to end, resulted in the transfer of villages that remained in separated denominations, while in Vellore and Coonoor, the members of the separated churches have become members of the same united church, in spite of controversy and forceful complaints about each other. In the negotiations between Arcot and Hermensburg, there is little evidence that consultation with the villages themselves took place. Membership in a denomination was a matter of mission policy rather than personal choice.

Should Polur be transferred to the Danish Lutheran Mission?

The Arcot Mission always enjoyed a cordial relationship with the Danish Lutheran Mission located on its southern boundary. A number of the Danish mission catechists and teachers had received their training in the Arcot Theological Seminary. The Danish mission also cooperated with the Arcot Mission in the founding of the Union Mission Training School for teachers in Viruthampet. In 1899, the Arcot missionaries in Tindivanam and Arni were overburdened with the large number of villages under their care. They were also conscious of the fact that there was a large area in the Polur Taluq (county) that they were not adequately covering. Therefore they proposed to the Arcot Mission that Polur Taluq be

40 Ibid.

handed over to the Danish Lutheran Mission that was adjacent to Polur. The Arcot Mission considered the matter carefully, but "decided that we should not abandon this field, that would bring an alien society within a few miles of Arni, but rather endeavor to strengthen our forces there. It is hoped that the Board will enable the Mission to properly work this large Taluq."[41]

The board was not able to respond positively to this request. On the contrary, at the end of 1900 the mission was once again informed that the appropriation to the mission for 1901 had to be reduced. One result of the reduction was the action of the mission to offer Polur Taluq to the Danish Lutheran Mission. In making the offer, the mission had three points of concern. First, because the Classis of Arcot had not yet acted, the mission feared that the classis might refuse to hand over the congregation in Polur. Second, the mission wondered whether the 150 members of the congregation in Polur might feel betrayed somehow in being transferred to be Lutherans. Third, the mission feared the reaction of members of the Reformed Church who were known to be opposed to church union when they learned of the mission's gift of the congregation to the Lutherans. The mission saw no alternative, however, in view of the need to reduce expenditures by 12.5 percent.[42]

All of these concerns became mute when the mission learned from the Danish Lutheran Mission that the offer was declined because the Danish mission was also short of resources.[43] The congregation in Polur remained a member of the Classis of Arcot.

Missionary Lifestyle and Inter-Mission Cooperation

The above review of the ways in which the Arcot Mission defended its position and negotiated boundaries in its area serves to make us aware of the details and technicalities involved in sustaining broad cooperation among the missions. In the first half of the

41 J. H. Wyckoff to Henry Cobb, August 22, 1899.
42 J. H. Wyckoff to Henry Cobb, January 15, 1901.
43 J. H. Wyckoff to Henry Cobb, April 4, 1901.

nineteenth century, there was more than enough room for all to operate. In a series of official and unofficial negotiations with each other, boundaries were laid out within which each mission bore its sole and exclusive responsibility to evangelize the area. In order to maintain such a system, it was necessary for each mission to recognize the basic Christian orthodoxy and faith of all the other missions. A series of missionary conferences in India provided occasions for mutual discussion, planning, and building of trust among the missionaries.

As the nineteenth century was nearing an end, more and more people came to feel the need for even greater cooperation among the missionary societies and churches. Not only were a number of Indians beginning to sense that the European and American divisions were counterproductive in India, but a number of missionaries began to take leadership in moving toward greater unity. One must not think that this movement toward unity came about largely because of deep theological reflection or was simply due to the pragmatic need for efficiency in working together, although both theology and pragmatism did provide incentives to that end. Rather, the common lifestyle, friendships, and sense of family that developed in the missionary community in India played a major role in encouraging cooperative efforts among the mission societies and churches.

Reformed Church missionaries in India found themselves in an awkward position on the social scale. On the one hand, they were part of the same English-speaking white race that had established British rule in India. To the people of India, they represented political power, western culture, educational knowledge, and Christianity. On the other hand, they knew themselves to be vulnerable to forces known and unknown. During most of the century, the United States was not yet a world power and was not particularly allied with England. England had burned the American capitol just six years before John and Harriet Scudder had sailed to India. Americans still felt themselves to be an appendix to European culture. The United States was as yet more a land of promise than a country of wealth. It took several decades for its economy to recover from the devastation of the Civil War. Reformed Church missionaries served in India with the permission of the British rulers, but they were not at all a part of the ruling elite.

All European missionaries in India knew themselves to be vulnerable to uprisings of Indians against the ruling race. The sepoy mutiny of 1857 had taught them that in the time of rebellion the sepoys and their allies did not distinguish between English and other Europeans. Closer at hand most of the time was their vulnerability to the diseases and epidemics of India. Death could strike quickly and often in missionary families. Beyond such physical dangers was their vulnerability to the emotional stress and loneliness of foreigners living among people of other languages and unfamiliar cultures. This sense of personal vulnerability served as a common bond with all Europeans living in India, whether or not they belonged to the ruling elite or the same social class.

In their need to cope with their vulnerable position, Europeans in India developed a lifestyle designed to facilitate their social life and to provide a sense of belonging and security. The English colonial leaders developed the pattern. Prior to the nineteenth century, the vast majority of those who went out under the East India Company were young, unmarried men who intended to stay for several years, establish their reputation, and perhaps make their fortune. Their death rate from tropical diseases, hard drinking, and sexually transmitted diseases was at times unbelievably high. By the time the Arcot Mission was established, however, English military and civil officers often took their wives with them and settled down to live as comfortably as they could in India. With the encouragement of their wives, they established habits that enabled them to avoid some of the diseases and to maintain the standards of genteel British society. With the exception of the British colonialist's enjoyment of beer, whiskey, gin, and similar alcoholic beverages plus their love of dancing, the missionaries saw much in that lifestyle that was attractive to them as well.

Three important components of British life in India were the cantonment or civil lines, the bungalow residence, and the hill station.[44] The missionaries adapted each of these to serve their own purposes. The first two components were developed in order to ward off exposure to diseases such as cholera, malaria, typhoid, and plague by isolating the British colonialists from the Indian population as a whole. The cantonment area consisted of civil lines of homes built along straight roads or streets and were available for Europeans and higher ranking employees of the company. It was always laid out at a separate but convenient distance from the city or town in which the Indian population lived. Even today it is possible for a visitor to recognize clearly the old cantonment area in Madras, Vellore, and other towns in the old Arcot Mission area. American and European missionaries recognized the advantages of locating somewhat apart from the close quarters in the Indian towns and villages, but they were not welcomed into the cantonment areas. Instead, they looked for a rather large piece of more-or-less vacant property a short distance away from the town on which they could erect a bungalow and buildings for other mission activities. This came to be known as the "mission compound."

The second component was the bungalow in which senior officers lived. The bungalow was usually constructed of brick and masonry, had high ceilings, several rooms, and a wide verandah. It served a number of purposes. It gave some protection against the hot climate. It was sited away from the reflected heat of other buildings and kept the occupants away from the noise, dust, and disease of India. It was surrounded by a wall, had a gate with a guard, and a long entry drive. It thus served to impress Indians with the power and authority of the British while at the same time regulating entry and providing a measure of security.[45] The compound within

---

[44] Metcalf, *Ideologies of the Raj*, 177.
[45] Ibid., 177-78.

Mary Lott Lyles Hospital

which the bungalow was situated usually also contained a number of small houses for the use of the Indian staff: butlers, maids, cooks, gardeners or those who worked in other positions.[46]

By the last quarter of the nineteenth century, most of the missionaries lived on a mission compound in bungalows. Mission bungalows were acquired or erected as mission stations were opened in the various towns. Several of them were large and had been converted into living quarters after having served the East India Company in other capacities. Mildred De Vries, in her memoir, remembered her move in 1930 into a bungalow at Arni that had been used from the early days of the mission.

> The old bungalow formerly was an Indigo Company. The verandah had a hundred feet to sweep and was happily used by David with his tricycle! People living there had added room after room. The dining-living room had 12 large outside doors with great hand-fashioned hinges and bolts and locks. It was a ritual to close up that massive house at

46 Ibid., 179.

night. It was repaired and reroofed when we (at a later time) were stationed there. Termites were many and the palmyra rafters were riddled. It took extensive cleaning every Saturday to make us comfortable.[47]

On the other hand, a number of bungalows were built by the mission itself, as was the case in the bungalow for Jacob Chamberlain's family in the 1880s and for the unmarried women missionaries in Mary Lott Lyle Hospital in Madanapalle. The bungalow planned for Dr. Hart and Kitty Scudder in Ranipet was funded by the Woman's Board in the amount of $1,800 in 1898. It had living quarters upstairs and a place for meeting people, Dr. Hart's office, and a dining room downstairs, with a large verandah around two sides of the house.[48]

The bungalow in Punganur was remodeled from a building on ten acres donated by the local Raja for a mission station. It was quite small, as described by H.J. Scudder:

It was a conundrum where to tuck away our boxes and trunks, goods and chattels. After much planning we are fairly well settled and are very "snug" in our little house. Our boxes were converted into chests by a pair of hinges and a clasp, and the front, back and two small side verandahs are lined with various boxes containing the things for which we could find no room inside. Our combined parlor and dining room is 12x12 feet and the children's bedroom is the same size, my study is 6x9 feet and our one large bedroom is 21x12 feet.[49]

---

[47] Mildred De Vries, *To Serve with Joy: My Life Story* (privately printed for her children and grandchildren; a copy is in possession of her son, David A. De Vries), 30.

[48] *Mission Gleaner,* November/December, 1898, 14-15. Wide and long verandahs made a bungalow comfortable because they provided a place to work and to meet people in a pleasant setting. They also served as a buffer for the inside rooms against the heat of the sun.

[49] Henry J. Scudder, "Building Up and Tearing Down in India," *Mission Field,* August, 1908, 135.

The third component for the welfare of foreigners in India was the hill station, located on or near the top of one of India's mountains. Within the Madras Presidency, Coonoor and Ootucumand were two of the most important. Hill stations were located at an altitude where malaria-bearing mosquitoes did not breed. Hill stations played an important role in providing rest and recuperation. There the missionaries regained their health and experienced recreation and social life in the British style. Late in the nineteenth century, Kodaikanal, located in the mountains about three hundred miles south of Vellore, became the leading hill station for missionaries. In the hot months of May and June, as many as five hundred missionaries representing all of the major missionary societies would be present in Kodaikanal. The social interaction of these missionaries in Kodaikanal played an important role in facilitating inter-mission strategy and cooperation, including moves toward church union.

The name of the Arcot Mission's committee that was responsible for its property and interests in Kodaikanal was *Sanataria*, because in the beginning the hill station was used primarily as a place for rest and restoration of health. We have already learned how often members of the Scudder families were afflicted with ill health and how they had to rest in the hills, take a sea voyage, or even return to America for a period of time. It is amazing how many of the missionaries, such as John Scudder, Sr., and Jacob Chamberlain, persevered in their work in India over years and even decades in spite of constant headaches, jungle fever, general weakness, eye strain, and other diseases.

Not only did medical problems become chronic in individuals, but they were also widespread among the members of the mission. In a single paragraph, William Farrar gave Henry Cobb the medical report on the members of the mission in May, 1902. His list included the fact that L.S. Scudder fell off his bicycle three times coming to Coonoor from Ooty, but the injuries were confined to the front wheel. Jacob Chamberlain had suffered a stroke but was improving. Jared Scudder was suffering from an injured foot and not able to wear a shoe. Miss K. Scudder was not well. James Beattie's wound was healing slowly. Harry Scudder still had his serious headaches. Mrs. John Scudder had dengue. Mrs. Walter Scudder's children were doing "poorly." Dr. Hart was presently disabled. He concluded with the comment that almost everyone was carrying too much responsibility.[50]

The medical history of John and Elizabeth Conklin during their ten years in India provides a striking example of missionary perseverance in the face of constant health problems. The Conklins arrived in India in March, 1881, and promptly became seriously ill in Madras before they could travel to the Arcot area. Elizabeth was pregnant at the time she arrived. When she gave birth, the baby died. In September, 1882, the mission recommended that the Conklins return to the States for health reasons.[51] But then they both experienced some improvement, so they did not leave India.

However, the Conklins continued in such poor health that they were sent to the Ootacumund hill station. After four months of rest, John began to feel guilty because they were an expense to the board and not able to do any work. He described their condition in a letter to J.M. Ferris:

> You will want to know how we are. My wife has been steadily gaining vigor, not very rapidly but surely. She was very much run down with the care and anxiety, but is now much better. Her eyes were very weak so that she could scarcely use them at all, but now they are almost as good as ever. I hardly know what to say about myself. I am encouraged. I can do more physically. I ride several miles a day on my pony and walk sometimes more than a mile. My head is also a little stronger, but my back troubles me—the effect of my stomach [sic!]. The doctors all told me I must

[50] William Farrar to Henry Cobb, May 21, 1902.
[51] J.W. Scudder to J. M. Ferris, September 2, 1882.

be very patient and that I would probably not see very much improving the first three months.[52]

In 1884, it is reported that John Conklin's health had improved to such an extent that he was able to carry on his work at the Arcot Seminary in Chittoor.[53] He and Elizabeth continued to struggle with poor health, however. At the end of December, 1885, he remained discouraged about their situation. Like others, he was concerned about the budget situation. He had calculated the annual costs of maintaining himself and his wife in India and believed that it was equal to that of maintaining thirty Indian helpers. He wrote,

> I believe that under some circumstances our work might be of more value than theirs. But as things seem at present, I feel that, if one or other must be dispensed with, it should by all means be ours. I do not want to leave the work. I am not tired of it nor discouraged. The bright side of life here has greatly overbalanced the dark. But I write in the interests of the work. I believe that without more money some one or more should go home that more funds may be available for "general purposes" here.
>
> I think that for some reasons we should go first. *My health has been affected more by the climate,* I think, than that of any other missionary. I have not regained my full strength and ability to work since my first attack of fever....I often feel the *limitations of my brain power* consequent upon illness. *I have not mastered the Tamil language.*[54]

Neither the mission nor the board was ready to accept the offer of the Conklins to be relieved of their duties in India. Whatever John Conklin himself may have felt about their weaknesses as

---

52 John Conklin to J. M. Ferris, May 22, 1883. He required eight months in the hills before he was able to return to his work in Chittoor.
53 "BFMR," 1884, 4
54 John Conklin to H. M. Cobb, December 15, 1885.

missionaries, the mission's confidence in them was growing. The following year, John was carrying heavy responsibilities in Chittoor and Arni. After the tragic death of Lambertus Hekhuis in 1888, he was also given the responsibility of carrying on the work at Arcot as well.

The Conklins suffered another blow in the summer of 1888, when their three children became ill with high fevers. The five and one-half-months-old daughter, Jean, died, but their two older children recovered.[55]

Still the work went on. Carman Scudder graphically described the immense burden of work that had been laid upon the Conklins:

> The extremes of these stations, Chittoor in the north, and the uttermost villages of Arni on the south, are seventy-five miles apart; Arcot being a sort of middle ground. The area of the whole field is immense, and yet over this whole area, the missionary in charge expects to go four times each year. The villages are widely scattered, and the roads to many of them were not made after the rule of Macadam! The helpers, though most of them faithful and hardworking, have, not many of them, had the educational and other advantages enjoyed by those now studying in or lately graduated from our various institutions of learning.[56]

John Conklin had supervision of forty-three Indian assistants, while Elizabeth supervised twenty women teachers and Bible women. The three pastorate areas had thirty-three villages occupied by catechists and teachers, with thirty-two schools. Among other responsibilities, John Conklin also served as clerk of the Board of Superintendents of the Arcot Seminary, as the examiner in biblical subjects of the boys in the Praeparandi School in Tindivanam, and as a member of the Committee on Bible Examination in Vellore.[57]

[55] John Conklin to Henry Cobb, August 4, 1888.
[56] "BFMR," 1890, 49.
[57] "BFMR," 1889, 45, 68.

The next year, the Board of Foreign Missions Report contains the information that Carman Scudder had reluctantly relieved Conklin in the three mission stations. Scudder reported, "Mr. Conklin, under whose charge these stations have been, is broken down from overwork, and cannot help much in making up this report."[58]

The Arcot Mission medical committee recommended that John and Elizabeth Conklin should leave India permanently for reasons of health, so they returned to America in early 1891. John went on to serve as pastor of several Reformed Church in America congregations. Between 1900-1906, he served as a foreign secretary of the Board of Foreign Missions. Elizabeth Conklin edited the *Mission Gleaner* for the Woman's Board of Foreign Missions from 1905-1917. Their daughter, Elizabeth Woodruff Conklin, returned to India in 1915 and served there until 1934.

Kodaikanal as a Center for Missionary Retreat and Renewal

Lambertus Hekhuis, as chairman of the medical committee of the mission, was profoundly concerned about the health of the Arcot missionaries in 1886, when he proposed to Henry Cobb that Kodaikanal would be a healthy place for missionaries to go for rest and restoration of health.[59] The main railway line to the southern part of India had been built in 1875, and there was a railway station at what came to be known as Kodaikanal Road. From there, one could travel about twenty miles to the base of the mountain on top of which Kodaikanal was located. Hekhuis believed Kodaikanal was a better place for missionaries to go than was Coonoor, which, he believed, was more for the government officials.[60] Kodaikanal was located at an elevation of approximately seven thousand feet, and it overlooked the plains six thousand feet below. It was above

---

58 "BFMR," 1890, 48.

59 Silas Scudder, soon after his arrival in India 1860, had forced through a ruling that all members of the mission must take a three-month holiday in the hills every year (Scudder, *A Thousand Years*, 135). Because other missionaries were reluctant to leave their work for a three-month holiday, they usually disregarded the rule.

60 L. Hekhuis to Henry Cobb, August 17, 1886

the mosquito line and therefore malaria free, with the average high temperature reaching seventy to eighty degrees in the hot season. The nights were always cool.

Three years later, Jacob Chamberlain was again in need of rest in the hills because of his illness. He went to Kodaikanal with the intent not only to rest but also to acquire property for the mission. At cost to the missionaries rather than the Board of Foreign Missions, he purchased a piece of property that became known as "Arcotia Compound," with space for building four houses for the use of Arcot missionaries.[61] By August of the following year, he had put the finishing touches on three Arcotia houses.[62] As the missionaries adopted the custom of going to Kodaikanal for the hot season in May, more houses were needed. Consequently, in 1905 a second compound, named "Woodville," was purchased for six thousand dollars, of which four thousand came from the Woman's Board. Woodville had a large central bungalow for use by the unmarried women missionaries as well as two cottages, and it included nine acres of land.[63]

As more and more missions purchased land and erected houses in Kodaikanal, it became a central annual gathering place for up to five hundred missionaries in South India. Some criticism of this annual trek developed. On one occasion, the Indian newspaper, the *Patriot*, complained that missionaries take to the hills in the hot season. J.H. Wyckoff defended the custom that was developing at the end of the nineteenth century. He wrote to Henry Cobb that because the work was so heavy, the missionaries needed time together for refreshment and for the possibility of religious and social nourishment.[64]

At the time Wyckoff wrote to Cobb, a number of the missionaries still looked upon their time in the hills mainly as an opportunity to

[61] J. Chamberlain to Henry Cobb, April 17, 1889.
[62] J. Chamberlain to Henry Cobb, July 7, 1890.
[63] J. H. Wyckoff to Henry Cobb, June 3, 1905.
[64] J. H. Wyckoff to Henry Cobb, June 11, 1896.

escape from the heat and recover from illness. In the years following the Panic of 1893, the board cut appropriations to the mission repeatedly, so, in 1897, the mission decided "that in view of the large cost to the Board of our visiting the Sanitaria, those coming out from home newly, or after furlough, be not expected to visit a Sanitarium the first season except under medical orders on account of sickness."[65] After thinking it over, however, it was felt that those who had recently arrived could well be as much in need of escaping from the heat as did those who had been on the plains all year. To force missionaries to live on the plains when the temperature remained above one hundred degrees Fahrenheit day after day was to open the door to illness and thus was a false economy.[66] The mission then relented and fully accepted the tradition that missionaries would go to Kodaikanal in the hot season. It even went so far as to plan to hold its summer meeting of the Arcot Mission there each year with the expectation that all missionaries would be present unless excused. By the turn of the century, Kodaikanal had become a focal point for missionary spiritual renewal and social life.

In the earliest days of missionary presence in Kodai, many informal social gatherings took place, with the Arcotia houses often serving as a social center for persons coming from other missions. As more missionaries arrived, however, there were many denominational groups living on compounds of their own and mixing only with their own. A group of missionaries, including J.H. Wyckoff, recognized the dangers of such separateness and took action to establish the Kodaikanal Missionary Union (KMU), which was at first centered in Arcotia Lodge. It then sought to locate near the tennis courts of the newly established "Highclerc" school. In 1923, it built its own large clubhouse that had a large central hall for social events and afternoon teas, six tennis courts, a reading room, and other spaces for meetings. The KMU brought

---

[65] J. Chamberlain to Henry Cobb, August 20, 1898.
[66] Ibid.

missionaries together for conferences on medical issues, spiritual life development, educational concerns, and industrial and agricultural uplift. It developed a social calendar for the vacation season that included an annual spiritual life convention, tennis tournaments, teas, and a series of concerts and stage plays.[67] In doing so, it played a major role in enabling missionaries of the various missions to come to know and trust each other, and it encouraged them to develop mission strategy and outreach in cooperation with each other.

The Kodaikanal hill station played an important role in the development of a widespread missionary subculture in India. Its role was in many ways ambivalent. It can be rightly criticized for the way in which it served to reinforce the missionaries' identification with their European and American cultures rather than their Indian context. In providing missionaries convenient access to each other, it encouraged inter-mission cooperation, but at the same time it also meant that missionaries were more likely to plan without having conversations with the Indian members of the churches. The role of the missionary hill stations is worthy of more careful study and analysis than it has received to date.

In any case, at the turn of the century missionaries clearly felt the need of a place such as Kodaikanal where they could go for renewal and rest. It must be remembered that at that time most Reformed Church missionaries spent ten years in India between furlough times in the United States. Such long terms in India meant that the focus of missionary attention and their important peer relationships would be located in India. While the Arcot Mission had from the very beginning denied that it was a "family mission," it became, like the other missions, an extended family. This was indicated by the fact that all of the children in the mission called all of the adults either "uncle" or "aunt," regardless of blood relationships.

---

[67] Charlotte Wyckoff, *Kodaikanal, 1845-1945,* (Nagercoil, India: London Mission Press, 1951), 21-23.

Kodaikanal became a place for the annual family reunion, and, as such, was important to maintaining personal and social stability.

Except for those stationed in the larger towns such as Vellore, the missionaries often felt considerable isolation. They worked, by and large, in places where practically no one spoke English, where there was no medical assistance near at hand, and where there were few people whose world reached much beyond the boundaries of their own daily rounds. Newly arrived missionaries in particular experienced such a sense of isolation. William Farrar was typical in the way he expressed his and his wife's feeling eight months after they arrived.

> Becoming acquainted with the new scenes and faces, the new manner of living, getting settled in our new home and beginning our study of the language, have all combined to keep us interested, and for the most part, free from homesickness. Still, at times, and especially on Sundays, there will often creep over us, in spite of our best efforts to keep it off, that indescribable, yet very real feeling of longing to see and speak once more with those we have left behind. Those at home scarcely ever realize, I suppose, what a privilege it is to be able to address any number of people, in stores, on the street, or anywhere, in their own language, or the blessing of hearing it spoken by the people all around one. The lack of *social* life is one of the hardest things to get used to.[68]

Missionary wives especially could suffer from the lack of social life and opportunities to talk with others in their own language. Upon her return to India in 1884, Sophia Scudder joined her husband, John II, in Tindivanam. Most of the time they were the only Europeans there, and weeks, sometimes months, would go by when she saw no other Europeans and had little opportunity to meet people who spoke English. Sophia Scudder commented on

---

[68] William Farrar to Henry Cobb, June 22, 1898.

her own actions when one such opportunity arose. "When I had not seen anyone for three months with whom I could speak English, I talked so much that I spent the next three months repenting."[69] In 1883 and early 1884, John and Emma Wyckoff were coping with their assignment to be in charge of both Tindivanam and Madanapalle, 160 miles apart. They spent one-half the year in one place, followed by six months in the other. John found one good thing about the assignment. Emma was not too well, but the opportunity to spend half her time in Madanapalle meant that she would have more companionship. That was helpful because "she does not really like life in India."[70]

Even those missionaries who were located in towns where there were a number of English officials present found themselves in need of social relationships with other missionaries. Although Ezekiel and Sarah Scudder served prior to the time when missionaries went to Kodaikanal, they felt the need for a more adequate social life. When they moved to Vellore, however, Sarah was embarrassed by her missionary poverty. When she thought about meeting the three English officials and their wives there, "She thought about her faded and mended wardrobe and wondered if she could possibly afford a new dress to wear when she met these officials and their wives."[71]

One of the highlights of being in Kodaikanal was the privilege of joining in worship in one's own language. Another was participating in the annual Kodaikanal Missionary Convention, which had outstanding speakers, Bible study, hymn singing, and worship. The missionary convention served not only the personal spiritual needs of the missionaries, but it also opened the door to biblical and theological conversation across denominational and theological lines and therefore encouraged cooperation among the mission agencies.

[69] Scudder, *A Thousand Years,* 140.
[70] J. H. Wyckoff to J. M. Ferris, April 25, 1884.
[71] *A Thousand Years,* 104.

Kodaikanal furnished a place for missionaries to promote their mission enterprises and organize sales for special purposes. Many of the missions brought articles with them to sell that had been made by their industrial institutions on the plains. Such articles ranged from lace, cross-stitched, or hand-woven kitchen towels to rosewood furniture, painted pottery, and sisal mats. Mothers of the children in Highclerc School organized an annual sale for the benefit of the school. They asked friends in America to send boxes of goods unobtainable in India, including hosiery, kitchen utensils, ready-made housedresses, and toys. A "white elephant" sale was also organized as a means of enabling missionaries to dispose of no longer needed items, such as children's clothing, furniture, books, and other materials that would be useful to others. All of these sales were for the benefit of Indian workers on the plains, for the school, or for other benevolent purposes.[72] Perhaps just as important, they enabled missionaries to come to know and respect each other across denominational and theological divisions.

Kodaikanal was also the place where missionaries played together. They held bridge tournaments, put on Gilbert and Sullivan operettas, orchestral concerts, art exhibitions, and a wide variety of stage plays. There was an annual tennis tournament whose result was reported regularly in letters to the United States. The first tournament was held in 1895 and was won by the team called "British Empire." L.R. Scudder and H.J. Scudder were two of the four members of the American team.[73] As late as 1934, C. Wierenga considered it important to inform William Chamberlain in New York that the missionaries had defeated the English Club, 109-67 and that the rest of the World had defeated the British Empire, 99-77.[74]

The missionaries also used their time in Kodaikanal to hike in the mountains. Some of their expeditions could be quite elaborate,

72 Wyckoff, *Kodaikanal,* 44.
73 Ibid., 17.
74 C. Wierenga to William Chamberlain, May 25, 1933. After William and Mary Chamberlain had to leave India in 1906 on account of the ill health of their daughter, William taught a short time at Rutgers College and then served in New York with the Board of Foreign Mission from 1910-1935.

taking several days. In 1922, Chris De Jonge, a graduate of Hope College in Holland, Michigan, serving his second year in India, wrote home with enthusiasm about one four-day hike. Six missionaries had left Kodaikanal accompanied by thirteen coolies (workers) who carried the food and other items needed on the hike. They hiked seventeen miles the first day.

> I 'spose some of you will think we missionaries are crazy going out on such a long hike but it is such a great change from the heavy mental strain we have been under all year that it is a most pleasant recreation. We slept that nite, or tried to sleep on the stone floor, and then the next morning started out for Kukal cave, a huge monstrous cave, some miles beyond. It was a very good walk, and the cave was just wonderful. We were fortunate enuf to see some wild animals, and that was great....Above the rock we were lucky enuf to find some real orchids, the American flower for which they pay some steep cash. Judging by the price of orchids which was prevailing when I left the States, I should judge that we had a bunch of orchids worth thirty or forty dollars.[75]

The Kodaikanal School for Missionary Children

John and Harriet Scudder sent their two oldest sons, Henry and William, to America to receive an education when they were just ten and nine years old.[76] The two boys did not see their parents again for more than twenty years. John and Sophia Scudder and their family of six children left India for America after seventeen years. Five years later, in 1883, John returned to India alone. One son, Lewis, remained on their farm to carry on the work there. Sophia went to the eastern part of the United States in order to care for her

[75] Chris De Jonge to "Dear Folks at Home," May 7, 1922 (correspondence located in Joint Archives).
[76] Scudder, *A Thousand Years*, 77.

Kodaikanal School

children while they continued their education. After John wrote a number of letters describing his loneliness without her, Sophia returned to India in 1884 and left her children in America in the care of others.[77] The other missionaries also felt the need to send their children to the United States for the sake of their education. For example, J.H. Wyckoff in 1893 informed Henry Cobb of his hopes to send his son John, aged twelve, to America to live with the John Scudder family in America.[78]

Two years previously, Wyckoff had brought his concerns about the education and health of missionary children to the Arcot Mission. He proposed that a school for missionaries' children be established in Kodaikanal in order to provide a healthy locality for them. Such a school "would obviate the necessity of those children being widely separated from their parents at so tender an age, and enable those parents to remain longer in India."[79]

---

[77] Ibid. 139.
[78] J. H. Wyckoff to Henry Cobb, July 29, 1893.
[79] Action of the Arcot Mission, "Proposed Boarding School in India for Missionaries' Children," October 13, 1891 (on file in mission correspondence with board, Archives of the RCA).

The resolution of the mission was sent to the Board of Foreign Missions and to the Madura, Jaffna, and Marathi Missions of the American Board of Commissioners for Foreign Missions. It requested those missions to join with the Arcot Mission in establishing the school. It also requested that the Woman's Board support such an institution as well as send a female teacher to be in charge. The mission action concluded with the affirmation that

> a school would increase the efficiency of the missionary families in the field, by relieving them of care and anxiety on behalf of their children with them on the tropical plains of India, and would in many cases obviate the necessity of so early a return to America on account of their children, while some who had gone home and who were detained on account of inability to find suitable homes for their children of from seven to ten years of age, would be enabled to return to the work for which previous experience and a knowledge of the language and the people had specially fitted them.[80]

Another ten years would pass before the school would be established in Kodaikanal. However, the Madura Mission did respond with the idea that a children's boarding home could be set up in one of its homes in Kodai and that the children could be tutored by one or more mothers or another person while they were still so young. This option was to be available first to children of the Arcot and Madura missions, and then to children of other missions as space was available.[81]

The two missions finally decided in 1901 to proceed to open a school at Kodaikanal for Arcot and Madura children, with others welcome as space permitted.[82] In its first five months of operation, the school had thirteen students studying with Mrs. M. L. Eddy,

[80] Ibid.
[81] Report received from the Madura Mission, June 30, 1892.
[82] J. H. Wyckoff to James Amerman, June 18, 1901. James Lansing Amerman was secretary-assistant treasurer of the Board of Foreign Missions, 1893-1915.

who had come to India to visit her son, Sherwood Eddy. She was asked to be the principal. Though her teaching days were far in the past, she responded to the needs of the children and organized the new boarding school, which ran like a two-room village school. Charlotte Wyckoff, aged eight in 1901, a daughter of John and Emmaline Wyckoff, still had happy memories of that school more than forty years later:

> The school was as informal and happy as a home. There were a rose garden and a pine grove where now the gymnasium stands, and a pear orchard all the way down to the road. Beyond the two tennis courts was a separate property, called 'Barton' where now Kennedy and Boyer Halls are; 'Airlie' was also separated by a hedge and was once a 'shop.'[83]

Mrs. Eddy returned to America enthusiastic about the need for the school. She went home to settle her affairs and raised Rs. 10,000 to buy the Highclerc property in the central location on which the school remains to this day. Within a very short time, the school was flourishing. Other missions supported the school by sending their children to study there and by providing personnel to teach in and funds to operate the institution. For a number of years, the school provided an American elementary education through the first eight grades. As a result, it was still necessary for missionaries to send their children to America for their high school education. For example, Galen Scudder, the son of L.R. Scudder, went to the United States at the age of fourteen after having completed his elementary school education in Kodaikanal.[84] The school was recognized as a middle school in 1916 and became a high school in 1920,[85] with a managing board composed of representatives of the cooperating missions.

---

[83] Charlotte Wyckoff, *Kodaikanal,* 37.
[84] L. R. Scudder to Henry Cobb, August 31, 1905.
[85] Ibid.

Establishing Inter-Mission Cooperative Institutions

As missionaries gathered together annually for rest, spiritual and social renewal, and recreation, they also learned to trust each other enough to formulate plans for inter-mission cooperative institutions. Some of these served the needs of the missions themselves, such as the committee for missionary language examinations, the South India Missionary Association that later merged in the Madras Representative Christian Council, and the Industrial Missionary Association. Others led to the establishment of major mission institutions. Among these were the United Theological College at Bangalore, the Union Mission Tuberculosis Sanatoriam at Arogyvaram, near Madanapalle, and the Missionary Medical College for Women at Vellore.[86] We will here note the origins of the first two of these institutions. The third will be discussed in the next chapter.

United Theological College, Bangalore.

An informal meeting of missionaries representing four different missions, including J.H. Wyckoff of the Arcot Mission, took place in Kodaikanal June 18, 1906, to discuss the need for a high-class theological school for South India. At such a school, college graduates could pursue their theological studies principally in English, with some of the training being done in the vernacular languages. The new school was not intended to replace existing vernacular theological schools such as the Arcot Theological Seminary.

> The scheme informally outlined at the meeting referred to, does not contemplate an interference with existing training schools or classes, which are doing admirable, and urgently necessary work in preparing village Pastors, Catechists, and Teachers for Mission service. The aim is rather to found an institution which will supplement the work of existing positions, such as Pastors of large Churches, Teachers in Training Schools, Bible Instructors in Colleges, or

[86] Wyckoff, *Kodaikanal,* 68-69.

Evangelists at important centers....It will be understood
that only the great essentials of our evangelical faith will be
taught in the school, leaving any special denominational
teaching to be supplemented by the Missions that desire
their students to have it.[87]

Six missions joined together in support of the new United
Theological College, which was located in Bangalore and opened in
July, 1910, under the chairmanship of J.H. Wyckoff.[88] The Board
of Foreign Missions and the Arcot Mission provided a representative
to the school's board and an annual grant for the theological college
for the next five decades. The United Theological College has
continued to serve as one of the leading theological schools in India
to the present day.

The Union Mission Tuberculosis Sanatorium.

The first steps toward the foundation of the Union Mission
Tuberculosis Sanatorium were taken in 1908, when a few medical
missionaries in Kodaikanal discussed the possibility of such an
institution. Dr. T. V. Campbell of the London Missionary Society
had returned to India following an attack of pulmonary tuberculosis.
He laid his concerns before the other missionaries, who were
becoming aware that tuberculosis was a growing problem in India.
The medical people laid the question before the South Indian
Missionary Association in 1909. A plan was drawn up in 1910 and
presented to the missions and government for support.[89] The
Arcot Mission agreed to the need and reminded the Board of
Foreign Missions of the importance of Reformed Church
involvement.[90]

The Arcot Mission gave strong support to the proposal of Dr.
Campbell for a tuberculosis sanatorium in 1908. Dr. Louisa Hart in
Punganur became increasingly aware of the prevalence of

---

87 J. Duthie and J. H. Wyckoff, *Divinity School for South India*, appeal letter to missions, dated
    June 22, 1906, Archives of the RCA.
88 L. R. Chamberlain to William Chamberlain, July 13, 1910.
89 C. Frimodt-Moeller, "A Survey of Ten Years' Work, 1915-1924," Annual Report, 1925, 1.
90 L. B. Chamberlain to William Chamberlain, June 21, 1910.

tuberculosis among the people of that area. It was affecting women especially, because they spent so much of their time indoors in stuffy rooms. A number of the Indian mission workers and members of their families had died of the disease. The mission doctors therefore decided to examine four hundred children in their boarding schools. They discovered that thirty-eight children between the ages of ten and eighteen were seriously infected, fifteen more were in an early stage, and many more were clearly disposed to becoming infected.[91]

Gertrude Dodd,[92] who was at the time an active member of the Woman's Board of Foreign Missions, learned about the problem and gave a large grant to found the Dodd Sanitorium in Punganur. It was opened with a capacity of about forty patients, but by 1910 there were already thirty-eight school children, two Bible women, and two mission family servants there. "This number is overtaxing our resources and consequently is being carried on in a very imperfect way, but even so it is doing much good. We can do nothing for the others, except that the school buildings have been and are being improved."[93]

The plan for the new union sanatorium was large. It called for the purchase of fifty acres of land, with a well and accommodations for

---

[91] "AAR," 1910, 51.

[92] See Mary Pauline Jeffrey, *Ida S. Scudder of Vellore, India* (published in India by permission of Fleming H. Revell, 1951), 38-39. Gertrude Dodd (1858-1944) was the daughter of a wealthy businessman and building contractor in New York City. She became a member of the Woman's Board of Foreign Mission in 1901 and after several years served as treasurer of the board. She decided to see India for herself and spent eight months there in 1908 as a guest of Ida Scudder. She returned to India in 1916 and remained a close companion of Ida Scudder until her death in 1944. She served for a long time as treasurer of the Vellore medical school. In addition to providing a grant for the founding of the tuberculosis sanitorium, she also gave a number of other grants to assist the work of the Arcot Mission. Since she was never officially appointed to be a missionary and always served in India without any remuneration, she was never listed as a Reformed Church missionary in India, even though she even served as a short time as treasurer of the mission. She is listed in the 1978 Reformed Church historical directory as "Miss. India 1916-1941; companion to Ida S. Scudder 1908-1944" [Peter N. Vanden Berge, ed., *Historical Directory of the Reformed Church in America, 1628-1978* (Grand Rapids: Eerdmans, 1978), 221].

[93] Ibid.

150 patients together with supporting buildings. The monthly expenditure for staff was projected at Rs. 832 per month. By the time Chamberlain sent the details of the plan to New York in early 1910, the experience of Dr. Hart at the Dodd Sanatorium had indicated that they must plan for 200-300 patients rather than 150. It was hoped that the government would meet much of the cost, but it was still necessary to ask the Reformed Church in America to accept its share of the starting expenses in the amount of ten thousand dollars. The mission believed it could ask for this amount because, if the union institution were opened, it would relieve the mission doctors and staff of a heavy responsibility and would place the major tuberculosis institution for all India within the Arcot mission area. Moreover, the cost to the Arcot Mission could well be less than it had been bearing by treating the patients in Punganur.[94]

The mission boards in America and Europe did not respond as generously as had been hoped. A plot of seventy-six acres of deforested land was secured partly by purchase and partly by assignment by the government. The seven cooperating missions had only Rs. 15,000, however, and the government granted another Rs. 30,000 for the erection of buildings. In 1913, the construction was begun under the direction of Ben Rottschaefer, an Arcot missionary. The convenor of the committee in charge of the project was L.R. Scudder, a physician whose wife had spent some time in a tuberculosis sanatorium in Germany and had recovered.

In the meantime, patients began to be accepted and housed near the Madanapalle mission hospital in temporary buildings with mud walls and thatched roofs. Dr. Hart's care and treatment of the patients showed good results in spite of the lack of medical knowledge about tuberculosis early in the century. The new facility was finally ready in 1915. Dr. C. Frimodt-Moeller of the Danish Mission then took charge of the work and provided outstanding leadership there for many years.[95]

---

94 L. B. Chamberlain to Henry Cobb, January 28, 1910.
95 Frimodt-Moeller, *Ten Years' Work,* 2.

H. M. Levick, a young, unmarried woman missionary doctor, was assigned in 1910 to take charge of the Madanapalle hospital when Louisa Hart went to the United States on furlough in that year. Levick had been working in Ranipet under the direction of L. R. Scudder since her arrival in India. Unfortunately, she became so weakened with illness that the mission's medical committee determined that she must return to the United States.[96]

The Christian Endeavor Society

The Arcot Mission was not only supportive of inter-mission cooperation in establishing union institutions. It also linked its youth organizations with those of other missions through its enthusiastic welcome of the Christian Endeavor societies into the life of the congregations. The worldwide Christian Endeavor movement had begun under the inspiration of Dr. Francis E. Clarke who made a visit to the Arcot area in 1898. A number of societies had been opened several years earlier in the area, but his visit created enthusiasm to start many more in the towns and villages of the Arcot Mission area. A number of delegates had attended the Christian Endeavor convention held in Madura in 1897 and come back eager to begin more societies. Christian Endeavor societies provided opportunities for younger people to lead in worship, prayer, and discussion. It encouraged them to take seriously the pledge daily to live a consistent Christian life for Christ and the church.[97]

The Christian Endeavor movement grew in importance over the next several decades in the Arcot area and beyond. By 1900, it claimed to have over 450 societies in India. Its societies began to carry out evangelistic work in Indian villages. J.H. Wyckoff reported on their important activities.

The society at the station has kept up its organized work, and its members have grown in Scripture knowledge and

96 "BFMR," 1910, xvii.
97 "BFMR," 1898, 53-54.

piety. The evangelistic services rendered have been greater than ever. The Narisinganur and Wandiwash societies have each organized a Bajani [a preaching/singing evangelistic group] which is a great attraction in their meetings as well as in their preaching work.[98]

The convention of the South India Christian Endeavor Union was held in Vellore in 1910. It was remarked that when that convention had last met in Vellore in 1898, only twenty-nine delegates had been present. In 1910 there were fifteen hundred in attendance. The theme of the meeting was "All ye are brethren." There were sessions on the National Missionary Movement, temperance, and a consecration service on the hill with the old Vellore fort ruins. There the members of the societies were encouraged once more to carry out the great work of "bringing the gospel of Christ by word and deed to all within our borders."[99]

The Christian Endeavor movement continued to thrive in the area. The president of the All-India Christian Endeavor movement in the 1960s, the Reverend Ebenezer Tychicus, resided in Vellore while carrying out his duties as head of the Arcot Seminary and chairman of the Western Area of the Diocese of Madras, Church of South India.

At the beginning of the twentieth century, members of the Arcot Mission were accustomed to inter-mission cooperation and to collaboration with a variety of Christian organizations carrying out evangelistic and benevolent activities in India. It is not surprising, then, that its missionaries were in the forefront of the movement toward church union. Before tracing that movement, which resulted in the formation of the South India United Church, it is important to note that in their cooperative activities the missionaries did not wish to compromise the Reformed theology that they continued to hold dear.

---

[98] "Christian Endeavor in the East," *Mission Field,* August, 1900, 126.
[99] "AAR," 1910, 29.

The Case of Henry Huizinga

The case of Henry Huizinga forced the members of the Arcot Mission and the Board of Foreign Missions to face the issue of theological boundaries, so far as working together in one united church and mission was concerned. Henry Huizinga graduated from Hope College in 1893 and Western Theological Seminary in Holland, Michigan, in 1896. He married his wife, Susan, was ordained by the Classis of Muskegon, and together they sailed to India to serve as missionaries with the Arcot Mission. It was intended that he would be assigned to be principal of Vellore High School and College, which had just been taken over from the Church of Scotland Mission. Before taking on that assignment, however, it was necessary for Henry to learn the Tamil language and gain a little experience with the church and culture.

It soon became apparent that Henry had a zeal for evangelistic touring and a gift for that type of ministry. As time went on, however, he began to have doubts about the doctrine of infant baptism. While in Kodaikanal in May, 1899, Henry informed his missionary colleagues that he had come to differ with the mission on infant baptism. He recognized that this would in all probability mean that he could no longer function as an ordained missionary in the Arcot Mission. It was also the case that to that time all of the male missionaries appointed to India by the Board of Foreign Missions were ordained ministers. Therefore, Henry stated, he was ready to demit from the ordained ministry and to be classified as an "evangelist."

A meeting with John, Lewis R., and Henry J. Scudder took place in Kodaikanal near the end of May. They were most kindly and considerately disposed to Huizinga but were firmly of the opinion that he could not remain in the mission. They advised him to consult with members of the American Baptist Missionary Union, who were in Kodai at the time, to see if tentative arrangements could be made for his speedy transfer to that body. Huizinga maintained that he loved the Reformed Church and would make such contact only with great reluctance. Nevertheless he followed their advice. He consulted with the American Baptist Missionary Union, following which there were additional consultations between members of the Arcot mission and the Baptists. The Baptists agreed that they would write to their board in the United States recommending that it accept Huizinga as its missionary.[100]

While these discussions were going on, the mission was aware that decisions concerning appointments and resignations or dismissals of missionaries was the prerogative of the board, not of the mission. Lewis R. Scudder had concurred in suggesting to Huizinga that he consult with the American Baptist Missionary Union; nevertheless, he suggested to Henry Cobb that the board take a little more time to consider whether Henry Huizinga could work in some other capacity in the Tamil area.[101] Huizinga had worked under Scudder's supervision in the Ranipet area while doing his Tamil study, and Scudder had a good impression of his abilities.

Within a short time, it became clear that a transfer to the Baptists would not happen. The secretary of the American Baptist Missionary Union responded that it was a Telugu field in India and that it was not financially able to take on Tamil work. Huizinga pointed out still another problem. He had learned that the American Baptists were "close communionists" who did not partake of Communion with those who differed from them, while he himself was an "open communionist" who did eat with those who differed. Consistent with his views on Communion, he believed that the Reformed Church constitution allowed a minister who did not believe in infant baptism to remain in good standing so long as he was ready to ask another minister to perform infant baptisms when the occasion arose.[102]

Henry Cobb sent Huizinga a cable July 19 that he would have to leave the mission. J.H. Wyckoff was on an evangelistic tour

[100] Henry Huizinga to Henry Cobb, May 29, 1899.
[101] L. R. Scudder to Henry Cobb, June 4, 1899.
[102] J. H. Wyckoff to J. Chamberlain, July 26, 1899.

accompanied by Huizinga at that time. By July 26, Wyckoff had come to believe that he had considered the case too abstractly before and that his first response had been too narrow and one-sided. Now he wondered whether there was any possibility that the matter could be reconsidered. After considerable prayer on the matter, his thoughts had taken a new shape.

> We are a preaching Mission, but during the past decade comparatively little has been done to give the gospel to the millions within our territory. I have just made 3 encampments in the Wandiwash Taluq. In the first we reached villages where neither missionaries nor native helpers have ever preached, and this only 30 miles from Tindivanam and Arni. The 2nd center, the gospel has certainly not been proclaimed for 25 years; and at the 3rd only 12 miles east of Gnanodiam no work had been done since Dr. John and I preached there in 1883. Verily we are not giving these people the gospel.[103]

Wyckoff went on to say that Huizinga was well fitted to serve in that neglected Wandiwash area, and that he not only wanted to stay there, but that he promised not to obtrude his views about baptism on those among whom he labored. He would refer all cases involving infant baptism to the Indian pastor in the area. Wyckoff did not believe that baptism either of infant or adult is the essential thing, since Paul believed that he had been called to preach but had not been sent to baptize. Wyckoff's passion on the subject apparently grew as he wrote. He pointed out how short the mission was of missionary help. He asked whether the Lord was not in this case endeavoring to teach them a lesson in tolerance and broadmindedness. He noted that four of the Arcot missionary wives, Mrs. E. Carman Scudder, Mrs. William Chamberlain, Mrs. James Beattie, and Mrs. L.B. Chamberlain, were all brought up Baptists and remained Baptists until they joined the mission.

[103] Ibid.

It is not to be supposed that these good ladies have abandoned in toto the belief in which they were born and trained. Like sensible women, and true Christians they have consented to hold in abeyance their traditional opinions and as far as they are able to act in harmony with their husbands and the church with which they are for the present identified. But is the tolerance all to be exhibited on the other side? Are we not called to exercise at times liberality in our opinions or practice? Must everyone who does not agree with us, be made to conform to our procrustean bed? Is the fear of its effect upon the native brethren sufficient in the present instance? A similar result was prophesied to take place because of difference of views on the kudumies question, but have the disastrous consequences as predicted been realized?[104]

Wyckoff's appeal to Jacob Chamberlain, with a copy of his letter to Jared Scudder to assist in reopening the case, did not succeed in persuading those two elder statesmen of the mission to change their minds. Huizinga had no alternative but to resign and return to the United States. In the search for ways to greater unity, infant baptism was not a line to be crossed organizationally. There would be no serious move in that direction for a hundred years. Wyckoff's letter to Chamberlain does, however communicate a sense of how far his great passion for carrying out the task of evangelism was also pushing him in his zeal for ecumenical cooperation and unity.

Wyckoff continued to be haunted by the fact that the Arcot Mission was not adequately reaching out to the whole of its area with the preaching of the gospel. Almost a decade after the case of Henry Huizinga, the issue of relations with Baptist missions again came up. This time it involved the fact that the Arcot Mission had proposed to the Board of Foreign Missions that it offer a portion of its mission territory around the town of Gudiyattam to the

104 Ibid.

English Strict Baptist Mission. The board had refused to grant permission to do so.

In response, Wyckoff, in his office as secretary and treasurer of the Arcot Mission, asked how many more decades we are to "exclude sister societies from our fields that we cannot and do not work, simply because they differ from us in external practices." He had just returned from a preaching tour in that area of twenty thousand people. The mission listed Gudiyattam as "occupied," but it had there only one small school in a low-caste hamlet on the outskirts of the town and one native evangelist who had to spend most of his time outside the town. Two other mission societies had expressed a willingness to place a missionary in Gudiyattam, which was the second biggest town in the whole Arcot area after Vellore. Wyckoff wondered whether the fault was that the mission had not pressed on the board and the members of the Reformed Church the need for more work in those fields. If so, he would be glad to press harder.[105]

The Formation of the South India United Church

The formation of the South India United Church was a two-stage process that culminated in its fruition in 1908. Impetus was given towards such a united church by developments in other countries. The United Free Church of Scotland, formed in 1900, fostered a sense of Presbyterian ecumenicity in the British Isles and elsewhere. Two missions of Presbyterian polity, the English Presbyterians and the Amoy Mission of the Reformed Church in America, had decided to combine forces in 1888. The Church of Christ in Japan

[105] J. H. Wyckoff to Henry Cobb, March 18, 1907. Since the missionaries never ceased taking every opportunity to impress upon the secretary of the board the absolute importance of sending more missionaries and more money for the work of the Arcot Mission, one may be sure that Henry Cobb did not fault Wyckoff or any other missionary for not having pressed hard enough. He would have agreed about the need for receiving more information to be sent on to the churches about the mission in India. The missionaries often excused their failure to send such information or to send it on time by stating that they were overburdened with work in light of the shortage of missionaries on the field.

had also recently been formed. Jacob Chamberlain had studied both of the latter two on his way back to India from the United States.

The South Indian Missionary Conference at Madras in 1900 had given further impetus to the movement. At that time, J.H. Wyckoff had been made convenor of its Committee on Comity and Co-operation. Wyckoff had also gained a real admiration for the Church of England and used the *Book of Common Prayer* from time to time. In this he had been influenced by the Reverend Meshach Peter, whose family had come from the Anglican area of Tinnevelly and who was to become a leader among the ordained ministers in the Arcot Mission area. Wyckoff brought the matter of Presbyterian union before the Arcot Mission, and, at the end of February, representatives of the Arcot Mission met representatives of the two Scottish missions, the United Free Church and the Church of Scotland. The representatives agreed that cooperation and comity were not enough; they aimed at a closer union of the three missions at an early date.[106] Since the churches in India were actually members of the overseas churches, the plan of union had to be submitted to the parent bodies. The Reformed Church and the United Free Church in Scotland approved it, but the Church of Scotland did not. The result was that in 1902 it was the churches related to the Free Church mission and the Arcot Mission who actually formed the South India United Church.[107]

[106] Bengt Sundkler, Church of South India: The Movement Towards Union, 1900-1947 (London: Lutterworth Press, 1954), 37.

[107] Relations among the Arcot Mission, the Church of Scotland Mission, and the Free Church Mission were complicated by the history of the church in Scotland. There had been two schisms from the Church of Scotland, the first in 1843 and the second in 1893. These two movements came together in 1900 to form the United Free Church. "When the disruption came in 1843, all the missionaries of the Church of Scotland cast in their lot with the Free Church. They gave up their property and started on a new foundation. The Church of Scotland sent other of her sons to man the stations thus deserted. So it came to pass that from 1843 both these Scotch churches have been working side by side in Madras" (R.C. Reed, *History of the Presbyterian Churches of the World* (Philadelphia: Westminster, 1915), 377. The United Free Church was reunited with the Church of Scotland in 1929. For our purposes, it is not necessary to distinguish

The South India United Church adopted the constitution of the Church of Christ in Japan. The Confession of Faith was based on the "Statement of Doctrine and Questions of the Ordaining of Office-bearers in the Native Churches of India," which was a shortened version of the Westminster Confession. That confession had been prepared by the Pan-Presbyterian Alliance between 1878 and 1883.[108] There were some difficulties about the place of ordained missionaries in the new church. They were to be "assessors" in the courts of the church with the right to speak and vote, but not subject to the jurisdiction of the courts.[109]

The South India United Church was formed at a provisional synod held at Vellore, October 1901, with Jacob Chamberlain as moderator. It had a total membership of more than twelve thousand, of which the Classis of Arcot had ten thousand at the time. The new church had avoided the name "Presbyterian," because the church in the United States associated that word with a particular denomination. The name was also chosen with the hope that other churches would also be assimilated into it. The formal transfer of the old Presbytery of the United Free Church and the Classis of Arcot was made to the South India United Church in September, 1902.[110] There were two presbyteries related to its synod, the Presbytery of Madras and the Presbytery of Arcot. Two churches of the former Scottish church became members of the Presbytery of Arcot, while Tindivanam and Ranipet (Arcot) entered the Presbytery of Madras. One of the ironies of the situation was that the town of Arcot was no longer in the Presbytery of Arcot.

By these actions, the South India United Church became a church organizationally independent of its parent bodies in the United

between missionaries who were in the Church of Scotland Mission and those in the Free Church Mission, since the Arcot missionaries cultivated cordial relations with both.
108 The Board of Foreign Missions report for 1891 includes the full statement of the Confession of Faith that was adopted by the Church of Christ in Japan in 1890, as well as some of the considerations which led to its being formulated and adopted (7-11).
109 Sundkler, *Church of South India,* 37.
110 Ibid.

States and Scotland. It was a self-governing Indian church. While all the missionaries rejoiced in the new step forward, Henry Scudder reflected their feelings that "this step has not been taken by those of us who have personal associations with the Home Churches without some feeling of regret."[111]

The formation of the South India United Church then entered its second phase, which was union with the Congregationalists, who were involved in a parallel movement among mission bodies. The London Missionary Society and the Congregationalist churches of the American Board in the Madura Mission area formed a joint committee in 1903 and thereafter met in 1905 as the First General Assembly of the General Union of the United Churches of South India, with a Christian community of 133,000.[112] Their union assumed that they were on the way to a wider union, as had been the case with the Presbyterian and Reformed union.

Formal negotiations about a further union began at Kodaikanal in June, 1905. The Presbyterians were not happy about the Congregationalist attitude to creeds, but both sides were ready to make some concessions. It was agreed to accept for the new church the brief "Madura Confession of Faith" as a general basis, with each church entering the union to be allowed to add much more detailed confessions as they pleased. Several other matters had to be negotiated. The term "church council" replaced "presbytery" and "classis." The Congregationalists accepted the General Assembly as "the representative body of the church," but the Presbyterians conceded that the General Assembly could assume no authority over the churches.[113]

While the negotiations were going on between 1903 and 1908 with the Congregationalists, the Arcot Mission and Church of Scotland Mission were also involved in discussions that were once again looking toward an organic union of all Indian Presbyterian

111 Henry J. Scudder to Henry Cobb, September 31, 1902.
112 Sundkler, *Church of South India*, 40.
113 Ibid., 42-44.

churches. In 1904, Reformed Church missionaries had agreed to become part of one single Presbyterian church for the whole of India and had participated in the first General Assembly of the Presbyterian Church in India. At that meeting, held in Allahabad, the Reformed Church missionaries had argued that the name should be, "The Church of Christ in India, Presbyterian." Their point was that, as other churches joined, the last word would be dropped, as a tail drops off a tadpole as it grows up, to use an analogy of Wyckoff.[114] Those who were from South India wanted to keep the door open to their further union in the south, so they joined the union with the reservation that they would be free to withdraw from it "in the interest of a more practical Union in South India."[115] However, it became apparent that it was not possible to move forward into union on both fronts at the same time. A choice had to be made between forming an all-India Presbyterian Church and moving forward to union with the Congregationalists in South India. In the fall of 1907, the South India United Church did withdraw from the Presbyterian movement in order to complete its union with the Congregationalists in the south.

The years immediately following 1905 saw a growing nationalist movement and increasing agitation in India for self-rule. At the time of the consummation of the wider union in 1908, the two moderators of the uniting churches, J. H. Wyckoff and J. P. Cotelingam, stood together on the platform as the delegates filed in. It was stressed by many that the new church must be truly Indian, a national church. Some regretted that the union had been brought about by the missionaries and that the Indians themselves had relatively little to do with its formation. Cotelingam declared, "There is undoubtedly a great future before the South India United Church, if the faint beginning of Swadeshism ["self-rule"] in it be wisely directed."[116]

[114] Ibid., 38.
[115] Ibid., 38-39.
[116] Ibid., 42-43.

The second General Assembly of the South India United Church was held in 1909, with J.H. Wyckoff as president. J.P. Cotelingam was elected president for the following two years. Much of the business had to do with possibilities for a still wider union. Of interest for our purposes is that the Arcot Council was reported to be ready to hand its Telugu churches over to the Cuddapah Council as soon as it organized. In contrast to what had been the position of some persons, Jacob Chamberlain urged that the move into self-government should go on even where self-support had not been attained.[117]

A leading Presbyterian, the Reverend J. H. Maclean, gave an address that allows us to feel some of the undercurrents present at the General Assembly—undercurrents that would be taken seriously by Arcot missionaries over the next several years. Maclean spoke of the growing maturity of the church that had been displayed in the General Assembly, but he believed that the church was still in an adolescent stage, with a desire for greater independence. He urged missionaries and Indians alike to be sensitive to the dynamics of the situation.

> The new life was showing itself in desires for independence. These desires might take unreasonable forms, yet missionaries must take them into account and try to win the respect of the Church by their character, rather than insist on being obeyed because they happened to represent the parent Church. Indians, on the other hand, must remember that they had not yet attained unto "full-grown man," and so be moderate in their demands, and ready to listen to advice. They must above all refuse to impute evil motives to missionaries, though they might sometimes hold— perhaps rightly—that they erred in judgment.[118]

---

117 *Mission Field,* April, 1910, 485.
118 Ibid., 486.

With the establishment of the South India United Church, the Reformed Church in America's ecclesiastical life in India came to an end, and the Classis of Arcot was transferred to the South India United Church. Nevertheless, the Arcot Mission continued to exist. It became imperative to work out the relationships between the mission and the church more carefully and sensitively than had been necessary in the past. That work presented one of the great challenges the mission faced in the twentieth century.

8

Moving Into the
Twentieth Century

Jacob Chamberlain, on March 2, 1908, fulfilled his vow to live and die in Madanapalle. "It was doubtless as he would have had it, and among his Telugu people he will sleep well till the morning of his resurrection."[1] He had served as a missionary in India since 1860, forty-eight years.

Jared Waterbury Scudder died October 17, 1910, at the age of eighty-one years. He had been born in India and served the last fifty-five of his years in India. "To him was granted the rare privilege of witnessing the growth of the Christian community connected with the Arcot Mission from a few score to nearly ten thousand, with an organized pastorate, a largely self-supporting church, and an elaborate organization of schools, in the development of all of which he had a large share."[2]

With these two deaths, the first generation of Reformed Church Arcot missionaries was all gone. The pioneer era had truly come to an end, and a new century in mission had dawned. The Reverend Dr. John Livingston, who was in many ways the spiritual father of

---

[1] Henry Cobb, "Jacob Chamberlain, M.D., D.D., L.L.D.," *Mission Field,* April, 1908, 445.
[2] "BFMR," 1911, 45.

the Reformed Church in America, had preached that the nineteenth and twentieth centuries were to be the great time of mission in preparation for the millenial return of Jesus Christ. The nineteenth century of preparation had now given way to the twentieth century. Europe and America entered the new century full of hope. A new Christian weekly magazine called the *Christian Century* was established and became a leading voice in American Protestantism.

In the year of Jared Scudder's death, the Arcot Mission was optimistic about the steady, quiet progress being made in every department of its work. By the power of the Holy Spirit, it knew that success was assured. The kingdom was coming not by sensational outbursts, but as yeast working in the dough works quietly and surely.

> We are impressed with the firm, sure, and upward trend that permeates all the work. There have been no very striking things taking place, such as cause emphatic outbursts of wonder or applause, but all along the line there have occurred very many of those quiet, ordinary, but telling events that indicate earnestness, patience, and power and point to ultimate success....The quiet service is God's way.[3]

The new century's male missionaries even looked different from the men of the previous century. The 1910 Arcot Mission report includes on its frontispiece a picture of Jared W. Scudder in his magnificent, flowing white beard, waistcoat, and vest, the very picture of dignity, authority, and wisdom. The same report contains a picture of the members of the Arcot Mission and guests who were at the mission meeting in 1910. The new century men are pictured wearing business suits. Only one has a short beard. Four wear mustaches, and one has full sideburns that join in a mustache. The others are all clean shaven.

[3] "AAR," 1910, 7.

At the turn of the century, the conveniences of modern life were becoming available to missionaries in India. No longer did they have to take sea voyages lasting three months. They now traveled between India and the United States on steamships rather than sailboats. Letters could arrive at their destination halfway around the world in less than a month. The Board of Foreign Missions and the Arcot Mission could communicate by cablegram. The board and the missionaries even had a codebook for use in cablegrams, in which a single code word could substitute for a whole sentence, enabling them to keep the cost down. The magic lantern was no longer a novelty. Jacob Chamberlain had two decades previously begun to use a typewriter in writing his letters—the first Arcot missionary to do so. In fact, Jacob Chamberlain learned to type before Henry Cobb, the secretary of the Board of Foreign Missions in New York, gained that skill. Chamberlain congratulated Cobb when the first typed letter was received from New York.[4]

The missionaries continued to introduce new technological marvels. A phonograph was brought to a harvest festival in 1909. American popular songs were played on it, to the awe and amusement of the villagers, many of whom had not seen a white face before.[5] By that time, however, many people were becoming more accustomed to the new machines brought to India by the Arcot missionaries. They had been especially impressed twenty years before, in 1889, when Carman Scudder had ridden through Punganur on his way to Madanapalle on his new bicycle that had just arrived from the United States.

> The bicycle was of the high wheel kind then in vogue, with the very high wheel in front, and through every village the people stared in speechless wonder at the sight of a man flying through the air on a "one wheel wagon." On some of the country roads women carrying heavy burdens on their heads, when they saw the apparition, dropped their loads

---

[4] Jacob Chamberlain to Henry Cobb, June 29, 1888.
[5] *Mission Gleaner,* July 1909, 9.

and ran across the fields shrieking. *"Pi-sah-su! Pi-sah-su!"* ("Devil! Devil!).[6]

The missionaries sometimes traveled long distances on bicycles. In 1902, L.R. Scudder traveled on his bicycle from Ootocamund to Ranipet, a distance of over 250 miles, in order to help Louisa Hart complete her preparations to leave for the United States for the sake of her health. Unfortunately, Scudder fell off his bicycle three times on the way, "but fortunately the injuries were confined to the wheel that was pretty badly used up."[7]

Most amazing of all, perhaps, was the first motor car to arrive in Vellore. It arrived September 23, 1909, in a crate and was destined for use by Ida Scudder. A mechanic had to be called from Madras, ninety miles away, to assemble it. It was a small French car, a Peugeot, which had just one cylinder, a high folding top, wire-spoked wheels, and two seats. Very soon after receiving it, Ida Scudder began to load it with medicines and take it on the roads to villages to administer medical treatment.

White uniform swathed in a duster, topee securely anchored by a long veil, Ida sat in front with the driver, Salomi and a religious teacher behind. They set forth gleefully, even the little car seeming to sense its responsibility and chugging gaily, if noisily, through the town, horn honking incessantly, bicycles, pushcarts, cows, bullock bandies, pedestrians, all scrambling madly to get out of the way. And wisely, for Hussain, the driver, had little more knowledge of the car's workings than the woman at his side, and slightly less of common sense.[8]

The arrival of the motor car for roadside clinics became an every-Wednesday event for the village people on the road from Vellore to Gudiyattam. Roadside clinics were the medical equivalent of

---

[6] *Mission Gleaner,* April, 1908, 11.

[7] W. H. Farrar to Henry Cobb, May 21, 1902.

[8] Dorothy Clarke Wilson, *Dr.Ida: Passing on the Torch of Life* (New York: Friendship Press, 1976), 127-28. The "topee" was the pith helmet worn by Europeans during the colonial era.

evangelistic touring. They combined love for the poor with the romance of mission. We can excerpt here part of Ida's sister-in-law Margaret (Mrs. H. J.) Scudder's description of a day on the road with Ida Scudder.

> Well it was a scene I shall never forget. The people crowding around the car, talking, gesticulating, elbowing one another, and yet with some order too….The patient then presented his or her slip of paper to Dr. Ida, who examined and diagnosed the disease, wrote her prescription, and passed it on to nurse Salome, who gave out the drugs….[At the next stop] It was the same thing again; old women and little children suffering from neglect and sin; so many helpless cases of blindness, tuberculosis, etc. that could only be tenderly treated, but not cured….One man, when asked by the Doctor if he had had any medicine before, held out his hand to her, saying, "Feel my pulse and see if there is any medicine in my stomach."…If I found myself so tired, with no responsibility, what do you think was the Doctor's condition, with all the strain on her nerves as well as her brain.[9]

The Arcot Missionaries Approval of Twentieth-Century American Colonialism

The improved speed of transportation and communication also made it possible for missionaries to keep in closer touch with events in the United States. They were much interested in the progress of the Spanish-American War in 1898. John Scudder was proud of the way in which the American army and navy were fighting the war. He wrote that the missionaries were hopeful that Santiago in Cuba would surrender in a day or two. "I don't see how they can hold out much longer. Then perhaps we shall hear of peace—when America

---

[9] *Mission Gleaner,* November, 1910, 8. For another description of a roadside clinic, see Wilson, *Dr. Ida,* 127-34.

will have her hands full, taking care of the new territory gained, a difficult work, but no doubt the Yankees will be equal to the task."[10]

Henry Cobb's letter of July 19, in which he expressed his joy at the American victory over Spain, reached India August 15. It was read aloud during a mission meeting. Chamberlain responded to Cobb, "Our joy equals yours at the speedy termination of the war, and over the splendid achievements of both the Army and Navy of our country. The God of Battles be praised, and may He guide to the securing from this war the best results for His Kingdom."[11]

Two months later, Jacob Chamberlain had two comments to make about the return of peace following America's victory in Cuba and the Philippines. The first was that he hoped that, with the end of the war, Reformed Church members would no longer be called upon to make loans to the government but instead would increase their contributions to the Board of Foreign Missions and avoid a deficit for 1898. "The fact that the loan called for by the government was taken up by the people with such marvelous eagerness in small sums and so much more than asked for shows that the people have money. May they now invest it in the Lord's War."[12]

His second comment shows that the Arcot missionaries were quite ready to support the entry of the United States into the community of colonial powers, in spite of the heavy responsibility that America would have to bear.

> Our country has a heavy responsibility not of its own making thrust upon it by the results of the war. We out here are hoping that the government will not give back any of the Philippines or Ladrones or Caroline Islands to Spain and Spanish misrule, nor hand them over to anarchy and barbarians. The Lord give wisdom to President McKinley and his advisors. We are watching with intense interest for

---

[10] John Scudder, Jr., to Henry Cobb, July 13, 1898.
[11] J. Chamberlain to Henry Cobb, August 20, 1898.
[12] Ibid., October 19, 1898.

some news from the Peace Commission in Paris. We have
a fine set of Commissioners. May they do good work.[13]

President McKinley rose to the occasion and set the United States
on a course to civilize and Christianize the Philippines. The need for
such civilizing and Christianizing of that country was clear to all
Protestants in the United States, who rejoiced at the end of three
hundred years of Spanish Roman Catholic misrule. McKinley was
applauded by missionaries and his fellow Methodists alike for
accepting the challenge. To a meeting of Methodists, he confided
his deepest convictions:

> I am not ashamed to tell you, gentlemen, that I went down
> on my knees and prayed Almighty God for light and
> guidance more than one night. And one night late it came
> to me this way....There was nothing left for us to do but to
> take them all and educate the Filipinos and uplift and
> civilize and Christianize them and by God's grace do the
> very best we could by them, as our fellow men for whom
> Christ also died.[14]

Wyckoff was less eager for the United States to take responsibility
for the Philippines. His hesitancy, however, was not due to a deep
opposition to colonialism but to the magnitude of the task. He
thought the United States would find Cuba and Puerto Rico about
all that it could handle. He commented, "We are awaiting with some
anxiety the decision as to the Philippines. I wish they could be given
to England. I doubt if Americans who favor their retention realize
what a responsibility the proper government of them would entail.
Cuba and Porto Rico [sic] will be quite sufficient for America to
experiment upon."[15]

13 Ibid.
14 Quoted in Sydney E. Ahlstrom, *A Religious History of the American People* (New Haven,
    Conn.: Yale Univ. Press, 1972), 879.
15 J. H. Wyckoff to Henry Cobb, October 20, 1898.

To the great sorrow of the missionaries and the Board of Foreign Missions, President McKinley was assassinated in 1901. The editor of the *Mission Field* wrote a eulogy printed in the October, 1901, issue. He praised McKinley especially for the speech that the president made at the Ecumenical Conference for Foreign Missions in New York City on the evening of April 21, 1900. In that speech, McKinley gave high praise to foreign missionaries when he said,

> I am glad of the opportunity to offer without stint my tribute of praise and respect to the missionary effort which has wrought such wonderful triumphs for civilization....They furnish us examples of forbearance and fortitude, of patience and unyielding purpose, and of a spirit which triumphs not by the force of might, but by the persuasive majesty of right."[16]

The Arcot Mission had been in India for a half century when President McKinley was shot, but its missionaries had not forgotten that America was still their homeland, to which they owed loyalty. By that time, they referred to the Board of Foreign Missions as the "Home Board." The phrase was for a number of decades used by other missions as well to refer to their own boards in Europe or America. Indian Christians who had never been to the United States also learned to speak affectionately of the Board of Foreign Missions as the "Home Board." As late as the 1960s, when no missionary used that phrase any longer, one could still occasionally hear the older generation of Indian Christians speak affectionately or critically of the "Home Board."

The Growth of National Hindu Feeling in India

As they approached the twentieth century, Reformed Church missionaries in India were confronted with a resurgent Hinduism and a growing sense of confident Indian nationalism. This represented a distinct change of mood from what missionaries had

16 *Mission Field,* October, 1901, 194.

met in the first half of the nineteenth century. In the early days of their presence in India, the Scudders, along with the British and other missionaries, constantly pointed out the ignorance and superstition in a Hinduism that practiced the burning of widows on their husband's funeral pyre (*sati*), intense caste discrimination, idolatry, child marriage, and the ill-treatment of widows. They were confident of the immense advantages of western civilization and education, as well as of the benefits of the English law codes that were being bestowed on the Indian subcontinent.

By 1885 the situation was changing at an increasing pace. In that year, the Indian National Congress held its first meeting. Its seventy-three members, representing districts from the whole subcontinent, were beginning to show signs that like-minded Indians should follow western political examples by uniting under a single umbrella organization that would represent their national feeling. The congress accepted the democratic ideals professed in the parliamentary and common law of England. Its basic objective was to hold Britain to its word, which was that the Raj existed for the benefit of Indians who, under its guidance, would advance to a state in which they could manage their own affairs. In its loyalty to England, the Indian National Congress for a number of years referred to Queen Empress Victoria as "mother," and her name was cheered. As late as in its 1900 session, one of its members, Achut Sitaran Sathe, expressed the general sense of loyalty present in the congress:

> The educated Indian is loyal by instinct and contented through interest. The English flag is his physical shelter, the English philosopher has become his spiritual consolation. The English renaissance has so far permeated the educated Indian that it is no longer possible for him to be otherwise than loyal and affectionate towards the rulers of his choice. He is the vanguard of a new civilization whose banner is love, charity and equality.[17]

17 Quoted in James, *Raj*, 352.

Indians after 1885 were no more pleased with Britain's insistence upon their colonial status than were the American colonialists after 1765. In America it was Stamp Acts and trade restrictions that spurred rebellion. In India it was British racism, British insistence that British and other Europeans in India be tried only before British judges, and restrictions on Indians entering the Indian Civil Service that were especially irritating. Lord Curzon's unilateral decision in 1905 to partition the state of Bengal with its seventy-eight million inhabitants into two states set off an uproar. It symbolized for the growing nationalist movement the impotence of Indians under British rule and the arrogance of British despotism.[18]

The changes taking place in India were hastened by a growth in admiration for Indian spirituality on other continents. Hinduism gained popular respect in America and Europe when Swami Vivekananda (Naarenddranth Datta) (1863-1902) made a lecture tour of America and Europe following his speech at the World Parliament of Religions, held in Chicago in connection with the 1893 World's Fair. Vivekananda was the founder of the Sri Ramakrishna Mission in India, which patterned its methods of communication and exercise of social concern on those of Protestant missionary societies. At the World Parliament of Religions, Vivekananda gave a brilliant address that affirmed the superiority of the spirituality of the East over the materialism of the West. He preached the unity of all existence, the divinity of the soul, the nonduality of the godhead, and the harmony of religions. He called upon the followers of other religions to accept the Hindu spirit of tolerance in place of their religious exclusivisms. His evident intellectual brilliance together with his impressive manner and exotic dress gained the admiration of his hearers. No longer could India be understood as a land of ignorance and superstition. It was the place from which true spirituality and tolerance emanated. The admiration that he had earned in the West gained for Vivekananda a new respect in India. His compatriots there accepted his

18 Ibid., 341-63.

admonitions that they cultivate faith in themselves and accept a life of renunciation and service for the sake of national ideals.

The Arcot Mission felt it necessary to respond in its annual report to Vivekananda's affirmation of the power of Hindu traditions and his attack on the work of missionaries. They told members of the Reformed Church that the very fact that Vivekananda needed to make a speaking tour in America provided evidence that the missionary effort was having a deep impact in India.

> Perhaps none more than Swami Vivekananda has insisted on the folly of supposing that missionary effort could change India. According to him, the hoary customs and deep and subtle philosophy of Hinduism need fear nothing from the futile, absurd, inefficient, yea even insulting attacks of the missionary body. He would have his hearers believe that these missionaries gifted with, perhaps, a little sentimental piety, but blessed with small brains and less tact and no common sense, were, by their ignorant attacks on Hinduism and by their willful misrepresentation of it, doing more to alienate the minds of thoughtful Hindus from Christianity than to win them to Christianity. If it were really so, why should he be at such pains to cry down and discourage their work?[19]

The missionaries declared that they were confident that the net result of the lectures of Vivekananananda and the full discussion that was following was serving "to vindicate the work of the missionaries and discredit the Hindu monk."[20]

While Swami Vivekananda and the Sri Ramakrishna Mission were having their impact in the western world as well as in India, the newly organized Theosophical Society was providing them with stronger competition in the Arcot Mission area. The Theosophical Society provided an organized alternative to the missionaries'

[19] "BFMR," June 1910, 19.
[20] Ibid., 21.

teachings because its western founders admired things Indian and Hindu while opposing Christianity. "Theosophy" ("divine wisdom") as a movement was developed by two unusual individuals, Helena Petrovana Blavatsky and Colonel Henry Steel Olcott, in 1875. The movement adopted ideas and symbols from Egyptian, Hindu, and Buddhist religions, as well as elements of Blavatsky's and Olcott's shared interest in nineteenth-century spiritualism. Olcott went to India in 1878, where he established contact with Swami Dayananda Saraswati and the Arja Samaj Hindu reform movement. An open break with Dayananda and the Arja Samaj occurred in 1881. The Theosophical Society was re-structured and formalized with three goals: "to form a nucleus of the Universal Brotherhood of humanity, without distinction of race, creed, sex, caste, or colour; to encourage the study of comparative religion, philosophy, and science; and to investigate the unexplained laws of Nature and the powers latent in man."[21] Tensions arose within the society between Englishmen and Indians over the question of caste distinctions and universal brotherhood, but the tensions did not lead to a break of relationships. Olcott and Blavatsky made lecture tours in India for several years. Charges of fraud against Blavatsky led to her permanently leaving India in 1885.

Olcott continued to give lectures praising aspects of Hinduism. He spoke glowingly of the glorious Hindu past with its magnificent achievements in all areas of culture and science. He said that India was "the cradle of European civilization, the Aryans were the progenitors of the Western peoples, and their literature the source and spring of all Western religions and philosophies."[22] Educated Hindus enthusiastically welcomed this dogmatic articulation of their great history, philosophy, and religion by a representative of the western world.

---

[21] Jones, *Socio-Religious Reformed Movements,* 170.
[22] Ibid., 173. It is well to remind Europeans and Americans that the "Aryans" had their origins somewhere in Asia in the region of modern Iran or the Indus Valley, but in any case not in Europe.

The Theosophical Movement gained renewed impetus after 1907, when Olcott died and was replaced by Annie Besant. She made her residence at the Theosophical Society headquarters in Adyar, now a part of Madras. Besant organized the Theosophic Order of Service with the goal of promoting practical, humanitarian work. It advocated brotherhood, national education, and an end to child marriage. It sought to abolish capital punishment, extend cooperatives, promote hospital visits, advocate prison reforms, support child welfare and aid to the blind, and oppose the "white slave" trade. Besant proclaimed that she was a Hindu at heart, and she became involved in the independence movement. She proposed Home Rule for India and was elected president of the Indian National Congress in 1917.[23]

Theosophical lodges were established in leading towns in the Telugu area. Madanapalle became a center of Theosophical educational efforts when the Besant Theosophical College, the Besant Theosophical High School, and a night school were established there. Theosophical activity was also strong in the area around Tindivanam in the southern part of the Arcot area. In the face of the work of the Theosophical Society and other Hindu reform movements active in the Arcot Mission area, missionaries found it increasingly difficult to cite superstitious practices and abuses against women as reasons to leave Hinduism and become Christians.

Colonel Olcott spoke to large audiences, especially to young men, and was enthusiastically received in Vellore in 1885. Jared Scudder proposed two reasons for his popularity. The first was that the Hindus saw that they must move beyond their ancient mythological religion. Theosophy with "its vague generalities, its occult mysticism and its specious ethics better suits the depraved moral appetite" than does Christianity that "is too pure and too radically destructive of their sinful inclinations to be palatable," while Theosophy

---

[23] Ibid., 174-75.

"serves to stay the longing for something more satisfying than their lately abandoned faith."[24]

The second reason for the colonel's popularity, according to Scudder, was his ability "to soft-soap the Hindus without stint."[25] Scudder believed that Olcott's popularity would pass as soon as thinking minds began to recognize the need for something more substantial. His disdain for Olcott's fawning speeches brought forth all of Scudder's eloquence:

> According to him Occidental Philosophy is yet in its teens. Sanskrit is the great repository of all true and perennial thought. Europe and America if they wish to arrive at certainties, must sit at the feet of the Hindu Gurus, and humbly submit their intellects to the Koot Hoomies of Thibet. All this wonderfully tickles the *amour propre* of men who are just emerging, with blinking eyes, from the darkness of a secular night. They have not yet had time to look about enough to see that the swelling sentences of the Colonel are but the outfoamings of a mind which is equally empty of Sanskrit and of Philosophy. But the fulsome flattery and fawning blandeloquence of the expounder of Theosophy have their charms, especially for the young and unripe.[26]

In spite of Jared Scudder's scorn for the eloquence and empty sentences of Colonel Olcott, the Theosophical Society's activities continued to disturb the work of the Arcot Mission for at least four more decades. J.D. Muyskens in Madanapalle in 1918 was still facing the competition of the Theosophical High School, which was taking away some of the students from Hope High School.[27] Sarella Te Winkel wrote about speeches made by Annie Besant in Chittoor in 1916. Thousands had flocked to hear her speak, and

[24] J. W. Scudder to J. M. Ferris, December 1, 1885.
[25] Ibid.
[26] Ibid.
[27] J. D. Muyskens, letter to the Hope *Anchor*, Dec. 12, 1918, Joint Archives.

some were saying that she was the goddess of wisdom incarnate. She told the people that they should no longer allow outside missionaries to come into their homes and prejudice their wives and daughters against the noble Hindu faith. She said that she had once been a Christian and knew that the Hindu faith was far better for them than was Christianity. She urged them to bring out their idols and give them a fresh coat of paint and take them for a ride around the city. As they did so, they should be sure to make as much noise as possible near the mission school.

Sarella Te Winkel, like other missionaries before her, took comfort in the fact that the zenana work was going on as before. She also had hope that after the summer vacation the children who had dropped out of the mission school would return. Perhaps the opposition was being used by God to bring about a positive result. She wrote, "We hope that during the coming vacation the zeal of our opponents will have burned out and the children who have been stopped from attending our schools will find their way back again, and that in time the silver lining to this cloud of opposition will become visible....Even Mrs. Besant's wrath may be made to praise Him!"[28]

Missionary Response to Resurgent Hinduism

The Arcot missionaries discovered that the resurgent Hindu movements and the teachings of the Theosophists were not confined to towns and centers of education. Even villagers were using the arguments of these movements when Christians came preaching the gospel:

> Begin to preach Christ and at once will be revealed the power of the enemy. Although the village may be far away from centers of learning, distant from the public highway and seemingly out of touch with the rest of the world, an

[28] Sarella Te Winkel, "The Encouragement of Opposition," *Mission Gleaner,* September 1916, 4.

argument on religion will bring one face to face with all the teachings of Hinduism, the iron rules of caste, the arguments of Theosophy and the new Vedantism and the latest theories of Mrs. Besant.[29]

Such opposition led Reformed Church missionaries in India to ponder how much strength remained in Hinduism at the end of the nineteenth century. Ever since the Scudder's arrival in India, missionaries had been saying that Hinduism was an outdated religion that would succumb to the power of the gospel. But resurgent Hindu movements seemed to be pointing in the opposite direction. Jared Scudder, like Sarella Te Winkel, believed that resurgent movements should be understood as some of the last vigorous kicks of a dying religion. He wrote, "Brahminism is now moribund, wounded to death by Western sciences and God's revelation. Educated Hindus are making efforts to resuscitate it, but their task is hopeless."[30]

Wyckoff was less optimistic about the decline of Hinduism. He told of his experience with opposition on one of his evangelistic tours. On a Saturday morning, he had been in two caste villages. In the first he began talking with an old Hindu teacher about the soul's salvation. When the Hindu teacher saw the women of the house listening, he became restless and asked them to leave. Then he asked Wyckoff to leave. He began stopping his ears and putting his hand to his mouth, saying, "Oh what sin! O what sin! Krishna, forgive me! Krishna, forgive me!" He begged Wyckoff to go away, saying that his devotion to his god was so great that he could not allow himself so much as to hear the name of another religion.

They passed on to a second village. "The street proved to be inhabited by Brahmins only, and a more insolent crowd it has seldom been my lot to meet."[31] One of the older men thought that

[29] "BFMR," June 1905, 24.
[30] J. W. Scudder to Henry Cobb, December 10, 1890,
[31] J. H. Wyckoff, *Notes of an Evangelistic Tour,* September 1893, board correspondence file, Archives of the RCA.

Wyckoff represented the government, so he invited him to sit on his verandah to talk. When Wyckoff began to talk about religion and the gospel, a young man came up and told the older man that his family was calling him. When the older man was willing to listen a few minutes longer, the young man began to shout that Wyckoff must not teach any religion in their street. He said that preaching in that street was contrary to custom and to law. Others joined the young man in his shouting, so Wyckoff left the verandah and began preaching in the middle of the street, saying that he was now on a government road where he had a perfect right to be. They could listen or not listen as they chose. They then accused him of defiling their street with his shoes and wanted to know who would pay the expiatory rites that would have to be performed because of the presence of Wyckoff and his low-caste helper. Wyckoff reflected on what had happened that morning, writing, "To those who think that Heathenism has but a superficial hold upon the Hindus, this illustration may be useful in ridding them of their delusion. The fact is Hinduism is still the living faith of thousands if not millions in India."[32]

Four years later, J.H. Wyckoff would make an even stronger statement as he reflected on the continuing hold of caste in the country. He commented,

> I do not think any European has yet fathomed the real character of the Hindu. He is more and more of an enigma the longer one studies him. If Satan has ever manufactured a more pernicious system than the religion of India, I have yet to see it. When an English educated Brahmin, member of the Legislative Council, publicly declares that the penal code is not binding on certain privileged persons, and quotes the Bhagavad Gita to prove it, one realizes the failure of mere education to regenerate men. And what a rebuke to Europeans who eulogize the Hindu philosophy![33]

32 Ibid.
33 J. H. Wyckoff to Henry Cobb, August 4, 1897.

Evangelism, Conversions, Persecution, and Tolerance

In an era when the Indian independence movement was beginning to gain momentum and resurgent Hinduism was posing new challenges to missionary activity, the Arcot missionaries continued to emphasize that evangelism must have priority. The Arcot Mission report for 1900 provides evidence for that fact. Evangelistic touring and street preaching remained important. In the Vellore area, the Indian workers had preached the gospel in 5,197 places, 11,342 times to 165,569 persons, and distributed 12,000 handbills. The number of women reached by the zenana women workers should be added to this to make a total of 193,292 persons who heard the good tidings. "The message has generally been well received, and many are ready to acknowledge that it is the truth and should be accepted, but as yet they are unwilling to do so."[34]

By 1900, evangelists in the Arcot area were learning to build on friendship and good relationships with the non-Christian community, in contrast to previous generations of preachers who often spent time attacking idolatry and what they considered immoral Hindu practices. The Young Men's Christian Association (YMCA), under the leadership of Dr. Sherwood Eddy, was assisting the churches in India to develop effective conversations with educated Hindus and Muslims. A local branch of the YMCA was organized in Vellore in 1900 in order to give opportunities for the college teachers and Christian men of all denominations to meet and work together in doing the Lord's work. Sherwood Eddy was invited in to give a series of lectures as a means to exert an evangelistic influence upon the educated and student population in Vellore.[35]

In many places, there was a marked change in people's thinking. James Beattie noticed that among the educated Hindus in the Chittoor area there was a kind of agnosticism that made the turn of the century a time of transition in matters of caste practices.

---

[34] "BFMR," 1900, 34-35.
[35] Ibid., 34.

A kind of agnosticism may describe the condition of the educated Hindus, and the restaurants on railways and in cities and shops, where the oilman's stores are sold, can testify how they break in practice the caste they defend in theory. This is a stage in which the mind of man cannot rest, and such a transition, as all history shews [sic], is prophetic of better things.[36]

Carman Scudder also noticed that open opposition to the gospel was less marked than it had been a few years before. Whether this was due to a change in attitude among the Hindus or to a change of tone in Christian preaching is not clear. It was probably both. In any case, the Christian evangelists were well received when they preached the positive message of Christ without attacking the Hindu deities. At the same time, the more positive attitudes on the part of all concerned was not necessarily leading to more conversions to the Christian faith. Scudder set forth a clear and full statement of his assessment of the situation.

Wherever our men go they are well received. I forbid useless arguing, and all abuse of Hindu gods, or even undue reference to them. It is enough for them to preach "Christ." To this rule I ascribe the present relations which prevail....The present attitude of the higher classes is one of friendliness, or at least not opposition to the Gospel. I feel sure there are many who read the Bible. I know of a few such, and though they are not disciples, they will in time become so. There are two great hindrances: (1) the caste difficulty, and (2) the fact that Christianity, as worked out practically by many of its exponents, does not commend itself sufficiently to compensate for the risks of a change of religion.[37]

[36] Ibid., 36. Beattie is saying that they "break caste" because they enter into close contact and dealings with persons of lower caste and thereby violate the standards of their caste.
[37] Ibid., 35.

The friendlier atmosphere did not mean that the street preachers would never meet opposition. Henry Huizinga reported in 1900 that on one occasion they had to discontinue their magic lantern program and preaching when a number of young men came out from behind trees and houses and temple walls and threw stones at the crowd and the evangelistic team. In another village near by, they met some mild opposition from a few Brahmins. One of them began to interrupt them and warn the people against listening. He tried to start an argument, saying, "Our god Vishnu became incarnate nine times, assuming the form of different animals, in order to save all creatures. Christ came only to save men!' This Brahmin volunteer followed us to another part of the town and by his noise considerably disturbed us. The people, however, sympathized as much with us as with him."[38]

In spite of the more friendly and positive atmosphere that was developing, the line continued to be drawn at the point of conversion and baptism. Baptism following conversion represents a much greater social change in a country such as India than it did within the Christendom that still could be assumed at the beginning of the twentieth century. Evangelicals in England and America called people who were within supposedly "Christian" countries to be converted to their own religious roots and the religious traditions of their surrounding environment. For them, conversion and baptism meant being welcomed fully into the community again. In India, it was possible for Hindus to become interested in Jesus Christ, to pray to Jesus, and sometimes even to confess faith in Jesus Christ without necessarily causing great offense. Baptism, however, signified a change of community, a leaving of the customs and caste practices and the worship of God through the use of the idols. That change was not easily tolerated. Near the turn of the century, there were several conversions and baptisms in India that stirred up considerable controversy. Perhaps the most famous of these came

[38] Ibid., 37.

Baptizing a new Christian

to be known as "The Madanapalle Conversion Case," and it was
widely reported in the press.

L.B. Chamberlain, the son of Jacob Chamberlain, was in charge
of the boarding schools in Madanapalle. One day he received a
letter from a Brahmin boy who was in boarding. It was a voluntarily
written declaration of faith in Christ. The boy was in the highest
class in the school. He wrote that he had been brought to his new
faith by the teaching and his study of the Bible in the school.
Chamberlain for two months kept the letter in his desk drawer
without taking any action, because he did not want to make the
conversion public. The boy was still afraid to face his relatives and
wanted to go away to be baptized.[39]

When the mission met in Tindivanam, 170 miles from Madanapalle,
the following January, the young man, whose name was Adiseshayya,
appeared and asked to be baptized. It was agreed that his testimony
and steadfastness was such that this request should be granted, but
it was decided to inform his relatives first. They instantly instituted
a suit in the court to stop the baptism from taking place on the

[39] *Mission Field,* April, 1896, 352.

grounds that he was a minor and had been seduced by the missionaries. A great hue and cry went up against all phases of mission work, and a violent attack was made on several mission schools connected with the Madanapalle station. The attacks on the schools were effective. The Hindu Girls' School lost 80 percent of its pupils, while the elementary school for boys lost 50 percent.

Prior to the point at which the case was coming to trial in the court, great efforts were made to lead Adiseshayya to recant his conversion, but he refused. The trial began on March 29 and went on until April 17, with some interruptions. The vital question was whether Adiseshayya had attained the age of majority, which in India at that time was eighteen. He claimed to be twenty, but his parents said he was fifteen. The local judge was partial to the Brahmins at crucial points in the trial. A number of legal technicalities and maneuvers complicated the trial, resulting in differing rulings by separate judges. The local judge declared that Adiseshayya must be delivered over to his parents, but the district judge declared that he was at liberty to go wherever he pleased. Meanwhile, some Christian friends in Madras, without consulting either the missionaries or his relatives, assisted Adiseshayya to go to Ceylon, where he lived for a time happily and safe from interference.

Then, on September 9, 1894, the mission's appeal of the local judge's decree was heard in district court and sustained completely. The Hindus and relatives decided not to appeal further. The young man returned to Madanapalle and was examined again as to the sincerity of his faith, which proved "eminently satisfactory." He was baptized in Madanapalle in January, 1895, and received a Christian name as well, becoming Paul Adiseshayya. His intellectual ability was recognized, so arrangements were made to enable him to continue his studies toward a bachelor's degree.[40] He became one of the leading Indian Christians in the Arcot area, including being named as the first Indian principal of Voorhees College near the end of his career.

40 Ibid., 352-53.

This case, which was followed in the newspapers throughout the Madras Presidency and even beyond, became important in establishing the legal status of young men who desired to be baptized, as well as in clarifying that in the case of minors such baptisms could not take place without the permission of the parents or legal guardians. It also reinforced for the missionaries that it was crucial for them to exercise restraint and observance of legal codes in regard to any calls to conversion among young men and women in the boarding schools.

Parenthetically, it may be noted that while, on the one hand, many Hindu parents desired their children to be enrolled in mission boarding schools in order to receive a good education together with good training in morality and social development, on the other hand, a residual fear of the boarding schools remained. Rumors continued to fly about why missionaries were ready to accept the children into the boarding homes. Jacob Chamberlain, as late as 1893, was surprised by the rumors he met while on an evangelistic preaching tour. He learned that the villagers among whom he was traveling seriously believed that, while passing through preaching and distributing literature, his real object was to kidnap their children and put them under Christian instruction away from their parents in the boarding schools. Moreover, there were at that time several large bridge construction projects going on in the area. Many of the villagers had accepted as true the rumor that Chamberlain was an agent of the British construction firms. They suspected he might be kidnapping children and putting them to dangerous work under water and on the scaffolding involved in bridge construction.[41]

One thing that irritated the Arcot missionaries was the way in which Americans accepted the thesis of men such as Swami Vivekananda and some western scholars, who were claiming that Hinduism was superior to western religions in that Hinduism was tolerant while the Christian faith was dogmatic and intolerant. The missionaries claimed that Vivekananda misrepresented missionaries

---

[41] J. Chamberlain to Henry Cobb, June 29, 1893.

and their work, on the one hand, and on "the other by drawing a picture of Hinduism, that no orthodox Hindu would recognize."[42] The Hinduism that the missionaries saw was oppressive of the "Pariahs," or outcastes, who had no hope so long as Hinduism did not change. When members of such outcaste communities became Christians, they became victims of persecution and intolerance. L.R. Scudder contrasted the portrayal of the tolerance of Hinduism with what he saw happening repeatedly.

> The beautiful pictures of the tolerance of Hinduism and of its spirit of brotherhood to which America has been treated of late have their foundation I fear only in the imagination of the champion of Hinduism. I have not seen it here. On the contrary in my short experience of five years of village work I could multiply severe instances of the most bitter persecution and intolerance and caste hatred. In fact, without exception so far, every effort on my part to enlighten, ennoble, and christianize a Pariah community has been bitterly opposed by the Hindu. And in nearly every case, the village officials have been the chief instigators. Persuasion, promises, threats, abuse, injustice and even violence have been resorted to.[43]

Scudder went on to report in detail on recent instances of Hindu intolerance and persecution of pariahs who had recently become Christians in the area of Ranipet. In the first case, there was a poor man who had borrowed six rupees for seed before he became a Christian. He paid back all but one-and-a-half rupees. The man from whom he borrowed it told him he would give the receipt for the repayment later, but he never gave it. When the man became a Christian, the caste man sued him in court for the full amount of six rupees, plus interest and costs. The man had no receipt to show, and his witnesses were all pariahs who were discredited as witnesses.

[42] "BFMR," 1897, 21.
[43] L. R. Scudder to Henry Cobb, February 26, 1895.

The judge ridiculed him for having become a Christian and gave the decision to award the full amount plus costs. Two other Christians in the same village were in the same predicament.[44]

In a second case, a young man who became a Christian was severely abused and beaten. His relatives joined with the caste people in turning against him. His own mother also joined with them. The village officials refused to listen to his complaints and brought a case before the same local judge, who ruled against him and deprived him of the larger part of his land. This case was appealed to a higher court. In still another case, new Christians were refused permission to remove a white ant hill next to their house. They had wanted to remove it because cobras like to live in the holes of such hills. Instead of giving permission, village officials placed a small temple on top of the hill and the cobra was worshiped daily. The people in the house were told that the cobra would not hurt them since it was being worshiped. "This is the sort of tolerance and spirit of brotherhood that we have out here."[45]

The missionaries recognized that Vivekananda would have agreed that such persecution should not go on. They also knew that Vivekananda would have argued that such intolerance is contrary to true Hinduism and that, just as there are Christians who do not live according to the spirit of Jesus, so there are Hindus who do not live as true Hindus. Therefore the missionaries wished him well in his campaign to reform Hinduism, but they believed such efforts were futile. They believed that "a highly educated and intelligent Brahmin," to whom the Government of Madras had committed the important duty of writing the Progress Report of the Madras Presidency, had been more accurate about the state of affairs when he pointed out, "from a Hindu standpoint, there was no hope for social amelioration of these outcastes within Hinduism. There was but one way for them to rise, and that was to renounce Hinduism and accept either Mohammedanism or Christianity."[46]

[44] Ibid.
[45] Ibid.
[46] "BFMR," 1897, 21

In its 1895 report, the Arcot Mission saw one other ray of hope for the Pariah community, many of whom were becoming Christians. That was that they would organize themselves to struggle for their own emancipation. It was this possibility that was raising the fears of the caste people, who saw that the outcastes who had become Christians were being trained up into educated, self-respecting communities that

> can compete on almost equal terms with the proud Brahmin....It has also awakened in them to assert themselves, and to struggle for their own emancipation. They now have a newspaper to represent their community, called the *Pariah*. And this year they, as a community, presented an address of welcome to the new Governor of Madras, praying for a sympathetic helping hand and they were received with sympathy and kindness.[47]

In the twentieth century, Jawaharlal Nehru also set forth the thesis that in India there was almost complete tolerance by Hinduism of the many religions that had come into the country. Then, the assertion of the tolerant nature of Hinduism played an important role in the program of the Indian National Congress. Since this thesis is at odds with the experience of those who were becoming Christians at the turn of the century, it is appropriate to examine the matter a little more closely, assisted by an analysis of the issues by Ainslie Embree. Embree maintains that in its earlier periods Hinduism was not tolerant of other religions such as Buddhism. The thesis that Hinduism is tolerant was first proposed by German philosophers, who used the thesis in opposite directions. Hegel and Marx spoke of such tolerance to show its deficiencies and "other worldliness" instead of facing the real issues in this world. Schopenhauer, on the other hand, popularized the idea that Indian religion was superior to the Semitic tradition of monotheism, which

[47] Ibid.

was responsible for fanatic crimes perpetrated in the name of religion.[48]

The emphasis upon Hinduism and Indian society's tolerance for other religions and systems of thought became an essential component of the nationalist movement, led by the Indian National Congress, which had to convince Muslims and Hindus, especially, and others as well, to work together for Indian independence and the unity of the nation. The Muslims always remained suspicious that the Hindu majority would ultimately not consent to share power with others.

> ...political issues involving the rights of minorities were being obscured by the assertion that Hinduism was uniquely tolerant and willing to absorb other systems into itself. That the Islamic community in India wanted neither to be absorbed or tolerated seems to have occurred to very few exponents of Hindu tolerance, but neither is it self-evident that Hinduism is really tolerant and absorptive in the sense that has so often been claimed.[49]

Embree's position is that Hinduism can best characterized as *encapsulation*, rather than by words such as toleration, absorption, or synthesis. By this he means that historically Hinduism appears to have been remarkably little influenced by outside forces. When the Muslims entered and ruled over India, the Hindus made no attempt to absorb them into their own frame of thought or to achieve a synthesis with Islam.[50] Their strategy was to encapsulate foreign religions and cultures within their own framework, while Hinduism remained the over-arching and dominant religion and culture of the land.[51] As an encapsulating religion that seeks to maintain the boundaries between castes and between Hindus and other religions

---

48 Embree, *Utopias in Conflict*, 20.

49 Ibid., 23-24.

50 In contrast, the Sikh religion is the result of precisely such an attempt to achieve a synthesis.

51 Embree, *Utopias in Conflict*, 25.

and cultures, Hinduism can become very intolerant of those who seek to change their religion or to move beyond the hierarchical structure of caste, as the pariahs and missionaries repeatedly discovered. In the twentieth century, it was M.K. Gandhi who struggled seriously with the issue of how to break through this impasse.

The Early Indian Independence Movement and the Arcot Missionaries' Anxiety

We commented briefly earlier in this chapter about the growth in the Indian independence movement up to 1905, when the viceroy of India, Lord Curzon, unilaterally ordered the partition of Bengal without taking into account Indian feelings on the matter. His reason for doing so has often been debated. His own explanation was that he had partitioned the state of 78 million inhabitants for the sake of administrative efficiency. Indians suspected less sincere motives. The partition line was so drawn as to give the Muslims in East Bengal a majority of more than six million to the Muslims. At the same time, it seemed to the Hindus to be a political move to undercut the power of the Hindu community in both parts of divided Bengal. The partition became the spark that enabled a more radical group of advocates for independence to gain greater influence in the Indian National Congress. There was a widespread feeling among the people of India that England's purpose was to keep India apart, divided against herself, so that she could never become a self-governing people.

Some of the radicals began to plan acts of terrorism, including the use of bombs. The first bomb to take British lives killed two English women in Bengal by mistake. It had been intended for Magistrate-Judge Douglas Kingsford, who was notorious for the pleasure he took in sentencing political offenders to being flogged. British reactions to the bombing were strident, with demands that all terrorists be arrested and punished and that ten Indians should be shot for every life they took. More violence ensued. A bomb thrown at the viceroy himself failed to go off. Meanwhile, the British were moving to provide for increased Indian membership in the Legislative Council for India and for direct election of the Indian representatives by a very small electorate. This electorate was composed of upper-class Indians enfranchised by virtue of the municipal property taxes they paid or the amount of higher education they had obtained. For the moment, these legislative reforms brought a measure of quiet and peace in the land.[52]

Reformed Church missionaries in India watched these political events with some anxiety. Although the British had welcomed the missionaries in India but grudgingly and had generally opposed their enthusiasm for calling people to be converted to Christ, the Arcot missionaries felt that the British Raj provided an umbrella of security under which they could work with considerable freedom and confidence. They were particularly distressed when the independence movement turned violent, and they were pleased when the British took firm steps against the agitators.

The annual reports sent by the Arcot Mission to the Board of Foreign Missions after 1905, as well as articles sent by missionaries for publication, can help us understand how they felt and what they thought.

An article in the *Mission Field*, written by J.H. Wyckoff at the conclusion of the war between Japan and Russia in 1905, provided its readers with missionary perspectives on the independence movement in India. The victory of Japan in that war was a turning point in Asian understanding of its position in relation to the western world. Japan's wonderful success raised the question of whether India could become self-governing and take a place among the nations. "Brahmin pride has been aroused, and it is asking how long the heel of the white man is to be allowed to crush the ambitious aspirations of the Oriental. If Japan can humiliate a great Western nation like Russia, what is to hinder the most enlightened

---

[52] For a brief report of the events between 1905-1910, see Wolpert, *History of India*, 274-85.

race on the face of the earth—the Brahmins—from becoming a world power?"[53]

Wyckoff's answer to this rhetorical question was that it was the caste structure of Indian society that stands in the way of the independence of India. He commented upon the impressive meeting and speeches he had heard at the great meeting of the Indian National Congress in Madras, where speakers talked eloquently of the need for national unity in India. Yet the speakers, almost all Brahmins, at the same time were clinging tenaciously to caste, refusing so much as a cup of pure water from their foreign rulers for fear of personal defilement. In Wyckoff's opinion, only when caste discrimination came to an end would India be ready for independence.

> That a man should clamor for political self-government who marries his son to an infant, condemns his widowed daughter to a life worse than slavery, and keeps his own wife behind zenana walls, is an anachronism. When caste shall have been dethroned; when woman shall be elevated to her rightful position; when the out-caste shall have been reclaimed; when polygamy, infant marriage, and idolatry shall disappear; when personal morality shall become a dominant factor in the life of the people; then, and not until then, will the Indians be competent to take the reins of government and rule a united India. [54]

Within a few years, M.K. Gandhi would return to India proclaiming essentially the same message. India must overcome caste discrimination if it were to become independent.

Eight months later, another article by Wyckoff was published in the *Mission Field*. The article was prompted by the rising temper of the independence movement following the partition of Bengal.

[53] J. H. Wyckoff, "Japan Stirring India—National Congress—the Retiring Viceroy," *Mission Field,* January, 1906, 312.
[54] Ibid., 314-15.

Wyckoff stated his concern about the "antigovernment movement that threatens to spread all over the country, and may lead to grave results."[55] He was of the opinion that, while the partition of Bengal was the immediate occasion for the protests, the underlying factor was the rise of a large body of educated Indians who had been raised upon the liberal democratic policy of the government itself.

Wyckoff was pessimistic about the developments. His basic concern was that it was the Brahmins who were by far the most influential class among the Indians in government positions. He did not trust the Brahmins. "The English have generously extended the policy of self-government until only a small proportion of public offices is reserved for Europeans. But the avaricious Brahmin will not be satisfied until he receives the largest emolument in sight, and hence there is a constant clamor for a larger participation in the affairs of the administration."[56] He believed that the slogan of the agitation, "Swadeshiism," ("India for the Indians") that was shouted in mass meetings when people went on strikes and boycotted English goods ultimately only served the Brahmin class. The Muslims recognized this and therefore had not taken part in the agitation, but on the contrary were parading their loyalty to the Raj.[57]

Wyckoff concluded with the comment that the present moment was very trying for the Indian Christian community. Always loyal to the English government, they were looked at askance by their fellow Hindus because they would not join in the party cry of *Bande Mataram* ("our own goods," meaning boycott English products) or follow in exhibitions of Indian patriotism. But he was sure that if only the Christians bided their time, their true patriotism would be recognized and rewarded. "The Brahmin may be at the top at present; but, unless his whole nature changes, he cannot remain

---

[55] J. H. Wyckoff, "Swadeshiism in India," *Mission Field,* October, 1906, 208.
[56] Ibid., 209.
[57] Ibid.

there. The testing day is approaching when it will be revealed who the loyal friends of India are."[58]

When one reads the articles by Wyckoff, it becomes clear that Indians antagonistic to the church had a point when they accused the church of being a foreign body in the nation, more loyal to England than to India. The missionaries were all too ready to overlook and forgive the sins of British colonials and to find reasons to criticize the agitators at the beginning of the twentieth century. They ignored or were unaware of the economic factors feeding the unrest. The financial panic of 1893 in the United States and financial troubles in Europe at that time had also resulted in a severe financial depression and famine in India. The opening of new silver mines in the United States had devalued silver in relation to gold, which resulted in an approximately 50-percent devaluation of the rupee in relation to the English pound. As a result, India's grain surplus had to be sold to meet the costs of maintaining the government in India. The Indian peasants were forced to sell their grain instead of using surplus in good years as a hedge against years when harvests were meager because of lack of rain. When the monsoon rains failed in 1896-97 and 1899-1900, the result was severe famine and outbreaks of plague throughout the country.[59] During the first decade of the twentieth century, the impact of those calamities was still reverberating through the land, but the Arcot missionaries apparently did not recognize the internal contradiction between Britain's economic policies and its concern to provide a benevolent rule for the good of the Indian people.

Nevertheless, a half-century and more later, the Tamil-speaking people of India would make many of the same complaints against the dominance of the Brahmins that are to be found in the words of Wyckoff. The *Dravida Muttetra Kazhagam* (DMK) "Dravidian Progress Party") would make the same complaints about the superstitions of idolatry, caste oppression, and Brahmin rule that

[58] Ibid..
[59] Wolpert, *History of India,* 267-68.

the Arcot missionaries made at the beginning of the century. The DMK defeated the Congress party, in which Brahmins played a leading role, and took over the Madras state government in the mid-1960s.

Other Reformed Church missionaries in India shared Wyckoff's views. Henry J. Scudder in Punganur had been counseling the boys in the mission high school to exercise caution in any support of the independence cause and to help to maintain law and order rather than join in the agitation against the Raj. His attempt to quiet the boys in the school led to considerable resentment against him.

> "Swadeshi," "Swaraj," "Bande Matram," which being interpreted means, "Own goods," "Own country," "Mother country," respectively, became the slogans of the people. As I rode on my bicycle through the streets even of distant Punganur, crowds of "hoodlums" followed me shouting these words. They were written with charcoal on the white walls of our churches, schools, hospitals and compound gates. They appeared in chalk on the blackboards of our schools. Seditious essays became the rage. One of my high school boys in the Arcot Mission High School at Punganur had to be disciplined for handing in such an essay and refusing to withdraw his statements.[60]

Feeling against the high school and Scudder ran high. While he was in Kodaikanal several months after the incidents described in the previous paragraph, the high school was set on fire and partially destroyed. To the credit of the Indian officials in the town, they acted quickly and saved much of the school's equipment and most of the building itself.[61]

The Arcot Mission, in its annual reports to the Board of Foreign Missions, consistently supported the British rulers as they took a firm stand to quell the disturbances. The missionaries agreed with

[60] Henry J. Scudder, "The Crisis in India," *Mission Field,* June, 1914, 45.
[61] Ibid.

the British secretary for India, John Morley, who affirmed in 1905 that Britain had a moral responsibility not to leave India. Should it leave prematurely there was certain to be great bloodshed. Sir Sayyid Ahmed Khan, the Muslim reformer, agreed, saying that in India, until the nation of Hinduism or the nation of Islam had conquered the other, peace could not reign.[62] Having accepted the opinion of Morley, the Arcot missionaries always supported the British in their harsh treatment of agitators. In their annual reports they stated their approval. Thus, in 1909, they reported,

> The firm attitude of the Government had the result of intimidating the agitators, and a more healthy condition has been produced throughout the province. The fiftieth anniversary of the Queen's Proclamation on assuming the sovereignty of India in 1858 was enthusiastically observed in all districts and the various towns vied with one another in evincing their loyalty to the throne.[63]

The following year the mission reported that the unrest had quieted somewhat due to the firm hand of the government.

> The firm attitude of the Government of India toward the agitators has had a salutary effect and only an irreconcilable minority has continued to stir up strife in some parts of India. Lord Morley's epoch-making Reform Scheme published in India, December 19th, 1908 has become a Law, and the people as a whole are satisfied with the privileges accorded them in giving them larger representation on the Legislative Councils.[64]

---

[62] Embree, *Utopias in Conflict*, 21-22. M.K. Gandhi recognized the force of Morley's assertion that the abandonment of India by England would lead to conflict and chaos between the Hindu and Muslim communities. For that reason, he struggled constantly and fasted often in his attempts to overcome the antagonism between the two. Ultimately, of course, he had to agree that it was necessary to divide the subcontinent between Pakistan, with a Muslim majority, and India, with a Hindu majority.

[63] "BFMR," 1909, 32.

[64] Ibid., 1910, 27.

The unrest that was occasioned by the partition of Bengal finally
came to an end following the death of Edward VII, when the new
King George and Queen Mary visited India in 1911. The king
canceled the partition of Bengal. "This was a bold and dramatic
stroke worthy of a king....It was a bid for the confidence and loyalty
of the people and has everywhere, apparently, evoked the response
intended."[65] King George took the further bold step of proclaiming
that henceforth the seat of the central government would be in
Delhi, the previous capital under Muslim Moghul rule, rather than
Calcutta, which the British had built for their reign in India.

This change from Calcutta to Delhi, while it has created misgivings
and criticisms in some directions, has no doubt appealed to the
glory of past history and is especially satisfactory to the Mohammedan
community. It is a question whether the King at this time could
have made any other proclamation which would have so thrilled the
solidarity of Mohammedanism on the one hand, and Hinduism on
the other.[66]

Persons more cynical about the benevolence of King George
than were the missionaries suspected that his movement of the seat
of government to Delhi was one more maneuver to play the Muslim
off against the Hindu in India. But in their anxiety about what the
future of the Indian church would be in the event that India became
independent the missionaries remained ready to give the British Raj
the benefit of the doubt.

As a consequence of their anxiety about the restlessness in India,
the Christians of India were inspired to renew their desire to spread
the gospel in their country more than ever before. Not only in the
Arcot Mission, but also in the majority of the missions in India there
arose a growing concern for the self-support, self-government, and
self-propagation of the Indian church. There was much discussion
about the devolution of responsibility from the missions to the
Indian church. Within the Arcot Mission area, a number of the

65 Ibid., 1912, 34.
66 Ibid.

churches signified their willingness to assume a larger responsibility for church and evangelistic work as well as for primary school education. "Thus indirectly the political unrest and the sufferings and death of many, have indirectly benefited the interests of the Kingdom of Christ and have had the effect of infusing new desires and ambitions into the hearts and lives of the Christian people in this land."[67]

Indian Workers in the South India United Church and the Arcot Mission

By the end of the first decade of the twentieth century, the annual report leaves a clear impression of an Indian church being served by a growing number of competent Indian leaders. The Arcot Mission area contained seventeen organized pastorates with a total of 165 congregations. It began the year with seventeen ordained pastors, but two died during the course of the year, leaving a total at the end of the year of fifteen. This number indicates the growing strength of Indian leadership, especially when one remembers that all of those ordained had been required to meet the high standards for ordination of the Reformed Church in America. In what had become by 1910 the Presbytery of Arcot, all of the ordained ministers were equal in rank and privilege of participation in the proceedings with the eight ordained missionaries. The total Christian community was 10,751. The Sunday schools had 371 teachers with 3,743 Christian boys and 2,428 girls enrolled. They also had 4,913 non-Christian boys and girls on the rolls. There were thirty-five senior Christian Endeavor Societies with 488 members and twelve Young People's Christian Endeavor Societies with 369 members.[68] Practically every one of the teachers was Indian.

A significant change in understanding also is indicated by the fact that in the statistical report of this year one no longer finds the category of "native helper." The phrase had served to indicate that the mission tasks really belonged to the missionaries, who were

---

[67] Ibid., 1910, 28.
[68] "AAR," 1910, 62-63.

helped by Indian workers. But, in 1910, the "force" was categorized as "missionaries" on the one hand and "Indian workers" on the other. The total number of missionaries included in all the subcategories was thirty-five and of Indian workers 593. The subcategories for missionaries are "ordained," "unordained," "wives," and "single lady"; for Indian workers "ordained," "unordained Indian Christian workers," "Female Indian Christian workers," and "Non-Christian Indian workers."[69]

The amount of work carried out by this overwhelmingly Indian "force" is impressive. The evangelistic work report for the first nine months states that preaching was done a total of 43,702 times to 636,815 hearers. The 29 Bible women had visited in a total of 1,183 houses, with 995 women under regular instruction. They had spoken 15,536 times to a total of 36,730 hearers.[70]

One need not look at the statistics alone to learn the extent to which the life and work of the church had become Indian in membership and leadership. The reports coming from the various churches and mission institutions provide much anecdotal information about the Indians' contribution to the growth and life of the church. Their understanding of the people in the villages often made it possible for them to deal more adequately with the pastoral and evangelistic issues than could the missionaries.

The ordained Indian minister in Madanapalle in 1910 was the Reverend Joseph John.[71] He reported a number of incidents that had occurred in his pastoral and evangelistic ministry. In one village he responded to the people's request to teach them to pray. He recognized that they needed a catechist to be with them for a day or two a week for that purpose, with the result that at the end of the year there were seven families worshiping there. They were planning

69 Ibid., 58.
70 Ibid., 58-59.
71 Joseph John was ordained in 1898 and died in 1929. He was the father of the Rev. Arthur John, about whom we will learn later. Joseph John of Madanapalle should not be confused with the other Rev. Joseph John, who was ordained in 1934 and served in the Serkadu area and eventually in Deenabundapuram.

to build a church. In another case, he was traveling between Piler and Vayalpad. He met members of two different castes having an argument. The Reddis (a landowner caste) were saying idolatry was of no use, but the Brahmins were maintaining that it was very necessary for all beginners and illiterate people. They also said that when Annie Besant came to Vayalpad, both the educated and illiterate people prostrated themselves before her and worshiped her as a goddess. Joseph John entered the conversation at that point.

> I had a very good opportunity there to explain to them the folly of idolatry, saying that although Mrs. Besant may deserve to be praised for her high calling, she is no more than a human being and that the Almighty God above is worthy of all praise and veneration, having revealed himself in the Lord Jesus. It was a very profitable conversation, and they were clearly made to understand that idolatry is nothing but folly.[72]

The Reverend Samuel Thomas was pastor in Palmaner. He reported that the members of their evangelistic team had compiled 1,042 miles on 170 days of touring in distant and nearby villages. The following passages from his report make it apparent that the people in the villages at times could raise rather original theological concerns:

> A Brahman priest said to us: The teachings of the Christians are very sublime, and although the heathen hear them, they do not do according to them.
>
> Only a few among the ignorant Hindus know about sin and salvation. A cowherd who heard us preaching about Heaven said, "If all went to heaven there would be no one to feed the cattle."[73]

[72] "AAR," 1910, 16.
[73] Ibid., 17.

The Indian evangelists and catechists often encountered problems on their travels that missionaries could avoid. The evangelists in the Chittoor area had great difficulty obtaining water, and their wives suffered additional problems at home.

> Our evangelists this year have had much to contend with....At one place the four evangelists have had many trials and hardships, the caste people have periodically refused to allow them to draw water from wells, and it was with great difficulty that any one could be hired to supply them with water. While the men were away on their tours, the women had trying times and untold hardships. Washermen have refused to wash the Christians' clothes and bazaar men have at times declined to give them supplies, and yet they stick to their posts of duty, enduring all as good soldiers for the sake of Christ.[74]

At times Indian pastors and catechists were ready to make considerable personal sacrifices for the sake of their ministry. At the beginning of 1910, the Reverend Lazarus Marian was serving two churches, one in Madanapalle, where he gave three-fourths of his time, and the other in Punganur, thirty miles away, for the remainder of his time. The Punganur church made the decision to have its own pastor full-time and called Marian to serve them. However, the church had little hope of his accepting, because the limit of the salary it could offer was considerably less than he had been receiving, and the church knew that his salary from the two churches had already been very low.

> But the needs of the Church and this new station appealed to him and his interest in the work here with which he had been connected for 20 years, and which he had been mainly instrumental in developing, drew him and greatly to the joy

---

74 Ibid., 21.

Lazarus Marian

of all he accepted the call, resigned his pastorate in Madanapalle, and took charge of the work here...."[75]

The report also provides evidence of the faithful work being carried on by the Indian zenana workers and Bible women. For example, there is a paragraph about what two Bible women, Elizabeth and Milcah, were accomplishing.

The Hindu women show their love for her (Elizabeth) in many ways, and when she was ill with fever they came very often to her house, saying how much they missed her visits

[75] Ibid., 25-26. Lazarus Marian was born of Roman Catholic parents and brought up in that faith. After finishing his education, he was accepted into the Survey Department of the government, which would have provided for him lifetime economic security. He came under the influence of Jacob Chamberlain, resigned his position, and studied at the Arcot Theological Seminary. He became the first Indian Bible teacher in the mission schools at Punganur in 1889. It was largely through his influence that the Zamindar of Punganur turned over the high school there to Arcot Mission management. He died September 3, 1914. For additional details of his life, see M. D. Gnanamoni, "A Tribute to the Late Rev. Lazarus Marian," *Mission Field*, April, 1915, 490-91.

and asking what they could do to help her. Milcah was here about eight months and worked entirely in the five villages of cultivators just on the borders of Madanapalle and she has succeeded in gaining their ear for her message as few can. Her zeal, courage, mental ability and fine character made her respected by men as well as by women, and often she had as many of one sex as the other to listen to her preaching and arguments. [76]

The above excerpts from the mission's 1910 annual report provide ample evidence that the mission begun by the Scudders was entering a new phase in which more and more responsibility was coming to rest upon the Indian leadership and workers. Collegial relationships were growing between missionaries and Indian Christians. It is therefore not surprising that in spite of political tensions; the death of the last member of the pioneering generation, Jared Scudder; and food scarcity in some places, the mission felt it could go forward with confidence. It began its report by stating,

The year 1910 has been marked by steady, quiet progress in nearly every department of our work. As we scan the record of what has been attempted and what accomplished, or rather that part of it that can be seen and written down, we are impressed with the firm, sure and upward trend that permeates all of the work....The steady firm, every-day service on the part of many, each in his place, unobtrusively, honestly rendered, may, yea does, produce results more far-reaching than a less number of so-called greater deeds; and the quiet service is God's way.[77]

The church in India had moved beyond its nineteenth-century beginning stages and was by 1910 fully engaged in its service in an India that was eager to emerge as an independent nation. The South

[76] "AAR," 1910, 53.
[77] Ibid. 7.

India United Church was beginning to fulfill its responsibilities as a church among the churches of the world.

Plagues, Vaccines, Hospitals, Dedicated Doctors

Those of us who live at the beginning of the twenty-first century can scarcely imagine the anxiety that came to whole towns and countries when epidemics of diseases such as cholera and bubonic plague entered an area. Both those diseases awakened the most profound concern at the turn of the nineteenth century. The medical personnel of the Arcot Mission were often called upon to take preventative measures against them and to treat people with the disease, often at risk of their lives.

Cholera

Cholera was endemic in the mission area in an era when an adequate vaccine was not yet available and people were largely unaware of what caused it. The annual mission reports as well as missionary correspondence repeatedly tell of cholera in the area. Throughout the decade of the 1890s, there were almost annual outbreaks in one place or another. At times anxiety would be particularly high because of deaths. For example, there was a serious outbreak in the female seminary in Chittoor in 1891, with the result that two of the girls died.[78] Cholera was even more prevalent in the surrounding villages at that time where the famine conditions were severe.

> The people, weakened and emaciated by insufficient food have fallen an easy prey to disease. But few of our Christians have fallen victims to its ravages. This famine spectre has added heavily to the burden of anxiety resting on our shoulders....The distress is daily increasing, and the outlook for 1892 is discouraging in the extreme.[79]

[78] J.W. Scudder to Henry Cobb, letters of November 18 and December 13, 1891.
[79] "BFMR," 1892, 27.

The pessimistic outlook proved to be well founded. The 1892 report includes the information that there were again many outbreaks of cholera, especially in the Telugu area. In the town of Piler there had been nearly 250 cases, of which 50 percent proved fatal. One of the mission's most promising theological students died of the disease in Palmaner, as did one of the Christian boarding school boys in Arni.[80]

Cholera again became more prevalent in 1898, when the area was emerging from famine conditions. (Financial disruptions following the panic of 1893 and depressed economic conditions in England had caused high prices and resultant food shortages in India.) The Arni area again suffered a large number of cases. In the last week in June there were fifteen cases, with eight deaths, in Christian villages. A second outbreak in August saw five more attacks among Christians, of whom three died.[81]

While cholera was more prevalent among the poor, whose resistance was already low because of malnourishment and other chronic conditions, the disease constituted a danger at all levels of society. From time to time the members of families of the Indian mission workers would become ill with cholera, and a number of them died as a result. Given the number of times missionaries were exposed to the disease as they cared for its victims, it is remarkable that few of them contracted it. As we have already noted, John Scudder, Sr., and his wife, Harriet, went among the sufferers, bathing them, burying their dead, and trying to relieve their distress in every way possible. Although at that time "it was not yet determined whether cholera was infectious, Dr. Scudder thought it best to disinfect the cookhouse. The other servants believed all the smoke was a propitiation to their master's god."[82] While the elder Scudders remained free of cholera, Katherine Hastings Scudder, the first wife of William Waterbury Scudder, died of it on the way

80 "AAR," 1892, 3.
81 "BFMR," 1899, 37.
82 Scudder, *A Thousand Years,* 22.

back home to Ceylon from visiting William's parents in India in 1849.

In the twentieth century, however, when the nature and causes of cholera were beginning to be somewhat better understood, two Arcot missionaries died of the disease. The first such death occurred in 1914, when Henry Honegger succumbed to it.[83] Annie Hancock, who had made an outstanding contribution to mission among women since 1899, died of cholera in 1924. The account of her death by Henry J. Scudder enables us to gain an impression of how quickly and unexpectedly the disease could strike and cause its victims to die. On Friday morning, February 29, she had visited women in the Vellore jail and was apparently in perfect health. In the afternoon she became ill and was taken to the Schell Hospital, whose director was Hancock's close friend, Ida Scudder. The hospital staff "exhausted every resource known to medical science to check the disease and prolong her life."[84] She had a most virulent type of cholera, so none of the treatment had any effect. She suffered from the severe cramps caused by the disease, and after two and one-half days of suffering, she died. During those two days, she resisted the idea of dying because of her great concern for the development of her social service center for women in Vellore. When she was about to die, they asked if there was anything they could do for her. Her response was, "Finish the building."[85]

Bubonic Plague

Cholera was the cause of great anxiety in the population. Nevertheless, it did not compare with plague in causing panic among the people. There was international fear and horror of the disease, particularly among Europeans and Americans who knew

---

[83] Henry Honegger had been born in Switzerland in 1870. While still a young man, he went to America and worked in a number of industrial occupations before pursuing studies at Rutgers College and New Brunswick Theological Seminary. He entered India as a missionary in 1807. A brief sketch of his life is included in "BFMR," 1915, x.

[84] Henry J. Scudder to W. I. Chamberlain, March 5, 1924.

[85] Ibid.

that the "Black Death" had wiped out perhaps one-third of the population of Europe in the fourteenth century. Its causes were not fully understood at the end of the nineteenth century, but the people knew that when dead rats began to be found in numbers in the marketplaces and elsewhere, it could be that bubonic plague was not far behind. Later it was discovered that fleas that lived on the animals transmitted the disease.

The Arcot Mission report of 1904 contains a graphic description of the measures people took when plague hit an area. The epidemic had begun in Arni and Vellore in November, 1903, and raged until April. In Arni all schools were closed and work stopped. People deserted the town and went to live in the open fields some distance away. In spite of that, many deaths occurred. Bazaars were closed and food supplies had to be brought from Ranipet, eighteen miles away.

> Rats and squirrels died everywhere, even inside the Mission bungalow; so many died in the Industrial School building that even the workshops had to be closed and all the stock, lumber, yarn, paper, etc., was spread out in the sun for several weeks. The missionary was not allowed to live in the bungalow, but had to camp in a tent on the compound while the Government disinfecters turned out all the furniture of the bungalow and disinfected it and all the buildings thoroughly.[86]

In that area, three Indian Christians died, including a pastor's wife who died in the plague camp after an illness of four days.[87]

The situation in Madanapalle was much the same. The people who could do so fled the town. Others camped in fields just outside the town in groups of five to ten families, each caste having its own camp. "Madanapalle was literally a city of the dead. Caste was forgotten and Brahmins in their fright left their dead to be buried

[86] "AAR," 1904, 2.
[87] Ibid.

by the lowest caste. The Government of Madras sent 100 sepoys to thoroughly disinfect the town and the work was thoroughly done. Trade was paralyzed. All schools were closed...."[88]

Bubonic plague had entered India at the Bombay Harbor from a Chinese ship in 1896. Arcot missionaries had been reporting on its progress toward their area since it was first known to be present in Bombay. A Dr. Waldemar Haffkine had been called to Bombay from Paris to work on a cholera vaccine, but when the plague arrived he gave attention to developing a bubonic plague vaccine. He knew that Hindus would almost certainly refuse to accept a serum made from animal tissues, so he devised a medium from clarified ghee, the clarified butter that Hindus use in their cooking.[89]

The British authorities took firm steps to stop the plague. They carried out intensive efforts in Bombay to disinfect whole neighborhoods and to examine people to see whether they were coming down with the disease. Their aggressive preventive measures alienated the population. Especially humiliating were the actions in some neighborhoods where British troops ordered men and women alike to strip to the waist and allow their armpits to be checked for the swelling that were the first symptoms of infection. These actions led to a general strike, attacks on Army doctors, murder of several soldiers, and the burning of a hospital. It enabled radical elements to intensify violent actions in the independence movement.[90]

By the time the plague reached Bangalore, seventy-five miles from Madanapalle, in October, 1898, wild rumors were in the air. One rumor that many believed was that England planned to sacrifice 700,000 Hindus to their God to stop the plague.[91] It was therefore not too surprising that when the government medical authorities came into the Arcot Mission area with their new vaccine,

[88] Ibid.
[89] Scudder, *A Thousand Years,* 143.
[90] James, *Raj,* 357-58.
[91] J. Chamberlain to Henry Cobb, October 19, 1898.

people were afraid to be inoculated. The government officials sought to counteract the rumors by holding meetings for the leading people in the towns and asking them to be the first to receive the vaccine. A fairly large number of people had agreed to participate in those meetings, but when the vaccine arrived many had lost their courage. In Madanapalle the Muslims and the Sudra Hindus held meetings, and both groups stated that they would excommunicate any of their members who agreed to be inoculated.[92]

When the vaccine actually arrived, the people were called to a meeting to be instructed about the vaccine and receive it. But no one except some of the Europeans in town came.

> But when I saw that the meeting was going to be an absolute farce, I pulled off my coat and bared my left arm and asked the doctor to inoculate me then and there. Yesterday the doctor came to our compound and in the large room of the Girls' School inoculated the other missionaries, both native pastors and some thirty or so of our teachers and helpers, Bible women, girls' school female teachers and boys and girls and today he is to inoculate others. The Brahmin headmaster of our town boys' school came forward and was inoculated yesterday with our other teachers, but he is the only non-Christian so far inoculated.[93]

In the other towns, the Arcot missionaries were also the first to be inoculated. John, Jr., and Sophia Scudder, H. J. Scudder, Margaret Beattie, and L. B. Chamberlain were among the first. After their participation, many others took courage to receive it until all of the serum was exhausted.[94] Since the serum supply was limited

[92] J. Chamberlain to Henry Cobb, November 9, 1898.
[93] Ibid.
[94] Ibid. The new serum was not without its risks. The 1899 vaccine was given in 10 c.c. doses in contrast to the later 3 c.c. doses. "These early vaccines could produce severe febrile reactions, and when Dr. John Scudder received his injection he developed enlarged glands in the axilla, which by some strange sequence of events, underwent malignant changes, which spelled 'cancer'" (Jeffery, *Ida S. Scudder,* 35). He died as a result of the cancer the following year, less than six months after Ida Scudder's return to India in 1900.

and many of the people continued to refuse to be inoculated, the plague continued from place to place in the area intermittently over the next few years.

Two Indian Doctors, Mary Gnanamoni and M.D. Gnanamoni

It has already been noted several times that, although many of the Arcot missionaries were medically trained, the mission had always given medical missions a subordinate place in its list of priorities. That was still true at the turn of the century. L.R. Scudder in Ranipet was both a medical doctor and an ordained minister and consequently suffered from overwork. He was torn constantly between his desire to do evangelistic and medical work in the surrounding villages and the need of the hospital to have him present. He wrote to Henry Cobb in New York asking that a woman missionary doctor be sent to free him to carry out both sides of his work. "I want help myself. The longing to do village medical work has grown constantly within me. But how to leave the hospital has always been the great problem. But if a lady doctor is here, she can always take charge during my absence and we could arrange to do a great deal of village work."[95]

Two years before Scudder wrote that letter, a group of women in the churches of the Synod of Albany in New York asked Jacob Chamberlain to find, if possible, a young Indian Christian woman of suitable character to be educated at their expense as a medical missionary to the women and children of the Telugu field. After searching for some time, his attention was called to Mary Rajanayagam, head mistress of a girls' boarding school in the Madura Mission of the American Board. She had been serving there with distinction and had shown her dedication to Christian work by declining an offer to enter government service with very high pay. She consented to undertake a course of medical studies. After a year of preliminary study with Chamberlain in Madanapalle in 1890, she

[95] L.R. Scudder to Henry Cobb, November 17, 1891.

Mary Rajanayagam Gnanamoni

entered the Madras Medical College, from which she graduated in 1894. She proved to be an excellent choice as the first Indian woman doctor to serve with the Arcot Mission. Everyone seems to have agreed with the comment made about her by Mary Chamberlain in her history of the first fifty years of the Woman's Board of Foreign Missions. "It is doubtful, indeed, if India (and I had almost said any other country) has ever furnished a more consecrated, spiritual, and intellectual type of woman than Mary Rajanayagam."[96]

In the year that Mary Rajanayagam graduated, Jacob Chamberlain's health was again seriously impaired to the extent that it was necessary for him to spend some time in the United States. As a result, she went to serve in Ranipet with L. R. Scudder. There she met and married Dr. M.D. Gnanamoni, an earnest Christian civil apothecary who was working as an assistant to Scudder. The couple

---

[96] Chamberlain, *Fifty Years,* 57-58.

enjoyed the hearty approval of the entire mission when they were married in 1897, and they continued to do excellent evangelistic medical work in the Tamil area until 1899.[97]

M. D. Gnanamoni was also a remarkable person. Born of Christian parents in the south in Tranvacore, he was cast on his own resources at an early age because of the death of his parents. He supported himself by finding work of various types, and he financed his education in college and then in the Madras Medical College at a time when no one else was known to have earned his way through school. After graduation he entered government medical service but was loaned to the hospital in Ranipet when L. R. Scudder requested his assistance there. Following his marriage to Mary Rajanayagam, he agreed with her desire to serve in the Telugu area. When he requested a transfer to Madanapalle, the government named him to be in charge of its hospital there. His skill and character won the confidence of people of all castes and creeds with the result that he was made mayor of the town by the government. One of his delicate responsibilities was to enforce the sanitary laws, a task that required a considerable sensitivity due to the great variety of religious customs regarding sanitation.[98]

When her husband was transferred to Madanapalle, Mary saw herself and was seen by others as an honorary unpaid medical missionary to the women and children of the Telugu mission field.[99] She worked daily in the dispensary of the government

[97] The fact that these two persons met each other and married in an era when it was the firm custom for marriages to be arranged by parents or guardians serves to indicate the progressive leadership qualities in both of them.

[98] L.B. Chamberlain, "Dr. M.D. Gnanamoni: Assistant Surgeon in Madras Medical Service," *Mission Field,* May, 1915, 4. L.B. Chamberlain, a son of Jacob Chamberlain, served as a missionary in the Telugu area from 1891 to 1914. Mary Chamberlain, quoted in the previous footnote, was the wife of William Chamberlain, a brother of Lewis. William and Mary Chamberlain served in India in the Tamil as well as the Telugu area from 1887 to 1906, when they returned to America because of the illness of their daughter. They had also suffered the death of a daughter through illness in Kodaikanal.

[99] Jacob Chamberlain's medical work was often carried out in close integration with the government medical program in Madanapalle. Hence this fusion of missionary and government service on the part of Mary Gnanamoni was not unusual at that time in Madanapalle.

hospital as an assistant to her husband and treated more than a thousand severe cases a year. There was a terrible outbreak of bubonic plague in Madanapalle in 1903. Within a two-week period two hundred people died. She and her husband labored long and hard to save those who became ill and managed to save many lives.

Mary took every precaution that she could to protect herself from the plague even while she was daily ministering to its victims and their families. At the same time, she seemed to have a premonition of her death. Contrary to the wishes of her husband, she sent their children to live with her sister in another town two hundred miles away. On March 10, 1904, she developed a fever that soon displayed itself to be the onset of the plague. In spite of the prayers of the whole Madanapalle and Christian communities, she died eight days later. In that year she was the last victim and only Christian to die of the plague. As she lay dying, she said to her husband, "I know that I am safe in the arms of Jesus. You are safe, too. You are safe. We shall meet again at the resurrection." Looking at a photograph of her sons, she kissed them fondly and said, "Tell them to be Jesus boys. Assure them that I have gone to Jesus and they must meet me there."[100]

M.D. Gnanamoni continued to give distinguished service. He served for a few years away from the Arcot Mission area, but in 1909 was again loaned by the government to serve in the Ranipet hospital, where he was placed for a time as the first Indian in charge of the entire hospital activity. In 1913 he was transferred to Punganur to replace Henry J. Scudder, the brother of Ida Scudder, as the doctor in charge of the new Mary Isabel Allen dispensary. Its building had been erected in 1912 with a gift of $2,500 through the Woman's Board from the Reverend Arthur Allen in memory of his wife. There he not only carried on the medical work, but also supervised the work of the mission station. He made evangelistic tours in the villages, managed the boarding schools, and disbursed

100 H.J. Scudder, "Mary Gnanamani [sic] (Rajanayakam) and her Triumphant Death," *Mission Field,* August, 1904, 147. See also Chamberlain, *Fifty Years,* 91-93.

Mary Isabel Allen Dispensary

all funds. He also served on many church committees in the area and became the vice-chairman of the Indian Church Board. In 1914, the Arcot Mission proposed to the Board of Foreign Missions that Gnanamoni be placed on the footing of a missionary in all lines in which he had responsibility. Unfortunately, after a very short illness, he died in early 1915.[101]

The impressive character and service of M.D. and Mary Gnanamoni were important to the lives among whom they ministered. They were also important in establishing confidence among the missionaries in the maturity of the Indians who were taking increasing responsibility for work that missionaries had done previously.

Medical Missions among Women

In a previous chapter attention was paid to the Woman's Board of Foreign Missions and the impetus it gave to medical mission among women in India. In the decade of the 1890s, when the Board of Foreign Missions suffered constant budget deficits and repeatedly asked the Arcot Mission to reduce its expenditures, the Woman's Board refused to give up its dream of improving the conditions of Indian women. On the contrary, it moved forward in its concern for

[101] For a more detailed biography of M. D. Gnanamoni, see Chamberlain, "Dr. M.D. Gnanamoni," 4-7.

their health by agreeing to support three women missionary doctors, Louisa Hart, Ellen (Nell) Bartholomew (Mrs. Walter T.) Scudder, and Ida S. Scudder. Louisa Hart arrived in 1895. Ellen Scudder and Ida Scudder were appointed in 1899. The vast improvement that would take place in medical services for women in the twentieth century was symbolized by the fact that Ida Scudder arrived on January 1, 1900, for her second term of service, but her first as a medical missionary.

It is important to follow the contribution made by each of these three doctors during the first decade of the new century. Of the three, Ida Scudder was destined to become world famous and one of the most loved persons in India, while Nell Scudder has been almost totally forgotten and Louisa Hart is today remembered fondly by but a few. Nevertheless, each woman in her own way made a very significant contribution to women's health and to the knowledge of Jesus Christ.

Ida Scudder and Nell Bartholomew were classmates in Philadelphia Woman's Medical School, but they decided to transfer to Cornell Medical School in New York for their fourth and final year.[102] They were among the first group of four women to enroll in that school. The male students needed a little time to adjust to their presence. A number of the male students were appointed to defend them from some of the less desirable actions of the other students. "In knightly fashion, they used to champion the cause of the women whenever it was getting worsted by students who often did things to make women feel as if they were 'foreign bodies.' When the women entered the (operating) theatre, some of the men used to stamp their feet and throw kisses, as if to create a great scandal in those puritanical days!"[103]

Nell married Ida's brother Walter T. after graduation and was appointed along with him for missionary service in that country. While Ida was engaged in pioneering the development of medical

---

102 Wilson, *Dr. Ida*, 51.
103 Jeffery, *Ida S. Scudder*, 28.

education for women in India, Nell, as a "missionary wife," dedicated herself for forty-three years to serving women in Tindivanam in the dispensary that she had established. The contrast between the financial support that each received could not have been greater. By the time of her graduation and return to India, Ida had already been promised ten thousand dollars to establish the Mary Taber Schell Memorial Hospital in Vellore, and she would eventually be receiving gifts for the Vellore Medical College and Hospital in the hundreds of thousands of dollars. Nell always had to carry on her work almost totally without outside financial support. Nevertheless, Ida and Nell remained united in their life's purpose to share the love of Jesus Christ with the women of India and to provide medical care for those who otherwise would not have been likely to receive it.

Following their arrival in India, Walter and Nell Scudder were stationed in Tindivanam, where he and Ida had lived with their parents, John and Sophia Scudder, Jr. Nell soon opened a dispensary in a small room with very little equipment. At first her patients averaged eight or ten per day. She was also often called out to make medical calls in homes. Her work increased so rapidly that the mission appropriated a small amount of money for her to buy some proper instruments and equipment. In the space of six months in 1903, she had made 150 home visits and treated 1,002 persons in her dispensary.[104]

> Without the convenience of a hospital she had many discouraging experiences. Patients were suddenly snatched away from her when on the way to recovery, in obedience to the whim of mother or grandmother. Called at the last moment to see a dying child, she would have to prescribe from the vestibule of the house in which the child lay because the family had just taken their evening ceremonial baths. Many, while desiring European treatment, yet sought

[104] "AAR," 1903, statistical report facing p. 38.

to keep on the safe side of the gods by employing native skill in secret. If the patient died, as under these conditions, she or he was only too prone to do, it reflected upon the Christian means employed.[105]

After a break of several years when they were stationed in Chittoor, Nell Scudder reopened her dispensary in Tindivanam in 1910. In 1913, with the assistance of the Woman's Board, a small building for her medical work was completed.[106] It then became possible for her to care for several in-patients as well as carry on her work in meeting out-patients in the dispensary and in their homes. Through her medical work, the conservative upper classes of the Hindus and Muslims in the Tindivanam area began to be more open to what the missionaries were doing. In 1915 she wrote,

> Today let us rejoice that since the 'yesterdays' of ten, twenty, and forty years ago there have been changes in the Hindu community making for tolerance and progress, which, we are glad to say, makes it possible to get nearer to the people of Tindivanam. Yesterday I went out to the dispensary after 'hours' and there sat two Brahmin gentlemen before a Sunday School picture listening to the Bible woman. The patient's medicines might have been renewed by sending the prescription. Instead these two gentlemen came to renew the medicine and stayed on to listen to the Truth of their own accord.[107]

Nell Scudder's faithful service in managing her dispensary for her more than four decades of service in India was typical of the self-effacing ministry of the missionary wives of that era. She went with her husband where the mission stationed them. Although a well-trained physician, she was willing to be moved as necessary and do whatever had to be done, whether that was managing boarding

105 Chamberlain, *Fifty Years*, 95-96.
106 "BFMR," 1913, 102.
107 "BFMR," 1914, 105.

schools, serving in various ways in the life of the local congregations, or simply assisting her husband in carrying out his duties. Nevertheless it is clear that she maintained her own identity as a medical doctor and played an important role in bearing witness to the love of Jesus Christ through her ministry of care and healing.

Although Ida Scudder is recognized as the founder of the Mary Taber Schell Memorial Hospital and the Christian Medical College and Hospital in Vellore, the idea for a woman's hospital there was first proposed by Louisa Hart, working in cooperation with L.R. Scudder. Hart had begun working in Ranipet under Scudder in 1896. When he went on furlough to America in 1899, she assumed charge of the Ranipet hospital with the assistance of M.D. Gnanamoni. Her duties were greatly increased that year because the government requested her assistance in its program to combat the bubonic plague. Her role was to inspect the women in their homes and to inoculate all who would cooperate. In one week while on that duty she inoculated one thousand people. Through her work in Ranipet, she became aware of the need for a hospital just for women and suggested the idea to the Woman's Board of Foreign Missions. The Woman's Board responded positively to her suggestion and authorized Ida Scudder to raise the money needed to open the hospital.

Louisa Hart was also involved in opening and managing other new medical work among women during the first two decades of the twentieth century. For a number of years she played a key role, along with Ida Scudder, in making periodic visits to assist the nurse named Agnes stationed in the dispensary in Punganur. Nurse Agnes had a very large practice. In 1911 she had made nearly seven thousand "treatments," besides attending to her dispensary patients and calling upon people in their homes.[108]

While Hart carried some responsibility for supervising Agnus in Punganur, along with her work at the hospital in Vellore, she also

---

[108] Chamberlain, *Fifty Years*, 157. It is not clear precisely what is included in the word "treatments."

became involved in the planning and management of the tuberculosis sanatorium that was built in Punganur in 1910. Gertrude Dodd had responded the presentation she and and Ida Scudder had made regarding the need for such a place to treat women and children who were ill with tuberculosis. One of the gifts that Louisa Hart and Ida Scudder both had was the ability to inspire others to work together to meet the needs of health care for women. In the cases both of the need for a woman's hospital in Vellore and of the need for a sanatorium for tuberculosis patients, they recognized that the problems were wider than the Arcot Mission area. In each case, Louisa Hart and L.R. Scudder met in "Arcotia" with other medical missionaries in Kodaikanal. There they secured the cooperation of other missions in these projects.[109]

The Woman's Board of Foreign Missions recognized throughout the first decades of the twentieth century that there was a great need for additional doctors in the Arcot area. It sent out Margaret Levick, who soon became ill with what proved to be tuberculosis and had to return to the United States. Two registered nurses, Delia Houghton and Josephine Te Winkel, were sent in 1909 to provide valuable assistance. It was becoming evident that there was a great need for a woman's hospital in Madanapalle. The Woman's Board designated the legacy of Mary Lott Lyles for that hospital. Louisa Hart was assigned to it, with Josephine Te Winkle named as head nurse. During its first year, the new hospital saw over five thousand different patients and gave out over fourteen thousand treatments [110] In her first three years in charge of the Mary Lott Lyles Hospital in Madanapalle, until the new union tuberculosis sanatorium buildings were completed in near-by Arogyvarum, Hart also was in charge of the tuberculosis patients housed in Madanapalle.

---

109 Wyckoff, *Kodaikanal, 1845-1945*, 69. "Arcotia" was one of the houses on the Arcot Mission's Arcotia Compound in Kodaikanal. Arcot missionaries on a number of occasions invited persons from other missions to meet there to discuss the need for cooperation among the missions on matters such as medical care, theological education, and teacher training.

110 Chamberlain, *Fifty Years*, 156.

While Louisa Hart was the medical missionary with a true sense
of the needs of women throughout the mission area, Ida Scudder
was working with tremendous energy in the first phases of the
developing mission of the Mary Taber Schell Memorial Hospital,
which opened in Vellore September 16, 1902. Since the story of her
life and work has been told admirably by several others, this
consideration of her amazing life and work in India can be quite
brief.[111]

During her first decade as a medical missionary, Ida Scudder
concentrated on the development of the Mary Taber Schell Hospital.
She enjoyed the support of her mother, Sophia Scudder, who often
worked with her in the dispensary on the mission compound in
Vellore while the hospital was being built. From the very beginning,
Ida Scudder displayed the enthusiasm, energy, scrupulous attention
to detail, and deep compassion for the suffering of women that
would mark her work to the very end of her life.

Those characteristics served her well in 1903, shortly after the
hospital was opened, when Vellore underwent an epidemic of
bubonic plague. Reformed Church missionary William I.
Chamberlain, in addition to his missionary responsibilities, was
serving at that time as Chairman of the Vellore Municipal Council.
He went with Ida Scudder on visits to homes with the intention of
encouraging people to take protective measures against the plague,
including inoculations. They found many houses to be deserted, or
worse, learned that families with a member who was ill had taken
the person to another village. There were about four hundred
deaths in Vellore that year, but without the missionaries' courageous
and strenuous efforts, the death toll would have been much
higher.[112]

The doctors in the Schell hospital were confronted daily with the
results of neglect or improper treatment of women with serious

[111] The reader is referred to the two biographies already cited, Mary Pauline Jeffery, *Ida
S. Scudder of Vellore, India,* and Dorothy Clarke Wilson, *Dr. Ida.* Dorothy J. Scudder, *A
Thousand Years,* also gives an excellent succinct sketch of her life and work, 184-222.
[112] Scudder, *A Thousand Years,* 193.

medical conditions. The stories that the doctors told about these cases could be tragic or filled with comedy. A woman came in with an ovarian cyst that weighed more than the woman herself. After the operation, she was given a private room to keep her quiet. The nurse soon reported to Ida that the woman was having many visitors—precisely what she did not need. Dr. Scudder went quickly to the room and heard the patient describing the operation, saying, "And she took out my lungs and scrubbed them with a scrubbing brush and soap and water and then replaced them. Now I can breathe so easily." The visitors were quickly sent from the room and the woman ordered back into bed where she was not to sit up for the rest of the night. She recovered uneventfully from that point on and presented the doctor with a goat as a thank offering.[113]

As we have previously reported, among Ida Scudder's innovations were weekly roadside clinics conducted along the road between Vellore and Gudiyattam. An account of an operation conducted during the return trip to Vellore was included in the Arcot Mission report for 1910. It had been an especially hot day in May, the hottest month of the year. The whole medical team was worn out from their work when they saw a man walking across the field and beckoning to them. His hand was in a sling and he obviously needed help, so they stopped. Ida Scudder described what happened after that:

> He had a fearfully infected hand and arm swollen to the shoulder, with high fever and intense suffering. There was but one thing to do to save that hand, and possibly that life and choosing a spot by the roadside for my operating table we set to work. My chaffeur, to whom I had to entrust the chloroform, had no idea where to find the pulse even. I gave him a short lesson and carbolized my instruments and operated on the worst hands I have ever seen. After all was over and I watched the man go away, I wondered if I would

---

[113] Ibid., 193.

see him again, for I had grave doubts about him. He made a splendid recovery, however, and was so grateful he promised a bag of rice to the hospital and I believe he will give it to us.[114]

Ida Scudder proved herself to be a worthy granddaughter of John and Harriet Scudder, Sr., in her firm belief that medical care was to be carried out as a witness to the love of Jesus Christ. Her strategy was quite different from her grandfather's in that she did not spend energy on attacking the superstition and idolatry of Hinduism, but instead made her witness through her words of compassion and telling the story of the gospel. She was clear about the purpose of the hospital. She wrote:

> The great purpose for which the hospital was founded is the pointing of sin-sick souls to a loving tender Saviour who can save them from their sins, and for this end and purpose we work. Every patient is told of Christ's love for them, and although we have seen no out and out results, we can see that this great Divine Love is entering into the lives and homes of many, and we believe that many a life had been brightened and uplifted by contact with those they have met in the hospital. [115]

The Bible women in Vellore noticed that the presence of the woman's hospital was making their work easier. One of them reported in 1906 that the hospital was a great help to her. "In many a home I recognize a face seen and known before in the hospital; or in another home a mother will bring her little one to show me, saying, 'This one was born in your hospital.' It is always true that if the doctor has been before me into a home to cure some sick one, I am cordially received."[116]

114 "AAR," 1910, 46.
115 "AAR," 1906, 29.
116 Ibid., 33.

Ida Scudder commented that a hospital that treats women only is at some disadvantages because men are reluctant to allow the women to go to it for medical treatment.

> The men when sick will expend much upon themselves, or go anywhere to get well, but there is not such good fortune for the poor women. They cannot leave home, as their husbands must have their food cooked for them, the children must be looked after. This is quite true, but some of these women go on through life dragging out a weary existence, because no arrangement is made to enable them to leave temporarily for much needed treatment. I am thankful that many of the educated Hindus of Vellore are beginning to take more kindly thought for their wives.[117]

In the first decade of the twentieth century in India, the nursing profession was still considered to be a degraded one, much as was the case fifty years earlier in Europe and America when Florence Nightingale was beginning to bring higher respect to it. Ida Scudder sought to overcome the need for nurses and to raise respect for their work by recruiting young women to be trained as nurses in Vellore. Recruitment was no easy task. Most Indians refused even to consider sending their daughters for training. Those who were ready to send their daughters on for any training wanted them to be teachers. At times a father would be more desperate to find a proper role in life for his daughter. One father wrote in submitting an application for his daughter, "My daughter has failed three times in second standard. I am sure she would make a very good nurse."[118]

Finally, a sufficient number of qualified girls was found, and, under the tutelage of nurse Lillian Hart, a sister of Dr. Louisa Hart, instruction was begun. Lillian reported that their progress in practical work had been fairly good but their classroom work was moving more slowly because Lillian herself had often been ill with

117 Ibid., 28-29.
118 Wilson, *Dr. Ida,* 123.

fever. One of the things that was proving hard for the students to realize was that an article that is clean may not be sterile. The nurses had to work hard. They began the day's work with prayers at 6:00 a.m., following which they had coffee and began work at 6:45. Each nurse had one half-hour off to eat and an hour and a half for a rest period. The day's work was finished at 7:00 p.m., after which the night nurses came on duty.[119] The hospital's pioneering work in the recruiting and training of nurses in India proved to be a success. By 1909 Louisa Hart was able to report that a graduation ceremony was held for those nurses who had studied in the hospital for three or four years. A large number of Indian ladies and gentlemen were present for the occasion. They seemed to listen carefully to all that was said by the two speakers, Miss MacNeill of the Free Church Mission Hospital, Madras, who spoke in English, and L.R. Scudder, who spoke in Tamil.[120]

At the end of the first decade of the twentieth century, the medical work of the mission finally rested on a firm basis. With the firm advocacy and support for medical mission among women by the Woman's Board of Foreign Missions and the steadfast work and dedication of women doctors and nurses sent to India between 1895 and 1910, hospitals and dispensaries had been established and were poised to give increased medical service within the framework of the love of Jesus Christ. With the possible exception of the hospital in Ranipet, the medical missionary activity of the male doctors was always more personal than institutional, subject to the vagaries of their time, health, and presence or absence away from their stations. Even when one or another of the men wanted to expand his medical activity, support and encouragement were only grudgingly given by the others. Louisa Hart with her wisdom and Ida Scudder with her compassion, personal drive, and winning

---

[119] "AAR," 1906, 32.
[120] "AAR," 1909, 54-55.

personality had broken through that reluctance and gained the other missionaries' firm approval of their work.

By 1910 the South India United Church was taking up its responsibilities as an Indian Christian church. The schools were enrolling ever more students. Indian leaders were ready to accept a larger role. The industrial institutions were beginning to find their place in the work of the mission. The Arcot Mission with its related institutions and the South Indian United Church had entered the twentieth century and were ready to move forward together in obedience to the will of God.

9

The Devolution of Mission
from Paternalism to Partnership

The Devolution of Mission and the Indian Church Board

The Arcot missionaries held firmly to the theory that the work of the mission must be turned over to a self-governing, self-propagating, self-supporting church. The phrase that was used to denote the organizational process by which the transfer of responsibilities would take place was "devolution of mission." Missionaries and Indian Christian leaders were in agreement that "devolution of mission" was a positive step inasmuch as it implied the successful accomplishment of the mission's goals.

By 1907 Indian Christians were eager to be allowed to participate in making decisions concerning the life of the church and its evangelistic outreach. They also believed that the work would move forward more rapidly if they were given more administrative responsibility. Following the example of Indian National Congress in the life of India, a group of representative Indian Christians met in 1907 following the annual Arcot Mission Workers' Conference to form a "Native Congress." They passed resolutions that included the following words:

Whereas, until now the American Arcot Mission missionaries
themselves have been responsible for the evangelistic work,
schools and finances in the bounds of our congregations,
but whereas the time has come when the native
congregations should undertake these responsibilities
themselves, Resolved that this Assembly gives its opinion
that the stronger congregations which are competent to
take up and bear such responsibilities should arouse
themselves and begin this work....Resolved that we express
to Sessions here represented our conviction that a larger
share of the raising and spending of church funds, of the
direction of church work, of discipline and of evangelistic
work should be given to and placed upon the members of
village congregations....[1]

The initiative of the Indian Christians gave impetus to the
movement of devolution of responsibility from mission to church.
The Arcot Mission decided to launch the scheme of devolution of
responsibility October 1, 1910, for forming the Indian Church
Board.[2] The Indian Church Board was made up of twelve members,
with three members elected by each of the four "circle committees"
that operated under the Indian Church Board. In 1910, five of those
elected were missionaries and seven were Indians, giving the board
an Indian majority. The Arcot Mission had no right of veto over the
actions of the Indian Church Board. It was given responsibility for
the employment and supervision of catechists and teachers in
village congregations, for the village elementary schools, and for
evangelistic work. All of these administrative responsibilities prior
to 1910 had been vested in the Arcot Mission and its missionaries.
Beginning in 1910, the village catechists, teachers, and other
workers in the villages were considered to be employees of the
Indian Church Board.

---

1 Quoted in Wyckoff, *A Hundred Years*, 50.
2 "BFMR," 1911, 68.

Issues of salary level, employment, discipline, and dismissal also belonged to the Indian Church Board. The funds previously held by the Arcot Mission for village and evangelistic responsibilities were placed in the hands of the Indian Church Board. In 1911, the budget for congregation and village programs placed in its hands was Rs. 42,308, but the financial administration of the evangelistic activities remained directly under the mission. The Arcot missionaries transferred congregation and village responsibilities with a measure of relief. They reported,

> Hereafter in our Mission minutes there will be found no reference to the employment of these workers, no thorny questions of increase or decrease of salaries and allowances, no questions of their discipline or dismissal. We, who have spent hours over these questions in the days gone by, will appreciate how great a change has been made.[3]

In 1910 the "circle chairman" replaced the "station missionary" as the person administratively accountable for the disbursement of funds for village and evangelistic expenditures. Under the Indian Church Board, the old pattern of nine "mission stations," each under charge of a missionary, was reorganized into four geographical "circles," each with its own chairman, who could be either an ordained Indian pastor or an ordained missionary. The mission reported on the significance of the change:

> The Circle, embracing two or more stations, is now to be the unit. If, in God's providence and with His blessings, this wider view is taken and maintained, we believe that the work will be developed more wisely and more proportionately and more successfully. With 1910 the time will pass away when any one missionary is to report for a station. Station boundaries have disappeared. The Native Church has taken its burden, which is the charge of all

3 "BFMR," 1912, 43.

congregational and village work in the Mission, and in
addition the Board is to conduct also the evangelistic work,
the finances of which, are for the present, still in the hands
of the Mission.[4]

Each of the circles had its own committee composed of
representatives from three or four pastorates. Each circle committee
had approximately twenty members, of whom no more than two or
three were missionaries. Thus within each circle committee, the
Indian members held the vast majority.

While these organizational changes were seen as a great step
forward, most of the power still remained in the hands of the
missionaries. L.R. Scudder remained chairman of the Indian Church
Board for the first ten years. Three out of four of the circle chairmen
were missionaries in 1910, and in subsequent years it was not
unusual for all of the circle chairmen, who held much of the power,
to be missionaries. Nevertheless, the new organization required an
attitudinal change on the part of missionary and Indian alike.
Missionaries who had formerly felt free to make decisions on their
own now had to consult with Indians and listen to their comments,
challenges, and criticisms. The Indians welcomed the change and
moved quickly to accept their responsibility.

> But now that the responsibility has been placed on them
> and they have assumed it, a new spirit is to be seen. They
> were employees. They are now members of the firm. They
> were working for others. They are now working for
> themselves. No one could attend the Circle and Pastorate
> meetings without seeing many indications of this new
> spirit."[5]

The establishment of the Indian Church Board defined more
clearly what was required for a church to be self-supporting. "Self-
support" now meant that the town and village congregations would

4 "BFMR," 1911, 68.
5 "BFMR," 1912, 43-44.

be responsible for the salaries of the pastors, catechists, village teachers, and congregational expenditures. The Arcot Mission would continue to be responsible for the financial needs of the institutions of education beyond the village level (grades 1-5), medical services, and the industrial institutes. In later decades, as the church came to take more and more of the responsibility that had formerly belonged to the Arcot Mission, it would become necessary to define the meaning of "self-support" further and to delineate the authority of the church in relation to the institutions.

Paternalism and Partnership in Mission

On the sixtieth anniversary of the founding of the Arcot Mission, in 1914, the authors of the mission's annual report were in a reflective and repentant mood. They listed their "mistakes in principles and methods," in inward life and outward conduct. They confessed,

> One-sided principles have lost valuable time; mistaken methods have wasted efforts. Sin and self have raised obstacles where love and sympathy simplicity would have smoothed the road. Impatient actions and untempered words, arrogant ways among Missionaries, more perhaps than among Indian workers, have hurt sensitive hearts and turned even seekers from the great quest. Christ's words come properly to our hearts and lips, "Even so say ye, We are unprofitable Servants."[6]

The mission recognized a number of contrasts between the past and the present. "In the earlier days the Mission was a big family. Missionaries were parents; Indians were children. Simplicity, directness, autocracy, characterized the administration. Although the Mission was a benevolent paternalism and not a despotic autocracy, the missionary's word was law, his wish a command."[7]

6 "BFMR," 1914, 48.
7 Ibid., 49.

The missionaries admitted that in previous decades there had been much friction with other missions as well as violations of comity agreements. They had for the first thirty years had little relationship with the government. The second thirty-year period was an era of growing cooperation with the government. Moreover, as a result of the normal course of development and of worldwide changes in principles and ideas, four additional contrasts required special mention. These four were (1) the role of women, foreign and local; (2) the role of the Indians; (3) the role of the male community, consequent upon the previous two changes; and (4) the role of cooperation between the Arcot Mission and the Indian church, as well as cooperation among the missions.[8] In each of these four areas the mission was moving from paternalism to partnership.

The 1914 report pointed out that the mission had gone through three periods during its first fifty years: "the initial period, 1854-1860"; "the village development period, 1861-1878"; and "the development of the institutional period, 1879-1903." It termed the sixth decade, 1904-1913, "the devolution, or cooperation, period."[9] One can always quibble about the division of history into periods. In this case, it would seem that the period of devolution could better be understood to begin with the establishment of the Indian Church Board in 1910, when changes were put in place from which there was no retreat.

Eight years later, in 1922, the mission's annual report began with a broad summary of the major political and social issues that were having an impact upon its work. Between 1914 and 1918, Indians had been involved in the support of the allied powers, expecting that after the war Indians would be rewarded with a greater amount of political autonomy. By 1922 the direction of the post-war nation and the church were becoming clear. In its annual report, the mission sought to inform people in the Reformed Church in America about its activities in relation to (1) the political situation;

8 Ibid., 49-50.
9 Ibid., 50.

(2) church unity; (3) mass movements; (4) inadequate funds; (5) further moves in organizational devolution of the work of the Arcot Mission, including issues of the relation of Indian Christians and foreign missionaries; (6) village education; and (7) cooperation with other missions.[10] We will now follow briefly some of the developments that took place between the two World Wars in these areas, reserving a discussion of church unity for a subsequent chapter.

The Response to Political Developments after World War I

It has been noted that, prior to World War I, Reformed Church missionaries in India were unanimous in their agreement that it would be necessary for the foreseeable future that British rule would continue over India. They agreed with English statesmen that India would degenerate into chaos if the British were to leave. They feared that the agitation for home rule could quickly degenerate into violence and repeatedly pointed out that the Christians in the land were of all people the most loyal to the queen or king. They also feared that Indian autonomy would mean the oppression of Christians as members of a foreign religion. Nevertheless, as World War I neared its end, several of the younger missionaries began to recognize the legitimate demands of Indians for home rule. They encouraged the church abroad as well as in India to face the new situation. F. Marmaduke Potter and his wife, Elsie, had arrived in India in 1913 and served at Voorhees College until illness forced them to leave India in 1917.[11] While the Indian troops were still fighting on the western front in Europe in 1918, he wrote an article for the *Mission Field* in which he encouraged members of the Reformed Church to understand the significance of the agitation for home rule in India.[12]

[10] Ibid., 1922, 26-3.
[11] Following his return to the United States, Francis Marmaduke ("Duke") Potter became a member of the staff of the Board of Foreign Missions. He served as full secretary of the board from 1935-1952.
[12] F.M. Potter, "India," *Mission Field,* September, 1918, 247-48.

He pointed out that England and the United States had themselves encouraged national aspiration for home rule. England had introduced western education, the English language as a unifying instrument of communication, newspapers for the exchange of ideas, and the concept of western democracy. England had put itself on record as prepared to introduce a more representative form of government in India. Not only that, but the aspiration for national home rule was in the spirit of the times. President Woodrow Wilson had clearly enunciated the principle of self-determination for all peoples. This principle meant home rule for India if the majority desired it, as seemed to be the case in 1918.[13]

In his article, Potter reinforced the opinion of his fellow missionary, J.H. Warnshuis, who also had arrived in India with his wife, Dr. Lillian Warnshuis, in 1913. Warnshuis had written an article for the *Mission Field* in 1917 in which he had discussed the somewhat surprising development that, contrary to expectations, some of the strongest opposition to home rule came not from Englishmen or from the government in India, but from other Indians. Potter with Warnshuis wanted it to be clear that opponents of home rule were suspicious that the movement was really an attempt by the Brahmin caste to gain control in India, "which non-Brahmins feel is more to be feared than the English Bureaucracy."[14] At the time Warnshuis was writing, the non-Brahmin movement was gaining in popularity, especially in the Madanapalle area.

> At Vayalpad, that ancient citadel of fanaticism and faction, the non-Brahman movement has gathered into one fold Christians, Reddis and other castes. They have sworn to stand by each other, attend each others' wedding and other social functions. They have compelled us to open a First Form [sixth grade—*auth.*] in our Elementary School to accommodate non-Brahman pupils. It is not so much the political side of it that appeals to us, nor the fact that the

13 Ibid.
14 J.H. Warnshuis, "Caste Levelling Movement in India," *Mission Field,* February 1918, 419.

British Raj has found a strong champion in the Indian people, but the missionary aspect of such a caste levelling movement, as this is something that staggers the imagination.[15]

Potter, like Warnshuis, believed that, in an India that enjoyed democratic home rule, the Brahmins would have to take into account the legitimate claims of the non-Brahmans. They were critical of Annie Besant and other foreigners who ignored such problems. Nevertheless, Potter also believed that "India will obtain Home Rule at no remote date, and that in the course of time the process of evolution will be completed and she will become a nation."[16] Furthermore, he took this to mean that Christian missions must move to evangelize India immediately, while they still had freedom under the British rule and while the government was still willing to pay one-half the net cost of the missions' educational work. Potter had a broad vision of what such evangelism and education could do:

Every form of our missionary work takes on a certain new significance as we see that we are not simply converting individuals of a subject race, but are molding the thoughts and policies of a nation of the future, vast in population, rich in undeveloped resources, and endowed with peculiar spiritual possessions....It is the solemn duty of the missionary enterprise to give to these nations of our best, and lay the foundations of future world peace, and insure that the world in coming generations will be "safe for democracy."[17]

M.K. Gandhi proved to be the real challenge to the missionaries' basic argument.

15 Ibid.
16 Potter, "India," 247.
17 Ibid., 248.

They maintained that British rule should continue for the foreseeable future because India would fall into chaos if the British left. The core of the missionaries' contention was that caste divisions in India ran so deep it was impossible for the country to be governed with justice for all. Moreover, the chasm between Hindu and Muslim was equally deep. Gandhi made it his life work in his leadership in the Indian National Congress to show that there were currents within the traditions of India itself that would enable Indians to live together with peace and justice as one nation. His translation of *Hind Swaraj* on the political level was "home rule" and on the individual level was "self rule." He maintained that only a people with "self rule" could maintain "home rule." "Self rule" required the practice of certain virtues, including temperance and chastity, truthfulness, justice (including freedom from possessiveness and greed), and courage to overcome fear, including the fear of death.[18]

It was Gandhi's emphasis upon self-rule and nonviolence that often confused his followers. He firmly maintained that the struggle for Indian independence required spiritual training in self-rule for all who were participating. When his followers began to engage in violence rather than nonviolence, he withdrew on a number of occasions to fast and call off his campaign. On one occasion he reported that "God...has warned me the third time that there is not as yet in India that nonviolent and truthful atmosphere that alone can justify mass disobedience, which can be at all described as civil, which means gentle, truthful, humble, knowing, willful yet loving, never criminal and hateful."[19]

Gandhi never forgot that a peaceful, free India required that all of the people in the land live together with full respect for one another across religious, caste, and racial lines. It was for this reason that he went to live in a village with the *harijans* ("God's people"

[18] Anthony J. Parel, ed., *M. K. Gandhi: Hind Swaraj and Other Writings* (Cambridge, England: Univ. of Cambridge, 1997), liv.
[19] Quoted in Wolpert, *History of India,* 307.

called untouchables, outcastes, pariahs, by others). It was also for this reason that he constantly took his spinning wheel with him. The spinning wheel was for him a symbol of many things—"of spiritual dynamism, of the importance of manual labor, of solidarity between the rich and the poor, of the protest against the tyranny of modern 'machinery' (technology) and the economic exploitation of the poor by the rich."[20]

Gandhi was the first Hindu who forced missionaries and the Christian community to reflect at greater depth on what it really means to live as a follower of Jesus Christ in India. In his affirmation that there was a common truth at the heart of all of the religions in India, he called upon Christians to live fully in accordance with the teachings of Jesus. Instead of keeping Christians at arms' length, he asked them to enter fully into the life of the people of India who were seeking to gain their rightful place among the nations.

In his message for India, Gandhi was promoting many of the same reforms that missionaries had been advocating for more than a century. Members of every caste and religion were welcome in his village. He was opposed to the abuses under which women had suffered for centuries. He advocated nonviolence and thereby was able to claim a higher morality than that favored by westerners. He opposed caste discrimination and desired that public places be open to everyone. In 1933 he took his stand in favor of opening the temples of India to the *harijans*. Arcot missionary W.H. Farrar, who was often critical of Gandhi, was not eager to give credit to Gandhi for his stand, but he could not avoid taking notice of it. He wrote,

> Mr. Gandhi's attempt to make the Hindus open the temples to the Pariahs has certainly stirred up the country as nothing else has. The very stirring and the fact that there are many who are on his side shows what the teachings of Christianity have done in India. Surely, as some of the Hindus say,

[20] Parel, *M.K. Gandhi*, liv.

Hinduism is being riddled to pieces by the advent of truth."[21]

Nevertheless, the missionaries remained fearful that Gandhi's call for noncooperation[22] with the British Raj inevitably would lead to violence and chaos. In its annual report of 1921, the mission asserted that the noncooperation movement of civil disobedience of that year constituted a threat to public order, as evidenced by the riots and rebellion that had occurred in several areas. The mission felt that one should not be misled by Gandhi's favorable comments about Jesus. Gandhi was still profoundly Hindu.

> Gandhi's appeal to India is intended to strike many and various chords, but it is essentially an appeal to the ancient forces of Hinduism....This movement must be viewed as Hinduism's effort to assert itself against the civilization of the west, and, from another standpoint, Muhammadanism's attempt to establish its supremacy.[23]

Missionaries were not the only ones who were suspicious of the noncooperation movement. In 1921 there had been considerable unrest as Hindus showed support for Muslims who were objecting to the western powers' actions in dismantling the Ottoman Empire and Khilafat.[24] The Reverend Meschach Peter, one of the most

---

[21] W.H. Farrar to William Chamberlain, January 17, 1933.

[22] The Indian National Congress, in its special session in Calcutta in 1919, called for a multiple boycott which would bring the wheels of British government to a halt. It included a boycott not only of British cottons and manufactured goods, but also British schools and colleges, courts of law, councils, titles and honors, and possibly even demands for taxes (Wolpert, *History of India,* 302).

[23] "BFMR," 1922, 26.

[24] There was a rumor in India that the western powers intended to abolish the Turkish Khilafat (Caliphat). The Ottoman emperor Caliph was understood by the Muslims in India to be the leader of the Muslim world, so the Muslims in India wanted to agitate against the British in defense of the Khilafat. The Indian National Congress decided to support the Muslims. When the young Turk Mustafa Kemal Pasha brought the Ottoman Empire to an end and became president of Turkey in 1923, the Khilafat agitation in India came to an end.

Meshach Peter

respected Indian pastors, who was chairman of the Western Circle, expressed his concern about the movement's impact on the church:

> The Counter-march of the Khilafat propagandists, the devoted followers of Mahatma Gandhi in his non-cooperation and Buddhist preachers in a number of our villages, has been injurious to the efforts by the Christian Workers, and members of the Congregations. Had not the Government authorities removed by force some fanatics out of our region or arrested and locked up some of the seditionists in prison the poor and ignorant of the masses would have been greatly deceived both in political as well as in religious matters.[25]

Nevertheless, many Christian students in the mission schools were enthusiastic about the movement toward home rule and were

[25] Ibid., 46.

eager to participate in the noncooperation movement of civil disobedience. The national consciousness had been awakened in young people. They felt that the movement toward home rule was pitifully slow. The principal of Voorhees College,[26] the Reverend Lambertus Hekhuis, who had arrived in India in 1916, reported that students in the college were very much fascinated by noncooperation, but that only one student had dropped out because he "could no longer attend a school that received government aid....While the majority of the students have taken no part in the movement, either directly or indirectly, they have not been altogether free from the effects of the movement and there has been an unrest and inattention to work that is akin to the unrest of the public."[27]

The issue of national independence continued to be on the mind of the Arcot Mission throughout the 1920s. In its 1922 report, the mission was pleased that with the imprisonment of Mahatma Gandhi the political unrest of the previous year had subsided, even though his spirit was still in the people. One can note, however, a somewhat ambiguous tone concerning the spirit of independence: "His teaching of a 'fundamental and enveloping distrust of the foreigner' has not been without effect on the Mission work. It is one of the factors that have made for change and progress....Furthermore, as one of our Indian Christians expressed it, Christianity has always been the forerunner of a greater independence of the people."[28]

Although the name of Gandhi is not mentioned in the report of the Arcot Mission to the Board of Foreign Missions for 1923, his challenge was still on its mind. It had heard his call to live according to the Sermon on the Mount and his question to the Christians

---

[26] Voorhees College was named after Elizabeth Rodman Voorhees after the Board of Foreign Missions received a major gift of twenty thousand dollars for the college in her honor from her husband, Ralph Voorhees. For further information about Elizabeth Rodman Voorhees, see Una A. Ratmeyer, ed., *Hands, Hearts, and Voices: Women Who Followed God's Will* (New York: Reformed Church Press, 1995), 165-67.

[27] Ibid., 51. This Lambertus Hekhuis, born in 1890, should not be confused with Lambertus Hekhuis who died of rabies in India in 1888.

[28] "BFMR," 1923, 27.

about whether they were really ready to live according to the spirit of Jesus. In the second paragraph of the report's foreword, one reads,

> More ready and more earnest are the listeners to the message of the Master. Not only has the teaching of the Sermon on the Mount been tried in a very practical way within her (India's) borders but on every hand there is the challenge raised, for with the Bible in one hand and life's problems in the other, there comes from the lips of men and women, from our school boys and girls, the cry, "Does Jesus really mean what He says? Does His teaching hold good and are we safe in entrusting ourselves to Him? What message has He to offer me in India?...The times demand renewed consecration and the best we can give. Political life surges with the ideals of service to the Motherland and with strugglings of the patriot or by the claims of the constituency that has elected him. The Swaraj Movement has made itself felt in the recent elections in returning large numbers to the legislative councils and local bodies....To be a lover of Mother India and to sacrifice for her interests has caught the vision of many...[29]

Gandhi visited Vellore in 1927. When he came, the Indian Christians of Vellore gave him a hearty reception. By this time, the Indian Christians and Arcot missionaries agreed that his sincerity was unquestionable. They also welcomed his affirmation that while continuing his noncooperation movement he would leave nothing undone to preserve its nonviolent character. At the time of the public reception, the leading Indian pastor, Meschach Peter, and the chairman of the Arcot Assembly, L.R. Scudder, spoke, while "this remarkable man, the leader of the land, was seated, a Kadar clothe round his waist, on a high table." Scudder made an irrefutable presentation of the all-saving power of the man of Galilee, whom

[29] "BFMR," 1924, 21.

the missionaries of the west had been teaching to their brothers and sisters in India. Peter spoke of the Christian message that he believed to be in line with the Mahatmaji's policy of selfless service to the country. Gandhi in reply said that he felt pleased and returned hearty thanks.[30]

Gandhi's visit to Vellore also made a deep impression on the students at Voorhees College. The mission was pleased to note that it made them think seriously about several of India's problems. One such problem was that all the students in college wanted to have "white collar" jobs after graduating and tended to look down on those who did manual labor. It was good for them to hear the "gospel of the spinning wheel" preached so persuasively by Gandhi. Even though his gospel of the spinning wheel might be declared impractical and visionary, it nevertheless hit exactly the need of the Indian college student, with its emphasis on work with the hands, care for the illiterate masses, and service for India.[31] Henry J. Scudder's letter in 1926 to William Chamberlain gives us an insight into the way missionaries could simultaneously seek to dismiss Gandhi and still recognize his achievements.

> With regard to your observations concerning Gandhi, I think all would agree with your feeling that "his peculiar doctrine of soul force" is, "too passive for an active world." His economics is childish. But his moral and spiritual influence on India is undoubtedly very great. He has lost much influence politically, but is still venerated as a devout godly man. His insistence upon the necessity of educating and treating decently the untouchables of India, and his openmindedness with reference to Christ and His teachings have undoubtedly done much good in this great land of castes and prejudices.[32]

---

[30] "AAR," 1927, 55.
[31] Ibid., 11.
[32] Henry J. Scudder to William Chamberlain, January 13, 1926.

By 1934, the Arcot Mission had accepted the hope that India continue to take steps to move toward the "ultimate goal" of dominion status in the British Empire, as Canada and other lands had done. The mission was confident that this is what the majority of the Indians wanted, even though the Indian leadership was not yet satisfied with the nature of the reforms proposed to them by the English Joint Select Committee. The mission was pleased that the cult of terrorism had been exorcised and that the country had experienced a period of quietness in which to consider more carefully the trend of its affairs.[33]

As Indian leaders and missionaries worked together in the Indian Church Board and the circle committees, they sought means to set forth the Christian message in ways that showed genuine respect for the great cultural traditions of India. Given the fact that those cultural traditions had developed in intimate relationship with the ancient religious systems of India, it took considerable effort to adapt cultural forms developed within Hinduism to assist in the living and communication of the Christian faith. We will take note of four efforts in that direction: the growth of lyrical preaching, or "kalachapams"; festival pilgrimages to worship on a hilltop; erecting church buildings in a Hindu architectural style; and the founding of ashrams.

In the context of rising aspirations for home rule coupled with an increasing number of people receiving education, the Indian Church Board realized that it was becoming important to employ more highly qualified men to serve as evangelists and catechists and to use Indian cultural forms in its communication. The evangelistic bands that went on tour included persons who were in tune with the Hindu culture. The "Jacob Chamberlain Evangelistic Band" in the Telugu area in 1921 had a leader who had studied in a college as well as a member who was a former Hindu Sanyasi (a holy man who practiced self-renunciation). It also had a young lyrical preacher who, with his combination of speaking and singing, could hold the

33 "AAR," 1934, ix.

attention of people for a couple of hours at a stretch. A drummer was part of the team. In addition to these indigenous Indian methods of communication, the team also took with it a magic lantern and a grammaphone.[34]

In contrast to some other nineteenth-century mission areas, where most of the music introduced by missionaries consisted of western tunes, the Arcot missionaries had available to them almost from the beginning indigenous Tamil lyrics in which the words were sung using simplified Tamil tunes and rhythms. In the twentieth century, a number of missionaries and Indian Christians began to study Tamil music in greater depth. The Reverend Popley, the evangelistic secretary of the National Christian Council of India, had made such a study, and the evangelistic band under direction of Henry Scudder invited him to join them. He presented the gospel in song, using the form of preaching called "kalachapam," a word that literally means a passing away of time. Audiences were willing to listen quietly to his preaching for two hours or more as he sang the gospel message in an Indian style and interspersed his singing with spoken explanations of the meaning of what had been sung.[35] J.H. Chamberlain wrote enthusiastically about how the hearts of people were touched through hearing their Indian music during a kalachapam, "Moreover, the adoption of this Indian method of teaching won the hearts of this race, so jealous of its own civilization and art. Christianity was no longer a thing of the west, the foreigner's religion, but a religion that spoke to them in a way they best understood and with a speech they loved."[36]

The Hindu practice of celebrating festivals and holding pilgrimages to a temple located on a high hill also began to be adapted to Christian use. Meschach Peter encouraged the Christians of the Western Circle to observe the festival of the birth of Christ by leaving their villages and going to the top of a hill. He realized that

[34] "BFMR," 1921, 40-41.
[35] "BFMR," 1923, 48.
[36] J.H. Warnshuis, "Musical Evangelism in India," *Mission Field,* August, 1919, 125.

the Christians in his area were very fond of festivals and pilgrimages, so he sought to provide them with opportunities to worship Christ in that way.[37]

A large cross was dedicated in 1938 on top of a hill located in the vicinity of a group of Christian villages of the Katpadi pastorate. At the beginning of Advent, Christians from the surrounding villages would climb to the top of the hill, singing Tamil lyrics as them came, and then raise the Christian flag as a symbol of the coming of their king. They would also climb the hill for Easter and came to call the hill "Easter Hill." "It was the crowning joy of a long series of services he [the pastor] had conducted during the years—this raising of the emblem of our faith. This is truly an Indian expression of service and consecration to the Master without the least danger of idolatrous practices creeping in and may well be encouraged."[38]

In spite of their hesitation about Gandhi's noncooperation campaign, the missionaries did not hesitate to make use of his positive comments about Christ on evangelistic tours. When the evangelism team under the leadership of Henry J. Scudder was on one of its tours, it stopped at a village named Ramasumudram. There the preachers made repeated references to Mahatma Gandhi's attitude toward Christ and his teachings. "After one of our meetings some Hindus expressed that what we said was true, and that the Christian religion is the only religion that can exalt the nation."[39]

The Reverend Joseph John, who became chairman of the Serkadu Circle in the 1930s, was a leader in seeking to adapt Hindu cultural and religious forms for Christian life and worship. As a student during the decade of the 1920s, he had become an admirer of the

---

[37] "AAR," 1922, 48.

[38] "AAR," 1939, 9.

[39] "BFMR," 1923, 41. M.K. Gandh's full name was Mohandas Karamchand Gandhi. As he grew in stature in India, he came to be referred to as "Mahatma," which can be translated as "Great Soul." The fact that already in the early 1920s the Arcot Mission could refer to him as "Mahatma Gandhi" rather than simply as M.K. Gandhi indicates that he was regarded with respect even while they objected to much of what he was doing. In 1927, when Gandhi visited Vellore, Meschach Peter apparently even referred to him as "Mahatmaji." Adding the "-ji" honorific suffix indicated even higher regard.

work of Gandhi in advocating for Indian autonomy and for the
overcoming of caste discrimination. He often wore simple khadir
homespun clothing instead of machine manufactured cloth.
Following his ordination in 1934, he adapted a number of Hindu
symbols, as can be learned from his 1937 report. The pastorate flag
in the Serkadu pastorate consisted of a red cross on a lotus flower
with a white background. The lotus plays an important role for
Hindus. Joseph John recognized that it could also stand for the
beauty of Jesus Christ. He was also interested in the Christian
ashram movement and arranged for the village workers of the
pastorate to hold a retreat at the Christian ashram in Tirupattur,
where they were given an opportunity to rededicate their lives to
Christ.[40]

Joseph John was also known for his advocacy of building
churches on the pattern of a Hindu temple. In this he was following
the example of the first Indian Anglican bishop in India, Bishop
Azariah of Dornakal Diocese, who had constructed a church on a
Hindu pattern with stone materials including carved pillars with
Christian symbols. The church in Dornakal had a dome patterned
after a Muslim mosque, but it also related to the Hindu temple
tower called a "goparam," again using Christian symbols rather
than Hindu statuary or Muslim calligraphy. Within the Serkadu
Circle area, a small church was built in 1938 in the village of
Kandipedu in which the sanctuary area was formed in the rectangular
basilica style familiar in the West, but the church had a goparam
instead of a steeple over its front entrance.

On June 19, 1940, a beautiful church in the South Indian
Dravidian style of architecture was dedicated on "Zion Hill" in the
Serkadu pastorate. The Reverend Sam Ponniah reported on the
dedication and the significance of the church building in the years
to follow:

---

[40] "AAR," 1937, 6-7. The Rev. Joseph John of the Serkadu Circle was not related to the
Joseph John who served in Madanapalle. All references to Joseph John in the
remainder of this book are to Joseph John who began his ministry in Serkadu.

Muttathur Church, built in Dravidian style, 1983

On that day a large number of men and women, after systematic instruction, made profession of faith. On a full moon majestically overhead those people partook of their first Lord's Supper. Since then, every month on full moon day, the Lord's Supper is celebrated there. For three days, during the full moon season in the month of May every year, a Christian festival is held in the place when thousands of people attend it in all its work.[41]

Arthur John,[42] like Joseph John, had been much impressed by the work of Gandhi and the aspirations for Indian independence

---

[41] J. Sam Ponniah, "The Contribution of the Reformed Church in America to the Church of South India" (thesis presented to the faculty of Western Theological Seminary, 1964), 94.

[42] Arthur John, ordained in 1930, was a son of Joseph John, pastor in Madanapalle, ordained in 1898. He was not related closely to Joseph John, ordained in 1934, chairman of the Serkadu Circle.

during his days as a student. Following Gandhi's example, he wanted to establish an ashram in Chittoor. In ancient India, ashrams were religious retreats for monks. Ashramites resigned from the world, and, contemplating themselves inside and out, waited for the end. Gandhi, however, had developed a new understanding of an ashram when he established his "Satyagraha Ashram" across the river from the city of Ahmedabad. It consisted of low, whitewashed huts in a grove of spreading trees, not far from slum dwellings located near smoking factories. His room in the ashram, where he lived for more than sixteen years, was about the size of a prison cell. People of all castes were welcome at the ashram, whose population fluctuated from thirty at its beginning to 230 at its maximum. Those who stayed in the ashram tended the fruit trees, spun, wove, planted grain, prayed, studied, and taught in the surrounding villages.[43]

Several Christian ashrams had been opened in India by the time Arthur John opened his in Chittoor. In order to profit from the experience of other Christian ashrams in India, John visited the one in Puri in north India and a second one in Tirupattur, about forty-five miles from Chittoor. He adopted for himself the term, *sevak*, which means "servant," to represent the spirit in which he wished to live.[44] He meant the ashram to be not only a social center but a home for religious and spiritual conversation and instruction. It was to be a place where his evangelistic work among educated Hindus could be carried on. He had a free reading room where men could come to read, reflect, and carry on conversation. The main room was decorated with pictures of Christ and of national leaders. There was a badminton court attached to the ashram as a place where men could come together to play.[45]

Arthur John's desire was to develop genuine Christian fellowship in the heart of Chittoor, in order to leaven the whole town with the

[43] Louis Fischer, *Gandhi: His Life and Message for the World,* (New York: The New American Library of World Literature, 1954), 55.
[44] "AAR," 1926, 32.
[45] "AAR," 1924, 26.

spirit of Christ. He provided opportunities for young men to gain help in their personal problems. He developed a program of Sunday classes for New Testament study as well as weekly lectures on the lives of great men and women. During the course of the first year, more than 130 well-attended lectures were given by eight different Christian leaders. In that year, two men, both of whom were Muslims, decided to accept Christ as their savior, but they were not baptized immediately. It was believed necessary to wait long enough to understand more about them and test their sincerity.[46]

Indian and missionary leaders in the Arcot area continued for the next several decades to encourage the ministry of Christian ashrams. Among the missionaries, Lavina Honegger emphasized the need for such ashrams. She joined Arcot missionaries John De Boer and Mason Olcott, along with E. Stanley Jones and members of other missions, in establishing an ashram in Kodaikanal. She also gave many years of leadership to the Ashram in Vellore.

In the time between the two world wars, missionaries and Indian Christians in the Arcot Mission area sought ways to adapt their preaching, music, and architecture to the Indian context. They also encouraged the creation of Christian ashrams. Through these developments an important shift can be discerned in the way the gospel was presented to the people of India. In the nineteenth century, the missionaries had been quite ready to point out the ignorance, superstition, and degraded customs of the Hindus, often by comparing the best of Christianity with the worst of Hinduism. By the 1920s and 30s, however, an appreciation was growing for the great cultural heritage of India. Missionary sympathies, encouraged by their Indian colleagues, were beginning to shift from loyalty to the British queen or king to participation in the building up of an Indian nation.

46 Ibid., 27.

The Response to Political Developments after World War I

The number of Christians under the care of the Indian Church Board more than doubled in the first decade of its existence. Between 1910 and 1920, its numbers grew from 10,751 to 21,851. In those ten years, more people entered the Christian church than in the previous fifty seven years between 1853 and 1910. L.R. Scudder, the chairman of the Indian Church Board, commented that this growth was not entirely due to the board. Much of the growth was due to the impulse of the evangelistic campaign of the years between 1914-1920. "But we may legitimately say that the training in leadership and in assuming larger responsibility that the Indian Church Board has developed among our Indian workers, has had a large share in making the campaign effective."[47]

Scudder went on to comment that the year that just ended (1920) was perhaps the most successful year in the history of the mission. Work had begun in ten new villages. Three hundred ten new families were added. Four hundred eighty-four had been received on confession of their faith into full communion. There were 616 additional Sunday school scholars and 292 additional members in Christian Endeavor societies. Contributions had increased by about 16 percent to Rs. 1,975. Moreover, the missionary force had been strengthened greatly during the course of the year by the return of Henry J. Scudder after an absence of six years and by the presence of the Reverend K. Lange of the Danish Mission, who had been made chairman of the Eastern Circle. [48]

Within a few months after the above report was filed with the Board of Foreign Missions, "this mighty movement into the Kingdom came to an abrupt cessation."[49] The next year's report records the lowest number of additions to the Christian community since 1914. In seeking the reasons for this change, the Arcot Mission report pointed to the tense political situation. The

47 "BFMR," 1921, 35.
48 Ibid., 36.
49 "BFMR," 1922, 29.

missionaries had decided that it was inadvisable to engage in evangelistic activities while the people were in such an excited state. More important, however, was the failure of the mission to do what was expected in caring for new converts:

> Promises have been given which we have been unable to redeem with our limited resources or have postponed fulfilling so long that villages have lost faith in us. Villages have come over expecting educational, social, and economic benefits and deliverance from caste bondage. When we fail to meet these expectations reproaches begin to meet us after a month or two, next the faint-hearted backslide, and soon evangelistic progress is at an end.[50]

This abrupt change in the situation was not a total surprise to the missionaries. They had seen it coming for several years and had been hoping that the necessary financial resources would arrive in time to avoid such disappointment. The comment was made that "once the problem was how to get a convert; now we might almost say the problem is how not to get them." [51] In order to see how the Arcot Mission and the Indian Church Board met this impasse in precisely the year of their greatest success, it is well to look back to the year 1905 and follow the developments between that year and 1921.

When many missionaries were gathered in Kodaikanal in May, 1905, their missions received a letter from the Indian National Council of the Young Men's Christian Association. The letter called attention to the fact that there were still vast districts in India, containing a total of over a hundred million people, that were unoccupied by present missionary efforts. The Indian YMCA, therefore, was calling upon the missionary societies of Great Britain and America to open new missions in those areas. Moreover, the YMCA believed that this did not necessarily require sending a large

[50] Ibid.
[51] Ibid., 31.

number of new missionaries from the west. There were hundreds of thousands of Protestants in India, many of them third and fourth generation Christians, who, it was feared,

> often with a growing worldliness because of a lack of outlet (have) lacked a sense of personal responsibility for the evangelization of their own country….It has been suggested by representative Missionaries that the Young Men's Christian Association as an international body working in all parts of India, should undertake a *forward movement* to encourage and help the native community in the establishment of indigenous Missions in unclaimed fields.[52]

It took several years for the missions to respond to this call to engage in a "Forward Movement" evangelism effort, but the challenge did raise their level of consciousness. They realized that not only were there large areas in which no mission at all was working, but also that within their own areas there were thousands of villages that they were not visiting. As usual, the Board of Foreign Missions and the Arcot Mission were under financial pressures for the next several years that left little to spare for beginning new evangelistic efforts. For example, in 1906 the mission's expenditures had exceeded its income by Rs. 3710 or twelve hundred dollars. The board informed the mission that the mission would have to find the twelve hundred dollars in its 1907 budget and cut back its other expenditures accordingly. The missionaries were disappointed by the decision, especially because the financial firm, Arthuthnot and Binny, in which they kept their personal funds, had recently defaulted. The mission secretary wrote, "We have reached a point where we cannot do any more cutting down of the work; and the recent losses of members of the Mission through Messrs. Arbuthnot and Binny's suspension, makes it impossible to meet the deficit personally, as we have done in past years."[53]

[52] E.C. Carter and G.S. Eddy to "Dear Sir," May 24, 1905.
[53] J.H. Wyckoff to Henry Cobb, July 3, 1907.

The situation began to turn around in 1910 after the Indian Church Board was formed and Indians began to feel a greater responsibility for the work of evangelism. By 1914, six evangelistic teams were making regular tours throughout the area. Usually, but not always, they received a friendly reception. The teams in their preaching emphasized plain, positive statements of the Christian faith while avoiding criticisms of false teachings and foolish practices. Indian music was used. Members of the teams were encouraged to make use of a traveling library of books to stimulate and nourish their own spiritual and mental lives.[54]

It was not unusual for the leader of opposition in a village later to change his attitude and become an inquirer.

> More than once on a first visit the Band [team] was invited to "move on" by those who on later visits sought to detain them. Once the Band was positively, though politely, expelled. Subsequently it was learned that stones and clubs were ready for use if the Missionary and the Band had not retired. It was on a dark night. Since then the leader in this expulsion has twice bought Gospels, and with others of the village is particularly friendly.[55]

Not only had the general atmosphere become friendly to the evangelistic teams, but in many cases offers of refreshment were "embarrassingly urged on the workers." Some very real friendships were being struck up, "especially with fine-spirited caste men and women."[56]

Until 1920, transportation for all evangelistic touring was by bullock cart, walking, horseback, or *jutka*, a very uncomfortable two-wheeled covered cart drawn by a horse. When Henry Scudder returned to India in 1920, he brought with him a car for touring. It became well known throughout the area by the name he gave it,

[54] "BFMR," 1914, 63.
[55] Ibid.
[56] Ibid., 65.

"Prince Henry." One can only wonder whether he had invented the first motor home. He wrote,

> I am rejoicing in the use of my car, "Prince Henry," which Mr. Rottschaefer has fitted out most comfortably for touring. The back of the front seat has been cut and put on hinges so that it falls back and makes a spacious and comfortable bed. By means of water-proof canvas spread over the top and extending five feet each side of the car, Prince Henry is converted into quite a spacious tent large enough for two persons. At the back there is a khaki cloth room for use as a dressing and bath room. I have just been out for ten days with my car and used the tent several times with great pleasure. It is a relief not to be bothered with and hampered by a bullock cart to carry my necessary samaan [baggage]. By means of the car I can do double work, and save expense, after the initial cost of outfitting the car has been met.[57]

Within a very short time after the Indian Church Board joined the evangelistic "Forward Movement" campaign in India, the number of persons asking for instruction in the Christian faith began to increase across the land. In the Arcot Mission area, the average number of converts for the three years prior to the opening of the campaign was 334, while the annual average for the next three years was 1,175. In 1919, John Warnshuis wrote that there had been a

[57] Henry J. Scudder to William Chamberlain, November 17, 1920. We can here remind ourselves again that technological and medical innovations in the United States reached India very quickly. Ida Scudder had imported the first car in Vellore in 1909. Henry Scudder was using his car in India at a time when most Americans did not yet own a car. Chris De Jonge, who had recently graduated from Hope College, lived in the bungalow in Madanapalle while fulfilling his three-year term as short-term missionary. He drove "Prince Henry" in a year in which most of his relatives in America did not yet own a car. He wrote, "Harry [Henry] kindly gave me the use of his Tin Lizzie, so I drove the inspector all around the place. Believe me, I am getting more auto rides out here than I ever did in the States. Hope to know a little about driving et cetera when I get home, as I expect all my relatives to be so wealthy that they will at least have a Lizzie" (Chris De Jonge to "Dear Folks at Home," October 23, 1921).

thousand converts in one month and that twenty-eight villages were in need of a teacher or catechist. The Indian church itself was taking responsibility for bearing witness to the gospel.

> The Indian Church has arisen and is beginning to feel its strength. These humble people who, before this Campaign was launched, had not the faintest conception of their responsibility in carrying the Gospel to their fellows, are now becoming alive with the evangelistic spirit. You say the movement will not last, it will die down. Possibly, but we are sure that next year it will be stronger than ever....Almost one-third of our present Church are converts of the last two years.[58]

The churches in the Arcot area were facing problems related to their rapid growth. The Reverend S. Sigamani, an ordained minister in the Yehamur pastorate, which consisted of twenty-seven villages, wrote to "Dear Friends" in America to appeal for financial assistance. Their central church needed repair; it was too small and in bad condition. Each of the four walls was cracked from top to bottom and was dangerous. When the bell was rung, the whole building shook. The number on the roll of the pastorate had grown to over twenty-four hundred. Sigamani reported that his congregation was advancing each year toward self-support, self-government, and self-propagation. The church was entirely self-supporting in its annual expenditures, even though the average income of the head of each family was only six cents a day. There were still 250 villages within the Yehamur area that needed to be visited by members of their evangelistic team. Last year five villages had asked for instruction in the faith. But as they tried to fulfill their evangelistic task, the additional effort to raise funds to enlarge and renovate the church was beyond their means, so they hoped help would come from friends in America.[59]

[58] J. H. Warnshuis, "A Pentecost in India: 1,000 Converts in One Month" *Mission Field,* January, 1919, 486-87.
[59] S. Sigamani to "Dear Friends," May 16, 1918.

Nevertheless, while the church was enjoying the fruits of the "Forward Movement" evangelistic campaign, the people of India were entering a new era of suffering brought on by World War I. At first, India supported England in the war, sending 1,200,000 of its citizens into the army. Great numbers of them were sent to the western front in Europe, where they suffered heavy casualties. There was a 300-percent increase in defense spending that had to be paid for in India by increased taxes or semi-compulsory war loans. A comment by the British governor in Bombay was picked up by the press and reported: "Large quantities of valuable fodder are being exported from here to Mesopotamia by the Army....Luckily the (*Bombay Chronicle*) have not tumbled to the fact that fodder is being exported while the Deccan starves."[60]

There was a drastic increase in prices of foodstuffs, cloth, salt, kerosene, and other materials essential for daily life. The price index doubled between 1914 and 1920.[61] The result was that the great bulk of the population no longer could sustain an adequate diet even by Indian standards, and among the village people famine conditions prevailed in many places. Even without the efforts of the Indian National Congress to stir up agitation for home rule, there would have been many strikes, riots, and other forms of unrest under the conditions arising due to the war.

When the population became physically weakened as a result of food shortages, cholera, typhoid, malaria, and/or plague became more prevalent than usual. It became necessary for the missionaries, pastors, catechists, and teachers to do what they could to help those in need of food and those suffering from diseases. L.R. Scudder learned from S. Sigamani about the heroic service of C.A. Jebamoni, the catechist in the village of Paramasathu near Ponnai. While the people were short of food, cholera broke out in the village. When the surrounding villages heard about the cholera, they exercised a

60 Sumit Sarkar, *Modern India: 1885-1947* (New York: St. Martin's Press, 1989), 169. The Deccan is a high central plain of in India. Madanapalle and Punganur are situated on the southern end of the Deccan plain.
61 Ibid., 170.

quarantine against the people of Paramasathu. When the people in that village tried to enter a market to seek work or to buy a little food, the people would drive them away with sticks and stones. Jebamoni, at risk to himself, insisted on going out and begging for rice for his poor people, and he secured enough to give a little to each family. He visited each house where cholera was present, gave simple remedies, and encouraged the people. He also sent for medicines and gave some to the people. But then the cholera entered his own home and took two of his children. He also contracted it and died. Sigamoni testified, "He faced and suffered a terrible death in loyalty to Christ and for love of those to whom Christ sent him."[62]

The famine conditions continued to grow worse after the war ended, due to lack of rainfall as well as dislocations in the economy caused by the war. By May, 1919, many of the people in the pariah villages were able to secure only one scanty meal a day.

> Some, the pastors assure me, go even two days without food. Herbs, roots, grass even forms the diet of many of the poorest. How many of them live is a wonder. Work in the villages is very scarce and hard to get. Those who in prosperous times hire labor now generally do it themselves. The rains have failed and the crops are very scant. There is a real scarcity of food in all of South India. Government is trying to help in importing food and distributing grain. But even then it is the more prosperous with money in hand who can secure it.[63]

The Arcot Mission had foreseen to some extent the rising threat of famine due to the rapidly increasing prices of food and other commodities. In May, 1918, it had appealed for an additional appropriation of three thousand dollars to meet the increased cost of food for the boarding homes and for the needs of the village workers. The Board of Foreign Missions wrote back to say it had

[62] L.R. Scudder to William Chamberlain, July 16, 1919.
[63] Ibid.

approved the amount requested. Unfortunately, by that time the mission realized that it had asked for too little. When it held a special meeting in April, 1919, the mission sought to meet the needs of the boarding homes and to give some relief to the catechists, teachers, and other mission workers. In light of its financial situation, the mission felt that it could give an additional bonus only up to Rs. 30, even though this was far below the standard set by other missions and the government who were giving Rs. 50. To give this bonus required an additional three thousand dollars. Fortunately, Gertrude Dodd was present and came to the relief of the mission by offering her personal donation of three thousand dollars, with the stipulation that it be used to give the mission helpers adequate relief and to begin to give relief to others in the villages. A realistic estimate of the needs over the next six months in 1919 would be about ten thousand dollars.[64]

Although good rains after 1919 brought in good harvests and an end to the famine, the underlying problem of how to supply pastoral care to new villages seeking to come under instruction in the Christian faith only continued to grow with the mass movement to the Christian faith. Joseph Mayou in the 1860s and John Conklin in the 1880s had already called attention to the fact that the system of supplying paid Christian workers to provide pastoral care and lead worship in each village was too expensive to maintain as the church grew in numbers. The problem was that the missionaries could find no adequate alternative. The new converts were for the most part illiterate, with no Christian background. They were too poor to be able to support a catechist.

In accepting an area the size of the state of New Jersey as its mission field in India, the Board of Foreign Missions had adopted a responsibility that was seemingly beyond the capacity of Reformed Church members to support. The missionaries could not believe it was beyond the means of Reformed Church members. They constantly hinted that it was a matter of lack of zeal to do so. In the

64 Ibid.

famine time, L.R. Scudder wrote, "We had a community of 18,635 at the end of last September; I believe we have over 20,000 now. But are there not 18,635 well fed, comfortably clothed, happy and grateful children of God in our beloved Church who would be willing to give at least one dollar to alleviate the hunger and nakedness of those who are suffering out here?"[65]

By 1922 the mass movement seemed to have come to an abrupt cessation, as was previously noted. A great limiting factor was the financial inability to invest fifty dollars in a church and school in each new village. Lack of funds also meant that the mission was not able to hire enough good teachers. "Since good teachers are more expensive than poor ones, the cheaper grade men are employed....The great majority of our helpers do not have a living wage or even 50 percent of what they require."[66]

The Indian Church Board decided to place responsibility for finding a solution to the financial crisis on the highly respected pastor and leader of one of the evangelistic teams, the Reverend E. Savarirayan.[67] He pointed out that a more rapid response to the need for a teacher or a catechist in a new village was crucial to the morale of the evangelistic teams. The evangelists invited people to accept Jesus Christ and be instructed in the Christian faith. The people believed the evangelists and accepted their offer in the face of the persecution that often came upon them. But if no person was sent to follow up the work of the evangelists, the villagers felt betrayed and the evangelists lost their credibility. Therefore, on behalf of the Indian Church Board, Savarirayan presented a request

---

[65] Ibid.

[66] "BFMR," 1922, 29.

[67] The Rev. E. Savarirayan was "the grand old man of the Indian Church in our area." During his half century of ministry 1898-1946, he served at various times as headmaster of the Arcot Seminary, as chairman of the Southern Circle, as pastor of the Vellore church, and as chairman of the Evangelistic Council. He raised a large family who gave many years of service to the church in India. We will meet two of his sons in the following chapters. S. J. Savarirayan was principal of Voorhees College in Vellore. Dr. Julius Savarirayan served as Medical Superintendent at the Scudder Memorial Hospital in Ranipet. One can hope that someone in India will write a monograph about the Savarirayan family's service to the church and country in India.

E. Savarirayan and family

for Rs. 6080, about two thousand dollars, to the Board of Foreign
Missions to enable the Indian Church Board to place teachers in
sixteen new villages beginning as soon as possible, at a cost of $125
per village.[68]

Savarirayan gave a second reason for the need to act. Conditions
in India were changing rapidly. The non-Brahmin political movement
in the area was making "pretension of anxiety for the amelioration
of the Panchama [Pariah] villages." The Brahmins also were echoing
Gandhi's cry for the removal of untouchability. In tune with these
competitive movements, the government was also beginning to
take a more active concern for the welfare of the pariahs.

> With a mistaken notion of patriotism, all classes of Hindus
> think they owe it to their country to resist attempts to

[68] E. Savarirayan to William Chamberlain, April 9, 1925.

christianize the village people and not infrequently make
overtures of help to them when they see such attempts.
Surely the motive behind all these is not love but more
policy based upon party spirit and selfish ends. But the
ignorant villager hardly sees the difference and he begins to
think that he can get on well socially without the help of the
Christian missionary. And the thought of the social uplift
which once strongly appealed to him when he came into
contact with evangelistic efforts is fast losing its old place
in his mind.[69]

In contrast to the missionaries who were often concerned about
whether villagers were seeking to be baptized because they were
"rice Christians" seeking economic gain, Savarirayan wrote from
his own family's experience. His father and mother had taught their
children how they had been among the poor, illiterate, oppressed,
and scorned outcastes of society. The gospel of Christ had come to
them not only in the form of preaching, but also in the form of
tangible love, such as protection from the local landowners and
caste people, as well as the opportunity for education and in time
of famine even food. For such villagers, "rice" and "Christian" were
not easily separated. He did not trust the sincerity of the new
political friends of the "pachamas" to deliver what they promised.
He believed it to be crucial for the Board of Foreign Missions and
the Indian Church Board to be true to their words about the love
of Christ for the people in the villages.

At this point we can stop to deal with a criticism that has often
been made against missionaries, which is that they use the wealth
of the West to induce people to become Christians and put pressure
upon the people to convert to Christianity. In the case of the Arcot
Mission, the field of work was so vast and most of the time there
were such a small number of missionaries that it lacked the power
to apply heavy pressure on people to convert. Instead of applying

69 Ibid.

pressure, the missionaries kept people who were asking for conversion waiting for months and sometimes even years as they tested their sincerity. In the case of mass movements, the mission responded so cautiously and with so few resources that it is subject to the criticism that it contributed to the movement coming to an end more than that it used improper inducements to bring people to conversion.

Mission among Muslims

The Arcot missionaries from the very beginning were intent upon calling members of the Hindu communities to turn to Jesus Christ. They learned the Tamil and Telugu languages, read some of the Hindu poets, sought to understand Hindu thought patterns, and compared Hindu and Christian teachings while on their evangelistic tours. Almost all of those who responded to their message had their family origins in the Hindu religion. The new converts knew to some extent what it meant to live as Hindus, even when they were members of the pariah castes and had been forbidden to enter Hindu temples. The missionaries and the Indian Christians alike agreed that India was a Hindu land, as England and America were Christian countries.

Missionaries did make the acquaintance of Muslims and, on an individual basis, did speak to them concerning the gospel. A few boys and girls entered the mission schools. There were even a very small number of Muslims who decided to follow Jesus Christ. However, from the time that John and Harriet Scudder first arrived in India and Ceylon until 1910, one finds very little evidence in the Arcot Mission annual reports or in its correspondence that there were any long-term efforts to reach out to Muslims with the gospel. This is not surprising in light of the fact that the missionaries were already overwhelmed with the need to bear witness to the Hindus who constituted perhaps 90 percent of the population. Furthermore, although the men among the Muslims knew the local vernacular language well enough to communicate easily in it, the language of the Muslim community as such was Urdu. Yet there was a considerable population of Muslims in the area. In 1910, it was estimated that there were twenty-six thousand Muslims in the Madanapalle area, four thousand in Punganur, and twenty-six thousand in Vellore.

An invitation was extended to the Reverend Canon Goldsmith, a missionary of the Church of England, to make a tour of the Madanapalle field in 1910. Goldsmith had long experience working among Muslims and gladly accepted the invitation. Accompanied by L.B. Chamberlain, he made a tour lasting about two weeks in the surrounding towns and villages. One of the purposes of the visit was to provide opportunities for the mission workers to talk with Goldsmith and learn more about how to carry on conversations with Muslims on religious matters.[70]

Much of Goldsmith's time was spent with the Muslims themselves. His meetings with them were extremely cordial in Madanapalle. Such cordiality may have been encouraged by the fact that recently a visit of Annie Besant and a Hindu Yogi had stirred up some antagonistic feelings that had seemed to threaten Muslims and Christians alike. There had also been some problems about the ringing of bells on religious processions and thereby interfering with worship taking place in one of the other religions. Muslims and Christians had come to an agreement on how to respect each other on such matters by not ringing bells or beating drums while on procession past a mosque. Six public meetings were held in Madanapalle in the mission school and the government Muslim school. Attitudes during the meetings were very conciliatory. Goldsmith and Chamberlain were garlanded by the Muslims in a farewell gathering.

The same cordial reception took place in several of the places to which they went on their tour. In the town of Mahal, they encountered a reception that was "more stiff and indifferent than actually antagonistic," possibly because some Kabuli men from

[70] "AAR," 1910, 13-15.

Afghanistan were at the head of affairs. They also spoke with
Muslims in Piler, where their reception was similar to what they had
received at Mahal. The Muslims there asserted that their saints had
wonderful miraculous powers and therefore they had no need to
listen to a message about Jesus Christ.[71]

Goldsmith's visit raised the consciousness of Christians in the
area to the presence of Muslims. They learned that some of the
Muslims were open to carry on more conversation about religious
matters. However, the mission made no special efforts to reach out
particularly to Muslims for the rest of the decade. Finally, in 1924,
a conference was held in Vellore that was led by Samuel M.
Zwemer, a Reformed Church in America missionary in Arabia.
Only one mission worker, David Kay, had a fair knowledge of the
Urdu language. Following the conference, a findings committee
gave a report. It concluded that evangelistic activity among Muslims
had not been initiated because successful work among Muslims
requires a working knowledge of Urdu and some knowledge of
Arabic, together with a full knowledge of some of the literature of
Islam. The mission did not have such workers because there were
greater results among Hindus and the pressure of caring for them
took many of the mission's resources. It further concluded that
there was a lack of enthusiasm because of the general feeling that
Muslims would not respond to Christian efforts and because the
Muslim community was more widely scattered and more difficult
to reach with visits.[72]

In order to make a start in special work among Muslims, it was
decided that two workers, David Kay and Mr. Jared, a converted
Muslim who had just been appointed, should be set apart for such
work under the supervision of Arthur John in Chittoor. Mr. Jared
knew only Tamil, so it was anticipated that he would work among
the *Lubbais*, or Tamil-speaking Muslims.[73] No progress was reported
on this plan in the following year, but interest in starting Muslim

[71] Ibid.
[72] "AAR," 1924, 29.
[73] Ibid., 29-30.

work continued. A request was made of the Reformed Church's Arabian Mission to loan the Reverend and Mrs. G.D. Van Peursem for a time to train persons for work among Muslims. The Arabian Mission said it could not spare the Van Peursems, but he conducted a three-day workshop for about twenty workers.[74] The following year Van Peursem gave three weeks of his vacation time to tour in the Arcot area. Van Peursem was able to speak in Arabic, but he needed an interpreter to communicate in Urdu.

Gudiyattam was the first town to which they went. There they met considerable opposition. They attracted a large crowd when they first went to the home of a Muslim friend of the mission. The other Muslim reprimanded the owner of the house for permitting Christians to be on his premises, so they had to leave that place. They then went to the village *maidan* or "commons" and used Henry Scudder's "Prince Henry" Ford as a pulpit. A very large crowd gathered and listened without any trouble so long as they spoke in Tamil or English, but when their words began to be translated into Urdu by one of the team, Mr. Nazruddin, a convert from Islam, there was pandemonium, with the people shouting, "There is no God but God," and, "Muhammad is the Apostle of Allah." Stones and sand began to be thrown and they had to leave.[75]

In other places the team received a good reception. In Arcot they were guests of a Muslim who was a member of the government's legislative council and who had just received special recognition by the government. A program very Islamic in character was given in Van Peursem's honor, and their host, Khan Bahadur, spoke as a Muslim to Muslims. Van Peursem pleased them by reciting several quotations from the Quran in Arabic. Henry Scudder reported, "In view of the communal strife and jealousy in India our plea was for Tolerance, Liberty, and Fraternity."[76]

---

[74] "AAR," 1925, 34-35. The Reformed Church missionaries in Arabia sent their children to Kodaikanal for their education. They also took their vacations there so that they could be with their children for a time.

[75] "AAR," 1926, 26.

[76] Ibid., 27.

The Van Peursem team also held four meetings in Vellore, arranged by E. Savarirayan. They also visited the Arabic College (or Quran school), where the members of the school were especially open to conversation when they learned that Van Peursem spoke Arabic. The meeting in the town hall was the climax of the tour, when six hundred people gathered. Nazruddin related the story of his conversion to Christianity while the audience listened intently. At the end of the meeting the Muslim chairman commented, "It is inspiring to think that Vellore had advanced far enough to allow one of another religion to present his cause and to be listened to without disturbance."[77]

The 1926 visit by Van Peursem led to some continuing work among Muslims by many of the evangelists in the area. They had seen that it was possible to receive a welcome from Muslims and carry on respectful conversations with them. Some efforts continued, especially in the area around Punganur by missionary Ralph Korteling and his coworkers. Korteling had originally been appointed as a missionary for the Arabian Mission but had been side-tracked to India, where his interest in Muslim work continued. Apart from his work and sporadic efforts on the part of others, little evangelism was carried out thereafter among Muslims.[78] C.R. Wierenga, secretary of the Arcot Mission, summed up the view of many in 1940 when he wrote to the secretary of the Board of Foreign Missions that the Arcot Mission had neither the men nor the money for Muslim work.[79]

The Devolution of the Arcot Mission and the Organization of the Arcot Assembly in 1922

The establishment of the Indian Church Board in 1910 had put in place a body where Indians and missionaries met together regularly to supervise and plan for the development of the work and

[77] Ibid.
[78] Ibid., 28.
[79] C.R. Wierenga to J.M. Potter, April 4, 1940.

witness of the churches and the elementary schools. The accomplishments of the Indian Church Board in the first decade of its existence were so positive that it came to be felt that the possibility for wider administrative cooperation between missionaries and Indians should be explored. After the end of World War I, external pressure for more rapid movement toward such cooperation grew as a result of the Indian National Congress's call for home rule in India. Internal pressure for an organization adequate to foster cooperation between missionaries and Indians was felt when the Board for Foreign Missions in 1922 experienced another of its chronic financial crises, and the Arcot Mission had to make decisions about where to reduce its expenditures. As a result of the experience with the Indian Church Board and the combined external and internal pressures for greater Indian involvement in decision-making in the Arcot Mission area, a new organization, "the Arcot Assembly," came into being in 1924.

A tentative move toward involving Indians in the whole scope of the work of the Arcot Mission took place in January 1922. That year, the mission invited two Indian leaders, Meschach Peter and Joseph John, to attend its meeting in order to take part in its discussions and "to present the Indian point of view."[80] It was almost immediately recognized that such small Indian representation was unsatisfactory, so plans were made for a joint session of the Arcot Mission with leaders of the Indian Church Board plus other Indian representatives from the mission station areas, in order to give full scope for Indian opinion. Three questions were put before the joint session: How should the lack of sufficient funds for next year be dealt with? How can we place a greater emphasis on evangelistic work? How can we educate our Christian community, which has doubled its numbers in the ten years?[81]

---

[80] Wyckoff, *A Hundred Years,* 75.
[81] Ibid.

The Suicide of the Arcot Mission

The joint session of the Arcot Mission and the Indian Church Board set in motion a process that would lead to what one of the missionaries with some feelings of ambiguity called "the suicide of the mission."[82] There was considerable nervousness at the beginning of the meeting on the part of missionaries and Indians. The missionaries were uncertain whether the Indians would respond with cooperation or antagonism. The Indians were hazy about what was expected of them, what the real purpose of the missionaries was in calling for a joint session at just that critical moment in India's political development, and how they were expected to respond.[83]

The first session went so well that a committee was appointed to draw up a constitution for a body that came to be called the Arcot Assembly. The constitution was approved at the second joint meeting in 1923 and sent to the Board of Foreign Missions for its approval. Upon receiving approval, subject to review after three years, the assembly was formally organized in 1924. In keeping with the goal that the assembly should be an organization where Indians and missionaries would consult together in making decisions concerning Christian outreach in the Arcot area, it had a very large membership. Its membership by 1926 included all forty-seven Reformed Church missionaries present in India, all twenty-two ordained Indian pastors, an Indian representative from each of the fifteen mission institutions, eight Indian members elected from the circles, and sixteen Indian coopted members, for a total of 108 members of whom sixty-two were Indian.[84]

---

[82] James H. Potter, "The Second Meeting of the Temporary Organization of the Arcot Assembly" (mimeographed undated report on file in India secretary correspondence, Archives of the RCA). James Potter was an Indian member of the Arcot Assembly and principal of the Arcot Theological Seminary. He was not related to F.M. Potter, who served as a missionary in India and later became secretary for the Board of Foreign Missions.

[83] Ibid.

[84] "AAR," 1926, v-vii.

The Arcot Assembly was given responsibility for the entire range of work which to that time had been the responsibility of the Arcot Mission alone. Its formation was understood to be an intermediate step on the way to the goal of a fully self-supporting, self-governing, and self-propagating church. The Board of Foreign Missions wanted the goal of full integration of the work of the mission into the self-governance of the church to be kept in mind. The secretary of the board, William Chamberlain, made this point clear when he wrote,

> Whereas it is distinctly stated in the Proposed Constitution of the Assembly that the purpose of the organization is to carry on the work now administered by the Arcot Mission looking toward an ultimate transfer of its functions and powers to the organized Church in India, and to this end it aims to carry on not only the Evangelistic, Economic and Medical activities necessary to the establishment of the Christian Church in India.[85]

The Arcot Assembly in 1924 replaced the Arcot Mission as the body to which the Indian Church Board and all of the mission's institutional and evangelistic activity was accountable. In order to fulfill its purpose, the constitution provided that the work of the assembly be delegated to a number of boards: the Educational Board, representing the various educational interests; the Medical Board, embracing the ministration to the needs of the sick; and the Economic Board, seeking the amelioration of the economic life of the community.[86] There was also a Women's Evangelistic Board, which carried on responsibility for the Hindu girls' schools, social centers, and zenana work as well for the work of the Bible women.

The Arcot Assembly was formed with the full recommendation and approval of the Arcot Mission. It was for this reason that the missionaries could look upon the devolution of the work from the

[85] William Chamberlain to H. J. Scudder, December 4, 1922.
[86] "BFMR," 1924, 24.

mission to the assembly as the self-willed "suicide of the mission." When, in the 1924 meeting of the assembly, several of the Indian speakers implied that the mission should make up its mind on an issue, Henry Scudder rose to remind the assembly "to bear in mind that the Arcot Mission as a legislative and administrative body was no longer in existence."[87]

After 1924, the Arcot Mission as an organization had responsibility only for matters related to the missionaries themselves, such as providing for their housing, their travel, health, language study, Kodaikanal property, and children's education. Since the mission was still the legally incorporated body, while the Arcot Assembly was not incorporated, the mission continued to be legally responsible for the management of the property which the mission had accumulated over the decades.

In 1924, the Indian Church Board, which had been organized in 1910, was also placed under the Arcot Assembly. It continued to have responsibility for the work of town and village congregations, evangelism, and elementary education. An important change was made in 1925, when the Indian Church Board was transferred to the control of the South India United Church through the Madras Church Council.[88] The South Indian United Church at that time had a unit called "Indian Church Board," so there were objections to the use of the term for a unit under the Madras Church Council. Therefore, between November, 1925, and 1940 the name of the board was the "Board of Administration," but the responsibilities of the board remained essentially the same. After 1940, the name of the unit once again became Indian Church Board. For the sake

[87] H. J. Scudder to William Chamberlain, January 17, 1924.

[88] In the South Indian United Church, the "church council" was the term used to designate what in the Reformed Church is a classis. After the Classis of Arcot had been transferred to the South Indian United Church in 1902, its name was the Presbytery of Arcot. After the 1908 merger of the Congregationalists with the South Indian United Church took place, the name "church council" replaced that of "presbytery," and the Presbytery of Arcot became the Arcot Church Council. In 1925 the Arcot Church Council amalgamated with the Madras Church Council to form the new and enlarged Madras Church Council within the larger framework of the South Indian United Church.

of simplicity, we will continue to use Indian Church Board throughout the whole period, 1910-1947, while bearing in mind that the Arcot Assembly annual reports use the title, Board of Administration.

The change of title was important as a reminder that the work of the old Indian Church Board in the Arcot area was no longer simply a continuation of the work of the Arcot Mission. It had become part of the work of several missions that were administered by a single body in the South India United Church. By placing the work of the Indian Church Board fully under the Madras Church Council, the Arcot Mission and Arcot Assembly showed themselves to be moving more rapidly in the course of devolution than the Church of Scotland Mission or the United Free Church of Scotland Mission, who had not yet placed their village work within the scope of the new Board of Administration.[89]

Perhaps the most sensitive point in the devolution of power from the mission to the assembly was the provision that henceforth the assignment of work responsibilities of missionaries and Indians alike was to be done by the assembly rather than by the mission. Since Indians outnumbered missionaries in the assembly's membership of approximately ninety persons, this provision provided concrete evidence that the missionaries were ready to trust the judgment of Indian leaders. The secretary of the board concurred with the missionaries' statement, "Nothing will do more to convince the Indian that we are here to serve him in the name of our Lord than to tell him that we are ready to listen to his judgment as to the most acceptable way in which that service can be rendered."[90]

The Board of Foreign Missions raised two concerns that it hoped would be addressed by the assembly. The first was whether the plan did not put so much power in the hands of the assembly that there would be little room left for the "living activity" of the church. "Will

89 "AAR," 1926, 4.
90 Ibid.

not all the real work be done by the Assembly so that the Church itself as such will discharge no living duties, but only formal ecclesiastical functions?"[91] This was not a new problem. The problem was there from the moment the Scudder brothers had organized both the mission and the classis. The initiatives, funds, and property had always been in the hands of the mission, with the result that the classis found itself in a dependency role for much of its work. For example, through the decades when the mission found it needed a missionary or Indian ordained pastor in a certain mission station for the sake of its mission outreach, the local church and the classis usually found themselves obliged to follow by calling and installing the person needed by the mission also to be pastor of the church. For the time being, little could be done to fully resolve the problem, but it was important to keep it before the assembly.

The board's second concern was that there was no provision in the assembly's plan for a gradual increase of Indian contributions toward self-support. Again, it was an old problem, but the board wanted the assembly to know that the Reformed Church in America was serious about the matter.

Indian representatives at the joint conferences in 1922 and 1923 felt very positive about these new developments in the process of devolution of control from the Arcot Mission to the Indian church. The report of the 1923 meeting by one of the Indian leaders, C. J. Lucas, provides insight into the feelings of the Indian representatives:

> One satisfactory feature of the Conference was, that it was through-out characterized by goodwill, fellowship and mutual sympathy. By the grace of God, every thing went off smoothly and well. We all felt that we were brethren and were conscious of the Divine presence in our midst. The attitude of our Missionary brethren towards the Indians was simply admirable. How tolerant and amiable they were! We all forgot that we were Americans and Indians, and one

91 Ibid.

and all approached the problems for our solution with the best of motives and intentions.[92]

Residual Power of the Mission and Missionaries

The formal transfer of power from the mission to the assembly meant that henceforth Indians had to be involved in the approval of all decisions. Nevertheless, considerable power did remain with the missionaries and with the mission. Since all of the physical property still was registered in the name of the mission, it could exercise considerable control through the way in which it regulated matters of the maintenance and erection of buildings and use of the properties. Another point at which missionary control remained strong was in the provision that the treasurer of the Arcot Assembly was responsible to the mission for the proper use of funds received from and through the mission. Since a missionary always occupied the office of treasurer throughout all the years of the life of the assembly from 1924 to 1940, Indian leaders still had to look to a missionary in financial matters.

In contrast to the accountability line of the treasurer to the mission, it was provided that the secretary of the assembly "shall be in direct correspondence with the Board" without going through the mission.[93] This provision became more important in later years when an Indian served as secretary. It came to be greatly appreciated that matters of concern between the church in the Arcot area in India could handled by direct correspondence between Indian leadership and the board in New York without going through a missionary.

[92] C. J. Lucas, "A brief report of the 'Joint Conference' of the Arcot Mission an the Indian Church Board, 1923," on file with board secretary's correspondence, Archives of the RCA. The word "brethren" here is used generically to refer to both sexes. There were a good number of women representatives in the assembly, which was a very large body. In the 1926 list of representatives eligible to attend there were seventy-five men and fifty-four women.

[93] William Chamberlain to H. J. Scudder, December 4, 1922.

The mission also retained more power in matters of missionary assignment than the formal transfer of power might indicate. The mission was permitted to make recommendations concerning such assignments, and there were always missionaries on the missionary personnel committee of the assembly. Indians were reluctant to oppose recommendations of the mission or individual missionaries, but at least no missionary assignment could be made without their approval.

Indian Concerns for a Just Minimum Wage

Even before the Arcot Assembly was formally instituted, the Indian members of the Joint Conference of the Indian Church Board and the Arcot Mission expressed their great concern that the wage scale of Indian workers be raised. Through their efforts, the conference resolved

> that every worker of the Mission or the I. C. B. is entitled to a living wage, that merit should be recognized as well as educational qualifications, and that a committee be appointed to consider a revision of the scale on this basis, the Mission to appoint five members and the I. C. B. to appoint five members to constitute such a committee."[94]

The committee was appointed and brought back its report to the joint conference.

The consensus was that the absolute minimum wage to enable a single person to live in decency was Rs. 15, or approximately $5 per month, with married couples with families at a proportionately higher minimum. The committee informed the conference that to bring people to this minimum level would require an additional amount of Rs 50,928 or approximately $16,500, annually. An amendment adopted by the conference brought the total need

---

[94] Report of the Findings Committee of the Joint Meeting of the Indian Church Board and the Arcot Mission, January 9-10, 1922, on file with board secretary's correspondence, Archives of the RCA.

higher, to $22,000. The joint conference sent this information on to the Board of Foreign Missions to learn to what extent the board was ready to respond to the need.

> While the Mission and the Joint Assembly felt this was a tremendous figure as it represented not the total salary but the amount of money needed above what we now have for salaries to grant a living wage, it was decided that it should be sent to the Board to place before them the real vital issue of a living wage for those who are working. [95]

There are two significant points to note here. First, Indian concern for the salary scale of workers brought to light their belief that the missionaries had not adequately addressed the issue of providing a just and living wage for those employed by the mission and the Indian Church Board. Second, the question of how to solve the problem, whether by a greater appropriation from the Board of Foreign Missions or by cutting back on the number of workers or by finding ways to raise the level of contributions in India, had become a matter of joint concern among missionaries and Indians, rather than a matter to be decided by the mission alone. The Board of Foreign Missions recognized the need to raise Indian workers' salaries, but it was faced with a deficit and actually had to decrease its appropriation for the year 1923 and to suggest that a further reduction might be necessary in 1924. The Arcot Assembly and the Arcot Mission did not know what to do in a time when the Christian message was being met with general acceptance. It could not believe that the Reformed Church would let them down. It asked,

> What are we to do? God's call in the conditions of India is to advance. Our home church says retreat. The only thing for us to do is to take our courage in our hands and call for the great advance. Loyalty to Christ will allow us to do nothing more. The word for us from the two lean years is

[95] Lambertus Hekhuis to William Chamberlain, February 14, 1923.

that we should plan a great drive. Let us respectfully inform our home church that in their name and at Christ's command we are going out in 1924 into the byways and hedges to compel them to come in....I cannot believe that our home church would tell us to stay our hand with the fields ripe for the harvest or refuse to care for those who are asking for the Bread of Life. Let us send the challenge home to them in no uncertain terms.[96]

We can be certain that William Chamberlain in New York felt some pangs of guilt as he read the appeal for increased appropriations, but the board had no funds to spare, so the workers could not hope for any substantial raises.

Assignment of Missionaries and Indians to Positions of Responsibility

From time to time, Indian representatives also asked that the missionaries become more open to considering appointment of qualified Indians to positions of responsibility. They particularly desired Indian ordained ministers to be appointed as circle chairmen and Indian educators to be entrusted with the management of schools.

For example, they suggested that experienced Indians be appointed to serve as principals of the high schools in Madanapalle and Tindivanam. That suggestion was made because the Board of Foreign Missions, at the request of the mission, had developed a practice of recruiting newly graduated unmarried men from Hope College to serve as high school principals in India for a period of two or three years. The young men could be sent to India at salaries as low as $400 a year plus room and board. They were energetic, usually related well to boys in the boarding homes, and in a number of cases agreed to become career missionaries following their short-term service. However, they did not know the local language or the customs of India and lacked experience in teaching and

[96] "AAR," 1923, 25-26.

administration. The Indian leaders who suggested that there were Indians more qualified for such positions had a good case.

In spite of all of the concern in India after World War I for Home Rule and the need for Indians to be appointed to places of responsibility, at the local level there remained an amazing readiness on the part of local Indians to place a missionary in a leadership role, however inexperienced he might be. An extreme example of a young missionary who was moved rapidly into local leadership is that of Chris De Jonge, although most other missionaries also received many heavy responsibilities very soon after their arrival in India. De Jonge was appointed to serve as principal of the Hope High School and to manage its hostel, where ninety boys lived during the school year. These positions were in themselves an adequate challenge. He wrote home that he had to be a sort of father to the boys in the hostel, even though some of the boys were almost as old as he was.[97]

In addition to these responsibilities, De Jonge also managed the Fort Elementary School, which had an enrollment of a hundred when he took it over but grew in his first year in India to 250. When the budget required that the mission reduce the scope of its work, it decided that the Fort Elementary School must be closed. De Jonge fought to continue its existence, and ultimately the school did remain open. When the first word came that the school had to be closed, De Jonge wrote to his family in America:

> All these boys will be denied an education, because it is a school especially designated for poor boys who cannot pay fees. It just breaks my heart to think of parting company with those two hundred and fifty naked little boys who assemble every morning. Such is the situation here on the Mission field. In addition to other troubles the Missionaries have to face the cold problem of the lack of money and it makes the work very unpleasant at times.[98]

[97] Chris De Jonge to "My Dear Mother and Sis," November 17, 1920.
[98] Chris De Jonge to "Dear Folks at Home," January 21, 1921.

As if these duties were not enough, he was asked to take on other responsibilities and, like other enthusiastic young men, did not seem to know how or when to say no. Four months after his arrival in Madanapalle, De Jonge was chosen to be the convenor of the committee to organize and run the annual Madanapalle church harvest festival with all its complications.[99] He was informed that as the new missionary, he was also superintendent of the Sunday school and chairman of the evangelistic campaign of the church. The latter job consisted of arranging evangelistic tours in the villages around Madanapalle. Meanwhile, he had arranged the "Hope High School Lecture Course" for the local intelligentsia. He gave the first lecture in the series, "The World War," complete with some stereoptican slides. He wrote that Hope High School's rival institution, the National College that had been taken over by the Theosophical Society, "which also has a lecture course, is a little peeved at me, but I trust they will soon get over it. The next number on the course will be to-morrow nite when an outsider will give a 'Kalachapam," a musical entertainment in Tamil."[100]

He was elected to be an elder in the church at the beginning of his second year in India, and then was made secretary of the consistory.[101] By that time, he had already served the first eight months of his term as president of the Madanapalle Christian Endeavor Union.[102] When he attended a meeting of the teachers of all the schools in Madanapalle, he was elected president of the Madanapalle Teachers' Association.[103]

Soon after he arrived in India, De Jonge joined the boy scouts in order to have more opportunity to mix with Hindu boys. He found a warm welcome among the fifty boys in the local troop. The ceremony of his investiture into the scouts was impressive. The scouts assembled in a horseshoe formation, with the British Union

[99] Chris De Jonge to "My Dear Mother and Sis," November 17, 1920.
[100] Ibid.
[101] Chris De Jonge to "Dear Folks at Home," October 23, 1921.
[102] Chris De Jonge to "Dear Folks at Home," January 26, 1921.
[103] Chris De Jonge to "Dear Folks at Home," October 23, 1921.

Jack in the center. He then stood in the center and took his oath to do his duty "to God, King and Country; to help other people at all times and to obey the Scout Law." Then the scouts paraded in the streets for about half an hour, halted, and sang the national anthem before disbanding.[104] It was not too long before De Jonge had become a district commissioner of the scouts, which gave him opportunity to travel throughout the district to meet with scout troops.

Chris De Jonge's brief career as a missionary was by all standards of measurement a happy time in his life. At the same time, he made a remarkably fine contribution to the educational and Christian needs of the people among whom he worked in Madanapalle. He had a genuine respect for the people and a way of winning their confidence. He went on to have a distinguished career as an educator in America.[105] Yet in hindsight one can see that, without casting any aspersions on all that he accomplished in Madanapalle, there was something unhealthy about the way the people in that city were so ready to elect him to tasks for which other persons in the town were also well qualified. De Jonge was the last such young man to be appointed to be the principal of a high school upon his arrival in India. In part, the Board of Foreign Missions found it difficult to recruit qualified young college graduates on a regular basis, but also the missionaries—with some prodding from the Indian representatives in the Arcot Assembly—agreed that it was time to look first to the growing pool of Indians who were qualified to serve as principals in the high schools.

The Boy Scout Movement in India

Chris De Jonge's involvement with the boy scouts was consistent with the Arcot Mission's support of the movement. In 1923 the Arcot Mission report provides the information that the movement

---

[104] Chris De Jonge to "My Dear Mother and Sis," November 17, 1921.
[105] A collection of some of his letters and papers together with a record of some of his later accomplishments are included in the Joint Archives.

was growing in interest and enthusiasm among the boys in the mission schools. It believed the boy scouts to be a worthwhile organization because it helped build character.[106]

The Boy Scout organization in India was not above criticism, however. It had been founded in 1908 by Baden-Powell, who had come to believe, on the basis of his experience with British young men in the Boer War, that the young men lacked discipline and self-reliance. During the years prior to World War I, the movement sought to inspire patriotism and to encourage the scouts to "be prepared" to serve their country and its empire in time of need. At the same time, it set forth an ideal of comradeship founded upon universal values of brotherhood and mutual understanding.[107]

When the movement spread to India, the government sensed the tension between the Baden-Powell notion of the British as an imperial race, with its implied contempt for "natives," on the one hand, and the scout's liberal ideal of multiracial harmony on the other. At first, the British Raj in India discouraged scouting on the grounds that it would expose Indian boys to potentially seditious "evil influences" that implied the equality of all men. Baden-Powell urged support of the Boy Scouts in India because he believed that Indian boys were "singularly without character by nature."[108] They were also lacking in training in a sense of honor, of fair play, of honesty, truth, self-discipline, and other attributes that make up a reliable man of character. In 1921, the government decided to support the Boy Scout movement as a means of checking the growth of rival organizations under the control of Indian nationalists.[109] The tension continued between the Boy Scouts' loyalty to the British Raj and its underlying liberal philosophy of universal brotherhood in character building. In 1938, a discouraged Indian scout movement severed its ties with imperial headquarters.[110]

[106] "BFMR," 1923, 57.
[107] Metcalf, *Ideologies of the Raj*, 219.
[108] Ibid.
[109] Ibid., 220.
[110] Ibid.

Although the Arcot missionaries were probably unaware that such policy discussions had gone on in the government, they were fully aware of the role of the Boy Scouts as an organization that not only built character but also fostered loyalty to the king and the British Raj. Participation in the Boy Scouts was encouraged throughout the Arcot Mission area. In 1922, it was reported that there were 268 scouts in the mission area. At that time, Chris De Jonge was serving as scout commissioner for the Chittoor District, and Lambertus Hekhuis of Voorhees College was serving in the same position for the North Arcot District. During the year, 157 of their cub scouts had gone to the city of Madras to greet the royal patron of the scouts, the Prince of Wales. Their participation

> meant a pledge of loyal citizenship in an empire that may be certain of its future. The scouts together with the cubs braved the petty difficulties that the non-co-operators stooped to perpetuate and courageously marched through the streets of Madras in honor of the Prince, Patron of India's scouts. Subsequently a new spirit for the movement has sprung up and while there are still large difficulties that face the movement it has secured such a footing that there is no danger of its losing its grip.[111]

It may be significant that, while the Boy Scout movement received significant inclusion in the Arcot Mission report in 1923, there is little if any mention of the Boy Scouts in annual reports sent thereafter jointly by the Arcot Assembly and the Arcot Mission. Boy Scout troops continued to exist in the area, but their absence from the reports may well indicate that the Indian representatives in the assembly felt some ambiguity about supporting the movement.

Urgent Issues in Village Education

As World War I was coming to an end, Indian Christians and missionaries agreed that the matter of improving standards of

---

[111] "BFMR," 1923, 57.

education was crucial to the future of the church and the land of India. The issue was especially crucial in the matter of village mission schools because the teachers in those schools often served as the catechist in charge of the congregation there. Government grants-in-aid for the school made it possible for the church to maintain leadership for the congregation as well. When a school was closed, it often meant loss of continuity in pastoral care and worship and could even lead to the abandonment of the congregation. In the changing conditions of India after World War I, it was inevitable that these issues would have to be faced regarding village mission schools.

In an article about education policy, Lambertus Hekhuis, principal of Voorhees College, used a vivid metaphor to describe the rising consciousness of nationhood in India at the end of World War I: "A mountain tumbling in great travail, throwing up dustclouds, and absurd noises, is visibly there; uncertain yet what mouse or monster it will give birth to."[112] He went on to say that the "increased attention on every hand to the trend of events augurs an awakening, potential of large progress in the advance of Christianity and of social consciousness, but likewise pregnant with poison of easy satisfaction and show, relying upon the appearance and unwilling to face the issues of truths's demands on individual action."[113]

Hekhuis recognized that during World War I India had taken some major steps toward industrialization as major industries were built up to sustain the empire's war efforts. He prophesied that in the near future young men would aspire not only to be the bureaucratic "clerks" for the Raj but that they would look toward employment in the production and distribution of material goods. These changes would require the government and the missions to think harder about the educational needs of India.

He suggested that the "township school" model for primary education in certain communities in the United States should be

---

[112] Lambertus Hekhuis, "The Birth of a Nation," *Mission Field,* October, 1919, 185.
[113] Ibid.

considered in India. That model contained two lines of school life, basic education and "practical instruction in some phase of livelihood," such as one or another of the industrial or agricultural arts and crafts.[114]

He also urged that more careful attention be given to the implications of the "Conscience Clause" being considered by the government. The Conscience Clause, if implemented, would mean that those students in the mission schools who had conscientious scruples against studying the Bible must be exempted from the requirement for such study. In the case of a school such as Voorhees High School and College, which had a majority of Hindu students who could apply for exemption, the clause could bring about a major change in the school's atmosphere. If the mission schools would not agree to exempt students from the study of the Bible, then, according to the Conscience Clause rule, the school would lose its government grant-in-aid. For Voorhees that loss would at least triple the amount of money required from the Board of Foreign Missions.[115]

At the end of World War I, these issues were still clouds on the horizon, rather than the storm overhead. Hekhuis's warnings were taken seriously, however, and for the next several decades much greater attention was given to improving education in the schools under the management of the Arcot Assembly. The Arcot Mission became the first mission in South India to set apart a person to devote full-time attention to re-evaluating and strengthening primary schools in the villages. The first missionary assigned to the task was J. H. Warnshuis, who served with great zeal and insight until serious trouble with his eyes forced him to return to the United States in early 1925. He was followed by Mason Olcott, who had arrived in India in 1915.

Warnshuis and Olcott each conducted a number of surveys to determine the nature of the problems that had to be faced in the

[114] Ibid., 188.
[115] Ibid., 189.

more than two hundred elementary village mission schools with more than six thousand pupils. Results of major statistical surveys were reported in 1923 and 1929, with fairly similar results. It was found that approximately 41 percent of the children in the villages with mission schools were actually enrolled in the schools. The Christian population had a somewhat higher percentage of 53 percent enrolled, with the percentage of boys higher than that of girls. At least 50 percent of the children in the villages were not enrolled in any school. The average daily attendance reported by the teachers was 74 percent of those enrolled, but visits by supervisors usually found only 60 percent of those enrolled actually present. In the 1929 survey, the percentage of Christian children enrolled had increased from 53 percent to 64 percent.[116] One encouraging note in the 1929 report was that in 71 villages, every Christian child of school age was in school.[117]

There were other statistics that caused concern. Literacy rates remained very low in the population at large. Nineteen percent of the population was literate, but the literacy rate was considerably lower in the villages than in the towns. "In as many as 161 villages it was found that there was not a single adult, man or woman, who could read or write. This may be partly due to the fact that those who can read or write often leave the village to find work that makes use of their ability."[118] One of the problems in encouraging literacy was that there was nothing to read in most of the villages. Moreover, the people who stayed in the villages did not see what advantage they gained by learning to read. "We have yet to discover in what way literacy benefits a village cooly or what use he makes of it."[119]

Another problem was that the children in school did not progress very far. Sixty-two percent of the children did not progress beyond the first grade. If they did not progress much beyond the second grade, they often forgot what they had learned and became illiterate

[116] For these statistics, see "BFMR," 1923, 61, and "AAR," 1929, 22.
[117] "AAR," 1929, 22.
[118] Ibid.
[119] Quoted from Warnshuis report in "BFMR," 1923, 62.

once more. It was not easy to solve the problem because parents did not encourage their children to remain in school. In fact they often discouraged attendance because the family needed the small amount of income the children could earn by working in the fields or tending animals. The low attendance discouraged teachers, who had to struggle to keep it up.

> (The problem) involves poverty, the ignorance of the people, and the difficulty of getting the unusual type of teacher who can work successfully in the very discouraging conditions of isolated villages, where his first task each day is to round up the children, and whose second task is to keep parents from taking the children out for work before the lessons have begun.[120]

When the Joint Conference of the Indian Church Board and the Arcot Mission met in 1923, it recognized that there were few issues facing it that were more urgent than that of the deplorable conditions prevailing in the village primary mission schools. As it dealt with some of the information in a preliminary report by J. H. Warnshuis, the conference came to two conclusions that are important to note here. The first was that the management of Christian schools was taking place in an environment different from what had previously been the case. Originally, the mission had been able to operate schools in the villages pretty much as it pleased with little supervision by the government. Following World War I, the government was taking considerable interest in the matter and moving toward a policy of compulsory education for all children. The second conclusion was that

> wherever Government is ready to take over the burden of providing elementary education, we should encourage it to do so. In the past this has been impossible. In the matters of girls' education and of the schools of the depressed

120 "AAR," 1929, 22.

classes, missionary bodies have been the pioneers for all India. The possibility of such education depended on us and us alone. That day is past, for here as in many other realms of thought, the vitalizing power of Christianity has made itself felt. Compulsory free education is yet far from being a fact, but it is the goal of Indian reform. Vellore introduced compulsory education in July 1922, being one of six towns in the whole Presidency to do this.[121]

The joint conference concluded that a three-year program should be set up to close some of the Christian schools in the towns and villages where the government was ready to step in. Teachers in the schools should be encouraged to take up positions in government schools or, if they wished, to continue the schools on their own personal initiative by charging fees and arranging with the government for continuing the grants.[122] At the same time, the joint conference looked to J. H. Warnshuis and those who were working with him to find ways to improve those schools that would continue to be under the Arcot Assembly's management.

In its recommendation to close some of the schools, the joint conference was acting on the perennial frustration that missionaries and Indian leaders felt with the inadequate quality of education in the schools, the lack of parental cooperation, and the low performance level of a number of the teachers. It was not too difficult for mission and church leaders gathered in a high-level joint conference to decide that it was not efficient to keep such schools open. The matter could appear in a very different light at the local level. There, pastors and pastorate committee members dealt with questions about how to maintain village congregations when such schools were gone. There, pressures developed to keep the schools open, both for the sake of the congregations and because, when a school was closed, the government alternative

---

[121] "BFMR," 1923, 33.
[122] Ibid., 34.

proved even less satisfactory. The value of the village schools as educational institutions and their place in the life of the church continued to be debated vigorously for much of the rest of the twentieth century.

Under the leading of Warnshuis and Olcott, several positive steps were taken to improve the quality of the schools. One step that they took in cooperation with the government was to encourage the establishment of "central schools." A central school was located on a plot of ground within a one-mile radius of several villages. The small schools in each of the villages were closed, and all the children would walk to the central school. The central schools made it possible for several teachers to work together and to encourage each other. They also made it easier to divide the children into ability and interest levels. These schools were also easier to supervise. Several of them were turned into "demonstration schools," where teachers in surrounding schools came to attend conferences on educational methodology and to observe good teachers at work with the children.[123]

Warnshuis and Olcott were introducing into the Indian environment a number of advances in educational management that they had seen in operation in the United States. While the central schools were urged as a replacement for the one-room school in each village, great emphasis was placed on the appointment of three or four supervisors for the whole area. It was the supervisor's duty to visit each of the schools and to encourage and assist the teachers to improve their educational quality. The supervisors were sent to visit schools in other areas in order to gain ideas that could be passed on to teachers as they visited. One of the hopes was that such cooperation between supervisor and teachers would make it possible, at least in the central schools, to strengthen vocational training suitable to village life. It was hoped that in their vocational periods of instruction, the children could learn to make bricks, tiles,

---

[123] "AAR," 1926, 38-39.

cotton tape, and many other articles, as well as to learn to tend the school flower garden.[124] On the whole, the teachers seem to have appreciated and profited from the increased support and encouragement they received in what had often been a lonely and somewhat thankless task. It is not surprising, however, that in some cases teachers were suspicious of the motives for appointing supervisors.

> Some teachers used to have the mistaken idea that the supervisors visited them merely to criticize and transmit bad reports. One supervisor tells how this attitude of suspicion and hostility was gradually replaced on successive visits by willingness to listen and then by glad welcome and keen eagerness for new ideas. [125]

However great the problems of the village schools may have been, there remained a basic confidence that much could be accomplished through them. In 1927, a dramatic production was presented at the South India Christian Endeavor Convention held in Vellore. The three acts portrayed the change of a "dirty school" into a "physically clean school" and then into a "spiritually pure school." The drama symbolized "the work of the Village School Department in changing the village through the school by flooding the minds and hearts of the people with God's sunshine, purity and salvation through the crucified Christ."[126]

During a decade when there was great concern about the state of the village schools, the Hindu girls' schools under the management of the Women's Evangelistic Council of the assembly were flourishing. Clara Coburn, who was living in Madanapalle, was also supervisor of the school in Punganur. She reported in 1929 that the headmaster and teachers were keenly alive to the opportunities they had in working with their 180 girls. Attendance was regular, and the

---

[124] "AAR," 1928, 23.
[125] "AAR," 1926, 40.
[126] "AAR," 1927, 21.

school was constantly growing more popular in the community. The school was making it possible for girls without much hope in life to look forward to a profitable career, since "among the girls there are several widows and deserted wives who are looking forward to careers as teachers."[127]

Ella Wierenga wrote a report in a similar vein concerning the school in Palmaner. The school enabled girls to live among friends of their own age and to benefit from the physical, social, and mental stimulation available to them that was not present in the villages. Ella Wierenga spoke of the girls' love for the school:

> That the girls love the school and are benefiting from education is exhibited by the case of some of the girls whose parents tried to arrange early marriages according to old custom. The girls pleaded they might remain in school until they were a little older and better prepared for marriage, and they are still in school.[128]

Equally enthusiastic reports were received in 1929 about the Hindu girls' schools in Chittoor, Vellore, Ranipet, Arcot, and Kaveripak. The schools also continued to enable zenana Bible women to hold contact with students after they had left the schools and become married. The 1929 report includes information about home visits in a number of places. It was pointed out that in Arni, for example, five Bible women were visiting women in 141 homes. While each home had at least one woman under instruction of some type, in almost every home there were at least half a dozen other women who gathered to sit and listen.[129]

Cooperation with Other Missions

The last of the major issues listed in the 1922 annual report was cooperation with other missions. That cooperation had become so

[127] "AAR," 1929, 24.
[128] Ibid.
[129] Ibid., 28.

extensive as to raise questions about whether the Reformed Church had overextended itself in India. Henry Scudder, who favored wide cooperation, nevertheless became discouraged when he saw cooperative activities flourishing while the Arcot Mission was having to cut back in its area because of a shortage of funds. This was having a detrimental effect on the evangelistic efforts in the area. He wrote,

> We are expanding outside of ourselves, but retrenchment is the repeated cry in regard to our own work. Men are being sent away from the care of our villages, children in our boarding schools are being dropped and only a limited number are being added; Hindu Girls' Schools are being closed and our evangelistic work is at a standstill for want of funds that are being devoted to other purposes. I hope all members of the Mission are not as discouraged as I feel these days.[130]

In its 1922 report, the mission recognized that the influence of the Arcot Mission was not limited to the field in which it had been planted. By that time, it had become linked with the work of other missions in a very complex manner. Its missionaries were much in demand elsewhere and at times were loaned to serve in other mission areas and to work in union institutions not directly under the control of the mission. The Arcot Mission was directly involved in providing grants to twelve union institutions, of which eight were located outside the Arcot Mission area. In 1922 the mission had received five additional distinct proposals for union activities with other missions. In terms of its size, the Arcot Mission may well have been engaged in more cooperative work than most or all of the missions then serving in India.

The problem was simply noted in 1922, without any attempt to resolve it. The Arcot Mission continued to live with the tension

---

[130] Henry J. Scudder to William Chamberlain, June 7, 1922.

between its specific calling in its mission area and the opportunities that could be met only through broad cooperation. It expressed its hope that in time the very nature of the cooperation would break through the tension. It wrote, "The great change which Indian thought and social institutions are experiencing at present, perhaps requires that mission societies should make their influence felt as a unit and it may well be that co-operation among Missions on a scale hitherto unconceived may prove a solution to many of our problems."[131]

By the end of the 1920s, the Arcot Mission had moved a long way down the road of devolution from paternalism to partnership. But the end of the road was not yet at hand. The issues that were recognized in the mission's report of 1922 had not faded away by the end of the decade. On the contrary, most of them had grown more urgent.

However, the decade ended with hope. The Board of Foreign Missions was in a stronger financial condition, thanks to prosperity in America, and there was peace in the world.

A new decade lay ahead, but in it hope would turn to depression, war clouds would once again hang over the world, and the call of Indians for independence would become ever more insistent.

---

[131] "BFMR," 1922, 30.

10

The Turning of the Times:
Toward Indian Nationhood

Can India be a Nation?

With the advantage of hindsight, we can see clearly that India was on its way to nationhood during the period between the two world wars. Nevertheless, whether India was or could be a "nation" was very much in dispute during that period. In fact, it was not and could not be a nation as defined by nineteenth and early twentieth century writers in the West. Such writers had maintained that in order to exist as a nation, people needed (1) a common language, (2) a proudly shared historical tradition, (3) a common religious tradition, and (4) a racial homogeneity. All of these were conspicuously absent in India. For this reason Ali Jinnah, who was the head of the Muslim League and was to be the first governor-general of Pakistan, claimed that India was not a single nation but that Hindus and Muslims were members of competing nations.[1]

The Indian National Congress, from its origin in 1885, had attempted to display the unity of the people of India by bringing into its annual meetings representatives from every geographical

---

[1] Embree, *Utopias in Conflict*, 60-61.

region and major religions. It had also welcomed the assertions of those persons who affirmed that there is an underlying unity at the core of all religions. Nevertheless, it remained subject to the criticism that the overwhelming preponderance of men in its leadership were Hindu and even Brahmin. Gandhi recognized that if India was to become a unified nation, the outcastes, whom he called *Harijans* ("God's people"), had to be allotted their full place and given their full rights as citizens.

Gandhi's Harijan Campaign and Opposition to Conversion

Gandhi opened his campaign for including Harijans fully into the Hindu community by starting an All India Anti-Untouchability League in September 1932, and the weekly paper, *Harijan,* in January 1933. He rode in third-class railroad compartments as a symbol of solidarity with the Harijans, and he campaigned for the abolishment of restrictions against their use of wells. He called for them to be given the right to enter temples, while advocating more humanitarian projects for them. He did not reject the caste system, however, and advised caution about interdining and intermarriage. One result of his caution was that the political leader of the Harijans, Ambedkar, resisted Gandhi on the grounds that "nothing can emancipate the outcaste except the destruction of the caste system."[2] By contrast, Gandhi's campaign to remove much of the discrimination practiced against the Harijans was welcomed among the Christians, most of whom were of the Harijan castes.[3]

---

[2] Sarkar, *Modern India: 1885-1947,* 328-29.

[3] This ambivalence about Gandhi's concern for the Harijans continued to be present among Christians after India became independent. For example, the Rev. M. Azariah, who in 1983 was general secretary of the Church of South India and later bishop in the Diocese of Madras, wrote:

> Just one generation after the passing away of the "Father of the Nation," his ideals are being forgotten by the educated and illiterate classes alike. Only a small band of economists and social workers are struggling to rediscover Gandhi's relevance for our national transformation. But, what are the reasons for the neglect so far of the Gandhian approach? Could it be because that in the *Gandhian system,* for all his identification with the rural poor and outcastes and untouchables whom he called the "Harijans" (people of God), these vast mass

Gandhi's challenge to his Hindu contemporaries to support the basic rights of the Harijans, provide for their uplift in society, and carry out more humanitarian work among them became a challenge to the Arcot missionaries and Indian Christians.[4] The two sides of the challenge appear in a sentence that Gandhi quoted from a Harijan named Sevak Sangh. He wrote, "The missionary propaganda bore fruit on account of the fact that the Harijans were extremely dissatisfied with their unbearable conditions and hoped to get rid of them by the change. The reasons, therefore, of conversions may be roughly described as economic or socio-economic."[5]

Gandhi's campaign on behalf of the Harijans intended, among other things, to make it unnecessary for Harijans to remove themselves from their unbearable conditions by converting to Christianity. The implicit charge that missionaries were using socioeconomic benefits to induce Indians to become Christians had some force, in spite of the missionaries' caution about accepting "rice Christians" for baptism. Gandhi's campaign had an impact. Christian village workers in the 1930s reported that Harijans were less likely to listen to the Christian message as Hindu caste people became more accepting of them.

The second challenge coming from Gandhi was his strong objection to the call for conversion and baptism in the name of Jesus Christ. He accepted conversion to the truth as a requirement

of over 200 million out of the 700 million people of this country—were condemned to their traditional "servitude" as the fifth caste (panchama), un-integrated and apart from the other four grades of castes within the Hindu Varnashrama Dharma which Gandhi wanted to be intact as a sacred social organisation?...But, as *Rabindranath Tagore* has asserted, unless the evil system of caste is abolished, there can be no salvation for the Indian society. And yet, we cannot deny the fact that the Gandhian approach is the most indigenous and people-oriented among the alternatives available to us. Hence the need for a serious theological reflection on Gandhian ideals in relation to the Christian faith by the Church in India [M. Azariah, *Witnessing in India Today* (Madras: United Theological Lutheran Churches in India, 1983), 71].

[4] For an Arcot missionary's evaluation of Gandhi's contribution twenty years after he opened his campaign, see Wyckoff, *A Hundred Years*, 90-91.

[5] M. K. Gandhi, "Harijan," June 6, 1937, in M. K. Gandhi, ed. Bharatan Kumarappa, *Christian Missions: Their Place in India*, (Ahmedabad, India: Navajivan Publishing House, 1941), 65.

for a person within his or her own religion, but he objected to conversion as a transition from one faith to another. In an address to a number of Indian Christians, he said,

> Conversion must not mean denationalization. Conversion should mean a definite giving up of the evil of the old, adoption of all the good of the new and a scrupulous avoidance of everything evil in the new. Conversion, therefore, should mean a life of greater dedication to one's own country, greater salvation to God, greater self-purification.[6]

He also stated:

I believe that there is no such thing as conversion from one faith to another in the accepted sense of the term. It is a highly personal matter for the individual and his God. I may not have any design upon my neighbor as to his faith which I must honor even as I honor my own. For I regard all the great religions of the world as true at any rate for the people professing them as mine is true for me.[7]

He called upon Christian missions to render true service to India:

> Christian missions will render true service to India, if they can persuade themselves to confine their activities to humanitarian service without the ulterior motive of converting India or at least her unsophisticated villagers to Christianity, and destroying their social superstructure which, notwithstanding its many defects, has stood now from time immemorial the onslaughts upon it from within and without.[8]

While missionaries and Indian Christians were in agreement with Gandhi that missions should render true service to India, they would have rejected his contention that conversions to Christ were

[6] M. K. Gandhi, "Young India," August 20, 1925, in ibid., 70.
[7] M. K. Gandhi, "Harijan," September 28, 1935, in ibid., 50.
[8] Ibid.

almost always basically for economic or social gain. In fact, those Harijans who were at that time converting to Christianity often found themselves in a less favorable position than previously. Not only did they have trouble getting employment from landowners, but they also lost certain educational prerogatives, such as scholarships, that would have been available to them had they not converted. They also remained suspicious of the sincerity of many of the followers of Gandhi, even if not of Gandhi himself. In the political realm,

> men in the communal basis of political representation do mean votes....The anti-untouchability movements and temple entry agitation are probably as much weapons in the hands of political agitators as they are means employed by the social and religious reformers to lighten the load of disabilities that have for centuries pressed the very life out of millions of depressed class sufferers.[9]

Gandhi's Harijan campaign reinforced the missionaries' growing realization that they had entered a new era in providing educational, medical, and industrial arts services in India, services that emphasized the needs of Harijans and impoverished Christians.

Twin Challenges: The Re-Thinking Missions Report and the Harijan Campaign

In the same year that Gandhi launched his Harijan campaign, 1932, a group of thirty-five Christian laymen under the chairmanship of the philosopher William Ernest Hocking, after two years of research, published a report, *Re-Thinking Missions: A Laymen's Inquiry after One Hundred Years*. Their report represented a challenge to the Reformed Church missionaries and Indian Christians at the same points as did Gandhi's campaign, but with the difference that the challenge was from a Christian rather than a Hindu perspective. The Laymen's Commission of Appraisal had five members from

9 "AAR," 1938, 15.

each of seven leading American Protestant denominations, including five from the Reformed Church in America. It had not included in its membership anyone who was affiliated with a mission organization. The commission's aim was to make an objective appraisal of the activities of the various missions on the fields in India, China, and Japan; to observe the effect of missions on the life of people in the Orient; and, on the basis of the first two, to offer recommendations concerning the future of missions.[10]

The Laymen's Commission wanted it to be clearly understood that in its project of rethinking missions, it was attempting to suggest future directions for missions, rather than to undermine or oppose missions. It affirmed that there is always a reason for mission because "there is always a valid impulse of love to men: one offers one's own faith simply because that is the best one had to offer….That these missions should go on, with whatever changes, we regard, therefore, as beyond serious question."[11]

The commission believed that in 1930 questions were being asked about missions that deserved a response. These questions were urgent not simply because the "nationals" of other countries or a number of people in Europe and America were asking them. They were urgent "by the turn of the times. Have these missions in some measure finished their work? Are there new channels for what they have been bringing? Is there a decline in their value to the Far East, in view of vast changes since their early days in the relations of peoples and the means of intercourse?"[12]

Re-Thinking Missions was a wide-ranging and detailed report. In broad outline, it wanted to reconsider missions on two basic points. First, it wanted to reconsider the relationship between Christianity and other religions, including the emphasis upon the atoning work of Christ as the one way of salvation. Specifically, the matter to be

---

[10] William Ernest Hocking, *Re-Thinking Missions: A Laymen's Inquiry after One Hundred Years,* (New York: Harper & Brothers, 1932), ix-xv provide information concerning the commission's procedures and aims.
[11] Ibid., 4.
[12] Ibid., 3.

reconsidered was the affirmation that there is just "one way of salvation and one only, one name, one atonement....it was committed to a certain intolerance, beneficent in purpose—in the interest of the soul it could allow no substitute for Christ. It came to proclaim truth, which is universal; but its truth was embodied in a particular person and his work."[13]

The second point that required reconsideration, according to *Re-Thinking Missions,* was the relation of the educational and other philanthropic aspects of mission to the work of evangelism. *Re-Thinking Missions* maintained that those aspects must be set free to be exercised in their own right, rather than as adjuncts to evangelism.

> We believe, then, that the time has come to set the educational and other philanthropic aspects of mission work free from organized responsibility to the work of conscious and direct evangelization. We must be willing to give largely without any preaching; to cooperate with non-Christian agencies for social improvement; and to foster the initiative of the Orient in defining the ways in which we shall be invited to help.[14]

The report went on to speak specifically about what should be the true nature of medical and educational missions:

> But the perception that the relief of suffering may be of itself a genuine interpretation of the Christian spirit, never absent, now increasingly if slowly wins its way. All that is an essential part of medical mission work will eventually be regarded as an end in itself, as one of the ways of liberating and enlarging life. And when this work is done "in the name of a disciple," the hospital, quite without any pressure of preaching and prayer in the wards, may be as truly a place where human and divine love are revealed as is the most religious sanctuary.[15]

13 Ibid., 35-36.
14 Ibid., 70.
15 Ibid., 71.

The truest type of education takes for granted that the spiritual quality should be interfused with every step of the educational process—interfused, not superadded. It comes into play best when it is present as an indefinable trait of life in the teacher and works all the time as an unconscious influence, an atmosphere which everybody breathes, a mode of interpreting that aspect of the world with which the teacher is dealing.[16]

The commission's report was "much discussed in the Home Church, as also on the mission field" in the year after it appeared.[17] The Board of Foreign Missions wanted the members of the Reformed Church as well as the missionaries to know that the report came from a number of mission-minded laymen, but that the board had given no money in support of the project and had been not been asked to take any responsibility for it. It had suggested to missionaries that they cooperate in the fact-finding activity of the Laymen's Commission.[18]

Since William Ernest Hocking, who chaired the commission, had played a very strong role at the 1928 Jerusalem Conference of the International Missionary Council, a number of positions in the laymen's report reflected positions already set forth in the 1928 conference. That conference had identified a Godless "secularism" as the enemy in the modern world. It set forth the thesis that, in the

---

16 Ibid., 71-72.

17 "BFMR," 1933, 4.

18 Ibid. Some of the Arcot missionaries resented what they felt to be the arrogance of the commission's assumption that it could make wide-ranging recommendations critical of the missionaries on the basis of brief visits to the fields. W. H. Farrar probably expressed what others were also feeling at a time when they had to deal with reduction in funds: "In the face of such difficult situations as we now face it is a pity that missionaries are such a poor incompetent lot as the famous Commission made us out to be....And we thank you especially that even if we are a bunch whose problems are too great for us, that we may feel that in our continued struggle to find a solution for some of them we have the confidence of those who know us, and we believe that you do know us better than any group of specialists who rush in and out and size us up on all sides by a glance of a day or two" (W. H. Farrar to William Chamberlain, January 17, 1933).

face of the growing secularism, the various religions of the world could regard themselves as friends defending the worship of God in opposition to the incipient atheism in modern life. In those same years, the battle lines were being drawn in American Presbyterian denominations between liberals, who held a position similar to that of Hocking, and conservatives, who wanted to sustain the theology of mission that had been articulated in the nineteenth century. The crucial point in the debate concerned the question of whether Christ was the only and unique way of salvation.

Leaders of North American missionary societies to which the Reformed Church related felt the need to respond to *Re-Thinking Missions* by reaffirming their commitment to the doctrine of the unique work of Jesus Christ. The Committee of Foreign Missions of the Western Section of the Alliance of Presbyterian and Reformed Churches met April 12, 1932. The committee, which included representatives of the Reformed Church in America, adopted a seven-point statement, "The Basis and Warrant of Foreign Missions." In it they reaffirmed their conviction in the uniqueness and universality of Jesus Christ as the way of salvation. Point 4 recorded:

> Their conviction that the uniqueness and universality and absolute significance of Christ and His Gospel must be unswervingly maintained by our Churches against all movements of syncretism or adjustment which compromise or imperil belief in the aloneness of our Lord Jesus Christ and the unique indispensableness of His Gospel and that nowhere save in this truth of Christ and about Christ is there any hope for the love and righteousness and power of redeemed human lives and a redeemed human society.[19]

The Arcot missionaries also wanted to go on record quickly to reaffirm their position "from which they have never departed...our belief in the absolute uniqueness of Christ and in the assurance that in none other is there hope of salvation....We are committed to

[19] Ibid., 1932, 6-7.

make Christ known to all as the only Way, the Truth, and the Life."[20]

The board returned to the theme in its 1933 report, when it reaffirmed the primary nature of the missionary calling to bear witness to the gospel. It stated:

> The missionary has received the revelation, and duty and privilege alike make him a witness. The primary duty of the missionary is to proclaim, both by word and deed, the Message he has received, but his marching orders carry him beyond that frontier; he must inevitably seek to lead others into the riches of the Revelation he himself has received. Fidelity to his own convictions demands this, and he surely owes it to the people he professes to serve to let them know that his supreme desire is that they might accept Jesus Christ and follow him. This aim seeks man's highest good as the Christian conceives it, and when the aim is followed under the compulsion of sincere and disinterested love it vindicates itself.[21]

Gandhi's claim that conversion should be a matter of turning toward the truth in one's own religion, rather than a change of community and faith from one religion to another, was closely related to his position that Jesus Christ was one who bore witness to the truth but was not to be considered uniquely to be the savior of the world. The missionaries vigorously defended their right and the necessity to call upon everyone to repent, believe the gospel, and be baptized in the name of Jesus Christ.

In chapter 11, we will consider this crucial matter in relation to the provision in the Constitution of India that guarantees the right to propagate one's faith and to convert to another religion. In this chapter, we will examine more carefully the response of the Arcot Mission and Arcot Assembly to the call to reconsider its humanitarian

[20] William Farrar to William Chamberlain, January 21, 1933.
[21] "BFMR," 1933, 5.

ministries in the fields of education, medicine, industrial and agricultural mission, and women's ministries.

Mission as Love and Compassion for Human Beings

Because of Gandhi's Harijan campaign and increased governmental interest in raising the levels of education and medical care, the Christian community was forced to improve the quality of its work in order to meet governmental standards. While the government in India was much more open to religious activities in institutions to which it gave grants than is the American government, it did not wish its grants to be used to support proselytizing intentions. Moreover, among the missionaries themselves, medical and educational personnel were beginning to question whether evangelism should always have the priority that the Arcot Mission had affirmed from the beginning.

Medical Work of Missions

The Board of Foreign Missions asked Reformed Church missionaries in each of its fields to study *Re-Thinking Missions* and report their conclusions to the board. The Medical Committee of the Arcot Mission met in June, 1933, and informed the board that the laymen's report failed to understand the real problems and needs of the people of India, and that its recommendations were ill-advised and superficial. The mission could not agree with the report that government subsidies should be relinquished, and it did not sympathize with the indiscriminate condemnation of smaller hospitals. These hospitals, the missionaries believed, enhanced Indian medical work "because they reach a need in the villages not otherwise met and because, under supervision of the larger hospitals they are of actual value in sending urgent and difficult cases to them and to the Government hospitals."[22] By defending the smaller

22 "Findings of the Mission Medical Committee on the Chapter MEDICAL WORK OF MISSIONS in *Re-Thinking Missions,*" June 5, 1933 (board secretary's correspondence file, Archives of the RCA).

hospitals, the medical committee was reaffirming the value of the medical work that was being carried on in places such as Wandiwash, Punganur, and Tindivanam.

Although they were not impressed with *Re-Thinking Missions,* the Arcot missionaries re-evaluated their justification for medical missions and what the nature of that work should be in the modern era. They remembered that, when Silas Scudder had begun his medical work in Ranipet, the purpose of the mission in starting a hospital was to break down opposition to the establishment of the Christian church in India through the ministry of healing. Once the church was well established, they thought, there would be no great objection if the government or other non-Christian organizations took over the burden of ministering to the sick. Now that that the church was well established and the government pronouncing itself ready to improve its medical services, the mission had to face the issue of whether to continue its medical mission.[23]

In his report on the Scudder Memorial Hospital in Ranipet to the Arcot Assembly in 1937, Dr. Galen F. Scudder, the son of L. R. Scudder, quoted the basic statement of the Christian Medical Association of India as the rationale for medical work in the life of the church. The statement reads, "It is our conviction that the Ministry of Healing is an essential part of the work of the Christian Church, whose mission it is to represent God as revealed in Jesus Christ."[24]

According to the new rationale, the care of the sick is an essential part of the whole Christian ministry. It should not be justified on the basis of its evangelistic intent but directly on its relation to the love of Jesus Christ for suffering humanity. Medical missions must be judged not simply on their effectiveness in bringing converts into the church. Their basic function is to show forth the love of God as revealed in Jesus Christ through the practice of medicine. Because the practice of medicine in a Christian hospital is done in

23 "AAR," 1937, 43.
24 Ibid.

the name of Jesus Christ, it remains important to help all who come to know the nature of the person in whose name it is done. As an institution working in the name of Christ, it must not hide the fact that it remains an evangelistic activity of the church.

The Scudder Memorial Hospital had set for itself the goal of proving to be the kind of Christian hospital which India needed in the "turn of the times." It had organized itself into a number of departments in order to meet efficiently a wide range of needs. Its department of medicine was engaged in treating diseases such as typhoid, malaria, dysentery, tuberculosis, and syphilis, which were prevalent in the area due to lack of adequate public health measures. It was also seeing large numbers of patients with anemia but was frustrated because it did not have financial resources to provide iron pills to people too poor to purchase their own supplies. Its radium institute had cared for sixty-five cases of cancer of the face and jaw and carcinoma of the cervix during the year, but most of the patients had come only when the cancer was too advanced to be cured. The obstetrical department was dealing with an upward trend of births in the hospital, while the department of surgery continued to be the busiest of all of the departments, in spite of the fact that the hospital had been unable to afford up-to-date equipment.

One of the major contributions of the hospital was its program for training nurses. The government of Madras was giving priority to hiring male nurses who had graduated from the hospital's school of nursing. One of its graduate nurses had just returned from rendering two years' service at the Reformed Church's mission hospital in Bahrain. As one of the leading schools of nursing in the Madras Presidency, it was "earnestly working and looking forward to the day when the nursing profession in India will reach the high standards it has reached in western countries."[25]

_____

[25] Ibid., 45. After 1937, graduates of the schools of nursing of the Scudder Memorial Hospital, along with similar schools in the Mary Lott Lyles Hospital in Madanapalle and the Christian Medical Hospital in Vellore, would be very much in demand in the hospitals of the Arabian Gulf. As a result, they were not able to supply a sufficient number of nurses for the hospitals in the Arcot Mission area.

Re-Thinking Missions had been critical of the "one-man hospital which the non-medical members may praise, but which the Commission feels should not be tolerated."[26] It also lacked enthusiasm for roadside medical clinics (such as those Dr. Ida Scudder had conducted each Wednesday) because it was impossible to maintain high standards of cleanliness, diagnosis, and treatment of the masses of people who appeared. The Arcot Mission Medical Committee believed that this criticism was superficial in its failure to understand the real problems and needs of the people. For that reason it continued to support Dr. Margaret Rottschaefer in her medical work until 1956, when she retired and was replaced by Dr. Susheela Ponniah, who had received specialized training in the treatment of leprosy.

Margaret Rottschaefer had first come to India in 1909 as a teacher, but at the end of her first term of service she took a medical course to become a doctor. After working for a time in Vellore Medical College and then in a mission hospital in Arabia, she came back to India to fulfill her desire to do village medical work. For a time she camped and toured through the Eastern Circle in the area, teaching the villagers about sanitation and health and attending to their ills, taking a Bible woman with her on her tours. In 1933 she moved to Wandiwash and established a dispensary in a rented house in town, with a nurse to help her. After some time, she gave up the rented dispensary and had a simple building erected on the church compound. She preferred to live in a tent rather than a house. After several years, she permitted the mission to erect a building around the tent, with the result that she lived in a simple home with a quality all its own, consisting of a inner tent surrounded by a screened, verandah-like living space. Later she also built two simple little houses for in-patients. In 1935, she began to drive out once a week for a roadside clinic.

On her return to India in 1938, after a furlough year in the United States, Rottschaefer began to take in obstetrical cases. At first no

[26] *Re-Thinking Missions,* 203.

one would come except in case of extreme need, but after a time she was able to do considerable prenatal work. In the last year of the full functioning of her dispensary she had over two hundred in-patients, of which seventy-seven were maternity cases. At the same time, she was receiving an increasing number of calls for roadside centers, especially for the treatment of leprosy. The need for such work became so great that she turned over her dispensary work to the small government hospital. In her roadside work, Rottschaefer came into contact with several hundred villages and found herself treating and administering medication to sixteen hundred leprosy patients each week. Since adequate drugs had not yet been developed for the treatment of leprosy, such treatment was probably more effective in relieving some of the symptoms of the disease than in treating the disease itself. Nevertheless, in an era when persons ill with leprosy were often rejected by those around them, her loving care was undoubtedly precisely what they needed.[27]

Few types of medical care require such dedication and love as does leprosy care. Because the nerves in various parts of the body become anesthetized as a result of the disease, patients suffering from leprosy do not feel the pain of cuts and blisters. Consequently, they do not treat their sores, and often gangrene sets in. Doctors and nurses are then faced with the terribly unpleasant task of taking off self-wrapped, unclean bandages, which when removed give off offensive odors and reveal gruesome wounds. Since most persons suffering from the disease are impoverished, very few patients can pay for any services. One can sense the dedication of Rottschaefer to her patients, as well as her sense of her work as a witness to the gospel, in this description of her work:

[27] For the above sketch of the work of Dr. Rottschaefer, see Wyckoff, *A Hundred Years,* 103-104. For an excellent account of the development of leprosy treatment and reconstructive surgery and rehabilition under the leadership of Dr. Paul Brand in association with the Christian Medical College in Vellore and the leprosy hospital at Karigiri near Katpadi, see Dorothy Clarke Wilson, *Ten Fingers for God* (New York: McGraw-Hill Book Company, 1965).

During the year 15,506 injections have been given to lepers, besides many intradermals and a large number of ulcer injections. Many burns, abscesses, wounds, ulcers and bone infections have been taken care of. This kind of treatment always impresses the people because they themselves would not lift a finger to help take care of such offensive conditions....We feel that the importance of the work is not valued in numbers treated but in the personal contacts which have been possible from day to day. We aim to make all our work serve the main purpose of preaching the gospel....We have tried in every way to heal the sick, cleanse the lepers, and preach the Gospel to the poor.[28]

Rethinking Education

The Arcot Assembly, under the leading of J. H. Warnshuis and Mason Olcott, had already been paying close attention to the need for strengthening the village schools. As one reads the chapter, "Education: Primary and Secondary," in Re-Thinking Missions, one senses that the report was influenced to some extent by some of the research of Mason Olcott. In its emphasis on improving the quality of the village schools and closing those which were below standards, it points in the same direction as do the earlier reports of the Arcot Assembly.

There is no record of any response to the report from the educational personnel of the mission and no reference to Re-Thinking Missions in the education sections of the Arcot Assembly reports. Re-Thinking Missions itself twice includes footnotes that commend the series of small books written by Reformed Church missionary Alice Van Doren. That series, the report suggests, "might easily, as it grows, amount to a traveling normal school built without bricks and mortar. It provides at one rupee each such books as 'Fourteen Experiments in Rural Education.'...Mr. Olcott has

28 Arcot Co-ordinating Committee Report, 1941, 52-53.

also added to the series, 'How We Learn,' by Professor William Kilpatrick."[29]

With regard to the Arcot Assembly's purpose in continuing to manage high schools and colleges, John De Boer, principal of Voorhees College, spoke of the relationship between educational and evangelistic goals. He understood evangelism to consist of the general influence of Christian education on the thought of the educated Hindu public more than the conversion of individuals. He pointed out that eighteen hundred of the three thousand students in the Arcot Assembly's eight high schools and one college were Hindus. Then he wrote, "Thus, while our primary purpose in higher education is to furnish the best type of Christian education that we can give to the youth of our Christian community, a second important purpose is an evangelistic one. The influence of our Christian schools upon the thought of the educated Hindu public has always been one of our most powerful evangelistic agencies."[30]

Five years later, in 1937, De Boer once again wrote about the purpose of Christian higher education, more specifically about the mission of Voorhees College. He used some of the language of the Jerusalem Conference of the International Missionary Council and of *Re-Thinking Missions* to contrast true religion with the advancing secularism in India. He wrote that Voorhees College

> is dedicated to the principle that religion is responsible for creating a higher moral and social order throughout the world. Our college was founded because of the conviction that Christianity has a world mission and that religion must be at the heart of true education. Secular education must always fail because it does not have at its heart the deep, eternal motives that true religion alone can foster.
>
> Here in this land of deep spiritual experience and quest we need the opportunity and freedom to help each other to

[29] *Re-Thinking Missions,* 135n; see also 132n.
[30] "AAR," 1932, 24.

the highest possible expression that the soul of India can find. It is our conviction that this expression is impossible apart from Christ, and that our main task is to interpret Him,—the meaning of his life, death, and resurrection. To that task may we rededicate ourselves.[31]

De Boer then went on to speak with great appreciation of the revision of the rules for elementary education which were being introduced into the Madras Presidency by the government's Department of Public Instruction. The government had decided to implement some of the proposals of the so-called "Wardha Scheme," which was set forth in a conference in the Indian city of Wardha. The conference at Wardha had endorsed M. K. Gandhi's proposals for "basic education" through the local vernacular language linked with manual productive work. Gandhi had enough popular appeal to force the government to implement his ideas on education in India in spite of the fact that many persons in the Indian National Conference did not favor them.

While embodying interesting ideals of simplicity, reduction of differences between mental and manual labour, and schools becoming self-sufficient through sale of their own manufactures, basic education never really became a viable alternative to conventional schools or colleges, and the link with cottage crafts was felt by many to be an unrealistic and archaic Gandhian fad.[32]

Despite the lack of enthusiasm for Gandhi's philosophy of basic education on the part of some of the members of the Indian National Congress, John De Boer was not alone in the Arcot Assembly in his appreciation of the government's position that the prevocational and vocational sides of education ought to be stressed more strongly than ever before. De Boer also commended the

[31] "AAR," 1937, 36.
[32] Sarkar, *Modern India*, 357.

government for its interest in encouraging the raising of cotton and of teaching the processes of manufacturing cloth by hand methods.[33]

In spite of the government's advocacy of elements of the Wardha Scheme, the new rules promulgated by the director of public education were not as helpful as had been hoped. Government grants, which had been gradually decreased since 1930 by an amount of Rs. 10,000, appeared likely to be reduced again. Although the Arcot Assembly had also gone on record that inefficient small village schools should be closed, experience had shown that where such schools were closed, the children of Christian families often had no alternative place to go.

Mason Olcott had learned that these children were generally not welcomed at the District Board schools. Government orders against caste discrimination were largely unheeded. The situation was perhaps the most serious challenge that had faced the congregations in the villages for eighty years. The village mission schools were being squeezed out by the new rules of the Department of Public Education. "The new popular Government, which is overwhelmingly Hindu, does not look on Christian teaching in school so favorably as the British officials used to do."[34] The result was that the Arcot Assembly believed it necessary to continue to make provision for the elementary education of the children in many villages. A further difficulty arose out of the practice of appointing village teachers as catechists. After the village schools were closed and the teachers gone, additional catechists had to be appointed to serve those villages.[35]

One other factor in the implementation of new approaches to education must be noted. At the Wardha Conference, Gandhi had insisted on prohibition of the manufacture and sale of alcoholic beverages. The missionaries and Indian Christians welcomed his influence as an ally in their opposition to strong drink. Drunkenness had been one of the most common reasons for disciplining

---

[33] "AAR," 1937, 37.
[34] "AAR," 1937, 17.
[35] "AAR," 1938, 16.

members of the church. The Reverend S. Ponnurangam, chairman of the Vellore Circle, praised the government for introducing prohibition: "A great boon has come to this area with the introduction of Prohibition in the North Arcot District. The Church and the Circle have welcomed the new innovation most heartily and have rendered every possible aid to its success. The Circle chairman and several other leading members of the Christian community were enlisted as members of the District Prohibition Board."[36] The Reverend H. E. Van Vranken, chairman of the Eastern Circle, also welcomed prohibition. He reported that people's lives were better for it. "Better dress, more food where hunger was before common, and happy homes have followed naturally on this great change."[37]

Unfortunately for the cause of education, taxes on alcoholic beverages were one of the major sources of income for the government. Thus the introduction of prohibition laws in the Madras Presidency militated against advances in education of the presidency's children. Hopes dimmed for receiving increases in government grants for education to keep abreast of the times.[38]

At the end of the 1930s, Arcot Christians gave mixed reviews concerning their village schools and their hopes for the future. Arcot missionary C. R. Wierenga was rather pessimistic. He saw that the government was changing the membership on its committees for the administration of schools in such a way that the missions would no longer be represented. He believed that public opinion was turning against mission schools because of the actions of "unscrupulous politicians." Moreover, "as disseminating centers of Christian influence they are not especially favored by another growing element of non-Christians who though fully appreciative of the service that is being rendered in the secular sphere are progressively more vocal in their assertion that so far as they are

[36] "AAR," 1939, 13.
[37] Ibid., 11.
[38] Ibid., 11.

institutions of foreign religious bodies they need not and ought not to lay claim to Indian help."[39]

On the other hand, the Reverend A. Ratnam, chairman of the Central Circle, reported that, while the government rules for elementary schools were exacting, they had helped raise the general tone of the schools in his area both in efficiency and in attendance. As a result, the schools had received a higher government grant. He concluded:

> It must be said to the credit of the teachers, most of whom are not very highly qualified, that they rose equal to the occasion and worked ungrudgingly to meet all the requirements of government, not merely in the progress of the children but also in properly keeping the records, which involves considerable clerical work. The good work done has attracted more children to our schools, in some places even in preference to their own caste schools, with the result, that we have had to employ four additional teachers.[40]

As the Arcot Assembly entered the 1940s, it had a sense of the direction it would like to see elementary education take. It remained to be seen whether the resources and the will would be forthcoming to meet the needs of the elementary schools.

Women's Education in a Changing World

From 1875 to 1946, when the Woman's Board of Foreign Missions merged with the denomination's Board of Foreign Missions, the Woman's Board steadfastly made it possible for the Arcot Mission to carry on a strong program for the education of girls and young women in India. During that period, the schools supported by the Woman's Board sought to improve the status of women in India and often proved to be pioneers in encouraging new avenues of service and in curriculum development.

[39] C. R. Wierenga to F. M. Potter, Secretary, Board of Foreign Missions, July 21, 1938.
[40] "AAR," 1939, 15.

Sherman High School

Over the course of the decades, the way in which the schools articulated their purpose went through considerable change. The first school for girls and young women, the Female Seminary in Vellore, was begun in 1855 with the purpose of training young women to become educated wives for the catechists and teachers who were employed by the Arcot Mission. By 1924 the purpose for providing an education for girls in the new Sherman Memorial Girls' High School in Chittoor was much broader and more ambitious:

> The purpose of the school is to give to the girls of the entire region a Christian education, which includes the building up of the body by exercise and hygienic living, the expansion of the mind through the acquirement of knowledge and the cultivation of the power to think and the establishing of character through the adoption of the ideals of Christ whose motto was "not to be ministered unto but to minister."[41]

[41] Chamberlain, *Fifty Years*, 228-29.

As it was becoming more apparent at the end of the 1930s that India would become an autonomous dominion within the British empire, or perhaps even an independent nation, further development took place in purpose statements. Esther De Weerd, missionary manager of Beattie Memorial Training School, the women's teacher training school in Chittoor, described the goals of the school in 1938:

> We have tried to make them teachers. Yes, but more than that. We want them to stand for the highest type of Indian womanhood. They have had a taste of the new freedom which is coming to Indian women today. We have tried to teach them to use that freedom with modesty and dignity. We wish them to be strong Christian leaders in whatever community they may be.[42]

The school's graduates were taught that they were called to play an important role in the growth of the nation. Esther De Weerd wrote, "Last year twenty-four of these students left us as teachers to join the ranks of India's nation builders, for isn't that a teacher's task?"[43]

Since the village primary schools in which boys and girls studied only went through the fifth grade at most, the Arcot Mission had developed a network of separate boarding schools and boarding homes for boys and for girls. Because there were government schools for boys but not for girls in some of the towns, boys from the village could be accepted into a boarding home while attending school in the town, as was the case in Chittoor. As time went on, the Arcot Mission established its own middle and high schools for boys in Madanapalle, Tindivanam, and Vellore.

---

[42] "AAR," 1938, 26.
[43] "AAR," 1940, 52. The use of the phrase, "nation builders," by De Weerd in 1940 is significant, as it indicates a change in missionary attitude toward Indian independence. After 1947, the conception of Christian participation in nation building helped shape the nature of Christian activity in India.

Since there were no suitable schools for girls, the girls' boarding homes were always related to the mission boarding schools, which were structured especially to meet the needs of the girls in the boarding homes. Such schools were ready to admit day scholars from the town as well. Village girls who entered boarding homes lived under a strict discipline in a confined environment. The boarding home was usually situated in a large mission compound surrounded by a wall. This arrangement insured a relatively clean and healthy environment, with space available to enable the girls to engage in recreational activities and sports. The girls were often also given responsibilities, such as helping raise and harvest vegetables from the garden, or other duties related to the needs of life on the mission compound. At the same time, they were not allowed to leave the compound except under supervision in groups.

When women were granted the right to vote in the Madras Presidency, Alice Van Doren and Charlotte Wyckoff believed that the girls in the boarding school in Ranipet should be taught how to exercise their responsibilities of citizenship. A constitution for the boarding school was adopted with a system of three courts. All cases of discipline in the boarding school were tried before the lower court of justice, composed of four teachers chosen by the girls and four girls in the home. Cases were tried following regular procedures and sentences decided by the court, with the right of appeal to the next higher court if the sentence was felt to be unjust. Ruth Scudder, the missionary in charge of the Girls' High School in Ranipet, observed, "We feel that the girls' growing dignity, sense of responsibility and fine discriminating justice are signs that self-government is a power for the character-development of which India is so much in need."[44]

The Female Seminary, which had been opened in 1855, was split into two different schools in 1895. The lower grades became the Primary Girls' School for Tamil girls and was located in Ranipet. The Chittoor Girls' School was established for the upper grades. It

[44] "BFMR," 1922, 57.

had two divisions, the middle school and the Normal class, which soon developed into the training school for teachers. Margaret (Mrs. James) Beattie was the missionary in charge of the schools in Chittoor. Margaret and James Beattie were originally from Scotland, where she had received her training in the field of education. Margaret Beattie continued to manage the school until her retirement in 1921. She and her husband had spent time on furlough in the United States in 1914-1915 and successfully raised money for a new building for the training school. They sailed on the ocean liner, *Lusitania,* for the first leg of their return voyage to India. As they entered into the waters off the coast of England, a torpedo from a German submarine struck the ship, and it quickly sank. James Beattie was drowned. Margaret Beattie was rescued and returned to India. When the new building was opened in 1919, the school received the name which it bears to this day, the Beattie Memorial Training School [45]

With the need to strengthen women's education to meet rising governmental expectations, the Ranipet Girls' School became a high school in 1919. The upper grades still used the English medium of instruction, since there was as yet little Tamil material available for courses such as physics and chemistry. In 1922 a new site for the school was purchased in Chittoor. That became the site of the Sherman Memorial Girls' High School, which opened in 1924.

The building and grounds plan for Sherman Memorial was a pleasant change from other girls' boarding schools, which usually consisted of a large hostel building in which the girls lived and a building attached or unattached for classrooms. The Sherman school grounds followed the Indian model and included a large inner courtyard, with light and airy classrooms, science laboratory, library, and large hall built around the central court. An innovation was that the girls stayed in cottages of the Indian bungalow type, each one designed for twenty girls and a resident teacher. The girls

[45] Chamberlain, *Fifty Years*, 223-25.

in each cottage were responsible for taking care of their own cottage, including planning meals and keeping accounts. The Ranipet system of self-government was continued in the new school.[46] The Sherman Girls' High School was intended for Christian girls, but a number of Hindu girls desired to attend and be a part of the boarding experience. The result was that one of the cottages was designated for Hindu girls, who were allowed to cook their own food and thereby maintain their own good standing in the Hindu community.

Re-Thinking Missions recognized that, in view of the great disparity of educational opportunity between girls and boys in India, there was little question of the continued need for mission girls' schools and colleges. In the year the Layman's Commission made its survey, it found that only 10 percent of the girls had access to schools, while 49 percent of the boys did. At the high school level, 50 percent of the schools in India were mission schools; 56 percent of the girl students were in mission schools. Forty-eight percent of the teacher-training schools for young women were under the management of missions, with 53 percent of the students attending.[47]

Re-Thinking Missions did report several concerns about what was happening in mission schools. One concern was that there was a great danger of westernization. The girls, the commission feared, were becoming educated in customs of western dress, amusements, and sports; in foreign forms of worship, music, and art; while lacking an appreciation of Indian values and customs. The hope expressed in *Re-Thinking Missions* was that the increase of Indian leaders in positions of higher responsibility would help solve the problem. A second concern was that the girls were segregated from normal community life while they were protected in the "purdah"-like atmosphere of a boarding school.[48] A third concern was that not enough attention was paid to the preparation of Indian girls for their life situations after they left the school, since most of them

46 Ibid., 229.
47 *Re-Thinking Missions,* 258-59.
48 Ibid., 263.

would become married and find their future careers in homemaking. The report worried that too much focus would be on the needs of the small minority who were preparing for further studies, such as teacher training.[49] *Re-Thinking Missions* did not want these concerns to imply that it was opposed to boarding homes. On the contrary, "The very great value of the boarding school, in developing Christian character, is by no means underestimated."[50]

Since most of the girls in the boarding homes came from the Harijan or *cheri* sections of villages, where they were usually married as soon as they reached puberty and had access to a very limited range of Indian culture, it is difficult to know how the boarding schools could have operated much differently from the way they did. The parents of the girls would not have trusted the girls to the boarding homes if there had not been a wall around the compound area for security purposes. Although the boarding homes may have seemed to have a "purdah"-like atmosphere to persons of western origin, many of the high-school girls regarded their time there as an era of freedom prior to being kept more closely confined to the home after marriage.

The third concern was well recognized by those who were in charge of the boarding school and home. Mary Chamberlain, who had served in India from 1891 to 1906, had often been asked "whether these Indian girls are not in some respects unfitted by education for the more humble and practical duties of daily home life, after they become wives and mothers."[51] This question, of course, was being asked in many areas of the world, including the United States, in the years following World War I, as people faced the question of the value of high school and college education for women.

Mary Chamberlain's response was that it was true that many of the young women who had spent eight or nine years in a boarding school often did find themselves at a disadvantage when they

49 Ibid., 260.
50 Ibid., 263.
51 Mary Chamberlain, *Fifty Years in Foreign Fields,* 83.

returned home. On the one hand, a girl was not so unfit for the home as some suggest. Girls in the boarding home in Chittoor were all taught to cook. "They did all the kitchen work by turns. Two of them for three days at a time left their classes, donned their working clothes and pounded rice, ground raggi, prepared curry-stuffs and cooked and served the meals."[52] But Chamberlain believed that the advantages for any girl far outweighed the disadvantages:

> She has become a wage earner, a bread winner. Her life is no longer circumscribed between four walls. Her brain is henceforth to count as well as her hands. Her heart, too is in tune with her head and hands. Whether as a teacher, training the children of other women, or as a mother, intelligently rearing her own, she is a strong uplifting factor in her community.[53]

The concern that the boarding schools and boarding homes were in danger of westernizing the girls was part of a much wider issue facing the Arcot Mission throughout its existence. Gandhi had raised a similar concern when he charged that converts to Christianity had become "denationalized." However, as was noted in the previous chapter, after World War I indigenous Indian cultural forms were intentionally introduced into the life of the Christian community. Indian forms of preaching, such as the kalachapam, along with use of the Tamil language and rhythms in the music of worship, were being used. Churches began to be built using Hindu and Muslim architectural forms. Ashrams were opened in Chittoor, Vellore, and Kodaikanal.

The girls' boarding schools began introducing Indian music into their curriculum in 1920. Sara Zwemer[54] had spent part of each of her vacations in Kodaikanal studying Indian music and was using

---

[52] Ibid.
[53] Ibid.
[54] Sara Zwemer and her husband, Theodore F. Zwemer, arrived as Reformed Church missionaries in India in 1923. Theodore died of typhoid fever in 1925. Sara continued to serve as a missionary in India until her retirement in 1961.

her knowledge to lead the girls in the boarding school in Madanapalle
to a better appreciation of India's musical heritage. Further
Indianization was taking place there by adding good Indian pieces
to the school's art collection.[55] Indian music had also been introduced
into the curriculum in Ranipet.

> We have taken lessons on the violin as well as on the Indian
> hand harmonium, and have lately added a veena to our
> school orchestra. The girls are becoming nationalistic in the
> constructive sense of the word. They are full of ideas for
> making the church service more oriental and hence more
> attractive to Hindus and are deeply desirous of giving their
> lives in Christian work for their country.[56]

Such attempts at indigenization could serve, however, to draw
attention to how much the culture of the Christian community had
been influenced by the western ways of the missionaries. Sunday
schools, Christian Endeavor societies, congregational singing in
worship, presbyteries, all eating together in Holy Communion, and
democratic forms of church life were all foreign to Indian culture.
Elementary schools, high schools, training schools, and colleges
were also foreign imports, as was the practice of modern medicine.
One of the problems in dealing with the issue of westernization
is that it is interwoven with the emerging modernization of the
world. The western world had already gone through the process of
modernization as it emerged out of the middle ages and especially
after age of the Enlightenment of the seventeenth and eighteenth
centuries in Europe. India became caught up in that same process
in the nineteenth century, especially through the growth of English-
language education and other contacts with the western world. The
missionaries, with their ideas of democracy and freedom, with their
technological marvels such as bicycles, magic lanterns, typewriters,

55 Sarella Te Winkel, *The Sixth Decade of the Woman's Board of Foreign Missions, 1926-1935*
    (New York: Woman's Board of Foreign Missions, 1935), 54.
56 "BFMR," 1923, 68.

and eventually motor cars, as well as with their modern medicine and education, were clearly a powerful modernizing and westernizing influence in India.

The concern about westernization, on the part of *Re-Thinking Missions,* and denationalization, on the part of Gandhi, found their validity in their rebuke of western arrogance. Westerners repeatedly and insultingly criticized the cultures and customs of other peoples as being rooted in superstition, ignorance, and sin, in contrast to the superiority of western culture and western religion. Missionaries could not answer these charges adequately in words, but only with new humility, sensitivity, and open hearts and minds to learn from those among whom they lived as guests in India. After independence, the major burden of dealing with the charges would fall on the Christians of India who, by virtue of becoming Christians, could not avoid accepting the legacy of western Christian missionaries.

While they were raising the standards of education for women in the Arcot area,[57] the Arcot missionaries and the Woman's Board of Foreign Missions had recognized the need for a college and a college-level teacher-training school. There, graduates of the schools in Ranipet and Chittoor could continue to pursue their studies. It was beyond the resources of the Arcot Mission to establish such schools within its area. Therefore, it cooperated with several other missions in founding the Women's Christian College in Madras in 1915 and the Teacher Training College, later named St. Christopher's College, in Madras in 1923. In the beginning, Alice Van Doren was loaned for a year to be principal of the Training College.[58] The mission continued to make annual grants to these two institutions until well after India became independent.

---

[57] In this chapter we are dealing especially with the Tamil-speaking area. The final chapter will look once more at education for girls and young women in the Telugu language area.

[58] Chamberlain, *Fifty Years,* 233-34.

Women's Social Service Centers

At the beginning of the 1920s, women's work in the Arcot area took a new turn when three of the women missionaries opened social service centers as a supplement to the zenana work, which had been going on for many decades. Annie Hancock, who had been appointed a Reformed Church missionary in 1900, had worked in Vellore and its surrounding area for two decades when she decided to open a women's social center in Vellore. By that time, she had gained an intimate knowledge of Indian women through her work with schools, visits with them in the zenanas, and through the Bible women who were visiting over four hundred homes in Vellore. As a close friend of Ida Scudder, Hancock also had made friends with many women while they were patients at the Mary Taber Schell Hospital. She became concerned about the isolation in which Hindu and Muslim women lived and believed that it was time to help them develop social relationships with other women and at the same time learn to take an interest in others who were less fortunate than themselves. The social service center provided an opportunity for them to come out of the seclusion of their homes to work and play and meet together.[59]

Annie Hancock rented a house in Vellore and persuaded Hindu, Muslim, and Christian women to join together in a "Social Service Society," which had the purpose of finding ways in which the women could help other women. She also invited good speakers to give lectures, planned musical programs and special programs for Christmas and Easter. Classes in sewing and English and other subjects were offered.[60]

Elizabeth Conklin, who had arrived as a missionary in 1916, opened a social service center in Chittoor and located it in Gridley School, so it could be open only in the evenings and on Saturdays. A British officer's wife headed the Red Cross Branch of the social

[59] Wyckoff, *One Hundred Years*, 73.
[60] Ibid.

center. Although the center there started somewhat slowly, it happened that the women of high caste who became active at the center then carried on much of the work of a "baby welfare center," which was started by the municipality. The social service center had helped them overcome their caste prejudices to the extent that they were ready to bathe and feed untouchable babies.[61]

Lavina DuMond Honegger arrived as a missionary in India in 1910, after marrying Henry Honegger, who had been serving in the Arcot Mission since 1907. Henry died of cholera in 1914, but Lavina remained to serve as a missionary in Ranipet and Vellore until she retired, after which she continued to live in Vellore until her death. She opened a social service center in Ranipet shortly after Hancock had opened hers in Vellore. She had rented a house in town and used the bottom floor for the social service center while she lived in the rooms above. The center sought to serve men as well as women. It provided space for Hindu women who conducted Red Cross meetings and made garments for the mission hospital in Ranipet. There were embroidery classes, entertaining programs, Bible classes, and Christian religious services especially designed for Hindu women and children. The center also had a reading room which was available to men.[62]

After Annie Hancock died of cholera in 1924, Lavina Honegger went to Vellore to continue the work there. Hancock had been in the process of erecting a building for the social center when she died. Honegger saw to the completion of the buildings in 1933. The center's main building was in a two-story Indian style with rooms surrounding an open courtyard in the center. The downstairs was for meetings and activities of various kinds, including a dining area. Since the center was also intended to be an ashram where women could come to stay for a time, the upstairs had rooms for guests as well as the apartment for the missionary. A beautiful chapel was also built in the style of a Hindu temple, with stone pillars, with no

61 Ibid., 72-73.
62 "BFMR," 1923, 76-77.

Womens Social Services Center, Ranipet

outside wall on three sides, and a Communion table in the place
where the idol would have been placed in a Hindu temple. It had
a *goparam* ("tower") in the shape of the lotus as a symbol of the
beauty of Christ's salvation, which lifts human life out of the mud
below. Lavina Honegger stated her hopes for life in the ashram:

> The name, "ashram" is a household word in the East and
> stands for a home of fellowship, prayer and peace. Of
> course, we have not yet attained all that our name indicates,
> but there has been an honest attempt to attain unto the
> ideal. There have been rich experiences of friendship,
> keeping in touch with old friends and making new ones.
> Since January a dear Hindu sister has taken up her residence
> with us, and we hope and pray for many more of her
> type....The social service work has reached out to touch
> many homes in the town.[63]

The Vellore ashram also managed the ashram higher elementary
school, which had a daily attendance of 250 pupils and a waiting list.

[63] "AAR," 1932, 49-50.

A number of the girls were already widows or married women. The school required high commitment from its teachers, who served on a "sacrificial basis" with low salaries. The ashram and its school represented a major attempt to bear witness to the gospel in a way that gave full respect to Indian life and culture. In 1934, Honegger reported,

> We have builded a temple to the Glory of God, and we are glad that the Hindu women together with the children enjoy worshipping in it. The Hindu people tell us that we have made a real contribution to the spiritual need of the people. Our daily chapel and religious meetings are Indianized as far as possible, and the people enjoy the simplicity of these gatherings.[64]

Rethinking Relationships and Self-support in an Era of Economic Depression

The year 1932 was not only "the turn of the times" in light of Gandhi's Harijan campaign and the Re-Thinking Missions report, but also because in that year the full impact of world-wide economic depression was felt. The impact on the Indian economy was catastrophic. The price index declined by 50 percent, and Indian exports declined proportionally. The Reserve Bank held the rupee at an artificially high rate in relation to sterling, which led to a further drain on India's foreign exchange balances. As people began to feel the impact of the depression, labor unrest became a serious problem. A number of major strikes took place, and Communists gained in influence.[65] Resentment against British rule was on the rise, with the result that when Gandhi began his "salt campaign" and his famous walk to the sea to manufacture his own salt from sea water, masses of people joined in his civil disobedience campaign.[66]

[64] "AAR," 1934, 41.
[65] Sarkar, Modern India, 258-60.
[66] Ibid., 284-96. Gandhi's "Salt Satyagraha" can be understood as the Indian equivalent of the American colonialist's Boston Tea party, although Gandhi's impact was the greater.

The impact of the Depression in the United States was equally heavy upon the income of the Board of Foreign Missions. Its receipts fell from $450,000 in 1930 to $265,000 in 1932. Its deficits during those two years totaled $71,958. Moreover, when America went off the gold standard in early 1933, the cost of foreign exchange rose and placed an additional burden on remittances overseas. Given its financial position, the board also believed it had no alternative but to inform its overseas mission and church partners that its appropriations would be stated in terms of American dollars with no adjustment for shifts in foreign exchange rates. This meant that the entire risk of increases in unfavorable foreign exchange rates would be taken by the mission overseas rather than by the Board in America.[67]

Due to the shortfall in income, the Board of Foreign Missions was forced to make drastic cuts in its appropriations to the missions. The reductions in appropriations forced members of the Arcot Assembly, including the Reformed Church missionaries, and the Board of Foreign Missions to face a number of complex and delicate issues. Among these issues were (1) whether older missionaries should retire early in order to make it possible for younger ones to return to India; (2) how the Arcot Assembly could reduce its number of workers and its activities with a measure of justice and without undue disruption of its work; (3) the relation of the cost of support of missionaries to the cost of support for Indian workers and mission work costs; (4) the authority of the mission in relation to the authority of the Arcot Assembly; (5) to what extent the Arcot Assembly favored the continuing appointment of missionaries; (7) the role of institutions in relation to the self-support of the church; and (8) in the relationship between the Arcot Mission and the Board of Foreign Missions, which was ultimately responsible for setting policy. We will now look more closely at this complex web of issues.

[67] "BFMR," 1933, 6.

The reduction in contributions to the Board of Foreign Missions in 1932 meant that the total number of Reformed Church missionaries had to be reduced by ten. Some missionaries on furlough in America were encouraged to seek other work. Among Indian missionaries affected by this decision were the Reverend Cornie A. and Francis De Bruin, who remained in America to serve the Reformed Church in Westfield, North Dakota, for two years. Funds permitted them to return to India in 1936. At first it seemed that Ralph and Anna Ruth Korteling, who were on furlough, would also have to remain in the United States. Missionary salaries were to be reduced by 8 percent in 1933, in addition to reductions of previous years. The appropriation for mission work, which covered salaries for Indian workers and for all types of work on the field, was reduced by 20 percent or more, in addition to the 15 percent reduction of the previous year.[68] These 1933 reductions were to be followed by additional reductions in succeeding years. The net result was that the appropriation that in 1933 had still been Rs. 200,000 for mission work, exclusive of missionary costs, had been reduced to Rs. 80,000 by 1936.[69]

Reformed Church missionaries in India were alarmed as they began to hear about the severe drop in contributions. Two of the older missionaries offered to retire early in order to enable the board to send the younger families back to India. Henry J. Scudder, who was known for his unselfish dedication, wrote December 14, 1932, to the board offering to resign so that the Kortelings could return to Punganur, where Anna's medical services were needed alongside Ralph's pastoral and evangelistic leadership. Scudder's plan was that he would retire in India, where he would voluntarily contribute his services. The board secretary, William Chamberlain, was reluctant to accept the offer but promised to place it before the board's executive committee.[70] W. H. Farrar followed Scudder's letter with

68 Ibid.
69 De Boer, *Story of the Arcot Mission*, 16.
70 William Chamberlain to H. J. Scudder, January 12, 1933.

his own offer to retire at the end of the year, since he was sixty-two years old. He said that it was important to have the younger men on the field and that C. A. De Bruin was more likely to be able to give many years of service.[71] Ultimately, the board allowed both L. R. Scudder and Henry J. Scudder to retire. Both of them remained in India to give voluntary service.[72]

The Arcot Assembly struggled with how best to manage the severe reduction in appropriations. Tindivanam High School, Scudder Memorial Hospital, and Voorhees College all agreed to go on total self-support by increasing fees to meet their loss of income. All of the Hindu girls' schools were placed on a self-supporting basis with the understanding that several of them might have to close. Eight Bible women were recommended for retirement and pension, eleven were reduced to half time, three to one-fourth time, and two were dismissed. All the other Bible women received a 15-percent cut in salary in addition to any previous cuts.[73]

In spite of the salary reductions, many of the Bible women and teachers continued to work with increased dedication. One of the Bible women in Arni, for example, gave most of her time to the lowly village women

> who toil from early morning until night for their existence, with a short rest during the heat of the day. The Bible woman visits them in their homes whenever possible. At other times she goes where they are at work in the fields and teaches them while they are resting. She assists them in times of sickness and troubles, night or day, and a change is slowly taking place, for the women and children look more tidy and are more friendly.[74]

When the Arcot Assembly had placed all the Hindu girls' schools on a self-supporting basis, it had implied that the schools could

[71] W. H. Farrar to William Chamberlain, January 17, 1933.
[72] "BFMR," 1934, 22.
[73] "AAR," 1933, 41.
[74] Ibid., 42.

continue by raising the fees of those enrolled. This proved difficult to accomplish, both because in an era of depression the families in India were also suffering from a shortage of income and because in some places there were government schools available that did not charge fees. This was the case in Punganur, which had recently been able to renovate its building and install a beautiful playground after receiving a special gift from the Woman's Board of Foreign Missions. It had good equipment and well qualified teachers. But the school was able to continue only because of the self-sacrificial service of the teachers.

> In connection with the self-support plan introduced in August, an effort was made to get fees from the children, but so far without success. It is true that the people of Punganur are poor, but if it were not for the fact that no Government or local school requires fees, we might after a while collect some. As it is, the parents know they can send their children to another school without paying fees, so why pay? Consequently the teachers elected to reduce their own salaries instead of risking the loss of pupils by demanding fees. The teachers are working now on 30 per cent less than they had last December....Although the little girls who attend our school might learn to read and write in a Board School, we believe we are teaching them much more than that. We try to put into their hearts a new idea of life as they may see it in Jesus. [75]

The Arcot Assembly's decision to discontinue financial assistance for the Hindu girls' schools contains within it old questions arising out of the original Arcot Mission policy that schools should be established only for the children of Christians. The different perspectives of the men and the women of the mission regarding the schools had continued to exercise their force.

[75] Ibid., 49.

As everyone related to the work of the Arcot Assembly was suffering from the impact of the budget cuts, Indian workers began to ask whether the missionaries were bearing their share of the burden. Indians had learned that missionary salaries were being cut back by 8 percent, while the salaries of most of the Indian workers had been reduced by far larger percentages. They suspected that it was not so much the Depression as the missionaries themselves that were behind the budget cuts. C. R. Wierenga wrote concerning a conversation he had with a young man,

> He was very frank and open and revealed the fact that behind all their thinking there is the suspicion, little short of conviction, that in the last analysis it is not so much the depression as the present missionary force which is ultimately responsible for the cuts....I told him that we were sharing the burden by receiving a living allowance reduced by 30 to 35 per cent over that of 1932, varying from time to time by the fluctuation of exchange. I have convinced him that the cuts are due to conditions in America, so difficult is it to overcome the belief that missionaries can still get money if they have the will to get it.[76]

The situation was complicated further when the Budget Allotment Committee presented its recommendations to the special meeting of the Arcot Assembly September 21, 1934. The budget committee had presented a budget that it hoped would keep most of the work intact and offer employment to the largest possible number of present employees, but it still had to include a number of additional reductions in salary or pension for some persons. The members of the assembly refused to accept the committee's report but instead voted that accrued interest of the "Jubilee Fund" be used to meet the remaining anticipated deficit for boarding schools for 1934. This action side-stepped the basic budget issue for the time being.[77]

[76] C. R. Wierenga to William Chamberlain, August 8, 1934.
[77] C. R. Wierenga to William Chamberlain, September 26, 1934.

Some of the missionaries had objected to using the accrued interest of the Jubilee Fund, which had been raised from contributions in the amount of Rs. 75,000 in honor of the seventy-fifth anniversary of the founding of the Arcot Mission. The fund had been established for the purpose of furthering the education of poor and deserving Christian children, especially those from the villages. In the vote that was taken, the missionaries tended to be on one side of the issue and the Indians on the other.[78]

The recommendation to use accrued interest from the Jubilee Fund raised yet another fundamental question. When the Arcot Assembly had come into being, one of the missionaries had spoken of the move as "the suicide of the mission," because henceforth financial and other decisions concerning the mission work were to be in the hands of the Arcot Assembly rather than the Arcot Mission. Yet the mission had remained the incorporated body; therefore, it was constitutionally the body legally responsible for integrity in use of funds. Since the Jubilee Fund was a restricted fund lodged with the mission, the question was whether the mission should not overrule the assembly in the case of the Jubilee Fund interest.[79] But if it were to do so, then it would be seen as claiming ultimate financial power to which the assembly would be subordinate. Since only the missionaries were members of the Arcot Mission and Indians were in the majority in the assembly, it would appear that the missionaries wanted to keep control in their own hands after all.

Between September, 1934, and the annual meeting of the assembly in January, 1935, the Board of Foreign Missions was consulted about its interpretation of the rules concerning the use of the accrued interest of the Jubilee Fund. The board had also heard hints that some Indian leaders preferred that no new missionaries be appointed for the time being in order to make more money available for Indian workers. The board responded that it did not

[78] Ibid.
[79] Ibid.

believe any breach of trust was involved in using the accrued interest as the assembly had voted, although it doubted "the expediency of such action." Nevertheless, it also recognized that the severe adjustments to the budget also made it important that there should be "the most sympathetic possible consideration of individuals" affected by the reductions.[80] The assembly accepted this interpretation of the board. It also heard a report from the assembly's executive committee concerning the history of the fund. It then requested the Arcot Mission to act as the custodian of the fund, so long as it was annually renewed by the assembly. It accepted that the purpose of the fund was to continue to be for the education of poor and deserving Christian children, especially those from the villages.[81]

Prior to the January, 1935, meeting of the Arcot Assembly, the Board of Foreign Missions had asked how seriously intended were the comments about not sending missionaries in order to provide more funds for Indian workers. In response to that question, the assembly placed in its minutes a letter of appreciation, which it voted to send to the board. Regarding its feelings about missionary personnel, it included the following paragraph:

> We fully appreciate your illuminating remarks on our words on Missionary personnel. It is far from the minds of the Indian members of the Assembly to prevent missionaries from coming out here. Not to speak of anything else, it is a most privileged association and comradeship we have had with them. Our suggestion merely meant to see whether a denial to a very small extent of that privilege would not open a way at this critical time for adding to the income for work. Your letter has now opened our eyes to the real situation and to the danger lurking in an expectation of that kind.[82]

[80] Minutes of the Arcot Assembly, 1935, 16-17.
[81] Ibid., 9-10.
[82] Ibid., 20.

Some grounds for Indian suspicions that the reduction in appropriation from the Board of Foreign Missions was not simply due to the recession can be found in the board's feeling that the assembly was too hesitant to explore possible ways to meet the pastoral needs of villages with fewer employed workers. The board was concerned that every new village was a permanent financial liability and that this was a limiting factor on the growth of the church. Board secretary William Chamberlain asked,

> Would it be not be possible for one well equipped young Indian, with heart aglow for service, to act like the old circuit riders in the early days of building up the church in America, for say ten villages, coming into the village on frequent visits and bringing possibly greater inspiration and uplifting power than one man in each village perhaps less equipped, and would it not be possible for such a one to depend for his maintenance upon the village churches to which he ministers?[83]

Chamberlain also commented that he was concerned because mission institutions and salaries had come to be looked upon "as permanent factors and that a great part of the life of the Christian community has been built around the steady work and income that these institutions furnished....[with the result that] any discontinuance of service presents personal elements that make the decision very hard."[84]

In raising these questions, Chamberlain undoubtedly knew that he was bringing the pressure of the Board of Foreign Missions to bear on complex and delicate issues that neither the Reformed Church missionaries nor the Arcot Assembly could face on their own. The assembly had become a large and unwieldy body by 1934, consisting of all forty-four of the Arcot missionaries and sixty-five

---

[83] William Chamberlain to John De Boer, corresponding secretary, Arcot Assembly, January 10, 1934.
[84] Ibid.

Indian members. Almost a hundred percent of the Indian members were employees of the assembly as pastors, catechists, teachers, Bible women, or similar positions, on the one hand, or employees of one of the other institutions, on the other. Chamberlain was seeking a way to decrease the heavy dependency relationship between the Board of Foreign Missions and the Arcot Assembly. Such dependency could be overcome only when the church had moved farther down the road to self-support and when the Arcot Mission was no longer regarded as the primary employer in the Christian community.

The Institutes for Economic Development

A self-supporting church in the United States was defined as a congregation in which the members themselves were able and willing to meet all of the expenses necessary to maintain life together. These included paying for pastoral services, the maintenance of the congregation's property, and meeting other costs of operating church programs. Many people would also want to include in their definition of self-support the ability to provide funds to strengthen the congregation's mission outreach both locally and globally. It was the local congregation rather than the classis or presbytery or conference that was responsible for meeting such costs.

American missionaries carried this concept of self-support with them to India. They did not explore seriously the ways in which churches in other centuries had been able to meet their financial needs. Roman Catholics, with their long history, had found other ways to sustain financial viability. At times, that church had encouraged people to contribute fees for the services of the priests at times of baptisms, weddings, funerals, and other significant life events. It sold candles for votive offerings and private masses, received offerings from people on pilgrimages. In Protestant Europe after the Reformation, when the civil authorities felt responsible for the maintenance of public worship, the government met many of the expenses of the church, such as payment of ministers' salaries and maintenance of buildings. In England and Europe, nobles and landowners often established their own private chapels and set up endowments with income to sustain the ministry at the chapel, and sometimes the local village church as well. Bishops rather than local congregations were ultimately responsible that the priests in the diocese received their salaries.

Missionaries in India were frustrated because the methods used in America and Europe for the self-support of the church were not working in India. They could not and would not appeal to the government for help in supporting the ministry. There were no members of the noble class available to provide large endowments. Because almost all of the Christians came from the lowest social and economic classes of society, their contributions to the expenses of the church were adequate only in rare cases, even when the people contributed willingly. The missionaries often complained that the people could give more, but, at the same time, they agonized over the fact that Christians lived in such abject poverty that they had nothing to spare. One of the innovations to encourage self-support was the annual harvest festival offerings, but this was but one small step on the way to self-support. William Chamberlain's encouragement, mentioned above, to consider employing fewer paid village workers can be regarded as another attempt to reducing the expenses of the church.

Over the decades, Arcot missionaries hoped to find ways to help village Christians improve their economic circumstances. They found land on which some could settle and grow their own crops. They fought in the courts for the economic and social rights of the lower-caste Christians. They encouraged children to get an education. After 1886, some of the missionaries began to explore ways to assist boys and girls to learn crafts that would enable them to increase their incomes throughout their lifetimes. The missionaries believed that these efforts would not only raise family incomes, but also that family contributions would increase and help the church become self supporting.

The first such effort had been teaching boys crafts as part of their primary education (see chap. 6). Reformed Church missionaries John Conklin and Lambertus Hekhuis had seen that Christian boys would not be able to learn crafts and trades because they were barred from such apprenticeship by reason of their caste. They advocated opening industrial schools where boys could learn rug-weaving, carpentry, weaving, blacksmithing, and other trades. They also agreed that such courses could eventually become self-supporting by selling the products made by the boys.

When the Arcot Assembly came into being, it established an economic board to act under its direction. That board was responsible chiefly for addressing the economic conditions of the Christian church in the area. The assembly acknowledged that earlier Arcot missionaries would not have foreseen such a board as a possibility, but times had changed. The Christian church rejected the fatalism that had for so long held India in its grip. The assembly accepted the doctrine that progress is a law of life, and that it was necessary to further economic progress in the life of a church in order to nurture self-government and self-support. The Arcot Assembly indicated the direction in which it wanted the economic board to foster the economic progress of the Christian community and the self-support of the church:

> The Indian Christian Church under God's blessing has by its rapid growth outgrown the financial resources the mother Church in America has been able to place at its disposal. It almost seems that financial assistance will be the limiting factor in the growth of the Church in the near future....Therefore the task of fostering and developing ways and means by which our Christian Community may be able and willing to assume contributing a larger share of the necessary finances for the work primarily is the objective

of the work carried on under the auspices of the Economic Board.[85]

Three institutions operating under the economic board played a major role in providing leadership in economic development of the Christian community and in encouraging a program of financial stewardship which would enable the church to become self-supporting. They were the Women's Institute at Palmaner, the Katpadi Industrial Institute, and the Katpadi Agricultural Institute.

The Women's Industrial Institute, Palmaner

The teachers in the girls' schools at the turn of the century were concerned about the young girls who did not show aptitude in the studies for becoming teachers and who were therefore returned to their villages, where they remained idle. In 1902, Ethel (Mrs. L. R.) Scudder volunteered to open a lace class for such girls. She had learned the art of making lace while on a visit in China. There were ten girls in her first class, and they stayed in the Scudder home in Ranipet until a building of their own could be secured. Using thread imported from England, they made ninety-three yards of lace in six weeks, of which eighty-two yards were sent to America to be sold. In 1904, the class size was increased to twenty-two, of whom two were personally supported by Ethel Scudder because the mission had allowed for only twenty in its budget. The goal was to make the lace class self-supporting. In the first six months of 1905, its income did exceed its expenses; the lace sold for Rs. 360 and expenses were Rs. 325.[86]

The lace class gained recognition from the government as a school and was able to increase its enrollment. By 1914, there were forty-three girls on its roll, and thirty-seven of its graduate outside workers continued making lace to supplement the family income. The lace workers earned from thirty-three cents to three dollars a

[85] "AAR," 1925, 65-66.
[86] Chamberlain, *Fifty Years*, 96-97.

month, amounts sufficient to make a difference in the standard of living of the family.[87] The lace class had proved its value by "giving (the girls) a means of earning a livelihood, grounding them in the first principles of Christianity and teaching them the much needed lesson of the dignity of labor and or true independence."[88]

Meanwhile, in 1912-13 the area around Palmaner was suffering from plague and famine. The Christian community had all moved into the mission compound to protect themselves from the plague. They remained there for three months in temporary sheds and held elementary school outside under the large tree. Julia Scudder, a daughter of Jared W. and Julia Scudder, was the only missionary located there in that period. While the people had nothing else to do, Julia saw an opportunity when a weaver appeared one morning and begged for work. She got him to agree to teach weaving to the people on the compound. By the time the rains came and the people could go back to their homes, a weaving industry had been established, and it became part of the Arcot Mission's industrial work for women program.[89]

In 1916, there were forty-two girls in the lace class, and many others had been refused admission because of lack of room. It was then decided to move the lace class from Ranipet to Palmaner, where it could grow under the leadership of Julia Scudder, who was already helping people enter the weaving industry. The curriculum would grow to include sewing, gardening, weaving, and basket making, as well as Bible lessons, reading, writing, and arithmetic. It took several years for the plan to be implemented, but in 1923 the move to Palmaner took place, and the lace class became the Industrial Home for Women. Alice Smallegan, who had arrived as a missionary in 1920, was placed in charge of it. She stated the threefold purpose of the Industrial School, "namely, to train and teach girls to make better homes, to cook, to sew, to be clean, to manage well, though poor: to train girls and women in a trade by

---

[87] A woman teacher at that time could earn approximately $3.50 a month (ibid., 242).
[88] Ibid., 159.
[89] Ibid.

Girls' sewing class, Women's Industrial Institute

which a livelihood may be earned: to carry on extension classes for
former students and any women desiring our aid."[90]

Smallegan went on to describe the school's facilities, which had
been renovated by the workers from the Katpadi Industrial Institute.

> We have for our own what is known as the Palmaner-Parry-
> Property; a large bungalow. Just what it was used for is hard
> to guess but we are told a treasury, offices and living
> quarters had laid claim to it. It serves us well, for in it we
> have three large, airy and spacious school rooms. These
> take up but two-thirds of the building. The remaining part
> is a most comfortable home for the lady in charge. This
> huge bungalow is far from being the best part of our school.
> Just back of it within four walls stand four double cottages.
> This small model village is the home of the girls....Each
> ["family" of six or eight girls] has its own front yard, a
> verandah, living-room, kitchen and store-room. Their
> backyards are adjoining and you ask, "Is there not danger

[90] "AAR," 1923, 112.

of family quarrels?" Oh yes indeed, but it is well thus, for the
girls leave the school to live even more closely with folks
with whom they have not so much as a common interest.[91]

The Layman's Commission, in *Re-Thinking Missions*, criticized
missionaries for giving inadequate thought to what happened to
girls who returned to their homes to be married after leaving school,
rather than becoming teachers or nurses. However, the development
of the Industrial Institute for Women indicates how the Arcot
Mission had been working at a solution to the problem in the three
decades preceding the publication of the report.

The Women's Industrial School became one of the most
important ways in which the people in the villages could be helped.
Most educational and vocational endeavors resulted in young
people leaving the villages and moving to towns in the hope of
finding jobs and more convenient living. The Women's Industrial
School was successful because its training made young women very
desirable as wives. Graduates of the school were able to use their
new skills to earn money in their own homes, and, by virtue of their
study of the Bible, Christian education, and worship, they often
became leaders in women's fellowship societies in their villages.

During the first ten years in Palmaner, many of the girls who came
from village schools had only a third-grade education, because that
was where the village school ended. In 1934, the government
refused to allow the Women's Industrial School to admit girls with
less than a fifth-grade education. When the school protested, the
government relented on the condition that the industrial school
itself would teach the fourth and fifth grades to such girls. This
meant that girls often boarded at the school for a total of six years.
During that time they received courses in sewing and drafting,
embroidery and design, drawing, child care, cooking, and care of
poultry and goats in addition to basic academic studies. At the
completion of their time at the school, they received certificates

91 Ibid., 112-113.

entitling them to be cottage workers earning money at home for sewing, embroidering, and doing cross-stitch work for the institute's extension department.[92]

The school developed a social service project in cooperation with members of the wider Palmaner community. Mina Jongewaard, who served for many years as director of the industrial school, had learned that girl day scholars in the mission school had very irregular attendance records because older children often had to stay home to take care of younger brothers and sisters while their mothers went out to the field to earn a little money to buy food. She proposed that a baby welfare center and "creche" (day-care center) be opened under the management of a local board of townspeople. Girls in the industrial school would go to the creche each morning to help bathe the children, prepare breakfast for them, and generally gain practical experience in child care. After the creche opened, the enrollment and attendance in the mission's day school improved a good deal.[93]

The school taught the girls how to raise vegetables and at the same time was able in good years to harvest a major portion of the vegetables needed for the girls' meals. The year 1935 was a good one, and the school reported harvesting a plentiful supply of tomatoes, beans, radishes, pumpkins, beets, various Indian vegetables, and peanuts.[94] Drought was only one of the hazards that could bring about the loss of a crop. As the time for harvest drew near, girls had to take turns doing guard duty against the encroachments of animals. The 1939 report gives an impression of what was required to harvest the crop.

> Work in the gardens has been carried on as regularly as possible, but the failure of rain at the right time has caused much discouragement. For some days the peanut fields looked as though they were practically dried up but when

92 "AAR," 1935, 48.
93 "AAR," 1934, 34.
94 "AAR," 1935, 49.

at last rain came a good part of this crop revived amazingly. Periodically, not less than once a week, great armies of monkeys descend upon our gardens and fields and rob us of the fruits and vegetables unless they are discovered in time and driven away.[95]

The Katpadi Industrial Institute

The Katpadi Industrial Institute is the oldest of the three industrial institutes in the Arcot mission area, and, in the early years, its predecessors were located in Ranipet and Arni. W. H. Farrar arrived as a missionary in India in 1897 and was soon made the manager of the school and "factory" in Arni. Later he proposed that Katpadi would be a better location, because the railway junction there made it easier to transport materials and completed products. The move to Katpadi took place in 1914. Benjamin Rottschaeffer became manager and remained related to the institution until 1955.

A primary goal of the Katpadi Industrial Institute was to enable the underprivileged boys whose families had become Christians to grow into economic self-reliance and thereby to grow in self-respect. It also hoped that as its graduates' incomes increased, they would increase their contributions to the church, enabling it to move toward self-support. In the beginning, the boys and their parents preferred that they be given a classical education in order to prepare for teaching or for clerical jobs with the government. By the 1930s, however, the number of village boys who wished to be enrolled in the institute's school and learn a trade or skill had become much larger. In 1936, for example, there were 120 boys enrolled in the school. But, "today we could easily obtain 300 lads who seek their first chance to rise above the low level of poverty and spiritual degradation that surround them in the villages. We try to do good to these under-privileged of the household of the faith. Little or no other opportunity is offered them."[96]

[95] "AAR," 1939, 35.
[96] "AAR," 1936, 42.

The industrial institute believed that even more important than teaching village boys a set of skills in areas such as carpentry, blacksmithing, and mechanical arts was the building of character, self-respect, and self-reliance.

> Our primary aim is not to produce mechanics, but to train boys for life, to give them right attitudes and ideals. Character is built on discipline and we believe that steady, intelligent toil provides one excellent form of discipline. But boys do not work for the joy of working—at least not until they get a taste of the joy of creating something....When a boy produces something worthwhile, something good to look at, possessing money value, he sets a higher value on himself,...Honest labour discourages a dependent spirit; it develops self-respect and self-discipline.[97]

In contrast to the Women's Industrial Institute, which expected most of its graduates to return to their villages after they left the school, the Katpadi Industrial Institute recognized that most of its students would not return to their villages. They would most likely gravitate to the country's commercial centers, where the demand for their skills was growing. The simplicity of village life would not be able to absorb their new skills. The industrial institute anticipated that its "work therefore contributes only indirectly to village improvement and that only in so far as family attachment prompts those earning better wages to help their less favoured village relatives." [98]

Just as the Women's Industrial Institute became known for the high quality of its cross-stitching, so the Katpadi Industrial Institute gained a reputation for excellent craftsmanship by producing high quality rosewood furniture, which the institute sold throughout India and to people in other countries. It was allowed to operate a commercial department as a business separate from the other

[97] "AAR," 1926, 72.
[98] "AAR," 1925, 68.

activities of the institute. The commercial department developed other activities apart from its production of furniture. Ben Rottschaefer's knowledge of building construction enabled the institute to serve as the building contractor for the many new building required by mission institutions between 1930 and 1950. In the 1920s Rottschaefer also acquired a Ford dealership, which continued to be operated until conditions changed in World War II. The course in auto mechanics proved very attractive to students during the years prior to the war because it opened to them the possibility that they could become drivers for commercial firms or private individuals. Missionary Ben De Vries described how the boys made progress in the mechanics course:

> Another smaller group of students you will find in the motor section. Beginners will be getting their first lessons by dismantling and assembling one of the old cars kept for the purpose but soon they are busy on road cars with instructors and experienced mechanics. American and European makes with imported or locally made bodies cover the pits. The blacksmith shop near at hand frequently lends a hand to straighten out fender bumps or bent chassis. A spray paint plant takes care of finishing the surface.[99]

From its beginning in the nineteenth century, the Arcot mission had always hoped that the industrial institute would become self-supporting through the sale of its products. This dream was largely realized between 1925-1947. Profits from the commercial department were used to help underwrite the costs of running the school in the hope that any subsidy from the Board of Foreign Missions could be kept as small as possible. In 1936, while the impact of the depression was still being felt, Rottschaefer reported.

> The Industrial school is not only a place of training for the under-privileged lads but also a place of employment for

[99] Arcot Coordinating Committee Report, 1941, 64.

many so trained. We have our commercial section attached
to the school. Our workers, trained in our school, establish
Christian homes in a neatly-kept Christian village and thus
help make the church strong and help the spread of the
'Blessed Gospel.'"...But for our commercial section we
should have to receive large annual subsidies for our school
and church work here....We have not sought and shall not
seek, unless forced to do so by the depression, financial
support from our American friends.[100]

The Katpadi Agricultural Institute

On the fiftieth anniversary of John and Henriette De Valois's
arrival in India to develop an agriculture institute, John looked back
at the attitudes he encountered when they arrived in 1920. The
dominant attitude among village farmers who sent their sons to the
boarding schools to further their education was that their sons
should later be employed in "white collar" or teaching jobs. That
attitude had begun to break down, to the extent that the industrial
institute was teaching crafts that enabled young men to get jobs that
let them reach a higher economic level than their parents had
enjoyed. But teaching boys to do agricultural work seemed to many
to be a backward step. De Valois remembered being confronted in
those early days by an irate pastor who said,

> What is all this nonsense of wasting money on agriculture
> or Rural Missions. The mother church in America has sent
> us wonderful missionaries in the past—Preachers,
> Evangelists, Doctors, Nurses, Teachers. They redeemed us
> from the village. Now attempts are being made to push us
> back into its filth and dirt and degradation. Let us put a stop
> to this absurdity!"[101]

[100] "AAR," 1936, 43.
[101] J. J. De Valois, "Message," *Golden Jubilee Souvenir, 1920-1970* (printed by the Agricultural
Institute, Katpadi, 1970).

John De Valois had received his degree in agriculture from Iowa State University, one of the leading institutions in the field of agricultural studies. He also had studied the role of agricultural cooperative societies, which were improving the capacity of farmers in America to have access to credit and to strengthen their role in the planting, marketing, and harvesting of crops. He had studied rural sociology and understood how local farmers must cooperate in the wider trends that set direction in a country as a whole. After his arrival in India, he soon gained an understanding of the importance of the "rural reconstruction" emphasized by national leaders such as M. K. Gandhi. As he looked back in 1970, he stated the philosophy which guided the agricultural institute through its first half century:

> The policy of the Institute from its beginning in 1920 and for the past fifty years has had the development of the total man, spiritually, physically and mentally and his well-being socially and economically as its goal. This, we believe is what Jesus meant in John 10:10 when he said, "I am come that they might have life, and that they might have it more abundantly." In doing so, we have consistently worked in the closest cooperation and in full accord with Mahatma Gandhi and other Christian and National leaders though the years.[102]

The DeValoises began their missionary work in India in a time when there was considerable agitation against British rule and in a period in which the Board of Foreign Missions was once again having to cut back on its appropriation. When they were finishing their introductory year of language study, the issue of below-minimum salaries for Indian workers was coming to the fore. As a result, there was nothing in the budget for the beginning agricultural work. Thus, their first several years were discouraging, but John De

[102] Ibid.

Valois soon proved to be a person who would not be diverted from a path once chosen.

He recruited a knowledgeable Indian Christian, Aaron Christian, to work with him. They succeeded in having the government assign to them two hundred acres of wasteland about three miles from Katpadi to use as a base of operations. Here, they planned an agricultural demonstration farm and a place to train boys in modern methods that could be introduced appropriately into village rural life. At first, it was extremely difficult to persuade anyone to attend a school for agriculture. De Valois convinced the Arcot Assembly to move the three upper classes of the Arni Higher Elementary School to the farm and to call it a "middle vocational school with agricultural bias." Such vocational schools were just beginning to be encouraged by the government.[103] Since there was no money appropriated in 1924 for a hostel at the new school, Ben Rottschaefer allowed what had been appropriated for the boys' boarding home at the industrial institute to be transferred to the new middle school. Henry Scudder, treasurer of the mission, informed the Board of Foreign Missions that the transfer was possible because the industrial commercial department was doing well:

> He (Rottschaefer) hopes to earn enough money through the Industrial Institute and his Sub Agency for the Ford Car, and the Agency for an American Type, to fully support his Boarding department, and is also aiming to save enough to repair and enlarge the Katpadi Church. Mr. Rottschaefer is using his gifts in every possible way possible to earn money here in India for the upbuilding of the Kingdom, and if our Churches at home are not able to better support our work, I sometimes wonder whether more missionaries had not better try to follow Mr. Rottschaefer's footsteps....[104]

[103] Wyckoff, *One Hundred Years*, 61.
[104] H. J. Scudder to William Chamberlain, January 17, 1924.

The first class started with sixteen boys. When it proved successful, the village people began to see the value of agricultural education and to enroll their sons in the agricultural school.

While he was engaged in developing the infrastructure necessary to a model farm, De Valois was also placed in charge of encouraging the organization of a network of cooperative societies. The government recognized the value of such a network and gave him an honorary appointment to a government position to carry out such activity in the district. Soon about fifty cooperative societies had been organized to enable cooperative buying and selling, insurance, and protection to farmers. By 1925, it was possible to hold a cooperative conference at the agricultural farm to deal with subjects related to Christian participation in the cooperative movement.[105]

Of all the projects that the agricultural institute carried out over the years, the most noteworthy was perhaps its efforts to improve the poultry stock and establish an egg marketing cooperative society. Most of the village people did not own land on which to grow commercial crops, but it was possible for them to raise a few chickens. Those who could manage to keep only a couple of birds could supplement their family diet with the eggs their hens laid, while those who could manage to keep more could thereby earn some income through the sale of the eggs. The chickens native to villages were a hardy breed and able to scratch out a living under adverse conditions, but they produced only a limited number of small eggs per year. Therefore, De Valois imported a dozen Rhode Island Red chickens and White Leghorn chickens from America. He wrote,

> The arrival of our "feathered missionary assistants" has created a good deal of interest. These messengers of good-will have set to work in right earnest. Their crowing and cackling is advocating one of the solutions to India's

[105] "AAR," 1925, 66.

economic need. A goodly number of setting eggs have been
distributed among our Christian people. We are busily
engaged in re-establishing a poultry breeding station from
which to dispense pure bred fowls and setting eggs. Our
school boys are taking a keen interest in learning the
intricacies of poultry raising.[106]

The institute was proud of its high quality White Leghorn
chickens. It claimed that in 1940 one of its hens had established the
record for India for the number of eggs laid in one year. Not only
was number of eggs impressive, but the size was also superior,
averaging over two ounces, in contrast to the village chicken egg
that averaged under one-half once. Two other hens almost were
almost equal to the first in terms of egg production, although
tragedy struck the third one-half of the way through the year: "Of
the three, one laid 336 eggs; the second 313 and the third 155 before
it died from a Cobra bite in mid-year."[107]

The Madras government passed the Co-operative Societies Act
VI in 1932. This act enabled the cooperative societies to receive
legal standing, whereas previously they had been unofficially
organized. The "Katpadi Co-operative Egg Marketing Society"
became the first such legally recognized society in the Arcot
District. In the same year a Co-operative Stores Society was being
organized to handle other produce and to supply family needs. The
poultry and egg-marketing project encouraged by the agricultural
institute through the cooperative society succeeded in its goal of
providing good market outlets for village egg producers. In 1939,
for example, it marketed 97,843 eggs.

The agricultural institute sought to assist in upgrading other
livestock as well as poultry. The village people came to appreciate
the upgrading of their cattle with the assistance of the pure bred
bulls acquired by the institute. Their services had resulted in 571

[106] "AAR," 1928, 37.
[107] Arcot Coordinating Committee Report, 1941, 69.

calves being born in 1939. The same upgrading was taking place in the improvement of the village milk goats. The institute's extension service had begun to set up branch centers where activities were organized to introduce vegetable and field crops, horticulture, and rural recreation programs in addition to animal husbandry services.[108]

From its supporters in America, the institute received gifts of a Plymouth automobile with a trailer, a 16mm movie projector, and a Homelite generator, as well as other related equipment. It used the car and trailer to haul its products. On some evenings they would load the generator and project in the trailer and go to a village for the latest version of evangelistic touring by showing the ten-reel movie produced by Cecil B. De Mille, *King of Kings*. In 1939, the movie was shown forty-five times to audiences estimated to total 55,000 people. The Tamil explanation and interpretation of the movie was always given by one of the institute's Indian staff. Their sound equipment was capable of being heard outdoors by a crowd of up to five thousand people.[109]

The Arcot Assembly had adopted a policy in 1935 that the agricultural side of the activity of the agricultural institute must become self-supporting within five years. In adopting this policy, it was following the example it set with the Katpadi Industrial Institute. It was not easy for the farm to achieve that goal, because drought conditions often prevailed in the area. Since the land on which the farm was located had been wasteland too dry for most crops, only by drilling large wells had it been possible to raise fruit trees and plant crops such as improved strains of rice, as well as grow fodder for the cattle. But during a serious drought the wells could go dry, as they did in 1939. In that year the farm lost several hundred fruit trees. The report went on,

> We had to send away the larger part of our goat herd because grazing was not available; we did not get sufficient fodder for our cattle and had to import hay; income from

[108] "AAR," 1939, 39-40.
[109] Ibid., 36-37.

crops was greatly reduced and many of them dried up and
withered away after all the investment of seed, fertilizer and
labour had gone into them; our wells went dry and had to
be deepened. War conditions in Europe have also interfered
drastically in the demand and sale of our produce particularly
pure bred poultry. [110]

Fortunately, at that time the agricultural institute had enjoyed
enough good years to weather the extremely difficult conditions of
1939 and restore what had been lost, but it remained difficult for the
farm to show a profit from year to year. John Conklin and Carman
Scudder had argued four decades earlier that the mission's demand
that the boys' industrial school and factory at Arni operate without
mission subsidy was unrealistic because of the conflicting needs of
a school and a factory. Again with the agricultural institute, the
missionaries faced an internal tension between the differing purposes
of a demonstration center and a working farm. A farm must
concentrate on the efficient production of the crops most likely to
show a profit, while a model farm must choose its crops to
experiment with new varieties of seeds and to test which new crops
can be grown under a variety of conditions.

Continuing the Search for a Self-supporting Church

The worldwide depression of the 1930s had the effect of forcing
the Arcot Assembly to take issues of self-support more seriously
than it had in the past. There were two separate but related issues:
the self-support of the church with its elementary schools, and the
support of the institutions. Some of the actions that were taken in
regard to institutions have already been noted. A number of the
institutions had to manage without any subsidy of funds from the
Board of Foreign Missions. Among them were all of the Hindu
girls' schools, the Scudder Memorial Hospital in Ranipet, Tindivanam
and Sherman high schools, and Voorhees High School and College.

[110] Ibid., 37.

These had to find the necessary income through grants from the government or charging fees for their services. Some of them did both. The Katpadi Industrial Institute likewise was to operate without subsidy. The other institutions had to manage on smaller grants than they had received in the past and were encouraged to find new sources of income. Mission boarding schools for Christians would continue to receive assistance.

Several institutions enjoyed some income from endowment funds that had been established on their behalf. The Arcot Theological Seminary had managed to meet its needs from a $50,000 endowment that had been raised for it when it became an official Reformed Church theological seminary.[111] The Scudder Association had provided an endowment of $50,000 for the Scudder Memorial Hospital in 1934,[112] while $15,000 had been raised as a endowment for the industrial institute following an appeal from the Arcot Mission.[113]

With regard to self-support of the church itself, we have seen that the harvest festivals began to play an important role. Weekly contributions from members in the village and town churches and special gifts from their members led to several pastorates, particularly Vellore, Serkadu, and Yehamur, becoming self-supporting. The agricultural institute developed several stewardship programs. It encouraged people, for instance, to give the first fruit of the harvest as an offering and to set aside "God's acre," or a small portion of the church's land around the church, for a crop whose proceeds would go to the church.

The contributions of the Indian workers themselves played an important and sometimes controversial role in efforts toward achieving self-support. On several occasions they themselves voted to make a self-denial offering for a special purpose. The most notable effort was the "deficit reduction self-denial," which was

---

[111] *Minutes of the General Synod, RCA,* 1889, 775-77.
[112] Lewis R. Scudder, *A History of the Ranipet Hospital* (printed in Ranipet, India, 1935), 15.
[113] J. H. Wyckoff to Henry Cobb, June 30, 1906.

voted in 1934 by the Arcot Assembly[114] and which eventually raised about Rs. 6,000.

More controversial was an action of the Arcot Assembly requiring that mission employees contribute to the life of the church one anna of each rupee they earned were eligible to serve as members of the Arcot Assembly. Since there were sixteen annas in a rupee, this meant that a minimum contribution was 6.25 percent of their salary. The wording of the assembly's action makes it clear that it is not simply the pledge to contribute that amount, but the actual contribution that was necessary. The resolution reads:

> Resolved that the Arcot Assembly express its opinion to the churches in the Arcot Assembly area that the payment of at least one anna on the rupee of their salary will be considered as co-operation in the activities of the Assembly and that free will offerings will be regarded as free will offerings only in case the one anna to the rupee or more is actually given. The giving of one anna per rupee shall be a qualification for membership in the Assembly.[115]

The assembly further voted that a credentials committee be immediately appointed to assist the assembly in observing its rule of one anna to the rupee for membership in the assembly. The resolution states that "it shall be the duty of this Committee to keep this matter before the members of the Assembly and to urge them to bring their giving to the level required for membership and to notify all that this is a requirement for the next annual meeting of the Assembly."[116]

This rule was not new. It had long been the practice of the Arcot Mission, as part of its stewardship education, that village teachers and catechists and Indian ordained ministers as well as missionaries follow such a rule. It was always considered a voluntary contribution,

114 "Minutes of the Arcot Assembly," September 1934, 8.
115 "Minutes of the Arcot Assembly," January, 1937, 10-11.
116 Ibid., 11.

even though there were strong pressures to conform, and personal circumstances had been taken into account. What was new in the assembly's action was that penalties came to be officially attached to noncompliance. The assembly's resolution meant that members of the assembly were forced to contribute; failure to do so would be taken to mean that the member was not cooperative and therefore would not be seated as a member.

More important, however, was the fact that strict application of this rule would fall most heavily upon the catechists and teachers and members of the congregations in the villages. The higher educational institutions who operated on a self-support basis had made a rule that they would not give reduced rates for their children's education to anyone who had not paid one anna per rupee as a contribution to the church. So the rule fell doubly hard on the village Indian workers. Their salaries had been reduced considerably as a result of the depression, and they were suffering great financial difficulties. It was hard for them to find anything to contribute. When educational institutions went on self-support, they increased their fees to make up for their loss of income, but those institutions had managed with government grant money to avoid cutting their staff members' salaries.[117]

There was considerable division on the matter in the assembly meeting and thereafter. Everyone agreed that it would be better if one could avoid using compulsion. However, those who favored the rule believed that if the church was ever to take seriously the need to move toward self-support, its entire leadership—including missionaries, the Indian Christians who staffed the institutions, and Indian pastors and village workers—had to take the lead with their own regular contributions of at least one anna to the rupee. Those who opposed the resolution of the Arcot Assembly in 1937 believed that the action was unjust because it was voted by a combination of missionaries who could afford it and members of

---

[117] C. R. Wierenga to F. M. Potter, September 2, 1937.

the staffs of institutions whose own salaries had suffered less adjustment downward.

The controversy continued. During the course of the next year, R. P. Nathaniel, a licensed medical practitioner, a co-opted member who had served as a doctor in the Scudder Memorial Hospital in Ranipet, presented a set of resolutions opposing several actions of the Arcot Assembly, including the rule about an anna to the rupee. The issue was debated on each of the three days of the 1938 assembly. Finally, it stated the rule in a softer way and left more room open for interpretation, when it ruled, "Every Christian employee of the Assembly shall be persuaded to pay toward the support of the work at the rate of on anna per rupee of total income including allowances."[118] There the matter ended so far as the assembly was concerned. There is no record that anyone was denied membership in the assembly because of the rule, and it was largely in the hands of various supervisors of the Indian workers to determine how firm one should be in persuading them to contribute one anna to the rupee. In any case, just as stewardship committees in the United States like to emphasize the importance of giving one-tenth as a tithe, so in India, the one anna rule remained a guideline, whether voluntary or somewhat compulsory, until the beginning of the 1960s, when India replaced the system of sixteen annas to the rupee with one hundred cents to the rupee.

At the end of 1938, the Arcot Mission was able to make one of the most optimistic reports in its entire history. With the depression coming to an end in the United States and India's economy improving, more funds were becoming available. The medical, educational, and economic development institutions were all presenting positive reports. Women's work was going well. The churches were reporting numerical growth again, with the total Christian community reaching the total of almost thirty thousand. Even the village Christians were taking new initiatives in building

[118] "Minutes of the Arcot Assembly," 1938, 13.

their own churches and school buildings without waiting for funds from America.

> In village after village plans for the construction of new church buildings are under way. One village contributed fifty rupees (nearly twenty dollars) for this purpose. This new sense of responsibility is of great significance as the Church in India faces the future. The way in which the Indian village Christian living constantly on the narrowest possible margin is setting aside his mite for the Church, should be an inspiration to us at home.[119]

A new day was dawning for the churches and institutions in the old Arcot Mission area. But as the year 1939 began with the bright rays of hope, it soon grew dark under clouds of war that first appeared in Europe and China and then began to threaten India and America.

Mission in Wartime

On September 3, 1939, the British viceroy in India unilaterally associated India with England's declaration of war on Germany without bothering to consult the Indian provincial ministries or any Indian leader. The Indian National Congress argued that, if the conflict was really about democracy, a fight against tyranny, then Indian leaders had to be consulted about India's future status and about matters such as a declaration of war by India. In response, Viceroy Linlithgow merely repeated old offers of dominion status in an indefinite and distant future.[120] When, in 1942, the Japanese invaded Burma and an attack on India seemed likely, the British government sent Sir Stafford Cripps to India to negotiate further concerning India's future status. His mission ended in failure in the month of April.

---

119 "BFMR," 1939, 22.
120 Sarkar, *Modern India*, 375.

During the summer of 1942, Gandhi called upon the British to leave India. On August 8, 1942, the congress passed its "Quit India" resolution and called for a mass, nonviolent struggle with the widest possible scale of participation. The British sought to paint the congress as having secret pro-Axis sympathies favoring Germany and Japan and to portray the British themselves as the defenders of India. These efforts were undermined by Indian refugees and soldiers coming from Burma. The Indian refugees told how the British in Burma had failed to help them be evacuated when the Japanese army was attacking. The soldiers, many of them wounded, also spoke of neglect and ill-treatment by the British military. This convinced many Indians that the policies of the British were racist.[121] Some of those Indians were Christians who had migrated to Burma to find work. Charlotte Wyckoff wrote, "Many of the ex-Arcot Christians who had emigrated to Burma and the Straits in search of work and settled there, had harrowing experiences trying to escape capture when the Japanese army invaded those lands. Some walked though forests from Mandalay to Assam, following a trail of corpses of those who had gone ahead of them...."[122]

In 1943 a terrible famine occurred in Bengal, leading to the deaths of between 1.5 and 3 million people. The famine was brought on because the British and American military forces gave priority to the use of the railways for military purposes rather than to transport food to meet basic civilian needs. They also failed to make any serious effort to check black market activities and extremely rapid rises in the price of food.[123] For a number of years after 1943, Americans perceived India as a poverty-stricken country that placed a low value on human life. To some extent, this perception was shaped by American servicemen stationed in Bengal, who reported seeing carts being taken along the streets to pick up the bodies of people who had died during the night. What Americans

---

[121] Ibid., 388-92.
[122] Wyckoff, *One Hundred Years*, 119.
[123] Sarkar, *Modern India*, 392-93.

were not aware of was that the death toll was not the result of Indian mismanagement or callousness, but of the low value placed on Indian lives by the allied governments seeking to save India from Japanese invaders.

The impact of the war on people in the Madras Presidency was not as great as it was on those living closer to the Burmese border. Food supplies in the south were not seriously disrupted, but prices for food and other items necessary for daily life did rise rapidly enough to cause serious problems. Fear that the Japanese would make a landing and invade near Madras brought about considerable disruption in the area.

When a Japanese fleet was known to be located off the coast of Madras, the government moved some of its operations inland. It requisitioned the buildings of Sherman Memorial Girls' High School in Chittoor, with the result that the school had to be closed between Christmas, 1941, and April, 1942.[124] There was also a large mobile military contingent with more than five hundred vehicles stationed in Ranipet, ready to move in any given direction at an hour's notice.[125] An "Air Raid Precaution" department commandeered the grounds of St. Christopher's Training College in Madras, and the training college was evacuated to Vellore, where the Christian medical college took it in for a year.[126] One Japanese bomb fell in Madras and then the Japanese fleet turned away, ending the threat.

The American consulate issued repeated warnings to all Americans to leave India when any transportation became available to them. Missionaries who were scheduled for furlough, such as the Kortelings and the Van Vrankens, handed their work over to Indians and left quite soon. Others made preparations to leave when it seemed necessary to do so. The missionaries had decided against a general evacuation, because that would have had a seriously demoralizing

---

[124] "Report of the Indian Church Board and Arcot Co-ordinating Committee," 1942, 18.
[125] J. J. De Valois to F. M. Potter, April 4, 1942.
[126] Wyckoff, *One Hundred Years*, 120.

effect on the whole Indian Christian community. The Board of Foreign Missions informed the missionaries of its general policy that each individual must make his or her own decision about when to leave places of serious danger. The policy, which continues to be in effect even today, stated that "each individual be permitted to decide for himself or herself whether to evacuate or remain in the present emergency."[127]

A matter of special concern to the missionaries was the welfare and safety of their children in the school at Kodaikanal. Of special concern to the Arcot missionaries were the children of the Reformed Church missionaries in Arabia who attended the High Clerc School for missionary children in Kodai. The letter from the American consul had caused people in Kodai to become somewhat frantic, and many began hectic preparations to leave. It happened that at this time the missionary chairman and missionary secretary of the school council decided to leave India, as did several members of the staff. John De Valois and several missionaries from other missions went to Kodaikanal to calm the remaining members of the staff, as well as parents and children in Kodaikanal. The delegation reassured them that they did not have to join a mass evacuation. With that the situation again became relatively calm.[128]

When she wrote her life story for her grandchildren thirty years later, Mildred De Vries told of her family's experience in responding to the rumors and the real dangers of a Japanese invasion. At that time her youngest son, John, was in first grade. Since missionary children could not be placed in boarding at Kodaikanal until they were at least seven years old, Mildred and the children stayed in one of the mission's houses there while her husband, Ben, worked out of their home on the plains. She remembered the events:

> Ben kept sending me cash. I didn't know why. We'd hear mysterious rumors, etc. This was in February, 1942. Our U.S. Consul was concerned and said that we should be

[127] F. M. Potter to J. J. De Valois, June 3, 1942.
[128] J. J. De Valois to F. M. Potter, February 25, 1942.

prepared to leave. Some missionary families did; for a ship
was ready to take them...(The fare was only $42, I think).
They left on a troop ship for New York. Ben promised me
he would keep enough gasoline (we were rationed) and if
we needed to leave he would come to get us, in case
evacuation was forced! One Monday he came and explained
what was about. The Japanese were in the Bay of Bengal
area....With haste, we packed, gathered up the Arabian
missionaries' children and we got off by train that
evening....There were 21 of us in our home the next A.
M....A couple of days later, the Arabian children left with
an escort...."129

With the departure of the Japanese fleet from the Bay of Bengal,
the De Vrieses learned that it was not necessary for them to leave
India after all.

Charlotte Wyckoff remembered that there was a marked difference
at the outset between the attitude of the American and British
missionaries toward the war and that of the Indian Christians. The
Americans and British wanted to participate, while the Indians did
not really feel that it was their war because it did not promise them
their freedom. "If the nation were free and under the complete
control of its own leaders they would fight to save their land from
invasion and voluntarily cast in their lot with the free countries.
They would not do it as a subject nation."130

Several of the missionaries were called to war service. Dr. Galen
Scudder and Johanna De Vries, a missionary nurse and sister of Ben
De Vries, left the Ranipet Hospital to join a medical unit that was
sent from Madras to Burma. They returned to Ranipet after the
British defeat in Burma. Mina Jongewaard served with YMCA
camps in Bihar, Chittagong, and Burma.131 The Arcot Mission

129 Mildred De Vries, *To Serve with Joy: My Life Story* (privately printed, in the possession
of David De Vries, Rockport, Mich.,) 39.
130 Wyckoff, *One Hundred Years*, 117.
131 Ibid., 118.

received reinforcements from China and Japan, however, when a number of unmarried women missionaries who had been evacuated from those countries were transferred to India. These included Jeanette Veldman, Anne De Young, Tena Holkeboer, and Florence Walvoord.[132]

A rather sensitive issue arose when the surgeon general in Madras wrote to the Arcot Mission requesting that Galen Scudder be loaned to him to serve as the district medical officer in Coimbature, about three hundred miles from Madras, in order to release a British doctor for military service. The Ranipet hospital council gave Scudder approval to accept. When the request was sent to the Arcot Mission, which was meeting in Kodaikanal, the mission rejected the request with a very clear no. The situation was complicated, however, because a number of the Indian leaders in the area were in favor of Scudder's going. There was suspicion that one reason the Indians favored his going was that it would give an opportunity for an Indian doctor, Julius Savarirayan, to run the hospital.[133] After some further discussion, permission was granted to Scudder to go to Coimbature, where he served until the British doctor could be released from his military service.

Regarding Scudder's appointment, John De Valois wrote to the board secretary in New York that he was concerned about one point of constitutional importance. In the relationship existing between the Arcot Mission and the Arcot Coordinating Committee,[134] the general policy was that a missionary was assigned by the Board of Foreign Missions and the Arcot Committee to work under the Arcot Coordinating Committee, which made the actual work assignment of the missionary within the bounds of the Arcot Mission area. In this case, the mission had at first refused to permit an assignment outside the area. If the disagreement had continued,

[132] Ibid.
[133] J. J. De Valois to F. M. Potter, June 12, 1942.
[134] In 1940 the Arcot Coordinating Committee had replaced the Arcot Assembly, but the functions remained very much the same, although with several important modifications (see chap. 11).

who would have had the final authority? De Valois believed that it was important that further thought be given to such a situation,[135] which in fact did arise after the establishment of the Church of South India in 1947.

Another and more urgent matter brought to the foreground by the Japanese invasion and the Quit India movement was the question of how long missionaries could or should remain in India and what arrangements should be made regarding the extensive property owned by the Arcot Mission. A sign of the times was the publication of an article entitled, "Missionary Action and the Present Crisis," in the *Guardian,* a Christian newspaper in Madras, August 27, 1942. The author stated that whatever one may say, to the Indian mind the missionary represents not only the country he comes from but also its governmental policy. He also asserted that missionaries continue to dominate the Christian community. Therefore the question had to be faced as to whether the missionaries must also "quit India." By doing so, they would make clear that they were standing on the side of democracy and for freedom.

On the other hand, it was not really the intention of the Indian Nationalist writer to imply that missionaries must leave India *en masse*, as if they were shaking the dust off their feet as a testimony against the country. What the writer actually advocated was that missionaries make

> a complete withdrawal from all places of leadership, headships of institutions, offices of administration and positions of trust so long ear-marked as specially designated for Foreign Missionary personnel. Bungalows and residential quarters which are considered special property meant only for missionary occupants may be interchanged with houses built for Indian colleagues. Basic salary schemes will have to be devised so that while adequate provision is made for differences in standards of living, all glaring disparity in the matter of stipends and allowances are done away with.

[135] Ibid.

Experiments in community living and sharing of financial resources should be undertaken.[136]

Over the course of the ninety-year history of the Arcot Mission, a great deal of property had come into its hands. Missionaries and Indians alike became concerned about what would happen to those properties if all the missionaries had to leave. The mission wrote to the secretary of the Board of Foreign Missions, F. M. Potter, about the matter. Potter, who had served as a Reformed Church missionary, was familiar with the issues. He responded July 31, 1942, by which time the immediate crisis of Japan's invasion had gone away, and the missionaries in India were feeling a little more secure.

Potter stated the position of the board by making four basic points. The first was that the board had anticipated all along that property used by the churches and village schools so closely related to the church should at some point be transferred to a responsible church body. The property should not be transferred to a strictly local body, but to an Indian church body capable of taking on the responsibility.[137] In taking this position, Potter was stating a principle well-known to members of the Reformed Church in America, which is that the property in the hands of a local congregation belongs to the classis of which the church is a member rather than the congregation itself.

This second point stated that the Arcot Coordinating Committee should be duly incorporated and that institutional property should be handed over to that body. Potter urged caution on this point. He was not sure that in the case of an international emergency there would be any real protection of the transferred property, because the committee included a number of foreign missionaries. An

---

[136] *Guardian,* August 27, 1942 (board secretary's correspondence file, Archives of the RCA). Missionaries from time to time included articles found in the Indian press for information of the Reformed Church personnel in New York.

[137] For this and the following paragraphs on the issue of property transfer, F. M. Potter to J. J. De Valois, July 31, 1942.

"alien enemy" would not be likely to view the Arcot Coordinating Committee as a fully Indian body.

His third point was that a distinction must be made between church and village school property, on the one hand, and the property used by institutions, on the other. Potter did not want the burden of financial responsibility for the property of some of the large institutions to fall on the church. Since it was likely that the mission and the Board of Foreign Missions would in any case have to bear much of that financial responsibility, Potter urged full consideration be given to all aspects of the transfer before anything be done.

Finally, Potter felt that the ownership of missionary residences was an altogether different question. The support of the foreign missionary himself or herself was entirely the responsibility of the Board of Foreign Missions. The board had never anticipated the need to transfer missionary residences. Potter did not want to write much more about that until he had more opportunity to discuss the matter with the board itself.

As the immediate crisis faded away, the matter of transferal of property became less urgent. It would be another decade before the issue was seriously addressed again, but in his letter Potter had laid some of the groundwork for later consideration of the transfer of mission property to a responsible Indian body.

When the war came to an end, the situation in India had been transformed. Everyone knew that India would not be satisfied until it was no longer under the British Raj. Matters had also been moving rapidly in the matter of church union. In the aftermath of the war arose an independent India and a newly united Indian church.

11

In Unity There is Strength

"Divide and conquer" has always been the strategy for emperors who have desired to rule over foreign tribes and nations. In spite of all their protestations about ruling India to preserve it from falling into chaos, the British understood the old adage well as they played one ruler off against another and one religion against another.

Eendracht maakt macht, "in unity there is strength," was the motto of the Reformed Church in America. It was a guiding principle for the Arcot missionaries. When the Arcot Mission was founded, the missionaries agreed that they would constantly work together in furtherance of the goals of the mission; they did not favor anyone who sought to go his own way without the approval of the mission. They also founded the Classis of Arcot in which every member, whether minister or elder, Indian or missionary, had equal voice and equal vote. They believed that in unity of task, unity of purpose, and unity of worship and doctrine the strength of the church and the power of Jesus Christ would be evident. Even when the missionaries favored the presence of the British Imperial rule in India, they were never imperialists at heart. They did not wish to continue their

575

dominance in the church and never sought to divide in order to maintain their power.

Nevertheless, when the time arrived that the Church of South India was established and a new manifestation of unity in the body of Christ became visible, the missionaries, Indian Christians, leaders in the Board of Foreign Missions, and the General Synod of the Reformed Church in America would all be challenged to accept all of the implications of that new-found unity. The fact that India had become a new and independent, or, unfortunately, two new and independent nations, India and Pakistan, served both to create for the church new anxieties and to provide a clearer sense of direction in a post-colonial context.

Reformed Church Deputation Recommends an Arcot Coordination Committee

Reformed Church missionaries in India believed that when they entered the Church of South India in 1947 the old Arcot Mission area was ahead of other mission areas. They had developed the Indian Church Board and the Arcot Assembly, organizational structures that facilitated partnership between Indians and missionaries in carrying out the mission of the church. They were ahead of other missions in the devolution of mission to the church.[1] By 1938, however, the missionaries and Indians recognized that the

---

[1] Indian leaders in other areas of the South India United Church recognized that the missionaries and Indians in the Arcot area had been pioneers in the process of devolution of mission as well as in the development of Indian leadership. In 1928, on the occasion of the seventy-fifth anniversary celebrations of the founding of the Arcot Mission, the Rev. C. Sundaram, the representative of the Madras Christian council of the united church, praised the Arcot mission for its progressive stance on devolution and leadership development. He stated, "...you have been among the foremost to devise and carry out a scheme of devolution not only in the Church but also in other departments. You have Revs. M. Peter and E. Savarirayan in positions of great responsibility, men who in an Episcopal Church would have adorned the Bishopric and you have Indian Principals for the Voorhees College and the Union Mission Training School. In this and other matters your procedure has given great satisfaction to the Indian Christian community, and I feel sure, I am voicing the thoughts of enlightened Indian Christians in making this statement" [*Jubilee Commemoration, 1853-1928: The Arcot Assembly and the Arcot Mission of the Reformed Church in America* (Madras: Methodist Publishing House, 1931), 78].

Arcot Assembly with its 110 or more members was too large and unwieldy a body to function efficiently.

It happened that two highly respected persons from the Reformed Church were coming to India at the end of 1938 to attend the International Missionary Conference at Madras Christian College, located in Tambaram, south of the city of Madras. One of them was F. M. Potter, secretary of the Board of Foreign Missions, who had served as a missionary in Vellore from 1913-1917. The other was Sue Weddell, secretary of the Woman's Board of Foreign Missions. The Arcot Assembly decided to ask the two to serve as a committee to make recommendations on modifying the structures of the Arcot Assembly in order to move forward in matter of devolution and to improve the group's organizational efficiency.

Potter and Weddell spent approximately a month visiting and meeting with people in the old Arcot Mission area following the International Missionary Conference, and they presented their twenty-nine page report to the Arcot Assembly in February, 1940. They stated their belief that the Arcot Assembly should be replaced by a new organizational structure that would give more weight to the church in relation to the institutions. The Arcot Assembly, in which all Reformed Church missionaries and all institutions held membership, tended to make the representatives sent from the churches into a minority whose central concerns could be overlooked. The report stated, "The assembly is in some respects just as much an artificial body as the Mission ever was. It was a step forward because it provided for expression of Indian opinion, but it is not the church."[2]

Potter and Weddell recommended that the new organization form six to ten "area councils," each of which would relate to all of the work within a given geographic area. By contrast, the Arcot Assembly structure had separate "boards" to bring together all those related to a specific type of work, such as education, medical

---

[2] "Report of the Deputation, Board of Foreign Missions, RCA," February, 1939, 2-3 (appendix to "AAR," 1939).

service, and economic and industrial concerns.[3] For example, the area council in Katapdi could include representation from teachers from the Katpadi Industrial Institute as well as the Katpadi and Gudiyattam pastorates; the Ranipet Council could include representatives from the hospital and the girls' schools along with the Ranipet and perhaps another pastorate. The report suggested the advantage of the new arrangement:

> It would preserve the vital contact of the Church with local institutions. There is already a tendency toward increasing local independence in some of our institutions which have become more or less self-supporting. This tendency we believe natural and inevitable. The example of similar developments in other countries warns us, however, that one result may be the increasing secularization of institutions. It is, therefore, essential that we make careful provision at this time, looking to the future, to ensure the close coordination of the Church with all the institutions which have in one form or another sprung from it.[4]

A second major change had to do with the size of the membership in the new organization, which came to be called the "Arcot Coordinating Committee." The Arcot Coordinating Committee (ACC) would have the task of coordinating the activities of the area councils. It was to have no more than thirty members, twenty of whom would be nominated by the area councils and appointed by the Madras Church Council, without distinction between missionary and Indian. The Madras Church Council of the South Indian United Church would appoint five additional persons, with the possibility that an additional five persons could be co-opted to be members. By providing that all of the members finally be appointed by the Madras Church Council, the South Indian United Church was given a key role in developing a stronger church

3 Ibid., 5.
4 Ibid.

consciousness rather than the old mission consciousness. Potter and Weddell wrote,

> It seems inevitable that this reorganization would therefore tend to develop a much stronger Church consciousness than is possible under the present organization in which everything is so largely directed by one large non-Church organization. The same emphasis is secured by the fact that in the proposed set-up no mention is made of the missionary. It is Church-centric. Because the missionary is related to the Church he will function in the organization, but it will be primarily because of his Church relationship.[5]

With the establishment of the Arcot Coordinating Committee, the process of devolution from Arcot Mission to Indian church had taken another step. Missionaries no longer served in positions of administrative power simply because they were missionaries. Although the Arcot Mission still had the privilege of making recommendations to the Arcot Coordinating Committee, it was the ACC that had the final authority to make missionary assignments. The ACC was also made ultimately responsible for formulating long-term plans as to the need for missionary personnel. At the end of a missionary's first term of service, the ACC also was the body that recommended to the Board of Foreign Missions whether the missionary's return was desired.[6]

Missionary and Indian Relationships with the "Home Board"

Indian leaders and missionaries were pleased with the recommendations of the deputation and made the suggested organizational changes. There are no indications that it was commented on at the time, but one of the things that the change brought about is that, in an era when power continued to devolve from the missionaries and from the Arcot Mission, the direct

5 Ibid., 7.
6 "Arcot Coordinating Committee Minutes," 1940, 38.

involvement of the secretary of the Board of Foreign Missions in the Reformed Church's mission in India was growing. In the early decades, the missionaries always conducted a polite and open correspondence with the board secretaries and held them in high regard. At the same time, they jealously held the management of the work of the mission to be their responsibility and protested whenever the secretary overstepped his bounds.

The relationship began to change when William Chamberlain, who had served so well in India, became secretary of the board. He was still regarded by the missionaries as a colleague who had the right to make suggestions concerning the internal workings of the mission and the Indian church. Potter had been given the same collegial welcome when he became secretary of the Board of Foreign Missions. However, in the recommendations of the Reformed Church deputations of 1930 and 1939 to the Arcot Assembly, the power previously enjoyed by the Arcot Mission could be seen to be in the process of shifting directly to the Board of Foreign Missions through its secretary.

Another change that was taking place was that Indians in the church were also developing personal relationships with the secretary and other members of the Board of Foreign Missions and of the Reformed Church in America. In 1926, the Board of Foreign Missions invited the Reverend Simon Cornelius, then president of the Arcot Assembly, to visit Reformed churches in America. He visited many churches and interpreted to them the new developments in India, assuring them that the devolution did not mean that the assembly wanted to cut loose from the church in America. Upon his return to India, he helped interpret the Reformed Church to the people of the area.[7] In 1937, C. J. Lucas, the Indian principal of the men's Union Training School for teachers in Viruthampet, had been sent to attend ecumenical conferences in Oxford and Edinburgh as a representative of the South India United Church. Following the conferences, he was invited by the Board of Foreign

---

[7] Wyckoff, *One Hundred Years*, 81-82; see also "AAR," 1926, ix.

Missions to be present at the meeting of the General Synod as well as to visit churches. He was warmly welcomed. The board's annual report states,

> Appreciation has come from every section of the Church of this opportunity of becoming acquainted with one of the outstanding Christians of one of the churches of Asia....Reports from various places visited by Mr. Lucas indicated that his messages and his roundtable conferences were very well received and contributed much to interest in missions and did much to create a better understanding of the problems of the work in India.[8]

Though visits of board secretaries from America and the visits of Indian Christians to the Reformed Church were few in number, they created warm personal relationships. Indians had often heard the missionaries speak of the "Home Board" with respect and even affection. The organizational changes coordinated with the personal encounters in such a way that Indians in the Arcot Area came to use the term, "Home Board," not simply as a shorthand way to refer to the Board of Foreign Missions but also with a sense that it was in some way their board. In later decades, when missionaries had ceased to use the phrase, one could still hear Indians of the older generation speaking of the "Home Board" with considerable nostalgia and affection.

The Objection of the Church of Scotland Mission

The decision to replace the Arcot Assembly with the Arcot Coordinating Committee met with objections from the Church of Scotland Mission, which was related to the South India United Church congregations and schools in the area between Ranipet and Madras. The Church of Scotland Mission believed that it was a mistake to place so much responsibility for managing schools on

8 "BFMR," 1937, 8-9.

the churches and their pastors. It feared that the demands of administration would overwhelm the spiritual side of their ministry. Reformed Church missionary C. R. Wierenga wrote to Potter that there was a clear difference of philosophy between the two missions.

> Where we do fundamentally differ is that whereas the Scotch [sic] people are prepared to take the responsibility of education under a mission centric programme and leave the purely spiritual programme to the Pastor and the church, some of us feel that the total programme in the village should be under one single administration, and that that should certainly be the church.[9]

The Church of Scotland Mission had other reservations as well. In the Presbytery of Arcot and in the Madras Church Council of the South India United Church the churches of Arcot Mission area had about five times as many members as those related to the Church of Scotland Mission. The result was that often unintentionally the agenda became crowded with items more specifically related to the Arcot area churches. Furthermore, because the Church of Scotland Mission had not placed nearly as much responsibility in the hands of Indian leaders, they were able to avoid some of the open differences of perspectives and vigorous debate that constantly arose in Arcot.

> Holding this view of a more autocratic mission regime they have obviated many of those unwholesome squabbles that have been our experience under a more democratic set-up. They are very frank to state that one of their misgivings in accepting the proposed constitution of the Indian Church Board is a fear of what they call the Vellore type of domination and mentality, and interference in the orderly procedure of their work. They want at all cost to prevent their people from being infected by this malignant "Vellore" virus.[10]

9 C. R. Wierenga to F. M. Potter, April 10, 1939.
10 Ibid.

It was not possible at that time to bring together in one organization the differing perspectives of the Arcot Mission and the Church of Scotland Mission on issues of devolution. Therefore, the India Church Board and the Arcot Coordinating Committee related only to the work in the Arcot area, rather than to the whole area of the Madras Church Council.

The Church of Scotland missionaries were correct in observing that in the more democratic set-up in the Arcot area, "unwholesome squabbles" and suspicions could develop, but the advantage of the Arcot structure was that suspicions and misunderstandings could be dealt with. For example, Indian leaders in the Arcot Coordinating Committee began to suspect in 1946 that certain personal requests for funding on the part of a missionary carried greater weight with the Board of Foreign Missions than did requests of the ACC. This suspicion was aroused when the board turned down a request from the ACC for an additional $4,000 appropriation for ACC work, but provided $4,000 for the purchase of a large piece of land for the Agricultural Institute under the direction of J. J. De Valois, even though the ACC had not yet requested the money. De Valois had made known his need for the money directly to the board in New York, thus bypassing the ACC. In responding positively to his request, the board likewise had bypassed the ACC. On February 12, 1946, C. A. Samuel, secretary of the ACC, sent a letter to Potter pointing out the suspicions that individual missionary requests for funds had priority over those of the ACC under Indian leadership.[11]

This was not the first nor the last time that De Valois received funds for the agricultural institute without having gone through all the proper channels of the ACC or its predecessors. In fact, had he carefully used the channels, a strong agricultural institute very possibly would not have come into existence. He was an effective fundraiser, and he had many friends in America who trusted him and believed in the need for a strong agricultural mission program in India. Potter responded to C. A. Samuel with a long letter in

[11] For this and the following paragraphs see F. M. Potter to C. A. Samuel, May 1, 1946.

F. Marmaduke Potter

which he said that a final decision had not yet been made and that
the board wanted to discuss the requests with the three-person
Indian delegation from Arcot Coordinating Committee that was on
its way to America. He wanted the ACC to know that the request
for the purchase of land for the agricultural institute seemed to
require a speedy response because sellers of land are not willing to
wait very long to close the deal.

Potter's reply was undoubtedly less than totally satisfactory to the
ACC, but because the suspicion had arisen within a larger relationship
of trust and respect, it was the kind of thing that could be handled
more personally when the delegation arrived in New York. And,
indeed, when the Indians arrived, they acquiesced in the decision to
send the $4,000 for the purchase of the land. When the Church of
South India came into being the following year, new questions of
organization arose, but Indians and missionaries in the Arcot area
put aside any remaining suspicions while they worked to preserve
the values in the organization they had created.

The Church of South India Comes into Being

The Arcot Mission may well have been the most consistent advocate of church union of all the missions in India. Already in 1879, Jacob Chamberlain was calling upon mission societies and churches to work together in unity. J. H. Wyckoff had played a leading role in the conversations leading to the formation of the South India United Church. He and others had also been instrumental in advocating for and establishing a wide variety of cooperative endeavors and union mission institutions. The Arcot Mission was also a strong supporter of organizations such as the YMCA, Christian Endeavor, the Bible Societies, the Boy Scouts, the American Tract Society, the Christian Literature Society located in Madras, and the National Christian Council of India.

A number of the Indian leaders in the Arcot area were also strong advocates for church union. C. J. Lucas, the Indian principal of the men's Union Training School, was sent to be the South India United Church representative to the Edinburgh Conference on Faith and Order in 1937. There he recounted his positive personal experience with a variety of denominations in India. His speech has often been quoted at length; below is a brief excerpt of his remarks on the part denominations played in his personal journey of faith:

> My father was a convert to Christianity and he is still a Lutheran. My mother was a convert too, but she was a Congregationalist and then she became a Lutheran. My mother was a woman of prayer, and at her knees I first learned to pray to and worship God. I was initiated into the mysteries of Luther's Smaller Catechism by my father and, later, of the Augsburg Confession just before my confirmation....At seventeen I was sent to a Puritan College, where I came under the influence of Calvinistic Puritanism. Later I went to a college staffed mainly by professors belonging to the United Free Church of Scotland. These two contacts made me like and appreciate the Presbyterian

service and form of worship, and paved the way for me to be easily reconciled to the form of worship in the Reformed Church.... As a boy and youth I immensely liked the services and worship conducted in connection with the Sunday School, Christian Endeavour Society, and, later, Young Men's Christian Association....In the city, while as a university student and later as a teacher in the college, I had great partiality for a Methodist Church service. Its rich hymnology and effective pulpits were my main attraction.

My wife belonged to the Anglican communion. Her parents were converts also, and they and some of her relatives are Anglo-Catholics; a few of her relatives are Roman Catholic. A brother-in-law of mine is a Methodist. Thus through marriage and geographical accident, I am connected with Christian people belonging to different persuasions and beliefs....[12]

Lucas's experience of personal family relationships with many denominations had come about because the missions had divided their responsibilities geographically and in the way they had set up educational institutions. The specific details of theological differences were less important to him than was his basic conviction of unity with others who claimed the name of Christ. His experience was not unusual among educated Christians. It is no wonder that such persons became ardent advocates for church union.

In 1919, a group of Indian leaders met at Tranquebar, about two hundred miles south of Madras, to attend the Tranquebar Conference on Church Union. Tranquebar holds a significant place in Indian church history because it was the site of the first Protestant mission activity. Meschach Peter of the Arcot Mission was one of the chief advocates for holding the conference. His father had been a pastor in the Reformed Church, his uncle was an Anglican, his grandfather

[12] Quoted in Sundkler, *Church of South India,* 31-32

a Lutheran as was his mother, and his wife came from a Congregationalist family.[13]

The Tranquebar Conference was attended by leading Indians in the Anglican and South India United Churches. It drafted a resolution in which it proposed union on the basis of four principles:

1. The Holy Scriptures of the Old and New Testaments, as containing all things necessary for salvation.
2. The Apostles' Creed and the Nicene Creed.
3. The two Sacraments ordained by Christ Himself— Baptism and the Lord's Supper.
4. The Historic Episcopate, locally adapted.[14]

These principles became the focal points for the long and tortuous negotiations that proved to be necessary for the next twenty-eight years before the union would actually be consummated in 1947.[15]

Arcot missionaries at times expressed reservations about some of the proposals, but they constantly expressed their desire for union for the sake of a more united witness and evangelistic outreach to the people of India. While they always remained firm advocates of Reformed theology and practice, they indicated at an early date that for the sake of unity they were ready to agree that the new church would have bishops, so long as that church would also recognize the validity of ordinations in the Reformed Church in America. Just how serious they were in their desire for unity became clear at a meeting in Madras in 1919 between bishops Azariah and Waller of the Anglicans and A.W. Brough and L. R. Scudder of the South India United Church. The Anglicans were suggesting that at the

13 Ibid., 98.
14 Ibid., 102. The defenders of the "Historic Episcopate" believe that the validity of the ordained ministry depends upon an unbroken line throughout history of bishops in succession to each other. There was debate within the Church of England as to whether the "Historic Episcopate" was of the "essence" (absolutely essential) or "*bene* essence" (essential for the well-being of the church but not absolutely essential). The Tranquebar Conference did not try to settle the issue.
15 For the definitive history of these negotiations, see ibid., 108-338.

time of union a "service of commission" would take place with a mutual laying on of hands by bishops and ordained ministers. Congregationalists and Presbyterians always viewed such a service as suspect, because it could be understood as a means to make valid the ordination of non-episcopally ordained ministers.[16]

L. R. Scudder accepted the Anglican desire for such a service by saying,

> I have prayed about this matter, and if it comes to it at the last moment I suppose I would submit to it for the sake of union and for the sake of the Indian Church. But should you require this of me? After forty years of ministry? Within the United Church where we would accept the Episcopacy and granted that hereafter all ordination shall be by Bishops—could you not license us as authorized to celebrate in any Church this organization where the pastor or local church may invite me?" Azariah was shaken by the earnest plea of the venerated old missionary. He (Azariah) adds, "I quote these words so fully because it shows the spirit of the demand made. I wish we could allow this (Azariah, August 20, 1919, to Mrs. Whitehead).[17]

While the union negotiations were slowly moving forward in India, opposition to church mergers grew within the Reformed Church itself. Major struggles within American denominations were going on about modernism, liberalism, and fundamentalism. These struggles were creating suspicion of ecumenical movements because many feared that, in the desire to bring about mergers of

---

[16] The churches that merged into the Church of South India agreed that the ordained ministry was to include the offices of bishop, presbyter, and deacon. For a full discussion of these three offices in the Church of South India in relation to the Reformed tradition, see Eugene Heideman, *Reformed Bishops and Catholic Elders* (Grand Rapids: Eerdmans, 1970), 90-150.

[17] Sundkler, *Church of South India*, 378-79; 108-109. At the service of union in 1947, the validity of the ordination of all ministers entering the Church of South India was accepted without such a "service of commission."

denominations, compromises of theology and practice would have to be made at points vital to the faith.

The Arcot Assembly decided that it should ask the advice of the Reformed Church General Synod about the proposed 1933 church union scheme in India, with particular reference to the matter of the Anglican demand that the Historic Episcopate be accepted in the new church. The General Synod responded at length. The Board of Foreign Missions wanted its supporters to know the position of the General Synod, so it quoted the synod action in full in its annual report of 1934. The issue was specifically the office of bishop, rather than any judgment of the faithfulness of the Anglican Church in India. Of that church, it said, "There can be no question as to the positive and genuine Christian character of the leadership and the membership of the Church planted and builded up in India through the direct agency of the Anglican Church. For nearly a century and a half they have walked humbly before God and boldly before men."[18]

The General Synod and the Board of Foreign Missions continued to have reservations about the office of bishop but recognized that it would be wrong to impose historic European church divisions on Asia. They accepted the fact that the proposal was for India and not for America. Furthermore, they were impressed by the fact that most of the Reformed Church missionaries in India "were willing and confident in making this bold venture of faith."[19] Therefore the General Synod and the Board of Foreign Missions both were ready to follow the lead of the missionaries on the matter of church union, but they wished the missionaries to hear their advice on six points, with the board adding a seventh point. Because the issue of the office of bishop and validity of ministries remains a very live question to the present day, we quote in full the guidelines in the response given to the Arcot Assembly in 1934:

[18] "BFMR," 1934, 6.
[19] Ibid., 5-6.

a. That the Ministries of all uniting Churches are recognized as equally valid Ministries of the Word and of the Sacraments.

b. That, while the office of Bishop, new to the South India United Church, is to be accepted, its function be constitutionally regulated and that the full spiritual equality and value of the Ministries of these uniting Churches be maintained.

c. That the Bishops be elected and their election shall be subject to confirmation by the Synod representing the clergy and the laity as well as the Bishops.

d. That the consecration of Bishops and the ordination of Presbyters[20] shall be performed by the laying on of hands of both Bishops and Presbyters.

e. That the Synod, composed of Bishops, Presbyters, and Laity, be fully recognized as the supreme government and legislative body of the Church and the final authority in all matters pertaining to the Church.

f. That the validity of communicant membership of the uniting Churches be fully recognized. In summary, the General Synod of the Reformed Church in America is constrained to urge its opinion that the members of the Arcot Mission and of the Arcot Assembly would do well to maintain the attitude that any agreement with regard to the Orders and Sacraments of the uniting Churches can only be based on the recognition of the equal validity of the Orders and Sacraments of the uniting Churches and of the equal standing of the accepted communicants and ordained ministers in each.

g. That the United Church retain communion with all the Churches to which the uniting churches owe their origin and at the same time hold forth hope of a future successful

[20] "Presbyter" was the word chosen to replace both "priest" and "minister" in the Church of South India.

approach in the matter of union to other Protestant Churches in India not included in the present scheme.[21]

After it had received the reply from the General Synod, the Arcot Assembly wrote back. The assembly told the synod that it deeply appreciated the synod's sympathy with Christians in South India in their desire for organic unity and also the synod's trust that the Spirit of Christ would determine for their Indian brethren on what lines the church would be unified and built up. It assured the Board of Foreign Missions that it was not prepared to accept any scheme of union that did not clearly incorporate the important elements stated in the resolutions of the General Synod. It also voted to inform the Madras Church Council of the South India United Church of its position on this matter.[22]

The negotiations concerning the union were successfully completed, with the result that a service consummating the union into the Church of South India took place September 27, 1947, six weeks after Indian independence from Britain. Reformed Church missionary C. R. Wierenga led the prayer of confession and later questioned the bishops about to be installed concerning their assent to the union. Indian layman C. J. Lucas read the scripture lesson from John 17.[23] Later in the service, F. M. Potter spoke as the representative both of the Reformed Church in America and of the Indian Committee of the Mission Conference in North America.[24] Following the consecration of the bishops, those gathered together celebrated by eating and drinking together at the service of Holy Communion. In this service the Christian community of previously divided churches was finally able officially to eat and drink together across denominational lines. That meal was a crucial matter to a church and missionary community that had insisted that its new converts eat and drink together across caste lines when they became united in Jesus Christ.

21 "Minutes of the Arcot Assembly," January 5-9, 1935, 18-19.
22 Ibid., January 6-8, 1936., 19-20.
23 Paul, First Decade, 22, 24.
24 Ibid., 31-32.

The inauguration of the Church of South India in 1947 marked the first occasion since the Reformation in which such a wide variety of Anglican, Presbyterian, Reformed, Methodist, and Congregational churches had merged into one body. It was also remarkable that all of the related overseas church and mission bodies had given their blessing to the union (although some Anglicans held reservations concerning the adequacy of the Church of South India's understanding of the Historic Episcopate).[25]

In terms of numbers, those coming from the Methodist tradition were approximately 220,000; Presbyterians and Congregationalists (South India United Church) 290,000; Anglicans 500,000; for a total of 1,010,000. The supporting missionary societies were the Church of England Zenana Missionary Society, (Anglican) Church Missionary Society, (Presbyterian) Church of Scotland Foreign Missions Committee, (Congregational) London Missionary Society, the Methodist Missionary Society of Britain, the Reformed Church Board of Foreign Missions, the (Congregational) American Board of Commissioners for Foreign Missions, and, to a more limited extent, the (Anglican) Society for the Propagation of the Gospel in Foreign Parts.[26]

The four basic principles for a united church were stated at the Tranquebar Conference. However, the life of the united church was set forth in more detail in the Constitution of the Church of South India. Several provisions in the "Governing Principles of the Church" section of the constitution incorporate concepts that the Arcot Mission had followed from the very beginning. One provision was that unity was understood to be desirable for the sake of the mission of the church. The purpose and nature of the union was stated thus:

> The Church of South India affirms that the purpose of the union by which it has been formed is the carrying out of

25 Ibid., 190-206.
26 Ibid., 209. The SPG-related churches in the Tinnevelli diocesan area entered the union, but a group of SPG-related churches in Nandyal refused to enter the Church of South India until several decades later.

God's will, as this is expressed in our Lord's prayer—"That they may all be one...that the world may believe that Thou didst send me." It believes that by this union the Church in South India will become a more effective instrument for God's work, and that there will be greater peace, closer fellowship and fuller life within the Church, and also renewed eagerness and power for the proclamation of the Gospel of Christ.[27]

The Church of South India further believed that the work of evangelization might be more completely fulfilled by the union. Its Governing Principles included Article 3 on "The Evangelistic Calling of the Church," that included the following:

It believes that the Holy Spirit has guided those Churches into this union in order that this same work of evangelization may be the more effectually fulfilled, in accordance with the prayer which Christ prayed that by the unity of His disciples the world might know that He had been sent to be its Saviour. Therefore the Church of South India purposes ever to be mindful of its missionary calling; and prays that it may not only be greatly used of God for the evangelization of South India, but may also take its due share in the preaching of the Gospel and the building up of Christ's Church in other parts of the world.[28]

The Church of South India recognized in its governing principles that the church's essential unity was grounded in the unity of Christ and that there were many points at which it was not yet really united. It understood itself to be growing into unity. The practices of the uniting churches that were brought into the union, including their forms of worship and their confessional statements, could continue to be used in the new church. Where such practices were in conflict

[27] *The Constitution of the Church of South India,* (Madras, The Christian Literature Society, 1956), 1-2, Art. 2.
[28] Ibid., 4, Art. 3.

with each other across denominational lines, the Church of South India believed that "a united Church would in due time be able to come to agreement on them."[29] Furthermore, while it anticipated that eventually all ministers would be episcopally ordained, it would for thirty years after the date of union recognize as validly ordained all those of the related churches or in the Church of South India who were ordained at the time of union.[30] As matters turned out, little notice was given to this thirty-year provision at the end of the period in 1977. The Church of South India continues to the present the policy of the Church of South India to recognize the validity of the ordinations of all the overseas uniting churches.

India Becomes an Independent Nation

As India approached its day of independence, August 15, 1947, Indian Christians were filled with a mixture of joyful anticipation and a measure of trepidation, because they did not know what treatment to expect from the majority Hindu community after the British left. The Reverend Joseph John, who was a proponent of independence, nevertheless alerted the Indian Church Board to possible rough waters ahead when he made his report as chair in 1946. He feared both the increasing tensions between Hindus and Muslims and the possibility of restriction of religious freedom and the propagation of the gospel. He wrote,

> The India which is emerging as Free India is not yet free from communal discord which seems to go from bad to worse. When Nationalism is the watchword in India, restrictions are placed on religious freedom and the propagation of the Gospel. Hard times are ahead for Christians. The temples are thrown open to all Hindus whether caste or outcaste and the villages so far served by our churches are being approached by National leaders.

[29] Ibid., 16, Art. 20.
[30] Ibid., 17, Art. 21.

How we are to meet this challenge and adopt new methods of approach, remaining true to the Message of our Lord, are some of the things that exercise our thought and Christian faith.[31]

C. R. Wierenga felt some of the same anxieties at the beginning of 1946. He too believed there were real problems ahead. He apparently took some comfort in the fact that, while the All-India Muslim League controlled the Muslim political world in India, the right wing Hindu religious and political Maha Sabba party had no political following worth mentioning. That meant that the Indian Congress would be the party in control after independence. He was not at all certain about what to expect from the Congress but he was sure that it would move quickly after it took over the government, and the Christian community would have to be prepared.[32]

When missionaries from the various missionary societies met in Kodaikanal in May, 1947, they decided to make a public declaration of their gratitude that the day of India's independence was at hand. They pledged themselves to support a free India and to identify with the people of the land. They declared,

We believe that this new freedom will usher in an era of progress and prosperity for this country and, further, that a free India will be an asset in the establishment of world freedom and peace. We pledge ourselves to help in every legitimate way to bring into being these possibilities. We would be servants of Christ and of India and would identify

[31] "AAR," 1946, 3.

[32] C. R. Wierenga to F. M. Potter, January 3, 1946. When India and Pakistan were divided into two separate countries after 1947, Pakistan was committed to being a Muslim country, while India's *Constitution* adopted the Indian National Congress position that India was to be a country with no established religion. In 1947, there were major riots when the two nations separated. It is estimated that more than six million persons had to move from their homes from India to Pakistan or vice versa and that as many as one million may have died or been killed in the riots between Hindus and Muslims. The Christian community in India played an important humanitarian role in caring for victims. The southern area of India remained relatively unaffected by the unrest in northern India.

ourselves with the people of this ancient land now coming
to a new birth—their sorrows our sorrows; their joys our
joys; and their future our future.[33]

The missionaries went on to declare their belief in the right of the
individual to outer conversion when there is inner conversion, but
that they had no desire to build up communal power for political
ends through making converts. They believed that it was debasing
to religion and to politics to use a religious movement to gain
political power. They pledged themselves to support the lawfully
established government set up to serve the interests of the people.
"We will give it our best. We would like Government to feel that
they can call on us to help toward making India the land of our
common hopes and of our prayers."[34]

After many decades in which they had expressed their fears that
India would descend into chaos if the British were to leave, the
missionaries had confidently given their support to a newly
independent India and stated that they were confident that a free
India would be a asset for world freedom and peace. A number of
Indian Christians spoke more soberly. The Reverend Arthur John
had also hoped for the day of independence. Nevertheless, in his
role as chairman of the Indian Church Board, he commented upon
challenges facing Christians in independent India. Several of his
comments are worth noting. First of all, he was pleased that a
number of leading Christians had been invited by the government
to shoulder responsibilities in shaping the future of India. He was
also pleased that a number of leading persons in India had borne
testimony to the fact that the religion of Christ had come to India
to stay and that the Christian faith exerted a healthy influence. Thus
on the national level, there were indications that Christians could
move forward with confidence.[35]

33 "A Missionary Declaration," issued at Kodaikanal, May, 1947 (copy in Archives of the
    RCA accompanied a letter sent by C. R. Wierenga to F. M. Potter, May 15, 1947).
34 Ibid.
35 "AAR," 1947-1948, 1.

Arthur John

Nevertheless, in the villages there was considerable confusion. Some non-Christians had been spreading rumors that all the missionaries would be leaving India and that the Christian religion would cease to exist there. John was pleased to hear from the villagers that they had responded to the rumors by affirming that Christianity is not of the West and that Christ would not leave India. Another problem in the villages was that, while the government had taken a definite stand against untouchability, the village caste people were still struggling to maintain their false prestige by refusing to give work to Christians and to deny to converts the same rights others enjoyed. John remained optimistic about the future, however. He believed that some of these things represent "only a passing stage in the development of the New India."[36]

The Right of Conversion in Independent India

The Indian church as well as the missionaries wondered whether in independent India the right to proclaim the gospel openly and the right of people to convert to another religion would remain. They were concerned that the Hindus would proclaim Hinduism to be the religion of the country, as the founders of Pakistan were declaring the Muslim religion to be the religion of their country. On this point, when the new constitution of the country was adopted,

[36] Ibid.

India declared itself to be a secular state that did not practice religious discrimination. There were three components of its concept of a secular state: freedom of religion, equal rights of citizenship, and separation of church and state.[37]

With regard to equal citizenship rights, the Indian Constitution did not outlaw the recognition of caste lines. On the contrary, it specifically ruled that certain privileges of "affirmative action," to use a more recent phrase, would be guaranteed to "Scheduled Castes" (that is, lower castes legally recognized as such).[38] What was ruled out was unjust discrimination. Article 15(1) reads, "The State shall not discriminate against any citizen on grounds only of religion, race, caste, sex, place of birth or any of them."

With regard to the separation of state and religion, Article 27 provided, "No person shall be compelled to pay any taxes, the proceeds of which are specifically appropriated in payment of expenses for the promotion or maintenance of any particular religion or religious denomination."[39] In its concept of the relation of state and religion, India does not hold to the rigid "wall of separation" that prevails in the United States. Following independence it continued to follow many of the policies that were in force during the era of British rule and still does today. It permits providing grants to many religious institutions such as schools and hospitals, but it does not permit such grants to be used for specifically religious purposes. For example, government grants must not be used to provide religious instruction within school hours in institutions receiving state funds.[40]

The issues of full rights of citizenship and separation of state and religion remained matters of real concern to Christians in India. However, in the time immediately following independence, missionaries and Indian Christians were particularly concerned that

[37] Donald Eugene Smith, *India as a Secular State* (Princeton, N.J.: Princeton Univ. Press, 1963), 102.
[38] Ibid., 136.
[39] Ibid., 137.
[40] Ibid., 137-38

there be freedom to propagate one's religion and that there be freedom to convert to another religion. They were greatly relieved, therefore, when Article 25(1) was finally adopted to read, "Subject to public order, morality and health and to the other provisions of this part, all persons are equally entitled to freedom of conscience, and the right freely to profess, practice and propagate religion."[41] By using the word, "persons," rather than "citizens," aliens including foreign missionaries who were legally in the country possessed the right openly to bear witness to their faith by word as well as deed.

The right to freedom of conscience together with the right to freely profess and practice one's religion meant that individuals were also free to convert to another religion. This was the most sensitive point, with a number of attempts being made in the years following independence to restrict the right to propagate and the right to convert. Since the call to conversion had been at the very heart of what the Scudders intended to do when they established the Arcot Mission, it is important at this point to clarify the issues related to conversion in India.[42]

On one level, the right to propagate one's faith and to convert to another religion is simply a matter of basic human rights. It has been recognized as such by the General Assembly of the United Nations in its Universal Declaration of Human Rights, adopted in 1948 with India as one of the signers. Article 18 reads,

> Everyone has the right to freedom of thought, conscience and religion; this right includes freedom to change his religion or belief, and freedom, either alone or in community with others and in public or private, to manifest his religion or belief in teaching, practice, worship and observance.[43]

41 Ibid., 102, 135.
42 For a further statement on conversion and proselytism, see Eugene Heideman, "Proselytism, Mission, and the Bible," in *International Bulletin of Missionary Research,* vol. 20, no. 1, January, 1996, 10-12.
43 "Universal Declaration of Human Rights," Art. 18, in *The United Nations and Human Rights: 1945-1995* (New York: Department of Public Information, United Nations, 1995), 154.

On another level, conversion represents a change of community. India was dominated by the solidarity of caste relationships and by the need of families to retain their property as well as to carry out a number of social obligations. In such a society, it is profoundly upsetting to the harmony of the family when one or more of its members decides to convert to another religion. The issue became even sharper when India became independent, because a shift of religious allegiance, especially in a mass movement, could also mean a shift of votes to another political party. It was for this reason that in the "Missionary Declaration" issued in Kodaikanal in May, 1947, the missionaries specifically denied any desire to use conversion to build up communal power for political ends.

On another level, many, like M. K. Gandhi, condemned conversion as manipulative "proselytism" that induced people to change their religion for the sake of gaining economic, social, or political advantages, or for other impure motives. Christians throughout India, including those in the Arcot Mission area and the Arcot missionaries, were placed on the defensive by the Niyogi Commission report submitted to the government of the state of Madhya Pradesh in 1956. Although the report is usually referred to by the name of the chairman of the committee, Dr. M. B. Niyogi, retired chief justice of the High Court in the state, the official name for the committee was, "The Christian Missionary Activities Inquiry Committee." The committee was appointed by the government of the state of Madhya Pradesh in 1954 to inquire into the charge that missionaries were converting illiterate and other backward people through the use of fraud, coercion, or monetary inducements. The missionaries denied these allegations and charged that local officials were harassing Christian communities in the tribal areas. From the moment that the names of the members of the committee were announced, there was opposition to its make-up as biased against missionaries and conversion.[44]

---

[44] Smith, *India as a Secular State,* 206.

The report provided statements of fact that since 1950 there had been an increase in the number of American missionaries in India, and that large sums of money were being spent in connection with educational, medical, and evangelistic work. It claimed that missionaries were engaging in "extra-religious" activities such as medical, agricultural, and village projects. It asserted that the West must realize that such activities are none of its business and that independent India needed no foreign help in solving its social and economic problems. It went on to make unsubstantiated charges, such as, "Conversions are mostly brought about by undue influence, misrepresentations, etc., or in other words not by conviction but by various inducements offered for proselytization in various forms."[45]

The Niyogi Commission recommended that those missionaries whose primary object is proselytization be asked to withdraw from India and that the influx of foreign missionaries should be checked. It further recommended that circulation of literature meant for religious propaganda without approval of the state government should be prohibited. Moreover, nonofficial organizations should be permitted to operate institutions only for members of their own faith, and only with the approval of the state.[46] The Niyogi Commission's report received strong support from the very orthodox Hindus and was widely discussed in the press.

It also aroused considerable anxiety among missionaries and Indian Christians. However, the commission's recommendations were so extreme that even those opposed to Christians propagating their faith saw the possible consequences of adopting the Niyogi recommendations. M. M. Thomas, a leading Indian Christian writing in the National Christian Council of India's journal, *Review,* criticized the report as "unashamedly totalitarian" and fascist.

> The philosophy of state and its relation to religion, culture and society underlying the report and advocated by it is

---

[45] Ibid., 208.

[46] Ibid., 212. The conclusions of the committee can be found in Blaise Levai, *Revolution in Mission,* (Vellore: Popular Press, 1957), 274-78.

unashamedly totalitarian....In fact, the writer of these comments is frankly more afraid of the political idea it represents and its effect on the future of the state in India than about the effect of the report on Christianity. Christianity is an anvil that has survived many hammers. It will outlive one more. But the infant secular democratic state of India has yet to find roots in the indigenous cultural soils and is imperiled by totalitarian ideas finding their place in government committees.[47]

Implied in Thomas's response to the report is the conclusion that, in defending their right to propagate their faith and to call people to conversion, the Christian church was also defending the human rights of all people in the nation.

Bills in favor of the Niyogi recommendations were introduced in the Central Government parliament as well as in various state assemblies. The Board of Foreign Missions, in its 1957 report, included several paragraphs about what was happening in India regarding opposition to conversions. It informed members of the Reformed Church that when a bill seeking to implement the Niyogi recommendations was introduced in the Indian parliament, Prime Minister Nehru took a strong stand against the bill as unconstitutional. In spite of strong attacks against missionary activities in the Indian press and elsewhere, the spirit of opposition was dying down and a large measure of freedom continued to exist. The Board of Foreign Missions was encouraged by what had happened during the course of the controversy as it wrote, "In the decisive defeat of the restrictive bill in Parliament, we have reason to take courage and look with confidence toward the Church in India, continuing with vigor and effectiveness her ministry of redemption, and with joy undertake to undergird her in every way possible."[48]

In a sense, the Niyogi Commission report was correct in its assumption that the right to conversion was a denationalizing

47 M. M. Thomas, quoted in ibid., 212-13.
48 "BFMR," 1956, 16.

concept in India. It could have pointed to the fact that it was a group of missionaries at the Madras Missionary Conference in 1876 who had defended the liberty of conscience and the rights of converts to both spiritual and material entitlements. They had approached British administrators and urged them to reconsider their cautious and conservative approach, in which they gave preference to Hindu community laws concerning property, marriage, divorce, and other customary law, even when such laws subverted the right to liberty of conscience and freedom of choice on the part of the individual.[49] The missionaries in that case were calling upon the experience of England and the traditions of John Locke, who had advocated liberty of conscience and the right to conversion as a means to break through the devastation of the religious wars that had raged in England for almost two centuries. In the face of such appeals made by missionaries, the Niyogi Commission could with some justification maintain that conversion was a foreign concept imported into India.

When the missionaries defended the right of conscience and the rights of converts to both spiritual and material entitlements, they were also affirming the idea that a nation can live with a pluralism of possibilities. They were advocating for a nation that is egalitarian, just, open, protective, and constitutional, and at the same time one that is committed to a legal leveling of religious differences. Whether they intended it or not, their position implied that, in terms of the unity and identity of the nation, the religion to which one converts is less important than is the right itself to change religions.[50]

The issues in the debate between Nehru and the proponents of the recommendations of the Niyogi Commission report have continued to haunt the country to the present day as the various political parties vie for votes and influence. The nation functions constitutionally in defense of liberty of conscience; the right to conversion; and in opposition to discrimination on the basis of

---

[49] Viswanathan, *Outside the Fold*, 75-76.
[50] Ibid.

caste, sex, or religion; but there continue to be strong currents of support for the idea that India is a religious Hindu nation within which other religions are encapsulated.

At the deepest level, however, the issue of the whether the missionaries were right in calling upon people to repent, believe the good news of Jesus Christ, and be baptized is not one of civil rights or right methods that avoid manipulation. The issue is that of the truth of the gospel that Jesus is God's only Son, the Savior of the world. It is whether Jesus is one great teacher among many, or whether the event of the cross and resurrection has a unique role to play in the salvation of the world. It is the difference between the affirmation of God's one incarnation in Jesus Christ and the affirmation that Vishnu has appeared in nine *avatars* to save the world from injustice.

At this deepest level, the decision cannot be made by means of historical research into missionary practices, such as whether the missionaries enhanced or destroyed the cultures into which they entered, whether the missionaries were respectful or arrogant, or whether they were on the side of freedom or of colonialism. The missionaries were sinners like the rest of humanity and most of them knew it, at least to a moderate extent. The issue at its deepest level does not revolve around the missionary or the church; it is the question of the truth of the message. This is the issue of faith rather than of historical research. At this point in our historical study of the mission of the Reformed Church in India, we have gone as far as we can go into the issue of conversion. To go further would be to move into a full-scale theological discussion rather than a historical study.

The First Five Years in Independent India and the Church of South India

Life did not change overnight for most of the people in the old Arcot Mission area after India became independent and the Church of South India was born. Life went on in the villages and towns pretty much as before. In the writing of history, one is forced for the sake of brevity to deal with turning points and new developments, while ignoring to a large extent those things important to the daily lives of people that go on generation after generation. As we focus on the points of change and of tension, we must not forget that most of the time missionaries and Indian Christians were dealing with the daily matters of life where it was being lived. Pastors were preparing and delivering sermons, administering the sacraments, baptizing, marrying, and burying people. Teachers were dealing with the subjects at hand and classroom discipline. Fathers and mothers were seeking to earn enough for their family's daily food and to pay the fees for their children's education. Medical people were caring for the sick, doing surgeries, praying with patients.

For the first five years after independence, 1947-1952, the village people in the area were faced with perhaps the worst famine in the history of the Arcot Mission. Others were worse for short periods, but this one went on for five years. During that whole time, the monsoon rains failed. The cumulative effect of so long a drought resulted in impoverishment and depopulation of village areas. The goal of self-support had to be pushed back once again as people "were reduced to the choice between beggary and starvation. Hundreds migrated to the Kolar Gold Fields, Mysore Coffee Estates, and other distant places. Those who took part in relief-work had an opportunity to demonstrate real Christian charity by the aid they rendered at the gruel-centers."[51]

Once again, Christians in the villages suffered the most. Arthur John in Chittoor observed, "They have neither the money to purchase grain nor land to produce it. Instead of sending their children to school they have to send them as servants to high-caste Hindu houses to earn their food. Supplies from Church World Service and famine-relief funds from the Reformed Church in America have come just in time to alleviate some of the suffering."[52] The same conditions prevailed in the Katpadi area, where church

51 Wyckoff, *One Hundred Years*, 126-27.
52 "AAR," 1949-50, 19.

attendance fell off because people had to engage in a desperate search for work and food seven days a week.[53]

John Piet, like other missionaries and Indian leaders, believed that providing relief in times of disasters such as famines is one of the most difficult things to handle. Wherever possible, food-for-work projects were established in place of direct food distribution programs in order to assist the recipients to retain a measure of self-respect.

People in the villages continued to ask to be instructed in the Christian faith and to declare that they desired to receive baptism, according to the report from Madanapalle: "Our great task seems to be Bible instruction in the new village waiting to be baptized. In one village where sixty persons became Christians the only literate person is a woman, who conducts evening prayers. Another village is asking for baptism because one woman there wanted something better for her children."[54]

In spite of India's new constitution, discrimination and persecution continued on the local level. Two such cases were reported in the Chittoor area. In one case, the Hindu headman of a village threatened the Christians when they began to raise money for a church building. He declared that he would build a temple on that very spot and force them to offer sacrifices to the idol. His activities led to a riot and a dispute that lasted for two years until his death, but the Christians went on gathering stones to be used in the construction of the church.

In the second case, false accusations were made against the Christians, and their village was burned to the ground one night in May, 1950. The people had to live in sheds and were prevented by the chief man among their enemies from rebuilding their homes. There was one high-caste Hindu man who was bold enough to give them employment, but his life was threatened for doing so.[55]

---

53 Ibid., 27-28.
54 "AAR," 1949-1950, 3.
55 Ibid., 19.

Some change for the better was noticed as people gained self-respect in an independent India. They took more responsibility for each other, for discipline of those who needed some correction, and for moving toward self-support. New cooperation among Christians was beginning to take place because the churches had been united. The report from Ranipet was particularly positive.

> The morality of the people is improved. Members are carefully and prayerfully watched that they may not get into the habit of illicit drinking. Disputes between Christians are settled in a *panchayat* [a local church court], not taken to a court of law. In spite of famine conditions the church has grown in the grace of giving....Some village congregations are saving money for new church buildings....Though a few Anglicans in the town continue to have separate communion service, the members feel that they are units of a larger church, and are beginning to realize their responsibility to that church.[56]

At the time of union, the Church of South India was organized to include fourteen dioceses, each under the leadership of a bishop. The pastorates that were in the old Arcot Mission area were assigned to two different dioceses. The Telugu pastorates of Punganur and Madanapalle were placed in the Diocese of Rayalaseema under the leadership of Bishop Sumitra, who also became the moderator of the Church of South India. The rest of the pastorates were placed in the Diocese of Madras, under the leadership of Bishop Michael Hollis. Bishop Sumitra had been reared in the congregationalist tradition of the London Missionary Society, while Bishop Hollis had been the Anglican Bishop in Madras prior to union.

In 1950 the government of India made the decision to divide the Presidency of Madras into two states: Madras State in the Tamil language area and Andhra Pradesh in the Telugu area. The border

56 Ibid. 22-23.

was drawn according to where the people usually spoke one or the other language. It was therefore drawn about half-way between Katpadi and Chittoor, with Chittoor District being included in Andhra Pradesh. Thus the pastorates of Palmaner and Chittoor, although consisting largely of Tamil-speaking members, were left in a different state from the rest of the pastorates of the diocese. This division created constant problems, particularly in the field of education where the two state governments at times operated with different rules and different salary scales.

It seems that the missionaries and Indians in the old Arcot Mission area came rather slowly to the realization that the union into the Church of South India was causing much greater organizational and relational changes than had the previous union into the South India United Church. The South India United Church had developed a strong sense of mutual identity in matters of church order, the nature of the ordained ministry, and mutual cooperation in many areas of mission. In its actual life it had remained very much a confederation. It operated with a great sense of loyalty to the old mission areas and little if any sharing of missionary personnel and resources across mission lines, except in the cases of certain union institutions. The Church of South India did not want to be a confederation. It was desired that old mission loyalties should be replaced by a new sense of being together in the one church. This required a far greater shift of loyalties and attitudes than had been necessary in the South India United Church.

Indian Leadership of Institutions

From the time the Arcot Assembly came into being in 1924, Indians had requested more opportunities to lead in the educational and medical mission, as well as by serving as circle chairmen in supervision of the work of the churches and elementary schools. One place where their leadership was accepted was as headmasters and headmistresses of the high schools. C. J. Lucas served for many years as principal of the men's Union Training School in Viruthampet.

In 1938, Dr. Chorley replaced Dr. Louisa Hart to become the first Indian to be superintendent of one of the mission hospitals. Following the sudden death of John De Boer in May, 1940, V. P. Adiseshiah (whom we have previously met as the young Brahmin in Madanapalle whose request caused such a stir) was named to replace him as principal of Voorhees College. He served for a little more than a year prior to his retirement and was replaced by S. J. Savarirayan.

When India became independent in 1947, all of the major institutions in the area with the exception of Voorhees College were under the leadership of missionaries who had come to India in the 1920s. Their retirements were expected in the late 1950s or possibly even later. In light of the general anticipation in the country that after independence Indians would be in places of leadership, this situation naturally created some anxiety among Indians and missionaries, since both were sensitive to public criticism on the matter.

Vulnerability of Missionaries in Leadership Positions in Independent India

The anxiety surrounding mission work and the necessity for Indian leadership in independent India was heightened in 1948 when a labor strike unexpectedly took place at the Industrial Institute in Katpadi. After the war, the institute had prospered. The facilities were being used with maximum efficiency. Many servicemen who had returned from the war had been re-employed. A system of overtime work made wages considerably higher than average in the community. When the labor law changed, the overtime system of payment had to be changed, so the basic wages were increased 12.5 percent instead.[57]

There were some undercurrents of dissatisfaction among the workers at the institute. Ben Rottschaefer was a creative and strong-minded manager. With the best interests of his workers in mind, he

[57] "AAR," 1947-1948, 60.

had built a new village, named "Bernicepuram" after his wife, a short distance from the institute's buildings. It was a model Christian village with well-built homes that the workers were allowed to purchase. In order to maintain its character as a village for the workers, there were a certain number of restrictions in place, including some restrictions on lifestyle. He was also concerned that families would have an adequate income, with the result that marital status was at times taken into consideration in matters of remuneration. All of these provisions had been put in place with the best intentions and appreciated at the time.

But times had changed. With its large number of employees, the institute had to work under the regulations of the factory act that governed matters such as wage scales and workers' rights. A worker had been dismissed "for irregularity of attendance and poor work that arose out of his bigamous life."[58] The mission for one hundred years had regarded such actions as clear causes for dismissal. In this case the man had been taken back on condition that he leave off all connection with his concubine and lead a life according to the usually accepted Christian moral standards.[59] Meanwhile, Communists who were active in the area entered the scene and convinced many of the workers that they were being exploited. They urged workers to put forth a number of demands about salary and other working conditions, as a result of which a work stoppage took place in early 1948.

There was disagreement about whether it was a strike, as the management claimed, or a lock-out, as the workers claimed. The labor conciliation officer termed it a lock-out. The Area Coordinating Committee met twice and suggested that the fundamental principles necessary to maintain a Christian atmosphere had to be upheld and that the management had the right to determine moral conditions of employment in a mission institution. In response to workers' concerns, the committee suggested that the differential wage rate

58 "Report of the Executive Committee, Arcot Coordinating Committee Minutes," August 18-19, 1948.
59 Ibid.

between married and single be dropped, since many of the single persons also had family responsibilities. These suggestions were not acceptable to the workers, who at that time were placing their trust in their Communist advisors.[60]

When the labor adjudicator ruled, "I think no employer should enter into matters concerning private life and it is not within my province to go into these matters,"[61] the Area Coordinating Committee and the missionaries realized that it would not be possible for one of their institutions to operate under the provisions of the factory act in the prevailing mood in India at that time. The missionaries as heads of institutions were too vulnerable as foreigners, and the labor agitators would be no less willing to act if an Indian manager were in place. The result was that the commercial division of the Katpadi Industrial Institute was closed down and the employees were dismissed. The boarding school was closed, and the training course in carpentry was stopped. The higher elementary day school continued to exist, but its attendance dropped by 50 percent because of the workers' opposition.[62] Ben Rottschaefer continued to carry out his other duties and to supervise building projects throughout the Arcot area by employing a number of persons and using subcontractors. In one such major project of erecting buildings at the Christian Medical Hospital in Vellore, he showed his continuing concern for the men who had lost their jobs when the industrial institute was closed:

> When we returned to Katpadi in November 1950 we found families starving in our own backyard. They were families who were suffering because they had been misled and deceived by the rosy promises of their Communist Advisors. Some were those who even threatened to manhandle me. Seeing the golden opportunity of proving that we harbored

60 C. R. Wierenga to F. M. Potter, March 2, 1948.
61 "Report of the Executive Committee, Arcot Coordinating Committee Minutes," August 18-19, 1948.
62 "AAR," 1947-1948, 61.

no spite and because we had well seasoned timber in large
quantity and because we were assigned to the construction
work of the Medical College we are today employing more
than 60 workers and affording them a living until the
Institute is finally liquidated and they shall have opportunity
to find more permanent work elsewhere.[63]

The substantial Katpadi Industrial Institute property remained to
be dealt with, but no clear course of action could be found for
several years. When Ben and Mildred De Vries were stationed there
in 1954, it was decided that it would be possible to reopen the
institute under "cottage industry" rules.[64] These allowed workers to
use their craft skills and their carving and carpentry training in
making furniture and other items for sale. Under cottage industry
rules, the workers were not employees of the institute but were paid
for the items they produced. These were the same rules under which
the women in the Palmaner area worked for the Women's Industrial
Institute extension department. The carpentry training school was
opened once more in 1958.[65]

The events at the Katpadi Industrial Institute caused great
concern among the missionaries as well as in the Katpadi church,
where industrial institute workers constituted 50 percent of the
congregation. The leaders of the church took their stand about the
moral issue involved but were not able to bring about any settlement
of the issues. The pastor of the church, the Reverend J. Ebenezer,
believed that the workers were being very much influenced by the
Communist agitators.[66] The case also raised concerns in certain
circles in the Reformed Church in America that India like China
might fall to the Communists.

Among the missionaries who felt deep anxieties about the role of
missionaries in independent India was Mina Jongewaard, who was

---

63 Ben Rottschaefer to B. Luben, letter received in New York, September 23, 1952.
64 Herbert Van Vranken to B. Luben, December 10, 1954.
65 "Minutes of the Economic Board, Madras Diocese," sent by Bishop's Chaplain to M.
    J. John, April 7, 1958.
66 "AAR," 1947-1948, 17.

the director of the Women's Industrial Institute in Palmaner. She felt vulnerable in light of her responsibility to supervise the women in the villages who were making articles for sale by the extension department. She felt that Rottschaefer had been very level headed and that he had handled the situation as well as anyone could have.

> The conditions are bad and Katpadi is the first of many other mission institutions that will fold up soon....This we fear will soon be true of schools as well as factories. They are passing so many rules that we as Christians can't keep and if we can't follow we may be ordered to hand them over....Well, there are so many problems we missionaries face and we are all very discouraged because of the communist influence everywhere.[67]

Indians Become Heads of Church-related Institutions

Although Indian Christians continually stated that they wanted missionaries to remain and while Mina Jongewaard was more pessimistic than most others, the senior missionaries who had been leaders of their institutions for decades also began to believe that the time was arriving when Indians should become the heads of those institutions. During 1954, three senior missionaries resigned their positions in order to make it possible for an Indian successor to be named. Galen Scudder, the last of the Scudder family serving in India, retired in 1954, and Dr. Julius Savarirayan was named as the medical superintendent of the Scudder Memorial Hospital. J. J. De Valois went on furlough for a year and M. J. John was named acting director of the agricultural institute. When De Valois returned to India, M. J. John was named director, while De Valois continued to serve by administering special projects. C. R. Wierenga resigned as principal of the Arcot Theological Seminary in favor of the Reverend E. Tychicus, who had been serving as a teacher there for

---

[67] Mina Jongewaard to F. M. Potter, June 10, 1949.

some time. Leadership in the Diocese of Madras also changed hands in that year when the Reverend David Chellapa became bishop, replacing the English missionary, Bishop A. Michael Hollis.[68]

The Role of the Arcot Theological Seminary in the Church of South India

When Christian denominations merge to form a new denomination, it often becomes necessary to decide how many theological seminaries for the training of ordained ministers should continue and which of the seminaries existing prior to union should be closed or dedicated to another purpose. This issue faced the Church of South India dioceses in the Tamil language area after 1947. To the disappointment of the people in the Arcot area, it was ultimately decided that the seminary to teach ministerial candidates in the Tamil language should be located at Nazareth in the ex-Anglican Tinnevelli area, rather than Pasumalai near Madura or in Vellore. This raised the question of what the continuing role of the Arcot Theological Seminary should be.

In order to recognize the importance of the question, it is important to review briefly the history of the Arcot Theological Seminary in its relation to the Reformed Church in America and in its place in the South India United Church. The General Synod of the Reformed Church made it a seminary of the denomination to operate directly under the General Synod, as was also the case with the New Brunswick Theological Seminary and Western Theological Seminary. The General Synod, rather than the Board of Foreign Missions, was responsible for support and management of the seminary. The General Synod raised an endowment of over $50,000 and asked the Classis of Arcot to appoint persons to its Board of Superintendents. It voted that the Reverend William Waterbury Scudder be installed in the office of Professor of Theology, to be assisted by Indian teachers and other missionaries as they could be made available.

[68] "BFMR," 1955, 16-17.

When the South India United Church was formed, the Arcot Theological Seminary served the church and mission agencies related to the Madras Church Council. When the Classis of Arcot was transferred to the South India United Church, the General Synod authorized the Arcot Mission to appoint three missionaries and two Indians to the Board of Superintendents, with other cooperating missions invited to appoint one from each mission. The General Synod was concerned that if it became a union seminary its theology would no longer be specifically Reformed in nature. The General Synod resolved that:

> inasmuch as the present endowment was provided exclusively by the Reformed Church in America, therefore the Chair of Theology originally founded by it should permanently remain at the disposition of the General Synod and the relations of the Professor to the Synod remain unchanged. To him it is, in fact, that the church looks for "soundness of faith" under the new arrangement.[69]

Students were sent to the Arcot Seminary by the Danish Lutheran Mission, the Church of Scotland Mission, and the London Missionary Societies, and other missions, in addition to those of the Arcot Mission. The missions paid monthly stipends to the students for the time they were at the seminary, since the students were too poor to pay for their own education and living costs. Most of its students went on to become catechists and teachers. Those of exceptional ability continued to study longer in order to meet academic requirements for ordination. The course of instruction was based very much on the curriculum for theological education that had developed in Great Britain and the Reformed Church in America. At times more recent developments in theology made their influence felt, although the professors of theology were all solidly orthodox

---

[69]Edward T. Corwin, *A Digest of Constitutional and Synodical Legislation of the Reformed Church in America* (New York: Board of Publications of the Reformed Church in America, 1906), 60.

From Mission to Church

by Reformed Church standards. But other winds did blow from time to time, as we learn in reading the 1934 Arcot Mission Report:

> Two streams of influence have touched the institution this year. The one influence of the so called group movement has left its imprint on many and though perhaps lacking in the true Oxford accent is no doubt responsible for the very excellent work of evangelism carried out in commendable methodical fashion by the student group. The other, though less perceptible is no less strong. The influence of Karl Barth has come to our institution with strong conviction. Both movements, one supplemental to the other, are bearing down upon the student body through members of the staff.[70]

Negotiations toward wider union were moving forward in 1936. In order to further the interests of such a union, the Scottish missions decided to dissociate themselves as contributing members of the seminary. Wierenga learned that the action had essentially been taken as the result of a recommendation from Dr. Maclean, who was involved in the union negotiations. Maclean was influenced by his hope that the theological school of the Madura Mission at Pasumalai near Madura would become the Tamil-language union school for theological training in the anticipated new united church. Pasumalai had the advantage of being more centrally located in the Tamil area, while Vellore was on the northern edge. Pasumalai was also located closer to the area where the large Anglican churches were present. Wierenga had considerable hesitation about a Pasumalai location. "The people of Pasumalai for one thing suddenly become too zealous Anglicans—in their services, dress, even their preaching they completely capitulated…."[71] The Anglicans did not enter into the movement toward Pasumalai at that time, so the impact of Maclean's hope for a union location there did not move

---

[70] "AAR," 1934, 51.
[71] C. R. Wierenga to F. M. Potter, December 30, 1936.

Ebenezer Tychicus

forward and the Church of Scotland Mission continued to send theological students to Vellore.

After the Church of South India was formed, it decided that there should be one theological seminary in the Tamil area and that it should be located in Nazareth, which was southeast of Madura in the ex-Anglican area. The Arcot Theological Seminary was transferred by the General Synod of the Reformed Church to the Madras Diocese of the Church of South India in 1954. It was anticipated that the seminary would continue to provide an excellent course of theological studies for catechists and teachers under the leadership of the Reverend E. Tychicus.[72]

New Forms of Missionary Service

Charlotte Wyckoff had been heavily involved in educational work from the time she arrived in India as a missionary in 1915. Her dream for many years, however, was to live among the people in the

---

[72] At this point I cannot refrain from inserting a personal note. During much of our family's time in India between 1960-1970, we lived next door to the Rev. and Mrs. Tychicus. He was serving as chairman of the Western Area of the Diocese at Madras as well as principal of the seminary of that time. His quiet wisdom and broad perspectives on the needs of the area prevented me from making mistakes and helped me grow into ministry in India. By 1960 the role senior missionaries had once played in orienting new missionaries to life in India was more and more being fulfilled by Indians such as Rev. Tychicus—eph.

Charlotte Wyckoff

rural area in which her parents, John H. and Emma Wyckoff, had lived in the southern area of the mission. Through the 1930s, the Arcot Mission was always short of missionary personnel and funds, so Wykoff promised the mission that, if she could continue to receive her missionary salary, she would start her new work living in a tent, using about Rs. 1,500 that friends in America had given her while she was on furlough.

By 1941, the arrival of additional unmarried female missionaries opened the door to Wyckoff's release to work in the southern area, but she was still lacking in funds to employ an Indian Bible woman to work alongside her. In that year, she was asked to be the main speaker at the big outdoor meeting of the Women's Gospel Extension Society, where five hundred women were present. The Women's Gospel Extension Society had been founded by Indian women in 1892 for the purpose of raising funds to support designated Bible women. In her speech, Wyckoff shared her dream of opening a center in the southern area but said that she had not found any Indian woman to accompany her and that, even if such a person came forward, she still lacked funds to support an extra person. After she had spoken to the women at the meeting, one of them came to the microphone and proposed that the Women's

Gospel Extension Society assist her to get started. That proposal was enthusiastically endorsed, and Charlotte Wyckoff was at last free to fulfill her dream.[73]

Charlotte Wyckoff knew how to write letters to bring people to make a positive response. One of her letters about medical needs in the area led I. J. Dhriviam, a nurse trained at Ranipet Hospital, to volunteer to work with her. The women of the area had developed "the Lord's handful" program, according to which a woman would place in a separate box the first handful of grain for the family's food for the day. That grain would then be her contribution for the women's project. By this means, women in India supported Wyckoff's work. In 1941, the women of Katpadi raised Rs. 32, the southern circle women raised Rs. 25, and the Chittoor women Rs. 50 in three months' time. Women in America heard about the project and contributed $1,500 for nonrecurring expenses that enabled her to build a small thatched building for a medical dispensary where Nurse Dhriviam could work.[74] She herself moved from her tent into a village-style thatched roof mud hut complete with a cow-dung floor.[75] The site she chose at Muttathur was one that had been abandoned a number of years earlier because of budget cut-backs, but it was on a main road with seven Christian villages in a two-mile radius. Joseph Mayou had been the first missionary to visit some of those villages.

A pioneer missionary project begun by a woman with great energy, love for the people, a sense of humor, and the ability to provide vivid descriptions of her work could not fail to attract goodwill and contributions. At the end of ten years, the project had

[73] Wyckoff, *One Hundred Years*, 113.

[74] "Arcot Coordinating Committee Report," 1941, 39.

[75] The cow dung floor is made from earth mixed with some cow dung and a few other ingredients. When installed in a village home, it can be kept very clean. It is a little softer and cooler than concrete, and therefore more comfortable, but it requires more maintenance and had some disadvantages. Esther De Weerd told me on several occasions that one year when Charlotte Wyckoff had gone on furlough, she had agreed to be assigned there for that year on condition that she would be allowed to install a concrete floor. That was agreed to. When Charlotte Wyckoff returned, she said she was pleased with her new floor.

Jothi Nilayam, Charlotte Wyckoff in her tent

grown to include many activities, but its buildings all remained very simple and efficient for their purposes. Her tenth-year edition of the *Jothy Nilayam* ("*Place of Light*") *Journal* tells of the enormous amount of famine relief work going on at Muttuthur in the fifth year of the famine. She had received generous sums from the Reformed Church in America and in England. CARE parcels, sacks of grain, barrels of milk and egg powder, cartons of multipurpose food, and dried fish powder all came to her place. In the worst days of the famine, she worked in cooperation with local authorities to provide one bowl of nourishing food per day to as many as five hundred people.[76]

A leprosy clinic was opened with about seven hundred people on the roll for weekly treatment. The schools that were operating there had students walking in each day from thirty-three surrounding villages. Nurse Dhriviam traveled to Madras to receive a medal from the Red Cross in recognition of her "outstanding work in nursing" for operating a dispensary for hundreds of people with no doctor available to them or to her. A Bible woman named Rhoda Bunyan was employed, and then a second woman, Booshnam

---

[76] Charlotte Wyckoff, *Jothy Nilayam Journal* (for private circulation) no. 11, 1952, 2-5.

Lazarus (not related to Kamala Lazarus whom we will meet below), was added. Wyckoff wrote of Lazarus, "She was very keen to do that sort of work and has proved herself an able evangelist, willing to tramp from village to village—as Rhoda does—and with the wisdom and tact to deal with Hindus. Since she is the mother of nine children, she pulls more weight than Rhoda, who is unmarried!"[77]

Over the years, Jothi Nilayam became a center for communicating the gospel. Film strips and moving pictures were shown in the evenings with the aid of a generator to supply electricity for the projector. The pastor sang the gospel message as the pictures were shown. Gospel portions were sold and people were encouraged to enroll in Bible correspondence courses.[78] The number of people in the congregation of Muttathur grew.[79]

When Charlotte Wyckoff retired in 1960, Muttathur was still a place to which an Indian doctor could go only at the price of personal sacrifice. The Reverend Henry Lazarus, who was pastor of the leading church in the Arcot area, Central Church in Vellore, was asked to go to Muttathur to serve as pastor and also to manage the variety of activities at Jothi Nilayam. His wife, Dr. Kamala Lazarus, resigned her position as a doctor on the staff of the Christian Medical College Hospital in order to take over the medical services at Muttathur. Their acceptance of serving as Charlotte Wyckoff's replacement represented a great sacrifice on their part, especially for Kamala's career and their family income. They made only two requests. One was that the Board of Foreign Missions would take responsibility for the debt of Rs. 5,000 left by Wyckoff, who was always notoriously generous beyond her resources. The second was that the board would grant them enough money to build a good parsonage. They found it very difficult to live in the thatched house that Wyckoff had used as a single person.[80] Fortunately, six months

---

[77] Charlotte Wyckoff to B. Luben, April 22, 1953.
[78] RCA missionary John Piet introduced the use of Bible correspondence courses as a means of evangelistic outreach, beginning in the 1950s.
[79] Ibid., 10-13.
[80] Henry Lazarus to B. Luben, April 4, 1960.

later a Reformed Church congregation made an extra contribution
of $5,000 to cover both needs.[81]

With the growing strength of Indian leadership, ordained Indian
pastors took over much of the responsibility for administering the
work of the pastorate circles under the Indian Church Board. When
the Reverend Ralph Korteling saw that an Indian leader was
available to chair his Northern Circle and to take over many of his
responsibilities of circle management, he realized that missionaries
could be free to engage in new forms of missionary service. He
believed that the church needed assistance in acquiring new
audiovisual materials for its Christian education and evangelism.
The pictures and "magic lantern" shows that had served so well a
quarter of a century earlier no longer were adequate.[82]

Soon the Arcot Mission had agreed to release Ralph Korteling for
one-half time to serve as "field director for audio-visual work for
South India" under the National Christian Council of India.
Among his responsibilities were the production of film strips, new
pictures, flannelgraph materials, and other audiovisual aids for use
by the churches and Christian workers in the whole of South
India.[83] Upon the Kortelings' return from furlough in 1951, Ralph
was also commissioned to develop for the centenary celebration in
1953 a three-reel, 16mm film portraying the history of the Arcot
Mission. This film was made available to the Reformed Church in
America. It was also shown throughout the Arcot Mission area as
a means of helping the people there to know the history and
significance of their church.

*Concentration, Diffusion, and Integration of Reformed Church Mission
in the Church of South India*

The changing role of senior missionaries provided a clear signal
that new thought needed to be given to the future of the Reformed

[81] B. Luben to Henry Lazarus, February 16, 1961.
[82] Ralph Korteling to Sue Weddell, October 6, 1949.
[83] "Report of the All-India Conference of Audio-Visual Education," April 3-5, 1948.

Church mission in India. For almost a hundred years, the boundaries of the Reformed Church's mission had been clearly marked, subject to minor adjustments through negotiations with other missions. Union institutions and cooperative work with other missions had become a way of life, but the boundaries had remained firm. Any missionary who was loaned to another mission for work outside the mission, or any missionary who wished to take furlough or vacation outside the "bounds of the mission," had to obtain approval to leave its bounds, even for a stay of a week.

When the Church of South India placed the Telugu language pastorate areas in the Diocese of Rayalaseema and the Tamil language pastorate areas in the Diocese of Madras, the "bounds of the mission" became less clear. At the very least, missionaries had to be free to travel within the bounds of their own dioceses, and possibly within the Church of South India's bounds, without gaining permission from the mission. Prior to 1947, missionaries had been appointed by the Board of Foreign Missions to serve in the Arcot Mission; the mission in turn had agreed that specific responsibility for assignment of missionaries within the mission area should be delegated to the Arcot Assembly. This arrangement gave Indian church leaders in the Arcot area a crucial role in placing missionaries in specific assignments. After the formation of the Church of South India, a question began to arise about this practice. Would it be better for the Board of Foreign Missions to assign missionaries to a diocese without the involvement of the Arcot Mission or a local body such as the Arcot Assembly?

The question was wider and deeper than that of the role of the missionaries. The whole question of the relationship of the mission calling of the Reformed Church in America to the mission calling of the Church of South India had to be reconsidered. Furthermore, questions arose about who in the Church of South India should be the Reformed Church's primary working partner. Should it be the Synod of the Church of South India as a whole, the two dioceses of Rayalaseema and Madras, or, within each diocese, should it be the district or area to which the Reformed Church had been historically related? Another question was whether the Reformed Church was still called to a mission of its own within the Church of South India, or to a mission alongside the Church of South India. Some people in independent India were suggesting that the missionary era should come to an end and the missionary should go home. Should the Reformed Church in America also agree that its mission in India was finished and allow or force the Church of South India to be a truly self-supporting, self-governing, self-propagating church?

With all of these questions as well as other issues rising to the surface, the Indian Christians and the missionaries asked that they be given time between 1947 and the year of the centenary celebrations in 1953 to think through some of the issues. Their request was consistent with the history of the Arcot Mission, which had used its fiftieth and seventy-fifth anniversary celebrations for similar reconsideration of the purposes and goals of the mission. The Arcot Mission, the Arcot Coordinating Committee, and the Indian Church Board planned to develop a set of policy papers that members of those bodies would discuss with the deputation from the Reformed Church at the time of the celebrations.[84] A set of nine papers was prepared on major themes. Each paper was developed by a committee of three to five persons, balanced between missionaries and Indians. Space does not permit consideration of all the papers, but we will take note of their contents as appropriate in this and the following chapter.

The Case for Reformed Church Concentration in its Particular Mission

The first paper was entitled, "The Future Relationship of the Reformed Church in America with Its Work in India." Its committee was composed of two of the most senior missionaries, C. R. Wierenga and B. Rottschaefer, and two leading Indian ordained ministers, Arthur John and E. Tychicus. Although the style of

[84] The set of policy papers, printed in 1953, is available in the Joint Archives and in the Archives of the RCA.

writing is clearly Wierenga's, the paper is consistent with the patterns of leadership that all four gave to the area over a number of years. Thus one can conclude that, while there were some clear reservations on the part of some of the other missionaries and Indians participating, those reservations were not between Indian and missionary leadership.

The paper began with a succinct statement of the policy that had governed its administrative structures in 1910. The statement is worthy of careful reading. It acknowledged that all of the organizations and administrative bodies that had been created over the course of time were intended to be succeeded by the organized church in India

> as soon as that Church could assume its functions and powers, without in the slightest being encumbered by any unworthy restraint on the part of those bodies at whose sacrifice the progress of the Church must necessarily be made. In order to accelerate that time, unlike most other Missions in India, the Arcot Mission kept distinct the life and function of the Church (under which was also grouped village primary education) and the Missionary institutional program such as High schools and College, Hospitals, Industrial and Agricultural establishments. These activities were kept distinct so as to allow the Church sooner to attain its independent status, not with the purpose of secularizing the institutions. Careful safeguards were laid down in the Constitutions of the Arcot Co-ordinating Committee, Area Councils, and indeed the Constitution of every institution to maintain an inseparable and vital link with the Church, both as a local institution and as a territorial body. The distinction was maintained solely to assure an early self-governing Church, unshackled by financial obligations which a multitude of beneficial but not absolutely essential institutions would entail.[85]

[85] "The Future Relationship of the Reformed Church in America with Its Work in India," 3-4.

The paper went on to point out that, consistent with this policy, the Indian Church Board, which had responsibility for the work of the pastorates and village elementary education, voted immediately after union to become aligned with the Diocesan Councils. On the other hand, the Area Coordinating Committee, which dealt with the needs of the institutions, had not been integrated so soon, lest the diocese and churches become overburdened with institutional and financial issues. What had not been adequately recognized in the Arcot area was that the other missions and churches that entered into the life of the two dioceses had not made the clear distinction between pastorate and institutional administration. Those areas had moved more quickly to align all their work into the diocesan administration.[86] As a result, the dioceses were urging the Reformed Church also to carry out its relationships with the Arcot area through the diocese rather than directly with the Area Coordinating Committee, so that all of the mission activity in the diocese could fall under a single diocesan administration.

The policy paper resisted such centralization of administration. It took the position that much work remained to be done in the Arcot area and that the great need there could continue to be met only by concentrating the Reformed Church effort there, rather than allowing it to be diffused over a much wider area. It was important to be able to say, "This is the work the Reformed Church in America sponsors in India." Its missionaries should continue to serve in its historic area; service outside the area should be considered temporary, as it had always been. "We consider it poor stewardship," the paper stated, "to jeopardize God's gifts of a hundred years to the craving of an unexplored ideal. This means full and complete identification with the Church within our own area. Funds should be made available to the Church within that area...."[87]

---

[86] Ibid., 4.
[87] Ibid., 6.

The Case for Integrated Church-to-Church Relationships

The deputation of the Board of Foreign Missions[88] did not present a report as such, but it responded to the papers by emphasizing the need to move in the direction of integration as soon as possible. It emphasized the need to work in "church-to-church," rather than "church-to-mission" or "mission-to-church" relationships. Its fully developed position was eventually set forth in a paper, "The Role and Relationship of the Missionary in the Light of the Nature and Mission of the Church," that was provisionally adopted by the Board for Christian World Mission May 8, 1959. The basic direction, however, was already in the minds of the board secretaries in 1953.

"Church-to-church relationship" was defined to mean that churches in the West and churches in Asia should now be acting as full partners in obedience to Jesus Christ.

Paragraph 4 of the "Role and Relationship" paper stated:

> 4.   In several areas where the Reformed Church has been giving her missionary witness, indigenous churches of maturity and responsibility have been established. It is recognized that in lands where such churches now exist, the Reformed Church, acting through the Board, shares with these indigenous churches as partners in the evangelization of all mankind and in bringing to bear on all human life the spirit and teachings of Jesus Christ in obedience to the Holy Spirit and in loyalty to the Word of God. [89]

There was no controversy about the concept of church-to-church relationships as such. Paragraph 8 in "Role and Relationship"

---

[88] The Board of Foreign Missions name was changed to the Board for Christian World Mission in 1958. In the remainder of this book, either name will be used, depending upon the year under discussion. In cases where the matter overlaps the years, the name which best applies will be used.

[89] "The Role and Relationship of the Missionary in the Light of the Nature and Mission of the Church" (paper adopted by the Board of Christian World Mission, May 8, 1959), 5 (hereafter "Role and Relationship").

spoke to issues that had been the subject of debate in India throughout the 1950s. It stated that where there are national churches of strength,

> the missions cease to function as administrative bodies, and all work and personnel are integrated into the life and work of the indigenous church. Unless there is such an integration, the integrity of the national church is not recognized and safeguarded. In this new church to church relationship the missionary is released from suspicion that he may be reactionary and out of tune with the mood of the people. The national worker can feel that he is a colleague, and that together he and the missionary are subject to the mind of Christ.[90]

The missionaries who had arrived in India between 1920 and 1945 could not help but feel somewhat demeaned by the implicit charge that that they "may be reactionary and out of tune with the mood of the people." They had good evidence that they had gone further in the devolution of mission than any of the other missionary bodies prior to the establishment of the Church of South India. The administrative structures in place at the time the Church of South India was established were those which the 1939 deputation from the board itself had recommended be put in place. The senior missionaries were well on the way toward leaving their positions as heads of institutions to their Indian colleagues. The policy papers developed for the centenary celebrations had been jointly written and agreed upon by missionaries and Indians. Indians were full colleagues in the Indian Church Board and the Arcot Coordinating Committee.

The Indian "national workers" in the Arcot area believed that their collegial relationship to the Reformed Church Board for Foreign Missions was being lost in the diocesan administrative framework, because the board desired to relate to them through the

90 Ibid.

diocese and its bishop in Madras rather than directly. The administrative structures in the area previously had given elected Indian leaders direct access to the secretary of the Board of Foreign Missions in New York. C. A. Samuel, headmaster of Voorhees High School, in 1950 was serving as secretary of the Arcot Coordinating Committee. S. J. Savarirayan, principal of Voorhees College, became its first treasurer in 1951. Questions of budget and policy therefore were officially handled by Indians rather than missionaries in relation to the Board of Foreign Missions.

Questions regarding the Arcot Coordinating Committee's responsibility to oversee missionary furlough and study plans and missionary work assignment also arose among the Indian leadership. The convenor of the Missionary Personnel Committee of the Arcot Coordinating Committee in 1950 was Arthur John. One of the duties of that committee was to advise missionaries concerning furlough plans and study in preparation for return to India. C. A. Samuel wrote to the board that Arthur John would soon be writing for its advice on missionary study while on furlough:

> The Convenor of this Committee is asked to have direct correspondence with you in regard to this matter. After the Personnel Committee meets, he will inform you of the plans for study in preparation for return to India of missionaries who have already returned home on furlough and who will soon be leaving the country on furlough. With regard to Mr. Blaise Levai if I have understood the Committee's plans aright, he is expected to come back to the Voorhees College unless he desires to have a change of work.[91]

The Indian leaders believed that they had more to lose than did the missionaries if full integration with the Diocese of Madras was implemented without full consideration of all the issues. In the thinking of the Board of Foreign Missions, as represented by its

[91] C. A. Samuel to F. M. Potter, July 10, 1950.

secretary, correspondence should in the future take place with and through the bishop in Madras, rather than with Indians or missionaries in the Arcot area. Their sense of loss was the greater because of the geography and demography of the Diocese of Madras. Vellore was ninety miles from Madras, more than three hours away by bus, with no convenient telephone service available. Madras itself was urbanized; the Arcot area was still largely rural. One can sense the hand of the Indian members of the committee on the future of Reformed Church work in India in this sentence from its 1953 policy paper: "For if in the recent past with accelerated adjustments it was sometimes difficult to maintain an effective connection between the field and the Church in America, how much more will that exigency arise when so much administrative work will in the future naturally *devolve upon such as are strangers to the Reformed Church in America?*" [author's italics].[92]

As the role of the Arcot Mission decreased or disappeared, a number of decisions that formerly had been made in India by the mission now were devolving to the board in New York rather than to the church in India. This was also a matter of concern. The situation could scarcely be avoided so long as financial requests for specific objects were being made. Previously, however, many of the requests had been screened by missionaries, with or without consultation with Indians. From the point of view of Indian leaders, the devolution of the place of decision from the mission to the board was an ambiguous development. Between 1940 and 1953, devolution meant an increase in the role of Indians, who could enter into direct correspondence with the board on specific items. For example, in a single letter to Arthur John, chairman of the Arcot Continuation Committee,[93] the board secretary conveyed his

---

[92] "The Future Relationship of the Reformed Church in America with its Work in India," 8.

[93] By 1954, as part of the integration process, the Arcot Coordinating Committee had mutated into the Arcot Continuation Committee, with essentially the same range of responsibilities but more closely related to the diocese than its predecessor. The difference is not crucial for our purposes.

response to eleven line items in the area's proposals.[94] It is not difficult to understand why the Arcot Continuation Committee appeared reluctant to become integrated into the framework of the diocese when all such correspondence on financial matters would become the responsibility of the bishop of the diocese.

The missionaries at times could express rather forcefully their objection to being left out of the communication loop. In order to improve communications, it was agreed that one of the missionaries should be appointed "mission representative or correspondent." That person served as a liaison between the Arcot Mission and the diocese and received copies of church-to-church correspondence. He would then inform other missionaries of important developments, interpret their feelings to the board, and help the diocese understand the perspectives of others in the United States or in India. C. R. Wierenga in the Madras diocese and Harold Vande Berg in the Rayalaseema diocese first filled this role. When Wierenga left, Henry Van Vranken was appointed.[95] The mission representatives helped improve relationships with the missionaries to some extent, but their presence only served to impress the Arcot area Indians with the fact that they also were being left out of the communication loop. J. C. Savarirayan wrote to B. Luben that the appointment of board correspondents was a retrograde step, since previously Arthur John, C. A. Samuel, and Savirirayan had fulfilled that role in the Madras diocesan area.[96]

In spite of all the attempts to achieve genuine sharing of power and true collegiality, the need or desire of the church and its related institutions to continue to receive funds from the Reformed Church in America made it virtually impossible to escape the remnants of paternalism that had so often been decried by all parties. Missionaries were never slow to point out that the paternalism of the mission had been replaced by the paternalism of the board.

---

[94] B. Luben to Arthur John, October 29, 1954.
[95] B. Luben to H. Van Vranken, December 26, 1956
[96] J. C. Savarirayan to B. Luben, December 23, 1955.

In a paper delivered in 1958 at Hope College at the request of the Board of Foreign Missions, Blaise Levai commented on the shift of power to the board.

> What I say here is not merely my idea as a "Westerner," but it is the considered opinion of several outstanding national leaders. To quote one, "We find ourselves now not only under an Indian Bishop, but also bishops of the Board." Another prominent Indian churchman said, "All that is necessary, would appear to be a private telephone line from the headquarters of 156 Fifth Avenue to the Bishop's residence." There must be a change in relationships between the younger churches and the authority at the home office. The Board has assumed authority in dimensions never known by missionaries on the field. For the home Board had always been a check on the final authority of the mission.[97]

The extreme to which board control could go developed out of a general Reformed Church in America policy that prior to making a loan or grant for a building, the lending body had to approve blueprints. This was a particularly important policy in cases of loans for new church buildings in North America, in that it provided careful review of all plans. When applied to overseas projects, it led to considerable delay and what looked like paternalism in relation to Indian builders.

Reformed Church missionary Harold Vande Berg called the policy into question on two counts. One was that the need to send blueprints for approval in New York led to unnecessary delay in the face of urgent needs. With regard to a request for funds to erect a doctor's house at the Mary Lott Lyle Hospital in Madanapalle, he wrote, "The urgency for building this has become even more acute;

[97] Blaise Levai, "The Task of the Reformed Church Missionary in the World Situation Today" (unpublished manuscript), 7-8. "156 Fifth Avenue" was the New York address of the Board for Christian World Mission in 1958.

since writing to you that part of the roof already has fallen, I now have to add that tiles are daily obeying the laws of gravity!"[98]

He also argued that just as the Arcot Mission was being urged to turn its work over to the church and to respect decisions of the church, so should the board of Foreign Missions. It should place more trust in the church's property board, rather than take to itself the authority that was previously in the hands of the mission.

> I think we can freely express our feeling that the Properties Board here on the field is the competent body to deal with estimates and blue-prints. The members know the type of building material required, the proper prices, and all details necessary for the erection of a good building. In fact, one member of the Board is the Chief Engineer of Andhra State. Perhaps further action taken by the Board in the States would be interpreted as a lack of trust in the judgment of the Field and a betrayal of the spirit of integration. At this stage such a feeling created in the minds of the church on the Field would be extremely harmful.[99]

Nevertheless, Barnerd Luben felt obliged to follow the policy by exercising careful scrutiny of building plans. In October, Vande Berg sent the blueprint approved by the diocesan property board for the doctor's house in Madanapalle. In November, Luben responded with a number of detailed suggestions and questions that needed to be satisfied.[100]

In April, 1957, Luben wrote to Vande Berg with questions about the new parsonage in Vayalpad, for which the Reformed Church had been asked to give a grant. He made detailed suggestions:

> Two baths are indicated, one for each bedroom. Bathrooms are generally expensive because of the plumbing involved. The dining room has no outside light—a door opens on to

what appears to be a verandha from the kitchen....Would
there be an advantage in putting the store(room) elsewhere,
instead of on an outside wall, next to the kitchen, so the
dining room will run all the way from the outside wall to the
bedroom....Then, should there be an opening of the size
indicated between the dining room and the drawing room—
should there not be only a large door, something of the kind
which will enable the two rooms to be thrown into one for
meetings?...101

Luben was not the last board secretary to look at blueprints for
buildings on the other side of the world. It is not easy to escape
paternalism when unequal financial relationship are involved,
whether that paternalism be vested in bodies in Asia or in America.

Assignment of New Missionaries in a United Church

During the transitional period between 1947 and 1953, questions
arose about the "bounds of the mission" and the extent to which
the authority of the mission had actually devolved to Indian
leadership with particular reference to the assignment of new
missionaries to their tasks. In the first place, there was a serious
generational issue that had to be faced. Because of the financial
difficulties caused by the Great Depression, no new missionaries
were appointed to India between 1930 and 1940, with the exception
of one nurse who remained in Indian only two years. No male
ordained missionary was appointed between 1925 and 1940, when
John Piet arrived in India. Five unmarried women arrived in 1940,
of whom two were religious education workers and three were
nurses. The education workers remained in India for only one term.
Three new ordained missionaries and their wives arrived soon after
the end of World War II, Blaise and Marian Levai, Eugene and Ruth
Ten Brink, and Harold and Yvette Vande Berg. The appointment
of these ordained male missionaries raised new issues of expectations

101 B. Luben to H. Vande Berg. April 20, 1957.

and of the nature of missionary service in the new Church of South India.

C. R. Wierenga had seen problems coming with regard to assigning work to new missionaries, given the expectations of the Arcot missionaries and those of the younger missionaries themselves. In 1945 he wrote that his efforts to have these questions discussed had been rebuffed in the nationalistic fervor of that year. Nevertheless, he wanted F. M. Potter to be alert to the issues ahead, so he wrote, "Then also it is time that the Missionary should understand just what is his place in this new day. It is quite easy to emphasize that his place is not the old, at the control of institutions and phases of work, but when a young man or woman comes to India it is also only fair to point out to him just in what areas he is to engage his activities."[102] Two years later, Wierenga returned to the theme when he wrote that the new missionary recruits were impatient with the old ways of doing things and no longer satisfied to be replacements for those who retired.[103]

Wierenga was not the only one who was sensitive to the emerging problem. After C. A. Samuel had been in contact with several of the younger missionaries, he also alerted Potter in New York to the situation. He observed that younger missionaries want to be involved in evangelism. He believed that they were making their views known before they had either adequately understood the role of mission institutions or shown proper respect for such institutions.[104]

David Chellapa, bishop in the Diocese of Madras, also recognized that there was a clear difference of mentality between the older and younger missionaries. Writing about missionaries not only in the Arcot area but also in the other mission areas, he commented that the older missionaries "have grown up in a particular set-up and are often loath to think that any change is called for; they are, as it were, wedded to a particular outlook, and are somewhat averse to any re-

[102] C. R. Wierenga to F. M. Potter, January 2, 1945.
[103] C R. Wierenga to F. M. Potter, May 15, 1947.
[104] C. A. Samuel to F. M. Potter, December 30, 1950.

orientation; the older they grow, the less open to change they appear to be." The younger missionaries

> come out with certain ideas and ideals, but they are unable to put them into practice....These younger men are often able and thoughtful men, with an ecumenical outlook and an easy manner with all and sundry, but one thing they often lack, and this must be admitted in all candour; they lack a sense of discipline. They want to do the work they *like* to do, not what the Church—whether the sending or receiving— *wants* them to do. They naturally chafe and fret under a system which brings out able-bodied men from across the ocean, only to tie them down as Correspondents of Elementary Schools, dealing with unfriendly Deputy Inspectors of Schools, to be in charge of Elementary Boarding Schools, and with no opportunity for spreading their wings.[105]

The younger missionaries were not ready to accept an assignment simply because the mission had a vacancy in a mission station or because an institution wanted a missionary on its staff. They believed that there should be room for some new and creative ventures in mission, while Indians should be encouraged to take over leadership in work already established. The older missionaries and experienced Indian leaders realized how much still had to be done in the long established work and wanted the younger missionaries first to gain experience in such activity before launching out into something new. The gap between the two perspectives was not easily bridged, as we can observe in the cases of Blaise Levai and Eugene Ten Brink.

The Needs of the Mission and the Aptitude of the Missionary

Blaise Levai had served as an unmarried missionary as a teacher in Voorhees College and also as the manager of its student hostels

---

[105] Levai, *Revolution in Mission*, 2-3.

from 1946-1949. On the one hand, he was enthusiastic about the potential of hostel life. He reported,

> The hostels endeavour to bring students together with God and other students. Hostels can become the mold of human personality. Here is to be found the intimacy of an interactive group. Rarely will students have such opportunities to live away from the surface of caste, class and creed and live in genuine fellowship over a long enough period of time to build them into their lives through close comradeship.[106]

Nevertheless, the crowded conditions in the hostels made for a somewhat discouraging picture. In his concluding paragraph, he urged that the need for better hostel accommodation be faced squarely: "I feel certain that a frank understanding of what the hostels face is needed. This report has no place for shallow optimism."[107]

Blaise Levai returned to the United States in 1949 to complete his doctoral work in the field of education. He also married Marian Korteling, the daughter of missionaries Ralph and Anna Ruth Korteling. Prior to their going back to India in 1952, she completed her medical training. In India, various suggestions were being made concerning their assignment. One possibility was that Blaise would return to Voorhees College. Another suggestion was to use his first full term in India to learn about a wider range of work than he would in Voorhees College. Potter heard that Wierenga preferred that the Levais be stationed in Ranipet, where Blaise could chair a circle and do evangelistic work, as well as manage the village schools.[108]

With Voorhees College as the likely possibility, Levai did something unheard of. In days gone by, it had been taken for granted that new missionaries in their first full term would respect the wisdom of their elders in the mission and in the church. Levai, however, wrote to Potter stating that he believed it would be impractical to put him

[106] "AAR," 1947-1948, 59.
[107] Ibid., 60.
[108] F. M. Potter to B. Levai, October 31, 1951.

to work managing village elementary schools after so much money
had been spent and so much effort and time put into his gaining his
doctor's degree in education. His real purpose in his letter, however,
was to ask that he not be assigned to Voorhees College. He had
enjoyed his time there under the creative leadership of S. J.
Savarirayan, but Savarirayan had become principal of American
Madura College in the American Madura mission area. Savarirayan
had written to Levai asking him to consider teaching there. Levai
did not wish to teach under the new principal at Voorhees College,
who lacked the creative gifts of Savarirayan. He was concerned that
the new principal in all probability would not give him freedom in
his teaching methods.[109]

Potter responded to say that he sympathized, but that he believed
Voorhees College was still the place for him if that was where the
people in India wanted to assign him. He said that he was pointing
out to every candidate for missionary service that

> he would not go out to a position where he could exercise
> strong qualifications of leadership, but that he would
> probably have to be a 'doormat before the entrance to the
> Kingdom of God.'...Such a period requires something
> perhaps greater and deeper than the call of a generation ago,
> and this has been very much in my mind as we have sought
> men who might be possessed of the necessary
> qualifications.[110]

The "doormat" image of the missionary was resisted by Levai as
lacking in collegiality and partnership. Marian Korteling then wrote
her own letter to Ruth Ransom, the personnel secretary of the
board, in which she expressed herself somewhat forcefully. She not
only provided more evidence about why her husband should not be
assigned to Voorhees College. She added another element to the
picture. In all the discussion, little attention had been paid to the fact

---

[109] Blaise Levai to F. M. Potter, February 7, 1951.
[110] F. M. Potter to Blaise Levai, March 7, 1951.

that she was fully qualified as a doctor. She was not sure that she was really needed in Ranipet. Her role in relation to the hospital in Vellore had not really been explored, while there was a need in the mission hospital in Madura for a person with her training.[111] While she did not mention it in her letter, one can speculate that she had observed that her parents had at times been shifted away from Punganur, where her mother's medical work was, to other mission stations to meet the need for her father's services as an ordained minister.

Ultimately the Levais accepted an assignment for Blaise to teach at Voorhees College and to serve as vice-principal. Alongside that assignment, he was assigned by the diocese to serve as presbyter-in-charge of the English language St. John's Church in the Vellore Fort. That assignment was made possible by the formation of the Church of South India. For a number of years, St. John's Church had just managed to exist as an Anglican Church. After it became part of the Church of South India, the diocese had at first assigned several pastors to lead worship here on a rotating basis. Levai's term of service at St. John's Church was a stormy one for a time, owing to the opposition against some of his actions by the secretary and treasurer of the pastorate committee. The congregation experienced rapid growth under his ministry, with more than 150 members received during his time. By the time he left in 1958, it had become a strong congregation with a sure sense of its identity[112]

Through his time in India, Levai continued to wrestle with issues of what he termed a "revolution in mission." He produced a book with that title in 1957. The book aroused wide interest in the missionary community in Kodaikanal that year, as it made available in convenient form an extensive number of articles on the subject of the missionary calling of the church and the role of the missionary in independent India. Many of the articles were critical of current

[111] Marian Levai to Ruth Ransom, July 31, 1951.
[112] See Eugene Ten Brink, *History of the Vellore Fort and St. John's Church* (privately printed, 1961), 57-59, for a brief account of the events of Levai's ministry at St. John's.

mission practice.[113] In light of the fact that Arthur John was the chairman of the Missionary Personnel Committee, which had the final responsibility to determine Blaise and Marian Levai's assignment, it is interesting to note that Levai included a report of that committee in his book. In it is the following statement concerning the way in which young missionaries should approach their assignments. They "should come prepared to face humbler conditions in the capacity of a colleague or servant....Though sympathetic consideration will be given to individual desire and particular aptitude, missionaries should be made to understand that their work and assignment will be determined by the Church on the field." [114]

In spite of the statement that "sympathetic consideration will be given to individual desire and aptitude," the cases of Blaise Levai and Eugene Ten Brink indicate that, in the 1950s, placing young missionaries in traditional roles still had priority over a new missionary's particular aptitude.

Where are the "Bounds of the Mission" in the Church of South India?

Eugene and Ruth Ten Brink had been appointed in 1946 to serve in India. After completing their language study, they were stationed in Katpadi, where Eugene served as Western Circle chairman and, for a time, while J. J. De Valois was on furlough, as acting director of the Agricultural Institute. One of the pastorates in the circle, Gudiyattam, under the leadership of the Reverend Wales Yesupatham, was growing rapidly in number. A new congregation was begun in one village with the baptism of 110 persons. There were indications that the whole village of more than 350 persons would soon become Christians. Ten Brink further reported that the old dilemma was faced once again in that area. There were no funds to provide pastoral care for new converts in villages ready to come

---

[113] Arthur John, "The Place, Function, and Training of the Future Missionary," in Levai, *Revolution in Mission*, 291.
[114] Ibid., 290-91.

under instruction. "There are at least six more villages where work could be started if funds were available for expansion. Thus the method of educational evangelism, that has been the basic approach to the villages, opens doors but the extension of educational opportunities is so costly that we cannot afford to enter these doors."[115]

After a year of furlough at the end of their first term, the Ten Brinks returned to India, and Eugene was assigned to serve as chairman of the Tindivanam Circle. While he performed his assignment faithfully, he was restless in it. He was not sure that it was necessary for a missionary to serve as circle chairman when there were Indian pastors available for that position. With Reformed Church missionary Dora Boomstra and Arthur John, he had been a member of the committee that had written the policy paper, "Limitations and Opportunities for Service by Missionaries of the Reformed Church in India" for the 1953 centenary celebration. That paper stated, "There is a new urgency in the task of building up an indigenous leadership in the fact that Government is becoming increasingly insistent that key administrative posts be taken over by Nationals. Every year each missionary has to face the question in his application for renewal of his residential permit: "Give reasons why your work cannot be done by a National."[116]

In contrast to some missionaries and Indian leaders who maintained that the Reformed Church mission in India should continue to concentrate on the traditional area of the Arcot Mission rather than be diffused through the whole Church of South India, Eugene Ten Brink believed that the old boundaries should now be opened up and that missionaries should be assigned where they were most needed and where their gifts could best be used. In 1954, he called attention to certain financial and other irregularities in the management of the Tindivanam High School. This occasioned

[115] "AAR," 1949-1950, 27.
[116] "Limitations and Opportunities for Service by Missionaries of the Reformed Church in India," *Policy Papers,* 52.

considerable controversy and raised questions whether the young Ten Brink family would not be better served by being transferred elsewhere. At that time, the Tamil Theological Seminary, which had been opened at Tirumaraiyur (Nazareth) rather than Vellore to serve the whole Tamil-speaking area of the Church of South India, needed a person of the Reformed tradition to serve on its faculty. It requested the services of Eugene Ten Brink. He would have been pleased to accept the assignment as one well suited to his personal aptitude.

We have noted several times that final responsibility for missionary assignments rested with the Area Coordinating Committee. That responsibility had not yet been transferred to the diocese in 1954. However, it had also remained the practice that the Arcot Mission was responsible for missionary housing and transportation, and in any assignment the need for adequate housing always had to be taken into consideration. In the case of this request from the Tamil seminary, the question of the "bounds of the mission" also came into play. Meanwhile, the controversy at Tindivanam had quieted down. The Arcot Mission voted not to release Ten Brink to teach at the seminary, because there was a continuing need in Tindivanam. The Area Coordinating Committee would not intervene without the recommendation of the mission. Ten Brink complained bitterly to Luben that the day had come when the issues of residence and the bounds of the mission should no longer be used to allow the mission to exercise authority in matters of assignment.[117]

In the meantime, an Indian teacher had been found to take the faculty position, so the case became mute. The following year a request came from the Student Christian Movement asking that Eugene Ten Brink be released to them to be one of its three secretaries, with special responsibilities for recruiting students for full-time Christian work. In addition it requested $1,600 for the expenses of the work he would be doing. It happened that Henry Bovenkerk, treasurer of the board, was in India at the time. He intervened by exploring the matter with Bishop Chellapa of the Diocese of Madras. At the time, the Area Coordination Committee had before it the recommendation that the Ten Brinks be stationed at Arni, but it tabled the resolution in order to allow the possibility of the other assignment. The way was clear for Ten Brink to take an assignment outside the bounds of the mission, although without the recommendation of the committee.[118]

Looking at it from our vantage at the end of the century, one can only be sympathetic with almost everyone involved in the complex of issues the mission faced in the transitional period of the 1950s. The policies of the government toward the church and the missionaries had not yet crystallized, with the result that Indian Christians and missionaries could not feel very secure about the future. China had fallen to the Communists. Communists were also active in India and agitating among the workers in the mission institutions. Older missionaries knew that it was time for them to hand over their responsibilities to Indians. They knew that within a few years most of them would retire, but they saw that the younger missionaries were restless and interested in new forms of missionary activity outside the old Arcot area. The Indian leaders in the area saw how much remained to be done and wanted to retain strong ties with the Reformed Church and still have missionaries to work as colleagues alongside them. The board secretaries and the bishop knew how crucial it was that the diocese come to a greater sense of unity and cooperation within itself.

Time and altered circumstances were needed to resolve the many issues in that era of transition. In 1950, F. M. Potter anticipated that the transition would take ten to fifteen years of hard going. As matters turned out, his prediction was remarkably accurate. He wrote,

> To me there is always something of a comparison here with
> political developments. So long as India did not trust

118 B. M. Luben to the Members of the India Committee, Board of Foreign Missions, January 13, 1956.

promises of the British government, there was fierce antagonism. When the promise was fulfilled, tension relaxed overnight. So, too, in Church-Mission relationships. There has never come full confidence that the Mission or the missionary is really relinquishing authority. Any attitude which encourages this suspicion lengthens the necessary process. Once there is full belief, tension should relax and there should come a time of more easy and natural relationships.[119]

The Call to Return to Evangelism

The Church of South India believed that it had a missionary calling. Its constitution provided that evangelization of South India was at the very heart of its life. In setting forth the duties of the bishop, it stated that

It is the duty of the bishop to take the lead in the evangelistic work of the diocese; and he should do all in his power to foster and promote it both by his own example and also by the encouragement which he gives to others; and therefore he should continually remind both ministers and people of their duty in this respect.[120]

The churches and leaders in the Arcot area constantly affirmed the original purposes as set forth by the Scudders, according to which evangelism was to be a priority concern. For that reason the Scudders had resisted establishing educational and medical institutions that they feared would divert them from their primary goal. Nevertheless, over the course of the decades, institutions were built in order that people might know and believe that Jesus Christ is Lord. These developments led to many debates about how best to do evangelism. On one side were many who believed that faithful

[119] F. M. Potter to John Piet, June 1, 1950.
[120] Church of South India Constitution, IV, 2, 21- 22.

pastoral and outreach work by pastors and congregations was the most effective way to reach out to neighbors in the name of Christ. Institutions helped provide a favorable climate for such evangelistic outreach. On the other side was a long tradition in the Arcot Mission that the most crucial thing was evangelistic touring and literature distribution, with a direct appeal to believe in Jesus Christ. Reformed Church missionary John Piet brought these issues into sharp focus during the 1950s.

In spite of the fact that almost everyone agreed that evangelism must be a high priority, in actual practice it was difficult to know what was and what was not evangelism. Much energy was going into the maintenance of the life of the Christian community, which had to be educated, assisted in its social and economic development, and enabled to worship God from week to week. Humanitarian work, such as medical care and famine relief, could not be avoided. In all of these activities, it could be shown that there were people coming to a knowledge of Jesus Christ and to request baptism. But throughout the 1930s and 1940s, the numerical growth had not been as great as one could have hoped.

The Board of Foreign Missions was coming under pressure from people in the Reformed Church in America. An especially vocal group of pastors in western Michigan complained that the denomination, in its pursuit of unity and favorable attitudes towards the Federal Council of Churches, had lost its zeal for evangelism. Questions were being raised about the number of institutions and the cost of running the institutions in India in relation to the numerical growth of the church in India.[121]

John and Wilma Piet were appointed in 1940 to serve as missionaries in India. He was the only ordained minister to be appointed by the Reformed Church to India between 1925 and 1946. Thus he did not belong to the old generation of missionaries, but he also was not quite to be reckoned among the ones who came after 1947. During their first term in India, John Piet served as vice-

121 F. M. Potter to C. R. Wierenga, March 6, 1947.

principal at Voorhees College and as manager of the student hostels—essentially the same role that Blaise Levai was to have later. His heart was in evangelism, however. After the Piets' return from a furlough year in 1946, John was assigned to serve at Voorhees College and to do evangelistic work in the Vellore area. He organized The Vellore Evangelistic Council in 1949.

One of the council's first activities was the production of a series of brief leaflet tracts: "Jesus Christ," "The Bible," "The Church," "Christmas," "Christian Social Work," and "Easter." Ten thousand copies of each tract were distributed bimonthly to every home and shop in Vellore through the cooperation of Christian students. In the first year and one half, 547,450 seriated leaflets were distributed. On the basis of the success of their first efforts, the council produced a series for the surrounding villages. A cycle boy was employed to visit four villages each day with a goal of completing a circuit of ninety villages in four weeks. Each village home and shop received a leaflet every month. Thirty thousand leaflets were used monthly, while forty-five thousand more were divided among nine other centers. In addition to the tracts, the council sold three hundred Bibles, two hundred New Testaments, and ten thousand gospel portions, as well as three thousand Christian booklets.[122]

John Piet was familiar with a method of newspaper evangelism that had been developed by Albertus Pieters while Pieters served as a Reformed Church missionary in Japan between 1891-1923. He decided to use that method in India, so he published intriguing ads about Jesus in the leading newspaper in the Madras and Vellore area. He received a large response to the advertisements. This led him to cooperate with TEAM mission, which had developed the Light of Life Bible Correspondence Course. Piet got permission to modify and translate the Gospel of John course into Tamil. He made arrangements with the World Home Bible League, based in the United States, and the Bible Society of Indian and Ceylon to have attractive gospels printed. Each of these was sold at a low cost,

---

[122] "AAR," 1949-1950, 29-30.

about one cent per gospel, and with each gospel came the first correspondence course lesson and an encouragement to enroll. Eventually courses were developed on all four gospels and the book of Acts. By 1960, about twenty-five thousand people per year were enrolling in the courses, of whom about 40 percent completed at least one course, with 85 percent of the enrollees being Hindu, 5 percent Muslim, and 10 percent Christian.

Potter in New York and John Piet in India had to struggle with a dilemma about financing the new evangelistic program. At the beginning, the costs were anticipated to be relatively modest. Piet had some friends outside the Reformed Church whom he could approach for contributions without violating the rules about missionaries soliciting gifts that had not been approved through proper channels. But because the program grew so rapidly, more contributions were needed. Since the Arcot Coordinating Committee was not able to meet the needs of the various institutions from its sources of income, which included the annual appropriation from the Board of Foreign Missions, it was not inclined to make room for anything new.

Then Piet had the idea of using a Jeep outfitted with audiovisual equipment to go into the villages to show films and slide shows combined with music, preaching, and literature distribution. He hoped, with this modern method, to revive the old evangelistic tours. In September, 1950, a Jeep arrived from some of his friends in Michigan who had heard about this idea. Within a short time, the agricultural institute would be using its van and trailer for a similar purpose, as would Ralph Korteling in the Punganur area. Jeep evangelism proved to be an efficient method of reaching a large number of people. Piet wrote, "The Jeep is now on the road. Every night, it reaches from two hundred fifty to three hundred people. Two nights, there were crowds of between five and six hundred. Conservatively, I would say that we will reach one thousand people a week through these means."[123]

123 John Piet to F. M. Potter, March 9, 1951.

The evangelism program developed by John Piet was widely praised as a creative new approach that deserved both personal encouragement and financial assistance. The problem was that the Indian members of the Arcot Coordinating Committee also wanted to provide more adequate funding for the schools and support of the church's ministry, especially the village workers. From the missionary perspective, there was a lack of interest in pushing hard for advancement in self-support, even in the town congregations where the effect of the drought was not felt in the way it was in the villages. In any case, the Arcot Coordinating Committee was designating very little money to be used for direct evangelism work. When it saw that Piet was able to raise funds through personal contacts in America, it was even less likely to do so.

The only way Piet saw to develop a strong evangelism program was to secure gifts through irregular channels rather than through the budget process. In this he was quite successful. The World Home Bible League, which had close ties with Reformed Church members in the midwestern United States, agreed to fund much of the cost of the Scripture-distribution program and of the Bible Correspondence Course office in Vellore. In the latter years of the decade, when the diocese played a larger role in framing the budget in India, the Board of Foreign Missions provided an additional amount for the evangelism program from designated contributions of friends through the regular budget channels. By the time John and Wilma Piet left India to teach Bible, missions, and evangelism at Western Theological Seminary in Holland, Michigan, agreement had been reached for funding at an adequate level.

While agreement was reached in this specific case, Piet continued to challenge the basic policy that the Reformed Church mission and evangelism work in India should be fully merged into the Church of South India. On the basis of his biblical study, he had come to the conclusion that evangelism and Christian nurture are two distinct programs of the church. Evangelism is the external activity, and Christian nurture is the internal activity. The needs for spiritual growth and pastoral care and education within the Christian church will always be so great as to absorb most of the church's resources. He believed that it was crucial for every church to meet its needs for nurture out of its own resources rather than from external sources. Therefore, he believed it was necessary for the Reformed Church and the Church of South India to agree upon the gradual but certain withdrawal of foreign funds over a period of ten years from the Church of South India's programs of nurture and maintenance of institutional activity that are primarily nurturing in nature.[124]

Piet maintained that the chief role of the Reformed Church in India was to support the programs of outreach and evangelism. If it desired to provide some funds for nurture to meet special needs within the Church of South India, it should be free to do so, but these should not affect in the least the amount allocated for direct evangelism. Moreover, when the Reformed Church supported programs of evangelistic outreach, it should not expect that the Church of South India would take responsibility at some future date for support of those efforts. Such expectations would overburden the Church of South India.

> The C.S.I. [Church of South India] must first make itself responsible for nurture before it can take upon itself any heavy budget with regard to evangelism....At every point the Church called into being by means of an evangelistic drive should be allowed to consolidate herself without too much help from foreign funds. This means that the combined efforts of the C.S.I. and the R.C.A. will be centered around the primary object for which they both exist, namely, the proclamation of the Good News in Christ Jesus.[125]

---

124 "The Reformed Church in America and its Evangelistic Mission," *Policy Paper,* 1953, 8-10. The Indian members of this committee were the Revs. S. Ponnurangam and H. Lazarus, but the paper clearly reflects the thought of John Piet. One can doubt whether the other two really made as radical a distinction between evangelism and Christian nurture as did the policy paper.
125 Ibid., 18.

The policy advocated at the centenary celebration in 1953 by John Piet would have limited the Reformed Church to the original purpose of the Arcot Mission, which was evangelism, while the Classis of Arcot would be given responsibility to deal with the inner life of the church. Piet believed that the Arcot Mission had correctly resisted becoming financially involved in maintaining educational and medical institutions. He had reformulated the old Arcot Mission policy in terms of his understanding of the situation in India in 1953. He like many others was pessimistic about the political situation there. The impact of the fall of China to the Communists was having a deep impression in India. He wrote in a letter to Potter that a missionary who had come from China told him she could see that India was moving rapidly in the same direction as had China. He also knew that 15,000 in Vellore had voted Communist in the last election.[126]

In another letter he wrote,

> The times in India are growing more difficult. One needn't see all the black clouds to be sure, but there are signs—at least the size of a man's hand, if not larger....If forces other than those in the Church take advantage of the present situation in India, it will be largely because we haven't had the courage or foresight to learn *one simple* lesson from China.[127]

The lesson from China was clear. One must be prepared for the fact that India might soon fall to communism. The Church of South India must move rapidly toward self-support and free itself from all dependence on foreign assistance. It must consolidate its programs of Christian nurture, so that its members will be able to stand firm in the time of testing ahead. At the same time, the Reformed Church should assist to a much greater extent programs of direct evangelism

---

[126] John Piet to F. M. Potter, January 31, 1952.
[127] John Piet to B. Luben, August 8, 1953.

to reach as many people as possible while the opportunity was still there.

Piet was not predicting that India would fall to communism, but he believed that it would be foolhardy not to prepare for the possibility. Later, in his book, *The Road Ahead,* he would apply his distinction between evangelism and Christian nurture to the church in the U.S., calling members of the Reformed Church in America to give priority to evangelism, even though the threat of communism was no longer the real issue in America.[128] In 1953, however, the fear that India could soon fall to communism helped stimulate him to action, just as the knowledge of sinners on the road to hell had stimulated John Scudder many years ago to focus so fully on his evangelistic calling.

Integration of Church and Mission in the Diocese of Rayalaseema

We have seen that missionaries and Indian leaders in the Tamil-language area of the Arcot Mission were hesitant in 1953 and for several years thereafter to move forward to complete integration of their responsibilities into the Diocese of Madras. The situation was quite different in the Telugu-language area, where a merger plan for the Madanapalle Division into the Rayalaseema Diocese was approved by the central committee of that diocese in April, 1954. The action reads:

Provided that the Board of Foreign Mission, R.C.A. gives its full consent to the transfer of the work, etc. as outlined above, that the Rayalaseema Diocesan Council will accept responsibility for the control and management of work, for the funds, and for the use of buildings formerly controlled, managed and used by the Arcot Coordinating Committee for the Madanapalle Division, and will give the assurance that for a period of five years they will use such funds only

128 John Piet, *The Road Ahead* (Grand Rapids, Mich.: Eerdmans, 1970), esp. 48-68.

for the items of work for which they have been allocated hitherto.[129]

There were several reasons why the Madanapalle Division moved more rapidly into full integration with the diocese. One was the fact that Harold Vande Berg, who had arrived in India in 1947, was playing a leading role in the Telugu area. He was a strong believer in moving rapidly to integrate the work of the Reformed Church fully into the Church of South India. A second factor was the strong desire for integration on the part of Bishop Sumitra, who was the highly respected moderator of the Church of South India as well as the bishop in Rayalaseema. Equally important probably was the fact that the Madanapalle area had not enjoyed strong Indian leaders who had been in personal correspondence with the Board of Foreign Missions, as had been the case with leaders in the Tamil area. Indian leaders in Madanapalle did have reservations about integration similar to those in the Tamil area, as Vande Berg recognized. He wrote, "You see, part of our trouble with devolution is that the Indians themselves are a little afraid of it."[130] In spite of their fears, they agreed to the integration.

Like Blaise Levai, Eugene Ten Brink, and John Piet, Harold Vande Berg was part of the younger generation of missionaries who believed that evangelism should be the focus in the work of ordained missionaries sent to India by the Reformed Church. Like the others, he rejected the idea that they should be restricted in their assignments to the geographical area historically related to the Arcot Mission. He also believed that decisions about the work of the established mission institutions should be in the hands of the diocese rather than a coordinating committee in the Arcot mission area. Most importantly, he rejected the position set forth by the Committee on the Future Relationship of the Reformed Church with its Work in India, which held that one should be able to say,

---

[129] "Merger Plan for the Madanapalle Division," April 3, 1954 (board secretary's correspondence file, Archives of the RCA).

[130] H. Vande Berg to B. Luben, February 3, 1955.

"This is the work the Reformed Church in America sponsors in India." In the context of the strong desire for Indian national identity following upon independence, Vande Berg believed that the entire mission in India must be understood to be the work of the Indian church.[131]

Vande Berg disagreed with John Piet's conviction that, in light of the fact that India could possibly come under communism, the church should put its efforts into developing its own programs of nurture and self-support, while missionaries would engage in "interim work" like Jeep evangelism. He favored Jeep evangelism, but he insisted that it should be a part of the church's work rather than "interim work" of a missionary. He wrote:

> In Jeep evangelism, for example, much good is being done that could not be done without it. Nevertheless, even Jeep evangelism must be planned to match the ability of the Church on the field to march along with the programme. As long as it is looked upon as an "interim effort," giving the missionary something to do while others are making up their minds about the future of missionary endeavor, then it is a doomed effort. I am not so much opposed to the efforts that may be carried on only with missionaries as I am to the tendency that such effort gives to missionaries and Indians alike to be satisfied with the status quo.[132]

When the full integration of the work of the Reformed Church into the Diocese of Rayalaseema was implemented, it was intended that missionaries and Indians would no longer be satisfied simply to keep on doing what they had always done. One of the policies to which the Board of Foreign Mission was committed was cutting

---

[131] H. Vande Berg was fully in accord with the merger plan for Reformed Church mission for the Madanapalle Division within the Diocese of Rayalaseema. He thereby rejected the idea that there should be an identifiable work of the Reformed Church; see H. Sumitra, "Merger Plan for the Madanapalle Division," February, 1954 (Archives of the RCA).

[132] H. Vande Berg to B. Luben, April 20, 1956.

back on appropriations for long-established work and using the funds thus saved for undertaking new work. One piece of new work was a program of women's evangelism. Vande Berg also proposed that a lay leaders' training instructor be appointed to prepare village people to provide leadership in villages where there was no teacher or catechist. However, pastors resisted his proposal, arguing that they could do such training themselves and thus save the expense of somone especially assigned to such a duty.[133]

The reservations that Indians in the Madanapalle area felt concerning moving quickly into full integration were shown to have merit in February, 1955. At that time, the Education Committee of the diocese decided that, in order to save some money, the Girls' Middle School (sixth through eighth grades) should be closed and the girls should be sent to the Sherman High School in Chittoor, sixty miles away. Reformed Church missionary Mary Geegh, who was manager of the Middle Girls' School, was on furlough in America at the time, but she protested the decision both then and upon her return to Madanapalle six months later.

Geegh took the position that the eighty girls in those three grades should not be asked to go to Chittoor because of the expense and the distance. She believed that the education committee, composed exclusively of men, was not interested in girls' education. She reported that the bishop had made the recommendation to close the middle school and that he had reported that the Board of Foreign Missions had recommended it, so no one present from the Madanapalle area had dared to oppose his recommendation. Nevertheless, there was a great need to educate the girls in the area. "We who try to teach the children daily—know the need—fathers and mothers both work—the children grow up as weeds in this poor area. Our school has been their chief Christian training."[134]

Apart from the expense of travel for the girls to and from boarding between Madanapalle and Chittoor several times a year,

[133] H. Vande Berg to B. Luben, January 25, 1955.
[134] Mary Geegh to B. Luben, September 21, 1955.

there were other prohibitive expenses. Mary Geegh presented her case with a considerable amount of emotion:

> Our school girls are now doing much of the work [here in the Madanapalle boarding home]. They can dress more simply at our school also. People in Madanapalle would send their children to the Gov't schools or the Hope Boys' school;—and the villagers (who make up 2/3 of the 80) would just keep their girls home. The Madanapalle area *has been backward*—That's why communism could get such a grip on the place. I have felt—the "Tamil" section of our A.C.C.—have not "cared" enough about the "backwardness" of the one area of our Mission. Of course everyone was <u>too busy</u> to think about it.[135]

In this case, one cannot help but sense that history does repeat itself. The men of the Arcot Mission had voted to close the Hindu Girls' School, including the one in Madanapalle, in the late nineteenth century, but the Woman's Board of Foreign Missions had intervened to keep it open. In 1955, women in America once again came to the defense of education for girls. The women of the Trinity Reformed Church in Holland, Michigan, heard about the way local people in Madanapalle and the teachers at the school had rallied to seek ways to keep the Middle Girls' School there. The American women offered to provided the additional amount needed to keep it open. They recognized that asking the girls in Madanapalle to go to Chittoor for their education was like asking girls in Holland to go to Grand Rapids for their elementary education. "The women of Trinity said they would so gladly make it possible for the girls in our area to have an 8th grade education.—and would do it over and above their regular contributions—if the Board would permit and if the Church in India were willing. (The church will rise no higher than its women)."[136]

135 Mary Geegh to B. Luben, Feb. 4, 1955.
136 Mary Geegh to B. Luben, September 21, 1955.

The diocese was impressed with the local support that was raised in Madanapalle, and it agreed to keep the school open. The women of Trinity Reformed Church were faithful to their word into the 1990s. The school continues to this day to provide a good education to the girls in the Madanapalle area.

The integration of the mission of the Reformed Church in America into the church of South India and the Diocese of Rayalaseema bore fruit when the Church of South India Executive Committee asked the Diocese of Rayalaseema to take responsibility for the work in the Adoni area, which was located at a considerable distance from Madanapalle. The area had been served by the Christian Reformed Church but was "orphaned," since it was no longer under the care of that denomination. Since the Rayalaseema area is one of the most poverty stricken areas in the Church of South India, Bishop Sumitra asked the Reformed Church to appoint a missionary couple and some financial assistance to enable it to take on this added responsibility, beginning in April, 1958.[137]

In responding positively to this request, the issue of whether Reformed Church missionaries and funds could be assigned beyond the old "bounds of the mission" was settled, at least for the Rayalaseema Diocese. Instead of appointing new missionaries, however, it was decided that the Adoni area needed the presence of persons with experience, so the Vande Bergs were sent there. The number of Christians in the five Adoni pastorates that entered the Diocese of Rayalaseema was quite large, although the number of communicant members was small. Vande Berg described the situation in the churches when he arrived; "Salaries of church workers are ridiculously low; no recognizable system for determining salaries and salary scales is in evidence; the ability merely to read and write is in many instances the qualification for employment. Stewardship, far from being practiced, is not even a word in their vocabulary."[138]

---

[137] H. Sumitra to B. Luben, January 25, 1958.
[138] Harold Vande Berg, "A New Name in the Reformed Church," *Church Herald,* December 12, 1958, 12-13.

A systematic approach was taken to the development of the life of the church in the Adoni area. A first step was to hold a conference for the church workers in the area. Because they had been out of touch with an organized church, they began with a study of basic doctrines of the church, especially the meaning of the resurrection, the ascension, and the Holy Spirit. Salaries were fixed at a level adequate to give the workers a minimum level of security. A public ceremony was held to recognize them as members of the Church of South India and to integrate them into the diocese as the Division of Adoni. An ordination service was held in which Pastor Gurram Joseph became a minister in the division. It was the first ordination service ever held in the area.[139]

By 1964, the integration and development of the District of Adoni had reached the end of its first stage, so it became possible to assign Harold and Yvette Vande Berg to Anantapur, which was also outside the old Arcot Mission area. There, they assisted the diocese in making a survey of its activities and in developing plans for future directions in its ministry. The Reverend Reuben, a respected minister who had been trained originally in the Anglican tradition, became chairman of the district.

Administration of the Sacraments and a Question about Ordinations in the Church of South India

From time to time during the 1950s, questions were raised about the nature of the ordained ministry in the Church of South India. We will take note of two of these. The first was raised in 1953, when the Board of Foreign Missions asked Bishop Hollis of Madras to clarify why presbyters were allowed to administer the Lord's Supper and baptism, while the deacons were allowed to administer baptism but not the Lord's Supper. Since in the Church of South India, the deacon held a lower rank than the presbyter, did this not imply that baptism was somewhat less than the Lord's Supper,

---

[139] Ibid.

contrary to the Reformed Church's theology of the equality of the sacraments?[140]

Bishop Hollis replied that this stipulation was not a recent action, but one that had been in the very first proposed draft of a constitution for a united church in 1929, and that it had been accepted since that time by all of the uniting churches. He admitted that the nature of the diaconate in the Church of South India needed further study, but that required some time. So far as Bishop Hollis knew, the rigid confining of the administration of baptism to the ordained minister was something that the Calvinistic tradition alone had maintained; the other churches entering into union had allowed a wider number of persons to administer baptism. Considering the matter practically, the Church of South India had a limited number of ordained presbyters in relation to the number of congregations. When a presbyter had to serve a large number of congregations, people could well have to wait a long time for him to come to perform a baptism.[141]

Bishop Hollis had checked with Bishop Lesslie Newbigin, who was from the Presbyterian tradition in Scotland, about the theology of the matter. Newbigin had responded that both sacraments are the means given to us in Christ for our participation in his dying and rising, and therefore are of equal value and importance, but they are related to the total life of the church in different ways. Because Newbigin's response relates to the theology and practice both of the Reformed tradition and the understanding of the Church of South India, one paragraph deserves to be quoted at length:

> The next important point, I think, is that the rule restricting the administration of the Lord's Supper to a Presbyter is a rule of order. That which is the continuing visible center of the common life of the Church must be so ordered that there can be no doubt as to whether any particular celebration of the Supper is the local expression of the whole fellowship,

[140] B. Luben to M. Hollis, May 25, 1953.
[141] M. Hollis to B. Luben, June 18, 1953.

or an act of schism. This seems to me to be the basic principle which limits the administration of the Supper to those ordained thereto. But Baptism applies Christ's dying and rising to the *individual*, and therefore there may frequently be situations (as you have said) in which the choice is between baptism by a non-presbyter and complete foregoing of baptism. This puts baptism into a different relation to the Church and Ministry from the relation in which the Supper stands. The rule of order may well dictate that baptism should normally be performed only by a Presbyter, but baptism by others would not create disorder, as would similar exceptions in the case of the Supper.[142]

The response given by Bishop Hollis, including his quote from Lesslie Newbigin, apparently satisfied the Board of Foreign Missions, since there was no further correspondence on the matter.

Another issue related to ordination arose when the Church of South India requested that missionaries who had not yet been ordained at the time of appointment should be ordained in the Church of South India rather than in the appointing church. This was not a totally new question, for the South India United Church had raised a somewhat similar issue in 1945. At that time, it was suggested by some that ordained ministers coming from other countries should transfer their ministerial membership to the church in India, rather than retaining their membership in their own churches in the west.[143] The matter had not been pursued in the South India United Church, however, so the Reformed Church in America was not called upon to respond to the suggestion. With regard to ordinations performed by the church in India, there was precedent for the Reformed Church to accept such ordinations for missionaries. William Farrar had been ordained by the Arcot Church Council in the South India United Church October 31, 1920.[144]

[142] Ibid.
[143] C. R. Wierenga to F. M. Potter, March 1, 1945.
[144] "BFMR," 1921, 35.

The issue was important to the Church of South India because to ordain missionaries would make a clear statement that the overseas churches fully accepted its ordinations as valid. This was especially important in regard to the high church side of the Church of England, which tended to raise questions about the validity of the Historic Episcopate in the Church of South India. On the other hand, presbyterian and congregational churches overseas continued to ask whether there were some in the Church of South India who regarded the ordinations of churches that did not have bishops as being somehow inferior. It is also possible that some of the classes in the Reformed Church who remained suspicious of ecumenical church mergers would have questioned ordinations done in a united church. It was because such questions remained beneath the surface that the Church of South India wanted to have it clearly known that there continued to be mutual recognition of ordinations of all who served within it. Its basic statement read,

> Plainly, if there is to be any question of a missionary being ordained within the CSI, it is essential that his home Church accept ordinations conferred within the CSI as theologically adequate in the same way the CSI accepts ordinations within that home Church as theologically adequate. But this would appear to us to be a basic condition of any real Church fellowship and cooperation.[145]

The question raised by the Church of South India did not receive a formal response from the Reformed Church in America because it was generally agreed that the issue of such ordinations could best be decided in individual cases. The Reformed Church had no objection in principal against encouraging newly appointed missionaries to wait until they were in India, so that they could be ordained within the Church of South India. Perhaps the major reason that the issue remained somewhat dormant was that only

---

[145] "A note on the Ordination of Missionaries," accompanying letter of H. Sumitra to B. Luben, September 30, 1959.

two Reformed Church ordained missionaries were ever appointed after 1959 to serve within the Church of South India, and one of those had been ordained six years prior to appointment.

By 1960, many of the initial questions about integration of the mission of the Reformed Church in America into the life of the Church of South India and the Dioceses of Madras and Rayalaseema had come to a more or less satisfactory resolution. Many of the original anxieties about what the role of Christians would be after the British left had also been quieted. A change of generation in leadership in the old Arcot Mission area was also taking place, as the Indians and missionaries who had so faithfully served since the early 1920s when the Arcot Assembly was founded were retiring. The stage was set for further refinement of the role of Reformed Church mission activity with the life of the Church of South India in the second decade of its life.

12

Renewal and Advance

The End of an Era

Dr. Ida S. Scudder, the last of the Arcot Mission Scudders, died May 24,1960, at the age of ninety years.[1] Crowds lined the streets of Vellore as she was carried to her burial place in the Vellore Christian Cemetery, where so many of her relatives and friends had found their resting places before her. In many ways, she was to India in her time what Mother Teresa was three decades later. She had dedicated her life to God and the women of India while still in her teens, at a time when women died in childbirth because there was no woman doctor available. She had been instrumental in opening the doors for women in India to study nursing and to become physicians and surgeons. The hospital outgrew the resources of the Reformed Church in America and the Arcot Mission. It became an independent body with its own board. Christian women of the world had united around Dr. Ida to support her dream that there would be a fully accredited medical school for women in India. In

---

[1] Her niece, Dr. Ida B. Scudder, continued to serve in Christian Medical College and Hospital after 1960. She was directly employed by the hospital and was not a member of the Arcot Mission or a missionary of the Reformed Church in America.

the year that India became independent, Ida Scudder was pleased when an outstanding Indian woman, Dr. Hilda M. Lazarus, was named to succeed her as director.[2] By the time of her death, approximately fifty churches and missions were providing financial support for her efforts. The hospital in Vellore had been established for the purpose of serving women in India. Ida Scudder, as well as her chief financial supporters in among women in North America and Europe, desired to keep its medical training exclusively for women and feared that opening training to men would erode the basic purpose for which the hospital had been established. In 1938, the Madras government ruled that all entering students for medical schools must be candidates for a college degree in an institution affiliated with the University of Madras. The new rule represented a great advance in the quality of medical training in India, but it brought about a major crisis for the hospital in Vellore. It meant that the medical college would need to hire at least twelve new professors with advanced degrees in medicine; add new pathological, physiological, and bacteriological laboratories; and increase its teaching bed strength from 268 to at least 500. To accomplish all that, the annual income would have to double, and additional funds would be needed for the cost of the new buildings required.[3]

Scudder and her associates faced a real dilemma. If they did not move forward to meet the government's requirements, the medical school would not be allowed to admit students. But the only way to gather enough financial support to move forward was to become a coeducational institution. After considerable hesitation about their future course, Scudder, who was already sixty-eight years old, wrote to her Vellore board December 14, 1938, that she agreed to move ahead to fully upgrade the Vellore Medical College and Hospital as a women's medical college.[4] Efforts to raise adequate

---

2 For information about the accomplishments of Dr. Lazarus prior to her coming to Vellore, see Wilson, *Dr. Ida*, 320-21, and Jeffrey, *Ida S. Scudder*, 180.
3 Wilson, *Dr. Ida*, 274.
4 Ibid. 286-87.

Christian Medical College Hospital

funds for the women's medical college did not meet with adequate success, with the result that, in 1942, Scudder and the hospital board agreed that the institution should become coeducational. With that decision, the campaign for financial support moved forward rapidly. The government, which had been patient in implementing its new requirements, gave preliminary approval to the medical program in 1944 and final approval in 1947.[5] The Christian Medical College and Hospital was on its way to becoming the finest medical institution in India.

In 1947, male students were admitted to the medical school for the first time. Other departments were added from time to time, including training facilities for physical rehabilitation, pharmacy training, medical dieticians, medical records management, and community health, among others. The hospital grew to include more than twelve hundred beds. Vellore Christian Medical College was the first in India to initiate recognized residency training in chest, brain, and heart surgery and the first in the world to develop reconstructive surgery for leprosy patients.

[5] Ibid., 309.

In May, 1960, Ida S. Scudder had gone to her reward. In the five years prior to 1960, many of the long-term Arcot missionaries had retired, including Sara Zwemer, Mina Jongewaard, Ralph and Anna Ruth Korteling, Margaret Gibbons, John and Bernadine De Valois, Wilhelmina Noordyk, Galen and Maude Scudder, Charlotte Wyckoff, Cornelius and Ella Wierenga, Bernard and Bernice Rottschaefer, and John and Dora Muyskens. With the death of Ida S. Scudder, an era had come to an end. At such a time, the words of Dr. Paul Brand at her funeral were appropriate not only for the people of Vellore and the members of the Christian Medical College and Hospital community, but also for those Reformed Church missionaries who continued to serve. The words that Paul Brand offered began with a passage of scripture from the book of Joshua:

> "Moses my servant is dead; now therefore arise, go over this Jordan, thou, and all this people, unto the land that I do give them....I will not fail thee, nor forsake thee." [Brand] closed the book and said, "I have been asking myself, 'What would Aunt Ida wish me to say on this occasion?" I am sure she would ask us to arise, press on and cross our Jordans.[6]

Seventeen missionaries had retired between 1955 and 1960; three other families had resigned in order to take up new positions in the United States. Among the twenty-six Reformed Church missionaries who remained in the summer of 1960, fifteen more would leave by 1965 by retirement or resignation. During the decade of the 1960s, thirteen new Reformed Church missionaries were appointed to serve in India, bringing about a change of generation. The new missionaries had no memories of the Indian Church Board, the Arcot Assembly, or the Arcot Coordinating Committee. The Arcot Mission existed to meet the personal needs of the missionaries, while matters of work assignment were the responsibility of the diocese. The mission was responsible for matters such as automobiles

[6] Jeffrey, *Ida S. Scudder*, 228.

for missionaries, language study, allocation of houses to be used by missionaries on vacation in Kodaikanal, and the annual physical examinations and immunizations required for all missionaries and their children.

A New Era in India

In the new era, India was moving forward with confidence as a nation. It was the world's largest democracy. By 1960, it had held two national elections in which the Congress Party had emerged victorious. Prime Minister Nehru was leading India to become a truly modern nation as he pressed forward with programs to develop the nation's industry and social programs. Compulsory education through the fifth or eighth grade was being given priority, along with increased medical facilities for all. More high schools and colleges were established. Diseases such as malaria were brought under control, and vaccines were available to protect people against cholera, typhoid, and bubonic plague. The population was growing rapidly as the death rate declined. The "Green Revolution" brought about by the introduction of new seed varieties, increased irrigation, commercial fertilizers, and new methods of cultivation, combined with improved distribution channels, meant that the specter of famine no longer was seen in India after 1960.

As the decade went on, the modernization of India went on apace. Progress was being made toward the goal of providing electrical service for every village in India. Bus routes were rapidly expanded into the village areas. In the mid-sixties, low-cost transistor radios became a status symbol to be carried about by young men. India's movie industry, the third largest in the world, produced movies on themes of romantic love and the conflicts between values of the older traditional generation and the restless young people. At the beginning of the decade, it was more or less assumed by all that India was a nation of rural villages. During the decade, with the advances in communication and transportation facilities, the villages were increasingly brought within the orbit of the towns, and modern ideas were altering ageless customs.

Gandhi continued to be revered as the martyred saint who had given his life for his country. Politicians running for office still wore homespun cloth to symbolize their loyalty to his ideals. There was still talk about land reform; wealthy landowners at times still responded to appeals to make some of their land available for use by the poor and landless. Nevertheless, Gandhi's ideals of self-sacrifice were no as longer popular as they had been in the days of the independence struggle. The traditional crafts of spinning, weaving, and carving, as well as the cottage industry movement, were still encouraged by the government, but in modern India their role was becoming increasingly marginal. Under Nehru's leadership, the nation was not looking back to its traditional crafts and customs; it was moving forward in building a new democratic and industrial modern nation that would provide liberty and justice for all.

One of the questions that had faced the whole Christian community in India in 1947 was whether it should follow other religions in forming its own political party. Should a Christian party represent the interests of Christians as the Muslim League claimed to represent Muslims and as several of the Hindu religious parties desired to serve Hindu concerns? The Christians decided against setting up their own party. They were advised to seek out political parties (including the Congress Party) through which they could work for equal rights and justice for all people. Their basic premise was that they should become full participants in nation building, living according to the Constitution of India. The Christian educational, medical, and socioeconomic institutions were particularly alert to serving the country while carrying out their historic Christian mandate.

Renewal and Advance in the Church of South India

The Church of South India knew that it was living in a new era in the history of India. It set up a self-study commission in 1961 "to make an appraisal of the existing work and to get a vision of new horizons, all in the context of the Church's task in India today."[7]

The commission's report begins with reference to the new opportunity that had arisen since India became an independent nation. It stated:

> The coming of independence gave the Church a chance it had never had before to present Christianity to the people, released from the handicaps it had suffered under as the religion of the ruling race. The Constitution of India gave the right to Christians—as well as to the followers of other religions—to practice, preach and propagate their religion.[8]

The commission went on to indicate that its survey of the situation prevailing in the church and the formulation of its 171 recommendations were intended to encourage the church to fulfill the task of evangelism that had been entrusted to it. It wrote:

> When the Constitution of the new Church was drawn up, it was felt that the Church should place its evangelistic task, its mission to the nation, in the forefront and should mobilize all its spiritual and material resources in order to accomplish that task. It was hoped that as a result of the union which had brought the new Church into existence there would come into the Church a fuller life, renewed eagerness and an increase of power for the proclamation of the Gospel.[9]

The commission concluded that, while the Church of South India was self governing and self propagating, it was still far from being self supporting. In its opening chapter, it presented a basic survey

---

[7] *Renewal and Advance: Report of the Church of South India Commission on Integration and Joint Action, 1963* (Madras: Christian Literature Society, 1963), xiii. Please note that, although the official name of commission was the Commission on Integrations and Joint Action, we will refer to it by the name of its report, "Renewal and Advance."
[8] Ibid., ix.
[9] Ibid.

with statistics of each of the fourteen dioceses within the church. The Diocese of Madras in 1962 consisted of a baptized community of 86,277, of whom 37,272 were communicant members. It had 77 pastorates, 808 congregations, 90 ordained presbyters, 323 volunteer lay preachers, and 225 full-time evangelists, of whom 88 were women. It was more urban than rural, with 48 of the pastorates located in the city of Madras and its suburbs.[10]

The Madras diocese managed a large number of institutions. It had 12 high schools for boys and 9 for girls, a school for the deaf, 231 elementary schools, 35 higher elementary schools, 4 nursery schools, and 13 boarding homes, for a total of 31,336 pupils of whom 7,130 were Christians. Its 6 hospitals and 6 dispensaries faced great staffing and financial difficulties, because the diocesan scale of pay was far below what Indian medical personnel could earn elsewhere, in spite of the fact that its medical work was being subsidized by missionary societies to the tune of Rs. 100,000 ($21,000) per year.[11]

The commission was concerned about the heavy reliance of the Diocese of Madras on financial assistance from missionary societies. Although the diocese, with its comparatively large urban population, had the largest financial base in the whole church, it also received the largest amount of financial help from overseas. In 1962, it received Rs. 55,135 from the Australian Presbyterian Board of Missions, Rs. 245,803 from the British Methodist Mission Society, Rs. 281,810 from the Church of Scotland missionary societies, and Rs. 327,617 ($69,000) from the Reformed Church in America. The grants from the overseas churches were not at that time integrated into a unified budget but were kept separate and distributed in the areas to which the overseas societies had been historically related.[12]

The Diocese of Rayalaseema brought together churches that had come into being through the efforts of the London Missionary Society, the Society for the Propagation of the Gospel, and the

[10] Ibid., 20.
[11] Ibid., 21.
[12] Ibid.

Arcot Mission. In 1962, it had 52,300 baptized members, of whom 12,410 were communicants. Eighteen percent of its members were literate. It had 563 congregations with 54 presbyters. It had 3 high schools, 2 hospitals and 2 dispensaries, and 6 boarding homes. Because the Andhra State government had decided not to support teacher salaries in elementary schools, almost all of those schools had been turned over to the government. The diocese received Rs. 141,229 from the London Missionary Society, Rs. 23,684 from the Anglicans, and Rs. 99,510 ($21,000) from the Reformed Church in America. These grants were placed in an integrated budget, except that some of the money received from the Reformed Church was specifically designated for the institutions in the Madanapalle District.[13] Since the Diocese of Rayalaseema was the most poverty stricken and rural diocese in the church, its financial situation remained precarious. Eighty-nine percent of its expenditures were met from grants from overseas missionary societies.

Transfer of Property from the Arcot Mission to the Church of South India Trust Association

In its concern for the unity of the church and independence from foreign control, the commission recommended that all properties owned previously by the missions should be managed according to the rules of the synod's executive committee and the Church of South India Trust Association (CSITA).[14] By the time the commission reported, almost all of the Arcot Mission properties had been transferred to the CSITA. The issue of property transfer to the South Indian United Church had been raised already in 1942, when there was fear that Japan would invade India and force all the missionaries to leave.[15] When the threat had receded and the

---

13 Ibid., 30-32.
14 Ibid., Recommendation 93, 194.
15 J. J. De Valois to F. M. Potter, February 25, 1942; F. M. Potter to J. J. De Valois, July 31, 1942.

merger into the Church of South India had become immanent, the issue had been put aside.

Following upon the establishment of the Church of South India, the Board of Foreign Missions began to press the Arcot Mission to move more rapidly in the matter of the transfer. It seemed to the board that in this case as in other matters the missionaries were reluctant to become fully integrated into the new church. John D. Muyskens, who was due to retire within five years, was asked to devote much of his time to completing the transfer of properties before he left India. He pointed out how difficult and extensive the task was and that time was needed. When he sent the list to New York in 1957, it included 318 pieces of property, ranging in size from one-tenth of an acre in many cases of village schools and churches to 303 acres at the Agricultural Farm in Katpadi.[16]

In order to compile the list, Muyskens had traveled throughout the area, visited government offices, and researched issues of ownership. He learned that one-third of the properties were not supported by deeds, although in many cases the ownership of the property was registered with the government. He also ran into cases in which the government had assigned property ownership to the mission for educational, medical, or other use and registered the property in the name of a missionary, rather than in the name of the Arcot Mission. In some cases, the missionary "owner" had died by 1957. In other cases, the property was listed in the name of an Indian, particularly in the name of Arthur John in the Chittoor area.[17]

Apart from the need to gather precise information concerning ownership and registration of the properties, it was necessary to await the decision of the government to waive the stamp tax duties that, according to the law, should be levied on each piece of property transferred. In view of the many small pieces of property

---

[16] "Properties held by the American Arcot Mission," October 10, 1957 (Archives of the RCA).

[17] J. D. Muyskens to H. G. Bovenkerk, September 26, 1957.

involved, this was an inordinately high-cost tax relative to the value of the property. After representations were made to the government by the Indian National Christian Council and other mission bodies, the government agreed that it would not be necessary to levy the tax. After J. D. Muyskens retired, C. A. De Bruin was asked to complete the task. With a few exceptions, such as the missionary residences and the properties in Kodaikanal, De Bruin completed the transfers by 1962.

Rethinking Institutions

One of the concerns of missionaries as India was moving toward independence was whether the educational, medical, and industrial institutions that they had built through great effort and even sacrifice would deteriorate after they left. The Commission for Renewal and Advance was concerned that the institutions built up by the missionaries were too expensive for the Church of South India to maintain. It also questioned whether a number of them had outlived their usefulness in the changed climate of India. Previous to the appointment of the Church of South India's Renewal and Advance Commission, the Diocese of Madras had already appointed a Commission on Diocesan High Schools to evaluate each of the schools within the diocese. The diocesan commission had stated its perceived purpose for Christian institutions:

> ...it must be admitted that a Christian institution exists mainly to serve a Christian purpose....The business of the Christian Church in this country is not to do the work which the State should do or to relieve the State of a part of its obligatory welfare work. Nor should the Church aim at, or be content with, being commended for the philanthropic work which is carried on under its auspices. The sole purpose for which the church has been placed in this country—as in every other country—is to "Christianize"

the country, to do "evangelistic" work in the broadest, deepest sense of the term....[18]

The Madras diocesan report concluded by saying that no institution should be continued simply because it was begun by missionaries and missionary societies. It recognized that times had changed and accepted the possibility, even the probability, that it was time to close some institutions.

> The time has come when we must call a halt to the policy of continuing institutions (including High Schools and Colleges) merely because they were started by venerable Missionaries and Missionary Societies and have been running so long and have come to be looked upon by the local Christian community as a part of their life and as something in which they have certain vested interests.
>
> No institution should hereafter be retained unless it serves a specific purpose—for the Church first, for the Christian community second, and for the general public third. Only institutions which directly serve the purposes of the Church and are directly useful to the Christian community should be financed from Diocesan funds. The third should be wholly supported, if at all, by public funds.[19]

Like the Diocese of Madras and the Church of South India's Renewal and Advance Commission, the Reformed Church in America's Board of Foreign Missions and other mission societies were also raising questions about how long they should and financially could support the wide range of institutional mission. Beginning after 1950, the major institutions and programs developed by Reformed Church missionaries in the Arcot Mission area came under this kind of scrutiny. As we review those developments, it will become clear that reports of commissions and questions from

[18] Report of the Commission on Diocesan High Schools (Madras Diocese), October 1960 (Archives of the RCA).
[19] Ibid.

overseas missionary bodies made an impression on the decision-
making bodies. However, the decisive elements in each situation
were the extent to which the leaders in each institution were able to
modify that institution's mission to meet the needs of people in a
modernizing India, and the extent to which they were able to locate
new sources of funding apart from the church in India or overseas
mission agencies.

One of the ironies of the mission situation in the Arcot Mission
area was that the Board of Foreign Missions was supporting
educational and medical institutions overseas that the Reformed
Church could not afford for itself in North America. It had never
established hospitals in America. Its first college, Rutgers, had been
turned over to its own board and the State of New Jersey. The
academies in Cedar Grove, Wisconsin, and German Valley, Illinois,
had been closed. It had always been a firm advocate for the
common school at the elementary level and, unlike its sister
denomination, the Christian Reformed Church, it was not a supporter
of the Christian school movement in America. It is not surprising
that questions arose about continuing support for such institutions
in India.

Turning to the Renewal and Advance report, we learn that the
commission had three basic concerns about the institutions:

> We need to be greatly concerned about our institutional
> work, first, because these institutions...are far beyond the
> resources of the Indian Church to run and they keep us
> inordinately dependent on foreign help in money and
> personnel. Second, these institutions are not, except in a
> few more or less exceptional cases, in any sense an expression
> of the love of the Indian Church for the Indian people. It
> is an undeniable fact that it is becoming more and more
> difficult to get suitable Indian Christians of sufficient
> spiritual calibre to take up life-time service in these
> institutions in a spirit of self-sacrifice....There is, thirdly,

the increasing difficulty in keeping the institutions Christian in their functioning.[20]

The Board of Foreign Missions also was concerned about the institutions' continuing need for financial support. Already in 1954, it asked for a response to a set of criteria for the measurement and evaluation of existing institutions that had been developed by the Division of Foreign Missions of the National Council of Churches in the United States. In that year, the board once again was faced with a financial crisis and cut its appropriation for the Arcot area by 10 percent for 1954 and 1955. The people in the Arcot area graciously accepted the need for the reductions,[21] but the board felt some urgency in the need to evaluate which institutions should continue to receive support and at what level. When it had faced the necessity of reducing its appropriation before, the board simply had informed the mission of the amount that would be sent and anticipated that the mission (or, after 1923, the Arcot Assembly) would decide how much should be allocated to each institution. The fact that the board was proposing criteria shows again that it was beginning to occupy the role that had once been filled by the Arcot Mission.

Among the criteria that were being proposed by the overseas mission societies, the first was that each institution "should unmistakably be an examplar of Christ and of his Church; and within itself, it should be a truly Christian community. The majority of its staff (and in the case of a school, the students) should be practicing Christians."[22] There was agreement in India on these basic points, but the schools in the Arcot and Rayalaseema areas could never anticipate that a majority of the students would be Christian.

Also included in the criteria was the thought that each institution should form an integral part of the church and should serve an

20 *Renewal and Advance*, 149.
21 C. A. Samuel to B. Luben, October 1, 1954.
22 Division of Foreign Mission, NCCC, "Basic Principles and Criteria for Missionary Institutions," May, 1953, 4.

essential place in the broader ministry of the church's worldwide outreach. Its character and development should be such that its support might eventually be taken over by the church on the field. It must do its job well and maintain first-class technical and scientific standards. It was especially important to avoid putting money into buildings in western style, since that fostered "institutionalism." Instead, money should be put into skilled personnel, tools, and techniques.[23]

While the comments of the Renewal and Advance Commission of the Church of South India Synod and the Board of Foreign Missions made eminent sense on a broad scale, they had but small impact at the diocesan and more local levels. For the most part, it was impossible for the institutions to meet the standards proposed. If the Reformed Church in America was unable to provide the financial resources necessary to maintain its own small number of educational institutions, it was even less likely that any diocese in the Church of South India would be able to do so. Few of the institutions could aspire to meet "first-class technical and scientific standards." Most of the schools in the old Arcot Mission area had been opened for the purpose of making opportunities available to the disadvantaged children of the lowest castes who otherwise would have no opportunity at all. With regard to the relation between the Board of Foreign Missions and the dioceses in India, the policy statements of the board informed the church in India what to expect in terms of assistance. Nevertheless, the fact that the financial power of the Board of Foreign Missions stood behind the policy statements could not be avoided, however much everyone wanted to work on the basis of full partnership.

Medical Mission in the New Era

The Renewal and Advance Commission found, in spite of the large expansion of government medical services, that there was still a need for Christian medical services in India. Therefore it

[23] Ibid., 4-5.

recommended that the number of hospitals and dispensaries not be reduced and that the schools of nursing be continued.[24]

Within the Diocese of Madras, the Scudder Memorial Hospital in 1960 was growing in strength under the strong leadership of Dr. Julius C. Savarirayan. The Reformed Church assisted in strengthening the Christian witness and service of the hospital by appointing, between 1960 and 1963, five new missionaries—Vivian Anderson, Dr. and Mrs. Frank and Ann Zwemer, and Reverend and Mrs. William and Mary Hoffman—to serve in the hospital. The new roles of missionaries serving under Indian leadership is exemplified by these five missionaries in Ranipet, each of whom made specific contributions prior to their returning to the United States. Nurses Vivian Anderson and Ann Zwemer provided assistance in the integrated public health nursing program that was started in 1962. One of the features of this program was that nurses went out to surrounding villages on bicycles. They visited homes and organized a record system to enable them to maintain a systematic public health program. [25] The "Wilhelmina Noordyk School of Nursing" building was erected with a demonstration room, library, and a small laboratory.[26] Ann Zwemer also helped develop the public health integration in the basic nursing course, including home visitation and domiciliary midwifery in Karai village.[27]

The School of Nursing at Ranipet that opened in 1923 was a pioneer in nursing instruction. As nursing superintendent, Arcot missionary Wilhelmina Noordyk was not able to find any Tamil parent ready to send a daughter for nurse's training, but she did find two men, who at first had no idea what nursing was. On the fiftieth anniversary of the School of Nursing, Lois Marsilje, dean of nursing, recalled their progress as she had heard about it:

[24] *Renewal and Advance,* Recommendations 131-133, 201-202.
[25] J. C. Savarirayan, "History of a School of Nursing in a Private Hospital—Scudder Memorial Hospital," in *Golden Jubilee Souvenir 1973, School of Nursing* (privately printed), 15.
[26] Ibid., 15-16.
[27] Alayamma Matthews, "Nursing Education," in *Golden Jubilee Souvenir 1978, Scudder Memorial Hospital* (privately printed), 33.

Capping and candlelight service for nurses

Of course, they would expect to give medicines, do dressing, assist at operations and help the doctor. But baths and bedside care were beyond their concept of nursing. However, they soon learned that this was their job too....They even learned to keep simple charts. But probably the most difficult thing these men had to learn was to take orders from a woman even if she was the Nursing Superintendent.[28]

The School of Nursing played a significant role in changing attitudes about the profession of nursing. As the years went on, it helped nursing become a respected profession for women as well as men in society. Wilhelmina Noordyk wrote a small manual of nursing that came to be widely used elsewhere in mission, government, and military hospitals in India.[29] Near the end of her time in India and after returning to the United States in 1970, Ann Zwemer continued the tradition and wrote a large textbook for nursing in India that has gone through a large number of editions and continues to be used today.

[28] Lois Marsilje, "Fifty Years of Growth and Development" in ibid., 1.
[29] Savirarayan, "History of a School of Nursing," 14.

William and Mary Hoffman were appointed when the hospital requested missionary assistance in developing a more efficient laboratory and religious work department. William served as chaplain and business administrator. He made improvements in the day-to-day administration of the hospital and maintenance of accounts and took a keen interest in the religious nurture of the staff and patients. Mary made improvements in the curriculum of laboratory procedures and modernization of equipment.[30]

When Julius Savarirayan retired in 1967, Frank Zwemer became medical superintendent of the hospital. He developed plastic surgery for the hospital, including a modern Zimmerman skin graft unit, and carried out the construction of a new community health block, pediatric ward, and multipurpose store room. Meanwhile, when Reformed Church missionary Lois Marsilje retired, Ann Zwemer became dean of the school of nursing.[31] Following the Zwemers' departure from Scudder Memorial Hospital in 1970, the hospital has carried on its ambitious program of medical service as a Christian hospital without missionary assistance.

The Mary Lott Lyles Hospital in Madanapalle also has continued to provide training for nursing students to the present day. It was for many years under the leadership of missionaries Harriet Brumler and Alberta Biegel, but since the latter's retirement in 1982 it has been under the direction of Indian nurses. This school and the one in Ranipet became known for the dedication and excellent training of their graduates. This created a dilemma for the hospitals. Their graduates were so much in demand and were offered such high salaries elsewhere that the hospitals themselves found it extremely difficult to retain their own graduates. The Ranipet Nursing Superintendent, Aley Matthews, wrote about the problem in 1977:

> Staff nurses keep flowing to foreign countries where remunerations are very attractive. They all want to go and of course they get 15 to 20 times the salary that they get here.

30 Ernest Basker, "A Review," in *Golden Jubilee, 1978,* 5.
31 Ibid.

Their families need money and the opportunities are there and therefore we cannot blame them. However, the hospital work has to go on….This year we are shocked to have several of our tutors resigning to go to Arabia. They are leaving their families here to work in Arabia to educate their children and they make plans for their future.[32]

New Sources of Financial Support

A new factor entered into issues of institutional self support after World War II, especially in the "development decade" of the 1960s. It became possible then for medical and other institutions to secure grants from governments, international agencies, and humanitarian organizations. As a result of such new sources of support, the various institutions could survive and even flourish with less support from the Indian church or from overseas missionary societies. Their challenge then became responding creatively to the new needs that were arising in India and convincing international humanitarian agencies or Indian government agencies that these new approaches to human need were important. The hospitals in the old Arcot Mission area responded to the challenges of the new era in several ways.

Julius Savarirayan at the Scudder Memorial Hospital in Ranipet entered into an agreement with the government to implement the Wallajah Leprosy Control Scheme as a pilot project in the Wallajah area. The incidence of leprosy in the villages in that area was as high as 3 to 4 percent. In the first eighteen months of the project, 8,224 cases came under treatment, with the cost per patient being approximately two dollars a year. Dr. R. G. Cochrane, who was a pioneer in the modern treatment of leprosy, pointed out that the project set an excellent example of how one could integrate a public health program for leprosy with the general work of a hospital. With regard to Savarirayan's hope also to integrate the program with the

32 Aley Matthews to Johanna De Vries, April 13, 1977.

religious program of the hospital, Cochrane was less optimistic but for the moment was ready to give the benefit of the doubt:

> If the opportunity is taken to display Christian literature, including the Scriptures, then those purchasing these booklets will undoubtedly in some instances be attracted towards allegiance to our Lord. The team, however, should include committed Christians who are wise enough and mature enough to deal with any enquirer who might approach one of the members of the team with a request to learn about Jesus.[33]

The Mary Lott Lyles Hospital in Madanapalle also benefited by receiving grants from a large number of organizations and individuals in addition to what it received through the diocese from the Reformed Church in America. A summary of what such assistance meant to the community of Madanapalle was provided in a report from the hospital to a general public meeting in 1975. The report provides evidence of the remarkable loyalty that missionaries who had served in Madanapalle continued to show. In 1973, the "Mejeur-Biegel Library" was opened following receipt of a legacy according to the will of missionary nurse Albertha Biegel's father. Her brother-in-law had visited the hospital, and, on his return to the United States, he had enlisted people in the Thorn Creek Reformed Church in Illinois to purchase a new generator for electrical supply for the hospital. Dr. Margaret Gibbons had provided funds to paint the new outpatient block, and a new laundry building had been constructed with assistance of another legacy.[34] Among other major donors over the two decades following 1960 were listed Oxfam, Bread for the World (the German, not the American organization), the Arogyavaram Development Society, and the Tear Fund.[35]

[33] R. G. Cochrane, in "Gleanings," *Journal of Christian Medical Association,* (n.d.), 499.
[34] "Report of the Church of South India, M. L. L. Hospital, Madanapalle, 1975" (mimeograph copy in Rayalaseema file, Archives of the RCA).
[35] Stanley Vander Aarde, "Medical Superintendent's Report" in *Seventieth Anniversary Souvenir, 1911-1981,* (printed for Mary Lott Lyles Hospital, Madanapalle, 1981), 33.

The Church of South India hospitals often found themselves working in close cooperation with the Indian government to meet the health needs of the nation. One of the major areas of cooperation was conception control and family planning. The public health programs instituted after independence had enabled the nation to gain control over the diseases that had regularly reached epidemic proportions, and its improved agricultural programs had removed the threat of famine. The result was an alarming population explosion, which in turn caused the government to institute family planning programs. One of the most important programs consisted of encouraging women with three children or more to have a tubectomy paid for by the government, in order to prevent them from bearing more children. It also offered vasectomies for men. In its report to the general public in 1975, the Mary Lott Lyles Hospital reported that it had performed 542 such family planning procedures in 1974 and 416 in 1975.[36]

The Union Mission Tuberculosis Sanatorium in Arogyavaram, four miles from Madanapalle, was able to provide a new form of service with the help of a new major donor. It found its mission changing during the 1960s and 1970s as public health programs combined with better medical treatment led to a decline in the incidence of tuberculosis. India did, however, continue to have a fairly large number of people who suffered from the effects of polio. The Scudder Memorial Hospital in Ranipet had entered into cooperative arrangements with organizations dedicated to provide rehabilitation and prostheses for victims of polio and had opened a boarding home for polio sufferers on the hospital compound. The Arogyavaram Union Mission Tuberculosis Sanatorium, with its large and airy compound, provided an excellent setting to assist children who were polio victims. In 1980, it received a grant of $180,000 from Kinder Not Hilf of Germany to establish a children's boarding home and rehabilitation center that continues to serve polio sufferers to the present day.

[36] "Report of the Church of South India, M.L.L. Hospital," 1976.

Rethinking Elementary Education

As we have noted repeatedly, in the Arcot Mission, the village elementary schools formed a base on which leadership for pastoral care and worship could be maintained. When the government implemented its grant-in-aid policy for mission-managed schools and, at the same time, allowed the mission to charge some fees for attendance, it was not unusual for 90 percent of the cost of the school to be met from sources other than the mission. As a result, the mission was able to establish a very large number of elementary schools and employ more than two hundred teachers, almost all of whom could also serve as leaders in the village congregations.

We have also seen, however, that the missionaries were uneasy about the policy that an elementary school should be placed in every village where there were at least three families that asked to be instructed in the Christian faith. They believed that, as the number of villages grew, the policy would prove to be too expensive and therefore a factor inhibiting church growth. When faced with the question of what else could be done, the missionaries could find no adequate alternative. They always hoped that, as the number of literate Christians grew, unpaid volunteer leaders could be found in sufficient numbers to lead the village congregations, but that hope had seldom been fulfilled. As a result, missionaries and Indian pastors felt deep frustrations about the system. At one moment, they would display a tendency to be sharply critical of the performance of the village teachers. At the next moment, they would sympathize with the difficult circumstances under which the teachers had to labor in villages where parents were noncooperative because they did not see much value in elementary education for their children.

The Arcot Mission was not alone in its frustration about village elementary schools. The same system had been implemented by missions throughout the whole area in which the Church of South India carried out its ministry. Therefore, the Renewal and Advance

Commission looked carefully at the village elementary schools that had come under the management of the dioceses. After conducting its survey, the commission was sharply critical of the schools and suggested that, except perhaps in a few cases where local conditions were difficult, "there is no need...for the Church to run elementary schools."[37] The commission had discovered that

> There is hardly any difference of opinion about elementary schools. Everyone who replied to our questionnaire agrees that these have become almost useless to the Christian enterprise and even to the Christian community in increasing its literacy....Except that we, in the C.S.I., still have about ten thousand teachers in our elementary schools, we are getting little direct benefit from them. But as we do not now have to pay all of them ourselves—whatever we pay is over and above what the government pays them—they are not really our employees; nor do they consider themselves as such.[38]

The commission boldly concluded, "The pastoral care of our village congregations and our evangelistic work in the villages must therefore from now on be planned and carried out without the help of the village school and the village teacher."[39] It recommended that the church increase the number of paid and honorary ordained presbyters and deacons in order to make it possible for them to visit the villages more regularly. It also recommended a vigorous training program for voluntary lay workers, recruited from the rural congregations, to give pastoral care to those congregations.[40]

Reformed Church ordained male missionaries tended to agree with the findings of the commission. It is less clear how several of the unmarried women missionaries felt about it, despite the fact that several of them were correspondents or managers for village

[37] *Renewal and Advance,* 151.
[38] Ibid., 150.
[39] Ibid.
[40] Ibid., Recommendations 29-32, 185.

schools and probably more familiar with the educational needs of the children than were the men. They also tended to be less critical of the expense of running the schools and to be more vocal about the need to repair the roofs and provide better equipment. Unfortunately, after the merger into the Church of South India, they did not leave written records of their opinions in regard to village schools.[41] So far as the men were concerned, however, C. A. De Bruin reflected attitudes that had been present for more than a decade. He advocated that elementary schools in Madras State be turned over to the government, as most schools in the Chittoor and Madanapalle districts in Andhra State had been transferred when that state had decided no longer to provide grants-in-aid to church-managed schools. He agreed with the commission that, since the government in Madras State was paying 100 percent of the teachers' salaries and the teachers worked under rules of service established by the government, the teachers considered themselves to be employees of the government rather than of the church.[42]

The Reformed Church Board for Christian World Mission also responded favorably to the Renewal and Advance report on elementary education. It had heard complaints for decades about the quality of education provided by the village schools. It was further influenced by a strong anti-institutional bias that was growing in the United States. It also believed that greater efforts toward self-support could be made in the villages as well as the town churches. As a signal of its intentions, the board implemented a series of reductions in financial support for elementary schools. In 1963, the grant was $11,700. It was gradually reduced to $10,000 in 1966, with a further decrease possible for 1967.[43] At the same time, the board complimented the Rayalaseema diocese, where only

---

[41] All eight members of the commission were men.

[42] C. A. De Bruin, "The Changing Situation," mimeographed statement, October 14, 1964.

[43] Staff report, "An Evaluation of India Program and Budget Priorities—January 21, 1966" (Archives of the RCA), 6.

minimum church subsidies were given to the schools at any level of education. [44]

In spite of these recommendations from the commission and support for them by missionaries and the Board for World Christian Missions, Indian ordained ministers and others who had responsibility for the schools and village congregations were hesitant to abandon or transfer the schools. The issue came before the Madras Diocesan Elementary Education Board, which appointed its own commission to study the issues involved. The convenor of the commission, the Reverend D. I. Vedanayagam, a pastor in the city of Madras, placed before the board a memorandum that was far less critical of the schools and teachers than was the Renewal and Advance commission.

He pointed out that the vast majority of the Christian people of the diocese lived in some eight hundred village congregations where there was no resident pastor. The main responsibility for the day-to-day care of those congregations and for the week-by-week ministry of the Word of God to them was carried on by the village teachers. He affirmed that, instead of being critical of the teachers' deficiencies, the church should be more faithful in caring for their spiritual needs as they labored under very difficult conditions. He wrote,

> We know how easy it is for the fire of love and devotion to die down if it is not continually nourished by the Word of the Spirit of God. For this reason it seems to me absolutely essential that the teachers in charge of congregations should be able to meet each month as a fellowship, under the guidance of the presbyter, to pray together about their work, to share news of new developments, set-backs, problems and victories, and to study the Bible together— not for the purpose of passing an examination but in order

44 Ibid. 9.

that their own souls may be fed, illuminated and comforted by the Word of God.[45]

Vedanayagam believed that if a village teacher said he was a teacher and not a pastor, he should be respected for that rather than forced to do pastoral work. On the other hand, it remained true that many teachers continued to view pastoral work as their calling as well, even though it was not required of them. Vedanayagam knew that in the Andhra State areas of the diocese there were many teachers who continued to do the pastoral work voluntarily, even though the government had taken over the schools. "We have no right to use financial or administrative power to force men into doing church work."[46] In line with such thinking, he believed that the diocese should "raise up an army of voluntary workers in our village congregations who will be willing and able to carry the pastoral responsibility when a paid worker is not available."[47]

The Diocese of Madras had formed five "area councils" within its bounds in order to allow for more local discussion and decisionmaking than was possible in the large geographical area of the diocese. Most of the pastorates of the old Arcot Mission area were placed in the "western area," while Tindivanam, Muttathur, and Gingee Pastorates were in the "southern area." The diocesan commission on elementary education asked each of the areas of the diocese for its opinion regarding the continuing need for village elementary schools. The areas affirmed a continuing role for the village elementary schools under the management of the church. They concluded that

The village schools are still points of contact with the community and therefore these help to relate the Gospel to the non-Christian. The usefulness of the School...depends upon the teacher personnel....The village schools are a

---

[45] D. I. Vedanayagam, "Memorandum for the Elementary Education Board," December 16, 1965 (Archives of the RCA).
[46] Ibid.
[47] Ibid.

leavening influence in the community and they have a part to play in community development. The closing of a particular school may mean the loss of the Church's place in a village community....The schools are a pastoral necessity.[48]

The western and southern areas of the diocese agreed that the schools had not lost their usefulness to the life and mission of the church. They believed that savings could be made by placing full responsibility for the village schools directly in the hands of the pastorates. They could then discontinue the practice of using central "correspondents" or superintendents to manage the schools, as well as the separate office that required financial assistance for the administrative work. They suggested that, if the pastorates gained a greater sense of ownership in the management of the schools, the people in the villages would also be ready to increase their support of the church's ministry.[49]

These suggestions from the diocesan areas revived an old controversy about the role that ordained ministers should have in relation to the village schools. On the one hand, it was contended that the pastors should be kept free from the many details involved in relating to the education department of the government and in the management of the schools. They should be free to devote themselves to the spiritual needs of their people and to the task of evangelizing the multitude of unreached villages within their pastorate areas. Those who held this position advocated that missionaries or qualified Indian lay persons should be made "correspondents" to manage the schools.

On the other hand, the pastors themselves maintained that teachers would be better off relating to one person for their responsibilities as teachers and as pastoral leaders, than to two different persons in a dual management for church and school. When the correspondent lived outside the pastorate area, he or she

48 Ibid.
49 Ibid.

often also had a multitude of other responsibilities besides managing the schools. In these situations, the correspondent often was not in a position to give adequate attention to the needs of the pastorate and the work of the churches in the villages.

While the issues in the controversy were never resolved, as time went on the western (Arcot) area of the diocese moved in the direction of appointing pastors to serve also as correspondents and managers for the schools.[50] As the overseas mission agencies continued to reduce their appropriations for elementary education and ultimately to eliminate the subsidy altogether, it was the pastorates that bore the major burden of financing schools. This proved to be an important step in the direction of self-support.

Rethinking Higher Education

In 1960, there were two teacher training schools, three high schools, and one college operating in the old Arcot Mission area under the direction of the Diocese of Madras, and the Hope High School in Madanapalle under the Diocese of Rayalaseema. Later in the decade, the De Valois High School, which had an agricultural bias, was opened on the grounds of the Katpadi Agricultural Institute, and the V.R.V. elementary school in Ranipet moved toward being upgraded to include a high school.

The Renewal and Advance Commission did not recommend that high schools be transferred to the government, but it did urge that every high school should be examined to see whether it continued to meet a real need in the church and community. Each school should also maintain high professional standards; have a headmaster or headmistress who was a good administrator, had imagination,

---

[50] The question about the role of ordained presbyters in the management of elementary schools continued to be subject to shifts of policy. After churches in the western area of the Diocese of Madras entered the Diocese of Vellore, Bishop Sam Ponniah reversed the policy of appointing presbyters to be managers and correspondents for the schools. "Another important step the Bishop has taken is to relieve Presbyters from the School work as Managers and Correspondents....Presbyters are free to use their time and talents for their Pastoral and evangelistic work in their pastorates" (*Vellore Diocesan News,* April-May, 1980), 6.

and was a Christian open to God's leading; and exhibit "a natural and unmistakable religious atmosphere." It also needed sound financial management that did not require an annual subsidy from the church.[51]

The commission continued to favor the operation of hostels for boys and girls at the high-school level and to allow overseas mission societies to continue to provide a subsidy for them. While the commission believed every student should be required to pay fees for his or her time at the school, the poor boys and girls from the villages could not be expected to meet the entire cost. The hostels should be viewed as places for Christian nurture and training. The commission believed that

> Systematic Christian nurture of the inmates of Christian Hostels should be attempted through morning worship, singing lessons (*bajans*), Sunday Schools and Youth activities and by inculcating the habits of daily Bible reading and prayer. The boys may also be sent now and then with evangelistic bands to help in the singing and incidentally get impressed with a sense of evangelistic responsibility.[52]

Reformed Church missionaries and Indian leaders in the old Arcot Mission area were in full accord with the commission's report on high-school education. Self-support was easier to achieve in the management of high schools than in most other areas of the church's mission, since the high schools were already almost fully self-supporting through their receipt of government grants. For example, in 1964 the Voorhees High School, with 1,500 students in Vellore, had a budget of approximately Rs.100,000, of which the subsidy from the Reformed Church was Rs.1,000, or $220, which was still being given by the church as a "management grant" to help meet maintenance costs. The major assistance in high-school education from overseas was to help meet the cost of running the

51 *Renewal and Advance,* Recommendation 120, 199.
52 Ibid., 158.

student hostels. Within a few years, overseas assistance for hostels would also disappear.

With regard to what would happen in India after the missionaries left, the high schools all were already under the leadership of Indian headmasters or headmistresses before India became independent. In 1997, when the Church of South India celebrated the fiftieth anniversary of its inauguration, the high schools had all remained strong and were carrying on their educational mission under the direction of the diocese and in cooperation with the government education agencies.

During the decade of the 1960s, the Tamil Progress Party (DMK) became powerful in Madras State and defeated the Indian Congress Party in an election to win control of the state government. One of its objectives was to make government more available to the people of the state by encouraging use of the Tamil language rather than English as the language of the government, including the courts. It also opposed the use of the Hindi language that was favored in the northern states. During its first years in power, the schools were encouraged to use the local Tamil language rather than English as the medium of instruction.

By the 1980s, however, the first enthusiasm for Tamil as the medium of instruction in higher education had faded. Previous to India's independence, the leading schools in the southern part of the country were run by missionaries who also encouraged study in the English language. Those who learned their English well enjoyed greater advantages in gaining employment with the government and in industry. After independence, when opportunities to study overseas became more available, good knowledge of the English language was usually a requirement. Aware of those advantages, by 1980 the desire for education with an English medium of instruction again became strong in the state of Madras, now renamed "Tamilnadu" (Tamil land).

Just as the old mission hospitals found that they could prosper by obtaining grants from foundations, humanitarian agencies, and individuals overseas when overseas missionary societies reduced their support, so it was for the high schools. There were persons interested in helping the church meet the educational needs of Indians through the establishment of Christian schools. A group of Christian laymen who were members of the Christian Reformed Church and Reformed Church in America founded an organization named "Worldwide Christian Schools." Through their contacts with Harry and Janet Pofahl, who had served as Reformed Church missionaries at the Katpadi Industrial Institute from 1963-1972, they responded to the need for assistance to schools in the Arcot area. Harry Pofahl put them in touch with the Rt. Rev. Sam Ponniah, bishop in the new Diocese of Vellore, who had come to believe that there was a need for a new kind of high school designed to serve young middle-class students in an increasingly urban culture.

Two of the Worldwide Christian Schools' major projects were to provide funds for the establishment of two new "matriculation level" high schools offering English as a medium of instruction, one in Chittoor and the other in Ranipet. They were to be managed under the new Diocese of Vellore, each with its own board. These two high schools were intended to be for students of families who could afford to meet some of the costs of their education and who showed promise of being able to "matriculate" into a college following their graduation. These projects represented a new venture in the field of education for a church in which there was a growing middle class of educated persons.

Voorhees Becomes a Four-Year College

The Renewal and Advance Commission made very little reference to policies about four-year colleges within the Church of South India. Nevertheless, it is important at this point to review developments at Voorhees College, which became a four-year college in 1957.

The Arcot Mission and the Board of Foreign Missions had always been slightly hesitant about the college, fearing that it would require considerable financial support. They believed, however, that the 1946 decision to accept the requirement of the Madras University Commission to separate the high school from the college, and to keep the college at a two-year level, had been correct. Upgrading the college to a four-year institution at that time could have cost as much as $500,000, an amount far beyond the resources of the Reformed Church in America. It was recognized that the University Commission had hinted that if Voorhees did not upgrade, another body might be permitted to open a college in Vellore. That could mean competition from the Roman Catholics.[53]

Throughout the first half of the twentieth century, Reformed Church missionaries consistently followed a policy of sending students who had the capacity to complete college education to Christian union institutions of higher education established in the city of Madras. For that reason, the Arcot Mission had been an enthusiastic supporter of Madras Christian College for men, located south of Madras at Tambaram, and for Women's Christian College and St. Christopher's (teacher) Training College for women, in Madras. The Indian Christian leaders in the Arcot Mission area had accepted that policy, but they had the same reservations about it that the people in Madanapalle had about closing the girls' school there and sending them to Chittoor for their education. That is to say, Madras was ninety miles from Vellore and the expenses for a person studying in Madras were necessarily higher than in Vellore. Furthermore, the students in the Madras colleges usually came from a more urbanized environment than did those from the Arcot area. Christians in the Arcot area continued to hope for a four-year Christian college in their own area, in spite of the contention that there were a sufficient number of colleges within the Diocese of Madras.

---

[53] C. R. Wierenga to F. M. Potter, October 21, 1946; F. M. Potter to C.R. Wierenga, November 20, 1946.

Dr. A. Lakshmanaswami Mudeliar, vice-chancellor of the Madras University, the leading voice of university education in the state, spoke at the golden jubilee celebration of Voorhees College in 1951. He paid a glowing tribute to the missionary work in the Arcot area, and he urged that Voorhees become a four-year college:

> Voorhees College had stood as an ideal college of its kind in the district for many years. Voorhees College occupied a very responsible position among the Intermediate Colleges of the state. What is needed now is good and efficient teaching and training of boys and girls. In this respect, Voorhees College has earned a reputation in this part of the country for giving efficient training to students.[54]

Already in 1945, the Board of Foreign Missions had heard a presentation on upgrading the school. It replied that it was sympathetic, but that much more study was required concerning the cost. It also feared that premature upgrading of a number of colleges in India "would result inevitably in the springing up of a large number of inferior institutions throughout the country, without due consideration to the overall situation in India."[55]

However, by 1954 the board had decided to make Voorhees a four-year college, based on far lower cost estimates than the first ones. Since the teachers' salaries were to be met by the government, the basic need was for building an addition to the school's main building in order to accommodate the additional classes of students. The Board of Foreign Missions agreed to provide a grant to pay for the addition. However, it was dismayed to learn from the area treasurer, J. C. Savarirayan, in the fall of 1955 that it would be asked for an additional Rs. 75,000 ($15,800) to meet the actual costs of constructing a building already in the process of being erected. Savarirayan informed the board that the construction project had been carried out by workers of the Katpadi Industrial Institute

54 "AAR," 1952-1954, 58-59.
55 F. M. Potter to C. R. Wierenga, June 8, 1945.

under the superintendence of Reformed Church missionaries Ben Rottschaefer and Ben De Vries.[56]

The problem of the overexpenditure was not unique in the history of the Arcot Mission. Rottschaefer always insisted upon building a quality structure that would last for ages; he refused to be bound by a strict contract that required him to remain within budget if that meant compromising on the construction of what he understood to be a good building. As one looks at the building now, after more than forty years have passed, it is clear that full value was provided. At the time, however, the cost overruns only served to make the board hesitate to respond to further requests related to the upgrading of the college. The board did, however, ultimately promise to provide $80,000 to complete other elements in the upgrading program on the condition that a substantial sum also be raised locally in India.[57]

Voorhees College opened its four-year program in 1957, and new issues arose. Some members of the faculty who had been hired with credentials to serve in a two-year college now had to operate in a four-year institution. In the course of its decision to upgrade, it had been understood that to the fullest extent possible, Christians should be employed as members of the faculty. However, a number of senior faculty members were concerned that they could be pushed aside as younger, better-trained faculty were added to the staff. Several of them believed that they were given promises by Mr. S. Jesuratnam, the principal of the college, that they would be first to be promoted as professors and to be heads of departments when openings arose.[58]

The situation became embarrassing in 1960 when several department chairmanships came open. There were two men on the faculty who had been kept on probation as teachers for four years, contrary to the rules of the Madras University, which specified that

---

[56] J. C. Savarirayan to B. Luben, September 29, 1955.
[57] B. Luben to Mrs. S. Jesuratnam, January 2, 1960. Mrs. Jesuratnam was the wife of the principal of the college.
[58] Ibid.

confirmation had to be made after a probationary period of two years.[59] These two men were qualified to be heads of departments, while the older men did not meet the academic qualifications. Unfortunately, one of the men was a Hindu and the other a Roman Catholic. The college had no choice but to consent to the rules of the university and appoint the Hindu to be head of the Physics Department and the Roman Catholic head of the English Department. When the governing board of the college hesitated, it sought an interview with the vice-chancellor of the university. Following the interview, a strongly worded letter was received from the registrar of the university

> demanding immediate implementation of the University's directive and at the same time indirectly threatening disaffiliation. The contention of the University was that after having taken those men from other colleges and kept them on year after year, with the approval of the Governing Board, thus spoiling their chances of promotion elsewhere, the college had no right to do otherwise than to appoint them as Heads of their departments. The alternative would have been trouble, not only from the University, but also possibly from the law courts.[60]

The employment of Hindu teachers not only in Voorhees College but also in other institutions continued to raise concern among the members of the Reformed Church in America. The Reverend Dr. Louis Benes, editor of the Reformed Church's denominational magazine, the *Church Herald,* made a world tour of mission fields. After returning to the United States, he raised with the Board for Christian World Mission some questions about the practice of

---

[59] In the Indian educational system, Voorhees was a college within the University of Madras, which was the umbrella degree-granting institution, rather than itself being a teaching institution. Being recognized as a college meant conforming to the rules established by the university.

[60] "Report of the Voorhees College Commission," attached to BCWM staff report to members of the India Committee, December 5, 1960 (Archives of the RCA).

hiring Hindu teachers to work in Christian high schools and colleges. C. R. Wierenga, who was in the United States following his retirement, wrote a letter to Benes concerning the matter. He began by saying that the Indian Christian management of such institutions was equally dismayed that it was necessary to hire Hindus to teach on their faculties, but that it was often difficult to find qualified Christians for subjects that had to be taught. He said that the situation was improving slowly, as the church was helping Christians with potential for teaching to go on for further study. He then went on to give his opinion about the importance of the high schools and colleges for Christian missions:

> Amongst many others, I seriously doubt whether Christian Missions would have a place in India today, were it not for the fact of thousands of deeply affected graduates of Christian High Schools and Colleges, both men and women, now in important administrative positions in Government. Now these are admittedly not the full conditioned products of such institutions as we have hoped for and prayed for, but their fact today is also not to be regarded too lightly.[61]

Benes also argued that it was deceptive to use "consecrated Christian money" to pay non-Christian teachers to teach non-Christian students. Wierenga called this a dangerous argument, because it seemed to imply that through the decades Christian money had been sent in sufficient quantity to maintain the educational institutions in their day-to-day work. He asked,

---

[61] C. R. Wierenga to L. H. Benes, August 10, 1960. In light of Wierenga's comments, it may be of interest to note that in 1960 Dr. S. Radhakrishnan, a former student of Voorhees and a graduate of Madras Christian College, was serving as president of India. On his visit to Voorhees College in 1953, S. Radhakrishnan wrote in the college visitor's book, "It was a joy to me to visit Voorhees College where I spent full four years, 1901-1904. I have vivid memories of my stay here and the influence it exerted on me which has stood me in good stead in later years. Work of the type done by the Voorhees College is of great use to the country. My prayer is that the College may grow in numbers and in usefulness" [quoted in I. Elangovan, *Elizabeth Rodman Voorhees College, Vellore Centenary* (printed for the Association of University Teachers (Regd.) Tamil Nadu: Elizabeth Rodman Voorhees College Unit, Vellore, 1997), 13].

Are you aware of the fact that the annual appropriations from annual Board income to Voorhees College for instance for years upon years bordered on nothing, and that for years also the Tindivanam High School, to mention only one institution that comes readily to mind, had nothing at all. And this is to be added to make the picture complete— were it not for the fees from non-Christian students and government grants we should not have had these institutions, at least during my term of forty years in India, to train the men and the women, who are now the leaders in Church and Mission activities.[62]

Although the initial investment in additional buildings and equipment required for developing Voorhees College into a four-year institution was large, it has become clear over the decades that the decision to move forward on this matter was the correct one. Within a few years, the annual appropriation through the diocese to the college was very small, and then it was phased out completely. It enabled many Christians and others in the area to gain a college education who otherwise would not have been able to do so. In 1998, the centenary anniversary of its having become an intermediate college, Voorhees College had eighteen hundred students and eighty teachers. It offered ten undergraduate majors and four postgraduate majors at the master's level. [63]

Industrial and Agricultural Mission in a Changing Environment

The Church of South India's Renewal and Advance commission did not examine specifically the role of industrial and agricultural institutions. In its own *Policy Papers*, presented in 1953 at the time of its centenary celebration, the Arcot Mission did provide guidance for the Women's Industrial School, the Katpadi Industrial School, and the Katpadi Agricultural Institute. The leaders of those

62 Ibid.
63 Elangovan, *Voorhees College*, 10.

institutions were keenly aware of the changing conditions in India
and proposed a direction for the future. They said,

> Changing conditions in India have made it obligatory to
> change from the factory system with its attendant rules and
> restrictions to that of a less institutionalized approach. This
> is especially true since each phase of work has developed a
> good "home base" from out of which the village and the
> community approach can be made. The development of
> cottage industries and workers Co-operative Societies should
> be stressed and encouraged. The Extension method of
> teaching, demonstrating and helping villagers in their
> agricultural, industrial and home problems should be
> developed more largely....There is need for a more
> comprehensive, all-sided approach in a rural development
> program and the fullest possible cooperation of the Church
> and all institutions and agencies is required.[64]

The Arcot Mission *Policy Papers* served the church and the
institutions well through the 1950s and 1960s.

The Women's Industrial Institute in Palmaner prospered under
the leadership of Mina Jongewaard and, following her, Gladys
Kooy. As we have seen (p. 551), Mina Jongewaard succeeded in
gaining the cooperation of the Palmaner community in setting up
a Child Health and Welfare Center that had its own local board and
was located on land that she had personally bought. Women in the
Reformed Church at times provided financial assistance to the
center from their "Cradle Roll" offerings. The program Jongewaard
described in a letter written in 1951 continued to serve the community
for decades following:

> At present we are bathing and feeding around 75 children
> every morning. We had for a long time depended on Army
> surplus and Church World Service for food for the children.

[64] "The Reformed Church and its Economic, Industrial, and Agricultural Mission," *Policy Papers: The Arcot Mission*, 1953, 39.

Now we have to buy the ragee and chollom which does increase the running of the center....At present the nurse attends on the average of nine maternity cases a month besides going out to visit homes every afternoon. The nurse is a graduate of Ranipet (School of Nursing)—one of Maude's orphan girls—married with three children and a good for nothing husband, who is in Madras.[65]

The Women's Industrial Institute was less affected by changes in India than were many other institutions because educational facilities and opportunities for girls continued lag behind those for boys. The need for employment for married women in the villages also continued. As the number of missionaries declined, the large number of items produced by village women that had been sold in Kodaikanal also declined, but the institute found new markets through Indian channels. Following the retirement of Mina Jongewaard, Gladys Kooy became the director. In order to smooth the transition in leadership, Gladys Kooy asked to be made assistant director circa 1977 in order that her Indian successor, Esther Petter, could become director. Petter could then lead the institution into the next stage of its service to the church and the women of the area. The need for the services of the Women's Industrial Institute continues into the present.

The direction proposed by the *Policy Papers* also guided the Katpadi Industrial Institute through the 1960s. The carpentry school had reopened in 1963, after having been closed for a number of years after the 1947 strike. The cottage industry operation of the institute did well as the demand for Katpadi furniture and carved wooden products remained high. Nevertheless, Reformed Church

---

[65] Mina Jongewaard to F. M. Potter, April 9, 1951. Ragee is a grain which is made into porridge. It is considered the "poor man's food" but more nourishing than many other grains. "Maude" was Maude Scudder, wife of Galen Scudder, superintendent of the hospital in Ranipet. A number of the women missionaries throughout the history of the mission were particularly concerned to help orphan or abandoned girls have places to live and educations.

missionary Harry Pofahl, who replaced Ben De Vries as director following the latter's retirement in 1964, realized in the last half of the decade that conditions were changing. A worldwide market for rosewood trees meant that the rosewood furniture for which the institute had become famous could no longer be produced at economical prices. The hand tools had to be replaced with modern machinery in order to remain competitive in woodworking, but the change was difficult to implement in a cottage industry environment.

As the carpentry was going through changes, Harry Pofahl was asked to open an electrician training course, and a major grant for the project was received from OXFAM. The first Indian director, James Balraj, took charge in 1969 and gave leadership in gaining government recognition for the electrical courses offered by the institute. His successor, A. S. Savirirayan, arranged for the institute's affiliation with The Evangelical and Relief Fund (TEAR FUND), which enabled many boys in the courses to receive free education, boarding, and hostel facilities.[66]

The institute still faces constantly the challenge of responding to the rapidly changing environment for teaching the trade courses that it offers. As trades such as carpentry and electrical services require ever more sophisticated equipment and facilities, the extent to which the institute will be able to respond in the new millenium remains to be seen.

The Katpadi Agricultural Institute similarly found itself working in a rapidly changing environment. Under the leadership of the first Indian director, M. J. John, it carried out a wide range of programs in the 1960s. One major project was a large poultry-hatching program with chick distribution to village farmers in cooperation with the Indian Council of Agricultural Research. The establishment of the DeValois High School, named after Reformed Church missionary John J. DeValois, with an agricultural bias in grades ten and eleven, fulfilled DeValois's dream to provide a higher level of

---

[66] "History of the Industrial Institute, Katpadi" in *Katpadi Industrial Institute: 1886-1986 Centenary Celebrations* (privately produced), n.p.

agricultural training. In cooperation with the government, the institute also established the first district Young Farmer's School, in which twenty young farmers, eighteen to twenty-eight years old, enrolled in the one-year residential training course.[67]

The agricultural institute had been a pioneer in providing extension services and crop demonstrations after the model of the agricultural county agent system built in the midwestern United States after World War I. Following independence in India, the government established rural community "block developments" that offered a wide variety of services in agricultural development. As a result, the need for such services from the agricultural institute began to decline in the 1960s.

The Roles and Relationships of Reformed Church Missionaries in the Church of South India

One of the concerns of the Church of South India and its related missionary societies was whether missionaries would be permitted to serve in India after independence. During the first five years after independence, the government remained opened to their admission. Eleven Reformed Church missionaries arrived to serve in India between 1947 and 1953, but during the year of 1953 the government stopped issuing entry visas to missionaries. At that time the communist threat seemed particularly strong and was added to Hindu political party objections to the presence of missionaries.[68]

Communist pressures remained particularly strong in the southern states of India in 1954. In New Delhi, the capital of India, questions were raised in Parliament about the right of missionaries to evangelize, and actions on applications for entry visas for missionaries were delayed. The church failed within a reasonable time to secure visas for the Reverend and Mrs. James Dunham to serve in India, so they were reassigned by the Board of Foreign Missions to the Arabian

[67] "Chronological History of Agricultural Institute, Katpadi," in *The Agricultural Institute, Katpadi, Golden Jubilee, 1920-1970 Souvenir,* (privately printed), n.p.
[68] "BFMR," 1953, 7.

Mission. In the case of the Dunhams, however, the application was not pursued to its final conclusion, so it did not necessarily imply that foreign missionaries would no longer be given entry visas.[69] Further study showed that, during the period 1953-1955, the government had actually approved the vast majority of applications. "About 90 percent of the applications for visas were granted, some of the 10 percent are still pending, and many refusals had no political significance but reflected some local situations."[70]

The central government publicly interpreted its policy in April, 1955. The interpretation provided that "new missionaries may enter only if they possess outstanding qualifications and if Indians are not available for their posts. Also, new work or extensions of old work may be begun only with government approval."[71] The Board of Foreign Missions expressed confidence that missionaries would continue to be admitted into the country according to the provisions of the policy and that India would continue to be a country in which there was freedom of worship. It stated, "While the danger of Communism is always there, we should be encouraged by the potent forces within India that make for the growth of the nation along democratic lines, with freedom of worship for all, including Christians."[72]

The Board of Foreign Missions was correct in looking optimistically toward the future. The threat of communism began to fade, and the Reformed Church again began to send new missionaries to India. Between 1958-1968, it appointed twenty-one recruits to serve in India. The issue that became important as the new missionaries were appointed was not whether they would be allowed to enter India, but what their role would be after they arrived. An amazing transition occurred in missionary perceptions of their roles and relationships after 1960.

[69] Ibid., 1954, 15.
[70] Ibid., 1955, 16.
[71] Ibid., 1956, 16. The text of the letter from the Ministry of Home Affairs of the Government of India to the secretary, National Christian Council of India, dated May 31, 1955, is to be found in Levai, *Revolution in Mission*, 280-81.
[72] Ibid., 17.

The Board for Christian World Mission of the Reformed Church in America sent a draft paper entitled, "The Role and Relationship of the Missionary in the Light of the Nature and Mission of the Church," to its missionaries for response in 1957. The paper raised a storm such as the board had seldom seen among its missionaries in every one of its mission fields. One of the implications of the document was that the existence of the old mission organizations should be brought to an end and that a "church to church" relationship should prevail in the future. Many of the missionaries suspected that by implying that the old mission organizations, such as the Arcot Mission, should be disbanded, the board was also calling into question the calling of the veteran missionaries themselves. It is important to remember that the paper appeared in India at a time when the missionaries themselves were struggling to understand their role in an independent India and a large united church. There was heavy correspondence between the missionaries and the board secretary about the paper, as well as dialogue about it at meetings of the Board for Christian World Mission and at furloughing missionary conferences.

One of the signs of the rapidly changing context in India was that the missionaries sent by the Reformed Church to work with the Church of South India after 1960 were scarcely aware of the existence of the paper, and most of them never read it. Given the fierce controversy around the paper, after 1960 there was also surprising unity of understanding between the younger missionaries and those who had been serving in India for a longer period. All of them were in accord with a statement that had appeared in the role and relationship paper:

> Though methods and manner of service may change, the role of the missionary continues to be to serve as one who embodies the spirit of Christ in his life, who witnesses effectively of Christ, and who works within the Christian Church wherever he serves. For such service and witness

there will be unlimited need and opportunity in the days ahead.[73]

There were several reasons for this rapid change in focus. A major one was that missionaries who arrived in India after 1960 were met by Indian leaders with long experience in the life of the church and its institutions. Indians were serving as directors of most of the leading institutions and as officers in the councils of the church. After 1960, when vacancies occurred, the issue was usually that of seeking the most qualified person who could be made available for the position, be that person Indian or missionary. This became evident in the naming of directors of hospitals. In Madanapalle, Dr. Crowley, an Indian doctor, had become director of the Mary Lott Lyles Hospital and was followed by other Indian directors. When Dr. Stanley and Mrs. Darlene Vander Aarde went to serve in Madanapalle in 1961, he worked under the direction of Dr. H. P. Gideon. After Gideon accepted an appointment as medical superintendent at the Diocese of Madras Kalyani Hospital in the city of Madras, Stanley Vander Aarde was named to that position in Madanapalle.

A similar transition took place in Ranipet. It will be remembered that in 1942 there were Indians who were ready to see Galen Scudder released temporarily to serve as district medical director, because they knew that would give Julius Savarirayan an opportunity to act as director of the Scudder Memorial Hospital. In 1954, Galen Scudder retired, and Savarirayan replaced him. In 1967, when Savarirayan retired, he recommended that Reformed Church missionary Frank Zwemer replace him. Zwemer then served as medical superintendent until he left India in 1970. He was replaced by an Indian, Ernest Bhaskar.

There is an old saying based on the three-self theory that a "missionary is a person who works himself or herself out of a job." With the exception of missionaries who served in certain technical

---

[73] "The Role and Relationship of the Missionary in the Light of the Nature and Mission of the Church," adopted by the BCWM, May 8, 1959.

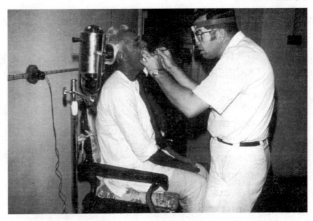

Dr. Stanley Vander Aarde examining patient

positions, the saying did not apply in India after 1960. Credence continued to be given to the idea that a missionary had to work himself or herself out of a job, because, in the application for a visa and a residence permit, the government required that the church show that it could not find an Indian to do the job. Each year when a missionary had to apply for renewal of the residence permit, he or she was bemused at the requirement to affirm that no qualified Indian was available for the job.

Reformed Church Mission Integrated within the Diocese of Madas, Church of South India.

In the previous chapter we observed that the mission of the Reformed Church was integrated fully into that of the Diocese of Rayalaseema, while it still retained a close relationship with the District of Madanapalle and the institutions within that district. We also saw that such integration moved forward with greater hesitancy in the Diocese of Madras. By 1960 the process of organizational integration was completed there also. All presbyters were paid from a central payment for presbyters fund. The fund was supported by assessing each pastorate 56 percent of its annual income while the overseas mission societies were still providing about 10 percent of the amount needed. All requests for overseas assistance had to be approved by the diocesan finance committee and all policies approved by the diocesan executive committee. The diocese had accepted the Methodist system of stationing presbyters in a pastorate for a period not to exceed five years, with rare exceptions. The place of service was determined by the diocesan stationing committee elected by the members of the Diocesan Council. Ordained Reformed Church missionaries also were assigned to their work by the diocesan stationing committee.

Grants from overseas mission agencies were still segregated according to old missionary boundary lines, however. Thus, funds received from the Board of Foreign Missions still were assigned to the old Arcot Mission area, while the same was true for funds received from the Church of Scotland Mission, the Australian Presbyterian Mission, and Methodist Missionary Society for their traditional areas. This remained a sensitive matter, particularly because after World War II the economies of England and Scotland needed a long time to recover from the devastation and disruption of the war while the American economy attained new heights. Although the Board for Christian World Missions remained chronically short of funds, its financial position was stronger than the British societies, hence there was a perception that the old Arcot Mission area received more than its share of overseas funding.

One of the questions facing the diocese was whether missionaries should be assigned work outside their traditional areas. We saw in the previous chapter that Harold and Yvette Vande Berg had been assigned outside the Madanapalle district to serve first in Adoni and then in Anantapur and that Eugene Ten Brink had fulfilled an assignment with the Student Christian Movement based in Bangalore prior to be called back to serve as pastor of the St. John's Church in Vellore. In 1963, Ten Brink was asked to serve as assistant director in the new ecumenical institute being established outside Bangalore and was released by the Diocese of Madras to serve there.

When Dr. Glenn and Carolyn Folmsbee were appointed in 1967 to be missionaries in India, it was at first intended that they would develop a public health ministry at Wandiwash, alongside the Madras diocesan leprosy work that was already a major activity there. As the situation developed, however, it was decided not to move forward with a program in public health there. The Erode Hospital in the Diocese of Coimbatore was eager to open a public health program, so the Folmsbees were assigned to locate there under direction of the Medical Superintendent. The Reformed Church provided a van specially equipped for public health work, with a special emphasis upon tuberculosis in the area surrounding Erode. The people in the area were very receptive to the program. Glenn also became the director of community services for the local Rotary Club, while Carolyn, a nurse, taught clinical services at the School of Nursing in the hospital. In 1972, the Reformed Church transferred them to service in Chiapas, Mexico, in order to lead a training program for church medical workers in small dispensaries located throughout the state, while the hospital in Erode continued to be responsible for sustaining the program in Erode.

Evangelism, Pastoral Work, and Assignment of Missionaries

After John Piet received a jeep and audiovisual equipment from friends in the United States, he carried out a very successful but expensive evangelism project. His touring of the villages with the Jeep, films and slides, preaching, and literature distribution was in the best tradition of Arcot missionaries who had regarded the primary work of missionaries to be that of evangelistic touring. He claimed that it was the type of "interim work" that missionaries should be doing alongside the church in a time when there was a real possibility that communism could take over India as it had China. The Jeep evangelism program had come to an end by the time Piet left India to teach missions at Western Theological Seminary in Holland, Michigan. The Light of Life Bible Correspondence Course had grown large and had become his major evangelistic effort. Its address, "Box 66, Vellore," became one of the best known addresses in the area.

New Reformed Church missionary Eugene Heideman was assigned by the diocese to become director of the Bible Correspondence Course in 1961. Accompanying the Bible Correspondence Course program was the India Home Bible League's distribution of separately bound gospels that were sold for five piase (1 cent) each by evangelists throughout the state of Tamilnadu. Much of the cost of the program was met by the World Home Bible League. Each gospel sold contained a first lesson of the Bible correspondence course on that gospel. In 1965, total enrollment reached 25,000. One of the somewhat amusing aspects of the program resulted from the practice of Communist Indians to name their children after famous Communists. Among those who received certificates for having completed a Bible course were "Joseph Stalin," "Lenin," and "Khrushchev." Several other missions opened aggressive Scripture distribution campaigns in India. As a result, the India Home Bible League assisted in the sale of more than 500,000 Bibles, New Testaments, and Scripture portions in 1965.

When Eugene Ten Brink left St. John's Church to take up his duties at the ecumenical center, Eugene Heideman was assigned to be the presbyter at St. John's Church in addition to his other duties. Two years later, in preparation for the furlough year of the Heidemans, the diocese assigned a new Methodist Missionary Society couple, the Reverend Peter and Ann Bishop, to assist in the Bible Correspondence Course office and St. John's Church. Peter Bishop took over full responsibilities when the Heidemans left on furlough in 1966. The Bishops were the first British missionaries assigned to the Arcot area by the diocese.

Another assignment of missionaries outside the traditional mission area took place following the Heidemans' return from furlough in 1967. They were at first assigned to live in Vellore, with Eugene appointed assistant director of evangelism for the Diocese of Madras under the Indian director, the Reverend S. Vedekan. He was also asked to lead a program of continuing education for presbyters called, "Corporate Sermon Preparation," in which the 125 presbyters of the diocese gathered monthly or bimonthly in the area of the diocese in which they served. In those meetings, they studied the lectionary passages for the following month in relation to their preaching and pastoral practice. When a vacancy occurred in St. George's Cathedral in Madras, it was decided to station Eugene Heideman as presbyter at the cathedral in addition to his other responsibilities.

Heideman was not only the first Reformed Church missionary to be assigned to Madras City since the formation of the Church of South India, he was also the first nonepiscopally ordained presbyter to be assigned to the St. George's Cathedral. This assignment required the diocese to follow a rule existing from the time of union that the first time a nonepiscopally ordained presbyter was assigned to an ex-Anglican church special permission from that pastorate committee was required. The acceptance of a nonepiscopally ordained presbyter at the cathedral that had been the seat of the Anglican bishop prior to union was one more sign that the Church of South India was truly growing into a united church.

Meanwhile, Peter Bishop continued to serve as director of the Bible Correspondence Course evangelistic program and as presbyter of St. John's Church in Vellore until he and his wife returned to England early in the next decade, when they were replaced by an Indian presbyter in each of the positions. In the 1970s, increasing postal rates and other changes in Indian society meant that there was less interest in enrolling in Bible Correspondence Courses. The World Home Bible League and its related organization, Project Philip, followed in turn by Bibles for India, began to develop a wider variety of materials and an all-India program of evangelism. That program was directed by persons not directly related to the Church of South India, but it remained available for use in that church.

Women's Fellowship in the Diocese of Madras

After the formation of the Church of South India, the work of the church among women went through a major change. The Arcot Mission had emphasized zenana work by Bible women and missionaries. In the villages, wives of teachers and catechists had primary responsibilities for the nurture of the women of the congregations. After entering into the Diocese of Madras, Reformed Church women missionaries such as Charlotte Wyckoff, Frances Be Bruin, Mildred De Vries, Esther De Weerd, and others became familiar with the way in which the British Methodist missionaries were conducting classes for village women. Frances De Bruin wrote about what she saw:

> I remember how pleased I was when I visited classes in the Nagari area and saw results of this instruction. And so the women in the Arcot Mission area decided to begin with a similar plan. That plan was to enroll all Christian women and girls over 12 years of age in a class for regular instruction in Christian doctrine, Bible stories, memory verses, prayers, lyrics, Kummies songs, health, Christian home and life.[74]

Three years after the Women's Fellowship work with the village women's classes was begun, 2,720 women participated in the classes, which were led by local volunteers following a syllabus that had been prepared. Great changes could be seen in some of the villages where most of the women in the classes were illiterate. Frances De Bruin described the kind of change that could take place:

> All the Christian women and girls over 12 years of age were enrolled in the class which met once a week, conducted by the wife of the village catechist. It was not easy for women to come to a class after they had been working in the fields

74 Francis De Bruin, "Ten Years of Village Women's Classes," typescript, 1958, loaned to the author by Joyce Dunham, Pella, Iowa.

all day, come home to prepare the evening meal and at nine or ten o'clock to come to the church for a class. Non-Christian women and girls were also urged to attend so these classes were an evangelistic agency. One Sunday morning when we attended service in a certain village, we witnessed 30 baptisms, including one entire family. When they came forward to receive the symbol of their conversion, the teacher whispered to me that this was a direct result of the Class.[75]

Each of the village classes followed a specific curriculum for the year and were given examinations at the end of the year. Mary Heideman described her participation in conducting the examinations for the womer's village classes:

> In the spring many of us go in pairs to give oral examinations to the classes in the villages. In April, I went to several villages to help with these examinations. I especially try to help with those villages which are not on a regular bus route and can only be reached by walking for one or two miles or more or by bullock cart or jeep. One day, eight of us went out to several villages when the temperature went up to 108. I drive the jeep and take each pair of examiners to their villages and then my partner and I drive on to the farthest village to examine the class there….The women enjoy having us come and even though most of them are illiterate and shy about answering questions, we try to be very sympathetic and encouraging and praise them for their efforts. The exam questions are graded and the results are printed. Each group hopes to be the highest in their pastorate.[76]

When the Diocese of Madras was bifurcated in 1976, and the pastorates in the old Arcot Mission area were brought together to

[75] Ibid.
[76] Mary Heideman to "Dear Friends," April 23, 1965.

form the new Diocese of Vellore, the women's fellowships in the area continued to play an important nurturing and evangelist role in the area, although all of the missionaries involved in that work had left India. Among the Indian women who provided especially strong leadership were Kamala Yesupatham and Mrs. E. R. Isaac. The last Reformed Church missionary to be heavily involved in the Women's Fellowship was Janet Pofahl, who continued her involvement even after returning to the United States with her family in 1972. When the diocese was short of funds for adequate support for the Women's Fellowship, she held regular garage sales at her home and sent the proceeds to India to support additional workers and to meet transportation needs for the village work.

Stewardship Development

During his last term in India before retirement in 1965, C. A. De Bruin was assigned to be director of stewardship in the Diocese of Madras, assisted by an Indian presbyter, the Reverend Wales Yesupatham. The leaders of the diocese believed that it was important that a senior and respected missionary should fill this position, which could play a crucial role in helping the diocese move further toward the goal of self-support. De Bruin wrote a small book, entitled, *The Challenge of Stewardship,* that was used along with statistical charts and other materials developed by Yesupatham. They entered into their work with a great amount of zeal and held workshops that were well attended and well received throughout the diocese. De Bruin wrote in their Christmas letter of 1965 that the program resulted in increased giving and that it had been one of the most satisfying tasks that he had undertaken in his forty years in India. In several places the gain in contributions was amazing. In one three-year period, a pastorate increased its contributions from Rs. 3,124 to 6,769.[77]

The fact that a missionary was appointed to this task illustrates a well established attitude within the Arcot Mission. From the

77 C. A. and Frances De Bruin, "Christmas Letter" to Dear Friends, 1963.

beginning, it was usually the missionaries who were the most zealous advocates of self-support. We have seen that missionaries from time to time lamented that they had not been more insistent that members of the church support their own catechists and pastors. The missionaries often hesitated to press the issue. At the same time, many of the Indians were fairly content to depend upon the Board of Foreign Missions to provide financial support.

John Piet's concern in 1954 that the Communists might gain control of India and cut off outside financial support led him to press especially hard for a new emphasis upon self-support. He produced a plan with statistics that showed that, if the plan were followed, the pastorates of Katpadi North, Gudiyattam, and Katpadi South could be self-supporting within three years. He addressed a letter to Arthur John, the area chairman, with details of the plan. He pointed out that teachers with salaries could contribute more than they were giving, since the government was giving them large "dearness allowances" in addition to salary in order to meet the costs of inflation. Despite these allowances, they were not increasing their level of contributions.[78]

Piet received a cool reception for his proposal. The effects of famine after five years of drought were still having an impact on the economic situation of the villagers, and the pastors and area leaders were not eager to call upon people to increase their contributions. In Piet's view, there would never be a real concern for stewardship development and self-support until the Reformed Church stated clearly that it would require the Indian church to take such matters more seriously. He expressed his opinion to Barnerd Luben, secretary of the Board of Foreign Missions, who had suggested during a recent visit that the Reformed Church would have to cut back on its grants to India.

> As I told you repeatedly and as several Indians told me after you left, self-support and self-determination and the

[78] John Piet to Arthur John, February 9, 1954.

willingness to do without R.C.A. funds for programs of Christian nurture will never come unless the church is made to face the fact by the donors of those funds, namely, the Board of the R.C.A. Why should they?...I have a high regard for some of the forthright statements you made while on the field, and all I ask is that these be now implemented. And that can only be done, as far as I see it, if the Board through you will express its determination and dictate to the church on the field that it *must* come to its senses and get its house in order.[79]

There was good reason for missionaries to be impatient in matters of self-support. In a survey that the diocese made in 1966, more than a decade after Piet wrote his letters and a year after De Bruin left India, it was discovered that the average contributions per year of all the members of the church was Rs. 3.10 (75 cents American). Persons who received a salary rather than doing day labor (coolie work) contributed at a higher rate, Rs. 17 ($3.75) per year, but only 15 percent of working adults received a salary. Moreover, 25 percent of all salaried workers were employed by the church and its institutions.[80]

In hindsight, one can see that the flow of overseas money was a clear hindrance to financial stewardship development and self-support. The claims of the Board of Foreign Missions and statements by missionaries that in the future there would be fewer funds available was not taken seriously so long as the institutions and projects under the direction of missionaries continued to receive special gifts, such as a jeep for evangelism or special equipment for a hospital or for the industrial and agricultural institutes. It was another decade before the Indian church would struggle seriously with issues of self-support.

---

[79] John Piet to B. Luben, February 19, 1954.
[80] Madras Diocese, "Report on the Survey of Central, Southern and Western Areas," 1966, 28-29.

The Arcot Mission Votes to be Dissolved

Powerful organizations do not die easily, and the Arcot Mission had been a powerful organization. It had been giving its power away ever since 1910 in the long process known as the devolution of mission. The board secretary, Barnerd Luben, had hinted strongly already in the mid-1950s that it would be better, perhaps, if the mission were dissolved. The idea began to be taken seriously by the missionaries in the 1960s, but there were a number of issues that had to be resolved before the mission could be disbanded.

When the property held by the mission was transferred to the Church of South India Trust Association, the Board of Foreign Missions had not given permission to transfer the mission residences. The board still remained directly responsible for missionaries' housing and did not want to have to build new houses or pay high rent when missionaries were appointed or moved to a new area. The mission owned the automobiles used by missionaries, as well as the vacation properties in Kodaikanal. It also still held a number of funds deposited with it by church bodies in India. In February, 1964, the secretary of the board for India, the Reverend John Buteyn, and the treasurer of the board, Robert Harrison, came to India to meet with Indian leaders and the Arcot Mission to see how best to resolve these issues. Excellent progress was made to the satisfaction of all concerned.

From the perspective of the church in India, perhaps the most important action was to transfer the old investments of stocks and bonds in the mission's "Profit and Loss Account" to CSITA to be a trust fund, "the interest of which is to be used to help build village churches, and that a Diocesan Committee shall select the churches and parsonages annually as most worthy of recipients, the grant not to exceed one-third the total cost involved."[81] We shall see how this action stimulated village stewardship as well as encouraging the erection of solid new churches in villages.

[81] "Arcot Mission Minutes," February 1964, action no. 64-133, p. 33.

It took another six years to work through other details: developing new patterns for payment of salaries to missionaries, handling ownership of automobiles, managing the properties in Kodaikanal, settling on how best to deal with matters of missionary income tax, and clarifying with the church various issues related to missionary residences, as well as other matters. On May 19, 1970, Albertha Biegel, secretary of the mission, was able to write to the board that the mission had voted to dissolve as a registered body in India.[82] Following this action, it was discovered that several items still had to be attended to, so the final dissolution took place only in 1972. Its passing was scarcely noticed. The old saying that death comes not with a bang but with a whimper had been proved true once again.

Building Churches in Towns and Villages

When the Arcot Mission established mission stations in towns such as Katpadi, Chittoor, and Vellore, it also built substantial churches in which the people could gather for worship. In the mid-twentieth century, those churches had begun to have serious structural problems, and their congregations had outgrown the buildings. From the perspective of the Christian community as well as the town and Arcot District as a whole, the most important of these buildings was the Central Church in Vellore. It was located rather inconspicuously on a side street not far from the bazaar. In the 1950s, proposals were brought forth that a large new church should be built in the old British Christian cemetery on the main street of the town. If one moved the old graves and stones, there was adequate space for a large church and parking lot within the old walled cemetery, which had been closed to new graves in 1866. It would give to the Christian community the kind of prominent presence that large temples provided for the Hindus.

The Board of Foreign Missions voted in 1957 to appropriate $15,000 toward the construction of the building. The Reverend

[82] Albertha Biegel to John Buteyn, May 19, 1970.

Joseph John wrote to the Reverend Henry Lazarus, pastor of the
Central Church, to say that the building was of importance not only
to the local congregation, but also to the churches of the whole area.
Therefore, it was crucial that it should be built in the model of the
indigenous India style used in building Hindu temples. He wrote:

> Time has come when we should relate our order of worship
> and the mode of our building programme to the non-
> Christians among whom we are living. Christ is the Saviour
> whom the Missionary Fathers brought to us and no one can
> take Him away from us and this dear land. But we should
> humbly acknowledge that our non-Christians have not
> followed intelligently our worship services and our Church
> buildings have not been witnessing to the fact that Christ
> belongs to us. There has always been a certain sense of
> "foreignness" in both our orders of worship services and in
> our Church buildings.[83]

Joseph John shared his letter with the relevant diocesan
committees, who rejected his proposal and asked Lazarus to inform
the board in New York of their opinion. They maintained that rapid
changes taking place in urbanized Indian life were making for a new
situation regarding architecture in India. The debate between the
two pastors sheds light on the nature of those changes and also
raises the question of what it means for Christian worship to be
indigenous or "contextual" in India today. Lazarus wrote:

> There are rapid changes overtaking Indian mode of life that
> do not favor the traditional 'Temple' structure. A
> congregation such as ours naturally participates strongly in
> these changes. Besides the temple idea is entirely foreign to
> the corporate worship of Christians. We must adopt our
> worship places to suit the functions they are to perform.
> The Vellore congregation is very strong on this point. We

[83] Joseph John to Henry Lazarus, December 22, 1956.

must not under any circumstances lose our Christian identity. We shall incorporate into our building as much of Indian architectural lines as possible. It does mean that we do not wish to substitute the distinctly Hindu for what is obviously required to maintain a Christian atmosphere and what is practical for a congregation such as Vellore. For instance, sitting on the floor is still practiced by Indians in the villages—it is not by town-people...Rev. Joseph John in the far away country cannot change these facts.[84]

Progress in the building project proceeded slowly. The congregation needed time to gather its own funds. Then politicians got into the act to curry favor with the Hindus. They agitated against allowing a large Christian church to be built in such a prominent location in the city. Hunger strikes were organized in protest in front of the cemetery. When the plans were submitted for bids, the price came in at Rs. 300,000, far above what had been anticipated. However, the Faith Reformed Church in Zeeland, Michigan, came through with an additional major gift, other funds were found, and the church was completed in 1965. Today the church stands in the cemetery, a focal point for activities in the Diocese of Vellore. Other buildings constructed in the area exhibit the same type of basic functional contemporary Indian architecture.

The growing strength of the churches in number and in the members' financial resources was shown a decade later in 1973, when the Bethel Church of South India in Vellore, with a small congregation, built a new building. The building cost Rs. 120,000, all of it raised locally.[85] Since that time, several more large, well constructed church buildings have been erected in the environs of Vellore with local funds.

The old Profit and Loss Account of the Arcot Mission also helped with the construction of new church buildings. Interest on the money invested from this account was used to provide grants for

[84] Henry Lazarus to B. Luben, January 4, 1957.
[85] Henry Lazarus to John Buteyn, December 26, 1973.

New village church under construction

the cost of the roof to village congregations who had themselves erected a well constructed, simple church building up to the roof level. The cost of the roof was usually about Rs. 3000 in 1970, one-third the cost of the building, so grants could be given for approximately six villages churches per year. The possibility of receiving a grant greatly stimulated the stewardship efforts of the villagers, and soon well-built, simple but attractive churches began to replace the old, inadequate mud-hut style structures.

The Inauguration of the Diocese of Vellore

Almost from the time the Church of South India was formed, there were undercurrents of hope in the old Arcot Mission area that at some time in the future it would be possible to have a diocese. There were some suspicions in the mid-1950s that some persons were carrying out a furtive campaign to gain such a diocese for the area. The bishop in Madras also made an accusation that even certain missionaries were part of such thinking.[86] Whether or not there was any substance to such rumors, it was the case that the

[86] D. Chellapa to B. Luben, April 1, 1959.

people in the area often felt that the urban location of the diocesan office and the bishop's residence in Madras was too distant from the towns and rural western area of the diocese. The Diocese of Madras was growing rapidly in members as well as in programs during the decade of the 1960s. At the beginning of the decade, it had within it approximately eighty thousand baptized members and seventy-five ordained presbyters. At the end of the decade, it numbered almost 125,000 members and 125 ordained presbyters. In the early 1970s, it was decided that the diocese had grown too large and complex to be served adequately by a single bishop, so an assistant bishop was chosen with special responsibility for the rural areas of the diocese. The person chosen was the Reverend Henry Lazarus, one of the most respected pastors in the western area.

Indian leaders in the old Arcot Mission area began to call for the bifurcation of the Diocese of Madras, with the new diocesan office and bishop's residence to be located in Vellore. Elsewhere within the Church of South India and within the Reformed Church in America, there was some hesitation about such a diocese. Because it would in all likelihood consist wholly of pastorates that had been started by a single mission, it would lack the ecumenical cross-fertilization of different traditions and the interaction among Christians in the city of Madras with those in the Arcot area. Nevertheless, the diocesan council of the Diocese of Madras agreed in January, 1975, to the formation of the new Diocese of Vellore.[87]

The Diocese of Vellore was organized in a service at the Central Church, Vellore, January 26, 1976, with Henry Lazarus as its bishop. John Buteyn of the Reformed Church mission staff was invited to be present to speak at the inauguration. He congratulated the new diocese for taking on its responsibilities. He also spoke about the unity of evangelistic purpose of the Reformed Church and the Diocese of Vellore within the Church of South India. He spoke of "the urgency of continuing evangelism and outreach. In

<hr>

[87] Bishop Sundar Clarke to John Buteyn, January 29, 1975.

the Reformed Church we consider this our 'number one priority.'
I hope and pray that all of us gathered here today may consider this
the number one goal of the Church, as truly it has been said, 'the
Church exists for those outside of it.'"[88]

Bishop Henry Lazarus led the diocese through its first two years
until he retired in 1976. The Reverend J. Sam Ponniah was then
chosen to be the bishop. Soon after he was consecrated as bishop,
he wrote a letter to several persons in the Reformed Church. In it
he reflected on his thirty years of service as a pastor in very rural
areas such as Wandiwash and Muttathur and on the service of his
wife, Susheela. She was a doctor who ministered to patients with
leprosy and other medical problems. He indicated his interest in
evangelism, the education of children, rural economic uplift, and
the need for training of voluntary lay leaders to serve village
congregations.[89]

Ponniah emphasized the importance of evangelistic outreach in
the villages. Throughout his thirty years as a pastor in the villages,
he had been remarkably successful in encouraging people to be
baptized as Christians.[90] His basic method of evangelism was very
simple, and it resulted from an experience he had early in his
ministry. He had noticed that the members of the village churches
had friends and relatives who were not Christians. One day he had
asked such a relative, "Why aren't you also a Christian?" The
response was, "Because no one ever asked me to become a
Christian." Ponniah then asked him to become a Christian, and the
man responded positively. From that time on, Ponniah asked

---

[88] John Buteyn, "A Great Heritage—a Glorious Hope," address given at the inauguration
of the Vellore Diocese of the Church of South India, January 26, 1976 (typescript,
Archives of the RCA).

[89] J. Sam Ponniah to Arie Brouwer, Glenn Bruggers, Harry Pofahl, and John Buteyn, June
20, 1978.

[90] Ponniah had baptized more than five hundred converts in the Wandiwash area during
the first six years of his pastoral service. During the same period, his wife was in charge
of the medical work with its leprosy program there (J. Sam Ponniah, "The Contribution
of the Reformed Church in America to the Church of South India" (thesis, Western
Theological Seminary, January, 1964), 123.

Bishop Samuel and Dr. Susheela Ponniah

people in the villages that question and discovered that there were many who appreciated being asked.

When he became bishop, Ponniah encouraged each pastorate to develop evangelistic teams to tour in their villages, to distribute Scripture, and to encourage people to take the Bible correspondence courses. Most important of all, he encouraged the people of the diocese simply to invite their relatives to become Christians as he had done. Within a short time, the diocese was experiencing remarkable growth in membership. Between 1977 and 1986, its membership almost doubled, from forty-seven thousand to ninety-two thousand persons.[91] We should not fail to notice that, within those ten years, the church experienced a growth in number almost equal to the entire 123 years of mission in the Arcot area. Since the only Reformed Church missionary in the diocese during that decade was Dora Boomstra, there can be no doubt that the churches in the Vellore dioceses had become truly "self-propagating."

During his first several years as a pastor, Sam Ponniah had worked closely with John Piet. Ponniah shared Piet's enthusiasm for evangelism, as well as his conviction that the number of villages that

---

[91] *Minutes of the General Synod, RCA,* 1986, 332.

had to be served by a presbyter in a pastorate was often too large to allow for effective ministry. For that reason, Bishop Ponniah moved to find more and better qualified men to send for theological training, and he thereby increased the number of ordained presbyters. The larger pastorates were bifurcated and in some cases even trifurcated. By 1981 the number of pastorates had increased from twenty-seven to forty-three,[92] and more pastorates continued to be added in subsequent years for the more than 350 village congregations and twenty-nine city and town congregations. The increase in number of presbyters and pastorates entailed a need to build parsonages for the pastors, since there often was no suitable housing available in a new pastorate.

In that time of rapid growth, the Reformed Church agreed to help finance the needed new church buildings in villages and to provide a small amount of assistance towards creating new pastorates and paying additional presbyters. A special appropriation of $10,000 per year for three years was given to the diocese, to be used for assistance grants to village congregations and pastorates who were constructing churches and parsonages. It was hoped that the amount granted, together with the income from the trust fund previously designated for village church construction, would enable the diocese to continue the policy of providing funds for the church roof after the villagers had finished construction to the roof level.

With the incentive of the grants, village congregations responded. By the 1970s, in most of the villages, there were men and women whose sons and daughters had been educated in mission or government schools and had gone to work in the cities and towns or in other countries. Appeals were made to them to contribute to the church building or parsonage in their home village. The people in the villages contributed what they could from their often meager earnings and also did much of the work preliminary to the construction themselves. The result was that the goal of erecting

[92] M. J. John, "A Note on Church of South India—Vellore Diocese Needs and Priorities" 17 May, 1981 (Archives of the RCA).

one hundred buildings was reached. In that same period, the Diocese of Rayalaseema was also growing and was in the process of erecting thirty-five new church buildings.[93]

The new diocese also moved to encourage volunteer lay workers to minister to the needs of the village congregations. This move had long been a necessity in the pastorates located in the Telugu area of Andhra State, where all of the village schools had been handed over to the state government by 1960. Many of the Christian teachers who had continued in employment by the government had also given voluntary service as leaders in the village congregations. By 1980, there was no paid worker in charge of a village congregation in the diocesan pastorates in the state of Andhra. The lay leadership developing in the Andhra area by 1980 was becoming an example for the pastorates in the Tamil-language Madras State as well.

> It is indeed a joy to see the great move in Andhra Pradesh (State) of Vellore Diocese, where no paid worker is in charge of a village congregation. But it has become a people's movement. When the spirit of the Lord is in operation, we are to co-operate with Him. We are grateful to God for the baptism of many hundreds of people including caste people. When at a time we handed over the Mission Schools to the Government in Andhra Pradesh, we did so with great apprehension. But the Lord is at work. The congregations grow strong in the faith, contribute liberally to the support of the Church and erect their own church buildings for worship. More than these aspects, they are genuinely interested in bringing their neighbors, relations and friends to the feet of our Saviour, Jesus Christ.[94]

The Mission of the Reformed Church Moves to "Regions Beyond."

When the Arcot Mission was organized in 1853, the Scudders already had a clear expectation that the lifetime of the Arcot Mission

---

93 *Minutes of the General Synod, RCA*, 1986, 332.
94 *Vellore Diocesan News*, April-May, 1980, 4.

would be relatively short. They anticipated that God would bring into being a church that was self-governing, self-propagating, and self-governing. When that had come to pass, it would be the responsibility of that church to continue God's mission in India. The Arcot mission would come to an end, and the Reformed Church in America would be free to move to other countries, to the "regions beyond," as the phrase of that time went, in obedience to God's call to preach the gospel in other lands.

In 1987, the last Reformed Church missionaries serving within the Church of South India retired, while one Reformed Church missionary family continued to serve in the Kodaikanal International School. Dora Boomstra, who had been appointed in 1948, served throughout her career in the Madras and Vellore dioceses in the field of education. Under her leadership the four schools, from elementary through high school to teacher training college, located on the single large compound in Ranipet, had grown to a total student body of over two thousand. Stanley and Darlene Vander Aarde[95] likewise had provided leadership and outstanding service for twenty-five years in the Mary Lott Lyles Hospital and the Madanapalle child care center and girls' schools located next to the hospital.

The end of the era in which there would be Reformed Church missionaries serving in India was not totally of the church's own choosing. The Church of South India still said repeatedly that it welcomed missionaries to work in partnership with it in carrying out the great unfinished mission task in India. The government of India, however, continued a strict interpretation of its policy that visas for missionaries would be granted only in cases where there was no Indian available or qualified for the position. In a church where there were now many qualified Indians, the practical effect of the government position was that no Reformed Church

---

[95] For further information about Darlene Vander Aarde, see Ratmeyer, *Hands, Hearts, and Voices*, 200-201.

missionaries were appointed to serve with the Church of South India after 1968.

With the difficulty of gaining visas for new missionaries to serve in India and the growing strength of the Church of South India, the Reformed Church took advantage of the opportunity to enter into new partnerships in missions and send missionaries to other countries. The world mission situation had undergone major changes over the century and half since the Scudders had first gone to India. In the beginning, Reformed Church missionaries were sent only to China and India. Foreign missionaries went from west to east, from American and Europe to Asia. After 1963, the phrase "mission on six continents" had come into wide usage. It indicated that all continents were in need of mission activity and that the flow of missionaries would in the future not only be from west to east, but that it would flow in every direction.

Thus, in 1987, when the last Reformed Church missionaries retired from service in the Church of South India, there was a Tamil-language congregation worshiping in a Reformed Church in New York City, and Indians were members of a number of Reformed churches. The Reformed Church Division of World Mission was providing assistance in mission outreach in more than twenty countries while, at the same time, congregations whose roots lay in the countries of Africa, Asia, and South America were entering the denomination in the United States and Canada.

The Continuing Presence of Reformed Church Missionaries in Kodaikanal

Dora Boomstra and the Vander Aardes were not the last Reformed Church missionaries to serve in India. In 1987, Keith and Marcine De Jong served on the staff of the Kodaikanal International School. The High Clerc School in Kodaikanal knew in 1969 that a crisis lay ahead. The policies of the government of India with regard to visas for missionaries meant that the number of missionary children needing education in India would soon be very small. Several suggestions were put forward about the school's future, including closing it within a few years. A number of overseas churches who had a long history of relating to the school believed that a wiser course would be to turn it into an "international school" that would be a member of the "International Baccalareate Association" and accredited in India and the United States. In 1974 it became such an international school with classes from kindergarten to grade twelve. The school presently describes itself as follows:

> Kodaikanal International School is a Christian School which serves children and parents of many different communities of Indian and international society. Guided by the spirit and teachings of Christ, the school explores new avenues for expression of the Christian faith. In community we strive to create a climate marked by a sense of God's presence and action in the world, love for one's neighbor, and a concern for social justice and the equality of all people.[96]

The government of India recognized the unique character of the school. It has continued to issue visas to missionaries who are appointed to serve alongside Indians as teachers or in other positions at the school in order to preserve its international quality.

In 1970, when intense discussions were being held concerning the future of the school, two Reformed Church families were serving as missionaries at the school. One of the families included Howard and Jo Ann Huyser. They had been appointed to serve in the school for two or three years, during which time Howard was to supervise construction of several new buildings at the school. Jo Ann taught in the elementary school. While there, Howard became interested in using his gifts to help the local inhabitants of Kodaikanal to improve their social and economic position.

Keith and Marcine De Jong had been serving at the school since 1958. He was on the faculty as head of the music department, while

---

[96] Undated brochure, "Kodaikanal International School," issued by the school.

Marcine assisted in a variety of tasks at the school, including teaching. Marcine had also begun a lending library of Christian and English language books and magazines in their own home. She also began a sweater project, by which sweaters sent to her by friends in the United States were distributed to needy persons to protect them in the chilly climate of Kodaikanal.

In 1970, the Reformed Church missionaries and others in Kodaikanal combined their energies to organize the "Co-ordinating Council for Social Concerns in Kodaikanal" (CORSOCK) to be a registered society in India with its own board, which drew members from the various religious communities in Kodaikanal. Marcine De Jong served as its president from 1975 to 1993, when she and her husband retired and returned to the United States. Under her leadership, CORSOCK became a wide-ranging organization. At present, it operates a cottage craft shop, a sub-unit named KOPEDEG (Kodai People's Development Group) that enables needy women to craft and market various toys and knitting and sewing items, the mercy home for elderly persons, and a goodwill center that offers clothing and gift items in exchange for a reasonable donation. It also provides more than seven thousand notebooks annually to needy students and supervised study centers for children to do their homework.[97]

The son of Keith and Marcine De Jong, Dr. Bruce De Jong and his wife, Tamar, began their service in Kodaikanal in 1989. He has served as the school physician and also as a doctor at CORSOCK's Van Allen Hospital, the only hospital in Kodaikanal. Tamar has been very active in providing leadership in KOPEDEG and other community outreach projects.

The other person serving in Kodaikanal is Rani Vande Berg, daughter of retired Reformed Church missionaries Harold and Yvette Vande Berg. After teaching for a number of years in Bahrain, Vande Berg returned to teach in the Kodaikanal International School, where she had completed her elementary and high school

<hr />

97 "CORSOCK: Serving the Poor since 1970," undated brochure printed for CORSOCK.

education while her parents were serving in India. She taught physical education for a number of years and in 1998 was made head of the elementary school.

Unity for the Sake of Mission

In planning to celebrate the fiftieth anniversary of its inauguration, the Church of South India showed that it was serious about two statements in its constitution:

> Again, for the perfecting of the life of the whole body, the Church of South India needs the heritage of each of the uniting Churches, and each of those Churches will, it is hoped, not lose the continuity of its own life, but preserve the life enriched by that union with itself of the other two Churches. The Church of South India is thus formed by a combination of different elements each bringing its contribution to the whole, and not by the absorption of any one by any other.[98]
>
> The Church of South India desires to be permanently in full communion and fellowship with all the Churches with which its constituent groups have had such communion and fellowship.[99]

Faithful to the above two statements in its constitution, the Church of South India believes that unity goes far deeper than organizational unity. It does not come to an end when churches no longer are engaged in sharing specific tasks or projects. The unity of the church is grounded in its unity in Christ manifested among us in Word and sacraments. Therefore, in 1997, it invited all of those churches and mission agencies with whom it had historic or present relationships to send representatives to join the celebrations of the first fifty years of its life as a united church.

[98] *The Constitution of the Church of South India,* II, 2, p. 2.
[99] Ibid., II, 14, p. 12-13.

In the celebrations, held at St. George's Cathedral September 26-28, 1997, it became obvious that the Church of South India had sustained its relationship to the overseas mission bodies who had served in India and that it valued the presence of the overseas participants in the festive activities. One could not miss the fact that the Church of South India leaders took the partner church and agency very seriously, for they played a very important part in the celebration. "Historic relationships were affirmed and partner voices were heard in key public events as well as in times of private conversations with CSI leadership."[100]

In affirming that it desires to be permanently in full communion with all of those churches and traditions that contributed to the union in 1947, the Church of South India also calls into question whether the early missionaries were correct to develop a theory that would help them know when their mission would come to an end in South India—when they could turn to mission in the "regions beyond." The CSI would certainly agree on the importance of being a self-governing, self-supporting, self-propagating church not dominated by foreign missionaries or mission societies. As a church with strong Indian leadership, a respected place in India, and an amazingly large range of ministries, there is no possibility that the foreign bodies could now exercise domination over it. It is a church with almost 3 million members and 10,114 congregations within 21 dioceses. It also has 1,930 schools, 38 colleges, 51 vocational polytechnic schools, 104 hospitals and clinics, and 512 hostels for poor children.[101]

In view of the unity of the church on all six continents, the mission relationship into which the Reformed Church entered when its first missionaries went to India can never finally come to an end. The Church of South India and the Reformed Church in America, together with the other churches whose traditions entered into the

---

[100] John C. B. Webster, "The Church of South India Jubilee," *International Bulletin of Missionary Research*, vol. 22, 2 (April 1998), 53.
[101] Ibid.

union, now have a worldwide calling to remain in mission together although the forms of cooperation undergo constant change.

It is well for us to conclude this review of the history of the Reformed Church mission in India by listening to the words that Bishop David Chellapa of Madras spoke to the Tamilnad Christian Council in 1957 after he had returned to India from a visit to the Reformed Church in America. He called American and Indian Christians to carry out their mission together for sake of the church, of their countries, and of humankind:

> It may be said, with some reservations, that America, by and large, is a Christian country, where Christians values may be assumed. It is, therefore, our Christian duty to interpret India to America and America to India. Indo-American friendship is one of the ways in which the forces working for world peace can be strengthened. Both Indian and American Christians are not only citizens of their own country but also members of a body which transcends racial and international barriers. We must stretch our hands across the seas for the sake not only of the Church but of our country and indeed for mankind at large.[102]

If there are some in North America who are even less certain than Bishop Chellapa that they live in a Christian nation, then the challenge that he issued in 1957 is even more worthy of a positive response today.

---

[102] David D. Chellapa, "The Church in America," 13 September, 1957 (typescript, Archives of the RCA).

Bibliography

Following its organization in 1853, the American Arcot Mission annually sent a printed report to the Board of Foreign Missions of the Reformed Church in America. Each annual report, in full or in abbreviated form, was in turn presented to the General Synod of the denomination. The annual reports from India became the responsibility of the Arcot Assembly in 1924 and then of the Arcot Coordinating Committee in 1941. After the responsibilities of the Arcot Coordinating Committee were merged into the Diocese of Madras and the Diocese of Rayalaseema, the annual reports were no longer sent. After 1950 an annual report about the progress of Reformed Church mission activity was compiled by the staff of the Board of Foreign Missions for presentation to the General Synod. The denomination merged its mission boards into its General Program Council in 1968. The General Program Council's subsequent annual reports are included in the *Minutes of the General Synod*.

The Reformed Church in America Archives and Gardner A. Sage Library, located at New Brunswick Theological Seminary, hold the following reports and minutes:

The Annual Report of The American Arcot Mission, 1853-1923

The Annual Report of The Arcot Assembly, 1924-1940

The Report of the Arcot Coordinating Committee, 1941-1950

The Report of the Board of Foreign Missions, 1857-1960

The Report of the Board of Christian World Mission, 1961-1968

The Acts and Proceedings of the General Synod of the Reformed Church in America, 1738-2000.

Information concerning the role of Reformed Church women in mission in India is to be found in volumes of the *Annual Report of The Woman's Board of Foreign Missions, 1875-1939*, which are also located in the Gardner A. Sage Library.

Many letters from missionaries and articles about the work of Arcot missionaries are located in the Reformed Church paper, the *Christian Intelligencer* and its successor, the *Church Herald*. the *Mission Field* was the periodical of the Reformed Church mission boards from 1887-1922. The Woman's Board of Foreign Missions published the *Gleaner* between 1883-1917. Complete sets of these four publications are located at Western Theological Seminary in Holland, Michigan, as well as in the New Brunswick Theological Seminary.

In addition to the above, a number of people have generously loaned personal papers and institutional booklets with permission to quote from such materials. Their names have been included in the author's preface to this book.

American Arcot Mission, *Jubilee Commemoration, 1853-1928: The Arcot Assembly and the Arcot Mission of the Reformed Church in America*. Madras: Methodist Publishing House, 1931.

Appadurai, Arjun, *Worship and Conflict under Colonial Rule: A South India Case*. New York: Cambridge University Press, 1981.

Beaver, R. Pierce, "Rufus Anderson, 1796-1880," in Gerald H. Anderson *et.al.*, *Mission Legacies: Biographical Studies of Leaders of the Modern Missionary Movement*. Maryknoll, N.Y.: Orbis Books, 1994.

Bosch, David J., *Transforming Mission: Paradigm Shifts in Theology of Mission*. Maryknoll, N.Y.: Orbis Books, 1991.

Brouwer, Arie R., *Reformed Church Roots*. New York: Reformed Church Press, 1977.

Chamberlain, Jacob, *The Cobra's Den and other Stories of Work Among the Telugus of India*. New York: Fleming H. Revell, 1900.

Chamberlain, Jacob, "Free Reading Rooms," in Margaret E. Sangster, ed., *A Manual of the Missions of the Reformed (Dutch) Church in America*. New York: Board of Publication of the Reformed Church in America, 1877.

Chamberlain, Jacob, *Sketch of the Arcot Mission*. New York: Board of Foreign Missions, Reformed Church in America, 1915.

Chamberlain, Mary Anable, *Fifty Years in Foreign Fields: A History of Five Decades of the Woman's Board of Foreign Missions, Reformed Church in America*. New York: Women's Board of Foreign Missions, Reformed Church in America, 1925.

Chamberlain, William I., *Education in India*. New York: MacMillan, 1899.

Chapin, Josephine, "Caste Girls' School at Vellore," in Margaret E. Sangster, ed., *A Manual of the Missions of the Reformed (Dutch) Church in America*. New York: Board of Publication of the Reformed Church in America, 1877.

Church of South India, *The Constitution of the Church of South India*. Madras: Christian Literature Society, 1956

Church of South India, *Renewal and Advance: Report of the Church of South India Commission on Integration and Joint Action, 1963*. Madras: Christian Literature Society, 1963..

Clarke, Sathianathan, *Dalits and Christianity: Subaltern Religion and Liberation Theology in India*. Delhi: Oxford University Press, 1998.

Corwin, Edward Tanjore, *A Digest of Constitutional and Synodical Legislation of the Reformed Church in America.* New York: Board of Publications of the Reformed Church in America, 1906.

David, Immanuel, *Reformed Church in America Missionaries in South India, 1839-1938.* Bangalore, India: Asian Trading Corporation, distributers, 1986.

De Boer, John J., *The Story of the Arcot Mission.* New York: The Board of Foreign Missions, Reformed Church in America, 1938.

De Jong, Gerald F., *The Reformed Church in China, 1842-1951.* Grand Rapids, Mich.: Wm. B. Eerdmans Publishing Co., 1992.

Devanandan, P. D. and Thomas, M. M., *Christian Participation in Nation-Building.* Bangalore: The Christian Institute for the Study of Religion and Society, 1960.

Elangovan, I., *Elizabeth Rodman Voorhees College, Vellore Centenary.* Vellore: Printed for the Association of University Teachers (Regd.) Tamilnadu, 1997.

Embree, Ainslie T., *Utopias in Conflict: Religion and Nationalism in Modern India.* Berkeley: University of California Press, 1990.

Fabend, Firth Haring, "Pious and Powerful: The Evangelical Mother in Reformed Dutch Households, New York and New Jersey, 1826-1876," in Renee House and John Coakley, eds., *Patterns and Portraits: Women in the History of the Reformed Church in America.* Grand Rapids, Mich.: Wm. B. Eerdmans Publishing Co., 1999.

Fassler, Barbara, "The Role of Women in the India Mission, 1819-1880," in James Van Hoeven, ed., *Piety and Patriotism.* Grand Rapids, Mich.: Wm. B. Eerdmans Publishing Co., 1976.

First Ten Annual Reports of the American Board of Commissioners for Foreign Missions, The. Boston: Printed by Crocker and Brewster, 1834.

Fischer, Louis, *Gandhi: His Life and Message for the World.* New York: New American Library of World Literature, 1954.

French, Hal. W. and Sharma, Arvind, *Religious Ferment in Modern India.* New York: St. Martins Press, 1981.

Gandhi, M. K., *Christian Missions: Their Place in India.* Ahmedabad, India: Navajivan Publishing House, 1941.

Gasero, Russell L., *Historical Directory of the Reformed Church in America, 1628-1992.* Grand Rapids, Mich.: Wm. B. Eerdmans Publishing Co., 1992.

Gasero, Russell L. "The Rise of the Woman's Board of Foreign Missions," in Renee House and John Coakley, eds., *Patterns and Portraits: Women in the History of the Reformed Church in America.* Grand Rapids, Mich.: Wm. B. Eerdmans Publishing Co., 1999.

Greenlee, James G. and Johnston, Charles, *Good Citizens: British Missionaries and Imperial States, 1870 to 1918.* Montreal and Kingston: McGill-Queen's University Press, 1999.

Harper, Susan Billington, *In the Shadow of the Mahatma: Bishop V. S. Azariah and the Travails of Christianity in British India.* Grand Rapids, Mich.: Wm. B. Eerdmans Publishing Co., 2000.

736 *From Mission to Church*

Harris, Paul William, *Nothing but Christ: Rufus Anderson and the Ideology of Protestant Foreign Missions*. New York: Oxford University Press, 1999.

Heideman, Eugene, "Proselytism, Mission, and the Bible," in *International Bulletin of Missionary Research*, vol. 20, no. 1, January, 1996.

Hocking, William Ernest, *Re-Thinking Missions: A Laymen's Inquiry after One Hundred Years*. New York: Harper & Brothers, 1932.

Hoff, Marvin, *The Reformed Church in America: Structures for Mission*. Grand Rapids, Mich.: Wm. B. Eerdmans Publishing Co., 1985.

Hollis, Michael, *Paternalism and the Church: A Study of South Indian Church History*. London: Oxford University Press, 1962.

Hudson, D. Dennis, "Arumuga Navalar and the Hindu Renaissance among the Tamils," in Kenneth W. Jones, ed., *Religious Controversy in British India*. Albany: State University of New York Press, 1992.

Hudson, D. Dennis, *Protestant Origins in India: Tamil Evangelical Christians, 1706-1835*. Grand Rapids, Mich.: Wm. B. Eerdmans Publishing Co., 2000.

James, Lawrence, *Raj: The Making and Unmaking of British India*. New York: St. Martin's Press, 1997.

Jeffrey, *Ida S. Scudder of Vellore, India*. Published in India by permission of Fleming H. Revell, 1951.

Jeyakumar, D. Arthur, "Christianity Among the Nadars of Tirunelvelly" in E. Hrangkhuma, ed., *Christianity in India: Search for Liberation and Identity*. Delhi: Church Missionary Society/India Society for the Promotion of Christian Knowledge, 1998.

Jeyakumar, D. Arthur, *Christians and the National Movement: The Memoranda of 1919 and the National Movement, with Special Reference to Protestant Christians in Tamil Nadu*. Calcutta: Punthi Pustak, 1999.

Jones, Kenneth W., *The New Cambridge History of India: Socio-religious Reform Movements in British India*. Cambridge: Cambridge University Press, 1989.

Jones, Kenneth W., *Socio-religious Reform Movements in British India*. Cambridge: Cambridge University Press, 1989.

Laird, Michael A., "Alexander Duff, 1806-1878: Western Education as Preparation for the Gospel," in Anderson, Gerald H. et.al., *Mission Legacies: Biographical Studies of Leaders of the Modern Missionary Movement*. Maryknoll, N.Y: Orbis Books, 1994.

Levai, Blaise, *Revolution in Mission*. Vellore: Popular Press, 1957.

Livingston, John H., "The Everlasting Gospel," in John W. Beardslee III, ed., *Vision From the Hill*. Grand Rapids, Mich.: Wm. B. Eerdmans Publishing Co., 1984.

Manual of the Board of Foreign Missions of the Reformed Church in America for the use of Missionaries under appointment and in their fields of Labor. Prepared and published in New York, 1895.

Marsden, George M., *The Evangelical Mind and the New School Presbyterian Experience*. New Haven: Yale University Press, 1970.

McGavran, Donald A., *The Bridges of God: A Study in the Strategy of Missions*. London, England: World Dominion Press, 1961.

Metcalf, Thomas R., *Ideologies of the Raj.* Cambridge: Cambridge University Press, 1994.
Millar, A. A., *Alexander Duff of India.* Canongate Press, Edinburgh, 1992.
Nehru, Jawaharlal, *The Discovery of India.* Garden City, N.Y.: Doubleday, 1959.
Oddie, Geoffrey, *Hindu and Christian in South-East Asia.* Wellesley Hills, Mass: The Riverdale Company, 1991.
Parel, Anthony J., ed., *M. K. Gandhi: Hind Swaraj and Other Writings.* Cambridge: University of Cambridge, 1997.
Pathak, Sushil Madhav, *American Missionaries and Hinduism: A Study of Their Contacts from 1813 to 1910.* Munshiram Monharlal, Delhi-6, India, 1967.
Paul, Rajaiah D., *The First Decade: An Account of the Church of South India.* Madras: The Christian Literature Society, 1964.
Pickett, J. Waskom, *Christian Mass Movements in India.* Cincinnati: Abingdon, 1933.
Piet, John, *The Road Ahead.* Grand Rapids, Mich.: Wm. B. Eerdmans Publishing Co., 1970.
Ponniah, J. Sam, *The Contribution of The Reformed Church in America to the Church of South India.* Master of Theology Thesis, Western Theological Seminary, Holland, Mich., 1964.
Ratmeyer, Una H., *Hands, Hearts, and Voices: Women who Followed God's Call.* New York: Reformed Church Press, 1995.
Robert, Dana L., *American Women in Mission: A Social History of Their Thought and Practice.* (Macon, Georgia: Mercer University Press, 1996.
Rufus, Mahimai, *Growth of Evangelism in the Arcot Mission from 1853 to the Formation of the C. S. I., 1947.* Master of Theology Thesis, Western Theological Seminary, Holland, Mich., 1977.
Sangster, Margaret E., ed., *A Manual of the Missions of the Reformed (Dutch) Church in America.* New York: Board of Publications of the Reformed Church in America, 1877.
Sargent, N. C., *The Dispersion of the Tamil Church.* Delhi: India Society for the Promotion of Knowledge, 1962.
Sarkar, Sumit, *Modern India, 1885-1947.* New York: St. Martin's Press, 1989.
Scudder, Dorothy J., *A Thousand Years in Thy Sight: The Story of the Scudder Missionaries of India.* New York: Vantage Press, 1984.
Scudder, Mrs. Ezekiel, "Village Work," and "Hindu Women," in Margaret E. Sangster, ed., *A Manual of the Missions of the Reformed (Dutch) Church in America.* New York: Board of Publication of the Reformed Church in America, 1877.
Scudder, Henry Martyn, *The Bazaar Book,* J. W. Scudder, trans. Madras, India: The Religious Tract and Book Society, 1869.
Scudder, J.W., "Historical Sketch of the Arcot Mission," in Margaret E. Sangster, ed., *A Manual of the Missions of the Reformed (Dutch) Church in America.* New York: Board of Publication of the Reformed Church in America, 1877.
Scudder, Mrs. J.W., "Chittoor Female Seminary," in Margaret E. Sangster, ed., *A Manual of the Missions of the Reformed (Dutch) Church in America.* New York: Board of Publication of the Reformed Church in America, 1877.

Scudder, John Sr., *An Appeal to Christian Mothers in Behalf of the Heathen*. New York, The American Tract Society, 1844.

Scudder, John Sr., *The Redeemer's Last Command*. New York: The American Tract Society, 1844.

Scudder, Julia, "The Chittoor Female Seminary," in Margaret E. Sangster, ed., *A Manual of the Missions of the Reformed (Dutch) Church in America*. New York: Board of Publication of the Reformed Church in America, 1877.

Scudder, Lewis III, *The Arabian Mission's Story: In Search of Abraham's Other Son*. Grand Rapids, Mich.: Wm. B. Eerdmans Publishing Co., 1998.

Smith, Donald Eugene, *India as a Secular State*. Princeton: Princeton University Press, 1963.

Sundkler, Bengt, *Church of South India: The Movement Towards Union, 1900-1947*. London: Lutterworth Press, 1954.

Te Winkle, Sarella, *The Sixth Decade of the Woman's Board of Foreign Missions, Reformed Church in America, 1926-1935*. New York: Woman's Board of Foreign Missions, 1935.

Ten Brink, Eugene, *History of Vellore Fort and St. John's Church*. Privately printed, on file at the Archives of the Reformed Church in America, 1961.

Thomas, Norman E. *Classic Texts in Mission and World Christianity*. Maryknoll, N.Y.: Orbis Books, 1995.

Vander Lugt, Gerrit T., ed., "The Heidelberg Catechism" and "The Belgic Confession," in *The Liturgy of the Reformed Church in America together with the Psalter*. New York: Board of Education, 1968.

Van Doren, Alice B., *Lighted to Lighten: The Hope of India*. West Medford, Mass.: The Central Committee on United Study of Foreign Missions, 1922.

Van Hoeven, James W., ed., *Piety and Patriotism*. Grand Rapids, Mich.: Wm. B. Eerdmans Publishing Co., 1976.

Viswanathan, Gauri, *Outside the Fold: Conversion, Modernity, and Belief*. Princeton: Princeton University Press, 1998.

Waterbury, J. B. *Memoir of the Rev. John Scudder, M.D.* New York: Harper & Brothers, Publishers, 1870.

Webster, John C. B., "The Church of South India Jubilee," in *International Bulletin of Missionary Research*. Vol. 22, 2, April, 1998.

Weddell, Sue, *Roadbuilders: A Study of the Foreign Mission Program of the Reformed Church in America*. New York: Department of Missionary Education, Reformed Church in America, 1932.

Wilson, Dorothy Clarke, *Dr. Ida: Passing on the Torch of Life*. New York: Friendship Press, 1976.

Wolpert, Stanley, *A New History of India*. New York: Oxford University Press, 4th ed., 1993.

Wyckoff, Charlotte, *A Hundred Years with Christ in Arcot: A Brief History of the Arcot Mission of the Reformed Church in America*. Printed for the Arcot Mission Centenary Celebrations, 1953.

Wyckoff, Charlotte, *Kodaikanal, 1845-1945*. Nagercoil, India: London Mission Press, 1951.

Index

739

Subjects

748

Philippines, 378-381.
Plymouth Brethren, 76, 100.
Portuguese, 15, 21, 70.
Praeparandi class, 81-82, 101, 209, 345.
Presbyterian Alliance in India, 317-321, 371.
Presbyterian, New School and Old School, 45-46, 197-204, 235.
Presbytery of Arcot, 409, 582.
Prohibition, 520-521.
Property transfer, 573-574, 670-672.
Racism, 106ff., 233, 314, 383, 490.
Raj, 74: missionary attitude toward, 103-110, 119, 402; and Christian community, 448.
Red Cross, 532-533.
Redeemer's Last Command, The, 217-229.
Regions beyond, 50, 725-726, 731.
Religious Endowment Act, 1863, 65-66.
Re-Thinking Missions Report, 506-522ff.
Rice Christians 112, 148, 471, 505-506, 600-604.
Roman Catholics, 15, 21-22, 70-72, 93-95, 111-115, 229, 330, 544, 595, 693; Jesuits, 70-71; "popery" 94-95.
Sabbath, 17, 40, 77, 79, 120-124, 130, 209, 232.
Sahodara Sangam Society, 244-245.
Sati, 58, 153, 170, 382.
Scripture and tract distribution, 25, 40-41, 42, 131, 646.
Self-support, 233-234, 243-251, 271, 440-441, 468-469, 482-483, 535-547, 552, 560-566, 680-683, 685, 706-707, 714.
Sepoys, 102, 105, 338.
Slavery, 59, 202-203.
South India United Church, 1, 44, 207, 313, 37, 367-373, 409, 414, 436, 480, 576-580, 587, 608, 614, 659, 670.
Stewardship, 243-244, 656-657, 713-717.
Student Christian Movement, 642-643.
Student hostels, 636-637.
Syrian Christians, 20.
Tamil: language, 22, 55, 62, 73, 157, 211, 607-608; lyrics, 73, 434.

Tamil Progress Society (DMK) 62, 405, 691.
TEAR Fund, 681, 701.
Telugu area, 55, 132-133, 211, 291-297, 309-310, 607-608; language, 55, 607-608.
Temple administration, 64-66.
Ten Commandments, 125, 126.
Theosophical Society, 384-389, 488.
Three-self theory, 49-52, 80, 110, 162-165. 171, 173, 251, 290, 312, 408, 437, 465, 479, 624, 625, 668, 731.
Tolerance/intolerance, 391, 396-401, 475.
Utilitarians, 57-58.
Villages: Aliandal, 120-121; Arnodaya, 129-130; congregations, 77, 243, 496, 683-688; day schools, 272-275; Gnanothiam, 124, 209, 229, 274; occupied, 77, 111, 229; pastoral care for, 461, 453, 684-688; Sattambady, 111, 116-127, 209, 229; Vellambi, 120, 146, 230; Yehamur, 145-146, 312, 465, 562.
Voluntary lay workers, 683, 725; lay training, 78, 654.
Wars: Japan-Russian War, 402; Spanish-American War, 378-381; World War I, 442ff., 446, 490, 492; World War II, 566-574, 707.
Woman's Board of Foreign Missions, 159-162, 165-171, 174, 189, 264, 292-293, 300-308, 359, 424, 425-435, 577.
Women: civilizing role, 166-167; Hindu, 165-166, 177-179, 218; widow-status, 178; Woman's work for woman, 169ff.; Women's Fellowship, 711-713; Women's Gospel Extension Society, 618-619; Women's Social Service Centers, 532-535; Women's Union Missionary Society, 161, 166.
World Home Bible League, 646-648, 710.
World Wide Christian Schools, 692.
YMCA, 391, 461-462, 570, 585.
Zenana, 151, 152, 169, 171, 182-187, 300, 391, 711.
Zion Hill, 456.